LONDON: HUMPHREY MILFORD
OXFORD UNIVERSITY PRESS

BACHRACH

ECONOMIC ESSAYS

BY

CHARLES JESSE BULLOCK

CAMBRIDGE, MASS.
HARVARD UNIVERSITY PRESS
1936

PRINTED IN THE UNITED STATES OF AMERICA

CONTENTS

INTRODUCTORY NOTE

WHEN Professor Bullock retired from active teaching, after serving thirty-one years as a member of the Department of Economics in Harvard University, his many former students and other friends were anxious to show their appreciation of his distinguished contributions to American scholarship in some appropriate way, and an informal committee was organized to consider ways and means. After considerable discussion the committee came to the conclusion that nothing would be so fitting as the publication in book form of the many important papers which had appeared over his name. So much of his best work was still scattered through the files of our learned journals, that such a volume would render double service: it would not only honor a great scholar but would make valuable material more conveniently available for his colleagues in the field. A preliminary survey soon made it obvious that this was too ambitious a plan—there were so many things which had a clear claim to being included. It was therefore decided to publish only a part of the papers and to include a complete bibliography as evidence of the amount and variety of the others.

The problem of selection was of course a difficult one. It was desirable, on the one hand, to make the volume as representative as possible of Professor Bullock's many-sided interests and activities, and, on the other, to include those papers which scholars would find it most helpful to have in this form. This double criterion entailed many omissions which were serious from one or the other of these points of view. There was also the puzzling question of articles and reports of joint authorship, and here a conservative policy was adopted, only one such item being included. The papers finally selected have been grouped under three heads roughly indicative of the balance of Professor Bullock's interests and arranged chronologically under each head. It is too much to hope that all the decisions will approve themselves to those familiar with Professor Bullock's work, and the committee begs the indulgence of those readers who miss some well-remembered item.

The editors have considered their task a happy privilege and join the committee in thanking the guarantors whose prompt and generous response made the volume possible and the several publishers who kindly permitted republication of the papers.

ECONOMIC ESSAYS

I

DIRECT AND INDIRECT TAXES IN ECONOMIC LITERATURE[1]

I

THE distinction between direct and indirect taxes seems to have originated in relatively modern times. In classical antiquity no trace of such a distinction can be discovered, while in mediæval and modern Europe the terms are first found in a work written during the last half of the sixteenth century.[2]

The Greeks, like all other peoples, had various words that meant impost or tax; but no trace can be found of any usage that resembles our expressions direct and indirect taxes.[3] The most common word for a tax, τέλος, was used at Athens for all the ordinary imposts,[4] some of which we should call direct, such as the personal tax upon the *metics,* while others would now be styled indirect, as the customs and market duties. A second word, φόρος, denoted primarily tribute from subject states.[5] The Athenians generally would not use this word for their own taxes.[6] In place of this hated term they often used

[1] Reprinted from *Political Science Quarterly*, Vol. XIII (1898), pp. 442-476. Reproduced by generous permission of the publishers.

[2] On the history of these terms see Roscher, Finanzwissenschaft, Sec. 37, note 4 (Stuttgart, 1886); Neumann, Die Steuer, pp. 417 *et seq.* (Leipzig, 1887); also in *Jahrbuch für Gesetzgebung, Verwaltung und Volkswirthschaft,* Vol. VI, pp. 955 *et seq.*; *Handwörterbuch der Staatswissenschaften,* Vol. VI, pp. 96 *et seq.* (Jena, 1890-95); Förstemann, Die direkten und indirekten Steuern (Nordhausen, 1868).

[3] *Cf.* Förstemann, pp. 1, 2.

[4] Gilbert, *Handbuch der griechischen Staatsalterthümer,* Vol. I, p. 331 (Leipzig, 1881), says: "Die Hauptquelle der ordentlichen direkten Einnahmen bildeten die τέλη, eine Bezeichnung, welche die Zölle und Steuern umfasst." Plato, Laws, viii, 11 [847], uses τέλος for export or import duties, as follows: τέλος δὲ ἐν τῇ πόλλει μηδένα μηδὲν τελεῖν μήτε ἐξαγομένων χρημάτων μήτε εἰσαγομένων. Aristotle, Politics, v, 11, uses ἡ εἰσφορὰ τῶν τελῶν for taxes in general.

[5] Gilbert, Vol. I, pp. 393, 394. See Thucydides, i, 96: καὶ 'Ελληνοταμίαι τότε πρῶτον 'Αθηναίοις κατέστη ἀρχή, οἳ ἐδέχοντο τὸν φόρον. οὕτω γὰρ ὠνομάσθη τῶν χρημάτων ἡ φορά.

[6] Yet Demosthenes, Against Aristogeiton, i, 21 [776, 9]: φέροντα τὴν τῆς σωτηρίας φορὰν πλήρη τῇ πατρίδι.

euphemistically the word σύνταξις.[7] But the common word for the extraordinary property tax at Athens was εἰςφορά.[8] This impost was levied reluctantly, and usually for war purposes solely. Thus it appears that the only distinction between these various words is that τέλος was the common word for the ordinary taxes, φόρος generally meant tribute and εἰσφορά denoted the extraordinary property tax.

In Roman usage the case is similar.[9] *Vectigal* was originally used to denote all dues and imposts gathered from lands or domains in the possession of the state: that is, tithes from cultivators of public lands, port dues, etc. Thus it was contrasted with *tributum civium Romanorum,* the property tax collected from the possessions of citizens.[10] Gradually the term *vectigal* broadened until it became the common word for a tax of any sort.[11] The *tributum civium Romanorum,* or *tributum,* was originally the extraordinary property tax levied upon Roman citizens.[12] Then in the provinces the *tributum soli,* or land tax, and *tributum capitis,* or poll tax, were imposed as the principal taxes.[13] When Diocletian extended the provincial *tributum* to the lands of Italy, *tributum* came to mean strictly the imperial land tax.[14] Yet the word was sometimes used for other taxes besides those enumerated above.[15] The absence of any single term for expressing the difference in the incidence of

[7] See Harpocration, σύνταξις. Also Demosthenes, On the Crown, 234 [305, 16 and 17]: χρημάτων δὲ σύνταξιν εἰς πέντε καὶ τετταράκοντα τάλαντα. *Cf.* Demosthenes, On the Peace, 13 [60, 11].

[8] See Gilbert, Vol. I, pp. 345 *et seq.* Thucydides, iii, 19, says: αὐτοὶ ἐσενεγκόντες τότε πρῶτον ἐσφορὰν διακόσια τάλαντα. See Xenophon, Oeconomicus, ii, 6.

[9] *Cf.* Förstemann, p. 2.

[10] Marquardt, Römische Staatsverwaltung, Vol. II, pp. 155, 156 (Leipzig, 1876).

[11] Thus we may mention the tax on sales, *vectigal rerum venalium.* See Marquardt, Vol. II, p. 269. Cicero uses the term for the land tax. *De Lege Agraria,* ii, 21, 57: *"agro pergrande vectigal imponitur"*; also *Brutus,* 36, 136: *"agrum publicum vitiosa et inutili lege vectigali levavit."*

[12] Marquardt, Vol. II, p. 157. For original references see Livy, xxiii, 31, 1, and 48, 8.

[13] Marquardt, Vol. II, pp. 178, 179, 191 *et seq.*

[14] *Ibid.,* pp. 217 *et seq.*

[15] Thus Pliny, Panegyricus, 37, says of the inheritance tax: *"vicesima reperta est, tributum tolerabile."*

direct and indirect taxes is well shown in the familiar passage in which Tacitus describes the effects of the remission of the old tax, formerly paid by the purchaser, of four per cent upon sales of slaves. Tacitus shows that the remission was merely nominal; since at that time the seller was taxed, and the tax formed part of the price which had to be paid by the buyer.[16]

In the literature of the Middle Ages we cannot expect to find contributions to the doctrine of taxation. For a large part of this period there was a dearth of writings upon economic subjects. Then the schoolmen began to discuss such matters as fair price and usury, but had very little to say upon financial subjects.[17] The few other writers of the thirteenth and fourteenth centuries whose works possess anything of financial interest merely touched upon questions of public expenditures, the management of domains, the farming of taxes and the like. In point of fact, financial problems were as yet seldom of sufficient importance to attract much attention from scholars.[18]

In the fifteenth and sixteenth centuries, in Italy, and especially at Florence, such writers as Ghetti, Carafa, Savonarola, Guicciardini, Matteo Palmieri and others discussed financial topics more thoroughly.[19] But it was in France that the germ of the distinction between direct and indirect taxes was first developed. Jean Bodin,[20] in 1576, used the words, "*payer les*

[16] Tacitus, Annals, 13, 31: "*Vectigal quoque quintae et vicesimae venalium mancipiorum remissum, specie magis quam vi, quia cum venditor pendere juberetur, in partem pretii emptoribus accrescebat.*"

[17] Upon the schoolmen in general, see Cossa, Introduction to the Study of Political Economy, pp. 138-148 (London, 1893); Roscher, Geschichte der Nationalökonomie in Deutschland, pp. 1-31 (München, 1874); Ricca-Salerno, Storia delle dottrine finanziarie in Italia, pp. 38 *et seq.* (Palermo, 1896). St. Thomas Aquinas may represent the views of the scholastics on taxes. See Baumann, Die Staatslehre des Thomas von Aquino, pp. 97-99 (Leipzig, 1873); Jourdain, Philosophie de Saint Thomas d'Aquin, Vol. I, pp. 429, 430 (Paris, 1858); Palgrave, Dictionary of Political Economy, Vol. I, p. 49 (London, 1894); Littlejohn, The Political Theory of the Schoolmen, pp. 184, 185 (New York, 1896); Brants, Esquisse des théories économiques professées par les écrivains des XIIIme et XIVme siècles (Louvain, 1895).

[18] Cossa, pp. 148-150; Ricca-Salerno, pp. 44-57.

[19] Cossa, pp. 156-160; Ricca-Salerno, pp. 47-54, 57-82.

(Mümpelgart, 1592); into English by Richard Knolles (London, 1606); into

tailles et autres imposts directement ou indirectement." It was, however, merely an incidental expression, applicable to nearly all taxes, which Bodin never thought of making the basis for a classification. This is apparent from his classification of public revenues, as follows: (1) from domains; (2) from confiscations; (3) from gifts; (4) from tributes; (5) from trade; (6) from tolls and customs, which he regards as paid by foreigners; (7) from taxes upon subjects. This seventh branch of revenue is again subdivided into: (1) extraordinary; (2) ordinary; (3) casual.[21] Although Bodin's work had a very great influence in Europe, his casual use of the phrase "to pay taxes directly or indirectly" made little or no impression upon subsequent writers, most of whom did not adopt it.

Giovanni Botero,[22] writing under the influence of Bodin's ideas, does not make use of this suggestion. He divides public revenues into extraordinary and ordinary. The former arise from escheats, fines, confiscations, etc.; while the latter are derived from the products of the soil or of human industry. These ordinary revenues may be either immediate or mediate, the first division including incomes derived from the lands of the prince, the second comprising incomes derived from subjects. Christoph Besold[23] favored what modern writers would call indirect taxes, holding that they are paid more easily than direct imposts; but he does not seem to utilize the suggestion of Bodin. The same is true of Antoine de Montchétien,[24] who, however, discussed taxation merely incidentally. But the case

Latin (1586), as well as into other languages. On the character and influence of this work see H. Hallam, Introduction to the Literature of Europe, Vol. II, pp. 204-230 (London, 1837). Roscher, Förstemann and Neumann have been unable to trace the expression further back than this work.

[21] See bk. vi, ch. ii. Cf. Hallam, Literature of Europe, Vol. II, pp. 226, 227. Hallam is mistaken in thinking that Bodin grouped excises with customs, and included only modern "direct taxes" under the seventh head.

[22] Della Ragione di stato (Venice, 1589). *Cf.* Ricca-Salerno, pp. 133, 134.

[23] Discursus de aerario politico (Tübingen, 1620). *Cf.* Roscher, Geschichte der Nationalökonomie in Deutschland, pp. 195-205.

[24] Traicté de l'économie politique (1615). Edited by Funck-Brentano (Paris, 1889).

is different with a number of other writers. Keckerman,[25] in 1607, wrote that indirect taxes are those which a state receives through artifices that it tolerates—as, for instance, public lotteries. Such authors as Lather, Faust and Klock,[26] in whose work the influence of Bodin may be seen, speak of payments "*per obliquum et indirectum.*"[27]

Yet it is certain that, until the time of Physiocrats, these vague expressions suggested to no one a new basis for a scientific classification of taxes;[28] while some writers did not use them at all. Thus Pufendorff,[29] who discussed taxes and argued that such imposts as customs duties are paid more readily since they are concealed in the prices of commodities, gives us no classification, and does not use the terms directly and indirectly. On the other hand, Seckendorff[30] wrote:

> . . . When taxes are not paid to the government immediately out of the purse of every subject, but a certain penny or share of the price is levied upon liquor, meat, salt, grain and similar objects of common use.

But such terms are not found in Broggia,[31] who formulated an elaborate plan for a system of taxes, composed of (1) a land

[25] Systema disciplinae politicae (1607). *Cf.* Roscher, Finanzwissenschaft, Sec. 37, note 4.

[26] Lather, De censu, tractatus nomico-politicus (Frankfurt, 1618); Faust, Consilia pro aerario (Frankfurt, 1641); Klock, Tractatus nomico-politicus de contributionibus (Nürnberg, 1634), Tractatus de aerario (Nürnberg, 1651). See Roscher, Geschichte der Nationalökonomie in Deutschland, pp. 165-167, 207-218.

[27] This statement is made upon the authority of Neumann, Die Steuer, p. 418. Of the works mentioned the writer has been able to secure only Klock's Tractatus de contributionibus.

[28] In Germany, at least, such a classification would have been hindered, at that time, by the fact that various terms were applied to the different kinds of taxes, and no single word was used comprehensively to denote all forms of public imposts. Up to the close of the eighteenth century the word "Steuer" meant what we would now call a direct tax. *Cf.* Neumann, pp. 419, 420; Förstemann, pp. 3, 4.

[29] De jure naturae et gentium (1672). Translated into English by B. Kennett (London, 1729). Bk. vii, ch. iv, Sec. 7; bk. viii, ch. v, Secs. 4-6. *Cf.* Roscher, Geschichte der Nationalökonomie, pp. 316-318.

[30] Teutscher Fürstenstaat (Frankfurt, 1656), part iii, ch. viii, Sec. 3. *Cf.* Roscher, Geschichte der Nationalökonomie, p. 251.

[31] Trattato dei tributi (Naples, 1743). Contained in Scrittori classici Italiani, edited by Custodi, Vol. IV (Milan, 1804). See chs. ii, iv.

tax, (2) a tax on manufactured articles and upon fixed incomes, (3) imposts upon internal consumption and (4) customs duties;[32] nor are they used by Pascoli and Bandini.[33] A similar expression,[34] however, occurs in the following passage from Montesquieu:[35] "L'impôt par tête est plus naturel à la servitude; l'impôt sur les marchandises est plus naturel à la liberté, parce qu'il se rapporte d'une manière moins directe à la personne." But, as Förstemann[36] has noticed, this seems to refer rather to differences in the legal relations of the taxpayers to the state in the two cases.[37] In any event, no idea concerning the shifting of taxes influenced Montesquieu's classification of imposts, which was: (1) taxes on persons; (2) taxes on land; (3) taxes on commodities.[38]

II

This brings us to the Physiocrats, who first formulated a scientific classification of taxes as direct and indirect, and gave these terms a definite place in economic terminology. The founder of the school, François Quesnay, developed the familiar Physiocratic doctrine of taxation in 1758. Holding that all imposts ultimately fall upon the *"produit net"* of the earth, he declared that taxes can be most cheaply and easily collected directly from the land. Therefore he called all taxes indirect except that upon land, and advocated *"l'impôt unique et direct"* upon the net product of the soil.[39] It is not necessary to follow

[32] *Cf.* Ricca-Salerno, pp. 228-234.

[33] L. Pascoli, Testamento politico (Perugia, 1733). *Cf.* Ricca-Salerno, pp. 217-222. S. Bandini, Discorso economico (1737, published at Florence, 1775).

[34] Neumann, p. 419, quotes from Boisguillebert and Vauban such passages as *"passer immédiatement de la main du peuple en celle du roi,"* etc. See Boisguillebert, Detail de la France (1695); Factum de la France (1706). Edited by E. Daire (Paris, 1851), pp. 237, 238, 266. But these expressions seem to refer to the costs of collection, as is apparent from the expression used on p. 238.

[35] L'esprit des lois (Geneva, 1748), bk. xiii, ch. xiv.

[36] *Op. cit.*, p. 7.

[37] In the same chapter Montesquieu explains that taxes on commodities are advanced by the merchant but really paid by the purchaser. He does not use the words directly or indirectly in this connection.

[38] L'esprit des lois, bk. xiii, ch. vii.

[39] The works of Quesnay in question are: Tableau économique (1758); Second problème économique (1767). These are contained in E. Daire's Physiocrates

this distinction of direct and indirect taxes through the works of all of the Physiocrats.[40] Turgot, however, may be mentioned briefly. He differed in some points from the other members of the school, although he held to their central doctrines. His use of the distinction between direct and indirect taxes is not always uniform. Sometimes he says that all taxes fall directly or indirectly upon the proprietors of land, and seems to regard the land tax as the only direct tax.[41] But elsewhere he says that there are three possible forms of taxes: (1) direct upon land; (2) direct upon persons; (3) indirect upon consumption.[42] Here he seems to have in mind the idea, suggested by Bodin, that some taxes are paid immediately or directly, while others are paid by other persons than the one who first advances the tax. With this notion he combines the classification of taxes formulated by Montesquieu. But he proceeds to discuss direct taxes[43] at some length, and explains that taxes on persons, so far as they fall upon any kind of income except that derived from land, are really indirect imposts. Thus his position is not inconsistent with the doctrines of Quesnay.

Various circumstances contributed to stimulate the discussion, started by the Physiocrats, concerning the relative merits of direct and indirect taxation. In the Constituent Assembly such questions were debated, and Physiocratic ideas exercised a demonstrable influence, especially in the reform of the land tax.[44] In January, 1790, an *instruction*, issued by the Assembly, defined a direct tax as follows:

(Paris, 1846) and Oncken's Œuvres de F. Quesnay (Paris, 1888). The passages referred to may be found on pp. 61, 83, 127-143 of Daire's edition and on pp. 312, 332, 696-718 of Oncken's edition. *Cf.* Henry Higgs, The Physiocrats, pp. 43, 44 (London, 1897).

[40] The most important citations are: Mirabeau, Théorie de l'impôt (1760); Dupont de Nemours, Origine et progrès d'une science nouvelle (1767); Mercier de la Rivière, L'ordre naturel et essentiel des sociétés politiques (1767). See Daire's Physiocrates, pp. 351-358, 474-524.

[41] Œuvres de Turgot, Vol. I, pp. 409, 416, edited by E. Daire (2d ed., Paris, 1844).

[42] *Ibid.*, Vol. I, p. 394.

[43] *Ibid.*, Vol. I, p. 396.

[44] See R. Stourm, Les Finances de l'ancien régime et de la revolution, Vol. I, pp. 136-143, 295-302 (Paris, 1885).

> Toute imposition foncière ou personelle, c'est-à-dire assise directement sur les fonds de terre ou assise directement sur les personnes, qui se lève par voies du cadastre ou des rôles de cotisations, et qui passe immédiatement du contribuable cotisé au percepteur. . . .[45]

This definition resembles the one formulated by Turgot, but contains an additional element—namely, the reference to the *cadastres,* or assessment rolls, by which direct taxes may be levied. This suggested an administrative basis for classifying direct and indirect taxes, which has been much favored by subsequent French economists and has become fixed in French public law.[46] The same idea was further developed in the *Code des Contributions* of 1811.[47] Direct taxes were there declared to be those raised *"par des rôles où les contribuables sont nominativement cotisés"*; while indirect were those collected *"en vertu des tarifs, sans dénomination de personnes."* The terms introduced by the Physiocrats lived on after their doctrines of taxation had been rejected.

Of French writers on economic science, Canard[48] may have been the first to formulate a new basis for the distinction of direct and indirect taxes, after Physiocratic doctrines had failed to gain acceptance. He held a tax to be direct when it reached the sources of an individual's income, as the income from land or from industry; while taxes collected from consumers, or from merchandise on the way to consumers, were indirect. A few years later J. B. Say[49] made a similar distinction, defining direct taxes as those demanded from an individual's real or supposed income, while indirect are demanded on each act of consumption of certain specified objects. In 1808 Montyon[50]

[45] M. Block, Dictionnaire de l'administration française, p. 636 (2d ed., Paris, 1881).

[46] *Cf.* the present classification in *"L'instruction generale."* Say, Dictionnaire d'économie politique, Vol. II, p. 25 (Paris, 1892).

[47] Handwörterbuch der Staatswissenschaften, Vol. VI, p. 97 (Jena, 1894); Neumann, p. 431.

[48] Principes d'économie politique, p. 154 (Paris, 1801).

[49] Traité d'économie politique (1803). 1st Amer. ed., Vol. II, p. 268 (Boston, 1821).

[50] J. B. R. A. Montyon, Quelle influence ont les diverses espèces d'impôts? (Paris, 1808). Contained in Mélanges d'économie politique, Vol. II, pp. 365-496 (Paris, 1848).

offered a similar definition, and the phrases direct and indirect taxes may then be said to have found a place in French economic terminology.

Through the influence of the Physiocrats the distinction of direct and indirect taxes came into general use in Italy, England and Germany. It is found in the writings of the Italian economist, Gaetano Filangieri,[51] who accepted many of the Physiocratic doctrines. He formally classified taxes as direct and indirect, and favored the single tax. Yet the terms were not used by Beccaria,[52] who discussed taxation incidentally, or by Verri.[53] The last-named writer treated at length the shifting of taxation, holding that taxes tend to diffuse themselves among all citizens in proportion to consumption. Occasionally he speaks of taxes falling "immediately" upon subjects, but he does not classify taxes as direct and indirect. Giuseppe Palmieri,[54] however, borrowed these terms from the Physiocrats, although he did not accept their doctrine that the single tax on land was the only proper form of taxation. Galanti,[55] who preferred the land tax to other imposts, but not as the only form of taxation, used the distinction; and the same is true of Di Gennaro,[56] who accepted the entire doctrine of the Physiocrats on this subject. The distinction occurs also in a work published at Naples in 1792.[57] After this date the terms direct and indirect taxes may be regarded as well established in Italian economic literature,[58] although the general rejection of the Physiocratic

[51] Delle leggi politiche ed economiche (1780). Reprinted in Economisti classici, edited by Custodi (Milan, 1804). See pp. 324-358.

[52] Elementi di economia pubblica (1769). Reprinted by Custodi (Milan, 1804). See Vol. I, pp. 21, 22, 278, 279, 285.

[53] Meditazioni sulla economia politica (1771). Reprinted by Custodi (Milan, 1804). See chs. xxx, xxxi.

[54] Riflessioni sulla pubblica felicità (1788). Reprinted by Custodi (Milan, 1805). See Vol. I, pp. 212, 213; Vol. II, pp. 149, 150.

[55] Discrizione delle stato antico ed attuale del Contado di Molise (Naples, 1781). Quoted by Fornari, Delle teorie economiche nelle provincie Napolitane, p. 413 (Milan, 1888).

[56] Piano per la riforma dei titoli dei legislazione relativi al tributo (Naples, 1792). Quoted by Fornari, Delle teorie economiche, p. 409.

[57] Esame critico delle due anonime operette. See Ricca-Salerno, p. 435.

[58] Thus they are used by Azzariti-Stella, in De mali e rimedi politici (Naples, 1806). See Fornari, Delle teorie economiche, p. 573.

doctrines had left no scientific basis for such a distinction. In 1813 Cagnazzi, the popularizer of Smith and Say, classified taxes as direct and indirect, in a manner which suggests the definitions formulated by Canard and Say. He called those taxes direct which are levied in proportion to income, and fall directly upon some source of wealth, such as land and industry; while he considered indirect taxes to be those which are levied upon the circulation or consumption of wealth.[59]

In Germany, Quesnay had a number of followers who advocated his doctrine of taxation.[60] Naturally writers of such tendencies used the terms direct and indirect taxes. Schlettwein may be cited as one of these.[61] But some economists, who did not accept the tenets of the Physiocratic school, made no use of this distinction: Lith, von Thiele and Fischer are cases in point.[62] J. H. von Justi, in a work[63] written prior to the publication of Quesnay's *Tableau Économique,* spoke of taxes being paid *"mittelbarer Weise,"* an expression which we have met in the works of earlier writers. Yet Justi never conceived of this as a basis for the classification of taxes. He applied the expression even to the shifting of the land tax, which he considered possible. In subsequent works[64] Justi refutes the theory of the single tax, and does not adopt the terminology of the Physiocrats; while he continues to classify taxes as (1) taxes on immovables, (2) taxes on persons, (3) taxes on business.

Other writers, however, adopted the language of the Physiocrats, even when rejecting their doctrines. Thus Pfeiffer, who

[59] L. Cagnazzi, Elementi di economia politica (Naples, 1813). *Cf.* Ricca-Salerno, p. 462; Fornari, Delle teorie economiche, pp. 579, 580.

[60] On Physiocratic influence in Germany, see Roscher, Geschichte der Nationalökonomie in Deutschland, pp. 480-500; Higgs, The Physiocrats, ch. v; *Jahrbücher für Nationalökonomie und Statistik*, Vol. XIX, pp. 1-63 (Jena, 1872).

[61] For a list of the works of Schlettwein, see Handwörterbuch der Staatswissenschaften, Vol. V, pp. 576-578. In particular see Schlettwein's Grundfeste der Staaten, p. 615 (Giessen, 1778).

[62] J. W. Lith, Abhandlung von denen Steuern (Ulm, 1766); C. G. von Thiele, Nachricht der märkischen Contributions- und Landessteuerverfassung (2d ed., Halle, 1768); F. C. J. Fischer, Lehrbegriff sämmtlicher Kameral- und Polizeirechte von Deutschland (Frankfurt, 1784-86).

[63] Staatswirthschaft (1755); 2d ed. (Leipzig, 1758), Vol. II, pp. 345-355.

[64] Politische und Finanzschriften (Kopenhagen und Leipzig, 1761); System des Finanzwesens (Halle, 1766).

attacked Schlettwein as the representative of the French school, used such expressions as *"direkte Auflagen," "direkt und indirekt besteuert,"* etc.[65] Sonnenfels, also, when rejecting the single tax and attacking the treatment accorded by the Physiocrats to indirect taxes, uses continually the expressions *"mittelbare Abgaben," "unmittelbare Gewerbsteuer,"* etc.[66] With these German writers we may group Bielfeld, who incidentally uses the words direct and indirect when treating of taxes.[67] Finally, J. J. Moser wrote that a certain tax was paid *"per indirectum,"*[68] while J. G. Hunger contrasted direct taxes with taxes on trade and consumption.[69]

Such discussions served to fix the words direct and indirect taxation in German economic terminology. Beguelin employed these terms in 1797.[70] Borowski used them, but with reference to Physiocratic discussions.[71] They occur in Bosse's *Grundzüge der Finanzwissenschaft,* published in 1804.[72] Kröncke[73] discussed the various meanings of these terms. Schlözer used the words in a different sense. He divided taxes into *"mittelbare"* and *"unmittelbare."*[74] The former he defined as taxes that fall upon the productive forces, gross income or production. Indirect taxes, in this view, would be those that fall upon consumption. Schlözer was a thorough student of Adam Smith's writings, and was acquainted with the works of Canard.[75] This last circumstance suggests that Schlözer's distinction was based upon that formulated by the French writer. In 1808 Eschenmayer wrote

[65] J. F. von Pfeiffer, Der Anti-physiokrat, pp. 212, 360, 361 (Frankfurt, 1780).

[66] Grundsätze der Polizei, Handlung, und Finanzwissenschaft (1763); 3d ed. (Vienna, 1777), Vol. III, pp. 269-272, 300-302, 309-311, 342, 343.

[67] Le B. de Bielfeld, Institutions politiques (La Haye, 1760). See part i, ch. xii.

[68] Landeshoheit in Steuersachen (Frankfurt und Leipzig, 1773), p. 686.

[69] Hunger wrote: *"Diese Handels- und Consumptionsabgaben waren bei Weitem nicht so drückend als jene direkten Steuern."*—Kurze Geschichte der Abgaben, ch. xi (Dresden, 1783). *Cf.* Neumann, p. 423.

[70] F. W. von Beguelin, Historisch-Kritische Darstellung der Accise- und Zollverfassung (Berlin, 1797).

[71] G. H. Borowski, Abriss des praktischen Kameral- und Finanzwesens (2d ed., Berlin, 1799). Quoted in Förstemann, p. 23.

[72] *Cf.* Neumann, p. 421, note.

[73] Das Steuerwesen (Darmstadt, 1804). *Cf.* Neumann, p. 424.

[74] C. von Schlözer, Staatswirthschaft (1805). Quoted by Neumann, p. 417.

[75] See Roscher, Geschichte der Nationalökonomie in Deutschland, pp. 795, 796.

that taxes may be divided into direct and indirect, according as they are raised mediately or immediately from the taxpayers.[76] Also Theodor Schmalz, "the last Physiocrat," insisted that the terms direct and indirect had no meaning, when applied to taxes, except in the Physiocratic sense.[77] In this year, finally, the words found their way into Prussian public law,[78] and their use in German economic literature may be regarded as established.

In England the terms direct and indirect taxes came into use at a late day, and gained acceptance but slowly. Bodin's *Six Books of the Republic,* with its allusion to taxes paid "directly or indirectly," was translated into English in 1606, and was read widely.[79] Montesquieu, who used a similar expression, was studied by such economists as Hume and Adam Smith. Yet the terms did not come into use from the influence of these French writers. German authors, moreover, were much less known in England, except as their works were accessible in Latin editions.[80] Probably the minor political writers and cameralists were never read. Pufendorff, who was well known through the Latin and English editions of his *Law of Nature and Nations,* does not use the terms direct and indirect. German influence may, therefore, safely be left out of our account.

In England discussions of the subject of taxation are old.[81] We may begin with Thomas Hobbes,[82] who treated of justice in taxation, favoring taxes on expenditure, but did not attempt

[76] D. H. Eschenmayer, Vorschlag zu einem einfachen Steuer-Systeme, p. 12 (Heidelberg, 1808).

[77] Handbuch der Staatswirthschaft, Sec. 410 (Berlin, 1808). *Cf.* Cohn, Finanzwissenschaft, p. 441 (Stuttgart, 1889); Roscher, Geschichte der Nationalökonomie, pp. 498-500.

[78] See Förstemann, p. 8.

[79] English translation by Richard Knolles (London, 1606). *Cf.* Hallam, Introduction to Literature of Europe, Vol. II, pp. 204, 205.

[80] This is well shown in Adam Smith's library, which contained works in Latin, Greek, Italian and French, but no German works, except in Latin editions. See J. Bonar, Catalogue of the Library of Adam Smith, pp. 57, 92, 102, 110 (London, 1894).

[81] See Ricca-Salerno, pp. 172-185.

[82] De cive (1642); Leviathan (1651). (English Works of Thomas Hobbes. Edited by W. Molesworth. London, 1839). See Vol. II, p. 174; Vol. III, pp. 333, 334; Vol. IV, pp. 216, 217.

any classification of imposts or use the terms direct and indirect. Sir William Petty, also, favored taxes on consumption. Holding that a land tax could be shifted only in part upon consumers of raw produce, he desired an excise on all consumption.[83] While he does not classify taxes as direct and indirect, he speaks, in one of his works, of taxes paid "insensibly and indirectly."[84] This is apparently the only case in which any English writer, prior to the time of Adam Smith, used any such expression. Thomas Mun, who devoted one chapter of his principal work[85] to the subject of public revenues, does not classify taxes or use the words direct and indirect. John Locke discussed taxation incidentally. Holding that all taxes "for the most part terminate upon land," he says it is vain for the landowner to desire taxes laid upon commodities, because, "though he pays not this tax immediately out of his own purse," he will ultimately bear the burden of such excise taxes[86] Charles D'Avenant, who accepted Locke's theory that all taxes are in the last resort a charge upon land, does not use the words direct and indirect.[87]

In the eighteenth century, discussions of the relative merits of a single land tax, a general excise system or a single excise upon houses, etc., continued; while the bitter controversies over Walpole's excise scheme of 1733 gave the question great practical interest.[88] Prominent among the writers of this period were Vanderlint, who, following Locke, favored a single tax

[83] Treatise on Taxes and Contributions (1662).

[84] Verbum Sapienti, Appendix to Political Anatomy of Ireland (London, 1691). The Verbum Sapienti was written in 1665. All editions have "insensibly and directly." Petty's manuscript shows this to be an error. For this fact I am indebted to Prof. C. H. Hull, who explains the matter in his forthcoming edition of the Economic Works of Sir William Petty.

[85] England's Treasure by Forraign Trade (1664). (Edited by W. J. Ashley. New York, 1895.) See ch. xvi.

[86] Considerations of the Lowering of Interest and Raising the Value of Money (1691). See Works of John Locke, Vol. V, p. 55 (11th ed., London, 1812).

[87] Ways and Means of Supplying the War (London, 1695); Discourses on the Public Revenues and Trade of England (London, 1698). See Political and Commercial Works of Charles D'Avenant (London, 1771).

[88] See Palgrave, Dictionary of Political Economy, Vol. I, p. 788, for Walpole's scheme. On the entire controversy see Ricca-Salerno, pp. 197-210; Seligman, Shifting and Incidence of Taxation, pp. 12-27 (Baltimore, 1892).

upon land,[89] and Sir Matthew Decker,[90] who desired a single excise upon houses. But this controversy did not result in the development, in English economic literature, of the distinction between direct and indirect taxes.

The immediate predecessors of Adam Smith now claim attention. David Hume[91] classified taxes as (1) upon consumption, (2) upon possessions, (3) arbitrary imposts; and did not use the terms direct and indirect. Malachy Postlethwayt, in his *Dictionary of Commerce,*[92] merely echoed Hume, and made the same classification. In another work[93] he spoke of "our Taxes laid directly upon Trade, or in any other intermediate Shape." But this does not seem to be similar to the technical use of the terms direct and indirect. Moreover, Postlethwayt made no classification of taxes upon this basis. Sir James Steuart devoted two hundred pages of his *Principles of Political Economy*[94] to the subject of taxation. He offered the following classification: (1) taxes on alienation, or proportional taxes, as customs, excise and stamp duties; (2) taxes on possession, or arbitrary and cumulative taxes, as poll, window, land taxes, etc.; (3) personal taxes, or "those exacted in service," as the road tax and militia duty. Steuart says that proportional taxes form parts of the prices of commodities, and are paid by the buyer. Taxes of the second class are intended to affect possessors in such a way that the taxes cannot be shifted.[95] Here he touches upon the very circumstance that forms a basis for a formal distinction

[89] J. Vanderlint, Money Answers all Things (London, 1734). *Cf.* Seligman, *op. cit.*, p. 22.

[90] Serious Considerations on the Several High Duties (1743). *Cf.* Seligman, *op. cit.*, pp. 17, 18; Palgrave, Dictionary of Political Economy, Vol. I, p. 519. The writer has been unable to secure a copy of this work. Decker also wrote Essay on the Cause of the Decline of the Foreign Trade (1744). This is contained in McCulloch's Select Collection of Scarce and Valuable Tracts on Commerce (London, 1859). In this later publication the terms direct and indirect do not occur.

[91] Essay on Taxes (1752). See Essays, Moral, Political, and Literary, by David Hume, Vol. I, p. 358 (London, 1882).

[92] Universal Dictionary of Trade and Commerce, Vol. II, p. 785 (London, 1755).

[93] Great Britain's True System, p. 307 (London, 1757).

[94] Inquiry into the Principles of Political Economy (1767). *Cf.* Works of Sir James Steuart (London, 1805).

[95] *Ibid.*, Vol. IV, pp. 173-175.

between direct and indirect taxes but does not use those terms. On the contrary, he uses the words directly and indirectly in a non-technical sense that is opposed to any such scientific distinction.[96] Finally, it should be noted that J. Cunningham, in the two works in which he discussed taxation, did not use the terms direct or indirect and did not classify taxes.[97]

To Adam Smith, or, more properly, to the influence of the Physiocrats upon Adam Smith, is due the use in England of the terms direct and indirect taxes. Although Smith was familiar with the works of Bodin and Montesquieu,[98] he had not, as late as 1763, adopted such expressions. In his lectures of that year he made the following classification: (1) taxes upon consumption; (2) taxes upon possessions, as land, stock, money.[99] Here the terms direct and indirect do not occur. In February, 1764, Smith started upon his journey to France, where he remained two years and a half. There he became acquainted with Turgot and other Physiocrats, and attended the meetings of the sect.[100] Although he rejected their doctrines of taxation, and could not have classified taxes as they did, he nevertheless retained the words direct and indirect taxes, using them in his most famous work. An examination of the passages in the *Wealth of Nations*, where these terms occur, leads to the following results:

(1) Smith did not formally classify taxes as direct and indirect. The classification adopted by him is: (*a*) taxes on rent; (*b*) taxes on profits; (*c*) taxes on wages; (*d*) taxes which fall indifferently upon all three kinds of revenues. In this last class he placed, first, capitation taxes and, second, taxes on expenditure.[101]

[96] Inquiry into the Principles of Political Economy, Vol. IV, p. 318. Here Steuart speaks of the impossibility of the land tax being shifted "directly," and considers whether it may be shifted "indirectly."

[97] Essay on Trade and Commerce, Containing Observations on Taxes (London, 1770). This contains the substance of an earlier work on taxes.

[98] See Bonar, Catalogue of the Library of Adam Smith, pp. 14, 70. Bielfeld's Institutions politiques was also in Smith's library. See Catalogue, p. 13.

[99] Lectures on Justice, Police, Revenue, and Arms, p. 239. (Edited by E. Cannan. Oxford, 1896).

[100] John Rae, Life of Adam Smith, pp. 174, 202, 215, 216 (London, 1895).

[101] Wealth of Nations. Edited by J. E. T. Rogers, Vol. II, pp. 413, 414 (2d ed., Oxford, 1880).

(2) The terms direct and indirect, as used by Smith, did not refer to the incidence of taxes. He applied the term direct to taxes upon the profits of stock and upon the wages of common labor, all of which, he held, are regularly shifted.[102]

(3) The distinction which Smith commonly had in mind seems to have been based upon the methods followed in the assessment of taxes. This will be evident from the following passages. He speaks of stock "taxed directly," "in proportion to the whole profit."[103] Again, he says that transfers of immovable property may be taxed directly, but that transfers of movables can be taxed only indirectly, either by stamp duties on legal instruments or by requiring a registration of such transactions and imposing duties upon registration.[104] In all these cases he considers taxes direct when they are assessed according to revenue or property. When Smith first uses the word indirect, he says: "The state, not knowing how to tax, directly and proportionably, the revenue of its subjects, endeavors to tax it indirectly by taxing their expense."[105] He therefore considers indirect taxes to be those which are assessed in proportion to expense. In accordance with this distinction, he speaks, in other places,[106] of direct taxes upon salaries of public officials; while he calls capitation taxes on "the lower ranks of people" direct taxes upon the wages of labor; and considers taxes upon interest and rent to be levied directly.

(4) But Smith suggested, in one passage,[107] another idea which was to be used by subsequent writers in defining direct and indirect taxes. He said that capitation taxes and taxes upon consumable commodities are imposts "which it is intended should fall indifferently upon every different species of revenue." The intention of the legislator was to play an important part in subsequent definitions.

[102] See *Ibid.*, Vol. II, pp. 440, 441, 460, 463, 466.
[103] *Ibid.*, Vol. II, p. 440.
[104] *Ibid.*, Vol. II, p. 453.
[105] *Ibid.*, Vol. II, p. 466.
[106] *Ibid.*, Vol. II, pp. 441, 442, 463, 466.
[107] *Ibid.*, Vol. II, p. 463.

Even after these suggestions by Smith, the words direct and indirect taxes were slow in making their way into general use. Thomas Mortimer, who had published, in 1772, his *Elements of Commerce, Politics and Finance,* did not employ these terms in the second edition, which appeared in 1780. The same is true of Sinclair in the various editions of his work upon the *Public Revenue.*[108] The words do not occur in the *Enquiry into the Principles of Taxation,* published anonymously, at Dublin, in 1791, although the incidence of taxes upon consumption is here discussed at some length. There were at that time, moreover, no settled meanings for such words as duties, excises, etc. The law of 1799, establishing Pitt's income tax, is entitled an act "granting certain duties upon income."[109] Similar terms are used in subsequent income tax acts,[110] and in the *Annual Register* for 1803.[111]

The slowness of the process by which the distinction between direct and indirect taxes gained general acceptance is shown in the various editions of the *Encyclopædia Britannica.* The first edition, published at Edinburgh in 1771, contained merely a brief treatment of the subject of taxation. The second and third editions, published in 1778 and 1797, show no trace of the influence of Smith's views. But the fourth edition, published in 1810, contains an article, nearly twelve pages in length, by Hugh Murray. Taxes are classified as follows: (1) assessed taxes,[112] "those which the subject is required to pay directly into the hands of the sovereign or commonwealth," *e.g.* income, capitalization and property taxes; (2) taxes upon commodities, which "are paid, in the first instance, not by the consumer, but by the producer, or importer," and "fall upon consumption."

In 1804 W. Frend[113] applied the term indirect taxation to

[108] J. Sinclair, History of the Public Revenue (Dublin, 1785; 3d ed., 1803).

[109] 39 George III, c. 13.

[110] 43 George III, c. 122.

[111] *Annual Register,* 1803, p. 633 (London, 1805).

[112] This term has no reference to the "assessed taxes" of the English tax acts. Murray considers the latter as merely one kind of the assessed taxes of his general classification.

[113] Principles of Taxation, p. 49 (London, 1804).

customs and excise duties. Ten years later John Craig[114] formally defined direct and indirect taxes in such a way as to suggest the influence of Murray's article in the *Encyclopædia*. Craig said that direct taxes are "paid without recourse on others"; while indirect taxes "affect the enjoyments of persons altogether different from those by whom the money is originally advanced." Yet Ricardo, writing in 1817, did not formally classify taxes as direct and indirect. Although he sometimes made use of these terms, it seems to be impossible to reconcile the various passages of Ricardo's writings in which such words occur with any one definition of direct and indirect taxes.[115] In 1821 James Mill[116] reverted to the usage of Adam Smith and spoke of "the direct mode of deriving a revenue" from rent, profits and wages, and of "the expedients . . . for deriving it from them indirectly." Thus Mill called taxes on rent, profits and wages direct; while he regarded taxes on commodities, etc., as indirect. From that time we may regard the distinction of direct and indirect taxes as established in English usage.

III

Without further consideration of the chronological details of its development, we may proceed to classify and examine critically the different views advanced concerning this distinction between direct and indirect taxes. Förstemann and Neumann have recognized three classes of definitions, exclusive of the Physiocratic usage;[117] but it seems impossible to reduce the divisions to so small a number, if all shades of opinion are to be included. In the following pages no attention has been paid to the long obsolete Physiocratic discussion. The reader will notice, also, that the names of some writers appear in more than

[114] Elements of Political Science, Vol. III, p. 12 (Edinburgh, 1814).

[115] See Principles of Political Economy and Taxation (1817) in McCulloch's edition of Works of Ricardo (London, 1886). See pp. 93-95, 119, 123, 141, 142, 144, 145. For example, on p. 141 Ricardo says that a rich consumer would pay a tax directly if it "were laid on income, on wine or on any other luxury."

[116] Elements of Political Economy (1821). See p. 241 (2d ed., London, 1824).

[117] Förstemann, p. 9; Neumann, pp. 425, 426.

one of the groups. This is because some economists have expressed different opinions in their various works, or have attempted to base upon several characteristics their definitions of direct and indirect taxes.

(1) The first of our groups of definitions is the oldest and the most familiar of all. Direct taxes are said to be those which are collected, in the first instance, from the persons who are to bear them, while indirect taxes are those which are collected from persons who shift the burden upon others. This distinction is an elaboration of the idea contained in the old expression, "to pay taxes directly or indirectly," and was first developed by the Physiocrats into a scientific classification of taxes. When the doctrines of the French school were finally overthrown, the terms direct and indirect remained in use,[118] and were employed by writers who believed that other taxes besides the tax upon the income from land were finally borne by the payer upon whom they were first placed. With the further development of the theory of the shifting of taxation, the classification of taxes as direct and indirect, according to their final incidence, remained a favorite one with students of finance.[119]

Such a classification seems to be logically clear and con-

[118] In Germany, in 1808, Theodor Schmalz, "the last Physiocrat," insisted that these expressions had no meaning apart from the Physiocratic doctrine of taxation.—Quoted by Cohn, Finanzwissenschaft, p. 441.

[119] D. H. Eschenmayer, Vorschlag zu einem einfachen Steuer-Systeme, p. 12 (Heidelberg, 1808); B. F. B. Weber, Lehrbuch der politischen Oekonomie, Vol. II (Breslau, 1813), quoted by Förstemann, pp. 21, 22; J. Craig, Elements of Political Science, Vol. III, p. 12 (Edinburgh, 1814); L. H. von Jakob, Staatsfinanzwissenschaft, Vol. I, p. 420 (Halle, 1821); W. Phillips, Manual of Political Economy, p. 276 (Boston, 1828); J. Schön, Grundsätze der Finanz, p. 86 (Breslau, 1832); H. Passy, "Impôt," in Dictionnaire de l'économie politique, Vol. I, p. 901 (Paris, 1852); R. E. Thompson, Social Science and National Economy, pp. 193, 194 (Philadelphia, 1875); H. Fawcett, Manual of Political Economy, p. 547 (5th ed., London, 1876); J. E. T. Rogers, Manual of Political Economy, chs. xxi, xxii (Oxford, 1876); J. L. Laughlin, Elements of Political Economy, p. 273 (New York, 1887); K. Umpfenbach, Lehrbuch der Finanzwissenschaft, p. 195 (2d ed., Stuttgart, 1887); C. Gide, Principles of Political Economy, p. 563 (Amer. trans., Boston, 1892). M. H. Baudrillart, Manuel d'économie politique, p. 501 (4th ed., Paris, 1878), combines this classification, to some extent, with the administrative classification discussed in the next group. W. Roscher, Finanzwissenschaft, p. 155, is inclined to follow this definition.

sistent. Moreover, it is based upon a most important economic fact. If our actual taxes could be classified with certainty as direct and indirect, the definition would prove most useful. But, unfortunately, it was soon apparent that difficulties must arise at just this point. Von Jakob pointed out, in 1821, that a wine tax might be direct, if collected from the consumer, and indirect, if collected from tradesmen or producers. The same is true, of course, of import duties. When consumers import goods directly, without resorting to middlemen, customs duties may be collected from the persons who finally bear them. But, more than this, the facts of incidence are often uncertain or varying. A house tax is surely direct, if the owner is also the occupier; but it may be shifted from the owner upon a tenant, especially if it is an exclusive tax. Such considerations long ago made it apparent that many taxes could not with scientific accuracy be assigned a definite place, in a classification based upon the actual facts of incidence.

A realization of this difficulty led to a modification in this definition of direct and indirect taxes: the supposition or intention of the taxing authorities was substituted for the actual facts of incidence. John Stuart Mill may represent the advocates of such a modification. He wrote:

> A direct tax is one which is demanded from the very persons who, it is intended or desired, should pay it. Indirect taxes are those which are demanded from one person in the expectation and intention that he shall indemnify himself at the expense of another. . . .

Such definitions as this have during the last forty years gained wide acceptance.[120]

[120] E. Baumstark, Kameralistische Encyclopädie, Sec. 487 (Heidelberg, 1835); K. S. Zachariä, Abhandlungen aus dem Gebiete der Staatswirthschaftslehre, p. 29 (Heidelberg, 1835); J. S. Mill, Principles of Political Economy, bk. v, ch. iii, Sec. 1 (London, 1848); K. H. Rau, Grundsätze der Finanzwissenschaft, Vol. I, pp. 441, 442 (5th ed., Leipzig, 1864); C. J. Bergius, Grundsätze der Finanzwissenschaft, pp. 263, 264 (Berlin, 1865); A. Walker, Science of Wealth, p. 312 (Boston, 1866); F. Bowen, American Political Economy, p. 436 (New York, 1870); A. L. Perry, Elements of Political Economy, p. 585 (New York, 1878); P. Leroy-Beaulieu, Traité de la science des finances, Vol. I, pp. 225, 226 (4th ed., Paris, 1888); H. Denis, L'impôt, pp. 136, 137 (Brussels, 1889); J. A. R. Helferich, in Schönberg's Handbuch der politischen Oekonomie, Vol. III, pp. 155, 156 (3d ed., Tübingen,

But this formulation of the distinction between direct and indirect taxes is open to criticism. It is urged correctly that the intention of the legislator is "too uncertain an element for the characterization of a scientific conception."[121] It is asked whether Congress intended to burden the producer or the consumer by the tax formerly imposed on bottles of patent medicine, and for whose benefit the tax was repealed. We must concede that the legislator often has considered not at all the incidence of taxes, but merely the easiest or quickest way of raising money. Moreover, it is certain that tax laws do not always operate in accordance with the expectations or intentions of the legislator. While Wagner[122] is right in claiming that the intention of the legislator has been an important element in shaping reforms in modern tax systems, it is true that the uncertainties of this classification are so great as to leave it no strict scientific validity.

This definition, accordingly, has been subjected to a second modification. Admitting that direct taxes are occasionally shifted from the people whom they are supposed to burden upon persons whom they are not assumed to reach, and conceding that our knowledge of the facts of incidence is sometimes insufficient to enable us to be certain that direct taxes will stay where they are first placed, it is claimed, nevertheless, that we may retain with advantage the distinction based upon the incidence of taxation. Thus Bastable writes:

Whether a duty is assessed directly on the ultimate bearer or is passed through various intermediaries before reaching him, may not be capable of being precisely determined in all cases. There are no hard and fast lines in fact, and the instances on the margin may be

---

1897); J. S. Nicholson, Principles of Political Economy, Vol. I, p. 214 (New York and London, 1893); K. T. Eheberg, Finanzwissenschaft, p. 150 (4th ed., Leipzig, 1895). Perhaps we should include here S. Newcomb, Principles of Political Economy, pp. 484, 485 (New York, 1885). J. Garnier, Traité de finances, pp. 47, 48 (4th ed., Paris, 1883), combines, in part, this distinction with the administrative classification mentioned in the second group.

[121] R. T. Ely, Taxation in American States and Cities, p. 67 (New York, 1888). See also Neumann, pp. 485 *et seq.*

[122] Finanzwissenschaft, Vol. II, pp. 244, 245 (2d ed., Leipzig, 1890).

numerous, but if we take the terms, not as giving a complete classification of taxes, but as marking the presence or absence of a certain characteristic, they may be employed with advantage, but rather to suggest reasons for discrimination than to definitely settle results.[123]

This is to admit that actual imposts can not be fitted into our distinction with absolute scientific accuracy. But there may still remain a justification for using the terms in this sense, to denote large groups of taxes that possess normally, in a large majority of cases, the same important characteristics. No error or confusion can arise, if care is taken to note all possible exceptional cases. Wagner well says:

In the most important practical cases this is not disputed. Income taxes, property taxes, direct taxes on luxuries, many taxes on transactions and inheritance taxes are demanded and formulated because we believe that we can assume, as a rule, that they finally fall on the payer and therefore are direct. Customs duties and internal excise duties are demanded and formulated in a given manner because we presuppose that they do not finally fall upon the actual payer, except in so far as he is also the consumer, but are shifted by him . . . upon the consumer.[124]

(2) The second group of definitions may be designated the administrative classification. According to it, direct taxes are those levied at stated periods by means of assessment rolls of names; while indirect are levied only under certain circumstances or situations, and by means of tariffs or schedules of charges.

The earliest suggestion of such a classification is probably found in an *instruction* issued by the French Constituent Assembly in January, 1790. This defined a direct tax as follows: "*Toute imposition . . . qui se lève par les voies du cadastre ou des rôles de cotisations.*"[125] This was practically repeated in the *Code des Contributions*[126] in 1811. French financial practice has

[123] Bastable, Public Finance, p. 326 (2d ed., London and New York, 1895). See also T. E. Cliffe Leslie, Essay on Financial Reform, Cobden Club Essays, Second Series, p. 188 (London, 1872).

[124] Wagner, Finanzwissenschaft, Vol. II, p. 244.

[125] Handwörterbuch der Staatswissenschaften, Vol. VI, p. 97.

[126] Neumann, p. 431.

retained a similar classification down to the present day,[127] while German administrative terminology has sometimes been influenced by the same idea.[128] Among economists, a number of French and German writers have followed this distinction,[129] and in France it has been used rather more often than any other.

This distinction is primarily of administrative importance. Its usefulness for economic purposes has never been demonstrated, as Block and Courcelle-Seneuil have admitted. The mode of administration is clearly an external matter that has little or nothing to do with the intrinsic nature and economic effects of tax systems. We may therefore reject this distinction as useless for purposes of economic investigation.

Moreover, it can be shown that the administrative definition leads to a grouping of taxes that is positively harmful for economic purposes. On this basis, taxes upon successions and gifts must be classified, with customs and excise duties, as indirect taxes. This is actually done in the administrative nomenclature of Prussia, Bavaria and Baden.[130] Little reflection is necessary to show the unfortunate results that must arise from grouping together taxes which differ so diametrically in their purpose, as well as in their economic effects.

Again, it may be noted, certain taxes do not always accommo-

[127] See M. Block, Dictionnaire de l'administration française, p. 1087 (2d ed., Paris, 1881); L. Say, Dictionnaire d'économie politique, Vol. II, p. 25 (Paris, 1891).

[128] Neumann, pp. 434-436; Handwörterbuch der Staatswissenschaften, Vol. VI, p. 97.

[129] L. F. Wiederhold, Wissenschaft der indirekten Steuern (Marburg, 1820), quoted by Neumann, p. 438; F. G. Schimmelpfennig, Die preussischen direkten Steuern (1831), quoted by Neumann, p. 439; F. J. Schmitthenner, Grundlinien des allgemeinen Staatsrechtes (Giessen, 1843, 1845), quoted by Neumann, p. 439; K. F. Dieterici, Ergebnisse der Verwaltung (1849), quoted by Neumann, p. 440; M. H. Baudrillart, Manuel d'économie politique, p. 501 (4th ed., Paris, 1878); E. de Parieu, Traité des impôts, Vol. I, p. 10 (Paris, 1866); J. G. Courcelle-Seneuil, Traité d'économie politique, Vol. I, p. 452 (2d ed., Paris, 1867); J. Garnier, Traité de finances, pp. 47, 48 (4th ed., Paris, 1883); M. Block, Progrès de la science économique depuis Adam Smith, p. 415 (Paris, 1890); P. Cauwès, Cours d'économie politique, Vol. IV, p. 293 (3d ed., Paris, 1893).

[130] See Wagner, in Schönberg's Handbuch der politischen Oekonomie, Vol. III, p. 169; Neumann, p. 435; Wagner, Finanzwissenschaft, Vol. II, p. 241.

date themselves to the administrative classification. Von Hock[131] has urged that some duties on consumption, which according to this definition are indirect taxes, may be paid by composition, and may therefore become direct in the administrative sense. Such cases are exceptional, and it may be claimed that the definition need consider only the conditions that prevail in a majority of cases. This may be conceded, as it was in the first classification of direct and indirect taxes; but it remains true that all actual taxes cannot be fitted into the administrative definition with perfect scientific accuracy.

A final point demands consideration. Baudrillart[132] and Garnier[133] have attempted to combine, in some measure, the administrative classification with the one based on the incidence of taxes. Such a procedure is manifestly impossible. Taxes upon inheritances or gifts are certainly direct, within the meaning of the first definition; while they are surely indirect, according to the criteria established by the administrative classification. In the case of these taxes the two definitions do not correspond at all, and they should not be combined.

(3) The third classification relates to the nature of the objects taxed—of the things which are made the bases of assessments. A. de Foville has stated it as follows:

> A direct tax reaches in the payer taxable elements which are of a durable, constant and continuous character, such as existence, possession or profession. To exist, to possess, to carry on trade or industry, these are permanent facts. . . . Indirect taxes do not reach qualities or possessions, but circumstances, particular or intermittent facts.[134]

In 1811 F. J. H. von Soden defined direct taxes as those which reach an object, and indirect as casual imposts which depend upon circumstances or events. In 1829 J. G. Hoffmann

[131] Die öffentlichen Abgaben und Schulden, p. 89 (Stuttgart, 1863). Wagner, Finanzwissenschaft, Vol. II, pp. 241, 242, has presented other difficulties of a similar sort.

[132] Manuel d'économie politique, p. 501.

[133] Traité de finances, pp. 47, 48.

[134] Quoted by R. Stourm, Systèmes généraux d'impôts, p. 281 (Paris, 1893).

wrote that direct taxes reach something that is, while indirect reach something that happens. In Germany, Murhard and Neumann, and in France, Parieu, de Foville and Stourm, have favored similar definitions.[135]

This distinction seems logically clear and admissible. But it is based upon criteria which, when applied to the facts of economic life, enable us to distinguish, in most cases, differences in degree of permanence only, not differences in the nature of the objects taxed. For this reason the practical application of the definition is not so easy as it might appear at first thought. Thus, production is considered to be a permanent or continuous fact, when taxes are classified upon the basis of this distinction. But it seems clear that a man's general activities in consumption constitute a fact of equal permanence, and that a general excise on consumption must be a direct tax within the meaning of the definition. Again, the systematic importation of raw materials from a foreign country seems to be a permanent and continuous part of the conduct of many productive enterprises. Why, then, are we not obliged to classify customs duties upon such materials as direct? Are they not imposed upon elements that are as permanent or continuous as the products, or net produce, upon which product taxes (*Ertragssteuern*) are levied?

The writers who favor this distinction consider that the use of a person's property or faculties in economic production is a fact of a permanent nature, and call taxes direct when they are levied on income or business.[136] It would seem that all taxes levied on producers as such, or upon goods regularly turned out by producers, must be considered direct, if this definition is to be consistently applied. This would necessitate the classification of excise taxes as direct when they are levied upon pro-

[135] F. J. H. von Soden, Die Staatsfinanzwissenschaft, p. 283 (Leipzig, 1811); J. G. Hoffmann, in *Preussische Staatszeitung*, Nr. 304, 1829; also in Nachlass kleiner Schriften, pp. 461-471 (Berlin, 1847); K. Murhard, Theorie und Politik der Besteuerung, pp. 170-173 (Göttingen, 1834); E. de Parieu, Traité des impôts, Vol. I, p. 118 (2d ed., Paris, 1866); Neumann, ch. x; R. Stourm, in Dictionnaire d'économie politique, Vol. II, p. 26.

[136] See Neumann, pp. 426-446.

ducers, as is the case with duties on beer, spirits and tobacco in the United States.

The adoption of this definition has never led to results that can be considered important for the investigation of economic questions. Further than this, it seems obvious that a grouping of taxes according to the criteria here suggested leads to unusual and even harmful consequences. By this method of classification we are compelled to call many customs and excise duties direct, while taxes upon inheritances and gifts must be considered indirect. Such a grouping under a common name of taxes whose economic effects are so diverse cannot conduce to scientific insight.

Some economists, as Stourm and Neumann, have sought to combine this third classification with the second, or administrative, definition of direct and indirect taxes. They hold that taxes on permanent facts are collected by means of periodical assessments and rolls of names, while taxes on intermittent facts are levied by tariffs of charges. This combination of the two definitions is inadmissible. Excise taxes levied upon producers, or upon commodities as they are produced, are imposed upon relatively stable and permanent facts, as has been shown. Such duties must be called direct, in the sense of the third definition. But in their collection tariffs of charges, not assessment rolls, may be employed; so that they must be considered indirect in the administrative classification. The same is true of such customs duties as strike regular and continuous importations.

(4) According to a fourth definition, direct taxes fall upon possession and indirect reach consumption. This classification considers the objects upon which taxes are levied—that is, things possessed or things consumed—and does not refer to the sources of taxation. It has been adopted by a number of economists in various countries.[137]

[137] F. J. H. von Soden, Die Nationalökonomie, Vol. III, p. 155 (Leipzig, 1805-1808); F. C. Fulda, Handbuch der Finanzwissenschaft, Sec. 154 (Tübingen, 1827); J. G. Hoffmann, Lehre von den Steuern, pp. 69-73 (Berlin, 1840); W. Roscher, Grundriss der Staatswissenschaften, p. 101 (1843); M. von Prittwitz, Theorie der Steuern und Zölle, p. 176 (Stuttgart, 1842); F. Wayland, Elements

This distinction may be assailed upon logical grounds. Possession and consumption, things possessed and things consumed, are not logical opposites. Our possessions include both capital goods, used in the process of production, and durable consumption goods, such as dwelling houses, furniture, clothing, carriages, etc. These durable consumption goods are not to be distinguished from food or fuel, except in respect of the length of time required to destroy or consume the satisfactions which they can afford. No scientific distinction can be based upon the criteria offered by this definition.

The objection just raised is fatal to such a classification, but it may also be pointed out that the definition is not sufficiently inclusive. In this grouping poll taxes can find no place. They are imposed upon persons as persons, not upon either possession or consumption as such. They may be paid by sacrificing property or by retrenching in one's consumption, but not necessarily in either way. Moreover, this definition considers, not the source whence arise the resources for paying the tax, but merely the objects upon which imposts are levied. The same difficulty occurs with inheritance taxes, which fall not upon property as such, but upon particular transfers of property. Similarly, taxes on sales occasion trouble. They are imposed upon acts, not upon property or consumption as such.

Some of these difficulties have been met by changing slightly the basis of the definition. Thus Soden, Levasseur and Cauwès include persons with property as the objects upon which direct taxes fall. Such a procedure may provide a place for poll taxes, but it does not obviate the difficulties that arise from the fact that possession and consumption are not logically opposite

of Political Economy, p. 391 (4th ed., Boston, 1851); E. Levasseur, Précis d'économie politique, p. 345 (Paris, 1883). E. Peshine Smith implies a similar distinction in his Manual of Political Economy, p. 265 (Philadelphia, 1853). E. Sax, Grundlegung der theoretischen Staatswirthschaft, p. 544 (Vienna, 1887), is perhaps to be classified with this group of writers, in spite of the pains he has taken to make his ideas appear so involved as to differentiate him from other economists. Finally, P. Cauwès brings this distinction into his definition of direct and indirect taxes: see his Cours d'économie politique, Vol. IV, p. 293 (3d ed., Paris, 1893).

terms. The same is true of Fulda's attempt to include income with possession as the basis of direct taxation.

Sometimes the word actions has been substituted for consumption, as in the cases of Soden, Hoffmann, Roscher, Prittwitz and Levasseur. Probably this has been done in order to make a place for taxes on sales, gifts, inheritances and various imposts on transactions. This change makes the definition more inclusive, but does not remedy the original logical difficulty. As applied to consumption, actions cannot be the logical opposite of possessions. My actions in acquiring and using a dwelling house differ from my actions in acquiring and using fuel only in respect of the length of time over which the use may extend. However this definition may be amended, it seems absolutely untenable.

(5) The fifth group of distinctions is based upon the opposition between production and consumption. Taxes which reach production are held to be direct, and imposts upon consumption are called indirect. Such a definition was partially formulated by Schlözer, in 1805, and has been adopted by several later economists.[138]

This distinction seems to be founded upon ideas that are logical opposites, but it cannot be made inclusive of all taxes. Poll taxes do not fall primarily upon production or consumption. Taxes on inheritances and gifts cannot, by any use of these terms, be brought under such a classification. Other difficulties arise when it is attempted to classify certain important kinds of imposts. Taxes on property that is not used in production certainly fall upon consumption goods. Hence, upon this basis, indirect taxes must include taxes upon dwelling houses, furniture, etc.—a result that is highly unusual and unfortunate. Taxes upon transfers must cause further trouble. These may be

[138] C. von Schlözer, Staatswirthschaft, p. 167 (1805), quoted by Neumann, p. 417; J. B. Montyon, Quelle influence ont les diverses espèces d'impôts? (Paris, 1808), contained in Mélanges d'économie politique, Vol. II, pp. 365-496 (Paris, 1848); J. F. E. Lotz, Handbuch der Staatswirthschaftslehre, Vol. III, p. 176 (Erlangen, 1821); T. C. Banfield, The Organization of Industry, p. 136 (London, 1848); P. De Luca, La Scienza delle finanze (Naples, 1858). See Ricca-Salerno, pp. 548, 549.

collected either from producers or consumers. While they may ultimately tend to burden the consumer, this definition does not allow us to consider the facts of incidence and to classify such imposts as taxes on consumption. Again, it is impossible to determine where taxes on checks or bills of exchange should be placed. These may be paid by producers or consumers in the first instance, and we are not allowed to consider their final incidence. It is clear, therefore, that the fifth definition offers no certain or useful classification of taxes.

(6) The sixth method of classification contrasts income and expenditure. It groups taxes that fall upon income under the head of direct taxes and applies the term indirect to imposts that fall upon consumption. This definition is found in the writings of Canard and Say, as well as in recent works upon finance.[139] This grouping of taxes is somewhat similar to that based upon the opposition between production and consumption; but it is more inclusive, since it makes a place for taxes on inheritances, gifts and all possible forms of acquisition. Perhaps even poll taxes may be considered as uniform taxes upon income. Moreover, this classification seems to be based upon criteria that are clearly logical opposites. Nevertheless, it is open to criticism in some directions.

First, it may be shown that some taxes fall, now upon income, now upon expenditure. Taxes upon checks and bills of exchange may certainly lead to such results. The same is true of many other taxes on transactions. Excise taxes, when collected from producers, fall primarily upon the acquisition of income. Such

[139] N. F. Canard, Principes d'économie politique, p. 154 (Paris, 1801); J. B. Say, Political Economy, Vol. II, p. 268 (1st Amer. ed., Boston, 1821); L. Cagnazzi, Elementi di economia politica (Naples, 1813); see Ricca-Salerno, pp. 461, 462. C. A. von Malchus, Handbuch der Finanzwissenschaft, Vol. I, p. 168 (Stuttgart, 1830); F. Lieber, in Encyclopædia Americana, Vol. XII, p. 155 (Philadelphia, 1832); C. Rusconi, Prolegomeni della economia politica (Turin, 1852); see Ricca-Salerno, p. 538. Perhaps, also, we should place in this group of writers, J. Mill, Elements of Political Economy, p. 241 (2d ed., London, 1824); J. R. McCulloch, The Principles of Taxation, Vol. I (London, 1845). L. von Stein holds that direct taxes fall upon net income, while indirect are imposed upon expenditure. Then he adds, as a third kind of impost, the general income tax.—Lehrbuch der Finanzwissenschaft, Vol. II, p. 499 (5th ed., Leipzig, 1885).

imposts may regularly be shifted upon consumers and may be called taxes on consumption. But this definition does not allow for the ultimate incidence of taxation; and, if this should be attempted, would lead to most singular consequences. Therefore, some excise taxes must be considered direct in this classification.

In the second place, the definition provides no satisfactory place for taxes on durable consumers' goods. If these are not a source of income, then imposts levied upon them must be considered as indirect; and thus taxes on houses and many other forms of property become indirect taxes—a result not contemplated or desired by the advocates of this definition. It may be argued, however, that such goods are a relatively permanent investment from which the owner draws part of his annual income, in the form of satisfactions derived from the use of such consumers' goods. But such a claim does not entirely remedy the difficulty. House taxes may be collected from occupiers in all cases, and many of the occupiers may be tenants. Such taxes, therefore, fall primarily upon the tenant's expenditure and must be considered indirect. In this case we are prevented by the definition from considering the question of final incidence; but, if this should be regarded, we know that house taxes often fall upon tenants—regularly so, in fact, if the taxes are exclusive and not parts of a general property tax. There seem to be sufficiently strong reasons, therefore, for rejecting as useless, if not misleading, this sixth definition of direct and indirect taxes.

(7) A seventh definition has been developed, perhaps out of ideas suggested by the last classification. It has been held that direct taxes reach ascertained ability to bear public burdens and therefore strike wealth in its immediate manifestations, while indirect taxes are based upon the mere presumption of such ability and touch wealth in its secondary manifestations. In the first case, the ability is ascertained directly; in the second case, indirectly and by inference from some external sign. Persons, property and income are considered the immediate manifestations of wealth, while transfers of property and acts of consumption are the mediate manifestations. Perhaps a suggestion of

such a definition is found in the following words of Adam Smith: "The state, not knowing how to tax, directly and proportionably, the revenue of its subjects, endeavors to tax it indirectly by taxing their expense."[140] Possibly one of Say's works has influenced somewhat the more recent writers who have developed this distinction.[141]

Such a definition seems logically clear and unassailable, but its scientific value must depend upon the ease with which actual taxes fit into the classification and upon the results obtained by a rigorous adherence to the criteria established for our guidance. Here objections arise at the very start. The various manifestations of wealth upon which taxes are assessed cannot be sharply divided into mediate and immediate. The possession of a funded income may be a more immediate manifestation of wealth than the purchase of common food and fuel, but in many instances the line cannot be so readily drawn.

Let us consider a few such cases. Is the possession of a dwelling house a more immediate manifestation of wealth than the purchase and use of such luxuries as velvets, diamonds or champagne? Is not such a transfer of property as is involved in inheritances or gifts an immediate manifestation of ability to pay taxes? Yet, in this definition, it is proposed to consider taxes on transfers as indirect. Is the ownership of property always a source of income and an immediate manifestation of ability? Clearly not, for men may be "land poor" and many investments may prove unproductive. In cases like these a property tax is

[140] *Wealth of Nations* (Rogers's ed.), Vol. II, p. 466.

[141] J. B. Say, Cours complet d'économie politique, Vol. III, p. 401 (ed. by H. Say, Paris, 1852); J. J. Clamageran, Histoire de l'impôt en France, Vol. I, pp. xiv, xv (Paris, 1867); Förstemann, *op. cit.*, pp. 12, 13; K. Knies, Lectures, quoted by R. T. Ely, Taxation in American States and Cities, p. 67; L. Cossa, Taxation, p. 66 (Amer. ed., New York, 1888); A. Roncali, Corso elementare, pp. 238, 239 (Parma, 1887). A. Schäffle distinguishes between direct and indirect methods of reaching a person's ability to pay taxes. According to him, direct taxes are assessed according to the measure of a person's average or general ability—that is, the size of a person's income; while indirect taxes reach facts connected with the processes of consumption or acquisition that indicate special or individualized ability. It is hard to see how this definition differs materially from those included in this class. At any rate, Schäffle classifies actual taxes in the same manner as Cossa and the other economists of this seventh group, calling taxes on inheritances, gifts, etc., indirect. See Die Steuern, Vol. I, pp. 58-73 (Leipzig, 1895).

levied upon the presumption that the possession of such property is a source of income. It seems impossible to call all possessions immediate manifestations of wealth or ability and to consider all transfers and consumption as mediate manifestations. Again, the advocates of this classification propose to consider the poll tax as direct, since they regard a person's existence as an immediate manifestation of ability. Here they do not adhere rigorously to the criteria established by their own definition. The uniform poll tax has been gradually discarded by civilized peoples, precisely because it does not regard differences in ability to bear public burdens. In its assessment the government does not consider manifestations of wealth, but proceeds on the assumption that the mere fact of existence implies ability to pay. Enough considerations have been adduced to show the impossibility of constructing a consistent and useful classification of taxes upon this basis.

(8) An eighth definition is based upon the old idea that imposts upon consumption are paid voluntarily, since they form part of the prices of commodities that citizens are free to purchase or to refrain from purchasing. Such a distinction between direct and indirect taxes was made as early as 1787.[142]

Criticisms of this distinction need be directed only at the alleged voluntary nature of indirect taxes, such as impost or excise duties and taxes upon transactions. Mill has shown that this notion is erroneous, and Leroy-Beaulieu has given it the *coup de grâce*.[143] Taxes on salt, sugar and staple articles of clothing cannot be altogether avoided by a retrenchment of one's consumption. In so far as the use of these articles is diminished, the imposition of the tax compels the citizen to sacrifice

[142] F. W. von Ulmenstein, Von Steuern und Abgaben, p. 161 (Erlangen, 1794); see Roscher, Finanzwissenschaft, p. 157; A. Ressi, Dell' Economia della specie umana (Pavia, 1820), quoted by Ricca-Salerno, p. 471; D. A. Wells, Principles of Taxation; see *Popular Science Monthly*, Vol. LI, pp. 173, 174 (New York, 1897). Förstemann, p. 27, quotes Prussian decisions, of the year 1837, to the same effect. In 1787 the same idea was advanced by Hugh Williamson, who wrote: "The capitation tax and land tax, such as are usual among us, are inevitable and positive taxes: they are not to be averted. . . . But the excise is a negative or indirect tax."—*American Museum*, Vol. II, p. 122 (Philadelphia, 1787).

[143] Principles of Political Economy, bk. v, ch. vi, Sec. 1; Traité de la science des finances, Vol. I, p. 279. *Cf.* Bastable, Public Finance, p. 330.

desired enjoyments. This is all that the payment of a direct tax necessitates, so that the position of the citizen is practically identical in both cases. The result is the same when taxes are levied solely upon so-called luxuries. Moreover, direct taxes can be avoided with equal readiness and in a similar manner. The citizen can live in a poor house located in an undesirable quarter, and can thereby avoid the direct tax levied upon the comfortable dwelling which he would otherwise have desired to occupy. He can cease to accumulate wealth, and may escape paying an income tax levied upon incomes that exceed five hundred dollars. Leroy-Beaulieu seems to be entirely justified in remarking: "*Mais, d'abord, c'est faire une plaisanterie que de dire que les impôts indirects soient volontaires.*"

(9) A ninth distinct group may be recognized, although it is of slight historical and even less scientific importance. Direct taxes are defined as those imposts which are demanded from citizens in definite amounts and indirect taxes as those paid according to special circumstances, without a determination of the exact sums due from each individual.[144] This definition has no significance for scientific purposes.

(10) Finally, it may be noted that our nine groups of definitions do not include all the economists who have employed this distinction. Thus, A. Marescotti[145] has defined direct taxes as imposts which fall upon immovables and indirect as imposts that reach movables—a definition which has no possible economic value and must lead to a most singular grouping of taxes.

Prof. R. T. Ely has retained the distinction, while he has appreciated the shortcomings of the various methods of formulating it. Without attempting to find a new scientific basis for the classification, he has called taxes direct when they reach

[144] G. H. Borowski combines this element with others in his definition of direct and indirect taxes. See Abriss des praktischen Kameral- und Finanzwesens (Berlin, 1799), quoted by Förstemann, p. 23. A. H. L. Heeren formulated the distinction more clearly in his Ideen über die Politik, Vol. I, p. 227 (2d ed., Göttingen, 1804), quoted by Förstemann, p. 23. M. von Prittwitz also used this definition in his Grenzen der Civilisation, p. 301 (2d ed., 1853), quoted by Förstemann, p. 24. Finally, J. B. Say and others have spoken of direct taxes as demands of definite portions of an individual's revenue, etc.; see Say, Treatise on Political Economy, Vol. II, p. 268 (1st Amer. ed.).

[145] Sulla economia sociale (Florence, 1856), quoted by Ricca-Salerno, p. 541.

real property or income and indirect when they are laid upon articles of drink, food and clothing. Around these principal taxes he has grouped as direct all taxes upon trades, occupations, persons and all forms of property except common articles of consumption, while he includes all imposts on transactions with the indirect taxes.[146] This classification seems to follow closely the usage that has been most common in the United States, and makes it possible to contrast the familiar points of difference in the effects of various forms of taxation; but it cannot be considered a rigorous, scientific definition.

IV

The difficulties and uncertainties of all attempted classifications have induced many economists to abandon altogether such a distinction. J. C. L. Simonde, as early as 1819, declared that the terms had no meaning outside of the Physiocratic doctrines.[147] A few years later Lieber, who offered a definition of direct and indirect taxes, admitted that the division was not a consistent one.[148] In 1862 Cherbuliez complained of the different meanings given to the words, and made no use of such a distinction.[149] Dudley Baxter then urged that the definition cannot furnish a trustworthy classification.[150] Henry Sidgwick abandoned the terms, considering that they were "liable to mislead the student, by ignoring the complexity and difficulty of the problem of determining the incidence of taxation."[151] W. Vocke adopted a similar course, because such a twofold division of taxes cannot be adjusted to his threefold grouping of public imposts.[152] Cohn says that, since the time of the Physiocrats, all writers have departed from this simple scheme of classification in proportion as they have acquired a greater knowledge of the facts of taxation.[153] Block concedes that the distinction has

[146] Taxation in American States and Cities, pp. 66-69.
[147] Principes d'économie politique, Vol. II, p. 479 (2d ed., Paris, 1827).
[148] Encyclopædia Americana, Vol. XII, p. 155.
[149] Précis de la science économique, Vol. II, p. 405 (Paris, 1862).
[150] Taxation of the United Kingdom, p. 21 (London, 1869).
[151] Principles of Poltical Economy, p. 567 (London, 1883).
[152] Die Abgaben, die Auflagen, und die Steuer, p. 7 (Stuttgart, 1887).
[153] Finanzwissenschaft, Secs. 326-332.

merely an administrative importance, while Cauwès holds that it is not precise enough to serve as a basis for a logical classification.[154] Most recently Eheberg has said that it would be best to abandon entirely this distinction.[155]

It has been shown that all attempts to distinguish direct from indirect taxes offer more or less serious difficulties and fail to attain that exactness and completeness which are necessary for purposes of strictly scientific definition. Some of the distinctions are not tenable for a moment; others promise well, but lead us into trouble sooner or later. Of all the definitions only those of the first group are based upon criteria that have sufficient economic importance to lead to useful scientific results. But the distinction here suggested cannot be applied with entire precision and consistency.

In view of such facts it would seem best for economists to abandon the terms direct and indirect taxes. But such a course is not free from difficulty. The words have been so long fixed in popular usage, and have been given such importance in administrative, and even constitutional, law, that it is doubtful whether the near future will see such a radical change effected in our terminology. Under such circumstances the economist may be obliged to retain these troublesome terms. If so, he should never fail to emphasize the difficulties and uncertainties of the definition. If such a compromise with popular and legal usage compels the retention of the distinction, it seems best to follow the definition based upon the usual and normal facts of incidence, as Wagner and Bastable have counseled. This definition offers convenient terms for describing large groups of taxes, and need not lead to error, if care is taken to consider individual cases. For American and English writers such a course offers a manifest advantage, in that it follows closely the usage that has prevailed since the early years of the present century.

[154] Progrès de la science économique, Vol. II, p. 415; Cours d'économie politique, Vol. IV, p. 346.

[155] Finanzwissenschaft, p. 153 (4th ed., Leipzig, 1895).

WAGE STATISTICS AND THE FEDERAL CENSUS[1]

IN THE United States, the Federal census presents the earliest official data concerning statistics of wages. The censuses of 1850 and 1860[2] made exactly the same inquiries upon this subject. In both cases the schedules[3] called for "the average number of hands employed," male and female, and the "average monthly cost" of male labor and of female.

It must be remembered that in these censuses, as well as in that of 1870, the enumeration was conducted by the United States marshals, who, upon their regular rounds, called upon manufacturers and gathered data. No prior schedules were used, and the marshals received only fifteen cents for each manufacturing establishment enumerated.[4] Under the circumstances the work of collecting data relating to employees and wages could not be carefully and intelligently done, except in the rarest cases, while the enumerators failed to visit any establishments that it seemed convenient to omit. No great value, therefore, can be attached to statistical tables based upon such uncertain materials.

In explanation of the schedules employed, the enumerators in the seventh census were given the following instructions.[5] "Under the general heading 'hands employed,' is to be inserted . . . the average number of each sex employed during the year in the manufacture or business. These numbers are to be esti-

[1] Reprinted from *American Economic Association, Publications,* New Series, No. 2, pp. 343-68. Reproduced by generous permission of the publishers.

[2] It is not necessary to refer to the questions asked in 1820 and 1840 concerning hands employed and total wages paid. For the schedules used in these censuses see Report on a Permanent Census Bureau, pp. 140, 145, Senate Executive Documents, Vol. I, 52d Congress, 1st Session.

[3] *Idem,* pp. 148, 152. See also Seventh Census, p. xxiv.

[4] See remarks of General Walker, in Ninth Census, Vol. 3, p. 391.

[5] Seventh Census, p. xxiv.

mated either by an average of the whole year, or by selecting a day when about an average number was employed, and inserting the number on such a day as the average." "Under heading 10 and 11, entitled 'Wages,' is to be inserted the average monthly amount paid for all the labor of all the hands, male and female, employed in the business or manufacture during the course of the year. In all cases where the employer boards the hands, the usual charge of board is to be added to the wages; so that cost of labor is always to mean the amount paid, whether in money, or partly in money and partly in board; and the average number of hands and the average monthly wages are to be returned, so that by dividing the latter by the former the result will show the average earnings of individuals. This is also to include the individual labor of a producer, working on his own account, whose productions are separately enumerated."

If the enumerators attempted to follow these instructions, it is evident that the average number of employees reported must be in most cases a mere estimate, not a true average. In the next place, the directions given for a determination of average monthly wages were highly unfortunate. In most cases the total yearly wages can be easily and quickly ascertained. To attempt to estimate average monthly wages with a staff of untrained and underpaid enumerators must lead only to confusion. Remembering, finally, that most of the marshals did their part of the work as carelessly and hastily as possible, we can conclude only that the number of hands employed and the average monthly wages could not have been ascertained with even reasonable accuracy. The average yearly earnings deduced from such data must have been grossly inaccurate. The study of subsequent censuses will serve to reinforce this conclusion concerning the wage statistics of 1850 and 1860.[6]

In addition to the materials just described, the seventh and eighth censuses provided, in the schedules of social statistics,

[6] In the census of 1850 the tables of manufactures have been found "arithmetically imperfect," but it is not known whether the errors are in the items, or the totals, or in both. See Ninth Census, Vol. 3, p. 393, note.

general questions concerning the average wages of farm hands, laborers, carpenters, and domestics.[7] In the eighth census the results were published.[8] Of course the answers consisted mainly of conjectural averages, and can possess but slight value, at least for purposes of comparison. In 1870 these inquiries were wisely omitted.

In 1870 the questions asked in the census schedules of manufactures were greatly changed, and alterations were made in the form of inquiry concerning employees and wages. General Garfield's report had recommended that a sharp separation of firm members and hired laborers should be enforced, and that the schedules should call for the "Amount of wages paid during the year."[9]

The wisdom of both recommendations is too apparent to need any discussion. The schedules finally adopted[10] called for the average number of hands employed, males above 16, females above 15, children and youth; and for the total amount paid in wages during the year.

In the ninth census, as in the eighth and seventh, the reports of the enumerators brought in results that were obviously defective. General Walker caused special investigation to be made by the Census Office, with the result that thousands of establishments omitted by the marshals were included in the report upon manufactures.[11] The final tables were admittedly defective, although much more complete than those of any previous census. This is apparent from the enormous increase in the total number of establishments reported.[12] We must now consider the

[7] Report on a Permanent Census Bureau, pp. 149, 153.

[8] Eighth Census, Mortality and Miscellaneous Statistics, p. 512.

[9] Report of Committee on Census, 1870, p. 55. House Report, Vol. 3, 41st Congress, 2d Session.

[10] Report on Permanent Census Bureau, p. 167; Ninth Census, Vol. 1, p. xxxi.

[11] Ninth Census, Vol. 3, p. 374.

[12] This number at each census was:

1850	123,025
1860	140,433
1870	252,148
1880	253,852
1890	355,415

Eleventh Census, Manufacturing Industries, Vol. 1, p. 67.

manner in which the statistics of wages were affected by the inclusion of this large number of establishments not previously enumerated. This is a matter of importance because the statistics collected by one census have been compared with those presented in the others. From such data, average rates of yearly earnings have been deduced, and misleading results have been reached.[13]

With the frankness characteristic of its superintendent, the Ninth Census states explicitly that the enumeration of industrial establishments had been much more thorough than ever before, although it was still far from complete. It was shown that in 1860 the census had returned, in its tables of occupations, 450,634 artisans employed as painters, carpenters, blacksmiths, and coopers.[14] Of these, only 39,389, or nine per cent, were accounted for in the statistics of manufacturing and mechanical pursuits. Now the total number of employees enrolled in the tables of all manufactures was 1,311,246. The omission of 411,000 skilled artisans in these four trades removed from the statistics of wages a number of high-priced laborers that amounted to 31 per cent of all the persons enumerated. The census returns showed an average wage of $289 for all persons employed: while carpenters received $429; painters, $415; blacksmiths, $307; and coopers, $311. It is evident, therefore, that the average wages computed from the eighth census are smaller than they would have been if these classes of skilled laborers had been more fully enumerated. Now in the ninth census General Walker took pains to secure more complete returns of persons employed in manufacturing and mechanical industries. As a result, 155,000 artisans were enumerated in these

[13] The census volumes usually have compared total wages paid and the aggregate number of hands employed from decade to decade. Prior to the eleventh census, the writer can find no actual computation of the average rate of wages of the entire country. See Eleventh Census, Manufacturing Industries, Vol. 1, p. 19. But many writers have computed average rates of wages from these census figures, and such computations have been widely quoted as official statistics. See Carroll D. Wright, in *Atlantic Monthly*, Vol. 80, p. 305, Industrial Evolution of the United States, p. 191; Mulhall, in *North America Review*, Vol. 160, p. 647; Jeans, in *Fortnightly Review*, Vol. 58, p. 752.

[14] Ninth Census, Vol. 3, p. 373.

trades as given in the statistics of manufactures. This was over 25 per cent of the whole number of such workmen included in the statistics of occupations. This fact, alone, must have tended to increase the average wage that has been deduced from the wage statistics of the ninth census, and to render difficult a comparison with the rates of the earlier censuses.

Great changes were introduced into the methods adopted by the tenth census in collecting the statistics of manufactures. The superintendent was authorized to withdraw the collection of such data from the regular enumerators, and to employ special agents where he considered such a method advisable. Accordingly, in 279 principal cities and towns, the statistics of manufactures were gathered by special agents.[15] As a result manufacturing establishments in these largest industrial centers were more fully enumerated than ever before.

From the copies of the schedules that have been published[16] it would appear that the tenth census asked for the "total amount paid in wages during the year" and the "average number of hands employed," males above 16, females above 15, children and youths. These questions were the same as those used in the preceding census. In addition, the tenth census called for the "greatest number of hands employed at any one time during the year," and asked for estimates concerning the "average day's wages" for a skilled mechanic and for an ordinary laborer. Such answers as were received to these last questions seem not to have been published.

Is it evident that the superintendent of the tenth census thought that the statistics gathered concerning the number of hands employed represented the average number for the census year.[17] But this was clearly a mistake. An examination of the original schedules of the tenth census has shown that the figures of the average number of hands employed, for nearly one-half of the establishments, were the same as the greatest number of hands employed at any one time during the year. In the re-

[15] Tenth Census, Vol. 2, p. viii.
[16] Report on Permanent Census Bureau, p. 167.
[17] Tenth Census, Vol. 2, p. xxviii.

maining establishments the statistics of the average number of hands represented the number employed during the weeks of the busiest season. As a result, the tenth census failed to get the average number of persons employed in manufactures; and, instead, secured a number "almost always more than the average and often several times the average."[18] This is conceded in the eleventh census, which states:[19] "The questions used in 1880 tended to obtain a number of employees that would be in excess of the true average, while it is believed that the questions used in 1890 have obtained, as nearly as possible, the average number."

A comparison of the tenth census with the Massachusetts census of 1885 will make it evident that the tenth census secured a number of employees far in excess of the average number. The Massachusetts census ascertained the total hands employed during the year, and the total wages paid to the 419,966 employees thus enumerated. From these figures an average wage of $351.02 was computed.[20] The census of 1880 enumerated 352,255 employees in the State of Massachusetts; and from its statistics, the average wages for the state appear to be $364.[21] These results correspond fairly well, when it is remembered that the Federal census secured in some cases a number of employees less than the total number employed during the year, and therefore used a smaller divisor than was employed by the Massachusetts census. Now, in 1886, the Massachusetts bureau began the publication of its annual reports upon manufactures. In these the bureau ascertained the average number of hands employed, and used this number as a divisor in computing average wages for the state. As a result, an average wage of $395.89 was computed in 1886,[22] or $44.87 more than the average wages in 1885 as shown by the state cen-

[18] Letter of Frederic C. Waite, who made the examination. Published in *American Journal of Sociology,* Vol. 3, pp. 360-361. See also the quotation from Carroll D. Wright, upon same page.

[19] Eleventh Census, Manufacturing Industries, Vol. 1, p. 14.

[20] Massachusetts Census, 1885, Vol. 2, p. xci.

[21] Tenth Census, Vol. 2, p. 15 (folio page).

[22] Statistics of Manufactures, 1886, p. 51.

sus. This difference is due, of course, to the employment in 1886 of a smaller divisor than was used in 1885. The state census of 1885 took pains to ascertain not only the total number of hands employed during the year, but also the number employed upon June 30, 1885.[23] If we assume that the number employed upon June 30 approximated the average for the year, and use it for a divisor, we can deduce an average wage of $389 from the census of 1885. This differs from the average wage computed for 1886, in the statistics of manufactures, by only six or seven dollars. A study of these figures will make it apparent that the Federal census of 1880, like the state census of 1885, really secured for Massachusetts a number of operatives far in excess of the average number, and differing but slightly from the total number employed during the census year.

One other matter should be mentioned at this point. The tenth Federal census did not ask for the number of "officers and clerks" except in a few of the textile industries.[24] Its figures represent, therefore, the number of laborers and the wages received by them in nearly all cases, except those in which the persons who filled out the schedules reported the number of officers and clerks with the other employees. When this was done, Mr. Waite found that the officers and clerks "were not credited with any wages except in exceedingly few cases."[25]

In addition to the data contained in the statistics of manufactures, the tenth census devoted a special volume to the sub-

[23] Massachusetts Census, 1885, Vol. 2, p. xci. The total number employed during the year was 419,966; while the number employed on June 30 was 379,328.

[24] In some of the textile industries the schedules called for information concerning the number of "officers and clerks." See Eleventh Census, Manufacturing Industries, Vol. 1, p. 13; *Journal of Political Economy*, Vol. 4, p. 89. In the cotton industry the number of such persons as "officers and clerks" is given as 2,115; but their wages are not included in the total wages, and they are excluded from the total number employed. Tenth Census, Vol. 2, p. 955 (folio page). In the woolen industry, on the other hand, 1,302 officers and clerks are included in the table of total employees, and probably their wages are also included. Tenth Census, Vol. 2, p. 967 (folio page).

[25] *American Journal of Sociology*, Vol. 3, p. 360. This point is discussed, but not clearly, in the Eleventh Census, Report on Manufacturing Industries, Vol. 1, pp. 13-14. See also *American Journal of Sociology*, Vol. 3, p. 626.

ject of wages.[26] This was prepared under the careful direction of Mr. Joseph D. Weeks. It related to wages in fifty-three of the more important manufacturing industries, and also presented much valuable information concerning methods of remuneration, regularity of employment, and similar subjects. Some of the materials were drawn from as early a period as the decade from 1830 to 1840, and possess considerable historical interest.

Mr. Weeks attempted to select, in each industry, typical establishments of recognized credit and standing, and to make the returns as accurate as possible. The various classes of employees were carefully distinguished, and only those classes were finally selected whose work had not materially changed in character during the period covered by the report. Thus it is probable that the data collected are thoroughly comparable. The schedules called for "rates of wages or average earnings" for each class of employees, by the day, week, month, or year, or by the piece. It was found that the "rates of wages at the several works of the same class in a given district do not vary much for a given class of labor"; and Mr. Weeks expressed the belief that the report would "furnish the means for obtaining a fair average for the whole country."

With all the care that was taken in selecting establishments for investigation, the first sets of returns were often unsatisfactory. In these cases Mr. Weeks called attention to defects, and asked for corrected data. The chief difficulty seemed to be in securing a uniform classification of employees in establishments of the same class, and uniform units of payment. Sometimes schedules were "passed backward and forward several times before a final adjustment was reached."

Mr. Weeks confined his attention to the collection of trustworthy and comparable materials, and did not attempt to compute average rates of wages for all establishments. Thus the report presents materials rather than final results. It collects

[26] Tenth Census, p. 20. Report on the Statistics of Wages in Manufacturing Industries.

as many facts as possible concerning wages in important establishments, and leaves to the reader the work of comparison and combination. The report undoubtedly deserves high praise. If any criticism can be passed upon the materials here presented, it grows out of a circumstance that was beyond the control of Mr. Weeks. The average wages of each class of laborers in each establishment were generally computed in the counting rooms; and under these conditions there must have been some danger that the book-keepers would select an arithmetical mean instead of computing a true average.

The eleventh census devoted no special report to the subject of wage statistics. The establishment of the United States Department of Labor in 1885 rendered such an investigation less necessary for the Federal census. The statistics of manufactures, however, contained the customary inquiries concerning employees and wages.

In 1890 the investigation into manufacturing industries was much more complete in towns and cities than it had ever been in earlier censuses. The superintendent was able to place 1,042 cities in the hands of special agents, as against 279 cities so treated in the tenth census. In country districts, on the other hand, the canvass was far less thorough;[27] and there is reason for thinking that in these cases the eleventh census was more defective than the tenth. The official who was in charge of this branch of investigation has written:[28] "I am confident that

[27] On this point the census says: "Under these circumstances, the canvass of the cities was more thorough than that of the rural districts, and the apparent decrease in some industries and some states is due, in part at least, to the less efficient canvass by the general enumerators. The defective canvass of the enumerators is more apparent in the totals for states in which there are comparatively few large cities, such as Nevada, or for industries conducted largely by establishments located in the rural districts, of which 'Leather, tanned and curried' is an example." Eleventh Census, Manufacturing Industries, Vol. 1, p. 1. Mr. Robert P. Porter says concerning the returns of manufactures furnished by the regular enumerators who operated in country districts: "Except in a few isolated cases the returns of productive industry secured by these enumerators have proved utterly valueless, and hence the Census Office, in order to obtain accurate data, has been subjected to heavy outlay in securing correction and reproduction of the returns." Report on a Permanent Census Bureau, p. 18, f.

[28] *American Journal of Sociology*, Vol. 3, p. 624. See also letter by Carroll D. Wright, quoted in *Journal of Political Economy*, Vol. 4, p. 89.

in the rural districts, as a whole, the canvass of 1880 resulted in securing a larger number of reports than did that of 1890." These facts have an important bearing upon the comparability of the wage statistics of the two censuses.

The schedules used in 1890[29] called for a more minute classification of laborers than had been attempted before that time. As published, the tables distinguish three classes of workers, (1) officers, firm members, and clerks; (2) operatives, skilled and unskilled; (3) pieceworkers. Each of these classes is subdivided into, (1) males above 16, (2) females above 15, and (3) children.[30] The schedules called for the average number employed throughout the year, and the total wages paid to each class of workers. The tenth census had called for the average number of hands, but had failed to secure such data. The eleventh census carefully defined what should be considered the average number; and probably succeeded, in large measure, in obtaining it.[31] This fact, also, is important in any comparison of the tenth and eleventh censuses upon these points.

The schedules called, also, for weekly rates of wages and the average number of hands employed at each rate, as well as for information concerning the number of months that the establishments were in operation.[32] These questions were more important than any of the others, for the student of wage statistics, and were in line with the best results of recent investigations. But to secure such data for the whole United States was a work of great difficulty, and one that went far beyond anything that had been attempted in previous censuses. The plan seems to have been carried out successfully in many of the more important industries. In the third volume of the report, classified wage tables are given for such industries as

[29] Eleventh Census, Manufacturing Industries, Vol. 1, p. 13; Report on a Permanent Census Bureau, p. 178, f.

[30] Eleventh Census, Manufacturing Industries, Vol. 1, p. 19. In Table 8 of Vol I, there is given a still more minute clasification of employees in selected industries. Clerks are separated from firm members and officers, while operatives are divided into skilled and unskilled.

[31] Eleventh Census, Manufacturing Industries, Vol. 1, p. 14.

[32] *Idem,* Vol. 1, p. 13.

woolens, cottons, silks, glass, petroleum, iron and steel, etc.[33] Such statistics possess great value for the student of wages.[34] For him the importance of the report lies mainly in these classified wage tables. The use which the census made of the statistics concerning yearly earnings and the average number of employees is open to criticism in one respect.

The eleventh census used its data concerning hands employed and wages paid, for the purpose of computing average yearly earnings. When this is done for all classes of laborers in the United States, the average thus obtained falls so far short of being typical that it possesses little value for scientific purposes. For this reason, perhaps, the eleventh census computed also the average earnings for each class of employees; and, within each class, gave separate data for men, women, and children.[35] Such tables are open to far less objection. The census then compared the data concerning average earnings in four different ways. First it presented tables that contrasted the wages paid to employees, men, women, and children, in fifteen industries that employed a large proportion of females, and wages paid in fifteen industries that employed a small proportion. Then it gave the average annual earnings of each class of employees in the various states and territories. Next it gave similar data for each class of workers by specified industries, and finally it presented in a single table the statistics for six of the largest industries. Such a treatment of the materials tended to secure more homogeneous classes of operatives, so that the wages computed are far less unreal averages, and must be more typical of the average condition of the laborers in each class. Moreover, since in these selected branches of business the statistics were, for the most part, gathered at centers of industry, and by competent agents, we may fairly assign considerable value to the investigation.

[33] *Idem*, Vol. 3, pp. 146, 150, 208, 230, 302, 338, 346, 356, 361, 372, 390, 397.

[34] In Table 8 of the first volume on manufactures, the census gives the average weekly earnings of each class of employees in selected industries, as well as the total yearly wages.

[35] *Idem*, Vol. 1, pp. 20-28.

In the report upon manufactures, however, there is one feature that calls for criticism. The average annual earnings per employee, exclusive of officials and clerks, are contrasted with the average annual earnings that may be computed from the tenth census. Thus we are told that the average annual wages in 1880 were $346.91, while in 1890 they were $444.83.[36] The report is careful to add that: "Owing to differences in the form and scope of the inquiry of 1890, as compared with that of 1880, previously referred to, neither of these average annual earnings for 1890 should be accepted as the exact increase during the decade." Some of these "differences in the form and scope of the inquiry" had been explained on a previous page,[37] where it was declared that "a comparison of the average annual earnings for all classes of employees as obtained from the reports of the two censuses" was "impracticable." But others were not sufficiently explained, so that it seems necessary to consider the matter at some length. If the census officials deemed the two sets of figures entirely incomparable, it was unfortunate to make any comparison of averages. For, although it is certain that any person who attempts to use the census should examine all the explanations that accompany the figures, it is equally sure that the average popular writer or newspaper scientist will not do anything of the sort. And, as a matter of fact, eminent statisticians have compared the average wages for 1890 with the census figures for 1880, 1870, 1860, and 1850. Folio pages of census statistics that invite comparison seem to possess

[36] *Idem,* Vol. 1, p. 19. Including officers and clerks, the average for 1890 was $484.49. But, as such persons were not included in 1880, they were excluded from this comparison. It is interesting to notice that Mr. Mulhall blundered into the very error against which the census had given warning. He takes $484.49 as the average wages for 1890; and compares this figure with $346.91, the average wages for 1880. See *North American Review,* Vol. 160, p. 647.

[37] Eleventh Census, Manufacturing Industries, Vol. 1, p. 14. In his report upon the textile industries, Mr. S. N. D. North makes a somewhat similar explanation: "The increase in wages and average annual earnings for each employee, as in other items, may be due in part to the change in the form of inquiry and the more perfect enumeration at the census of 1890. The large decrease in the number of children employed also has considerable bearing on the increase in the average annual earnings." *Idem,* Vol. 3, p. 10.

powers of attraction that no amount of caution and explanation can be expected to exercise.

The errors and omissions of the returns of manufactures in 1870 and previous census years are so notorious that it cannot be necessary to repeat what has already been said concerning the mistakes that must arise from the attempt to compare rates of yearly wages deduced from such materials. With the tenth and eleventh censuses, however, greater accuracy and completeness were secured, so that the incomparable character of their statistics of wages is not so easily seen. But the writer believes, nevertheless, that the attempt to compare the average wages computed for 1880 and 1890 can lead only to most erroneous and mischievous results.[38]

The first reason for considering the wage statistics of 1880 wholly incomparable with those of 1890 is that the later census was far more complete in the cities and large towns, while the earlier census was probably more complete in the country districts. Upon this point the facts have already been stated. The necessary result is that the average wages computed from the eleventh census are based upon figures that include a far larger proportion of city laborers, who receive higher money wages; while the census of 1880 probably included a larger proportion of country laborers, whose money wages are lower.

The importance of this consideration can be shown most readily by studying the average wages for the various counties of Massachusetts, as given in the state census of 1885. The figures are as follows:[39]

Plymouth county	$396.97
Suffolk county	369.13
Essex county	365.61
State of Massachusetts	*351.02*
Franklin county	348.56
Norfolk county	348.11

[38] Thus Mr. J. S. Jeans, using such data, came to the conclusion that wages had advanced more during the decade from 1880 to 1890 than they had in the thirty years prior to 1880. *Fortnightly Review,* Vol. 58, p. 752.

[39] Massachusetts Census of 1885, Vol. 2, p. ci.

Worcester county	$342.85
Hampden county	341.61
Middlesex county	330.77
Bristol county	324.16
Berkshire county	305.68
Hampshire county	283.38
Nantucket county	277.98
Barnstable county	238.97
Dukes county	106.79

Plymouth county, which heads the list, is only in appearance an exception to the statement that the highest wages are found in the counties having the largest proportion of urban population. In that country there is one large city, Brockton, where the average wages were $433. In the rest of the county the average was $65 less than in the city of Brockton. The same thing is noticeable in Worcester county, where the city of Worcester is the only large center of population. In this city wages averaged $382; while in the rest of the county they average only $324. It is evident that if one census of the state should be made far more complete for the cities than any previous census, while its enumeration of country laborers should be less complete, there would result an apparent increase of the average wages for the state in a period when wages might actually have remained stationary.

In the Federal census of 1890 a comparison of the average earnings in the fifty principal cities with the average for the entire country [40] shows that thirty-six out of the fifty cities were credited with wages that exceeded the average for the country. Of the fourteen cities where the average wages were less than the average for the United States, many showed figures that were far above the wages for the rest of the states in which they were situated. If we select the principal class of wage-earners, males above sixteen years, and exclude officers and clerks, the results are still more striking. The writer has made such a computation for the eight largest cities, with the following results: The United States, $498; Baltimore, $503; Philadelphia, $568;

[40] Eleventh Census, Manufacturing Industries, Vol. 2, p. xxxviii.

St. Louis, $569; Chicago, $587; Brooklyn, $636; Boston, $654; New York, $702; San Francisco, $709. In Baltimore, where the wages show the smallest excess over the figures for the United States, it appeared that the average for the city was $226 higher than the average wages for the same class of workers in the rest of the state.

The class of employees last mentioned, viz., males above sixteen years, is the more important in this connection because it was among just such laborers that the enumeration of the eleventh census was especially complete. The census explains[41] that: "The great increase shown in statistics for industries known as 'hand trades' is largely due to the fact that no previous census has obtained so complete a report regarding such industries as masonry, carpentering, blacksmithing, cooperage, painting, plumbing, and similar trades using machinery to a limited extent." In four classes of laborers, viz., masons, painters and paperhangers, plumbers, and carpenters, the eleventh census enumerated 357,000 persons, against 97,000 enumerated in 1880.[42] This was an increase of 260,000 laborers, or 266 per cent, during a decade when the whole population of the country increased less than 25 per cent. Now these particular trades receive wages that are far above the average for the United States. Excluding officers and clerks, the average wage of the country is given as $444.83. In these four trades very few women and children are employed; and the males above sixteen years, who form nearly the entire number of workers enumerated, are credited with the following wages: plumbers, $627; masons, $628; painters and paperhangers, $644; carpenters, $648.[43] We find, therefore, that the eleventh census enumerated more than 200,000[44] workmen who were omitted from these trades in 1880. These 200,000 or more workers

[41] *Idem,* Vol. 1, p. 2.

[42] *Idem,* Vol. 1, pp. 74, 79, 80, 81.

[43] *Idem,* Vol. 1, pp. 23-27.

[44] This figure allows for more than fifty per cent increase in these particular trades. The employees in all manufactures increased fifty per cent from 1880 to 1890, excluding officers and clerks.

formed 5 or 6 per cent of all persons engaged in manufacturing occupations in 1890, excluding officers and clerks. Their wages exceeded the average wages of all classes of laborers by amounts that varied from $182, in the case of plumbers, to $203, in the case of carpenters. This one body of employees, excluded in 1880 and included in 1890, would tend to increase the average wages for all persons engaged in manufactures by ten to twelve dollars, if not more.[45]

But there is a second reason, of still greater weight, for holding the results of the two censuses to be incomparable. There is no room for doubting that in 1890 the total wages paid were divided by a number of employees that was much smaller than it would have been if the same methods had been followed that were used in 1880. Upon this subject the census says:[46] "The questions used in 1880 tended to obtain a number of employees that would be in excess of the true average, while it is believed the questions used in 1890 have obtained, as nearly as possible, the average number." Attention has already been called to this fact. It is the more important since it had the same result as the first cause of difference between the figures of the two censuses. It tended to produce a larger average wage in 1890.

We have seen that the Massachusetts census of 1885, using as a divisor the *total* number of hands employed during the year, computed an average wage of $351.02 for the year 1885. It has also been shown that in 1886, when the publication of the annual reports on manufactures was begun, the *average* number of employees was taken as a divisor, and the average wages were thereby increased to $395.89. Precisely the same thing occurred in the Federal statistics when the eleventh census actually ascertained the average number of employees, and used this as a divisor. Further light is thrown upon this question

45 Since the writer made this estimate, the official who had charge of these statistics in the eleventh census has stated that, if the trades that were imperfectly enumerated in 1880 should be excluded from the tables for 1890, the average wages for the United States would be $429 instead of $444. See *American Journal of Sociology*, Vol. 3, p. 627.

46 Eleventh Census, Manufacturing Industries, Vol. 1, p. 14.

by the Massachusetts census for 1895, which has appeared during the past year. This census ascertained the total wages paid to all employees in manufacturing industries, and divided this sum by the *average* number of hands employed. Thus an average wage of $446.41 was computed.[47] This shows a magnificent increase over the average rate of $351.02 computed in 1885; but the larger wage was secured by using a smaller divisor, and the later census makes no attempt to compare the two results. No one would claim that the wages of laborers employed in manufacturing industries in the state had increased from $351 to $446 between 1885 and 1895. In the very year in which the last state census appeared, the bureau of labor statistics published the results of an investigation into comparative rates of wages paid in 1881 and 1897.[48] This covered twenty three industries, and showed an increased average wage in fifteen cases and a decreased wage in the eight other instances. These results may justify the claim that wages in Massachusetts showed on the whole a tendency to increase during the period in question; but they demonstrate also the atrocity of the error that would be committed by any one who should compare the censuses of 1885 and 1895, and should then claim that wages had increased on the average by $95 during the decade.

There has been considerable discussion of the question whether the average number of employees, or the total number of persons employed during the year, should be selected as the divisor in determining yearly earnings. It is clear that if the total number is taken, the divisor will be swelled unduly by the transient laborers who drift from one establishment to another, and are sure to be enumerated more than once. Such a divisor would give average yearly earnings that would be too low. On the other hand, when we select the average number employed, we use as a divisor the average number of positions filled throughout the year. This gives average yearly earnings

[47] Census of Massachusetts, 1895, Vol. 5; pp. 240, 280.

[48] Twenty-Eighth Annual Report of the Bureau of Statistics of Labor, pp. 1-42.

that represent what the individual laborers would receive if employment were continuous throughout the year. Average wages computed in this manner are more than the actual income of individual laborers, especially in trades where employment is irregular. It does not fall within the scope of this article to consider whether the census ought to inquire for the average number of employees, or for the total number. The statistics of manufactures are not designed primarily to furnish statistics of annual average wages. This particular question should be framed in such a manner as will be most useful for the primary purposes for which the investigation into manufactures is conducted. But we must insist that wage statistics computed with one kind of divisor must not be compared with data secured by the use of a different divisor.

Some of the criticisms that have been directed against the wage statistics of the eleventh census can be accounted for by remembering that the rates of annual wages given there represent, not the actual earnings of all persons employed, but the amounts paid annually to the occupants of a certain number of positions. Thus the average wages of carpenters in New York city are computed at $896. This would mean $3 per day for nearly 300 days of employment. A critic who has exceptional facilities for securing information concerning actual conditions in that city, writes: "The average wages of good, steady, thoroughly competent carpenters never exceeded $650 for the entire year."

Some of the results of comparing the average wages given in the two censuses are so ridiculous as to show the absolute incomparability of the two sets of data. Thus the same critic points out that, according to the census data, carpenters' wages in New York City increased from $640 in 1880 to $896 in 1890. For the city of Poughkeepsie we are asked to believe that carpenters' wages advanced from $357 in 1880 to $729 in 1890. These results are so absurd as to show that we are dealing with data that are either totally erroneous or else collected by such different methods as to be wholly incapable of bearing comparison.

It remains to be considered what the twelfth census should attempt to accomplish in this field of wage statistics. The writer will assume that the purpose of such statistics should be to investigate the conditions under which the large masses of our population who are dependent upon the receipt of wages are actually living. In the present condition of statistical science we can not hope that such investigation will throw much light upon what is technically called the problem of share distribution. Moreover, since the census can not well undertake to collect comprehensive statistics concerning the prices of commodities, it must confine itself to the question of money wages.

At the outset the question may fairly arise whether, in view of the establishment of the Department of Labor at Washington, the Federal census should continue to gather statistics of wages. This bureau was created for the purpose of investigating labor problems. It has already published much information relating to wages; and is, at the present time, preparing a report upon wages paid in the leading countries of the world.[49]

If a permanent census bureau should be established and should undertake the systematic collection of wage statistics, it would appear to be duplicating the work of the Department of Labor. If, on the other hand, the Census Office should remain a temporary affair, we may fairly doubt whether this particular field of investigation could not be covered more satisfactorily by the Department of Labor with its permanent organization. There is reason for thinking that even the special agents appointed by the census to collect statistics of manufactures do not always have the time or training for the work of gathering accurate data concerning wages. It seems probable that better results could be secured by placing additional funds at the disposal of the permanent labor bureau. Such an investigation might not cover as much ground as the census, but the improved quality of the materials might well counterbalance the greater quantity of the census returns. This would be especially

[49] Am. Stat. Ass'n *Publications*, Vol. 5, p. 373; Eleventh Annual report of the Commissioner of Labor, Vol. 5.

true of that portion of the census statistics that may have to be left in the hands of the ordinary enumerator.

One other point is worthy of consideration. The census returns necessarily cover but single years at intervals of a decade. The periods when the census materials are gathered may happen to be abnormal, so that by this fact alone any comparison of results from one decade to another may be vitiated. Then, too, important fluctuations may take place within each decade, and upon these the census can give no information. Such considerations induced Massachusetts to provide for annual statistics of manufactures. Finally, the publication of census returns seems to be necessarily such a slow process that no inconsiderable advantage might result from the prompter methods of the Department of Labor.

Assuming, however, that the census, in its investigations concerning manufactures, is to continue to gather data concerning wages, we may consider what should be attempted. In doing this, we should remember that the principal purpose of the census investigations is to gather information concerning manufactures. The questions relating to total wages and employees should, therefore, be framed with this primary object in view.

For this last reason, the census should continue to investigate the total wages paid, as an important element in the expenses of manufacturing industry. But it may be doubted whether the data thus gathered should be used for the purpose of computing average yearly earnings of laborers. In any event, the utterly incomparable character of the statistics of the eleventh and preceding censuses should be set forth so clearly as to offer no possible excuse for the further misuse of their figures.

If the computation of the average yearly earnings is continued, the twelfth census should carry on the work, commenced by the eleventh, of ascertaining the average earnings of workers in each occupation, separating in all cases men, women, and children. Such data could be used for some purposes, since the averages thus computed would be based upon units of some degree of homogeneity. The results would be further improved if they could be more fully classified by sections of the country. Furthermore, a separate table might be prepared, from which the notoriously incorrect materials gathered by the ordinary enumerators outside of the cities and towns could be excluded. This was accomplished in the eleventh census in the separate volume devoted to the principal industrial centers. For all these purposes it would matter less whether the divisor should be the *average* number of employees or the *total* number, provided that future censuses should adopt a uniform method of procedure.

It has been suggested that wage statistics should investigate only the earnings of laborers steadily employed in each establishment, because other workers are largely migratory or incapable.[50] It is urged that we should endeavor to ascertain primarily the earnings of capable laborers who are steadily employed during the months that each establishment is in operation. The importance of studying the numbers and condition of transient employees is not denied, but it is considered best to make this the object of an independent investigation. This point seems to be well taken, provided that it is feasible to separate the two classes of laborers. But it may be impossible to introduce such a feature into the investigation concerning manufactures, and an independent inquiry might be needed in order to accomplish such a result.

The writer has already expressed the belief that the most valuable wage statistics contained in the eleventh census are to be found in the tables of classified weekly rates. The advantage of such a method is that it deals largely with actual facts, and does not employ averages that may be unreal and misleading. Such statistics, when properly tabulated, enable the student to ascertain exactly what rates of remuneration the great mass of the laborers is receiving.

Besides tabulating such returns so as to show, for each class of laborers, the numbers employed at each rate, and the per cent

[50] See Mayo-Smith, in *Quarterly Journal of Economics,* Vol. 2, p. 397, f.; Von Meyr, in *Allgemeines statistisches Archiv,* Vol. 2, p. 135.

which such numbers bear to the total number of persons in each group, the results might be presented graphically according to the method suggested by Dr. Venn.[51] This consists in drawing a base line that shall represent the different rates of wages, and then constructing ordinates denoting the relative numbers of laborers receiving such specified rate. This plan would make it possible to plot a curve that would represent accurately the condition of the wage earners at a given time. Between different periods, changes in the shape of the curve would indicate the course of weekly rates of wages.

Tables of weekly wages need to be supplemented by statistics showing the number of weeks of full working time the operatives are able to secure in the course of the year. Such inquiries fall easily within the scope of the census of manufactures. With their use, the tables of weekly rates would furnish most valuable information concerning the course of wages in manufacturing industries.

[51] *Journal of Royal Statistical Society*, Vol. 64, p. 445.

THEORY OF THE BALANCE OF TRADE[1]

THE rapidity with which exports of American products have increased in recent years has served, naturally enough, to stimulate discussion concerning the unprecedented balance of trade which now stands in "favor" of the United States. Not a few writers seem to believe that the extraordinary excess of exports over imports has made our foreign trade peculiarly profitable to the country, and there has been a marked revival of some of those theories which are associated with the name of the mercantile school of the seventeenth and eighteenth centuries. Such conditions will justify renewed study of that time-worn topic, the "Balance of Trade."

I

Mercantilism arose in the period when the precious metals discovered in the New World began to find their way into circulation in the various countries of Europe. One cardinal tenet of the school was that the statesman must exercise especial care to secure for his country a sufficient stock of treasure in silver and gold. Spain and Portugal received directly from their colonies the riches that the treasure ships brought each year from the Indies; but England and other countries, whose dependencies contained no mines of the precious metals, could, manifestly, obtain new supplies of specie only by way of trade. For this reason, an excess of exports over imports, which might be settled by an inflow of gold or silver, was considered a "favorable" balance of trade, and became an object of solicitude to statesmen and to writers upon economic subjects.

Two circumstances aroused endless discussion of the balance

[1] Reprinted from *North American Review*, Vol. 173 (July, 1901), pp. 111-33. Reproduced by generous permission of the publishers.

of trade in England from the early decades of the seventeenth century. The East India Company was obliged to export specie each year to pay for the goods it obtained from the East, where there was little demand for English products. Then, the trade with France was believed to result in a balance unfavorable to England, so that it was thought that her traditional political rival was draining the country of its treasure. Partisans of the East India Company, such as Thomas Mun, insisted that the exportation of treasure to the East did no harm, because it was exchanged for products that were sold, at a still larger gain, in many countries of Europe; but the unfavorable balance in the French trade occasioned serious anxiety. Several times, commerce with France was absolutely prohibited; and at all periods heavy duties were imposed upon the staple imports from that country. Yet this branch of trade was long viewed with jealous eye; and writer after writer made elaborate calculations of the amount of treasure lost by the dealings with France, prophesying the utter ruin of the kingdom. "Make a law," they said, "to prohibit French trade: you need no wine and few of his commodities; and France will grow poor, while we grow rich."

Meanwhile, various Tory writers, such as Child, North and Davenant, less hostile to France, had argued that an unfavorable balance in dealings with a particular country need cause no alarm, because commerce with other countries resulted in a net excess of exports on the entire trade of the nation. But the theories of the mercantilists were not effectually controverted until the time of David Hume and Adam Smith. Hume contended that money, whenever the means of communication are open, brings "itself nearly to a level," and that its purchasing power cannot vary greatly in different nations. Spain and Portugal, he said, could not by any laws keep within their borders all the treasure brought from the Indies, since such a course would merely lower its purchasing power in those countries, and hasten its export to other places where it would command more commodities. Prices south of the Pyrenees could not be much higher than in France, since otherwise gold and silver would flow northward in exchange for cheaper products. He said that, if the various states of the old Saxon Heptarchy had maintained separate existences, each kingdom would have worried over the balance of trade. Moreover, Hume attacked that insane "jealousy of trade" which marked the commercial relations of the various European states; and insisted that, since a wealthy man or country is a better customer than a poor one, "the increase of the riches and commerce in any one nation, instead of hurting, commonly promotes the riches and commerce of all its neighbors."

It remained for Adam Smith to deal the death-blow to the theories of the mercantilists. He contended that all natural trade is profitable, and that its profit consists, not in the specie it may bring into the country, but in the addition it makes to the annual produce of the land and labor of the nation. The mercantilists, he said, had prophesied the ruin, through an unfavorable balance of trade, of every commercial country in Europe; and their forecasts had been discredited invariably. All the treasure that flowed from Peru and Brazil could not be retained by Spain and Portugal; and every attempt of those countries to check the outflow of specie merely tended to increase prices and to give other nations "double advantage" in their commerce with the Peninsula, by raising the prices obtainable for imports sent thither, while making domestic products dearer and more difficult to export at a profit. Since the publication of the "Wealth of Nations" few economists have thought it necessary to trouble themselves over imaginary evils resulting from the balance of trade.

But recent developments in our foreign trade have led to the expression of views that differ but slightly, if at all, from the theories of the old mercantilists. We are said to be now creating a favorable balance of trade equal to $1,300 for every minute of the day; while England, Germany and France are "writing a total of over one billion on the wrong side of the ledger" for each year's transactions. In foreign trade, we are told, it is, as in the philosophy of Mr. Micawber: "Annual income twenty pounds, annual expenditures nineteen six, result happiness. Annual income twenty pounds, annual expenditures twenty pounds ought and six, result misery." Then we read passages like the following:

> Never before in the history of the United States were the profits from foreign business so large as in 1898 and 1899. By profits, I mean the excess in value of the goods sold—that is, exported—over those bought—that is, imported.

When the country imports more than she exports, she is said to be "a loser by her foreign trade," and "all the great nations of the earth," with the exception of Russia and the United States, are declared to suffer enormous "losses" by importing more than they export. True, an occasional writer recognizes that our excess of exports is offset, to some extent at least, by invisible items of international indebtedness; while sometimes it is realized that the unfavorable balances of older countries mean cheaper food and raw materials for the people, and represent also the return upon foreign investments of capital or the earnings of merchant marines. But the revival of mercantilist theories is sufficiently marked to deserve recognition as a general tendency in the thought of the day.

II

With this general subject of international trade, it is notoriously true that the average man does not look with great favor upon reasoning based upon principles of a general and abstract character; while immediate results or events lying upon the surface of things create a far more powerful impression than the ultimate consequences of underlying forces. For this reason, the attention of the reader is now invited to a survey of the foreign exchanges of the United States during the years that have elapsed since the establishment of American independence. By such a study of simple historical facts, it may be possible to enforce more successfully than in any other manner some elementary truths concerning the real significance of the balance of trade.

A preliminary word is necessary regarding the sources of information. Statistics of international commerce always contain an element of error, and this is especially true of the only data available for the early decades of our national existence. Prior to 1821 imports admitted free of duty were not reported at all, and the rest were not valued in a satisfactory manner; while the valuation of exports did not receive sufficient attention from the customs authorities. The statistics now accepted as official for this period were made up in 1835. Beginning in 1821, the Annual Reports on Commerce and Navigation were published with greater or less regularity, and there has probably been a constant improvement in the character of our commercial statistics. For many of the items, other than exports or imports of merchandise, that contribute to the international dealings of the United States, no official data are obtainable, and we are compelled to rely upon mere estimates that sometimes have a decidedly conjectural character. Precise computation, therefore, is impossible. The most that can be done is to demonstrate what the general tendencies have been in each epoch investigated.

(A.) The first period that we shall study extended from 1789 to 1820. It witnessed a rapid growth of our commerce up to the year 1807, when such events as the Embargo, Non-Intercourse Acts, and the War of 1812 affected all industry most injuriously. After the restoration of peace in 1815, a period of wild speculation, fostered by an inflation of the currency, encouraged large importations of foreign products. These were viewed as a sign of prosperity while the "boom" lasted, but were styled an inundation of European goods as soon as the speculative fever abated. The reaction, however, lowered prices and checked the flow of imports, which decreased automatically from $147,000,000 in 1816 to $74,000,000 in 1820.

For the entire period of thirty-one years, the estimated imports of merchandise and specie amounted to $2,350,000,000, while exports were placed at $1,839,000,000, an "unfavorable" balance of $511,000,000. Nor was this our only item of international indebtedness. Foreign capital was largely represented in the debt of the federal government, and had been invested in the stocks of the first Bank of the United States and in other enterprises. For interest on all such investments we owed, for the entire period, a sum that is estimated at $200,000,000 or more. But the amount due for the excess of imports and the interest on foreign capital had been balanced readily by the earnings of our merchant marine. The tonnage of the ships registered for the foreign trade amounted for the entire period to 20,000,000 tons engaged in traffic for one year. One estimate places the "balancing power," or international earnings, of our shipping at $20,000,000 annually from 1789 to 1815; and another reckons the earnings at $800,000,000 for the period now under consideration. The neutral position of the United States during the wars that engaged the attention of Europe for so many years had enabled American vessels to carry the larger part of our exports and imports, besides earning large sums in trade between different foreign ports. By this means, therefore, we had paid our international indebtedness, and had been enabled probably to import a considerable net balance of gold and silver.[2] So far, then, from the country being drained of its money in payment for the balance of imported merchandise, the banks held not less than $20,000,000 of specie in the year 1820; while Gallatin and Crawford estimated that there had never been more hard cash in circulation.

The situation was analyzed correctly by Timothy Pitkin in 1817. He showed that a cargo of flour shipped to Spain in an American vessel would be valued at $47,500 at domestic prices, and would figure at this amount in the returns of our exports. If the flour were sold in Spain at the usual advance necessary to cover freight, insurance, commissions, and a fair profit, it might command as much as $75,000. Then, if the proceeds from the sale were invested in a return cargo that would be valued at our custom houses according to the prescribed methods, the final result of the voyage would be the importation of com-

[2] The balance of $511,000,000 due on the excess of imports does not show the facts regarding the movement of specie, since the estimates do not separate the two items of merchandise and specie prior to 1821.

modities that exceeded very greatly the value of the original exports. Therefore, he contended that, if the imports had not shown an excess, our ships would have incurred a loss on their voyages.

(B.) From 1821 to 1830, our commerce showed no material increase over the first period. For this decade, imports of merchandise aggregated $729,000,000 and exports were placed at $694,000,000, an "unfavorable" balance of $35,000,000, which was slightly reduced by a net exportation of $2,400,000 in specie. The indebtedness of the country was increased still further by whatever sums were due to foreign investors. Although the United States was reducing its public debt and returning considerable amounts of capital to foreign owners, the States had began to contract debts, and borrowed during the decade $26,469,000. We may assume, therefore, that the sums returned to foreigners by the federal government were reinvested in State securities, and that the annual interest charge against the country remained nearly stationary. Moreover, Americans were beginning to indulge more extensively in foreign travel, so that a new item of indebtedness affected the exchanges. The sums expended by our travellers, however, were offset in part by the money brought here by immigrants, who numbered 150,000 during the decade.

Whatever the indebtedness of the country may have been on these various accounts, the earnings of our merchant marine sufficed to pay it, and to turn the exchanges in favor of the United States at the close of the period. After 1821, we have statistics showing the amounts of exports and imports carried in American and in foreign vessels. From this time, the net result of the carrying trade can be computed upon the following basis. Since American consumers must bear the expense of bringing merchandise to this country, the freight charges on goods brought in foreign vessels will be reckoned as an element in our international indebtedness; while the sums earned by American vessels in the import trade will be considered to have no effect upon the foreign exchanges. Similarly, with our exports, we shall estimate that other countries are indebted to the United States for freights on goods carried in American vessels, and that cargoes shipped in foreign bottoms may be omitted from our computations. Estimates of the probable proportion between freight charges and the values of the products carried range from ten to fifteen per cent. We may, therefore, place the cost of ocean carriage at twelve and a half per cent; and this estimate may continue to be used until, for recent decades, it becomes possible to replace it by a better one.

From 1821 to 1830, exports carried in American vessels aggregated $666,090,000, on which the freight charges would be about $83,000,000; while imports brought in foreign bottoms were placed at slightly more than $51,000,000, which would be subject to a charge of something more than $6,000,000. Thus, our merchant marine earned from foreign countries about $77,000,000, which would be somewhat increased by the profits from carrying goods between foreign ports. Again, therefore, our ships earned enough to balance the indebtedness incurred on other accounts; and, in 1829 and 1830, the net imports of specie amounted to $8,400,000, while foreign exchange was quoted in favor of the United States.

(C.) The third period extends from 1831 to 1840. For the first six or seven years the country was engaged in an extraordinary speculative movement, which was followed by the inevitable reaction and business depression. Population advanced at a rapid rate, immigration became very large, and sales of public lands increased greatly. The State banks were enabled to expand their note issues from $61,000,000 in 1830 to $103,000,000 in 1835, the notes being used in payment for the lands occupied by settlers. Then, in 1836, the federal government distributed $28,000,000 of surplus revenue among the States, this money finding its way into the banks which increased their issues to $149,000,000 by the year 1837. Such an inflation of the currency raised prices and invited large importations of merchandise. Thus, our imports rose from $62,720,000 in 1830 to $176,579,000 in 1836; while exports increased much less rapidly. When the speculative mania ended in the crisis of 1837, imports immediately decreased; but, for the entire decade, importations of merchandise exceeded exports by $159,700,000.

More than this, the movement of specie showed for the ten year an excess of imports amounting to $50,650,000; so that on these two accounts the balance of importations was not less than $210,000,000. This sum was far larger than the earnings of our merchant marine, which amounted to $90,000,000. How shall we account for the unsettled balance of $120,000,000?

The explanation is found in the large investments of European capital that were placed in the United States during this period. Between 1830 and 1838, various States that had undertaken internal improvements created debts amounting to $147,835,000. For this purpose, bonds were sold in other countries, and foreigners became indebted to America for the principal of the loans. Two circumstances, however, contributed to reduce the claims which the country held against foreigners on this account. The debt of the federal government, which amounted to $39,123,000 in 1831, had been paid in full by the year 1835; and a considerable part of these securities had been owned in Europe. As a result, foreign investors had been able to purchase some of the State bonds by the simple reinvestment of funds already standing to their credit in the United States. In the second place, no small amount of interest had accrued upon federal and State securities during the decade, and this item may have amounted to thirty or forty millions.[3] Foreign investors, therefore, owed the United States $147,835,000, less that part of the principal of the federal debt, and of the interest accruing upon all securities, for which this country was indebted to European capitalists. After making such deductions, it is evident that our large imports of merchandise and specie had been made necessary by the movement of foreign capital toward the United States.

[3] Lest this estimate should appear too small, it will be well to add that, of the $147,835,000 invested in state bonds, $107,823,000 was placed in this country after 1835.

(D.) The next decade opened with two or three years of continued depression, but conditions improved after 1844, and subsequently the foreign commerce of the country began to show a decided increase. In 1847, the exchanges were affected greatly by the famine that followed the failure of the potato crop in Ireland. This event caused a remarkable increase in our exports of breadstuffs, which rose from $7,445,000 in 1845 to $53,262,000 in 1847. The result was that our exports of merchandise exceeded imports, in the year last mentioned, by $34,317,000. Such a sudden disturbance of trade caused a net importation of specie amounting to $22,214,000. This large inflow of money altered the condition of the exchanges; so that in 1848, imports increased by $26,000,000, while exports declined more than $18,000,000, and a balance of $9,481,000 of specie was exported.

From 1841 to 1850 the imports of merchandise aggregated $1,180,000,000, and exports were estimated at $1,195,000,000. Thus a small balance of something less than $15,000,000 stood to the credit of the United States. At the same time, imports of gold and silver had exceeded exports by $21,830,000; so that the movements of merchandise and specie had reached approximately a condition of equilibrium. From this fact, one would infer that the invisible items of exchange must show a similar balance. Now, what are the facts?

The panic of 1837 had checked the growth of State debts. In 1841, the aggregate indebtedness of the State and local governments was not much more than $216,000,000. When the States retired from industrial undertakings, the field was left open for business corporations, which constantly increased in number, and began to find in Europe a market for a part of their securities. Thus investments of foreign capital, which were estimated at $200,000,000 in 1840, were supposed to amount to $261,000,000 in 1853. For the decade they may have averaged $225,000,000, upon which the aggregate interest charges would amount to $135,000,000.

But this debt to holders of American securities was diminished by the $40,000,000 or $50,000,000 of new capital that sought investment in this country; so that our foreign indebtedness on this account was $85,000,000 or $95,000,000.

Upon the other hand, our merchant marine carried away from our shores exports that exceeded by $690,000,000 the imports that were brought to this country in foreign vessels. Therefore, on account of ocean freights, the United States was entitled to a credit of $86,000,000, which would balance approximately the interest due to foreign holders of American securities. Cargoes carried by our ships between foreign ports increased the earnings of the merchant marine; and were sufficient, perhaps, to balance any foreign outlays occasioned by the operations of our army during the Mexican War. Since specie exports exceeded imports in 1850 and 1851, we may conclude that some debts remained unadjusted at the close of this period.

(E.) In the ensuing decade our foreign commerce increased nearly 125 per cent over the figures for any previous period of equal length, and merchandise imports exceeded exports by $355,800,000.

Passing over, for the moment, the movement of specie, we find that State and local debts increased by $100,000,000 during the decade; while 21,000 miles of railroad were constructed, for which large amounts of iron rails were imported in exchange for newly issued securities. Foreign investments may have amounted to some $300,000,000 or $350,000,000, upon an average; but it is difficult to secure any satisfactory estimates. The annual interest charges may have been some $18,000,000 to $21,000,000, and, if we deduct $80,000,000 for new investments, we may place the debt due to foreign capitalists at from $100,000,000 to $130,000,000 for the decade. Thus, the United States was a debtor for $355,000,000 of imported merchandise, for $100,000,000 to $130,000,000 on interest charges, and, perhaps, for an unsettled balance from the year 1850.

To meet these claims, the profits of the merchant marine proved wholly inadequate. The net earnings of our ships amounted to no more than $158,000,000. Evidently, some new cause had been operating to disturb the exchanges, and to increase our obligations beyond the point where the earnings of our ships could establish an equilibrium.

We must now return to the movement of gold and silver. Upon the opening of the California mines, our domestic gold output suddenly rose, from insignificant proportions, to $50,000,000 in 1850; and subsequent years showed a still larger product, which was several times as great as the amount secured annually from all countries of the world prior to 1845. From 1851 to 1860, the aggregate production of gold in the United States equalled $550,000,000, and this was five or six times the estimated specie circulation of the country in any year before the discoveries in California. The money in circulation in 1850, including bank notes as well as specie, was no more than $285,000,000, or about $12 *per capita.* If the new gold could have been retained in the country, our circulating medium would have risen to $835,000,000 for the year 1860, or $26.60 *per capita.* Such a sudden inflation as this would have raised prices far above the level prevailing in other parts of the world, put an end to the exportation of many products, and attracted imports from all quarters of the globe. Therefore, the new gold began to flow out of the country, after prices had been raised to a point at which the import trade could increase sufficiently to produce this result; and, from 1851 to 1860, we exported a net balance of $417,608,000. By 1860, our specie circulation had risen to $235,000,000, an increase of $81,000,000 in ten years; while the issues of bank notes had grown to $207,000,000, giving the country a supply of money that averaged $14.06 *per capita.* The United States had become one of the leading gold producing regions, and the course of the exchanges was inevitably altered.

(F.) Even more instructive was the period that extended from 1861 to 1873. The fiscal year 1860 had been marked by great prosperity, and both exports and imports were larger than at any former time. But the Civil War wrought havoc with our foreign trade, which, in the space of two years, shrank to little more than one-half of the proportions reached in 1860. Especially marked was the decline in our exports of cotton, which decreased from $191,800,000 in 1860 to an average of $11,700,000 from 1861 to 1865. But in 1863 the volume of foreign trade began to increase; and, after the restoration of peace, the expansion was very rapid.

In 1862, the federal government began to issue inconvertible paper, which produced an inflation of the currency, raising prices and intensifying the speculative movement naturally induced by the enormous public expenditures for military purposes. The inevitable result was a large increase of merchandise imports, which rose from $243,000,000 in 1863 to $642,000,000 ten years later. While it is true, as Cairnes contended, that high prices in inconvertible paper would not tend to favor the growth of imports because foreigners did not exchange commodities for depreciated greenbacks but received payment in gold, it is certain, also, that the speculative mania had raised gold prices somewhat above the level prevailing in other countries, so that the inflow of commodities was greatly stimulated. For the thirteen years ending in 1873, imports of merchandise aggregated $5,107,00,000, while exports were placed at $3,952,000,000, a balance of nearly $1,155,000,000 against this country.

But this was not the only account which foreigners held against the United States. Our merchant marine had suffered irreparable damage from the ravages of the Confederate cruisers, and the proportion of our foreign trade carried in American vessels had greatly decreased. For this entire period the imports brought to our shores in foreign ships exceeded the exports carried in our own vessels by $1,500,000,000. This gave rise to a debt of $187,500,000. For the first time in our history, we were indebted to foreigners on account of the carrying trade; and the aggregates of our obligations for merchandise and freight amounted to $1,342,000,000.[4] Moreover, it was esti-

[4] The sum due for freight should, however, be considerably reduced; because many American vessels had been registered under foreign flags, and the earnings of such ships should not be credited to foreign account.

mated by David A. Wells, in 1869, that American travellers were then spending $25,000,000 annually in foreign countries, and the money brought here by immigrants could not have counterbalanced such an outlay. But there were other international transactions that restored the exchanges to an equilibrium.

In the first place, the net exports of specie during the thirteen years had amounted to no less than $677,822,000, this sum representing nearly nine-tenths of the output of our mines at this period. The rest of our foreign indebtedness was settled by the flow of European capital into the United States. From 1861 to 1863, there seem to have been large withdrawals of foreign investments on account of the disturbed conditions caused by the war, but, during the next ten years, the movement of capital turned in the other direction. The federal government had incurred an interest-bearing debt of $2,381,000,000, State and local indebtedness had increased by some $500,000,000, while 39,642 miles of railways had been constructed. Foreign investors were attracted by the securities issued for these purposes.

In 1868, Secretary McCulloch estimated the foreign investments at $850,000,000, exclusive of railway stocks. The following year, Mr. Wells computed that $1,100,000,000 of federal and local securities were held in other countries, while $365,000,000 of European capital had been placed in railway and other enterprises. Even if this estimate was too large in 1869, we may be certain that not less than $1,500,000,000 of foreign investments had been made by 1873; because the inflow of capital had been very rapid during the interval, amounting to $100,000,000 for the first eight months of the latter year. Now, if we place the withdrawals of the years 1861 and 1862 at $200,000,000, it may be considered that foreign capitalists were indebted to the United States for $1,300,000,000 on account of the principal of new investments. This debt would be decreased by the interest charges that had accrued prior to 1873, but the precise amount of this allowance cannot be determined. Remembering, however, that most of the capital came to the country after 1863 and that the interest was stated at $88,000,000 in 1869, we may estimate it as equivalent to some $80,000,000 annually for a period of six years. Thus, the aggregate indebtedness of foreign investors would be reduced to about $820,000,000. This was the item, therefore, which, in addition to the $677,000,000 of specie exports, furnished the means of settling the enormous balance due on merchandise, freights, and travellers' expenses.

Manifestly, such a condition of the exchanges could not continue. Even if nothing had occurred to check the inflow of foreign capital, the growing interest charges would have exceeded ultimately the annual investment of principal. In 1869, Mr. Wells had prophesied that exports of merchandise must increase, sooner or later, in order to pay for the interest accruing to European capitalists. More explicitly still, in 1873, Professor Cairnes wrote:

> These considerations lead me to the conclusion, that the present condition of the external trade of the United States is essentially abnormal and temporary. If that country is to continue to discharge her liabilities to foreigners, the relation which at present obtains between exports and imports in her external trade must be inverted. . . . This, it seems to me, is a result which may be predicted with the utmost confidence. The end may be reached by an extension of exportation, or by a curtailment of importation, or by combining both these processes, but by one means or the other reached it will need to be.

Proceeding a step further, Cairnes showed that the excess of exports over imports could not be established unless the high prices then ruling in this country should be materially lowered, or prices in Europe should show a considerable advance; and he considered it probable that the change would come about by a fall of prices in the United States sufficient to make importation more difficult and exportation more profitable. Such a decline of the price level would probably "come with a crash," so that he looked forward "to the immediate future of American trade as a period of much disturbance and fluctuation, culminating, it is possible, from time to time, in commercial crises."

Before his book appeared, these prophecies were in course of literal fulfillment.

(G.) The last period extends from 1874 to 1896, subsequent years being reserved for discussion in our final paragraphs. In September, 1873, the whole fabric of ten years' speculation utterly collapsed, while prices fell to a point at which imports must decrease and exports could expand. In 1874, for the first time in twelve years, exports of merchandise exceeded imports; and this condition was maintained in eighteen out of the next twenty-two years. By the close of the fiscal year 1896, the exports for the entire period stood at $17,479,000,000, while imports were placed at $15,190,000,000, a "favorable" balance of $2,289,000,000. In addition to this, exports of specie showed an excess of $529,000,000 over imports; so that the United States was entitled to a total credit of $2,818,000,000. This meant simply that the country had assumed its normal position as a debtor nation on the various items of invisible exchanges, and was paying annually something like $122,500,000 on such accounts.

In the first place we owed foreign nations for interest upon a mass of invested capital, which was not less than $1,500,000,000 in 1874, and increased to some $2,000,000,000 before the close of this period. The rate of interest upon these investments decreased from six to perhaps four per cent, as the years passed, and may have averaged about five per cent. This would make the annual interest charge stand at $80,000,000 or $90,000,000 upon the average amount of capital invested; so that, for the twenty-three years, this country owed from $1,840,000,000 to $2,070,000,000. But this sum would be decreased by the new investments made during the period, which aggregated $500,000,000.

Secondly, our foreign merchant marine showed a continual decline, so that imports brought in foreign vessels exceeded exports carried in American ships by $9,267,000,000. At the present time it is thought that freight charges upon imports are about ten per cent of the value of the cargoes, while upon exports the estimated charges are as high as fifteen per cent. Upon this basis, the net earnings of foreign ships would aggregate $805,000,000. This item of indebtedness tended to increase, as the proportion of imports in American bottoms declined.

Finally, there were several kinds of debt that cannot be ascertained with much accuracy. In 1869, the annual expenditures of American travellers were placed at $25,000,000, but for recent years they have never been estimated at less than $50,000,000. Upon this account, however, a certain reduction should be made for the money brought into the country by immigrants and foreign travellers. Then, it is known that considerable amounts of real estate are owned by foreign capitalists, and that the rentals upon such property are no small item. Also, various foreign corporations, such as insurance companies, conduct a large business in this country; and their annual profits go to swell the volume of our international indebtedness. When all allowances are made for the uncertainty of the data, enough facts have been presented to account for the constant excess of exports of merchandise and specie from 1873 to 1896. At the close of the period under consideration, the invisible elements of indebtedness must have amounted to $80,000,000 interest upon $2,000,000,000 of foreign capital; $52,000,000 due to foreign ships; something less than $50,000,000 expended by American tourists; and indefinite sums that must have carried the debt up to $200,000,000 per annum.

III

From this survey of the progress of American commerce, certain important conclusions may be drawn concerning the theory of the balance of trade.

(1.) Exports and imports of merchandise may throw no light upon the movement of specie, so that a favorable balance may not result in an inflow of gold nor an unfavorable balance cause an outflow. From 1831 to 1840, merchandise imports exceeded exports by $159,900,000, while the net imports of specie amounted to $50,650,000. On the other hand, from 1873 to 1896, a favorable balance of trade amounting to $2,289,000,000 was accompanied by a net exportation of $529,000,000 in specie.

(2.) Many items that are not included in the customs statistics enter into the determination of the foreign exchanges; and over a period of years, all these elements regulate themselves in such a manner that the total credits of a nation equal the aggregate of the accounts upon which it stands a debtor.

(3.) Whether imports shall exceed exports or exports rise above imports, depends wholly upon the position of the country as a producer of precious metals, or as a debtor or creditor on account of the movements of capital, of the carrying trade, of foreign travel, and the like. If capital is seeking investment in a new country, as was the case in the United States from 1831 to 1837 and from 1863 to 1873, imports must exceed exports; and this condition will be desirable or undesirable according to the advantages or disadvantages of the situation that invites foreign investments. When the inflow of capital ceases, exports must be sent to pay for the interest that accrues each year; and a favorable balance of trade caused in this way will point simply to the fact that the country is able to pay its debts, and will not indicate a peculiarly profitable condition of trade. If a country engages extensively in ocean carrying, imports of commodities will tend to exceed exports; and the unfavorable balance will be the measure of the profits derived from the merchant marine. Finally, in a country that mines an unusual quantity of the precious metals, gold and silver will be exported constantly to other nations where they are less abundant; and this will force larger imports of commodities. This was the condition produced by the Californian discoveries, and it continued until our growing indebtedness to foreign capitalists and ship-owners exceeded the annual product of our mines and caused an enormous excess of exports after 1874.

(4.) In all cases, the precious metals are used chiefly to pay balances, and they form but a very small element in the international exchanges. From 1821 to 1896, the merchandise exports and imports of the United States aggregated more than $53,000,000,000, while the entire shipments of gold and silver were less than $5,000,000,000.

All of these conclusions could be reinforced by a study of the commerce of other countries. In general, it is the younger and poorer nations that show an excess of exports over imports, while the opposite condition prevails in older countries that possess greater accumulations of wealth. Great Britain has had an enormous "unfavorable" balance of trade for many years, and must continue to do so as long as the earnings of her merchant marine and the interest on her foreign investments remain as large as they are at the present time.

The general conclusion is, therefore, that the movements of merchandise indicate nothing more than the position which a country occupies as a debtor or a creditor upon account of the invisible exchanges that form so important an element in international transactions.

But this statement of the case is not wholly complete, and needs to receive one important qualification before it can be accepted by the practical financier. From his point of view an excess of imports or of exports is frequently a matter of great important. Both domestic and foreign exchanges are conducted by means of a complicated system of credit, the volume of which greatly exceeds the reserves of ready money that serve as its foundation. At those seasons of the year when our exports of staple products are largest, exchange usually turns in favor of this country, and gold imports are to be expected. At other seasons, when imports of merchandise are heaviest, exchange may turn in the opposite direction and cause an outflow of gold. Such fluctuations in the exchanges have always existed, and are natural and inevitable under any system of monetary or commercial policy; but they may be important to the world of finance.

A favorable turn in the exchanges that results in a temporary inflow of gold, increases the reserves of the banks, making money plentiful and cheap in the financial centers; and such conditions are favorable to business activity. Upon the other hand, a movement of specie away from the country tends to decrease the reserves, harden the money market, and raise the discount rate. All this, however, is a matter of temporary importance if the currency of the nation is upon a thoroughly sound basis, and if the general condition of business is healthful. When gold imports lower the rate of discount, prices of merchandise and securities rise, and conditions are favorable for increased importations of foreign goods. Moreover, this tendency is accentuated by the concomitant fall in the rate of sterling exchange, which increases the profits that importers derive from their transactions. The result is that the tide soon turns in the opposite direction, and the inflow of gold is checked automatically. When, however, exchange rises to the point that makes gold exports necessary, discount rates are increased, prices tend toward a lower level, foreign bills drawn against exports yield a larger profit, and trade is given a counter impulse that restores the equilibrium.

But the case may be different. If business has been moving onward upon a course of mad speculation, straining to the utmost the delicate mechanism of credit, an unfavorable turn of the foreign trade may cause exports of gold at a time when specie reserves are all too small to withstand such a strain. Thus it is that panics are precipitated. If, in addition, the currency of the country is unsound, the importance of a rise in sterling exchange is greatly magnified. From 1878 to 1893, the United States was engaged in reckless experiments with its paper and silver money. The federal treasury had undertaken to circulate, at a parity with gold, a mass of debased currency the amount of which steadily increased under the operation of our laws calling for purchases of silver; while the banks, which had formerly supplied whatever specie might be needed for export, felt compelled in 1892 to draw upon the precarious gold reserve which the government endeavored to maintain. As soon as this occurred, every demand for gold needed in foreign shipments caused a drain on the slender reserve upon which the stability of our monetary system depended. Under such circumstances, an unfavorable turn of the exchanges was fraught with the direst peril.

But with these qualifications, the conclusions reached in the earlier part of our discussion will stand as correct beyond all reasonable doubt. There can be no greater error than to measure the advantages derived from the commerce of a nation by the excess of exports over imports, or to suppose that an unfavorable balance is a certain proof that the trade has become unfavorable. At the same time, a highly speculative market may well apprehend the consequences of an adverse turn in the exchanges; while a nation with an unsound monetary system will always be the sport of every fluctuation in foreign transactions. Moderation in business activity and the establishment of a standard of value that cannot be shaken, would rob the balance of trade of its last vestige of significance.

IV

It remains for us to consider briefly the tendencies that have manifested themselves in our foreign commerce during the last five years. Exports have increased enormously during this period, while there has been no corresponding movement in the import trade. Nearly all branches of exports have shown a noteworthy increase; but the most remarkable phenomenon has been the expansion in the sales of domestic manufactures, which have risen from $183,595,000 in 1895 to $433,851,000 in 1900. For the four fiscal years ending June 30, 1900, our total exports aggregated $4,903,000,000, while imports amounted to no more than $2,927,000,000, a balance of $1,976,000,000 on the side of the exports. Moreover, the returns for the first eight months of 1901 show a further excess of exports to the amount of $491,000,000.

No statistical data that have been produced offer an adequate explanation of this phenomenon. For the four fiscal years ending in June, 1900, exports had exceeded imports by $1,976,000,000;

while the net importation of specie had amounted to only $94,670,000, leaving a balance of $1,881,000,000. This would be reduced by the interest due on foreign investments, which may have ranged from $80,000,000 to $100,000,000 per annum, a total of $320,000,000 to $400,000,000 for the four years. The sums paid to foreign ship-owners aggregated some $191,000,000 during this period. In recent years, the expenditures of American tourists may have risen above $50,000,000 a year, so that, for the four years under consideration, our indebtedness on this account may have equalled $250,000,000. If the other items of invisible debts averaged $25,000,000 a year, we can make a further deduction of $100,000,000. But all of these items, even if we place interest paid to foreign investors at the highest figures, would amount to no more than $941,000,000, against a balance to our credit of $1,881,000,000.

Events growing out of the Spanish War may have contributed somewhat to reduce the unsettled claims standing apparently to the credit of the United States. For about two and one-half years, we have maintained an army of some 60,000 men in the Philippines, and have incurred in this manner debts which have been increased by the $20,000,000 paid to Spain and by the expenditures of American warships on foreign stations. Yet with this deduction, there would remain a balance, apparently unsettled, of over $800,000,000 upon the trade of the four years.

In financial circles, two explanations have been offered to account for this extraordinary situation. In the first place, it has been suggested that the official statistics have overestimated the value of our exports. As a general thing, customs statistics undervalue both imports and exports, and this tendency is usually more marked in the case of the latter than of the former. But when domestic prices are very high, it is easy to estimate the exports at higher figures than are realized upon the actual sales in foreign markets. Yet a study of the export prices officially reported shows that our statisticians have, in most cases at any rate, valued the exports at less than domestic prices; and it would be hard to demonstrate that overvaluation has actually occurred. We know, however, that many of the trusts have sold their surplus stocks in foreign markets at prices that are very far below the charges exacted from domestic customers, and that some manufacturers not connected with combinations have done the same thing. This would make it probable that exports may have been overvalued to a certain extent.

A second explanation is that, in recent years, American money has been seeking investment abroad, while a considerable amount of foreign capital has been withdrawn from the United States. Since March, 1900, no less than $118,000,000 of British, German, and Swedish securities have been sold in this country, and it is entirely possible that other investments have gone unrecorded. Concerning the alleged withdrawal of capital formerly invested in the United States, no reliable information is accessible in the writer, but leading financial authorities have declared that Wall Street has had no knowledge of such an influx of securities during the last two or three years. Upon the whole, it seems probable that this country now holds unsettled claims to a considerable amount against foreign nations. But, since it is not to be supposed that we have given away the surplus of exported commodities, our outstanding credits cannot exceed greatly the balances carried by international banking houses.

A word concerning the probable development of American commerce during the next decade may not be out of order. In the first place we may enquire whether conditions will remain such as to allow the enormous balance of exports to continue. There are only three forces that may operate to produce this result. If the accumulated wealth of the United States has now become so great that our investors can find better openings in other lands, as, for instance, in colonial dependencies, an excess of exports will result from the outward flow of capital, until the time is reached when the interest charges exceed the annual increment of principal. This force, therefore, will, at the most, prove to be of comparatively short duration. Another possibility is the withdrawal of foreign investments now placed in the

United States, which would be a second cause of an excess of exports. This force, however, would spend itself in the course of a few years; and, moreover, the removal of uncertainty concerning our standard of value ought to lessen the motive for the withdrawal of capital. Finally, there is the chance that our new foreign policy may entail the continued support of large armies in distant parts of the globe, which would tend toward a balance of exports. But the desire for strenuous living seems, upon the whole, more likely to show an abatement than an increase; and, if this forecast proves correct, military outlays will not intensify permanently the forces making for an excess of exports over imports.

Upon the other hand, counteracting causes may develop that will contribute to reduce our annual indebtedness to foreigners on account of the invisible items of the exchanges, and eventually will make an excess of exports an impossibility. First among these influences will be the revival of our foreign carrying trade.

The flourishing conditions of our merchant marine from 1790 to 1855 was mainly due to our possessing a cheap and abundant supply of ship timber. With the advent of the iron and then the steel vessel, this industry was certain to decline, so long as the American price of iron ranged above that prevailing in England. Recent years have reversed conditions in this respect, and the astonishing development of our iron and steel production will furnish shipbuilders with an opportunity which, as recent events show, they are likely to improve. To the extent by which, during the next decade, American vessels recover their share of the carrying trade, our indebtedness to foreigners upon this account will tend to decrease, and one cause for an annual excess of exports will be removed. A second influence will become operative if investments of American capital in other countries show, as they are likely to do, a tendency to increase. Temporarily, this movement will cause an outflow of commodities; but, sooner or later, the annual interest will be sufficient to produce an opposite tendency. So far, then, as indebtedness on account of capital is concerned, we may expect that conditions in the United States will come to resemble those which prevail in older nations which receive each year large imports of commodities that represent the earnings of invested capital. Finally, it should never be forgotten that this country furnishes a large part of the world's annual supply of gold and silver. If the interest upon our own foreign investments and the earnings of our ships ever equal or exceed the claims which are due to other countries upon these two accounts, then the product of our mines will turn the scale in favor of imports and put an end to the present excess of exports.

Upon the whole, it may be predicted that the existing condition of our foreign exchanges cannot continue for many years, and that, possibly before the present decade has passed, the relation between our import and export trades must be radically altered. This is not to say that exports must necessarily show an actual decrease, since the exchanges may be corrected by an increase of imports. But if conditions are such as to make the latter process difficult or impossible, then the former alternative will be forced upon us. Every dollar earned by foreign investments of American capital, or by a renascent merchant marine, will cancel an equal debt now owed to other nations upon these accounts, and will make it impossible to sell our present volume of exports without receiving a larger quantity of imports. The present balance of exports is due to our position as a debtor country on the many invisible accounts of the foreign exchanges; and, as we advance to the rank of a creditor nation, we must consent to receive our payment in the products that will represent the profits of our ships or of our capital.

Our recent unbounded prosperity has culminated in a speculative movement that has surpassed previous records. Unquestionably the rage of speculation has exceeded all reasonable bounds, and is likely to be followed by a reaction of equal intensity. While prudent men are even now putting their houses in order, the larger number will continue their overtrading until the storm bursts upon them. At such a time the foreign exchanges will assume a position of great temporary significance. While various European markets have experienced for some months the reaction that is certain to be felt in this country before the accounts of recent years can finally be closed, our own prosperity has suffered no material abatement, and we are able as yet to detect no certain signs of danger. To the firm condition of our markets the recent developments of our foreign commerce have contributed most powerfully, because our international position is so strong that no slight shock could start an outflow of gold sufficient to test the strength of the gigantic fabric of speculation; and, as long as present conditions continue, our day of reckoning may be postponed. In such matters it is usually the unexpected that happens, and no one can foresee the precise course of the events that will ultimately precipitate the crisis; but of one thing we may be assured. Unless untoward domestic occurrences intervene to cause the initial shock, the next turn of the foreign exchanges will put to the severest test our highly sensitive markets, in which the substantial profits of prosperous years have been given fictitious valuations. Whenever our excess of exports falls to a point where it will not counterbalance the debts incurred on the invisible foreign transactions, we shall probably witness the end of the present era of speculation.

THE VARIATION OF PRODUCTIVE FORCES[1]

NEARLY a century has elapsed since the law of diminishing returns became an integral part of classical political economy; and, despite all criticisms, it remains today one of the corner-stones of the science. But important additions have been made, notably during the last twenty years, to the accepted statement of the theory. In some industries the existence of a tendency to constant or increasing returns is predicated, so that commodities are now divided into three classes,—those produced under the conditions of diminishing returns, those which can be supplied with a constant expenditure of labor and capital, and those obtained at a decreasing cost, as the supply is enlarged. Such a mode of classification is widely employed in current discussions of value, monopolies, and the incidence of taxation, as well as in the study of the law of population.

It is the opinion of the author that, in developing what are now known as the laws of diminishing, constant, and increasing returns, economists have fallen into serious confusion of ideas at several points; and not a few writers have shown some appreciation of this fact.[2] But as yet no one has undertaken a critical examination of the relation of modern theories to the substance of the old doctrines, and offered a systematic statement of the results reached by a century of discussion.[3] To this end it is hoped that the present essay may contribute something of value.

[1] Reprinted from *Quarterly Journal of Economics,* Vol. XVI (1901-02), pp. 473-513. Reproduced by generous permission of the publishers.

[2] See Marshall, *Economics,* 4th edition, pp. 511, 512; Hadley, *Economics,* pp. 154, 155; Seligman, *Shifting and Incidence of Taxation,* 2d edition, pp. 199-201.

[3] For the best effort yet made in this direction, see Commons, *The Distribution of Wealth,* p. 116, *et seq.*

I

A brief survey of the early development of the theories in question will throw no little light upon the nature of the problems to be attacked, and will suggest, furthermore, a convenient method of procedure. Thanks to the labors of Mr. Cannan, it will be possible to state very briefly the history of the doctrines down to the year 1848.[4]

As every economist is now aware, the law of diminishing returns was originally formulated in the course of the discussions aroused in England by the high price of corn that ruled during the early years of the nineteenth century. As stated by Malthus, West, and Ricardo, the principle was applied to agriculture; and it was held[5] that, "in the progress of the improvement of cultivation, the raising of rude produce becomes progressively more expensive, or, in other words, the ratio of the net produce of land to its gross produce is continually diminishing." In manufacturing industry, however, it was believed that a different law prevailed, so that additional investments of labor and capital would yield a proportionate increase of product.[6] And, until comparatively recent times, economists have continued to express similar opinions.

But, as originally stated, the law of diminishing returns admitted of two interpretations: it might mean that, *at any given stage of agricultural knowledge or skill*, a point is soon reached at which increased investment begins to yield a smaller proportionate product; or it might be considered to imply that, *as a matter of historical fact*, mankind has had to expend a larger relative amount of labor and capital in order to provide

[4] E. Cannan, *History of Theories of Production and Distribution*. See also *Economic Journal*, March, 1892; Palgrave's, *Dictionary of Political Economy*, Vol. I, pp. 585, 586; *Quarterly Journal of Economics*, Vol. IX, pp. 179 *et seq.*

[5] West, "Essay on the Application of Capital to Land" (1815); Malthus, "Nature and Progress of Rent" (1815); Ricardo, "Essay on the Influence of a Low Price of Corn on the Profits of Stock" (1815).

[6] This is true of Malthus, West, Senior, McCulloch, and Mill. Palgrave, *Dictionary of Poltical Economy*, Vol. II, p. 381. In treating of the rent of mines, it was held that diminishing returns were the rule. Note Ricardo, *Principles*, chap. iii.

the additional food necessary to support a growing population. Upon at least one occasion Ricardo made the former application of the principle, basing his argument upon the assumption that no improvements are introduced in agricultural methods; but usually the early writers adopted the latter interpretation of the law, and held that, despite all discoveries and inventions, the growth of population must ultimately increase "the quantity of labor and capital necessary to procure the last addition that has been made to the raw produce of a rich and advancing country."[7] Against such a dismal view of the future of the race, several protesting voices were raised before many years had passed.

Thus, in 1828, Senior declared that, while unwise laws might have such an effect, "under wise institutions" the tendency was not what economists had alleged, but precisely the reverse.[8] In 1832 Thomas Chalmers contended that, while the law of diminishing returns may have driven men to the utilization of inferior soils, nevertheless improvements in the arts of agriculture have made the labor now employed upon poorer margins of cultivation as productive as that formerly expended upon lands of superior fertility.[9] Finally, Henry C. Carey attacked the assumption, often implicit in the statements of Ricardo and others, that the richest soils are historically the first to be occupied, and that the growth of numbers forces men to utilize less fertile lands.[10] But all such criticisms did not prevent most economists from holding to the belief that, although the opening up of new countries and the progress of invention might serve to retard the process, yet, in the end, a continuous increase of population would inevitably result in a decreased return to the labor and capital devoted to the production of the additional food supply.

[7] The quotation is from Malthus, *Nature and Progress of Rent,* p. 45. But citations might be given to the writings of West, Ricardo, James Mill, and McCulloch.

[8] Senior, *Two Lectures on Population* (1828).

[9] *Political Economy,* chap. i. (1832).

[10] H. C. Carey, *Political Economy* (1837-40); *Past, Present, and Future* (1848); *Social Science* (1858-59).

Although Senior, in his *Political Economy* (1836), made important additions to the statement and applications of the law of diminishing returns, we may pass on to the consideration of the views of John Stuart Mill, who adopted Senior's ideas, and made further contributions to the subject. The attention of the reader is invited, therefore, to Mill's treatment of agricultural production, large-scale industry, value, and taxation.

"After a certain, and not very advanced, stage in the progress of agriculture," says Mr. Mill,[11] "it is the law of production from the land that, in any given state of agricultural skill and knowledge, by increasing the labor the produce is not increased in equal degree." Here the application of the law is limited to "any given state of agricultural skill and knowledge," that is, to static conditions. But most of Mill's discussion relates to the actual or prospective progress of population and of agricultural production; and, although his statements may not always seem consistent, there can be no doubt that he considered that discovery and invention could control only temporarily the tendency toward diminishing returns, so that ultimately additional food must be procured "on progressively harder terms."[12] And this he believed to be true of mining and other extractive industries, as well as of agriculture.[13] With manufactures, however, the case was supposed to be different.[14] So far, indeed, as the supply of raw materials is concerned, manufacturing industry was admitted to be subject to the law of diminishing returns; but the labor of converting materials into finished goods was thought to tend "constantly and strongly towards diminution, as the amount of production increases," so that "the causes tending to increase the productiveness of industry, preponderate greatly over the one cause which tends to diminish it."

A second topic, which has played an important part in subse-

[11] *Principles of Political Economy,* Book I, chap. xii, Sec. 2 (1848). Note the similarity to Senior's statement in his *Political Economy,* p. 82.

[12] *Principles,* Book I, chap. xii, Sec. 3; Book IV, chap. iii, Sec. 5.

[13] *Principles,* Book I, chap. xii, Sec. 3.

[14] *Principles,* Book I, chap. xii, Sec. 3; Book IV, chap. ii, Sec. 2. *Cf.* Senior, *Political Economy,* pp. 81-83.

quent discussions, was treated by Mill in a separate chapter devoted to a comparison of large-scale and small-scale production. The subject was suggested to him, perhaps, by the well-known work of Mr. Babbage, who, better than any previous writer, comprehended the economic effects of the factory system.[15] Drawing many of his facts from this source, Mill discussed the advantages and disadvantages resulting from the enlargement of the size of an industrial undertaking,[16] and held that, as a general rule, "the expenses of a business do not increase by any means proportionally to the quantity of business." In referring to such industries as railroads and gas or water companies, he said that all "enlargement in the scale of production is generally an unqualified benefit," thus anticipating the modern theory of natural monopolies.

In presenting the theory of value, Mill divides commodities into three classes: (*a*) those "of which it is physically impossible to increase the supply beyond certain narrow limits"; (*b*) those "which are susceptible of indefinite multiplication without increase of cost"; and (*c*) those "which are susceptible of indefinite multiplication, but not without increase of cost."[17] This classification, which is but an elaboration of distinctions drawn by Ricardo,[18] is based, obviously, upon particular applications of the theory of monopoly, the economy of large-scale production, and the law of diminishing returns. With more or less important modifications, it has played a significant part in modern discussions of the theory of value.

And, finally, in treating of the incidence of taxation, Mill makes an important distinction between the effects of a tax

[15] Babbage, *Economy of Machinery and Manufactures* (1832).

[16] *Principles,* Book I, chap. ix.

[17] *Principles,* Book III, chap. ii, Sec. 2. *Cf.* also the table of contents.

[18] Ricardo recognized commodities "the value of which is determined by their scarcity alone," and commodities which "are procured by labor." The second class would subdivide into manufactured products and raw produce, the latter being secure under conditions of decreasing returns. I shall pass over Senior's somewhat peculiar classification, which has not been followed by later writers. *Political Economy,* p. vii. But, in discussing the effect of increased demand upon supply, Senior distinguished between raw produce and manufactured commodities.

imposed upon raw products, secured under conditions of diminishing returns, and other commodities that are free from such limitations of supply.[19] Here, again, subsequent theories have found a new point of departure.

For two reasons Mill's discussion of these topics possesses peculiar significance. In the first place it summed up nearly all the results reached by earlier writers; and then it left the theory in a position that was certain, in the course of time, to lead to important modifications and extensions. It is evident that the subjects treated by Mill included two things that far transcended the scope of the original law of diminishing returns. That principle had related to the productivity of labor and capital when employed in the cultivation of land or the utilization of other natural resources. But Mill proceeded to discuss the efficiency of productive agents when organized in manufacturing establishments of varying size, thus introducing a very different problem, as economists are now coming to realize. Finally, in treating of the law of value and the incidence of taxation, Mill looked at the process of production from still another point of view,—the conditions that govern the entire supply of any particular commodity; and this involved a third set of considerations that needs to be carefully distinguished from the other two. Subsequent writers have discussed all three problems, but have seldom appreciated the fact that different principles are involved in every case, and that, in each instance, we are obliged to study the process of production from a different point of view. For this reason, in presenting the later history of the theories in question, we shall treat separately each of the three problems considered by Mr. Mill.

II

First in order of both logical and historical development comes the law of diminishing returns. This principle, as we have

[19] *Principles*, Book V. chap. iv. In this matter, Mill follows the argument of Senior. *Cf.* Senior, *Political Economy*, pp. 120 *et seq.* Cournot, in his treatment of taxes on commodities, had considered the influence of diminishing and increasing returns. Curnot, *Théorie des Richesses* (1838).

seen, admits of two interpretations, the static and the dynamic, of which we shall now consider the former.[20] Assuming a particular state of the arts of production, economists have had little difficulty in recognizing that in the extractive industries the continued investment of labor and capital upon any given tract of land will, after a certain point is reached, yield a diminishing proportionate return. But, in considering manufactures and commerce, most writers have followed Senior and Mill in holding that these industries are governed by a different law.[21]

Yet, as Professor Commons has so clearly shown,[22] when we study the investment of labor and capital *upon a given tract of land,* we find that all industries show a diminishing return after the investment of labor and capital has been carried to a certain point.[23] Under given technical conditions, factories, and even office buildings in large cities, will not be raised beyond a certain number of stories, since better results can finally be secured by resorting to construction upon other land. Oversight of this fact is due to a failure to consider agriculture and manufactures from the same point of view, namely, the possible extent of investments upon a given area.[24]

[20] Ricardo, in his "Essay on the Influence of a Low Price of Corn," considered static conditions. So did Senior and Mill when they made the assumption, "agricultural skill remaining the same." Senior, *Political Economy,* 82; Mill, *Principles,* Book I, chap. xii, Sec. 2. For later writers see Marshall, *Economics,* p. 227; Nicholson, *Political Economy,* Vol. I, p. 152.

[21] Cairnes, *Leading Principles,* pp. 118, 132-134; Sidgwick, *Political Economy,* 2d edition, p. 144; Walker, *Political Economy,* 3d edition, pp. 38, 39; Gide, *Political Economy,* p. 329; Clark, *Philosophy of Wealth,* pp. 97, 100. Some writers, without expressly stating that manufactures are governed by a different principle, apply the law only to agriculture and mining. Fawcett, *Manual of Political Economy,* 6th edition, p. 74; Newcomb, *Political Economy,* p. 242.

[22] Commons, *Distribution of Wealth,* pp. 116, 117; also, in *Publications of the American Economic Association,* Vol. VIII, p. 101.

[23] This is recognized by Marshall, *Economics,* pp. 246, 247; Nicholson, *Political Economy,* Vol. I, pp. 159, 160; Commons, *Distribution of Wealth,* pp. 132-134; Bullock, *Introduction to Economics,* 2d edition, pp. 167-170.

[24] Ricardo and Malthus applied the law of diminishing returns to the cultivation of given tracts of ground, when they spoke of land of the first quality, land of the second quality, etc. Senior explicitly applies the law to "additional labor employed on the land in a given district." *Political Economy,* p. 82. Mill discusses "the quantity of produce capable of being raised on any given piece of land." *Principles,* Book I, chap. xii, Sec. 1. Later writers do the same thing. Walker, *Political Economy,* p. 35; Newcomb, *Political Economy,* p. 242; Hadley, *Economics,* p. 43; Clark, *Distribution of Wealth,* p. 165; Palgrave, *Dictionary*

Without doubt an important difference exists between the industries in question. In agriculture it is possible to invest only a small or moderate amount of labor and capital upon a definite area before the point of diminishing returns is reached, while in manufactures and commerce enormous investments can be made even upon a single acre. Yet the only difference is one of degree, and the same law ultimately applies in both cases. No exception can be taken to Mr. Cannan's statement[25] that the "fact that a certain amount of space is required for productive labor in other branches of industry is of little practical importance as regards the effect of variations of population on the productiveness of all industry taken together, because these branches of industry require very little space compared with agriculture." But for the study of other questions it is very necessary to remember that investments upon a given area of land are subject to diminishing returns in all industries.

This will become evident when we consider that the classical theory of rent is based upon a comparison of the productivity of investments made upon definite tracts of land. So far as agricultural rent is concerned, this statement is a mere commonplace. But the traditional formula for the determination of rent could not apply to land used in manufactures and commerce unless a law of diminishing returns governed investments made upon given areas employed for such purposes.[26] For the study of distribution, therefore, the static aspect of this principle is of most fundamental importance.

Under static conditions, then, the law of diminishing returns governs investments of labor and capital made in any

of Political Economy, Vol. I, p. 585. But, when manufacturers are considered, no such limitation is implied; and writers consider either a *manufacturing establishment* that is free to extend its operations over additional land or *the industry of manufactures* as a whole.

[25] Cannan, *Elementary Political Economy*, pp. 24, 25. *Cf.* Hadley, *Economics*, p. 155, note.

[26] This is recognized by Marshall and Commons. The former (*Economics*, pp. 246, 247), after showing that "building land does give a diminishing return," says that "the theory of ground rents is substantially the same as that of farm rents." The latter (*Distribution*, p. 134) says that, if "diminishing returns apply only to agriculture, there can be no law of rent for manufacturing and mercantile sites."

industry upon a given area of land.[27] This principle has usually been proved by showing that, if it were not true, all production would be conducted upon a few favored tracts,[28] but there are not wanting actual experiments that seem to confirm the law.[29] This much, at least, of the traditional body of economic doctrine has successfully withstood both earlier and later criticism.[30]

Passing now to the dynamic applications of the law of diminishing returns, we find that this aspect of the principle has always been of the greatest interest to economists, who have been especially concerned with the probable effects of an increase of population upon the conditions that control the supply of food. Even when they have not believed that the productivity of agriculture has actually decreased in the past, writers have generally held that the future growth of numbers must ultimately compel mankind to procure the means of subsistence upon "progressively harder terms."[31]

But it is evident that, in order to study the influence of increased population upon social prosperity, it is necessary to

[27] Few economists, probably, would refuse to accept the law as stated. Professor Patten's "law of limited returns" has been criticized by Sidgwick, and has been rejected by one of his own disciples. Patten, *Premises of Political Economy*, pp. 155, 182; Sidgwick, *Political Economy*, p. 293; Devine, *Economics*, pp. 346, 347.

[28] Professor Patten says that Mill "was the first to try to prove the law of diminishing returns." But Senior had advanced in 1836 the line of proof referred to in the text. *Political Economy*, p. 85. To this method of proving the law, Professor Patten objects that his own "law of limited returns" would explain the fact that men have recourse to poorer soils. This may be granted. *Premises of Political Economy*, pp. 152-154. But if, as Professor Patten contends, the returns increase proportionately up to the point where no additional product can be secured by any increase of the investment, then men would not resort to poorer lands until the absolute limit of productivity had been reached on the better soils. And this is not the case.

[29] For pertinent estimates by Von Thünen, see *Der isolirte Staat*, Vol. II, chap. i, p. 179 (quoted by Roscher, *Political Economy*, Vol. II, p. 17, note 5). See reference given by Marshall, *Economics*, p. 232, note.

[30] It is impossible to consider here Professor Commons's application of the principle to the *value* of the product of a given area as well as to the *quantity*. *Distribution of Wealth*, pp. 138-140. I believe, however, that the essential facts for which Commons here contends can be stated satisfactorily without introducing this refinement of the theory. *Cf.* Marshall, *Economics*, pp. 229, 230.

[31] Mill, *Principles*, Book I, chap. xii, Sec. 3; Book IV, chap. iii, Sec. 5; Cairnes, *Leading Principles*, p. 119; Walker, *Political Economy*, pp. 313, 314; Macvane, *Political Economy*, p. 314.

pass from our present standpoint,—the productivity of investments made upon a definite tract of land,—and consider the productivity of the agricultural industries of an entire country or of the civilized world. When the latter question is raised, we at once involve ourselves in problems that cannot be solved by the sole aid of the laws applicable to the investments upon any given area. Manifestly, these principles are one factor in the situation; but they are not the only thing involved, so that we cannot hope to discuss adequately the question of social prosperity from the narrow point of view now under consideration.

All that can be done, so long as we confine ourselves to the productivity of investments upon a given area, is to say that in agriculture the point of diminishing returns seems to be reached when a relatively small amount of labor and capital has been expended, so that, as population increases, a much larger amount of land must be taken into cultivation. And, upon the other hand, in manufactures and commerce the intensity of profitable investment upon a small area is so great that the need of resorting to additional land in order to secure more standing room, is not likely to exercise any material influence upon the productivity of these industries. To the question of social prosperity the study of our first standpoint can contribute nothing more decisive than this; but for the theory of distribution, which involves primarily the static aspects of the principle, the law of diminishing returns from investments upon a given area is of far-reaching importance.

In order to avoid any possible confusion in the use of terms, the expression "diminishing returns" will be applied hereafter solely to the productivity of labor and capital upon a definite tract of land. In discussing the problems that remain to be considered, we shall find that the operation of other principles is involved besides the law just mentioned. For these other principles different names should be used; and it is hoped that a consequent gain in clearness of thought and presentation will justify our insistence upon the need of greater precision in terminology.

III

After the publication of Mill's *Principles* it became almost the fashion for treatises on economics to devote one or more chapters to the subject of production upon a large and upon a small scale,[32] and in recent years many special studies have been made of the "size of the modern business unit" or of "the structure of modern industry."[33] As Professor Commons has clearly shown,[34] and one or two other writers have suspected,[35] this problem is very distinct from that involved in the law of diminishing returns. Instead of studying the results obtained from investments upon a given area of land, we have now to investigate the efficiency of the productive process when carried on in establishments of various sizes that occupy as much or as little land as may be required. The important difference between the two points of view will be made increasingly apparent in the following paragraphs.

The growing importance of capital, especially of the fixed variety, during the nineteenth century led to a marked increase in the size of the average business unit; and, naturally enough, attracted the attention of economists. In recent years this enlargement of the scale upon which single firms or companies operate has gone so far as to produce actual monopoly in many industries, and to appear to threaten it in many others. No one doubts that, within certain limits at least, "the expenses of a business," to use the words of Mr. Mill, "do not increase by any means proportionally to the amount of business done." But diversities of opinion exist concerning the extent of the economies realized after an undertaking has assumed a certain size.

[32] Fawcett, *Political Economy*, chap. vi; Gide, *Political Economy*, Part II, chap. i; Marshall, *Economics*, Book IV, chap. xi; Nicholson, *Political Economy*, Book I, chaps. viii and ix.

[33] Taylor, *History of the Factory System;* Wells, *Recent Economic Changes;* Schultze-Gaevernitz, *Der Grossbetrieb;* Hobson, *Evolution of Modern Capitalism*. The earlier work of Babbage has already been cited. See, finally, Willoughby, in *Yale Review*, Vol. VII, pp. 72-94.

[34] *Distribution of Wealth*, Vol. 117, pp. 130-132.

[35] Marshall, *Economics*, pp. 511, 512; Hadley, *Economics*, pp. 154, 155, note.

Doubtless differences exist between the various classes of undertakings. In the field of transportation and of the so-called distributive industries, probably no economist would question that "the industrial units which are necessary for proper utilization of labor have become so large as to produce actual monopoly."[36] In manufactures the existence of the same tendency is maintained by the advocates of the modern trust; but, upon the other hand, not a few economists believe that a point of maximum efficiency of plant is attained before a single establishment becomes so large as to monopolize the whole field.[37] In agriculture the case seems to be materially different, so much so that the whole drift of recent opinion is that the movement towards concentration has made no headway in this industry.[38]

So far as our present experience is concerned, therefore, it seems impossible to formulate any single law that will be applicable to all classes of business. In the distributive industries it is clear that increased investment of labor, capital, and land in a single enterprise results in continued economies up to a point at which a single company secures control of the entire supply.[39] In agriculture, however, the advantages of production on a large scale generally disappear after the business unit attains a very moderate size. Concerning manufactures a con-

[36] Hadley, *Economics*, p. 153.

[37] For a survey of the literature and an estimate of the results the writer will refer to an earlier paper published in this journal. See Vol. XV, pp. 191-203.

[38] In England there has been a tendency towards a less favorable view of "small farming" than Mill entertained. *Cf.* Mill, *Principles*, Book I, chap. ix, Sec. 4, with Nicholson, *Political Economy*, Vol. I, pp. 138-150. In the United States, one or two decades ago, the growth of a few "bonanza" farms led some writers to express the opinion that the tendency towards production on a large scale was strong even in agriculture. See Wells, *Recent Economic Changes*, Vol. 99, pp. 461-465. But events of the last ten years seem to point in the opposite direction, and it is now asserted that the small farm is more than maintaining its own. Spahr, in *Outlook*, November 4, 1899; Ely, *Monopolies and Trusts*, pp. 192-195; *Publications of American Statistical Association*, Vol. VI, p. 306. A recent socialistic writer, although naturally "inclined toward the concentration idea," admits that the farm of moderate size is growing at the expense of the two extremes. Simons, *The American Farmer*, p. 101.

[39] Obviously, there is some ultimate limit to these economies, else all cost would disapear. We mean simply that no limit is reached before a monopoly is established.

troversy now exists, and economists are divided in opinion as to the extent to which the enlargement of the scale of undertaking increases the efficiency of production.[40]

The purpose of this paper is not to formulate a law governing the economy of large-scale production in manufactures or in any other industry, but rather to show the nature of the problems here involved. It is clear that we are now dealing with the efficiency of industrial organization as it relates to the size of the business unit, without any restriction as to the area of land over which investments may be extended. In order to avoid confusion of terms, it is proposed to refer hereafter to the principle or principles governing large-scale production as "the law of economy in organization."

If doubts are still entertained concerning our contention that the law of economy in organization differs in nature very widely from the law of diminishing returns, a single illustration will serve to make the point entirely clear. Professor Marshall cites the following experiment in proof of the law of diminishing returns. Four plots of land "of an acre each were treated exactly alike, except in the matter of ploughing and harrowing, with the following result":—

Plot.	*Cultivation.*	*Product per acre.*
1.	Ploughed once	16 bushels
2.	Ploughed once and harrowed once	18½ "
3.	Ploughed twice and harrowed once	21⅔ "
4.	Ploughed twice and harrowed twice	23¼ "

[40] Cournot, in constructing the "supply schedule" of a single producer or firm, seemed to hold that, as the volume of business increased, the cost of production generally decreased indefinitely, in manufactures, at least. *Mathematical Principles of the Theory of Wealth,* American translation, p. 59. Such a condition, of course, would inevitably result in monopoly. Marshall notices this (*Economics,* p. 514, note), and presents reasons for thinking that, as a matter of fact, the growth of a single firm or company will be arrested before monopoly is attained. *Economics,* pp. 364-366, 394, 395. Ely holds that, after a business has attained a certain size, "new fixed charges emerge" with any further enlargement of the output. *Monopolies and Trusts,* pp. 65-66, 165. Seligman makes a similar contention, but does not state clearly whether the new fixed charges appear before or after the point of monopoly is reached. *Shifting and Incidence of Taxation,* p. 201. See, finally, *Quarterly Journal of Economics,* Vol. XV, pp. 198, 199.

With this table let us compare another which can be constructed from data given by Mr. Wells concerning the economy of large-scale production on the Pacific coast. The figures are drawn from a doubtful source, and their accuracy is open to question; but they illustrate perfectly the character of experimental proof relating to the law of economy in organization:—

Size of ranch.	*Cost of each unit of product.*
1,000 acres	92½ cents
2,000 "	85 "
6,000 "	75 "
15,000 "	60 "
30,000 "	50 "
50,000 "	40 "

But, although the two principles are distinct, nevertheless a relation exists between the law of diminishing returns and the law of economy in organization. The former principle is one, but only one, of the factors upon which the second depends. In industries where only a small amount of capital can be concentrated upon a given area of ground the difficulties of organizing business upon a large scale are materially increased.[41] In agriculture, for instance, if a farmer wishes to enlarge his output, he must increase greatly the size of his farm; and this adds materially to the cost of supervision, and renders difficult the study of the varying capabilities of each small tract of land. But many other factors besides diminishing returns from a given area enter into the determination of the efficiency of production upon a large scale.

First comes the all-important factor, economy in fixed capital, which usually makes for concentration. Then there is the need for skilful business management, which requires far greater ability as an establishment grows to colossal proportions. Again, the problem of finding a market for the increased output is sometimes an important consideration, especially in the case of commodities that are "specialties," appealing to a fickel public taste or a local demand. Doubtless other factors

[41] This is clearly stated by Mr. Marshall. *Economics,* p. 366.

could be mentioned, but we have suggested a sufficient number to show that the law of diminishing returns from a given area is only one element that contributes to a complex result.

If this view of the case is correct, it is evident that we cannot co-ordinate the law of diminishing returns and the law of economy in organization. Yet this is what many writers appear to do when they say that agriculture is subject to a law of diminishing returns, and that a law of increasing returns governs most branches of manufactures. Such a statement confounds two distinct problems,—investment upon a given tract of land and investment in business units that extend over any requisite area; and it co-ordinates two principles that are not of the same order, of which the former is but one of the number of factors upon which the operation of the latter depends. It is in order to avoid even the implication that the two principles are co-ordinate, or that they relate to the same problem, that we have suggested the adoption of a change in terminology, by which "economy in organization" will be substituted for "increasing returns."

IV

It has been shown that Mill, in his discussion of the theory of value, elaborated a classification of commodities which was based upon the three sets of conditions that were believed to control the supply. In one form or another a similar method of procedure has been adopted by most subsequent writers, and this tendency of economic thought is especially marked at the present day.

We have already intimated that Mill's classification raised a third distinct problem which must be distinguished carefully from those presented by the investment of labor and capital upon a given area or in a given business unit of any particular size. Mill refined his statement of the laws of value by considering the circumstances under which the entire supply of any commodity is secured, and in so doing adopted a third point of view for studying the efficiency of the process of production. A failure to recognize this fact has caused no little confusion in several directions, and has led to one erroneous application of modern theories of value.

It is important to notice, first of all, that the conditions controlling the supply of any commodity may be studied from two points of view,—the static and the dynamic. In the first case,[42] we assume that the conditions of production remain stationary, and then inquire what the circumstances are under which the commodity is supplied. In the second, we suppose that one cause or another changes the state of the industry, and proceed to investigate the consequent alteration of the terms upon which production will be carried on. It is from the static point of view that we need to formulate the theory of normal value, while the dynamic aspects of the question must be considered when we study the effects that changes of demand will exercise upon the conditions of supply. Both aspects of the problem must now be treated, and in the order just mentioned.

A. Supply under Static Conditions—If we assume that the arts of production remain stationary, the supply of any commodity may be secured under two conditions,—monopoly and competition. In the former case it is evident that all the units of the supply will be furnished at what must be regarded as a uniform cost.[43] This does not mean that all units of the monopolist's capital are equally efficient, but simply that our methods of bookkeeping compel us to average up the results, and to assume that each unit of product is furnished at the same cost.[44] This cost may, and often does, vary with the

[42] Note Marshall, *Economics*, pp. 439-441.

[43] This presupposes, of course, an absolute monopoly. Usually, some residual competition remains; and differences of cost appear in this portion of the supply. But the theory of monopoly value disregards the small amount supplied in this way.

[44] In the case of a single establishment which extends its scale of operations until it monopolizes the entire field, this conclusion is obvious. If, however, the monopoly is formed by the union of a number of different establishments, then, at the outset, it would be possible to recognize that the various factories had different costs. But the monopolist would endeavor, even in this case, to raise the several plants to the same scale of efficiency; and this process would finally eliminate the differences that might have existed at the start. With an established monopoly, therefore, we may affirm that the separate units of product will be supplied at a uniform cost.

amount of the commodity that is produced. But for each quantity of the supply it must be regarded as uniform.[45]

The reader will observe that, when we assume a monopoly to exist, this third standpoint for viewing the process of production becomes the same as the second, since the conditions controlling the entire supply of the commodity are, by hypothesis, identical with those which determine the efficiency of a single firm.[46] But the similarity ends as soon as we assume that an industry is controlled by competition; for, under such circumstances, we assume that there are several or many independent firms, no one of which can represent precisely the conditions under which the whole supply is produced.[47]

Now, when competition exists, the supply is furnished under conditions that bring it about that the various units are produced at different costs. Mill and many other economists have often reasoned in a manner that would lead one to suppose that they believed in the existence of a large class of commodities furnished by competing producers at the same cost. Thus Mill states that commodities of his third class, which includes "all the raw produce of the earth," have "not one, but several costs"; while goods of his second category, which embraces "the large class" of manufactured articles, are supposed, by fair implication, to be supplied at a uniform cost.[48] The value of products of the former class is governed by the cost of producing the most expensive unit, while that of the latter class depends simply upon "cost of production." Sidgwick expressly states that there may be cases "where the cost of production can be assumed to be the same for all producers," and contrasts this condition with that represented by "Mill's third class, of which the cost of production must be taken to be different for different portions of the aggregate amount pro-

[45] This is recognized by Seligman, *Shifting and Incidence,* pp. 195, 196.

[46] *Cf.* Commons, *Distribution of Wealth,* p. 130.

[47] *Cf.* Marshall, *Economics,* pp. 511-514.

[48] See Mill, *Principles,* Book III, chap. ii, Sec. 2; chap. iii, Sec. 1; chap. v, Sec. 1. I am aware that Mill is not always consistent on this point. See Book III, chap. vi, Sec. 1, par. vii. But, unless he really means that his second class of goods is produced at a uniform cost, his remarks concerning the third class are meaningless.

duced."[49] And other writers have interpreted Mill in a similar manner.[50]

Professor Marshall approaches the problem in a somewhat different way, but his statement of the case is influenced evidently by Mill's method of classification.[51] In treating of the value of raw produce, he recognizes the existence of different costs, and says that value depends upon "the cost of production on the margin of the profitable application of capital and labor." Then, when he considers other commodities, he introduces the device of "the representative firm," and holds that the value of an article "may be taken to be its normal expenses of production (including gross earnings of management) by that firm." The same method is followed by Mr. Flux, and, perhaps, by President Hadley.[52] Now the "representative firm" of which these writers speak is defined as a firm free from the disadvantages of some struggling new producer, and not enjoying the unusual advantages of an exceptionally efficient company, but one that is managed with "normal ability" and "fair success."[53] This definition is plainly inconsistent with the assumption that all producers furnish their supplies of manufactured products at a uniform cost, and is a recognition of the fact, for which we are now contending, that all products, manufactured as well as agricultural, are, under competitive conditions, supplied at varied costs.

And this is the view that not a few economists have taken when discussing the simpler problems connected with normal value.[54] When scores or hundreds of independent producers are

[49] *Political Economy*, pp. 196, 197.

[50] See Fawcett, *Political Economy*, pp. 315, 316, 325, 339; Adams, *Science of Finance*, pp. 390-392; and *Outline of Lectures on Poltical Economy*, 2d edition, p. 25. Nicholson, also, distinguishes commodities "continuously and permanently produced at different costs" from those that can be "increased indefinitely at the same cost per unit." *Political Economy*, Vol. II, pp. 54, 56.

[51] *Economics*, pp. 479, 480, 422.

[52] Palgrave, *Dictionary of Political Economy*, Vol. III, pp. 607, 608; Hadley, *Economics*, pp. 88, 89. Hadley does not use the expression "representative firm." For this he substitutes producers who have neither "the advantage of old locations" nor "the disadvantage of old methods."

[53] Marshall, *Economics*, p. 397.

[54] Seligman states this most explicitly. *Shifting and Incidence*, pp. 193-197. Some writers, in treating of value, assume different costs of production for

engaged, under natural or other conditions that result in inequality of advantages, the chances would be indefinitely great that the various units of supply must be procured at different costs. If doubts could have existed upon this subject a decade ago, the question would be finally settled now in view of the almost universal fact that our trusts have found that their constituent plants were, prior to consolidation, of very unequal efficiency.

The only difference that can be admitted between agricultural and manufactured products is that the former may show a much greater range of variation between the lowest and the highest costs. This is because the point of diminishing returns is so quickly reached in agriculture that increased production calls for the utilization of many grades of land possessing widely differing advantages of fertility and location. Even with manufactured products the possible differences of cost would not be the same for all commodities. In a branch that does not favor production upon a very large scale the variations would be wider than in another that permitted the concentration of production in a few large factories.[55]

If the case were otherwise, if all producers of manufactured commodities enjoyed equal advantages and supplied their goods at the same cost, there would be no room for those differential gains, recognized even by Mill,[56] which have played so important a part in modern theories of distribution.[57] We conclude therefore that, in competitive industry, under static conditions, the rule is that producers possess unequal facilities and unlike abilities, so that we may affirm the existence of a law of varied costs.

---

every commodity. Walker, *Political Economy*, p. 100; Hobson, *Economics of Distribution*, pp. 93, 97, 98; Commons, *Distribution*, p. 20. Hadley says: "If the demand for the products of any industry is too large to be met by a single organized source of supply, however great its natural advantages, we shall be likely to see a system of differential gains, due to the independent competition of men who make goods for the same market at different expense." *Economics*, p. 286.

[55] Seligman, *Shifting and Incidence*, 197, 198; Patten, *Stability of Prices*, p. 49; Bullock, *Introduction to Economics*, pp. 204, 205.

[56] *Principles*, Book III, chap. v, Sec. 4.

[57] It is unnecessary to refer to authors, but note Hadley, *Economics*, p. 286.

B. Supply under Dynamic Conditions.—The dynamic conditions of production have been studied by economists mainly when they have had occasion to consider the terms upon which the supply of commodities can be increased. Such questions arise in the study of economic prosperity and of the effect of changes of demand upon normal value.[58] In both cases the problem investigated is the productivity of land, labor, and capital in furnishing an increased supply of some given commodity.

Under conditions of monopoly, evidently, this question is identical with the one considered in our study of large-scale production; for we have to deal, in each instance, with the results of enlarging the output of a single industrial enterprise. But when competition exists, the problem becomes less simple.

Competition, as we have seen, results in varied costs for the several portions of the supply furnished at any time by different producers. Now when production increases, the important question is whether the cost of the marginal, or most expensive, unit rises or falls; for it is this unit that determines the normal value of the enlarged supply.[59] Most economists now recognize three possible conditions under which an increment of supply may be secured,[60]—increasing, constant, and

[58] Economic prosperity has been studied principally in connection with the law of population. The effect of changes in demand upon value was studied by Senior (*Political Economy*, pp. 119, 120) and by Mill (*Principles*, Book IV, chap. ii). The importance attached to the subject has increased rather than decreased in recent years. *Cf.* Marshall, *Economics*, pp. 446-452, 523-536; Nicholson, *Political Economy*, Vol. II, pp. 54-58; Hobson, *Economics of Distribution*, chap. iii.

[59] For some purposes it is important to consider also the extent of the differential gains received by the producers who furnish the less expensive units. But this is apart from our present inquiry.

[60] Mill, although he saw that increased production of some commodities tended to lower the cost, made no use of that fact when he divided reproducible goods into two classes,—those that can be increased at constant cost and those not susceptible of multiplication except at increased cost. In this he was followed by Fawcett. So far as the writer has been able to determine, Professor Henry C. Adams was the first to make a place in the classification for a third kind of commodities—those of which the supply can be enlarged at a decreasing cost. *Relation of the State to Industrial Action*, p. 55 (1887). For later writers see Marshall, *Economics*, pp. 524, 525; Commons, *Distribution*, p. 124; Nicholson,

decreasing returns. For the word "returns" we shall substitute "cost" in the following discussion, in order to avoid any possible confusion with the law of diminishing returns, which applies to a very different problem from that which is now under consideration.

Passing over the immediate effects of an increased demand,[61] it may be said that, when changing conditions call for a permanent enlargement of the supply, several different influences may be brought into play. As a consequence, the marginal cost of production under the new set of circumstances will be the resultant of a number of contending forces.[62] When due allowance is made for the effect of each of these, we shall see that it is more difficult than is ordinarily supposed to assign any particular commodity or industry to an invariable position in any scheme of classification.

One of these forces is the law of diminishing returns. If the product or industry in question does not permit the intensive application of labor and capital to any given area of land, then the increased demand will have a tendency to force producers to utilize inferior natural agents. Counteracting causes may prevent such a result from occurring; but, undoubtedly, whenever the point of diminishing returns is quickly reached, the tendency will be towards a higher marginal cost for every increment of supply. This principle is most important in the case of extractive industries, and is of little or no significance for manufactures and commerce. But it must be observed that we are dealing with nothing more than a *tendency*. So far as anything yet said is concerned, it would be premature to conclude that agricultural or mining industry is in any given case likely to show an increased cost for an increment of supply.

A second factor is the law of economy in organization. If the conditions of an industry are such that an enlargement in the

Political Economy, Vol. II, p. 54; Seligman, *Shifting and Incidence*, p. 199; Palgrave, *Dictionary of Political Economy*, Vol. III, p. 489.

[61] The immediate result may be to raise the marginal cost of producing any commodity. See Marshall, *Economics*, pp. 442, 443.

[62] Note Marshall, *Economics*, p. 398; Sidgwick, *Political Economy*, p. 190; Seligman, *Shifting and Incidence*, p. 202.

size of the average business unit will make for economy in production, then an increased demand for its products may give a stimulus to improved business organization, and lower the marginal cost at which the supply will be produced. This is, doubtless, often the case with manufactured commodities; and it may seldom happen in agricultural industry. Yet it is merely a tendency, and may or may not actually produce a lower marginal cost, even in manufactures. To say nothing of other counteracting influences, it may happen that the increased demand may cause an excessive investment of new capital *in additional establishments*. If this should occur, the average size of a business unit might remain practically the same as before, so that there would be no reduction of marginal cost due to superior organization. In the woollen industry in the United States it has been asserted by manufacturers that our tariff has had this precise effect in several instances.

A third cause may be found in the stimulus which increased demand may give to inventions and all other improvements of method. These, obviously enough, may occur in agriculture and mining, as well as in manufactures; and tend in all industries to lower the marginal cost in times of prosperity caused by the growth of demand.

And, finally, a fourth consideration should not be overlooked. If monopolized materials enter into the manufacture of a commodity that is the product of a competitive industry, an increased demand for the finished article may not lower the money cost of production. The enlargement of the output of the industry in question would lead to an increased demand for the monopolized materials, and thereby raise the price which the monopolist can exact. This increased cost of materials would tend to counterbalance the economies which an increase of demand would make possible in other directions.

When all four factors are taken into account, it becomes difficult to predict what the precise result of increasing the production of any particular commodity will prove to be. It is certainly unsafe to assume, without much more careful investigation than has been made up to the present time, that in agriculture or mining an increased supply will regularly be produced at a greater marginal cost, and that manufactured commodities can be multiplied at a decreasing cost. We must recognize that any case may involve the operation of more than a single cause, and that, furthermore, the actual result may vary according to the extent to which the supply is increased.

In agriculture it is tolerably certain that a great increase of the product will force men to resort to inferior margins of cultivation. But this fact, as Chalmers rightly insisted,[63] does not necessarily imply that there will be an actual increase in the marginal cost; for, "as the fresh soils that had to be successively entered on became more intractable, the same amount of labor, by the intervention of tools and instruments of husbandry, may have become greatly more effective." Without doubt, as economists have argued, an indefinite increase of population might ultimately force the margin of cultivation down so far that no improvements could counteract the operation of the principle of diminishing returns. But this is not the same as saying that the marginal cost has risen in the past, or that it will rise under the pressure actually exerted by any future growth that population is likely to show. Economists at the present day have recognized this fact, and are decidedly less inclined than were their predecessors to take a pessimistic view of the situation.[64] When we consider that scientific agriculture is merely in its infancy, and that improvements in mechanical trades react upon extractive industry, we are justified in demanding serious proof before we concede that any given increase in the demand for food will necessarily raise the marginal cost of production. Undoubtedly, it may have

[63] *Political Economy*, chap. i.

[64] Marshall says merely that "a continued increase in the application of labor and capital to land must ultimately result in a diminution of the extra produce." *Economics*, p. 230. Nicholson says that "the law gives no countenance whatever" to the assertion that "the absolute cost of production of corn must increase." *Political Economy*, Vol. I, pp. 163, 164, 173. "What may happen at the end of time," he considers "a matter for prophecy and beyond the range of science." Commons says that, in the past, agriculture "has constantly shown increasing returns." *Distribution*, p. 119. Note, also, Devine, *Economics*, p. 360.

that effect; but we have no proof that agriculture is always governed by a law of increasing cost.[65]

In the case of mining the situation is nearly the same, and the chief point of difference is that in the production of minerals the forces that tend to increase the marginal cost may be further neutralized by the economies that come from concentration. Fixed capital plays such an important part in modern mining operations that a definite increase of demand may, by increasing the average scale of production, tend powerfully to lower the marginal cost. Beyond all question the ultimate exhaustion of mineral deposits, as well as the operation of the law of diminishing returns from a given area, would cause a higher marginal cost if the demand should increase without limit. But whether any particular increase of output will be obtained with greater or with less difficulty must be settled by an investigation of the actual conditions of the case, and not by reference to an arbitrary classification of mining as an industry that inevitably shows increasing marginal cost.[66]

In manufactures the strength of the forces that make for a decreasing marginal cost is, doubtless, at a maximum. Even when the raw materials must be procured at an increased cost, the growth in the size of factories and the constant progress of invention would often result in cheaper production in the finished commodities. Yet it would be dangerous to say that in manufacturing industry a larger supply can always be furnished at a lower cost. There may be at any time a limit to the size of a factory of maximum efficiency, and the progress of invention may not necessarily keep pace with every increase of demand. Such conditions might result in a higher marginal cost for an increased supply, even apart from a possible rise

[65] The tendency of economists to classify agriculture as an industry governed by increasing cost is due in some measure to a failure to discriminate between the two standpoints recognized in this essay—the productivity of investments made under static conditions upon a given area and the productivity of an entire industry under dynamic conditions.

[66] In England it is possible that a very large increase of the output of iron or coal would be attended with an increased marginal expense. In the United States it would be very dangerous to predict that such would be the inevitable result.

in the cost of raw materials. All that can be claimed is that manufactures are subject to a law of decreasing cost more often than agriculture or mining, and that the rate of decrease in this industry is often greater that it is in the others. Then also, it is necessary to remember that the results will vary according to the extent to which the supply is to be increased. When an increase of 20 per cent can be secured at a lower marginal cost, an increase of 40 per cent may lead to a higher marginal cost of production. In any event the reduction of cost could not continue indefinitely, else the commodity would finally become a free good.

In current discussions it is usually assumed that there will be many cases in which the marginal cost will remain stationary as the output of an industry is increased, so that we may have a law of constant cost. But such a result could be brought about only by an accidental equivalence of the various contending forces which are set in operation by an increased demand for any commodity.[67] In almost all cases the chances would be greatly against a precise balancing of these opposing influences, so that, in strictness, we must conclude that the usual result of enlarging the output is to raise or lower the marginal cost.[68] But in practice the change in the position of the marginal producer may often be so slight, especially when the supply is increased to only a moderate extent, that no material error is involved in speaking of a condition of constant marginal cost. Even in such cases, however, it would be better to recognize that the conditions are those of increasing or decreasing cost, and then to make allowance for the fact that the change is so small as to be negligible.

Our conclusion is, therefore, that under dynamic conditions we find a law of decreasing and a law of increasing marginal cost, when we consider the efficiency of land, labor, and capital employed in the production of the entire supply of a commodity.

[67] This is perceived by Sidgwick, *Political Economy*, p. 190.

[68] Professor Carver, in discussing the incidence of taxation, mentions only two classes of commodities produced under competitive conditions,—those supplied under increasing and those furnished under decreasing "returns." *Yale Review*, Vol. V, p. 259.

It seems to be impossible, however, to assign to any particular commodity or industry a fixed place in schemes of classification based upon these laws; and it is especially important to remember that the result of any alteration of supply may depend upon the extent of the change that is to be effected. Before applying these laws to any concrete case, we need far more serious study than has yet been made of the actual conditions of the industry in question. Without such particular investigation, attempts to utilize the laws of increasing or decreasing cost are as likely to cause error as to conduce to scientific insight.

V

It remains for us to consider the manner in which the various principles above formulated have been applied to the problems of monopoly, value, and the incidence of taxation. In treating the first of these subjects, economists have often said that the so-called "law of increasing returns" is the primary cause of the growth of modern monopolies. Professor Adams, for instance, has divided industries into three classes,—those showing constant, diminishing, and increasing "returns,"—and has declared that in those cases where the "law of increasing returns" prevails there is an inevitable tendency towards monopoly.[69] Similar views have been expressed by not a few other writers.[70]

It is at this point that the distinction which we have drawn between the law of economy in organization and the laws of increasing or decreasing cost proves most helpful. The writers to whom reference has been made pass unconsciously from the standpoint of a single establishment to that of an entire industry, and apply the same principle, which they call "increasing

[69] *Relation of the State to Industrial Action,* pp. 55, 59, 60.

[70] Seligman, *Shifting and Incidence of Taxation,* pp. 202, 203; *Yale Review,* Vol. V, p. 270; Ely, *Outlines of Economics,* p. 297. In his *Monopolies and Trusts,* pp. 61-65, Professor Ely makes some changes in the statement of the principle. Professor Commons classifies industries in a similar manner, but does not say, except perhaps by implication, that where an industry shows "increasing returns" there will be an inevitable tendency towards monopoly. *Distribution of Wealth,* p. 124. English writers have, generally, at least, avoided the statement that a condition of "increasing returns" in an industry necessarily implies monopoly.

returns," to both cases.[71] But it is clear that an industry can show a decreasing cost for the marginal unit of an increased supply without exhibiting, necessarily, any tendency towards monopoly.[72] The cost of the marginal unit may be lowered by the general stimulus to inventions caused by an increased demand, and this may happen even in the case of agricultural products that are not produced by the methods of large-scale production. Moreover, even when the decreased cost is due wholly or in part to the fact that the growth of demand has made it possible for the average establishment to enlarge its scale of operations, it is probable that in many industries any one establishment will reach a point of maximum efficiency before it develops into a monopoly. By maintaining the distinction between the law of economy in organization and the laws of increasing and decreasing cost, the possibility of confusion at this point is easily removed.

In studying the theory of value, it is necessary to adhere rigidly to the consideration of the conditions that govern an entire industry, and then to discriminate between the static and dynamic problems involved. Our law of normal value should be formulated first of all for static conditions of supply and demand, and we should then study the changes of value that result from dynamic conditions.

Modern theories of value have succeeded in co-ordinating the principle of marginal utility, which governs demand, with the old doctrine of cost of production, which related to the conditions of supply.[73] Since, however, this essay is concerned with

[71] Thus Professor Adams begins with a discussion of the laws applicable to "industries," and then proceeds to examine the situation of "an established business" or "an expanding enterprise." *Relation of the State to Industrial Action*, pp. 55, 57, 59. Professor Commons, in spite of his usual care to separate the two standpoints, explains the condition of "increasing returns" in an *industry*, by saying that the "larger the enterprise," the "cheaper the cost per unit of quantity of product." *Distribution of Wealth*, p. 124. *Cf.* Ely, *Economics* p. 297.

[72] This was stated by Professor Seligman in the first edition of his *Shifting and Incidence*, p. 146, note.

[73] This, I take it, is the service rendered by Professor Marshall's treatment of the theory of value. *Cf.* Commons, *Distribution of Wealth*, chap. i; Hadley, *Economics*, chap. iii; Hobson, *Economics of Distribution*, pp. 68-70.

the question of the efficiency of the process of production, we shall, in our study of static conditions, neglect altogether the laws governing demand, and consider solely the terms upon which supply is furnished. Under a régime of monopoly, it has been shown that the cost of production must be considered to be uniform for all the units of the supply. But, under competitive conditions, the universal rule is that the different portions of the supply are produced at varying costs.

Now it is this law of varied costs that must be applied in determining the normal value of any commodity, under conditions of competition. At any given stage of production the normal value must correspond to the cost of furnishing the marginal, or most costly, unit of the actual supply. It is not the average cost or the cost to a representative firm, but the marginal cost of production that is decisive in fixing the normal value of all commodities. In this respect, manufactured goods differ in no way from the products of the farm or the mine,[74] and it is at this point that our law of varied costs finds its all-important application.

Passing now to dynamic conditions, we shall consider the subject that has received most attention from economists,—the effect of changes in demand upon the terms on which commodities are produced, and hence upon their normal value. In this connection, attention is usually directed mainly to the results of an *increased* demand; and it is at this point that the laws of increasing and decreasing cost find their principal application. We need not hesitate to accept the current doctrine that an increased demand for a commodity that can be furnished at a decreasing cost for the increment of supply actually required will have the effect of lowering the normal value, and that the opposite effect will be produced when the industry in question conforms to the law of increasing cost. But the results of our earlier discussion lead us to insist that the actual result in any concrete case must be determined by a careful consideration of

[74] For illustrations of the confusion arising at this point, from the failure to discriminate between static and dynamic conditions, see Gide, *Political Economy*, pp. 67, 68; Hadley, *Economcs*, pp. 88, 89.

the situation of the industry, and that it is impossible to make the general assumption that manufactured articles can be multiplied uniformly at a decreasing cost, while agricultural or mineral products are necessarily supplied under the opposite conditions. Moreover, we have found reason for doubting whether it is possible to assume the existence of a class of industries of which the output can be increased at a strictly constant cost.

But, when we turn to a consideration of the effects produced by a decrease in the demand, we find that the theories generally accepted lead to an erroneous conclusion. The current doctrine is that, when an industry conforms to the law of decreasing cost, a reduction in the demand, which enforces a curtailment of the supply, will raise the cost of production, and consequently the normal value of the product.[75] Upon the other hand, it is contended that, in industries subject to a law of increasing cost, the reduction of the supply will lower the marginal cost of production and decrease the normal value. This last doctrine is undoubtedly true; but we shall endeavor to prove that the first conclusion is incorrect, and is based upon a confusion between the conditions that control the output of a single establishment and those which govern the product of an entire industry.

Economists who believe that a reduction in the supply of a commodity subject to the law of decreasing cost will raise the marginal cost of production, tacitly assume that the decrease of the product affects all competitors in proportion to their outputs, reduces the scale upon which the average establishment is conducted, and therefore increases the cost. In so doing, they assume that what would be true if one establishment furnished the entire supply, will be true when the product comes from scores or hundreds of competing enterprises. This assumption is wholly inadmissible. The necessity of reducing the entire supply will generally have the effect of forcing out of business the marginal producers, who labor under the greatest disadvantages; and, after production is decreased in this manner, the

[75] See Nicholson, *Political Economy*, Vol. II, p. 56; Marshall, *Economics*, pp. 525, 526.

remaining establishments will be able to conduct their operations upon the same scale as before. This is the precise result which these writers assume to occur in the case of industries that are subject to the law of increasing cost; and there is no reason why the situation should be different in the one case from what it is in the other. Mr. Sidgwick seems to be the only economist who has appreciated this fact, and his statement of the case is worth quoting:[76] "It does not follow from this that a fall in demand will have a similar tendency to increase the cost of production: in most cases the effect of such a fall would, I conceive, rather be to diminish the number of separate establishments in which the branch of production in question was carried on."

It may be conceded that in an industry where there were only a few large enterprises, of nearly the same grade of efficiency, the *immediate* effect of the reduction in the demand might be to decrease the output of all the establishments in almost similar proportions, and therefore in some cases to raise the cost of production. But, if the reduction in demand proved to be permanent, and did not drive the producers into a combination, competition would ultimately eliminate the weakest establishments, and leave the stronger in the same position that they had formerly occupied. Such a case would differ from any other only in respect of the ease and promptness with which the industry adjusted itself to the change in business conditions. The difference is certainly worthy of notice, but it does not affect the ultimate working of our principle.

The erroneous views that have been entertained upon this point are caused by the failure to discriminate between the law of economy in organization and the law of increasing or decreasing marginal cost. Even if the reduced cost of the larger supply resulted solely from the fact that the increased demand had enabled the various establishments to produce upon a larger scale, it would not follow that a subsequent decrease in the demand would compel all competitors to curtail their operations. This, we believe, has been sufficiently demonstrated. But, as a

[76] *Political Economy*, p. 195, note.

matter of fact, the lower cost of an enlarged supply may be the result of general improvements which are introduced throughout the industry in consequence of the stimulus imparted by a growing demand. Now it is evident that no future reduction in the output will drive producers back to the use of discarded machinery and methods; so that in all such cases there is no reason for thinking that a decreased demand will raise the marginal cost. As a general rule, therefore, we must hold that a curtailment of supply will force the weakest producers out of the field, and will not ultimately restrict the operations of the remaining competitors.

The error involved in the current theories will become evident when we consider the diagrams usually employed to illustrate the point in question. Mr. Marshall, for instance, presents the following diagrams in order to show the effects of the laws of increasing and decreasing cost:[77]—

The first figure, which applies to an industry of increasing cost, calls for no comment. But the second, which illustrates the

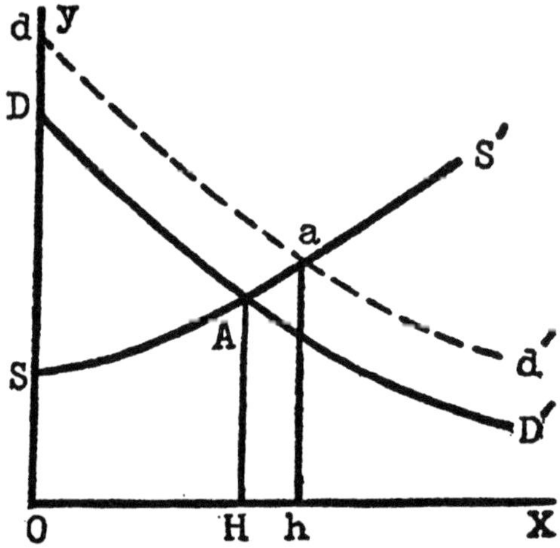

FIG. 1

law of decreasing cost, is open to criticism. For our purpose it is sufficient to examine the supply curve, SS′. This curve begins to decline after the supply is increased beyond OH units, and it

[77] *Economics*, p. 525.

represents nothing more than the rate at which the cost of *the marginal unit* decreases as the output is enlarged. It does not

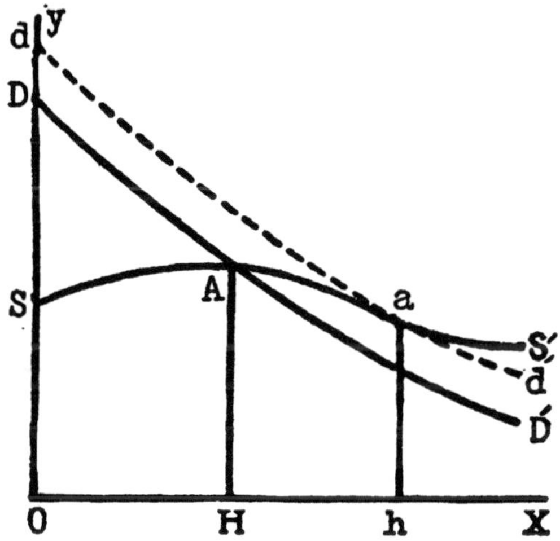

FIG. 2

represent the cost of producing *all* the units of the commodity, and can give us no idea of what will happen when the supply is reduced.

In order to show the effects of the law of decreasing cost upon

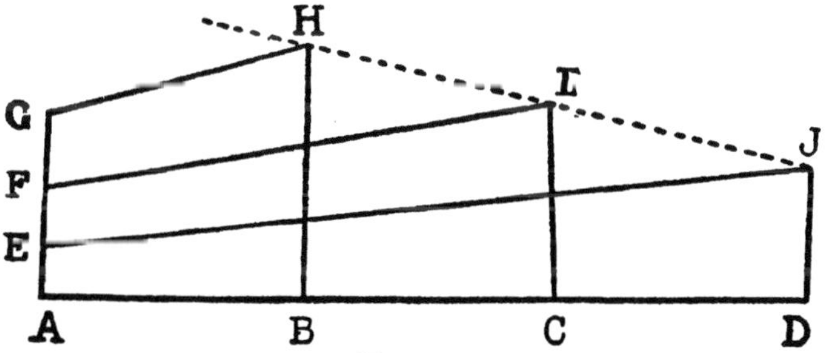

FIG. 3

the conditions of an industry,—*i.e.*, upon the entire supply of a commodity subject to the operation of competition,—the supply curve[78] must be constructed as shown in Fig. 3.

[78] For the sake of simplicity, I shall omit the demand curve, and assume an equilibrium of supply and demand at BH, CI, and DJ, under the various conditions assumed.

Here we assume that AB units can be produced at a marginal cost of BH, and that producers possessing superior ability or facilities will furnish their portions of the supply at varying costs represented by the line GH. Then we assume that, if the supply is increased to AC or AD, the marginal cost will fall to CI and DJ, respectively; while the superior producers will furnish their outputs at costs represented by FI in the first case and EJ in the second. For each stage of production the normal value will depend upon the marginal cost.

If now we assume that an increased demand has enlarged the output from AB to AC, and reduced the normal value from BH to CI, we are in a position to detrmine the effect of a subsequent reduction of the demand. When such a change occurs, the supply will be reduced to something less than AC; and the marginal cost will also recede from CI to some other point along the line FI. In other words, a decreased demand will lower the normal value by forcing out of business the weakest producers, whose costs of production approximate or equal CI. We are able also to demonstrate the precise nature of the error to which Mr. Marshall's diagram leads. His supply curve, SS′ (Figure 2), is the same as the line joining the points H, I, and J (Figure 3). It represents merely the rate at which the marginal cost falls when the supply is enlarged, and does not show the cost of production of the various units of any given quantity of the product, AB, AC, or AD.

For studying the effects of an increasing demand the supply curve drawn by Mr. Marshall will suffice, since all we need to know in that case is the position of the marginal cost of production. But when we consider the result of a subsequent decrease in the supply, it is necessary to draw the lines GH, FI, and EJ, which represent the varying costs at which all except the marginal units are supplied. When this is done, it becomes evident that a decreased demand will lower the marginal cost, and hence the normal value, of commodities subject to the law of decreasing cost as well as of those governed by the law of increasing cost.

And, finally, we come to certain problems relating to the

incidence of taxes imposed upon commodities. It was the theory of Ricardo that[79] "the taxing of all commodities, whether they be necessaries or luxuries, will, while money remains at an unaltered value, raise their prices by a sum at least equal to the tax." But Senior made a distinction between manufactured goods and raw produce, holding that[80] "taxes on manufactured commodities ultimately raise the price, and that by an amount exceeding the amount of the tax. Taxes on agricultural produce in its unmanufactured state do not necessarily occasion any ultimate rise of price, and raise it, if at all, by an amount less than that of the tax." His reason for this opinion was that a tax upon manufactured goods would raise the cost of production by decreasing the quantity produced: whereas, in the case of raw produce, the consequent reduction of supply would throw the poorest lands out of cultivation, and so lower the cost. In this direction, Senior was followed by John Stuart Mill.[81]

Later writers have made use of the laws of increasing and decreasing cost, and have held that a tax upon commodities subject to the law of increasing cost will raise the price by less than the tax, while a tax upon articles produced at a decreasing cost will increase the price by more than the amount of the tax.[82] But such a statement of the laws of incidence depends upon the erroneous inference from the law of decreasing cost which we have criticized in previous paragraphs.

We have seen that, even if the supply of a commodity can be increased at a decreasing cost, it does not follow that a reduction in the output, such as would be caused by a tax, would raise the marginal cost of production. The tax would drive the marginal producers out of the field, and would lower the cost of the marginal unit produced under the altered conditions. Therefore, there is no ground for discriminating between manufactured goods and raw produce or between commodities furnished at a

[79] *Principles of Political Economy*, chap. xvii.

[80] *Political Economy*, pp. 120-124.

[81] *Principles*, Book V, chap. iv, Secs. 2 and 3.

[82] Marshall, *Economics*, pp. 526-530; Nicholson, *Political Economy*, Vol. II, p. 57, Vol. III, pp. 310, 341; Seligman, *Shifting and Incidence*, 207-209; Daniels, *Public Finance*, 71; Davenport, *Outlines of Economic Theory*, p. 220.

decreasing cost and those supplied at an increasing marginal outlay.[83] In all cases we must assume that a certain stage of production has been reached at the time the tax is imposed, and that the tax merely drives the weakest competitors out of the industry. It is true that taxation may restrict the subsequent development of an industry in various ways, and that it may prevent a future reduction of the marginal cost through an increase which would have occurred otherwise in the demand. But this is a different question. There seems to be no reason for thinking that the imposition of a tax will raise the marginal cost above the level that formerly prevailed, and therefore increase the price by more than the tax. In all cases it would seem that the result must be to increase the price by something less than the amount of the tax.

The error which Mr. Marshall and others make in the use of the supply curve drawn to represent the condition of decreasing cost becomes very apparent when this question of incidence is considered. Thus Marshall draws a curve[84] parallel to the original supply curve, SS′ (Figure 2), and assumes that this represents the conditions of supply after the imposition of a tax. But his original curve, SS′, does not represent the cost of any except the marginal units of successive increments of supply; and the cost of the units furnished by superior producers must always be less than that of the marginal unit. The conditions subsequent to the levying of a tax can be represented only by drawing, in Figure 3, lines parallel to GH, FI, or EJ, according as the supply, at the time when the commodity is taxed, is AB, AC, or AD. When this is done, the resulting diagram becomes precisely like the one which Marshall uses in studying the effects of taxing commodities subject to the law of increasing cost, and the incidence of the tax is seen to be the same in both cases.

A single point remains to be considered. When a tax causes a reduction of the supply, it may happen that the marginal producers who are forced out of business will remove from the

[83] This discussion relates, of course, solely to competitive conditions. The incidence of taxes upon monopolized products is not now considered.

[84] *Economics*, pp. 527, 530. *Cf.* Seligman, *Shifting and Incidence*, p. 209.

market a larger quantity of the product than needs to be withdrawn in order to establish a new equilibrium between the demand and the supply. In any case when this happens, the remaining producers will be able to increase their sales before the deficiency in the supply offered under the new conditions is made good. Whenever this condition occurs, therefore, the tax may result in an enlargement of the size of the remaining establishments and a further reduction of the marginal cost.[85] Whether this is anything more than a mere theoretical possibility need not now be considered.

The three problems just discussed are far from exhausting the possible applications of the principles with which this essay has dealt, but they are sufficient to show the importance of the distinctions for which we have contended. In conclusion, it may be suggested that the various laws which we have presented should be looked upon as the special forms in which a more general principle manifests itself. This larger principle may be called the law of the variation of productive forces,[86] and the final results of our argument may conveniently be summed up in the following table:—

Laws of the variation of productive forces.	I. Of a given area of land.		Law of diminishing returns.
	II. Of a single plant or establishment.		Law of economy in organization.
	III. Of an entire industry.	1. Under static conditions.	Law of varied costs.
		2. Under dynamic conditions.	Laws of increasing or decreasing cost.

[85] This has been noted by Professor Carver in *Yale Review*, Vol. V, p. 263, note. Something similar is noted by Professor Seligman in discussing license taxes. *Shifting and Incidence*, pp. 292, 293.

[86] This law, as Professor Clark suggests, may be correlated with the law of diminishing utility under the general designation of the laws of the "variation of economic results." *Distribution of Wealth*, p. 209.

It is not claimed that this classification includes all the forms in which the operation of the general law of variation is manifested. But it is hoped that the results that have been reached will remove the confusion that has existed at several points, and prepare the way for future investigations of the working of this most fundamental principle in economic science.[87]

[87] Some further account of the subject is presented in the author's *Elements of Economics* (1905), pp. 74-96.

ADAM SMITH'S VIEWS ON NATIONAL DEFENCE[1]

THE opening chapter of the fifth book of the Wealth of Nations presents the first philosophical account in the English language, and perhaps in any other, of the important and comparatively neglected subject of public expenditures. According to Smith's "system of national liberty," the sovereign "has only three duties to attend to; three duties of great importance, indeed, but plain and intelligible to common understandings." The first is that "of protecting the society from the violence and invasion of other independent societies," which "can be performed only by means of a military force." Therefore the first branch of expenditures treated by Smith is the "expense of defence."

The full force and significance of what Smith has to say upon this subject, which fills some sixteen octavo pages, cannot be understood without reviewing the circumstances under which it was written. Ever since the invention of firearms had turned the scale in favor of the professional soldier, Great Britain had been "muddling" along through a tedious and ineffective debate concerning its military system. The Wars of the Roses had left Englishmen with a deep-seated hatred of professional soldiery, which made them averse to anything that looked like a standing army.[2] The insular position of the British Isles made it possible to trifle with questions of national defence, and the long contest required to establish the supremacy of Parliament over the Crown naturally fostered the belief that a standing army was dangerous to civil liberty. Even at the

[1] Reprinted from *Military Historian and Economist,* Vol. I (1916), pp. 249-57. Reproduced by generous permission of the publishers.

[2] More gave expression to this feeling in the Utopia. He argues that, since England need never have a war except when she pleases, it is unnecessary to maintain armies in time of peace; that the French army is a dangerous set of cut-throats; that untrained Englishmen often prove too much for the trained soldiers of France; that in order to keep their forces in training, the French sometimes seek occasion of war, as, according to Sallust, the Romans used to do.

close of the seventeenth century, the Tories remembered Cromwell while the Whigs could not forget the army of 30,000 men which James II had maintained without the consent of Parliament. Meanwhile other countries had developed large standing armies and military genius had transformed the art of war; so that except for the navy, which was often neglected, Great Britain was without adequate means of offence or defence.

The eighteenth century, by force of sheer necessity, brought some improvement; and very slowly the basis for a permanent army system was laid. Yet in every interval of peace Parliament sought to reduce the army to an inconsiderable force, so small as to render impossible both continuity of policy and sustained efficiency. It long refused to give the Crown the right to control the army by articles of war enforceable through courts martial; declined to provide the troops with barracks, preferring to billet them out, in a manner demoralizing to discipline and efficiency; and from time to time, when something happened to alarm the country, made feeble efforts to develop an even feebler militia system. During the Seven Years' War the successes finally achieved by the elder Pitt made the army somewhat less unpopular with the people; but the old opposition to a standing army continued, and the militia system found numerous and influential supporters.

Thus, in 1760, Lord Bath lamented the growing tolerance of large armies, deplored the erection of barracks, and expressed regret that members of great families were adopting the army as a profession. Blackstone, in his Commentaries, evinced fear that the Mutiny Act would prove dangerous to English liberties, and opposed the barrack system because he thought the army ought to live "intermixed with the people." Even after the American War politicians of note continued to harp upon these timeworn themes, while army administration remained corrupt and inefficient. The year 1793 found the British Army still muddling along, counting upon the dogged bravery of the enlisted men to offset unskillful handling, wretched administration, imbecility of politicians, and indifference of the people.

This was the practical situation when, from 1751 to 1764, Smith lectured at Glasgow College upon ethics, jurisprudence, and economics. His point of view and method of approach were wholly philosophical. That it was the duty of rulers to defend the state, political philosophers had always agreed. Plato had declared that the business of war is a separate profession which, in accordance with the principle of division of labor, must be turned over to a professional warrior class, carefully trained for its work. His exposition of the subject very clearly influenced the views of later writers; and from the sixteenth century onward was a natural and convenient *point d'appui* for political philosophers who, in treating of the subject of arms, advocated the substitution of standing armies for the older *levée en masse*.

Thus Bodin, after showing the necessity of military training, said that it is impossible to train all citizens, and that, therefore, it is necessary to maintain a permanent military force, as France had done since the fifteenth century.[3] Pufendorf contented himself with the simple statement that rulers should keep up and improve the courage and military skill of their subjects, and provide in good time fortifications, arms and men.[4] But Hutcheson, who was Smith's teacher, had an unfavorable opinion of standing armies. He taught that the military virtues and arts are accomplishments highly becoming honorable citizens, that arms should be no man's exclusive profession, and that all of the more honorable citizens should take their turn at military service. He was able, however, to suggest no method by which this result might be accomplished.[5]

When Smith succeeded to the chair once occupied by Hutcheson he considerably expanded the treatment of jurisprudence, dividing the subject into four parts: justice, police, revenue, and arms, which he termed the "four great objects of law." In the lectures dealing with arms he recognized that standing armies might be dangerous to civil liberty; but showed that

[3] *Six livres de la république,* Vol. V, p. 5.
[4] *De jure naturae et gentium,* Vol. VII, p. 9.
[5] *A Short Introduction to Moral Philosophy,* Vol. III, p. 8.

in modern commercial states, like Great Britain, the general run of people are unfitted for military service, and, without the protection of standing armies, would be "an easy prey" for their enemies.[6] "In the year 1745," he remarked, "four or five thousand naked, unarmed Highlanders took possession of the improved parts of this country without any opposition from the unwarlike inhabitants. They penetrated into England, and alarmed the whole nation, and had they not been opposed by a standing army, they would have seized the throne with little difficulty. Two hundred years ago such an attempt would have aroused the spirit of the nation. Our ancestors were brave and warlike; their minds were not enervated by cultivating arts and commerce, and they were all ready with spirit and vigor to resist the most formidable foe." His conclusion was: "However much standing armies may be exclaimed against, in a certain period of society they must be introduced." He found also that the British method of organizing the army minimized the danger to civil liberty.

It is a reasonable conjecture that the irruption of the Highlanders was responsible for the important place which Smith assigned to the subject of arms when he came to lecture upon jurisprudence at Glasgow College.[7] Following the defeat of the British at Fontenoy on the 11th of May, 1745, the young Pretender landed in Scotland; and with the aid of Highland chiefs raised a force with which he was able to overrun the whole country north of the Tweed in something less than two months, entering Edinburgh on the 11th of September. By the end of October he was ready to invade England, and on the

[6] *Lectures on Justice, Police, Revenue, and Arms*, pp. 26-30, 257-264.

[7] The Lectures on Justice, Police, Revenue, and Arms, in the form in which they have come down to us, were probably delivered in 1762 or 1763. In 1759, however, Smith's *Theory of Moral Sentiments* promised at some future time a treatise upon law and government, "not only in what concerns justice, but in what concerns police, revenue, and arms." John Millar, whose attendance upon Smith's lectures must have antedated by several years the publication of the *Theory of Moral Sentiments*, stated in his celebrated account of the lectures that Smith "considered the political institutions relating to commerce, the finances, to ecclesiastical and military establishments." It seems probable, therefore, that from the beginning of his professorship the subject of arms occupied an important place in his lectures.

15th of November captured Carlisle. Thence he marched through Lancashire as far south as Derby, reaching that point with about six thousand men on the 4th of December. Great Britain was wholly unprepared, the king being in Hanover at the time and the greater part of the army in Flanders. At length, however, forces were gathered to oppose the Pretender who, retreating, won two indecisive victories over incompetent British commanders before he was decisively defeated at Culloden, on the 16th of April, 1746. All this occurred during Smith's term of study at Oxford, where he was in continuous residence from the 7th of July, 1740, to the 15th of August, 1746. His mother, however, was in Scotland, probably at Kirkcaldy, so that his last year at Oxford must have been an anxious one.

In his preference for a standing army Smith differed not only from his teacher, Hutcheson, but probably from current opinion in Scotland, where a project for establishing a national Scotch militia aroused from time to time general interest and enthusiasm.[8] In 1759 French raiders appeared in Scottish waters, and this led to a general demand for a Scotch militia, which Parliament, mindful of the uprising of 1745, was unwilling to grant. In 1762, Smith appears to have been one of the original members of the Edinburgh Poker Club, which was organized apparently for the purpose of agitating the establishment of a militia. Perhaps this accounts for the apparent concessions Smith makes to the militia system at one point in his published lectures,[9] a concession the exact force of which is difficult to determine from the brief report that has come down to us. Of Smith's contemporaries, Adam Ferguson and Dr. Carlyle were among the strongest supporters of the principle of a national militia; and the former, after reading the Wealth of Nations, upbraided Smith for his advocacy of standing armies.[10]

[8] Cf. John Rae, *Life of Adam Smith*, pp. 134-140.

[9] *Lectures on Justice, Police, Revenue, and Arms*, p. 263.

[10] Rae, *Life of Adam Smith*, p. 138. Ferguson, *History of Civil Society*, Vol. III, p. 5, contends strongly for the militia system; and in 1792 his *Principles of Moral*

In the twelve years that intervened between his retirement from the professorship at Glasgow and the publication of the *Wealth of Nations,* Smith had ample opportunity to review the whole question. Meanwhile the Prussian army, under Frederick the Great, had reached its highest perfection, and "the acknowledged superiority of the Prussian troops."[11] must have tended to strengthen Smith's earlier convictions. He therefore concedes nothing to the militia system, and argues stoutly for the superiority of a standing army.

His treatment of the subject in the Wealth of Nations is based fundamentally upon the principle of division of labor. In the first book he maintains that the application of this principle is chiefly responsible for the improvement that has taken place in the productive power of labor in modern times. But in commercial states division of labor is carried so far that the general run of the people spend their whole life in the performance of a few simple operations, and tend to become ignorant, sluggish, and unwarlike, unless the government takes effective methods to combat this tendency.[12] Thus it comes about that, whereas in early stages of society the ordinary life of the people sufficiently prepares them for fighting, in the later industrial and commercial stages the people lose the martial virtues and become thoroughly unfitted for war. "An industrious, and upon that account, a wealthy nation," he remarks, "is of all nations, the most likely to be attacked; and unless the state takes some new measures for the public defence, the natural habits of the people render them altogether incapable of defending themselves."[13]

Under these circumstances, he says, there are only two methods by which provision can be made for the public defence, the militia system and the standing army. His definition of these terms is based wholly upon the idea of division

---

and Political Science, Vol. II, p. 6, sets forth in strong terms the dangers of entrusting military affairs exclusively to professional soldiers.

[11] *Wealth of Nations,* Cannan's edition, Vol. II, p. 194.

[12] *Wealth of Nations,* Vol. II, p. 267 *et seq.*

[13] *Wealth of Nations,* Vol. II, p. 192.

of labor. Any system that undertakes to "enforce the practice of military exercise" upon all or nearly all of the citizens, thus requiring them "to join in some measure the trade of a soldier, to whatever other trade or profession they may happen to carry on," is a militia system. Upon the other hand, the maintenance of a body of professional soldiers, which makes "the trade of a soldier a particular trade, separate and distinct from all others," constitutes a standing army. This definition was satisfactory enough in the eighteenth century, but it would have required Smith, had he lived in the next century, to classify as militias the so called national armies of Prussia and many other countries.

In Smith's opinion the conclusive objection to the militia system is that "in a militia the character of the laborer, artificer, or tradesman, predominates over that of the soldier," greatly to the detriment of the service. Before the invention of fire arms individual skill, strength, and dexterity counted for more, and this circumstance minimized the disadvantages of militias;[14] but under modern conditions, "regularity, order, and prompt obedience to command" are the qualities upon which success depends, and in these respects a militia, "in whatever manner it may be either disciplined or exercised, must always be inferior to a well disciplined and well exercised standing army."

A further consideration is that the "art of war, as it is certainly the noblest of all the arts, so in the progress of improvement it necessarily becomes one of the most complicated among them." Its improvement depends, of course, partly upon the general progress of the mechanical arts; but it cannot be carried to the degree of perfection which the existing state of the mechanical arts makes possible, unless it is made "the sole or principal occupation of a particular class of citizens" who can devote all their energy to perfecting it. "Into other arts," he says, "the division of labor is naturally introduced

[14] It merely minimized them, however. Smith believed professional troops to be much superior to others in the management and use of arms.

by the prudence of individuals, who find that they promote their private interest better by confining themselves to a particular trade, than by exercising a great number"; but "it is the wisdom of the state only which can render the trade of a soldier a particular trade, separate and distinct from all others."

These conclusions he seeks to reinforce by a historical review of military systems. This reveals the fact that his definitions of a militia and standing army are not always easy to apply. As Bastable has very justly observed,[15] the "whole discussion, in short, amounts simply to this: that the better disciplined and trained force will generally defeat its opponents, and that it ought to be called a standing army." Smith, indeed, at one point remarks that a militia "which has served for several successive campaigns in the field, becomes in every respect a standing army," and adds that if the war with the American colonies[16] should "drag out another campaign, the American militia may become in every respect a match" for the regular troops of Great Britain.

The possible dangers to civil liberty Smith considers briefly. A standing army may be dangerous if so constituted that the interest of the commander and his principal officers "are not necessarily connected with the support of the constitution of the state." In Great Britain, at least, he believed this condition was satisfactorily met, and he concluded that there a standing army "can never be dangerous to liberty," but may "in some cases be favorable to liberty."

In a later portion of the chapter on public expenditures,[17] Smith approaches the subject of military policy from another point of view, and expresses certain opinions which, on their face, appear hardly consistent with his earlier unconditional approval of standing armies. In treating of the education of youth, he says that with the progress of civilization the martial virtues gradually decay, unless governments take effectual means of combatting this tendency. Just what can be done

[15] *Public Finance*, 3rd edit., p. 62.

[16] The *Wealth of Nations* was published early in March, 1776.

[17] *Wealth of Nations*, Vol. II, pp. 271-272.

he does not make clear, but his references to the Greeks and Romans justify the inference that he had in mind systematic effort to encourage "military and gymnastic exercise." That something should be done to prevent the general body of citizens from becoming wholly unwarlike, is evident from his remarks that "a coward, a man incapable either of defending or of revenging himself, evidently wants one of the most essential parts of the character of a man"—a thoroughly accurate and philosophical description of a pacifist. "Even though the martial spirit of the people were of no use towards the defence of the society," the "serious attention of government" should be given to the task of preventing such "mental mutilation" as cowardice involves; just as "it would deserve its most serious attention to prevent a leprosy or any other loathsome and offensive disease" from spreading its contagion among the people."

These passages, however, are not incapable of reconciliation with the opinions expressed earlier in the chapter; and Smith indicates, though very briefly, how such reconciliation may be effected.[18] The "security of every great society," he says, "must always depend, more or less, upon the martial spirit of the great body of the people." Under present conditions, however, "that martial spirit alone, and unsupported by a well-disciplined standing army," would not suffice for defence and security. But "when every citizen had the spirit of a soldier, a smaller standing army would surely be requisite." Smith did not intend, therefore, to oppose military training for the people at large, or any other means of combatting such a "loathsome and offensive disease" as the decay of military virtue. Such training is good in itself, he thinks, as a part of the citizen's ordinary education; and if it is effective in preserving the martial spirit of the people, it will enable a state to get along with a smaller standing army than would otherwise be necessary. The idea that he combatted was that by a militia system, a standing army could be dispensed with. That was the practical question for the British people in the eighteenth century, and upon it Smith spoke in no uncertain tone.

[18] *Wealth of Nations,* Vol. II, p. 271.

THE NEED OF ENDOWMENT FOR ECONOMIC RESEARCH[1]

THIS is a time of economic unrest, and therefore of economic inquiry. Existing conditions are the object of incessant criticism, the fundamentals of the present order are often called in question, and nothing seems exempt from discussion, criticism, assault. Whereas a generation ago a mere handful of books and a few magazine articles represented the annual output of the United States in economics and sociology, today the output rises to approximately 1000 volumes, which is nearly one twelfth of the total book crop of the year; while the magazines and newspapers flood the market with their articles by the thousands and tens of thousands, to the despair of the cataloguer and expert indexer.

Recent conditions may have been unusual; perhaps another decade will see a change in popular interest. But it is not to be doubted that economic problems will continue to absorb their share of attention, and that economic inquiry will continue on a larger scale than was ever known before the 20th century. Equally clear is it that the importance of such inquiry cannot be gainsaid. If the 19th century was the century of the natural sciences, it cannot be doubted that the 20th, whatever else it may be, will be a century of social and economic inquiry. Modern life will doubtless grow more complex rather than less, more delicate and difficult economic adjustments will doubtless be necessary, projects for the reform and perfection of mankind will not become less numerous, and there will be great need of scientific investigation in economics and the other social sciences. Upon the success or failure of such inquiry, indeed, may depend in no small measure the future of western civilization.

[1] Reprinted from *The Harvard Graduates' Magazine* (June, 1915), pp. 601-610. Reproduced by generous permission of the publishers.

To meet the need of the times, our existing equipment for scientific economic research is inadequate. For serious investigation in this field two agencies, and only two, are now available. On the one hand, we have the individual investigator working with such private means as are at his command, and in such leisure as he can snatch from his regular vocation. On the other hand, we have governmental agencies like statistical bureaus, commissions of inquiry, and certain administrative departments having to do with such matters as taxation, railroads, corporations, labor, commerce, agriculture, and the like. These yearly become more numerous, and perhaps more influential; and they supply materials of the greatest value to the private investigator. Undoubtedly, the economist of today commands a far larger mass of data than his predecessors.

But the greater part of this material is in very raw state, some of it is untrustworthy, and most of it requires careful verification, analysis and interpretation before it is fit for scientific use. Therefore the resources of the individual investigator are as inadequate as ever; indeed, not the least of his troubles is the enormous mass of material,—valuable, doubtful, or worthless,—which must receive patient and critical examination at his hands. On the whole, he is hardly better off than the economist of the last generation, and there can be no doubt that the progress of scientific economic investigation is greatly hampered at every turn by the lack of such provision as has been made in generous measure for the study of the physical and natural sciences.

In the latter field it was long ago learned that the resources of the individual investigator, even when he coöperated with his fellow scientists, were inadequate for the work at hand; and it is today a matter of comparative ease to secure generous endowments for scientific research in physics, chemistry, biology, psychology, and medicine. But for economic science similar endowments are almost entirely lacking, and seem hardly to be regarded as necessary. For the most part the economist is expected to make bricks without straw, or at least with such few wisps as he can supply from his private resources, which are seldom large; and yet economic research, when conducted properly, is as expensive as research in any other field, and more expensive than in most others. The collection of the primary materials is often wholly beyond the ability of an individual investigator under present conditions, and must be entrusted to governmental agencies, which alone can gather comprehensive data concerning population, resources, production, commerce, labor, finance, and many other subjects. But such data frequently need to be supplemented by private inquiry, and they always need most searching and painstaking criticism; so that governmental agencies leave much to be done even in the collection of trustworthy primary materials. Then after the data are at hand must begin the process of analysis and interpretation, which is difficult and time consuming. Here, as in all other fruitful scientific inquiry, economic investigation is always reaching into new domains; and in any given domain must probe more and more deeply, and make its analyses increasingly minute. In all these respects the task of the economist is as difficult and exacting as that of his colleagues in any other branch of science. His province is vast, and a field for endless labor opens before him.

In some particulars, indeed, the task of the economist is even more difficult than that of the student of physical or natural science. The elements in any economic problem, the materials with which the science deals, are exceedingly mutable, and frequently change even while the economist is analyzing and classifying them. Work done by the mathematician, if well done, abides forever. The chemist or physicist may make his determinations so accurate that they will remain the closest approximations to the truth; and the biologist, even though he knows that species are not immutable, can safely assume that his beasts and plants are not going to change before his investigation is completed. But the economist's phenomena are in the highest degree mutable. Some things, indeed, may not change. The law of diminishing returns is not likely to be modified in the near future even by act of Congress; nor does human nature, however modifiable by environment, change over night or even reconstitute itself within a year. But such things as laws and institutions, methods of production, available natural resources, the numbers and distribution of population, are in constant state of flux; and many an economist who lightheartedly begins a study of current problems presently finds himself writing a treatise on ancient history. Indeed, the economist's task is never done. His materials must ever be collected anew, and his work must ever be repeated; the economic order changes, and the living specimens of today become in a few years the fossil remains of a bygone age. It will be noticed that I am speaking not of changes in theories about given economic phenomena, but of mutations of the phenomena themselves. In every field of science theories change, but in no field do the phenomena themselves change so generally and rapidly as in the social sciences.

A further difficulty is that the materials with which the economist deals are peculiarly liable to perversion, distortion, and even deliberate falsification. This fact enormously increases the investigator's difficulties, and greatly adds to his labor. For this reason alone, the resources of the private investigator would surely be inadequate; and when to this is added the mass and complexity of the materials and their extraordinary mutability, the need of greater facilities than the individual economist can command is too apparent to require further comment.

One conceivable solution of the difficulty is to turn all large undertakings over to the State. Already the United States government is spending large sums for research, and the total cost of such work must amount to several million dollars annually. The Department of Agriculture, the Department of Commerce, the Bureau of Labor, the Census Bureau, the Bureau of Corporations, and the Interstate Commerce Commission have done, and are doing, work of the greatest importance to the economist, much of which, especially in the field of statistics, would be absolutely beyond the capacity of any individual investigator or private organization. In a similar manner various states and an occasional city are carrying on work of great importance, usefully supplementing the scientific work of the Federal government. Why not, then, depend upon these public agencies for such economic research as lies beyond the power of the individual investigator?

I have not the least desire to disparage governmental research; on the contrary, as indicated in the previous paragraph, I believe it to be highly useful, and in some fields indispensable. I believe also that the last 10 or 15 years have seen a distinct improvement in the quality of the work done in the United States, although such improvement has not everywhere kept pace with the increase of output. But after giving the most generous recognition to what the State is doing for the promotion of economic research, we must recognize that it would be highly unfortunate, and even dangerous, to permit the State to monopolize all economic inquiries that lie beyond the power of the individual investigator.

For, in the first place, even scientific research, when turned over to a governmental agency, is brought directly within the domain of politics. I do not mean, of course, that all of our departments or bureaus carrying on scientific work are headed by practical politicians and manned by political workers. This sort of thing, as we all know, is becoming less common; and there are not a few cases in which it is possible to say that politics, in this sense of the word, has been largely, and for considerable periods even wholly, excluded. To be sure, even a president of Mr. Wilson's antecedents has been guilty of placing in charge of an important bureau, the only work of which is of a scientific character, a man whose principal qualification evidently was that he had been chairman of the party committee of a certain state. But such occurrences are becoming less frequent, and we may fairly anticipate continued improvement in the matter of treating scientific positions as mere political spoils.

But even with the grosser forms of political influence eliminated, it is true, and must remain true, that political considerations or purposes can never be wholly eliminated from governmental research. Even such an apparently non-political bureau as the Geological Survey may become the storm centre of the conservation movement if official determination has to be made of the apparently simple question of the effect of forest destruction upon soil erosion, and the Weather Bureau may become surcharged with political lightning if a loquacious chief expresses uncalled-for opinions concerning the influence of forests upon rainfall and the flow of rivers. Even chemical and physiological inquiries take on a political tinge if they relate to the use of benzoate of soda, the wholesomeness of oleomargarine, and the products of the Chicago stock-yards. In fact, a clever politician can extract a surprising amount of political capital from such scientific inquiries as these, and a scientific investigator may risk his official head if his inquiries lead to an unwelcome conclusion. Some years ago a physiological chemist who was so unfortunate as to determine that good oleomargarine is a perfectly healthful article of food was told that his institution need expect no further support from the State if its professors were to antagonize the farmers in this manner. Equally hard might be the lot of any other investigator whose scientific determinations in this, or any allied field, should prove unpalatable to the conservationist, the pure-food crusader, the farmer, the social reformer, or the big corporation that produced the articles subjected to scientific analysis.

What happens to such peaceful and apparently non-political sciences as chemistry and physiology when they come into contact with politics, is much more certain to happen to a science like economics, which from the very nature of the case must deal with questions that are political in character. Even if we grant that it is possible to eliminate absolutely the spoils system, it would still remain true that economic research under Republican auspices would necessarily be a somewhat different thing from economic research under Democratic guidance, or under the control of a Progressive, Socialist, or Prohibition administration. Messrs. Redfield and Davies, for instance, inevitably give a different tone to economic inquiries under their charge from that imparted by Messrs. Cortelyou and Smith. This is not by remotest implication a reflection upon the honesty or fairness of any of these gentlemen, but it is merely a statement of a condition that inevitably results from the personal equation and the political creed. Nor is it a reflection upon governmental research as such, for such work may be highly useful in spite of the allowance that has to be made for the personal or political equation. I maintain simply that we must not blink the patent fact that governmental research can never wholly lose a political character. Such research may be highly useful, and, in fact, is becoming increasingly necessary; but we should not on that ground indulge in any illusions concerning it. "Official statistics," the "impartial findings" of a Federal commission, the "final and authoritative" determinations of a government bureau, are indeed entitled to respectful reception and careful consideration; but they do not give us necessarily the last word upon any subject.

I have spoken so far only of the inevitable defects that arise from personal or political bias, such as is bound to exist among the best of men, and is least harmful when frankly admitted. But beyond this, there is the possibility of deliberate perversion of governmental investigation for partisan purposes. Some branches of Census work have suffered seriously from this cause, particularly the statistics that used to be published concerning the average wages paid in manufacturing industries. The most notorious case occurred in 1890, when, by manipulating the divisor used in computing average wages, the Census was able to announce that the average remuneration had risen from $347 in 1880 to $445 in 1890. On the eve of the presidential election the Census issued a series of bulletins relating to wages paid in the leading cities of the country, and exploiting in the most conspicuous manner possible the increase alleged to have occurred during the decade ending in 1890. These bulletins purported to show that wages had increased nearly 53% in New York, 35% in Chicago, 45% in Boston, 52% in Philadelphia, 73% in Atlanta, 77% in Richmond, 77% in Syracuse, and so on through the list. It seemed as if the campaign committee had mobilized its forces at the Census Office, and was directing a hail of deadly statistical shrapnel at the enemy's trenches. This may have been good politics, but it certainly was not good science; and even from the political point of view, it led to awkward consequences. The average wages for 1890 were placed at such a high figure that it was a foregone conclusion that, without deliberate falsification of the data, the statistics of 1900 could not exhibit a further increase. As a matter of fact, they showed a decrease, computed by the old method, from $445 to $438, which was perhaps a fortunate result in that it demonstrated the dangers of political wage statistics. It is gratifying to be able to add that there has been no time since the Census was made a permanent bureau when such a performance as that of 1892 would have been conceivable.

Another celebrated feat of official statistics was the so-called Aldrich Report of 1893, which purported to give, among other things, statistics showing the general course of wages in the United States from 1840 to 1891. These statistics were immediately accepted as "official," and incorporated in the economic literature of this and other countries; but it later developed that they had been gathered and handled by methods that would not bear the slightest careful criticism, and that some of the things done by the makers of the Report were so preposterous as to bring in question the investigators' honesty of purpose. In one establishment, a brewery, the investigators found a brewer whose wages had increased from $6.39 a day in 1860 to $23.96 in 1891, or something like 285%; and they adopted a method of averaging which made the wages of this typical proletarian count for as much in determining the general result as those of 133 common laborers found in another industry whose wages had increased only 29% during the period of 31 years.

These examples show what official investigators can do even with such comparatively simple and definite things as statistics.

When it comes to inquiries into complicated industrial conditions and the investigation of large questions of public policy, the opportunity for deliberate bias is greatly increased. Some 14 years ago, we had a Federal Industrial Commission which investigated almost every conceivable subject except white slavery and the recall of judges, but was particularly concerned with the trust problem and the protective tariff. The final report of the commission, in some 19 formidable volumes, has been widely used by both American and European investigators as a repository of economic information. Yet it was perfectly evident to the discerning at the time, and today would probably not be questioned by anybody, that, so far as the trusts and the tariff were concerned, the work of the commission was fundamentally partisan and political, and that its report contains fully as much misinformation as information. Certainly an economist with a professional reputation to maintain would today be chary of citing the findings of this commission as high authority upon either the trust or the tariff problem.

At the present writing, we have with us another industrial commission appointed a year or two ago as a result of the recent social unrest. In the closing months of his administration, President Taft named a commission, but his nominations aroused violent protest on account of the alleged conservative views of the nominees; and they were not confirmed by the Senate. President Wilson a few months later named another commission, against which the charge of conservatism can hardly lie; and this body is now making an official investigation of social conditions. On the eve of an important investigation the chairman, in a public address, denounces roundly the institutions he is about to investigate. Some months before the commission's inquiries are concluded he announces that the country can never prosper "as long as the banks handle the wealth of the nation purely to make it pay the largest dividends," and makes the "definite" suggestion that "autocracy in business" must go. When such performances arouse discussion and criticism, the grand inquisitor then announces that his "position is not a judicial one," and that "judicial poise" is "a great bar to human progress." Yet two or three years from now we shall be asked to accept the findings of this commission as "official."

Cases are not wanting where investigations that yielded inconvenient results have been wholly suppressed. This happened, for instance, with an investigation of the sugar beet industry in the United States, which was made for one of the departments of the Federal government only a few years ago. And other similar, but less well authenticated, cases will doubtless occur to persons familiar with Washington affairs. Actual suppression, however, is probably a comparatively rare thing. What usually happens is that the administration in charge of national or state affairs is committed to certain policies, and that the expert investigators of such an administration are unlikely to reach inconvenient results. This is true not only of the political policies of national or state administrations, but also of the general policies of public departments in matters that are not immediately of political moment. A scientific student who turns to the reports of any public department, whether it has to do with taxation, banking, railroad administration, labor, or any other economic interest, must always be careful to make due allowance for the settled policies of the department. This is not a reflection upon the integrity of administrative departments, but it is a necessary allowance for the personal equation which enters into all human affairs, public and private.

A final difficulty with the scientific work of governments is that it is generally confined to what are considered practical ends, by which is usually meant undertakings that give promise of immediate practical results. This is seen in appropriations for state universities which readily obtain money for agricultural, engineering, and other practical subjects, but have difficulty in securing meagre allowances for pure science, philosophy, and the humanities. It is evidenced also by the large appropriations the Federal Government makes for agricultural research, labor, and similar practical interests. In time, conditions may change, but for the present there is slight prospect of securing public support for research outside of economic questions of immediate practical concern.

Useful and even indispensable as it may be, therefore, governmental research in the field of economics needs to be supplemented by adequate private agencies. We need to place beside the Census Office, the Bureau of Labor, the Interstate Commerce Commission, the Bureau of Corporations, and the other excellent boards and bureaus, both state and national, now engaged in economic research, a number of private agencies that shall be free from political stress and disturbance, relieved from the necessity of confining themselves to investigations of immediate practical value, and amply equipped for the most thorough, painstaking, and accurate research in both pure and applied economics. Since scientific work of such a character cannot possibly be remunerative in the pecuniary sense, it is evident that such agencies can be provided only by endowments.

It also seems clear that a university devoted to scientific studies and dedicated to the pursuit of truth is a most fit institution to receive such endowments. Here the investigator will not be obliged to confine himself to inquiries that promise immediate practical results. Here he may be free from political or other pressure, and may benefit from association with scientists engaged in other fields of work, especially the older and more exact sciences.

The work that might be accomplished by such endowments can hardly be overestimated. Never yet in the history of the science has the economist been given the resources and equipment really necessary for his work. To fashion bricks without straw were a light and attractive task compared with his. If Harvard University could receive during the next few years an endowment adequate to make even a respectable beginning of organized research, it might within a generation do more than any private agency has ever done to advance the frontiers of economic science.

Such a tremendous vista of useful investigations would open before a department properly equipped for economic research that a very large endowment is thoroughly justified and even urgently needed. This may not be the time for undertaking large enterprises that call for money, but it is possible to begin the work in a modest way by the endowment of one or more research assistantships, which would permit the Department to prospect the field. Such endowment would enable the University to provide a professor with competent assistants like those provided for investigators in other fields. The sum of $30,000 would endow such assistantships and provide for the incidental expenses that always arise in connection with scientific work. They would certainly justify themselves by their results, and further endowments would then be easier to secure.

Another excellent plan would be the provision of funds for the investigation of particular subjects. There is great need, for instance, of searching investigation of the recent increase of public expenditures in the United States, an undertaking that would certainly prove fruitful in both theoretical and practical results. Even greater is the need of a searching investigation of the present world-wide increase of prices, which, like similar price movements of former times, is producing economic disturbances of vital practical moment and the greatest theoretical interest. Then there are the troublesome problems of the day,—socialism, single tax, labor legislation, the extension of public industries, public regulation of private industry, the tariff problem, the problem of large-scale production, and all the others,—that occasion so much discussion at the present time. We hear much about what other countries have done in this direction or that, but we have comparatively little first hand investigation, impartial and absolutely scientific, of the actual results of such experiments. At every hand topics of fascinating scientific interest and great practical importance abound. Competent workers are not numerous, and their resources are painfully inadequate.

In a new undertaking of this character, the first step is usually the hardest. The endowment of economic research at Harvard University is a thing that can be finally and conclusively justified only by its results, and such results in turn are impossible without an endowment. The Department of Economics, however, believes that a strong case can be made out in favor of an experiment in this direction. It is now in quest of endowments for research assistantships and funds to defray the expense of particular investigations. I am grateful for the opportunity to bring this matter to the attention of the *Harvard Graduates' Magazine*.

COMMODITY PRICES DURING THE PRESENT DECADE[1]

SINCE 1914 business has been subject to grave hazards the like of which have not been known since the Civil War. Upon the whole, conditions have improved since the armistice; and it is clear that, especially in the United States, the world is returning to a more normal status. The war strained western civilization almost to the breaking point, but did not destroy it; and we may set it down to the credit of the existing economic order that it has withstood stresses that would have wrecked any institutions not fundamentally sound.

The fact that, in spite of all difficulties, the general trend can now be clearly seen to be toward more normal and prosperous times has recently produced a marked improvement of business sentiment, which is such a vital factor in economic prosperity. Trade is better throughout the western world, economic reconstruction by the method of revolution is no longer a source of apprehension, money conditions have grown easier, and it is becoming possible to make intelligent plans for the future. On one point, however, considerable apprehension still exists, with the result of retarding to some extent recovery from the recent business depression. This point is the probable trend of commodity prices during the next five or ten years.

When the armistice was concluded it was very generally expected that prices would decline to something like their prewar level, and there did actually ensue a brief depression which seemed to confirm such fears. But in the spring of 1919 flush times returned and carried prices to a higher point than had ever been reached. This naturally led many people to conclude that the war had raised prices to a high level which was cer-

[1] Reprinted from *Harvard Economic Service,* Vol. I (June 10, 1922), Weekly Letter No. 24. Reproduced by generous permission of the publishers.

tain to be maintained for many years and might even prove to be permanent. The events of the last two years have shown the second theory to be erroneous, but have not yet proved the first to be correct. Prices declined very severely, but their general average is still far above the figures for 1913; and in recent months the trend has, upon the whole, been upward. Under such conditions it is not strange that a sharp division of opinion exists concerning the probable trend of prices during the next decade.

The Historical Evidence

Since business conditions are affected by price movements more than by any other single factor, the precedents offered by the past have been anxiously examined in the hope that they might disclose what the future has in store. For this purpose the most interesting and pertinent evidence is that afforded by the history of price movements in England and the United States since the year 1800; and wide currency has been given to such data as are shown in the chart on the following page.

This chart shows wholesale prices for a period of 122 years. For England from 1797 to 1820, and again from 1914 to the present time, prices were in terms of inconvertible paper money. For the United States the same is true for the years 1814-17, and for the years 1862-79. With these exceptions the chart records the movements of gold prices, which of course were substantially the same in other countries.

It will be noted that the high prices prevailing during the first half of the second decade of the nineteenth century, which were due to inflation caused by war, were followed by a long period of declining prices which continued, with temporary interruptions, until 1849, when the gold discoveries in Australia and California enormously increased the production of the yellow metal and inaugurated a period of rising prices. In the United States this upward swing was succeeded by currency inflation during the Civil War; and this, in turn, was followed by a period of drastic deflation which, by 1878, had brought prices back to a level lower than that prevailing in 1861. During the sixties gold prices in England pursued the even tenor of their way, but in the early seventies they entered upon a long decline which lasted until 1897. In the United States, which had returned to a specie basis in 1879, a similar movement was recorded; and like developments occurred in all other countries which had a gold standard. The upward swing of commodity

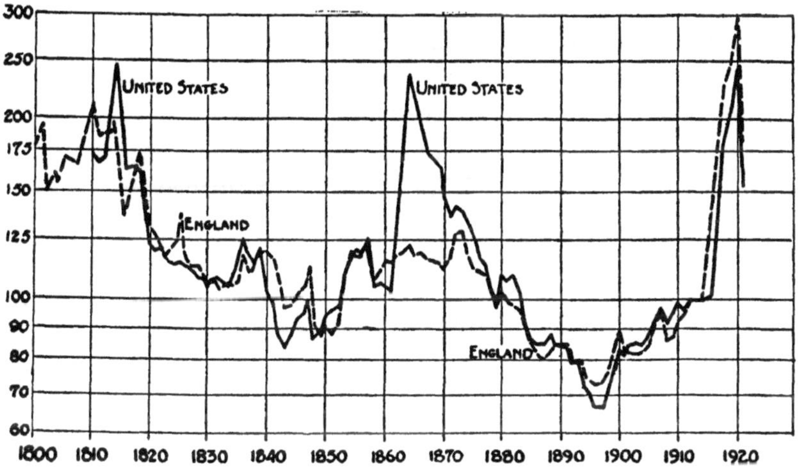

COMMODITY PRICES IN THE UNITED STATES, 1810-1921, AND ENGLAND, 1800-1921
Prices in 1914 = 100

prices from 1897 to 1914 was due to another phenomenal increase of gold production, resulting from the opening of the South African mines and the introduction of new and improved methods in quartz and placer mining. The inflated prices of the last eight years require no comment except that the great increase in the United States was due to the expansion of bank credit, not to inconvertible paper money, and to prodigious imports of the yellow metal which enabled credit to expand without causing a departure from the gold basis. From this historical record the natural and plausible inference has been drawn that just as prices after the two previous periods of currency inflation reverted to their former levels, so in the present instance they must return to something like the level that obtained in 1913.

Interpretation of the Evidence

But historical parallels are likely to mislead unless care is taken to determine whether all important conditions are the same. From 1815 to 1848, and from the late sixties to 1896 they seem to have been so; but some of the leading factors in the present situation are very different from those operative in the previous instances, so that judgment should be suspended until these points are carefully examined.

The war which came to an end in 1815 left England and the United States with a heavy burden of debt, but a burden which subsequently was greatly lightened by rapid industrial development. By 1836 the United States had extinguished its national debt out of the proceeds of customs duties and public land sales. England made no such progress in the reduction of her debt; but industrial development and the increase of population brought it about that by 1860 the debt had ceased to be a factor of serious importance. In both countries falling prices were attended with hardship, but did not require sacrifices too great to be endured. The same thing was true of the United States after the Civil War. Industrial development proceeded apace; vast areas of new land were made available for settlement; and the revenues derived from customs duties and moderate internal taxes upon liquors, tobacco, and a few other articles enabled the country to reduce its debt rapidly. No similar conditions can be expected today to alleviate the burden that would result from a return of the 1913 level of prices. Both countries will doubtless increase their industries and wealth, the United States more rapidly than England. But neither can expect that the natural growth of industry and population will enable it to make headway with the reduction of its debt without heavy internal taxation, so severe as to have a depressing effect upon industry and certain to become intolerable if the real weight of the debts is enhanced by a continued fall of commodity prices. In fact, deflation resulting in a return to former price levels would have consequences so serious as to produce dangerous political developments, and in all probability would lead to a sharp reversal of financial policies. Of this we have already had a foretaste in attacks upon the federal reserve system, the revival of the War Finance Corporation, and the recrudescence of paper money heresies.

When we turn to other countries, as we must because the problem involves the future of gold prices throughout the world, a return to the pre-war status appears even more improbable. The United States never abandoned the gold standard, the pound sterling never depreciated so far as to make it idle for Great Britain to attempt to return to the 1913 parity, and the European neutrals are, in general, not so deeply involved as to prevent them from restoring their currencies to the former status. But the continental belligerents seem to be left in a condition that precludes restoration of the former gold parities without partial or total bankruptcy. In cases where their currencies have sunk to an insignificant fraction of their original value this has already become evident; and it is noteworthy that the Financial Commission of the Genoa Conference, in recommending the ultimate restoration of a gold standard, says that this "will not necessarily be at the former gold par."

Countries like France and Italy occupy an intermediate position. The franc and the lira have so far depreciated that there can be no thought of immedate return to the pre-war parity; but instinctive repugnance to "redefining" their monetary units, fear of impaired credit and prestige, and absorption in problems of more pressing importance have resulted in a temporizing policy and disinclination to face the hard facts. These are, as we see them, that restoration of the franc and lira would involve, respectively, something more than doubling and trebling the weight of the domestic debt, while national budgets are not yet balanced and may not be for years to come. A deflationist policy has been proclaimed by all governments holding office in France since January 1920, and the banknote circulation has actually declined from 39 to 36 billions. But at the same time the issue of national defense bonds has increased by some 20 billions; and we are now told that these bonds, issued in denominations of 100, 500, and 1000 francs, have to some extent acquired the character of currency and are offered and accepted in transactions at fairs, markets, shops, lawyers' offices, and other places, so that there has been no real deflation. Reparation payments may yet improve the situation; but there will even then remain the problem of foreign indebtedness for which no provision has yet been made. Whether such indebtedness will be, or ought to be, canceled is a question that cannot be considered here; but it is obvious that debtor countries which adhere to policies that must have the effect of increasing enormously the burden of their domestic debt are not in a good position to ask the indulgence of foreign creditors. Official "devaluation" of the franc is unpleasant to contemplate, and as yet finds few advocates; but concerning it such a competent authority as Professor Jèze[2] has recently said: "This is a solution to which we shall perhaps have to resign ourselves, as has been done in many countries at various periods of history." Obviously the conditions left in Europe by the Great War are very different from those obtaining in England and the United States in 1815 or 1865.

Drastic deflation and restoration of the former gold standard were possible in England and the United States after 1815, and in the United States after 1865, because conditions were not as critical as they are today in most of the belligerent countries. Even so, the policy entailed many years of falling prices that involved long periods of deep depression and caused intense suffering. Favorable economic developments made it possible to endure the strain; but the history of those years is not pleasant reading, and all who remember the trade depression of the seventies and the history of the middle nineties can have no desire to see such experiences repeated. For most of the European belligerents restoration of currencies to the pre-war standard would mean suffering too great to be endured and would probably end in total or partial national bankruptcy.

[2] *Manchester Guardian Commercial* for April, 1922, pp. 23, 24.

Gold Production and Consumption

But after all, it will be asked, is the future course of gold prices a matter of human volition, and does it not rather depend upon the volume of gold production which, as we all know, has declined materially since 1915? The question is pertinent and vital, but before answering it we may well examine the present status and future prospects of gold production and consumption.

The last thirty-five years have seen the most remarkable increase of gold production in the history of the world. From an average annual production of less than $100,000,000 for the quinquennial period ending in 1885, the annual production rose to an average of nearly $163,000,000 for the similar period ending in 1895, and to over $322,000,000 for the similar period ending in 1905. The year 1906 showed an output of $402,000,000, by 1910 the figure had increased to $455,000,000, and in 1915 the peak was reached with a production of $468,000,000. Since then the output of the mines has declined, as a result of increasing costs, labor difficulties, disturbance of transportation, and the gradual exhaustion of deposits in certain fields. In 1920 the entire output was $334,900,000, and for 1921 it may be estimated at about the same figure. Labor difficulties in the Transvaal may result in a somewhat smaller production during 1922; but, taking the gold industry as a whole, it is reasonable to believe that the present decline has about come to an end, and that the next few years will bring at least a moderate increase in the output. Mr. Joseph Kitchin estimates conservatively that for the decade 1921-30 the production of gold will average about £70,000,000; and this figure coincides almost exactly with the conclusions reached in an article published in *The Review of Economic Statistics* for July, 1920.[3]

From these data one may conclude that the annual output of gold has declined from a peak production of $468,000,000 in

[3] Mr. Kitchin's estimates may be found in *The Review of Economic Statistics,* 1921, p. 259, and the *Manchester Guardian Commercial,* April, 1922, pp. 45, 46.

1915 to something like $350,000,000 at the present time. With these figures we may next compare estimates of the consumption of gold for non-monetary purposes. Industrial consumption had been rising for many years before the war; and probably continued to increase until the recent period of deflation, although exact data are unobtainable except in the United States where it is known that the increase was very large. In *The Review of Economic Statistics* for June, 1920, the available data were reviewed; with the result that the world's industrial consumption for 1912 was placed at $124,000,000, to which it is necessary to add $110,000,000 representing the net gold exports to British India. For that year it appeared that, with a gold production of $466,000,000, $234,000,000 was required for non-monetary purposes, leaving a balance of $232,000,000 available for monetary uses. Mr. Joseph Kitchin estimates that, for the decade ending in 1929, the world's production will average £70,000,000, industrial consumption of gold will average £23,800,000, and £15,400,000 will be exported to India, China, and Egypt, where the greater part of it will be lost so far as monetary uses are concerned. From this it results that something like £30,000,000 of new gold will be available for monetary purposes each year until 1930.[4] We may conclude, therefore, that the annual increment to the world's stock of gold money has been reduced from $232,000,000, the figure for 1912, to $150,000,000 at the present time.

In sum, the evidence shows that the annual increment to the world's monetary supply has fallen from a pre-war level of $232,000,000 to $150,000,000. This is a substantial decrease, but it does not justify alarm concerning the future course of gold prices. Before the war commodity prices were increasing at a very substantial rate, with an annual gold increment of $232,000,000; and there was general complaint of the increasing cost of living, which had led to the appointment of numerous parliamentary and legislative commissions to investigate the

[4] See *The Review of Economic Statistics,* August, 1921, pp. 250, 260, and *Manchester Guardian Commercial,* April, 1922, pp. 45, 46.

problem. In view of this fact it would seem that an annual increment of $150,000,000 should be ample to prevent a decline of gold prices during the present decade.[5] This is the conclusion which we reached when we studied the subject early in 1920.

What may occur after 1930 cannot be considered here and may be beyond our present ken. Mr. Kitchin, than whom we have no more competent authority, thinks that the permanent decline of South African production, uncompensated by sufficient increases in other fields, will reduce the annual output below £70,000,000, and may lead to a considerable period of falling prices. On this subject we prefer to reserve judgment until we see what happens to gold mining when conditions become normal throughout the world. Until 1930, at least, we see no prospect of shortage of gold, even though the conditions may have passed which prior to the war were tending to increase commodity prices.

This brings us to the second important point of difference between the conditions prevailing today and those which obtained after 1815 and 1865. As ill luck would have it, in both of the earlier instances return to a specie basis coincided with a period of declining production of the precious metals.[6] Gold production, which was then comparatively small, had averaged $11,815,000 per annum during the decade ending in 1810; and then declined to an annual average of $7,606,000 for the decade ending in 1820, and amounted to no more than $9,448,000 for the next decade. At the same time the annual average output of silver declined from $37,168,000 in the decade ending in 1810 to $22,479,000 in the following decade, and to $19,144,000 in the decade ending in 1830. In other words, between 1810 and 1830 the combined annual production of gold and silver shrunk from an average figure of $49,000,000 to an average of

[5] Of course the cyclical movement of prices will produce movements both above and below the general trend.

[6] Data for both gold and silver production need to be given for the period following 1815, since the United States at that time was on a bimetallic basis and most of the hard money in actual circulation consisted of silver. England, of course, by the law of 1819, adopted gold monometallism.

$28,600,000. During the decade ending in 1830, production could hardly have exceeded materially industrial consumption plus exports to the East. For the period following our Civil War it is necessary to consider only the figures of gold production, since silver was in process of "demonetization" and the course of prices was related to the output of the yellow metal. During the quinquennial period ending in 1860, when production of the early Californian and Australian mines was at its peak, the annual output of gold averaged $134,000,000. During the next five years production declined slightly, but thereafter it increased sufficiently to show an annual average of $129,600,000 during the quinquennial period ending with 1870. After this it steadily declined until in the five years ending in 1885 the average fell to $99,116,000. Meanwhile industrial consumption had increased to nearly $60,000,000, so that when allowance was made for treasure exported to the East it was estimated that very little new gold was available for monetary purposes.

One does not need to accept the so-called "quantity theory" of money in order to follow our reasoning at this point. Upon any tenable theory, a prolonged decline in the production of gold accompanied by increasing use in the arts and large exportation to the East must increase the value of that metal and therefore tend to lower commodity prices. After 1815 and 1865 conditions would have favored declining commodity prices even if there had been no contraction of paper currencies issued during long and exhausting wars. In both instances the return to a specie basis had to be accomplished under unfavorable conditions which bear no resemblance to those obtaining today. Against an annual combined production of gold and silver averaging $28,600,000 for the decade ending in 1830, and an average annual gold production of $99,100,000 for the quinquennial period ending in 1885, we now have an annual gold output of something like $350,000,000 for the present decade, and a clear surplus above industrial uses and exports to the East that will probably average $150,000,000. These considerations lead to the conclusion that inferences drawn from the periods following

1815 and 1865 must be absolutely misleading in so far as the movement of commodity prices depends upon the production and consumption of gold.

There are other elements in the gold problem which are not so easily determined and are, in fact, quite undeterminable. Upon the one hand, the uncertainty prevailing in Europe since 1914 is said to have had the effect of stimulating the hoarding of gold. It is true that during the war governments succeeded in concentrating in their central banks a large part of the known supply of the precious metals, but it is believed that hoarding took place none the less, and that it still continues. On the other hand, there is the counteracting influence of the large hoards of gold that have been seized, and are even now in process of seizure, in Russia. Some portion of these is supposed to be finding its way to other countries, including the United States, through various channels which make identification difficult. It is significant that large imports of gold into the United States during the last two years do not appear to have decreased the gold reserves in the central banks of Europe, and that, in fact, during this period there has even been a substantial net increase of these reserves. Between January 1920 and November 1921, the banks of France, Germany, and the Netherlands appear to have lost some $44,000,000 of gold, while those of Great Britain, Italy, Switzerland, Sweden, and Spain appear to have gained $164,000,000. During this period the gold holdings of the United States increased by $947,000,000, which is nearly three times the production of new gold; and the Bank of Japan increased its holdings by $266,000,000. Evidently with gold, as with other commodities, there have been "reserve stocks," due to hoarding or other causes, which must not be left out of the reckoning.

Upon all the evidence, then, we conclude that monetary stocks of gold will continue to increase at the rate of approximately $150,000,000 per annum during the next eight years, and this means a larger annual increment than the world has ever had except during the few years prior to 1915. If, therefore, the general trend of commodity prices declines during the present decade, this will be due to the financial policies pursued by the leading commercial countries, and not to a shortage of the yellow metal. These policies, of course, are wholly subject to human volition, although they are not within the control of any single country unless it be one that occupies a position of commanding influence. Perhaps, as the leading creditor nation, the United States might exert such an influence on financial policy, especially if it should oppose measures calculated to depress prices and so to increase the burden of indebtedness inherited from the Great War.

The Effect of Financial Policies

The policies of chief moment will obviously be those relating to the resumption of specie payments in Europe, the operation of the federal reserve system in the United States, and the adjustment of international indebtedness. Concerning the first of these, we have already indicated that we believe that, even if resumption at pre-war parities is conceivable in most of the belligerent countries, this would bring with it such a train of disastrous consequences as to make it practically impossible. Where paper currencies are so far depreciated as to be almost worthless, the slates will ultimately have to be sponged clean; and a return to the old parity will become possible as it was in the United States when our Continental paper was consigned to oblivion, or, as one historian put it, "expired in delirium tremens." But this is merely another way of stating the impossibility of returning to the old parity without national bankruptcy. For most of the belligerents, some sort of a compromise is the only feasible solution, and it is probable that sooner or later this will become evident to all. There is no doubt that, if it were possible for Europe to return to the 1913 status, by the old-fashioned method of contracting paper currencies and accumulating large reserves of gold, the general trend of commodity prices might decline in spite of the prospective increase of the world's supply of free gold. But the practical impossibility of carrying through such a policy justifies us in dismissing it from consideration.

When gold payments are resumed in Europe it will be necessary to follow methods calculated to avoid violent disturbance of the *status quo,* and to economize the use of gold as far as practicable. Gold-exchange standards, utilization of securities as an important part of reserves behind convertible notes, measures to prevent the use of gold coin in domestic transactions, and the larger use of silver, are already the subject of serious consideration by those closely in touch with the situation; and all these expedients—with perhaps others—will have to be employed if the formidable task is to be accomplished at all. Only Great Britain and the neutral countries can meet their present obligations and at the same time return to the 1913 parities.

Concerning the policies of the Federal Reserve Board little need be said at this time. Such deflation as has been accomplished since 1920 has resulted in a somewhat violent reaction which makes it tolerably clear that the adoption of measures designed to restore the purchasing power of the dollar to its 1913 level would cause political upheaval. Stabilization of commodity prices upon something like their present basis and prudent action to diminsh the intensity of the upward and downward fluctuations of the business cycle seem to be the probable course of federal reserve policy. This is said without any pretension to "inside knowledge," and is premised only upon such facts as are familiar to competent observers. At the time of writing it seems, perhaps, more probable that our enormous stocks of gold and the latent power of credit expansion possessed by the federal reserve system may lead to inflation than that the financial policy of the United States will incline toward further deflation.

The problem of international indebtedness is here pertinent only in so far as it may affect the price situation. Cancellation of all such debts would obviously help the debtor countries to carry through policies of drastic deflation, but would not necessarily mean that such policies would, or could, be adopted. Upon the other hand, if these debts are to be paid, it must inevitably happen that prices of international commodities will be higher in creditor than in debtor nations, since otherwise payment cannot be made. Deflation in the creditor nations must, therefore, mean severe pressure upon debtor countries; while inflation leading to higher prices would obviously ease the strain of international payments. At the present time so little progress has been made in dealing with international debts that it is almost idle to speculate upon the subject; but it is safe to observe that the United States, by virtue of the fact that it is the predominant creditor nation, is in a position to influence greatly the financial policies adopted in Europe. If we are prepared to accept, as apparently we must, the present price level, as substantially that around which the fluctuations of the business cycle must play during the coming decade, we can contribute powerfully to financial stability throughout the world. And, finally, if we adhere consistently to this view, we can make it clear that little indulgence can be expected by debtors who adopt policies calculated to increase inordinately the burden of debt inherited from the Great War.

BUSINESS OPINIONS AND BUSINESS CONDITIONS[1]

IN NOVEMBER 1918 the business community expected that the conclusion of the war would be followed by a more or less violent reaction in business. Prices were very high, credit was inflated, foreign demand for American products was abnormally large, and war industries—which had come to include nearly all essential ones—were greatly expanded. A drop in prices seemed inevitable the moment inflation came to an end. Foreign trade, it was argued, must return to a normal basis and war industries must be deflated with everything else. For such developments the business community was fairly well prepared, and it was generally expected that 1919—perhaps also 1920—would be a period of deflation, readjustment, and more or less severe depression.

There were, indeed, a few who knew that *post-bellum* inflation was conceivable; and there were also at Washington a number of officials who looked forward to several years of wartime control of industry, which they believed to be necessary during what they termed the "period of reconstruction." But such views were uncommon in business circles, where the general expectation, and probably the desire, was that the country should return to "normal" as quickly as might be possible without too violent disturbance.

Then, after a brief reaction, came the surprising development of 1919—another boom of greater proportions than its predecessor, which gave us twelve months of feverish prosperity and inevitably unsettled business opinion. Since the expected reaction had not materialized, something was obviously wrong with the reckoning; and it became necessary for

[1] Reprinted from *Harvard Economic Service Weekly Letters*, Vol. II (1923), pp. 1-8. Reproduced by generous permission of the publishers.

almost every one to try to get his bearings again under very difficult circumstances. Such conditions proved fertile ground for a crop of diverse opinions, and converted into reckless optimists in 1919 some executives who were extreme conservatives in 1918.

Theories During the Post-War Boom

Of these theories, one, which lured many to their ruin, was that in foreign trade the United States had suddenly found a new El Dorado which would insure its prosperity for years to come. Another was that the war had made this country the financial center of the world, and thus had laid a new basis for permanent prosperity. A third was the theory that years would be required to repair the ravages and make good the losses occasioned by the war, and that work of reconstruction and rehabilitation would insure active trade for many years. Out of these opinions, and perhaps others, in which the majority of people shared in some degree, came the belief in a new era of unexampled prosperity, which, although recalled with a smile today, played an important rôle during the twelvemonth that preceded the recent depression.

Of course a minority of business men kept their heads, and believed that inflation, however prolonged, must ultimately bring a day of reckoning. How far the inevitable reaction would go and what consequences it would entail might be difficult to foresee; but the prudent course was obviously to refrain from expansion, keep out of debt, and invest surplus funds in good securities. In some cases thoughtful conservatives adopted the view that war inflation must be followed by complete deflation to substantially the pre-war level, upon which, after the inevitable had happened, business could once more build with safety. Thus the theory of a new era found its counterpart in the theory of a return to 1913, and between these extremes the observer could distinguish at the end of 1919 a large number of divergent opinions.

Meanwhile the combined reserves of the federal reserve

banks had fallen nearly to the minimum prescribed by law, and it was evident that the brakes must be applied if the country was to remain upon the gold standard. In November 1919 came the first increase in rediscount rates, a danger singal which brought a reaction in security markets but was unheeded by a large part of the business community. There seemed to be no end to the demand for goods, profits in many lines were running larger than ever, and the opinion was widely entertained that only the "speculators" had been hit and that "business" would remain good for a long time to come. The next six months brought the inevitable reaction in commodity markets, and inaugurated a period of severest industrial depression.

In the main the difficult situation was well handled by the federal reserve authorities; credit was extended in increasing volume at rising interest rates until acute needs were satisfied, and an old-fashioned panic was avoided. Perhaps, after liquidation had got well under way, rediscount rates should have been reduced earlier than they were; and perhaps also too little attention was given to the psychology of the situation; concerning these matters opinions will always differ. But it is certainly true that during the trying period of readjustment the business community was left without definite information as to the ultimate objectives of federal reserve policy. Whether it was the intention to deflate prices to the level of 1913, whether without any such intention it was believed that the inevitable trend was toward the pre-war level, or whether it was believed that at some intermediate point prices could or would be stabilized and the process of liquidation completed—upon all these points and many others no clear word was vouchsafed; and every one was left to his own conjectures. Perhaps it could not have been otherwise; the reserve system was a new institution and had not fully found itself; its responsible heads faced conditions which were world-wide and in many respects unprecedented. It is easy to criticize today, but would have been difficult to advise at the time. Few, if any, would desire to undertake similar responsibilities. It is to be hoped, however, that before another depression occurs, policies will be formulated which can be generally understood and will dispel such uncertainties as clouded the outlook in 1920 and 1921.

Theories During the Depression

Left to its own devices, the business community in 1920 indulged in a variety of surmises and conjectures which naturally resulted in opinions widely divergent. There were, in the first place, those who, taking an international view of the situation, concluded that no improvement, or substantially none, was possible until European conditions had been stabilized and the trade of the world restored to something like a normal status. For fifty years or more Europe had imported foodstuffs and raw materials from all quarters of the earth, and paid for them in manufactured commodities. Her power to purchase had been greatly curtailed, underconsumption was prevalent and likely to continue for years, her productive capacity had been reduced, and the trade of the world seemed wholly out of joint. Under such conditions many believed that the foreign trade of the United States must remain depressed, and other lines of business could hardly expect to prosper. This view naturally appealed strongly to those who were disappointed at our failure to enter the League of Nations, cancel or scale down foreign debts owed to the United States, make new loans to Europe, and participate actively in European affairs. In some cases at least there seemed almost to be the desire that business in the United States should not improve until the country had been forced to do what was believed to be its duty in Europe. Those who had first-hand contact with European affairs were naturally impressed with the gravity of the situation, and in some cases were so profoundly depressed by what they saw in Europe that they failed to give due consideration to the great recuperative power of the United States.

Equally pessimistic was a second group, which held to the theory that liquidation could not be arrested until everything had returned to the pre-war level. For six years, it was said, the entire world had been undergoing inflation which had lifted everything to an abnormal level that could not possibly be maintained. Inevitably, as night follows day, deflation must follow inflation; and the process could not, and should not, be arrested until we had returned to the point from which our troubles started in 1913. In support of this theory history was invoked to show that after wars of the Napoleonic period, and again after our own Civil War, commodity prices, after being greatly inflated, fell to pre-war levels and then considerably lower. It was argued that in the present instance history would inevitably repeat itself, and as time went on the stages of the journey back to 1913 were definitely mapped out. By the middle of 1921 agricultural products were selling at something like 1913 prices, and in some cases were actually lower, so that the farmers had already been deflated. Speculation had been killed, and the stock market looked like the devastated war areas. Profits had not only been deflated, but had been submerged in a sea of red ink. It only remained, the argument ran, to deflate other prices, liquidate labor, reduce taxes, and thus complete the readjustment. If all things could be brought into line, normal relations between different factors would be restored and industry would enter upon a period of convalescence which would presently be followed by complete recovery. Viewed from certain angles the theory was plausible enough, and it seemed to be supported by persuasive historical evidence. It appealed strongly to many thoughtful men, and was widely held in influential circles. In conjunction with the theory of the internationalists, it tended naturally to produce an atmosphere of deepest gloom which has only gradually lifted during the past year.

In agricultural districts a return to 1913 might have been acceptable if wages, freight rates, and retail prices could have been deflated immediately, and some painless method could have been devised for dealing with a heavy load of debts. But these things were impossible; and the inevitable outcome was an insistent demand for relief, which resulted in the revival of the War Finance Corporation and other measures designed to aid the class which had been most thoroughly and successfully liquidated. Labor proved another intractable element which, by virtue of strong organization or otherwise, managed to retain a considerable part of its war-time gains. Taxes also were difficult to deflate; and, in view of the interest and other charges inherited from the war, could be clearly seen to be a factor which at the very best admitted of only gradual reduction. Manifestly the theory of an immediate return to 1913 failed to reckon with refractory elements which were certain to offer insuperable difficulties.

Gradually a third theory began to influence business opinion. General liquidation and acute industrial depression are always overdone, and are certain to be followed by at least a partial recovery. Production declines sharply with the downward swing of the business cycle; but consumption declines much less, and cannot be long supplied at prices that are below the cost of production. Therefore, about the middle of 1921, wholesale prices began to be stabilized and production to increase. It was then realized that a country with large natural resources and over a hundred million inhabitants can and must carry on a large business, even though some of its important foreign customers are temporarily impoverished. Export business, after all, accounts for only a small proportion of our total production; and although some industries arc dependent upon it for real prosperity, the United States does not depend for its living chiefly upon foreign commerce, and therefore finds itself in a position vastly more favorable than that of a trading country like Great Britain. The war had indeed strained our financial and industrial organization, and the subsequent depression had brought widespread loss and suffering; but our recuperative power was still enormous, the domestic market very large, foreign business on the whole compared favorably with anything known before the war, and there was no good reason why we could not look forward to a return of moderate prosperity. Upon some such analysis of the situation business men who did not lose their heads and were not too much concerned with European affairs were able to premise the opinion that liquidation had about run its course and that better business lay ahead. In most cases those who proceeded upon this theory have had no occasion for regret.

If opinion and sentiment had been controlling factors there is no telling how far the recent liquidation would have gone; at the height of a boom and in the depth of a depression the crowd is always wrong, and it is the exceptional man who avoids the prevalent illusions. But economic facts will not be denied; and during the summer of 1921, in defiance of widely accepted opinion, business began to improve, very slowly and unevenly at first, with halting gait, with little confidence, with temporary reactions, and in volume too small to bring immediate profit. Without much help from opinion, and in the face of most pessimistic predictions, it has continued to recover until today few observers doubt that 1922 brought substantial improvement and that 1923 opens with fair prospects. Opinions still differ, however, as to the nature and extent of the recovery which has taken place, and as to its probable duration. Under these circumstances it may be helpful to review the divergent opinions which the business man is now encountering in the street, at the club, at his bank, in his industry, and in responsible publications.

Present Theories

The internationalist is still with us. European conditions remain chaotic, we are not yet in the League, no real "settlement" has been reached in regard to debts owed the United States, and we have done nothing to promote the solution of the vexed question of reparations. Until these matters are attended to no real prosperity can prevail in the United States, and it is maintained that such improvement as has occurred during the past year is a mere "flash in the pan." Unless we coöperate heartily and actively, Europe faces a certain *débâcle,* perhaps during the present winter, and worse things lie ahead of us than we have yet known. Such is the gloomy outlook of the internationalists. Our own views are well known to subscribers, and need not be argued at length in this *Letter*. European conditions are bad in many respects, and react unfavorably upon the United States. We should be glad to have the United States do the right thing, but question the wisdom of some of the proposals of the internationalists. Perhaps if sentiment could be laid aside, and this country could consider what it ought to do as an intelligent creditor, it might exert a helpful influence upon European policies. Of this we may have something to say in a subsequent *Letter*.

We still have, also, those who hold that commodity prices and everything else that moves with them must ultimately return to the pre-war status, and therefore regard the improvement of the last eighteen months as a temporary interruption of a long downward swing that will ultimately land us about where we were in 1913. The extremists of this group have sometimes appeared to regard every favorable development since June 1921 as a misfortune which could only tend to postpone the inevitable and deceive the business community into thinking that nature could be prevented from taking its own course. In our *Letter* of the 10th of last June, we presented our reasons for thinking that during the present decade commodity prices are more likely to play around present levels than to decline to the level of 1913; and we therefore allude to the theory just mentioned merely for the purpose of giving a complete review of the opinions with which the intelligent executive must reckon.

A third opinion, somewhat widely prevalent, is that we have entered upon a period of "secondary" inflation: the war gave us our first and great inflation which was inevitably followed by drastic deflation, and this in turn has been followed by a "secondary" inflation such as sometimes occurs after great wars. Instead of accepting the deflation of 1920 as an accomplished fact and readjusting affairs accordingly, we have seen fit to revive the War Finance Corporation, undertake an ambitious program of public works financed with borrowed money, and carry on what is termed "prosperity propaganda," with the result that artificial stimulants have been applied and "secondary" inflation has begun. Large gold imports have favored this movement, and may presently be expected to carry it to greater lengths. The whole process is believed by these theorists to be unnatural and unhealthy, and unless checked it will produce nothing but undesirable results. In this view of the case, we may have before us a short-lived period of fictitious prosperity which will end in another collapse, perhaps more serious than that of 1920 because many concerns have lost the reserves which absorbed a large part of the previous shock. According to this view there is little that is natural or healthy in the business improvement of 1922, and the present outlook is therefore one that should cause serious misgivings if not alarm. In recent months rather less has been heard of "secondary" inflation, but when the present business cycle enters upon its final phase—that of recession of prices and business activity—we shall doubtless be told that such inflation has run its inevitable course, and that the country is suffering the natural results of the artificial stimulants applied during the past two years.

A fourth theory was gradually evolved during 1922, and is now held somewhat widely in banking and other influential circles. According to this, liquidation ran its natural course in 1920 and 1921, and was followed by a natural rebound of business which is gradually bringing prosperity. The improvement which has taken place is substantial and encouraging, but there is now danger of inflation. Gold imports and the expansive power of the federal reserve system are the dangerous factors, and it is important that during 1923 speculation should be held in leash and business kept on an even, conservative course. Prosperity is returning, but there is serious danger that bullish enthusiasm will lead to another boom which, as the result of an apparently strong banking situation, may lead to a repetition of the excesses of 1919. Gold reserves are large, but we hold considerably more of the yellow metal than we can hope to retain permanently, and there is danger of unwise credit expansion leading to another period of inflation. This view is in some respects like our own, but it does not make allowance for the inevitable upswing of the business cycle. It assumes that it is possible, through corrective action of the reserve banks or otherwise, to eliminate speculative and business enthusiasm, and thereby flatten out the curve of the business cycle and keep business on what may be termed an even course, enjoying access to what is called a stable volume of bank credit but receiving prompt correction the moment it departs from the golden mean. If human nature were something different from what it is, if enthusiasm could be largely eliminated from any form of successful activity, and if there were some agency generally recognized to be wise enough to administer corrective treatment in the right amount at precisely the right time, this opinion might have its attractions; but with things as they are, we do not believe that regulative measures can do more than moderate the extremes of business expansion and depression. With some misgivings, therefore, such as can never be eliminated from human affairs, but with confidence in the soundness of the present situation, we look forward to a continued upswing of the business cycle.

There is still a fifth theory, which must not be left out of account. It holds that, while business has undoubtedly improved very materially and will continue to advance for several months to come, there are certain maladjustments in the present situation which will bring a reaction some time between the spring and fall of 1923. The first trouble is that prosperity is unevenly distributed, and that while the condition of the farmer has improved, his purchasing power has not been completely restored. The second difficulty is that the prices of cotton, wool, construction materials, and other basic commodities have all risen to high levels, and that wages are beginning to advance, so that operating costs are on the increase before a satisfactory margin of profit has been restored. It may be possible to advance the prices of finished products to an extent sufficient to compensate for higher cost; but in many lines, notably textiles, it is believed that stubborn resistance will be encountered from consumers, who, especially if they be housewives, will ultimately have their way. In addition to this resistance of consumers, it is believed further that business will suffer from car shortage and other transportation difficulties which will slow up the movement of goods and increase credit requirements, which are already rising as the result of higher prices and of expanding business activity. The prospect, therefore, is believed to be for rising costs, meagre profits, and increasing credit requirements, which will result in a definite reaction before the end of the present year.

This last opinion seems to us to lay undue stress upon difficulties which may not prove as serious as anticipated. Consumers' resistance is always encountered when prices swing upward, except in times of wild inflation and extravagant spending, such as obtained in 1919. It may be serious in some lines of industry this year, but upon the present evidence it cannot be assumed at this time to be a condition that will generally prevail. Purchasing power is certainly upon the increase and may suffice for such a volume of production as we are likely to have. Labor shortage is already developing, and transportation difficulties are likely to persist; but such factors have not been a controlling influence in the last two business cycles, and may not control at the present time. Credit requirements will undoubtedly increase during 1923; but unless an actual boom develops, stringent money conditions are not likely to be encountered. It seldom happens that a business situation is free from troublesome elements, and it would be surprising if they did not exist today. At every stage in the recovery which has been under way since the middle of 1921, numerous difficulties have always been seen ahead; but some of these have not materialized and others have been overcome; so that until we see definite evidence of credit shortage we shall believe that business will continue upon the up grade.

Conclusion

Our own views are familiar to subscribers, and have been partially indicated in the above discussion of prevailing theories. We believe that, just as European complications have not prevented the development of a normal cyclical movement up from the recent depression, so they will not (barring another war) prevent the completion of this movement. We believe that the general trend of prices during the present decade will not be downward to the 1913 level; and that, even if, in some subsequent decade, that level is ultimately reached, we shall reach it only after the completion of a number of business cycles which will need to be included in the reckoning if the probable course of business is to be correctly forecast. We have found that the war did not destroy the old landmarks, and that it has been possible since the spring of 1919 to forecast the major movements of business by the use of familiar statistical data. In January 1923 we are somewhere near the middle of a tolerably normal business cycle which began in the middle of 1921 and should be completed within three or four years from the date.

The recovery of business has already been substantial, and rests upon a solid foundation. The fact that buying is still conservative and confined largely to current needs is not a reason for pessimism, but evidence of the healthful character of the movement of the last twelve months. When buying becomes excited and feverish and credit becomes strained, we shall expect a reversal of the present upward tendency in general business. Money is now in some demand and rates are somewhat higher; but we are only four months away from the low point reached by our money curve after the recent liquidation, credit is in no way strained, and the banking situation is absolutely sound. Business conditions are uneven and at some points unsatisfactory, but they are always so after a depression of such severity as that through which we have passed. A return of prosperity is the best and the only possible means of bringing into line the factors which now suffer from maladjustment. Renewed liquidation, even if it could be forced at this moment, would surely fall with chief weight on producers of foodstuffs and basic materials, as it usually tends to do. We see no "boom" in sight, and none may develop during the present business cycle. This has sometimes occurred in times past, and we hope it will be so in this instance. Current opinion would have been a poor guide at almost every stage of the present business cycle, since it is largely the creature of the moment and does not reckon sufficiently with the significant underlying factors. The only safe course has been to follow the old landmarks and appraise current developments in the light of fundamental conditions which seem to govern the business cycle. Not because business sentiment is generally hopeful at the present moment, but because the underlying conditions reflected in our statistics indicate continued improvement, we look forward to a year of good business in 1923. Leaving out of account unexpected developments in Europe, we believe the movement of money rates is the significant factor at the time of writing. Until this indicates the approach of credit stringency, we shall expect a continuation of the upswing in business which developed naturally and inevitably from the profound depression in which industry was gripped in the spring of 1921.

THE AMERICAN MONEY MARKET[1]

IN THE strict sense of the word, there is not and perhaps never will be an American money market. The great size of the country and wide diversities of local conditions produce marked diversities of interest rates which are not and perhaps never will be brought to a common level by nation-wide movements of money and credit to the places where they are in the greatest demand. But it is to be remembered that there are few perfect markets for commodities and that, with the commodity money, the differences in prices obtaining in different localities are less than the nominal rates of interest suggest. When allowance is made for differences of risk, it is clear that real interest rates vary considerably less than nominal. When, furthermore, we remember that there are different kinds of money and that comparisons of rates should be made only for money of the same kind, the local differences in nominal rates become less important and significant. Even within a single bank at a given time there may be the small customer who is always charged 6 per cent, the large borrower who may pay 5, the exceptional concern maintaining unusual balances who may pay 4¾, and the outside paper bought from note brokers at 4½ per cent; while, in addition to all these commercial rates, there are the rates on collateral loans which are different for time and for call loans. Even in the same city the average interest rates secured by particular banks on their total loans will vary according to the kinds of money their customers require; and between different sections of the country such average rates must vary even more on account of the greater differences in the kinds of money which local conditions demand. When these things and others are taken into account, it is evident that quotations of nominal interest rates exaggerate the differences which undoubtedly exist

[1] Reprinted from a pamphlet published by the Harvard Economic Society (1930). Reproduced by generous permission of the publishers.

in the real prices which money and credit command in various parts of the United States.

After all allowances are made, however, we are left with the undoubted fact that the United States is divided into a large number of areas within which local differences of supply and demand produce natural differences in money rates, which, so far as we can see, will long obtain. If a nation-wide market for this thing which we call money (and is mostly credit) exists, it can be produced only by the flow of funds from one section to another into those kinds of loans which can be handled on a national scale because they are sufficiently homogeneous to make a nation-wide distribution possible. The requirements of the small borrower, and doubtless other local needs, can be met only by local bankers thoroughly acquainted with local conditions and credit risks. But some kinds of credit requirements can be and are being handled in a different way; today money and credit flow more freely than ever before to the locality where they are in greatest demand, with the result that local barriers to competition are broken down and the distribution of credit is more and more assuming national proportions. In saying this, I am not referring to anything that branch banks or chain banking may be doing in certain parts of the country, but to competition between independent banks without branches except in their own city or immediate locality but competing for such business as can be done upon a national scale.

In 1789, when our national government was organized, there were but three banks in the United States—in Philadelphia, New York, and Boston—which, beside accommodating the territory naturally tributary to them, did business with each other, with London, and probably with a few merchants in outlying parts of the United States. By 1860 the country had a large number of commercial banks, and balances moved regularly towards the principal centres (and back again in case of need); while the circulation of bank notes had become nation-wide and it sometimes happened that, when banks in one locality had suspended specie payments and their notes had become utterly discredited, the most available medium of exchange was the notes of banks located in other parts of the country and enjoying better credit. Seventy years ago, therefore, bank credit, flowing over or breaking through some of the barriers separating local markets, had already become nationalized in some of its movements, even though there did not yet exist anything that could be called an American money market.

From 1860 down to the establishment of the Federal Reserve System, while the country continued to be served by independent banks, the flow of certain forms of credit became increasingly nationalized and the independence of local money markets was gradually decreased. New York became increasingly the financial centre to which money flowed in periods of slack demand and from which it was recalled as seasonal or other requirements dictated. Commercial paper handled by well-known firms of brokers gained wide distribution and became an important influence tending toward nationalization. Then came the growth of large corporations doing a nation-wide business and naturally doing their banking on a national scale. Beside these, and doubtless other factors that could be mentioned, it is probable that there was some increase in the practice of rediscounting, even though this was practiced on a very limited scale prior to the establishment of the Reserve System; while in time of great need, when outlying regions were thrown back upon our money centres, the issue of clearing house certificates, especially in New York, became a means by which relief could be given not only for local but for nation-wide demands, and at such times all parts of the country were acutely conscious that they were members one of the other and that credit was not and could not be a purely local affair.

Before passing to more recent times, I venture to point out the resemblance between the process by which an American money market came into existence and that by which an American government was evolved. We start with a number of local areas largely independent of each other in their economic life and having their separate financial arrangements. Then in the course of time, as trade overstepped local bounds and broke down local barriers, financial methods, like governmental institutions, tended to become national in scope; so that by 1860 both were in process of nationalization, even though state rights in the field of government and state banks in the field of finance were the order of the day. Finally, the last four decades of the nineteenth century and the first of the twentieth greatly strengthened the forces making for nationalization, and brought it about that, even before the Federal Reserve System was established, one could recognize an American money market in the process of making.

The last sixteen years have brought changes which now make the term "American money market" more than an academic phrase for a thing which in actual life exists only in vague and indefinite form. In the first place, we have the Federal Reserve System which, besides greatly increasing the practice of rediscounting, has established a uniform rate of discount within each Reserve District. Beyond this, we have found that the twelve Reserve Districts influence each other; so that, although rediscount rates may vary, there is a tendency for all to move in the same direction, while in case of need Reserve Banks may rediscount for the Reserve Banks of other Districts. Rates charged by commercial banks do not conform exactly to the rate at which Reserve Banks rediscount; but they are strongly influenced by it, even in cases where it used to be thought that the rediscount rate was ineffective. In regions where 7 or 8 per cent is the customary rate for commercial loans (and there are districts where it is even higher), the difference between a 3 per cent and a 6 per cent discount rate at the Reserve Bank of that region is at least indirectly felt. The most remote banks charging the highest rates are dependent upon connections with banks in larger cities that are not remote, and are directly and strongly influenced in their operations by the rate at which they can borrow at their Reserve Bank. Even during the last decade, when conditions have been so abnormal in many ways that it is still hazardous to say exactly what the Reserve System may and may not accomplish, we can see that rediscount rates have been a powerful factor tending to nationalize money and credit conditions in the United States.

In the same direction the open market operations of the Reserve Banks have tended. One smiles today when he reflects that in 1922 it was generally supposed that only by changes in discount rates could or would the Reserve Banks influence money and credit conditions. The next year taught us that, by increasing or decreasing their holdings of government securities, the Reserve Banks could ease or tighten the money market and thus prepare the way for changes in rediscount rates. With the acceptance, the lesson was harder to learn; and until 1927 or 1928 it was generally thought that the acceptance market was a thing apart from the general money market. We now know that substantial purchases of bills in the open market or the cessation of purchases which presently leads to a decrease of Reserve Bank portfolios, affect money immediately in New York and may influence all financial centres. As the acceptance business has grown, we have seen a factor developing which, in a most effective yet quiet way, ignores differences of geography and is slowly nationalizing certain important kinds of the most liquid bank credit. The Federal Reserve System may never destroy the barriers which create local differences in natural rates of interest; but its acceptance operations have gone far toward nationalizing money and credit. If the market for acceptances ever broadens and ceases to depend so largely upon the favor of the Reserve Banks, an important further step will have been taken in developing an American money market.

To give definiteness to the picture I have drawn, the American money market, as I visualize it today, consists of a central pool of money and credit, which is connected by pipe lines, now spanning a continent and reaching the large number of smaller pools constituting our local money markets within which geographical and other differences produce different natural rates of interest for business of a purely local character. Through these pipe lines money is pumped out from the central pool, or drawn back, as conditions may require, by the flow of currency and the movement of such forms of credit as have a common national character and therefore admit of nation-wide distribution.[2] These are:

(*a*) discounts or rediscounts granted by Reserve Banks to member banks or, in case of need, to each other;

(*b*) other Federal Reserve funds invested in acceptances and government securities of longer or shorter maturity, which not only equalize the flow of money by differences in distribution among the twelve Reserve Districts but are also an important factor in tightening or relaxing credit throughout the United States;

(*c*) acceptance credit and outside commercial paper circulating outside the Reserve System through agencies operating on a national scale and tending to produce uniform rates for credit sufficiently liquid to permit of national distribution;

(*d*) the deposits and the borrowings of large industries distributing their products or services upon a national scale, transferring deposits as business may require, and shopping around the entire country for loans which are placed wherever a difference of one-quarter or even one-eighth per cent can be secured in response to telegraphic inquiry;

(*e*) foreign funds, handled by the larger banks both at the

[2] My friend Mr. Paul Warburg, who has been good enough to read this paper, suggests that it might be better to describe the money market in terms of the credit risk involved. Thus he would begin with bank deposits with solid banks, prime bankers' acceptances, treasury bills, and similar gilt-edged short-term obligations, in which short-term money is invested in a fluid form and practically without credit risk. On this foundation he suggests the interest structure for other short-term investments is built up, by requiring a premium of varying amount for each credit risk and for varying degrees of fluidity in the investment. In this manner he arrives at a picture of the money market consisting of various categories of loans, classified according to fluidity and credit risk. Mr. Warburg's suggestion is most interesting; and I venture to express the hope that he will elaborate it in an article that will give us a picture of the American money market as seen by one of our great bankers who has contributed so greatly to the developments of the last two decades. I venture also to suggest that the resulting picture would not differ so widely from the impressionistic sketch which I have presented, because differences in credit risk and liquidity go far to determine whether any form of credit can take on a national or international character.

seaboard and in the interior, which flow back and forth as world-wide conditions may dictate;

(*f*) other items of which I will mention only one, namely, the recent flow of clearing house balances by over-night movements between banks within the same Reserve District or even city banks in different Districts.

The central pool to which I have referred must be thought of as a single pool in which money always *tends* to come to a common level and would do so if conditions remained unchanged for a sufficient time to permit this to occur. Upon closer examination, this pool proves to be divided into compartments in which money at any given time maintains different levels which deceive those who do not know that, far below the surface of the water, all are connected by a system of pipes, varying in their diameters, which bring it about that any funds turned into any part of the pool or drained out of it will affect the levels in all compartments if time is given to permit them to produce their natural result. Between the acceptance compartment and the rediscount compartment there is a special connection expressly designed to produce a difference of level which will favor the growth of the acceptance business. Between the acceptance and the treasury certificate compartments the connection is ordinarily close and immediate. The compartment containing outside commercial paper exhibits peculiarities of its own, because its contents play a special role in American banking and may receive most favored or least favored treatment according to the general credit situation. The brokers' loan compartment is unique, since in no other country does call money play such a role in speculation or does speculation at times, through the call money market, exert such suction upon credit resources not only at home but abroad. Time fails for a complete enumeration or full description of the various compartments of the central pool; and I must content myself with this brief sketch of its structure and contents. The important thing is to note that there is such a pool; that it is divided into compartments which, though they may seem to be separate, are really connected; and that nothing which occurs in one compartment can, if conditions remain the same, fail to affect the level maintained in all the others.

This account of the structure of the American money market may be concluded with a brief statement of some of its general characteristics which in this paper cannot receive the attention that is their due. In the first place, on account of the size of our country and its diversity of conditions, there are greater local differences than exist in the other leading commercial countries. In the second place, thanks to the good offices of the Federal Reserve System and the Comptroller of the Currency, we have more statistics and other information about money conditions than are available in any other country of the world. In the third place, we now have an all-American stock market which makes credit demands such as the world has never before known and is able, as we now know, to affect credit conditions throughout the world. Fourthly, our system of central control is comparatively new, is much more cumbersome in its organization than the central banks of other countries, and from its inception has been operating under peculiar difficulties due to the great war and the subsequent disturbances resulting from it. And, finally, unusual responsibilities greater than any ever attaching to financial leadership rest upon those who, within and without the Federal Reserve System, determine our credit policies. The war left us a creditor nation; and never yet have our debtors been in a position in any year to pay us what they owe on income account. What they could not pay has come to us in gold or has been settled for the time being by foreign loans or investments, which, of course, increase the amount subsequently payable on income account. Thus we have become the custodian of a very large part of the world's gold supply at a time when our position as international creditor makes the rate of interest at which dollar exchange can be obtained a factor of vital consequence to all the rest of the world. To the study of the American money market, which has developed so rapidly in recent years and must undergo further changes before it can function as it should, it is well for us to devote continuing attention for many years to come.

FOREIGN TRADE AND THE BUSINESS CYCLE[1]

OUR foreign trade provides several of the longest continuous series of statistics relating to economic conditions in the United States. In this article they are studied with a view to determining what light they throw upon the business cycles through which the country has passed since 1790, but such study has naturally brought to light other matters of economic interest.

The available data, like all statistics of international commerce, always contain an element of error; and this is especially true of the early decades of our national existence. Before 1821 imports admitted free of duty were not reported at all, and those subject to specific duties were reported by quantity, not value; moreover, reported values were reckoned arbitrarily at 10 or 20 per cent above the cost of the articles at their port of origin, in order to allow for the value gained in transportation, *i.e.*, freight charges and importers' profits. The statistics which now pass as official for this period were made up by the Treasury Department in 1835, and are based largely on estimates and comparisons.[2] In 1821 the *Annual Reports on Commerce and Navigation* began to be published, and with them came constant improvement in our statistics of foreign trade. Until 1843 the series relate to years ending on September 30, but in that year and subsequently relate to years ending June 30. The result is that in 1843 the statistics cover a period of only nine months, and therefore have to be omitted from comparisons. Although our official statistics of foreign com-

[1] Reprinted from *Review of Economic Statistics*, Vol. XIII (1931), pp. 138-59. Written in collaboration with H. L. Micoleau. Reproduced by generous permission of the publishers.

[2] See *Review of Economic Statistics*, Vol. I, p. 215, for further explanations and references to sources of information.

merce are admittedly imperfect, the following analysis shows that they yield results which correlate fairly well with information drawn from other sources, and may therefore be accepted as useful evidence concerning economic conditions in the United States during the last 141 years.

Chart 1 presents: (*a*) statistics of combined exports and imports, (*b*) statistics of imports, and (*c*) a third curve showing the course of wholesale commodity prices in the United States.[3] Curves (*a*) and (*b*) are plotted on a logarithmic scale, and show that there have been fairly obvious changes of trend, which are indicated by the trend lines superimposed upon the curves. Curve (*c*), also on a logarithmic scale, is included because there are clearly marked relations between prevailing trends of commodity prices and the trends determined for curves (*a*) and (*b*). It will be useful also in studying the business cycles revealed by the movements of our foreign trade shown by the curves on Charts 2 and 3.

In determining the trends shown for curves (*a*) and (*b*) on Chart 1, it was necessary, first of all, to treat the years from 1790 to 1820 as a separate period. The data available for that time lump together the movements of merchandise and specie, whereas in 1821 these items began to be separately reported. For the first period, therefore, the two curves show combined values of merchandise and specie, whereas from 1821 onward they show only values of merchandise.

The movement of curve (*a*) from 1790 to 1820 is highly ir-

[3] Curve (*c*) is a composite made from the following indexes, with proper adjustments for differences in level:

1795-1802, an unweighted index based on prices at Boston, constructed by W. M. Smith and published in *Review of Economic Statistics*, Vol. IX, pp. 171-83.

1803-1809, an unweighted index on prices at Boston, constructed by A. H. Hansen and published in *Bulletin of the United States Bureau of Labor Statistics*, No. 367, p. 235.

1810-1889, an unweighted index based on prices at Boston from 1810 to 1825 and at New York from 1825 to 1860, published by the *New York Times Annalist*, April 11, 1921, p. 425.

1890-1931, weighted index of all commodities of the United States Bureau of Labor. The 1931 figure is, of course, estimated.

regular, but exhibits two well-defined tendencies. For the first seventeen years there was an abrupt rise to a peak never again reached during this period, so that we have first a sharp rise and then a decline of combined exports and imports. If the statistics were more accurate, if they distinguished between movements of commodities and those of specie, and if the rising and declining trends were not connected with the great European war and then the war upon which we entered in 1812, it might be profitable to refine our analysis and break this period into two, one of them showing a rising, and the other a declining, trend. But such attempts to refine analysis of imperfect statistics relating to a period largely dominated by war would be unprofitable, and it has therefore seemed better, omitting the first four years,[4] to determine a trend for the period 1794-1820, setting aside the year 1814 when the British blockade of the Atlantic seaboard reduced foreign trade to insignificant proportions.

For this period, which is free from the influence of the first four years, a straight-line trend fitted by the method of least squares to the logarithms of the data showing combined exports and imports gives as good a result as can be obtained. Since it is fitted to the logarithms of the data, it is a compound-interest curve; and the rate of annual increase is 0.9 per cent.

This line of trend is not necessarily the one which would best show the normal level around which cyclical fluctuations would play, but it is the line which best expresses the average rate of growth of our total foreign trade for the twenty-six years in question—a period during which a sharp upturn was followed by a decline, which resulted in a small average annual rate of increase. This average rate of increase will be employed as a normal in the construction of Chart 2 which undertakes to measure cyclical fluctuations in foreign trade in the manner that

[4] The statistics start from a low level in 1790, a year which hardly felt the stimulus imparted to trade, domestic and foreign, by the adoption of the Constitution and the establishment of a stable government. To include the first four years would depress unduly the line of trend at its beginning, and so would produce an average rate of increase which it would be absurd to regard as normal for the period from 1795 to 1820.

was employed in the article upon "Postal Revenues and the Business Cycle," published in the May issue of this REVIEW.[5]

Curve (*b*) shows movements generally similar to those of curve (*a*), the only significant difference being that the peak reached in 1807 was slightly exceeded in 1816; but this does not change the fact that the general movement was strongly upward from 1790 to 1807 and thereafter irregularly downward. Omitting the first four years, a trend has been determined for the period from 1794 to 1820 by the method followed in the case of curve (*a*), with a single point of difference. In the case of curve (*a*), only the year 1814 was omitted from the computation, but in curve (*b*) the year 1813 also was omitted, because the decline of imports in that year was so much greater than the decline recorded by curve (*a*). A compound-interest curve for imports during this period results in a trend rising at the annual rate of 1.6 per cent—this moderate figure being due to the decline after 1807.

The difference which the omission of the first four years makes in the trends computed for curves (*a*) and (*b*) can be made sufficiently clear by computing for either of them the trend that we should get if we began with the year 1790. For combined exports and imports, for instance, a compound-interest curve fitted to the figures from 1790 to 1820 would give an annual increase of about 3 per cent. On *a priori* grounds such a rate of increase would not be rejected as abnormal; but inspection of curves (*a*) and (*b*) shows that from 1794 to 1820 the increase was small or moderate, and that to assume a 3 per cent rate of increase as normal would render invalid the analysis presented in Chart 2, of the cyclical fluctuations of our foreign trade during the difficult period with which we are now concerned. The trends we have used for curves (*a*) and (*b*), let it be said again, are not those which best exhibit the actual growth of foreign trade from 1790 to 1820, but those which best express the normal rate of increase during the twenty-six year period which began in 1794.

[5] In this connection, see *Review of Economic Statistics*, Vol. XIII, p. 47, fn. 2.

CHART I—Foreign trade and commodity prices.*

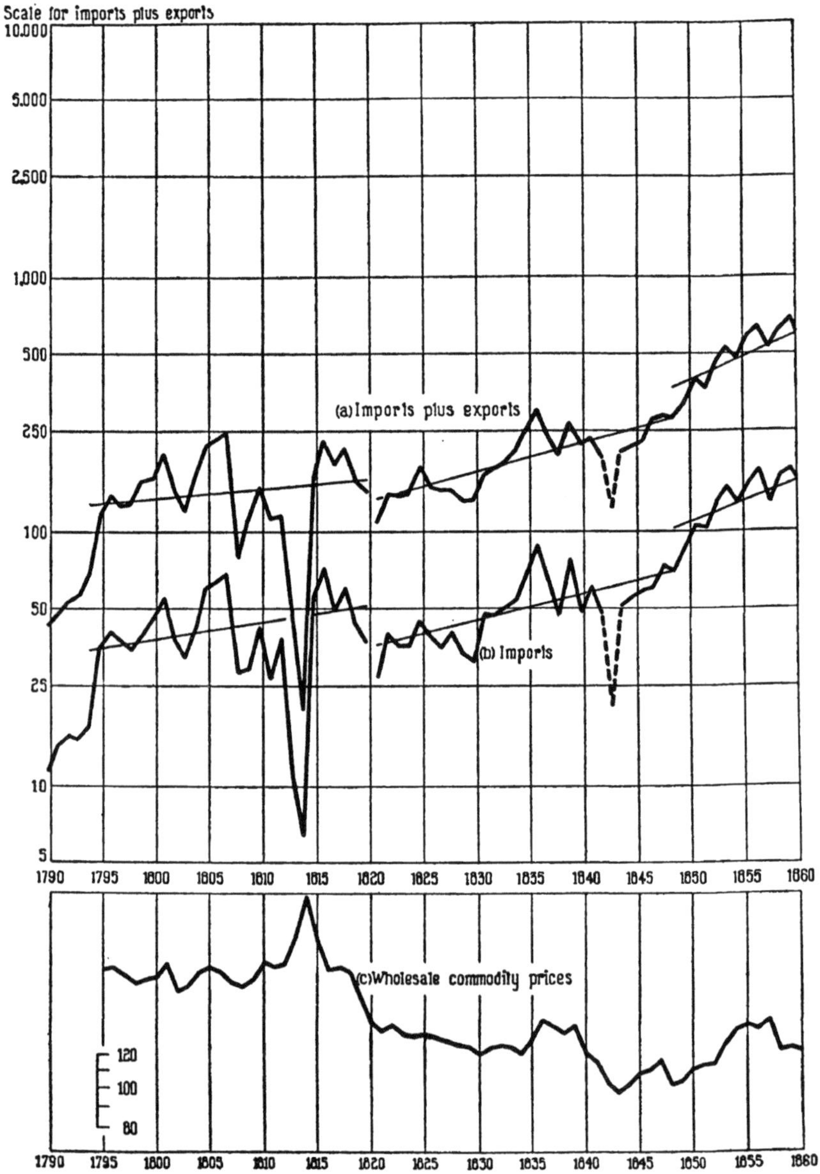

* (*a*) Value of Combined Merchandise Imports and Exports, 1790-1931; (*b*) Value of Merchandise Imports, 1790-1931; (*c*) Index of Wholesale Commodity Prices, 1795-1931 [together with lines of normal growth for (*a*) and (*b*)].

CHART I—(*Continued*)

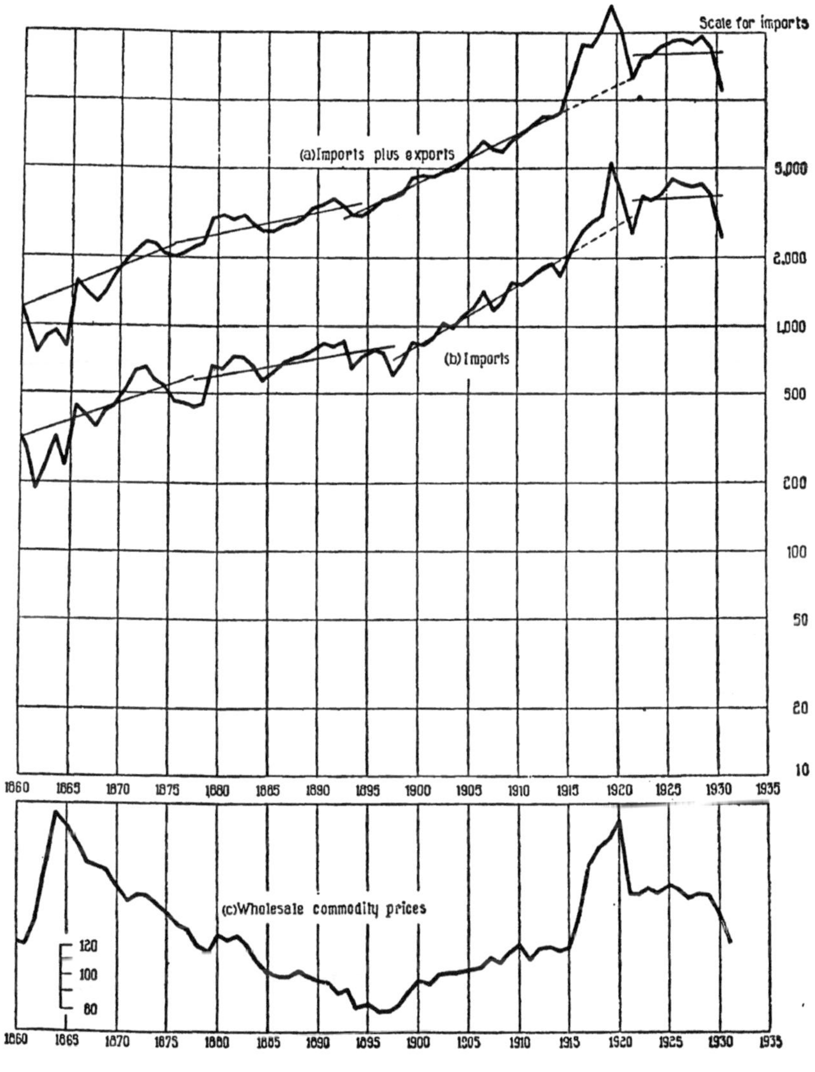

(*Logarithmic vertical scales. Unit for (a) and (b): million dollars.*)

The data for imports and exports include gold and silver prior to 1821; and relate to fiscal years ending September 30, 1790-1842, and to fiscal years ending June 30, 1844-1931. Figures for 1843 are for a nine-month period from October 1, 1842, to June 30, 1843. Curves (*a*) and (*b*) are on different vertical scales simply for convenience. The distance between them, therefore, is not a measurement of exports.

In considering the movements of curves (*a*) and (*b*) during this period and the trends determined for them, it is interesting to note the movement of wholesale commodity prices recorded by curve (*c*). From 1795 until 1812, prices moved irregularly in a generally horizontal direction, and do not seem to have been greatly influenced by the war which had raised commodity prices in England and some other European countries. The next two years brought inflation of prices in the United States, and then in 1815 came the inevitable decline which continued long after the end of the period we are now studying. It is clear, therefore, that the sharp rise in curves (*a*) and (*b*) occurred during a period when prices in this country were not declining and European prices were rising, while the sharp declines of these curves in the closing years of the period came at a time when commodity prices were declining not only in the United States but also in Europe.[6] Similar connections between commodity prices and changes of trends in curves (*a*) and (*b*) will be noted in subsequent periods.

The second period begins in 1821 and ends in 1849. Starting at a low level, curves (*a*) and (*b*) gradually rise, though their movements are very irregular and broken by sharp declines. In 1843 occurs the change of year to which the statistics relate, resulting in a nine-month "year" which must be ignored. It will be recalled, too, that the data now relate to merchandise solely, specie being excluded.

In computing the trend for this period, we must omit the years 1821 and 1843. The latter was a nine-month fiscal period, and the former was a year of deep depression, which, if included, would unduly depress the left end of the line because the period terminated with a number of normal years and not with a severe depression which would restore the balance. A compound-inter-

[6] During the War of 1812, commodity prices and our volume of foreign trade showed an inverse correlation, because the blockade of our seaports decreased the physical volume of exports and imports so greatly that higher commodity prices could not offset this influence. In 1815, with foreign intercourse again open, and belligerent countries in a position to restock shelves, curves (*a*) and (*b*) rose very sharply, in spite of the considerable decline reported by curve (*c*) in commodity prices.

est curve computed by the method herein followed, gives an average or normal rate of increase for combined exports and imports of 2.7 per cent. For imports a similar determination of trend results in a rate of 2.4 per cent. In both cases it is noticeable that the high point for the period was reached in 1836, when a record was made which was not again equalled.

Turning to commodity prices, we find that, neglecting such irregularities as always occur, the general course was downward until 1843, after which they became stabilized—the level for 1849 being a trifle above that for 1843. Curves (*a*) and (*b*) exhibit, first, a very moderate recovery from the low level reached in 1821, and then a sharp increase during the boom that ended in 1837, while commodity prices moved sharply upward in 1835 and 1836. Thereafter all three curves declined irregularly for a number of years; and then between 1843 and 1849, when commodity prices stabilized, curves (*a*) and (*b*) moved upward until they reached a level only slightly lower than that of 1836. Since our trade figures are value figures, they are inevitably affected by price movements; but it is probable that there is a connection between price movements and the physical volume of foreign trade, so that it is not surprising to find the movements of the three curves correlated as closely as they seem to be.

Up to this point, nothing has been said about the possible influence of changes in the tariff upon the volume of foreign trade. So far as yearly movements are concerned, there have certainly been years when the prospect of change in the tariff has affected imports, and others in which marked increases or decreases of rates may not unnaturally be supposed to have had the same result. In the study of trends, however, it is much harder to draw conclusions from the statistical evidence. The higher tariff of 1816 may have had something to do with the decline of curve (*a*) in 1817, but did not prevent a partial recovery in 1818. The higher tariff of 1824 was followed by an increase of imports in 1825, and the higher tariff of 1828 was followed by a decrease in 1829. But much more study than is possible at this time, or necessary for the principal purpose of this article, would be needed to justify any generalization.

It might be argued that, following the depression year of 1821, imports reached a point in 1822 which was higher than the figure recorded for 1830, and that between the two years the high tariffs of 1824 and 1828 had been operating to restrict imports. But it is also true that during this period commodity prices were gradually declining, and this factor may partly or wholly explain the decline in the import figures.

Again in 1832 and 1833, reductions in the tariff were made, and these were immediately followed by a great increase of imports. But in these years commodity prices had stopped declining and then between 1834 and 1836 entered upon a sharp rise of a distinctly inflationary character, so that the evidence is again inconclusive. Moreover, it could be pointed out that the year 1831, during which the tariff of 1828 was still in operation, recorded a greater increase of imports than any subsequent year except 1839.

In 1842 the tariff was raised and, omitting the nine-month period which constitutes the "year" 1843, we find imports higher in 1844 than in 1842, and still higher in 1845. In 1846 came a lower tariff which was followed by a sharp rise of imports in 1847 and 1848 and a slight decline in 1849. So far as this period is concerned, it is very difficult to establish any connection between tariff changes and the movement of imports; and we are therefore thrown back upon other factors, such as movements of commodity prices and general business conditions, with which it is possible to observe a definite correlation.

The third period began in 1850, and brought a marked rise of trend for both curves (*a*) and (*b*). For combined exports and imports, the trend can be best determined by regarding the period as closed in 1876, when the decline that followed the depression of 1873, came to an end and the figures began to increase again but at a reduced rate. A compound-interest curve fitted by the method we have adopted to the years 1849 to 1876, inclusive, gives a trend increasing at the annual average rate of 4.3 per cent. For imports, the third period naturally ends in 1878, when the same conditions obtained which the curve showing combined exports and imports reached in 1876. A compound-interest curve fitted to the import figures from 1849 to 1878 results in a trend showing an annual average increase of 3.7 per cent. In these computations the years 1861-65 are omitted, because the Civil War reduced temporarily the area and population to which the figures relate and made the data useless for our purpose.

Reference to curve (*c*) shows that, as in preceding periods, there was a distinct correlation between foreign trade figures and the movement of commodity prices. In 1849, the Australian and Californian gold discoveries enormously increased the supply of the yellow metal, and caused a world-wide increase of commodity prices. Then, in 1862, the United States began to issue greenbacks, and paper-money inflation ensued which accounts for the abrupt rise of curve (*c*) between 1861 and 1864. In 1865, with the end of the war, gradual deflation of commodity prices began, but this for several years did not check the rise of curves (*a*) and (*b*). One principal reason for this inconsistent development was that the credit of this country was firmly reëstablished and foreign capital was again flowing into the United States, resulting in large imports.[7] Exports also continued to rise until 1874, presumably as the result of the extension of foreign markets for American agricultural produce in the years following the Civil War. From 1850 to 1865, therefore, the upturn of foreign trade was due in considerable part to the rise of commodity prices, and after that date to special factors which offset the decline of prices which began when inflation came to an end.

So far as the tariff is concerned, the sharp rise of imports shown by curve (*b*) from 1849 to 1860 might be taken as an indication that the low tariffs of 1846 and 1857 favored import trade, and to that extent, at least, increased total foreign trade. But the higher tariffs established in 1862 and 1864 did not prevent

[7] See *Review of Economic Statistics,* Vol. I, p. 223.

curves (*a*) and (*b*) from rising sharply between 1868 and 1870, their influence being outweighed by special factors previously mentioned. The movements of curves (*a*) and (*b*) throw little light upon the relation between protective tariffs and the volume of foreign trade.

The fourth period for curve (*a*) extends from 1877 to 1895. Combined exports and imports recovered from the effects of the depression of 1873, but their trend, shown by the method we have adopted, is a compound-interest curve rising at the average rate of 2.2 per cent per annum, which is to be compared with a figure of 4.3 per cent for the previous period. For imports, the the fourth period extends from 1879 to 1898, and the trend is best expressed by a straight line representing a compound-interest curve rising at the rate of 1.7 per cent per annum, which compares with a trend of 3.7 per cent during the previous period. Once more curve (*c*) exhibits a movement that correlates well with the reduction in the annual percentage increases shown by curves (*a*) and (*b*). In the late sixties gold production had begun to decline, and this led to a long decline of commodity prices throughout the world. In the United States deflation of paper currency also contributed to the decline in curve (*c*), but in 1879 the country returned to a gold basis and the later decline of prices was due to the same forces that were operative elsewhere.

Tariff policies did not change sufficiently in the seventies and eighties to lead one to expect them to influence materially the movements of curves (*a*) and (*b*). The higher tariff enacted in 1890, while decreasing some imports, did not affect either of these curves significantly during the next two years, and the same may be said of the lower tariff resulting from the Act of 1894. The depression of the seventies, which was almost world-wide, and that of the nineties, almost equally widespread, naturally checked the growth of foreign trade and must have contributed to the decline in the percentage of increase shown by the trends determined for curves (*a*) and (*b*). But whatever other factors were operative, we must attribute great importance to the long decline of commodity prices.

The fifth period for combined exports and imports extends from 1896 to 1921, and for imports it runs from 1899 to 1921. In computing the trends for this period, we must omit the years 1916 to 1921, which were affected by the war. For curve (*a*) it was found necessary to use a trend-interval beginning with 1893 and ending in 1914. A compound-interest curve based on this interval gives results which are most nearly in accord with historical knowledge of the period. A similar curve based on the figures from 1898 to 1915 is used for imports. The trends so computed are then projected forward to the year 1921, not with the purpose of indicating a single trend-line for the whole period, but merely to provide a convenient working base for studying the movements recorded in the years of war and post-war inflation. The trend for curve (*a*) rises at the rate of 5.0 per cent per annum, and that for curve (*b*) rises at the annual rate of 6.3 per cent. This sharp increase in the rate of growth is again related to price movements recorded on curve (*c*). In 1897, as a result of the large and growing output of the South African gold fields, commodity prices in gold-standard countries turned upward and continued to rise at a moderate rate until 1916. Then came the World War with its very great inflation of commodity prices, which carried curve (*c*) to the high level shown in 1920. Such a revolution in prices could not be without effect upon the dollar volume of foreign trade, and it is recorded significantly by curves (*a*) and (*b*).

So far as the tariff is concerned, we may note that, disregarding the effect of anticipatory imports, the higher tariff of 1897 and the later tariff of 1909, which averaged only slightly lower, did not prevent an increase of imports and of combined exports and imports. The lower tariff of 1913 did not materially alter the direction of curve (*b*) in 1914, and whatever effect it may have had subsequently was entirely lost in the years of war inflation.

Having observed the relations between price movements and the trends of foreign trade during the five periods which curves (*a*) and (*b*) record, it is interesting to summarize the results. Three periods (1795-1820, 1821-49, and 1876-95) were characterized by falling prices. For these periods the average annual increases of curve (*a*) shown by the compound-interest curves we have used were 0.9 per cent, 2.7 per cent, and 2.2 per cent—the average percentage being 1.9. For the two periods characterized by rising commodity prices, the percentages of increase were 4.3 and 5.0—the average being 4.6. For imports during the same three periods of falling prices the percentages of increase were 1.6, 2.4, and 1.7—the average being 1.9. For the two periods of increasing prices, the percentage increases of imports were 3.7 and 6.3—the average being 5.0 per cent. In short, curve (*a*) showed an average increase of 1.9 per cent in three periods of falling prices and an average of 4.6 per cent in two periods when prices rose, while imports showed an average increase of 1.9 per cent in times of falling, and of 5.0 per cent in times of rising, prices. The differences, therefore, between the annual rates of increase in times of rising prices and such rates in times of falling prices are 2.7 per cent for curve (*a*) and 3.1 per cent for curve (*b*). Since these are rates of *compound* interest and apply to periods averaging twenty-five years in length, it will be seen that the influence of falling prices upon the dollar volume of foreign trade is very striking. What these figures mean when applied to periods averaging twenty-five years in length will be evident when we consider that $100 compounded annually for twenty-five years at 1.9 per cent will increase to $160.05 at the end of the period, whereas the same amount of money compounded annually for the same period at 4.6 per cent will increase to $307.79.

Since the period from 1790 to 1820 is a difficult one to interpret, it may be well to leave it out of account in considering the relation between price movements and the growth of foreign trade. At the same time, the figures presented for the later periods can be made more significant by relating them to statistics of population growth, since obviously the constant growth of population is one of the reasons why foreign trade of the United States has steadily increased during the last 141 years. From 1820 to 1849, when commodity prices were declining, the curve for combined exports and imports rose at the rate of 2.7 per cent compounded annually, while population increased at the rate of 3.0 per cent, so that the growth of our total foreign trade was less than that of population. During the third period, 1850-77, when the trend of prices was upward, curve (*a*) rose at the rate of 4.3 per cent, while the rate of population increase was 2.6 per cent. In the fourth period, when prices were declining, curve (*a*) rose at the rate of 2.2 per cent, which was exactly the percentage by which population moved during the same years. In the fifth period, when prices showed a rise in trend, curve (*a*) rose at an annual average rate of 5.0 per cent, while the rate of population increase was only 1.7 per cent. In other words, during two periods of falling prices the rate of growth of combined exports and imports was either a little less than or just equal to the rate of increase of population, whereas during two periods of rising prices it exceeded greatly the rate of increase of population.

The sixth period covers the decade ending June 30, 1931. The dislocation of world trade and violent deflation of commodity prices in 1921 brought the figures for the fiscal year ending June 30, 1922, to such a low level that it seemed unsafe to use it in determining trend for such a short period as ten years. A better result can be obtained by beginning with the fiscal year 1923 and ending with 1930; but this gives us a still shorter period, so that we cannot have much confidence in the result. Whichever period we select, we secure for both curves an upward trend, and this is consistent with the experience of the United States during all its previous history. We should probably be justified, therefore, in adopting for each curve the least upward trend resulting from our measurements, and using this provisionally, recognizing that it is probably too early to determine with safety a proper trend for the post-war years and that the results obtained are only provisional. Another method would be to resort to the makeshift of using a horizontal line, while recognizing that some sort of rising trend will probably be substituted when further data make it possible to reach a satisfactory

CHART 2—Combined Imports and Exports: Annual Percentage Changes* Adjusted for Normal Rate of Growth. (*Unit: one per cent.*)

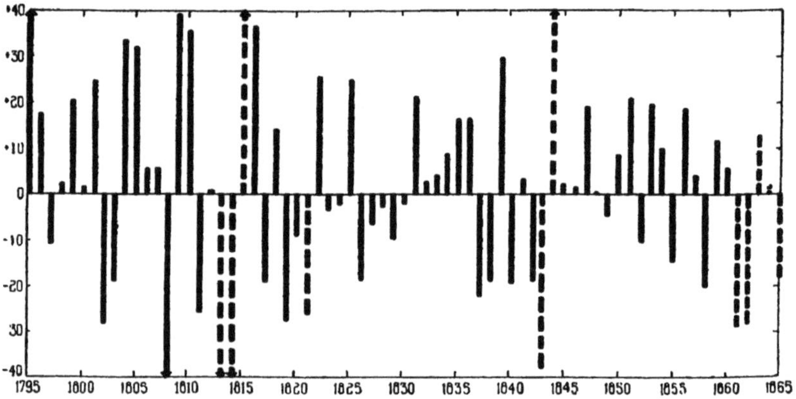

CHART 3—Imports: Annual Percentage Changes* Adjusted for Normal Rate of Growth. (*Unit: one per cent.*)

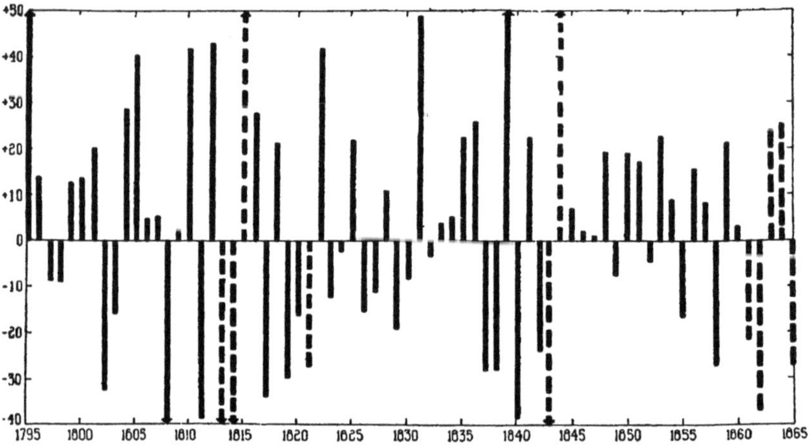

* For explanation of broken bars see text, p. 195. The bars, 1795-1842, show percentage changes for fiscal years ending September 30; the bars, 1845-1931, for fiscal years ending June 30.

CHART 2—(*Continued*)

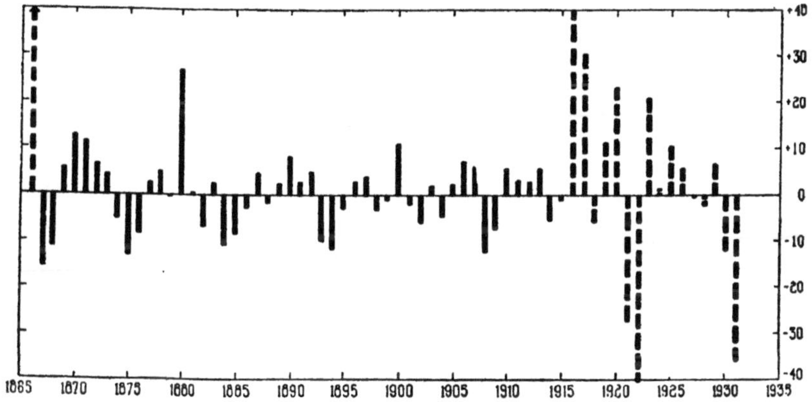

CHART 3—(*Continued*)

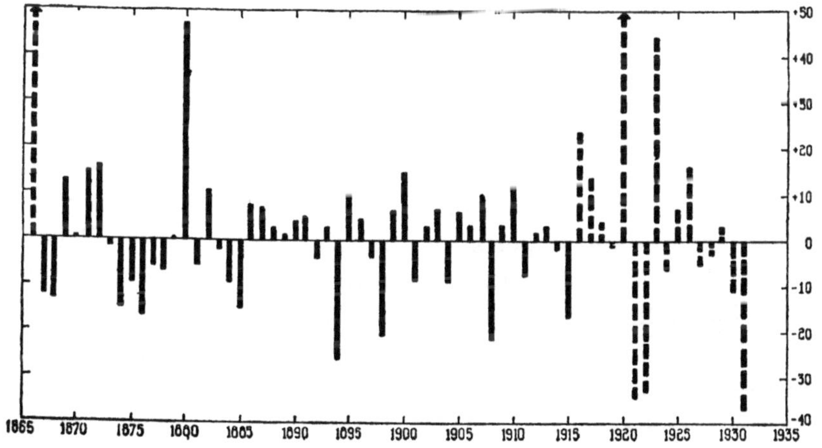

conclusion; but we have preferred to adopt the least upward trend resulting from our measurements, chiefly in order to keep our present curves homogeneous throughout their extent. For combined exports and imports from 1922 to 1931 the annual increase was 0.3 per cent, and for imports it was 0.4 per cent, both percentages being determined for the period 1922-31.

Here again it is interesting to refer to the movement of commodity prices. From 1922 to 1925 there occurred an irregular rise, and then in 1926 began an irregular decline, at first moderate, but after 1929 very sharp. Curves (*a*) and (*b*) reveal that up to 1926, when commodity prices were rising, there was a sharp upturn in the dollar volumes of imports and of combined exports and imports. They also show that during the next three years, when prices declined moderately, curve (*a*) increased only slightly and curve (*b*) turned slightly downward; while finally, in the last two years of sharply declining prices, both curves fell precipitately. In epitome, these ten years reveal the same facts disclosed by the previous century and a quarter. Rising prices mean a sharp increase in the dollar volume of foreign trade; moderately declining prices do not prevent an increase but greatly reduce the rate of growth; while precipitate price declines, which of course do not last long, always bring an actual decrease as long as they continue.

Having determined the varying trends of series showing imports into the United States from 1790 to 1931 and combined exports and imports for the same period, we shall now undertake to determine cyclical movements. In our analysis we shall follow the method used in dealing with postal revenues of the United States in the article published in the May number of this *Review*. That method consisted of studying the annual percentage changes after making adjustment for trend by subtracting (algebraically) the normal yearly growth from the actual percentage change for each year. In the case of imports and combined exports and imports, we shall first adjust the dollar figures for trend in the customary manner, and then examine the annual percentage changes of the adjusted figures.

Chart 2 gives the results for combined exports and imports. Each vertical bar above the base line represents the percentage by which a given year-to-year change in our total foreign trade exceeded the normal annual increase determined for the period in question. Each bar which falls below the base line, but by less than the amount of the normal increase, exhibits the amount by which the yearly gain fell short of the estimated normal amount. Finally, bars which fall below the base line by more than the amount of the normal percentage increase record an actual decrease in the combined exports and imports of the United States. Reference to curve (*a*) of Chart 1 will provide a check upon those years when actual decreases in the volume of trade were recorded.

There are a few years which need to be left out of account, namely, 1813 and 1814 and the years from 1861 to 1865, inclusive, since the chart records war disturbances so great as to make it impossible to study cyclical movements. The bars including these years are drawn as broken lines. For different reasons, we have decided to draw in the same manner the bars relating to the period from 1916 to 1931. The movements recorded in these years are not left out of consideration, but difficulty in determining trend makes it desirable to differentiate them from other years. Broken lines are also used for the year 1821, when for the first time the figure excludes specie and refers only to merchandise, and for 1843 and 1844, when a change in the fiscal year resulted in a transitional "year" of nine months.

As pointed out in the previous article concerning postal revenues, the time at which the chart begins was one when economic conditions in the United States were very dependent upon foreign trade. The great war which broke out in Europe in 1793 enabled our ships, as neutrals, to secure a large part of the carrying trade of the world, and great prosperity resulted. Chart 2, therefore, shows for 1795 and 1796 increases in combined exports and imports that greatly exceeded the normal percentage. In the latter year, however, a reaction in business began which presently deepened into depression.[8] In 1797, our index records depressed conditions resulting in an actual decrease for total foreign trade. In 1798, an increase something more than normal was recorded, but nothing like the amount registered in 1796. The year was one of depression, but the movement on our chart indicates recovery from the low level of 1797.

The following year brought a return to prosperity, and combined exports and imports registered an even larger percentage of increase than in 1796. Then came two years of percentage increases greater than normal, which were years of general prosperity. In March 1802 the Peace of Amiens deprived our ships of their advantage as neutral carriers, and another business depression resulted.[9] Our chart records a tremendous decline in the total volume of foreign trade in 1802 and another, though smaller, decline the following year. Renewal of the war in Europe brought a rapid recovery of trade and a return of prosperity which is recorded by the large percentage increases of combined exports and imports in 1804 and 1805, and the substantial, though much smaller, increases of the two following years. In this connection it may be noted that for such a period of continued growth of foreign trade the results recorded by our chart are cumulative. Therefore, after two such great increases as were shown in 1804 and 1805, it is natural that, even with continuing prosperity, much smaller percentages of further increase should be shown in the next two years. The year 1807, therefore, which records a moderate excess above the normal percentage increase, is actually the peak year shown in curve (*a*) on Chart 1, when combined exports and imports reached a level not again attained for years.

Thus far Chart 2 has shown a close correlation of combined exports and imports with economic conditions as recorded by historians. It is interesting, also, to compare it with the movement of commodity prices recorded by curve (*c*) of Chart 1.

[8] W. L. Thorp, *Business Annals* (New York, 1926), p. 114.
[9] Thorp, *idem*, p. 115.

That curve records a decline of prices in 1797 and 1798, the years of business depression, and then an upturn in the subsequent years of prosperity. The year 1802, which brought a decline in foreign trade and a business depression, brought, also, a sharp decline of prices, and subsequent prosperity then brought an increase. In 1806, prices showed a moderate decline which did not interfere with business prosperity or reflect a recession in foreign trade. This movement continued, however; and by the end of 1807, with war threatening and an embargo under consideration at Washington, business receded and prices showed further decline.

January 1, 1808 brought Jefferson's famous Embargo, which reduced our total foreign trade from 246 to 79 million dollars. This meant business depression,[10] and our chart records a collapse of export and import business. A partial modification of the Embargo, effected in March 1809, permitted foreign trade to recover; but conditions remained so disturbed that it could not return to the 1807 peak.

The years 1809 and 1810 were marked by prosperity which our chart records by percentage increases far greater than the normal expectation. In the same years, curve (*c*) of Chart 1 records an upturn of prices. In 1811, the Non-Importation Act was revived, so far as Great Britain was concerned, and therefore Chart 2 records a large actual decrease in the volume of foreign trade. The price curve of Chart 1 also showed a decline, but this year is not regarded by Thorp as one of depression. He characterizes it, indeed, as a year of moderate prosperity, but his data, which are not statistical, record numerous disturbing developments and very few favorable ones. On the basis of the evidence furnished by movements of foreign trade and commodity prices, as well as the unfavorable developments mentioned by Thorp, it might be safer to characterize it as a time of recession.

The period from October 1, 1811, to September 30, 1812, to which the statistics for 1812 relate, brought a slight increase

[10] Thorp, *idem*, p. 116.

which lifted foreign trade only a little above the low point to which it had declined. War with Great Britain was impending, and its outbreak in June is said to have caused a temporary check followed by some increase in activity. A high price for wheat and a small cotton crop very likely account for the fact that commodity prices averaged slightly higher than in the previous year. On the whole, 1811 and 1812 seem to have been years which saw neither prosperity nor depression, and with war always impending could not have been comfortable to live through. Chart 2, therefore, records a period of disturbance, which perhaps is best characterized as one of mild recession.[11]

At this point, it is desirable to consider Chart 3 which presents percentage changes of imports determined in precisely the same way as the percentages shown for combined exports and imports on Chart 2. Here is recorded an increase substantially exceeding the usual percentage in 1796, followed by two years of actual decrease, which coincide with the depression of 1797 and 1798. Then came three years of recovery, followed by two years of sharp decrease in 1802 and 1803; four years of increase substantially exceeding the normal expectation, and the great slump which in 1808 followed the Embargo; finally two years of recovery and the great decline of 1811. In 1812 a great percentage increase of imports is shown, whereas Chart 2 recorded only a trifling excess of combined exports and imports above the normal percentage. This is one of the few points at which Charts 2 and 3 have differed thus far.[12] Of course, since imports from 1790 to 1820 exceeded exports substantially, the statistics shown in Chart 3 contribute more than half to the total shown in Chart 2. Nevertheless, exports, on an average, contributed nearly 44 per cent of the total; so that it cannot be supposed that the movements recorded in Chart 2 are so far dependent upon those shown in Chart 3 that they have no independent significance. Considering the very technical character of the methods employed in this analysis, as well as the consider-

[11] Thorp calls the year 1811 a year of "moderate prosperity" and 1812 one marked by "brief recession; uneven prosperity." *Idem,* p. 117.

[12] In the two other cases, the year 1798 showed a difference in direction of movement while the year 1809 showed a substantial difference in amplitude.

able margin of error that must be present in the data themselves, the concurrence of results shown in Charts 2 and 3 is conclusive evidence that our early statistics of foreign trade, however imperfect, do, when properly analyzed, yield valuable results.

During 1813 and 1814, foreign trade was so far dominated by war conditions that its movements should be left out of account. In 1815, the return of peace brought swift recovery of the total volume of foreign trade as spectacular as the decline of the previous year, and this was followed by further increase in 1816. Imports contributed much more than exports to this result, but the increase of exports was great. Moreover, the exchanges of the country had long been accustomed to a substantial excess of imports over exports, such excess representing the profits made by our ships and merchants in the carrying trade. Great increases in both exports and imports were inevitable when trade channels were reopened, since both this country and its customers probably came out of the war understocked in many lines of goods and proceeded to make up deficiencies. Yet there is evidence that imports of manufactured goods checked the activity of domestic manufactures, and such a condition led to the enactment of a higher tariff in 1816. Whatever the cause, the prosperity which the return of business brought was undoubtedly short-lived. Inflated commodity prices of the war period had begun to decline, and 1815 closed with recession deepening into depression. Under such conditions the large increase of combined exports and imports in 1816 is hard to understand, but the data relate to a year ending September 30, and would probably have been smaller if they had related to the calendar year.

A decline both in imports and in total foreign trade is recorded on Charts 2 and 3 in 1817, the percentage decline in imports being sufficient to outweigh a slight increase of exports. Upon the whole, the movements recorded on Charts 2 and 3 agree fairly well with the known facts—that the return of peace brought a short period of prosperity which was followed by a recession that deepened into depression in 1816 and 1817. If we had accurate monthly data instead of somewhat inaccurate annual data, the figures of our foreign trade would certainly record these developments with greater accuracy than can be expected from the figures we are obliged to use.

According to Thorp,[13] between 1815 and 1822 the country went through a business cycle of seven years' duration. He characterizes 1816 with the word "depression," characterizes 1817 and 1818 with the words "mild depression," and characterizes 1819 with the caption "severe depression; financial panic";[14] thus indicating that he believes that 1817 and 1818 brought some improvement over 1816 and were then followed by a renewed depression in 1819. He presents no statistics, but the developments which he notes indicate that 1817 brought some improvement which lasted through a considerable part of 1818; while at the end of the latter year financial and other difficulties caused a decided turn for the worse, which brought the deep depression of the following year.

The movements recorded by Charts 2 and 3 raise the question whether, between the early part of 1817 and the very last part of 1818, there was not sufficient recovery to indicate a return to something like normal. While our total foreign trade declined substantially in 1817, imports declined greatly and there was a moderate increase of exports. In a year of financial strain, an increase of exports and decline of imports makes for improvement, so that whatever influence foreign trade exerted in 1817 was on the side of a revival of business. Following this, in 1818, Chart 2 shows an increase in the total volume of trade, which would indicate that the improvement that started in 1817 continued and became more marked in 1818. In the latter year, however, the increase in imports was greater than that in exports, so that from the short-run point of view the net result was not favorable to restoration of financial stability. That very substantial improvement occurred in 1817 and 1818 is indicated by commodity prices. Curve (*c*) of Chart 1 shows that, after precipitate declines in 1815 and 1816, prices rose ever so

[13] Thorp, *idem*, pp. 50, 117-19.

[14] Thorp, *idem*, p. 118.

slightly in 1817, and then declined moderately in 1818, the two years marking a very definite halt in the process of price deflation which was resumed again severely in 1819. Our recent study of postal revenues[15] showed that 1818 registered substantially more than the normal percentage increase, and tends therefore to confirm the conclusion drawn from the foreign trade figures. That study also shows that 1819 barely made the normal percentage increase, and was followed by a tremendous decline in 1820 and 1821. Altogether our data suggest the need of further study of other kinds of evidence before accepting the view that between 1815 and 1822 a seven-year cycle occurred. If that view should be substantiated by all the evidence, it would probably appear that 1817 and 1818 brought substantial improvement which was negatived by unfavorable developments at the end of the latter year, which threw business back into deeper depression than ever. Such "double-headed" depressions have been recorded in at least two other periods of our history.

From the deep depression which Charts 2 and 3 record in foreign trade from 1819 to 1821,[16] the country emerged in 1822 with increases in both total trade and imports, recorded by Charts 2 and 3. During the next two years, which were characterized by at least fair prosperity, our total trade recorded a small decrease in 1823 and less than the normal percentage increase in 1824. Both developments resulted from the movement of imports, because exports were showing a small increase.

Commodity prices reflected improvement in trade. Their precipitate fall was arrested in 1822, when a slight increase occurred. In 1823, there was a moderate decline; in 1824, almost no decline whatever; and in 1825, a very slight increase. The four years 1822-25, inclusive, brought another temporary halt, like that which had occurred in 1817 and 1818 in the post-war deflation of commodity prices, the net decline registered by the price index for those years being very slight indeed. Postal conditions also showed improvement, but did not register the

[15] See *Review of Economic Statistics,* Vol. XIII, p. 52.

[16] In the last year the decrease is exaggerated on account of the fact that specie movements are excluded from the figures.

normal percentage increase until 1825, when rate increases occurred which disturbed comparisons. Both the foreign trade and the price figures for this period confirm Thorp's findings.[17]

In the summer of 1825, a reaction began which assumed serious proportions by the end of the year and brought depression in 1826.[18] This is duly recorded by the sharp decline both of total foreign trade and of imports shown on Charts 2 and 3. Commodity prices also resumed a decline which lasted for several years, although proceeding at a fairly moderate rate. Thus, our charts give a correct report of the business cycle which began with the recovery of 1822.

According to Thorp, 1827 brought a return to moderate prosperity, and the following year saw continued activity until summer or fall, when another recession began.[19] Since our figures relate to years ending September 30, they would show only part of the recovery that occurred in 1827 and very little of the recession that developed toward the end of 1828. Chart 1 shows that combined exports and imports made no recovery at this time; and Chart 2 in 1827 and 1828 shows a check to the rate of decline but nothing that could be called prosperity. Chart 3 shows that imports reflect the depression of 1826 and a substantial recovery in 1828 followed by a depression in the following year; but curve (*b*) on Chart 1, which shows the actual figures, indicates only a very moderate recovery in 1828 at a level which certainly does not reflect prosperity. Exports, which registered a little improvement in 1827, actually declined in 1828. If the country enjoyed real prosperity in 1828, it certainly is not reflected by the movements of foreign trade by fiscal years.[20] To some extent this result may be attributed to the decline of general commodity prices, which decreased dollar volumes; and it is worth noting that Thorp records a poor cotton crop sold at low prices in 1827 and a low price for a

[17] Thorp, *idem,* p. 119.

[18] Thorp, *idem,* p. 120.

[19] Thorp, *idem,* p. 120.

[20] Postal revenues record the depression of 1826, and in the calendar year 1828 made substantially more than the normal gain; while in 1829 they record another mild depression.

good cotton crop in 1828. Cotton then bulked so large among exports that the low price of this staple might explain the failure of Charts 2 and 3 to record more clearly the prosperity phase of the business cycle with which we are now concerned.

The year 1829 was one of depression duly recorded on both Charts 2 and 3. Thorp notes that revival began at the end of the year, but this would hardly affect statistical series ending on September 30. He states that 1830 brought moderate prosperity.[21] Chart 2 records for that year an increase of foreign trade, but one that did not equal the normal percentage; while Chart 3 shows that this was due to an actual decline of imports, though one of moderate proportions. Perhaps this is explained by the restrictive effects of the tariff of 1828, but further investigation would be needed to establish this conclusion. In any event, 1831 brought substantial increase of both total trade and imports, such as points clearly to prosperity. In 1832 and 1833 further increases occurred in total trade, and postal revenues show large increases; so far the record is of continued prosperity. Again referring to curve (*c*) of Chart 1, we find that commodity prices turned slightly upward in 1831, and retained this gain during the next few years. Again, therefore, improvement in prices accompanied prosperous business.

In the autumn of 1833, Thorp records the beginning of another recession, which again would hardly affect trade figures relating to a year ending September 30. He characterizes 1834 as a year of mild depression, which, however, saw revival in its closing months. Since the improvement of the last quarter of 1834 would not affect our foreign trade statistics, we should expect Charts 2 and 3 to reflect a depression; but this they failed to do. Both charts record in 1834 increases substantially exceeding normal, though less for imports than for the total trade. For this there is no easy explanation. It is true that the spread of the population into the Mississippi Valley had made the country considerably less dependent on foreign trade; but, even so, such trade ought to show the effects of a real depres-

[21] Thorp, *idem*, p. 120.

sion. Since commodity prices declined in 1834 after three years of stabilization, we must conclude that our foreign trade figures failed to register the depression of 1834, but may also conclude that they strengthen Thorp's conclusion that this depression was, indeed, a "mild" one.[22] In the light of what followed, it may be viewed as a temporary halt in a great boom which culminated in the panic and depression of 1837. This is confirmed by the movement of postal revenues, which in 1835 showed an increase slightly less than the normal amount, but failed to record an actual decrease.[23] Probably the chief consideration[24] is that the country had entered upon a period of great internal expansion, which would account for a continued favorable showing in foreign trade and a fair showing of the postal revenues at a time when the country was passing through a very brief period of readjustment that might be recorded as a mild depression. Possibly further study of all pertinent data might show that recession rather than depression would better characterize the conditions that prevailed in 1834.

In 1835 and 1836 large increases of total foreign trade are recorded, which were actually more important than Chart 2 might seem to indicate, because they are the last of a series of six successive increases, which gave them a cumulative effect. Chart 3 shows that imports rose in considerably greater proportion than total trade—a condition likely to develop in the concluding years of a great boom. Curve (*c*) on Chart 1 shows a rapid upswing of commodity prices in these years, which, in view of the great increase in bank note circulation and the other conditions of the time, may be considered of an inflationary character. Thus, the stage was set for another business depression, the only severe one which had occurred since 1821 and

[22] Thorp, *idem*, p. 121.

[23] See *Review of Economic Statistics*, Vol. XIII, p. 54.

[24] In 1832 and 1833 reductions were made in the tariff, but only partisans of free trade or protection could attribute to these responsibility for the favorable showing of curves (*a*) and (*b*) between 1832 and 1836, or the generally unfavorable showing of the five following years. The great boom that led to the panic of 1837 and the subsequent depression are the only factors which this analysis of foreign trade indicates. The curves of our charts move as they would be expected to move during a great boom and subsequent depression.

one of the greatest in our history. As is often the case, the fatal year opened with great activity, both business and speculative, which in the second quarter was followed by signs of reaction.[25] Our data still relate to years ending September 30 and so do not give an adequate measure of the setback which foreign trade experienced, but yet they show in 1837 a great decline which Chart 3 reveals to have been decidedly sharper in imports than in the total foreign trade.[26] Inevitably, commodity prices declined, as is shown by curve (*c*) of Chart 1, though the decline was not nearly so precipitate as that which occurred in the great depression of 1819.

For 1838, Charts 2 and 3 register further declines, again greater for imports than for the total. Once more our foreign trade figures have given an accurate record of the final phase of a business cycle, one of the most spectacular and disastrous in our history. In 1839, according to Thorp, there came a revival which was not of long duration.[27] This our chart records in a percentage increase of total foreign trade much greater than the normal amount, which was due to a large increase of imports in a year when exports made only a slight gain. Such increased imports were natural after stocks had been reduced by two years of small importations, but their effect for the time being upon the financial situation could not have been favorable. Postal revenues improved, making nearly the normal percentage increase in the fiscal year 1839. Curve (*c*) of Chart 1 records a slight upturn of commodity prices in this year, so that the evidence justifies the conclusion that there was a real revival, even though it did not last.

While our data tend to confirm Thorp's conclusion that between 1837 and 1839 the country went through a three-year business cycle, further investigation might justify the alternative theory that the moderate recovery of 1839 was merely a

[25] Thorp, *idem*, p. 122.

[26] Postal revenues made a better showing in 1837, falling only a little short of the normal percentage increase; but the data relate to fiscal years ending June 30, so that they are not strictly comparable with the trade figures which include the third quarter of the year.

[27] Thorp, *idem*, p. 122.

short-lived improvement in a long period of depression that really lasted until 1843. In other words, the complete record might show a "double-headed" depression in the middle of which there occurred a brief recovery suddenly brought to an end by a renewal of adverse developments that plunged the country into even deeper depression. Such developments in the latter part of 1839 were renewed suspension of specie payments except in New England and New York, a decline of prices, and a threat of war with England over a boundary question.

The year 1840 brought a depression which lasted until the end of 1843[28] when our trade figures relate to a nine-month period ending on June 30. Total foreign trade showed a large actual decrease in 1840, a percentage increase somewhat greater than normal the subsequent year, and then a large actual decrease in 1842. Chart 3 shows that the movements of imports in these years corresponded in direction with those of total foreign trade, but that their amplitude was much greater. Curve (*c*) of Chart 1 shows that commodity prices, which had temporarily stabilized in 1839, plunged sharply downward during these three years of severe depression. Postal revenues recorded a series of substantial decreases.[29]

In the fall of 1843, that is, during the first half of the fiscal year ending on June 30, 1844, to which our statistics relate, signs of revival appeared, and the calendar year 1844 brought a return to prosperity. This Charts 2 and 3 probably record, but since our figures for 1844 were compared with a preceding "year" of only nine months' duration, they show a prodigious rate of increase far exceeding reality. Postal revenues improved, but fell far short of a normal percentage increase. Commodity prices turned upward.

Prosperity continued in 1845, Charts 2 and 3 registering something more than normal percentage increases. It must be remembered, however, that these charts now relate to fiscal years ending June 30, and do not reflect conditions prevailing

[28] Thorp, *idem,* p. 123.
[29] See *Review of Economic Statistics,* Vol. XIII, p. 52.

in the latter half of any year. Late in 1845, Thorp records the beginning of a recession which developed into "mild depression" the following year[30] which brought in May the beginning of the war with Mexico. Charts 2 and 3 record in 1846 percentage increases exceeding normal both for imports and for combined exports and imports. Commodity prices continued the rise which began in 1844. The testimony of postal revenues cannot be adduced because their movements were controlled by very great rate reductions made in 1846, but the movement of foreign trade and that of commodity prices do not point to a depression or even a serious recession in business in 1846. This conclusion is confirmed by Prof. Arthur H. Cole's index of the volume of trade.[31] For domestic trade this rose from 102 in 1845 to 104 in 1846, and for foreign trade it rose from 98 to 99, the combined average for domestic and foreign trade increasing from 101 to 102. Thorp records slackening of activity in some lines of business, severe pressure in the money market in certain months, a falling of security prices, and declaration of war with Mexico, but he also records favorable factors; and the statistical evidence now available does not justify the conclusion that a "mild depression" occurred in that year.

In 1847, Chart 2 records a large and Chart 3 a moderate increase, both movements being cumulative in character and therefore the more indicative of prosperity. Postal revenues in that year increased by much more than the normal amount, and Cole's index of domestic trade rose from 104 to 108, while his combined domestic and foreign trade index rose from 102 to 105.[32] Thorp records that the year brought prosperity, but ended with a panic in November and a decline in security and

[30] Thorp, *idem*, p. 124.

[31] See *Review of Economic Statistics*, Vol. XII, p. 172.

[32] In 1847 and 1848, foreign trade and the exchanges were greatly affected by crop failures in Europe, which increased our exports of breadstuffs from $7,445,000 in 1845 to $53,252,000 in 1847. The result was that exports of merchandise in the latter year exceeded imports by $34,317,000 and thus caused net imports of specie amounting to $22,214,000. This very large inflow of money naturally affected the exchanges, and in 1848 imports increased by 26 millions, while exports declined more than 18 millions, and a balance of $9,481,000 of specie was exported.

commodity prices. This decline he records as ending a two-year business cycle which began in 1846.

It is worth noting that his data led him to record a business cycle of only one year's duration beginning in 1845, and a second of two years' duration beginning in 1846. Since his measurements of business cycles in the United States[33] record no other cycle lasting but a single year, and since the one-year cycle beginning in 1845 was followed by a very short two-year cycle that began in 1846, there is further reason for doubting his conclusion that even a mild depression occurred in the year last mentioned. The movements of foreign trade, postal revenues, and commodity prices concur in pointing to a four-year business cycle from 1843 to the end of 1847. Cole's index points to the same conclusion, but it records a drop in the volume of business in 1845 from which there was prompt recovery.

In 1848, Thorp records a mild depression.[34] Charts 2 and 3 show increases for the fiscal year 1848 and then actual decreases for the fiscal year 1849. Allowing for differences between fiscal and calendar years, these movements support Thorp's conclusion. Curve (*c*) of Chart 1 records a sharp decline of commodity prices in 1848, and Cole's index shows a sharp decline from 105 to 98 for the volume of combined domestic and foreign trade. Postal revenues failed to make the normal percentage gain in the fiscal year 1849 which includes the latter half of 1848, and therefore probably point to disturbed business conditions at that time. We cannot doubt, therefore, that 1848 registered depression which marked the end of a business cycle.

Developments in the California gold fields and other factors brought recovery in 1849, which is manifest in the upturns recorded in Charts 2 and 3 for the fiscal year ending June 30, 1850. A similar upturn is recorded in the postal revenues, and commodity prices turned upward. Cole's combined index of the volume of domestic and foreign trade registered a decline from

[33] Thorp, *idem*, p. 50.
[34] Thorp, *idem*, p. 124.

98 to 92 in this year, and declined further to 91 in the following year, so that it is quite out of line with the other data. Thorp characterizes 1849 as a year of prosperity, and records substantially no unfavorable developments. Therefore, in spite of the conflicting evidence of Cole's index, we may believe that a cyclical upturn occurred in 1849.

During the fiscal years 1850 to 1854, Charts 2 and 3 show four years of increase and only one of decrease, the latter apparently being nothing but a temporary interruption of the sharp upswing of foreign trade which began in the third period shown on Chart 1. Postal revenues record large increases in 1849 and 1850, but their movements for the next few years are dominated by rate reductions which make them useless for purposes of comparison. Cole's index rose from 91 in 1850 to 105 in 1854, while commodity prices started upon the upswing resulting from the Californian and Australian gold discoveries. Thorp records that the prosperity which came in 1849 continued until the latter part of 1853, when a recession occurred.[35] This conclusion is consistent with the other evidence.

For 1855, Thorp records a depression followed by a revival at the end of the year.[36] Both Charts 2 and 3 reflect this disturbance, since they register substantial actual losses. Postal revenues show a very slight excess over the normal percentage increase for the fiscal year 1855 and a decrease in 1856. Commodity prices registered a slight increase in 1855, only to turn down slightly the following year. This time their movements are out of line with the other figures, but are such as to support the conclusion that the depression of 1855 was indeed mild. Cole's index records a slight improvement in combined domestic and foreign trade in 1855, which accords with the movement of commodity prices. Perhaps the conflict of evidence is explained by the fact that the trouble started with a financial panic in September 1854, and, as Thorp's record reveals, did not have any severe repercussion upon industry. Perhaps it would be

[35] Thorp, *idem*, p. 125.
[36] Thorp, *idem*, p. 126.

better to call it a recession rather than a depression, and in any event it was merely a temporary interruption of a great boom which did not come to an end until 1857.

For 1856, Thorp records the return of prosperity, and Charts 2 and 3 show increases in trade greatly exceeding the normal percentage. Postal revenues registered an increase only moderately less than the normal percentage, and Cole's index records an advance in combined domestic and foreign trade, but at the same time shows a substantial loss in domestic trade. The unimportant downturn in commodity prices has already been mentioned. Upon the whole, the evidence points to prosperity.

The year 1857 opened well, but the end of the boom was approaching. In August, a panic brought difficulties to a head and depression ensued.[37] The foreign trade figures, which relate to the fiscal year ending June 30, 1857, naturally do not show the depression, but in 1858 Charts 2 and 3 record severe declines. Postal revenues reflected the disturbance when in the fiscal year ending 1858 they registered only a slight actual increase, having failed to show any substantial part of the normal percentage gain. Cole's index showed sharp declines in all its elements. Commodity prices, while averaging higher in 1857 than in 1856, showed in 1858 the first sharp decline they had experienced since 1848. The events of 1857 were of such a character as to mark indelibly the statistical data for the year.

Thorp characterizes 1858 as a year of depression, and finds a revival in 1859, with restoration of prosperity in the early part of 1860.[38] Charts 2 and 3 record a recovery of foreign trade in the fiscal year ending June 30, 1859, with further improvement in that ending June 30, 1860. Postal revenues for both years show percentage increases slightly exceeding normal. Commodity prices in 1859 recovered a little from the drop they experienced in 1858, but lost this gain in 1860. Cole's index is lower in 1858 than in 1857, but rises sharply in 1859 and shows further increase in 1860. Thus, the various statistical indicia point to fairly rapid recovery from the depression of 1857 and

[37] Thorp, *idem*, p. 126.
[38] Thorp, *idem*, p. 127.

to the restoration of prosperity by the end of 1859 or the opening of 1860.

For the war period which followed, the statistics of foreign trade show sharp declines, as recorded on Charts 2 and 3, for the fiscal years 1861 and 1862. Then come two years of improvement, followed by sharp downturns in 1865. Little meaning attaches to these percentage changes, on account of the temporary loss of property and population occasioned by the war; and the same is true of the tremendous increases recorded by Charts 2 and 3 in the fiscal year 1866, which were due largely to the restoration of the Southern States to the Union.

Reaction from war activity brought a recession at the end of 1865, which in 1866 was followed by a mild depression[39] to which, no doubt, financial unsettlement in England was a contributing factor. Charts 2 and 3 record a downturn of foreign trade in the fiscal year ending June 30, 1867, and postal revenues registered a fairly sharp decline in 1866. Commodity prices, which were now expressed in paper money, reached their peak, so far as the annual averages go, in 1864, turning downward the following year, and also declined in 1866. The year 1867 brought continuation of the depression,[40] and this is registered on Charts 2 and 3 for the fiscal year ending June 30, 1868. Postal revenues made a slightly better showing, but commodity prices continued to decline, although less sharply. That a depression of two years' duration began in 1866 is confirmed by all the evidence.

From 1867 onward, statistics of foreign trade for calendar years as well as fiscal years ending on June 30 become available. It would have been possible to use these in our charts; but since we are dealing with annual figures it would usually make little difference in the general result, and we have decided therefore to continue to use figures for fiscal years and then in our text refer to calendar years in the few cases where it proves desirable to do so.

In 1868 a revival came, and this was followed by renewed

[39] Thorp, *idem,* p. 129.
[40] Thorp, *idem,* p. 130.

prosperity clearly shown by the movements on Charts 2 and 3 for the fiscal years 1869-72. Postal revenues made a similar showing, recording percentage increases equal to, or exceeding, the normal rate in every year. Commodity prices moderated their downward movement in 1868 and 1869, and then in 1870 renewed the sharp decline which lasted until 1872. Thorp records a recession and "mild depression" in 1870, but his data record no developments that are not consistent with the conclusion that nothing more occurred than a temporary recession. The Civil War had left many troublesome legacies, and even years of undoubted prosperity brought occasional developments in commodity prices, credit conditions, on the stock market, which must have made them uncomfortable to live through. Further investigation of all the statistics now available would be needed to justify a confident answer; but such investigation might well substantiate the conclusion to which Charts 2 and 3 lead, that 1870 was a year of temporary recession that ought not to be considered a depression ending the business cycle which commenced with the revival of 1868.

We have now reached a period in which statistical material becomes more abundant, and it is possible to chart with greater certainty the cyclical movements of business in the United States. Prior to the Civil War, the data are scanty; and it is not strange that we have found periods concerning which there is conflict of evidence and opinions differ. From now on our task will be simply to compare movements of foreign trade with the course of business which has been pretty well charted.

The panic of 1873 and the subsequent depression are duly recorded on Charts 2 and 3, which show, in the first place, three years of actual decrease in combined exports and imports, and, in the second place, five years of actual decrease in importations. Postal revenues for the period also make a generally unsatisfactory showing. There is no doubt that foreign trade records a long-continued depression.

At this point, it is interesting to note that, if we omit the period from 1861 to 1865, the movements recorded by Charts

2 and 3, in both good and bad years, became gradually less as the nineteenth century progressed. Until 1816 war conditions produced the widest fluctuations ever recorded. Thereafter the changes moderated decidedly. From the close of the Civil War down to 1914 a further moderation evidently took place; and then since the outbreak of the European War fluctuations have regained amplitudes which somewhat resemble, but by no means equal, those recorded between 1795 and 1816. For the moderate movements recorded from 1867 to 1914, diversification of exports must have been an important contributing factor, but further investigation would doubtless disclose others beyond the scope of the present article.

We are now able to compare the movement of our foreign trade from 1875 to 1913 with the movement of general business recorded by the index with Professor Persons constructed in 1927.[41] This index shows that bank clearings stabilized in 1878 and that the third quarter of that year brought a temporary upturn in both clearings and commodity prices, which, although followed by a brief decline of both series, proved the forerunner of business revival. Resumption of specie payments came on January 1, 1879, and deflation of the paper currency was at an end. The next twelve months brought a return of prosperity which kept the curve on the Persons chart above normal until the second quarter of 1884. Combined exports and imports, according to Chart 2, recorded some recovery in 1877 and 1878, preceding that of general business, but in the fiscal year ending June 30, 1880, recorded the full return of prosperity; with a further gain, though a small one, in 1881. Declining in 1882, they recovered in 1883, and therefore move in general harmony with Curve B on the Persons chart.[42] Chart 3 records a great

[41] See *Review of Economic Statistics*, Vol. IX, pp. 20-29.

[42] Postal revenues made a similar satisfactory showing from 1879 until 1883, and then in 1884, dropped sharply as the result of important changes in rates. (*Review of Economic Statistics*, Vol. XIII, p. 52.) Since postal revenues have been referred to in this article only because they supplemented the scanty statistical evidence available for earlier decades and their movements are described in the article to which reference has frequently been made, we need make no further mention of them.

upturn of imports in 1880, with irregular movements on a fairly high level during the next three years.

According to the Persons chart, the peak of prosperity during this period was really reached in the last half of 1881, and then about two years later a recession began which brought on the depression of 1884 and 1885. Combined exports and imports registered substantial losses in the fiscal years 1884 and 1885, with a very small further recession in 1886. Imports also declined sharply in the fiscal years 1884 and 1885. Clearly the picture given by Charts 2 and 3 is that of a business depression with improvement beginning during the fiscal year ending June 30, 1886. Turning to the figures for calendar years, we find that the low point was reached in 1885 and that combined exports and imports increased 101 millions, or about 8 per cent, in 1886; so that the result is of the same nature as, though distinctly clearer than, that given by statistics for fiscal years.

The Persons chart records a revival of business in 1886, and subsequent restoration of prosperity. His business curve (Curve B) did not reach a peak as high as that attained in 1881, but does record a long business cycle beginning with the recovery of 1886 and ending with the depression of 1893. Thorp records a slight recession in 1888 and a depression in 1891, but here as elsewhere presents an annalistic account without undertaking statistical measurements. His depression of 1891 is followed by revival the same year, and therefore could at most have been a mild one. The Persons index shows early in 1888 a decline of Curve B which did not carry it below the normal level, and in 1891 a sharp downturn in bank clearings which, however, at all times in the year remained above normal. A later index of industrial production and trade constructed by the same author shows a brief dip below normal in 1888 and another in 1891.[43] The difference in results is due to the inclusion of pig-iron production with outside bank clearings at this period in the second chart, and therefore the two charts do not give inconsistent pictures. Both record disturbances in the two years in question,

[43] W. M. Persons, *Forecasting Business Cycles* (New York, 1931), p. 8.

but not such as to justify the term "depression" unless that term is taken to mean any slight and brief decline of a curve below the normal level. By the same reasoning, boom would mean any brief and temporary rise of a curve above the normal level—a result which would lead to confusion both in theory and in practice. Evidently disturbances occurred in 1888 and 1891—that of the later year evidently being connected with the severe financial crisis in London. But on the evidence now available, it seems best to consider these developments as temporary interruptions in a long period of prosperity.

For this period, combined exports and imports show percentage increases substantially exceeding normal in every year except 1888 when the increase recorded was something less than one-half the normal amount. Imports also register increases in every year until 1892. Incidentally it may be noted that postal revenues made a favorable showing in every year. Also, it should not be forgotten that the changes noted on Charts 2 and 3 are cumulative in effect so that they mean a sustained increase in foreign trade for a period of six years. They tend, therefore, to confirm the view that in these years the country went through a long business cycle interrupted by temporary recessions in 1888 and 1891.

The depression which came in 1893 lasted until the end of 1898, when revival finally began. It saw, however, a temporary revival in 1895 when all the indexes note improvement that carried business well up toward a normal level. Professor Persons' first index, which related to general business conditions, showed the B curve below—but only slightly below—normal during the latter half of 1895. His later index of industrial production and trade shows it rising definitely above normal at the end of that year. If the slight dips below normal recorded by that index in 1888 and 1891 are taken as registering depressions, this slight rise above normal in 1895 must be taken to mean a boom. In the later episode, as in the two earlier ones, it is safest to conclude that we have nothing but a temporary interruption of a longer movement for which an explanation is easily found. In 1895 business recovery was well under way, but then came a run on the Government's gold reserve, President Cleveland's celebrated Venezuelan message, and in 1896 the campaign for free coinage of silver. Such developments quickly reversed conditions, and brought renewed depression about as severe as that of 1893.

Combined exports and imports show losses in the three fiscal years ending June 30, 1895, which, being cumulative, meant a decline of foreign trade to a depression level. The moderate increases in excess of the normal percentage recorded in the next two years mean recovery from the low level reached in an exceedingly severe depression, and do not point to a flourishing condition of trade.

The recovery which began in 1898 brought the country back to prosperity the following year, as is shown by all statistical indexes. In 1900 occurred another reaction which Thorp, in his annalistic account, calls a "brief recession," but elsewhere evidently classifies as a depression terminating a four-year business cycle.[44] Professor Persons' index of general business conditions shows the business curve falling slightly below the normal level during the latter half of the year, while his later index of industrial production and trade shows a more substantial decline, although one of very brief duration. This it would naturally do, since it includes pig-iron production, which declined sharply that year. It seems safest, on the basis of the evidence now available, to regard the episode as a "brief recession" and not a real depression, although that point is not material for this article because we are concerned primarily with foreign trade.

Chart 2 shows that combined exports and imports made nearly the normal percentage increase in 1899, and substantially exceeded it in the fiscal year ending June 30, 1900. The following fiscal year shows an increase somewhat less than normal, which perhaps reflects the temporary recession that is known to have occurred. Chart 3 shows that imports, which may have been disturbed by tariff changes in 1897, made more than normal percentage gains in 1899 and 1900, and then recorded an actual loss in the fiscal year ending June 30, 1901,

[44] Thorp, *idem*, pp. 50 and 138.

this loss being the result of the business reaction. The decline shown in the fiscal year 1901 is as severe as those recorded in certain years of mild business depression. The figures for calendar years give no indication of any disturbance in the year 1900. Combined exports and imports registered a large increase in 1900 and a moderate further increase in 1901. Imports increased substantially in 1900, and still more the following year. The conclusion is, therefore, that the disturbance was sufficient to be reflected in foreign trade figures for the fiscal year 1901 but made no impression on the figures for the calendar year.

After the disturbance of 1900, business remained prosperous until 1903 brought the "Rich Man's Panic" which was followed by a mild depression in 1904. Of this period Chart 2 gives an unsatisfactory account. Combined exports and imports showed an actual decrease in 1902 when business was good, and remained stationary in 1904 when business was depressed. Figures for calendar years also show an actual decline in combined exports and imports in 1902, but in 1904 record a small actual increase, though one much less than the normal percentage gain. Import figures make a better showing, since Chart 2 reveals in 1902 and 1903 increases substantially exceeding normal, and an actual loss in 1904. Again the import figures give the better record of the business cycle.

Prosperity returned in 1905, and lasted until the end of 1907 when a depression of considerable severity began. Chart 2 records substantial excesses of combined imports and exports over the normal percentage increase in the three-year period ending June 30, 1907, and then a marked decrease in the fiscal year 1908. Imports, as shown by Chart 3, made an exactly similar showing. For this business cycle, therefore, the correlation between foreign trade and general business in the United States was very close indeed.

Business remained depressed during 1908, but improvement occurred during the last part of the year and 1909 brought a return to prosperity which, however, was not of long continuance and was comparatively moderate while it lasted. In the second quarter of 1910 recession began, and 1911 was a year of mild depression. That the disturbance of this year should be classified as a depression all writers agree, but it was of a mild character.

Combined exports and imports show improvement in foreign trade that resulted in a substantial increase above the normal percentage in the fiscal year 1910, a period of prosperity; but they also show a smaller, though similar, excess in 1911, and therefore do not record a depression. The fact that they show this excess may, however, be taken as additional evidence of the mildness of the disturbance. Imports tell a better story. They record a larger increase for 1910 and register an actual decrease in 1911, so that for this business cycle, as the last, they correlate much better with general business conditions than do combined imports and exports. That this should sometimes be the case is not surprising since exports may be affected by changing crop conditions and prices for agricultural staples, as well as the state of demand in foreign countries; while imports reflect conditions in the United States.

The year 1912 brought a return to prosperity which, like that of the previous business cycle, was of moderate extent and limited duration. A recession in business came in 1913, which the events of 1914 deepened into a depression. Combined exports and imports, according to Chart 2, made a favorable showing in the fiscal year 1913 and an unfavorable showing in the year next following, which agrees with the movement of general business in those years. Imports showed an increase slightly exceeding the normal percentage in 1912 and 1913 and then an increase only slightly less than normal in 1914. In direction, therefore, their movements resemble those of general business, but the changes recorded were of very slight amount. The fiscal year 1915, which included the last half of the calendar year 1914, registers a substantial decrease undoubtedly attributable to the depression of 1914.

Recovery from the depression of 1914 is shown by the sharp increases of combined exports and imports in the fiscal year 1916 and 1917. The fact that the fiscal year 1918 showed a slight decrease from the previous year is not of significance, since the foreign trade of the country was then under war control, and since, furthermore, it was only a slight actual decrease after two years of great expansion so that it represented a very large volume of trade. Imports, as shown by Chart 3, registered increases exceeding the normal percentage from 1916 to 1918, but naturally did not exhibit as great changes as exports at that period.

In 1919 the country quickly recovered from the brief reaction that followed the Armistice, and entered upon a brief period of expansion which brought a recession in 1920 and severe depression in 1921. These occurrences are well reflected in the substantial increases of combined exports and imports recorded in the two fiscal years ending June 30, 1920, and even more significantly in the sharp decreases recorded in the two years ending June 30, 1922. Imports, as shown by Chart 3, also give a good record of this business cycle, but they show an increase slightly less than normal in the fiscal year ending June 30, 1919, and in the following year one of the greatest percentage increases shown on the chart. The next two fiscal years clearly enough record an extremely severe depression.

Recovery from the depression of 1921 and general prosperity continuing for a number of years are indicated by the favorable showing of combined exports and imports from the fiscal year 1923 to that ending June 30, 1929. Only once do they fail to register an increase, and in that case, the fiscal year 1928, the decrease was slight. Moreover, since this followed five years of increasing trade which had cumulative effect in determining the base from which the percentage change in 1928 was computed, the decline is less significant. Finally, in the fiscal year ending June 30, 1930, a substantial decline is recorded, which was followed by a spectacular drop in 1931.

Chart 3 shows that imports exhibit greater irregularity. In the fiscal year 1923 a very large percentage increase is recorded, and smaller, though substantial, increases are shown in the fiscal years 1925, 1926, and 1929. But slight or moderate percentage decreases are shown in the fiscal years 1924, 1927, and 1928. Thus we have four years of increase and three of decrease, the percentage changes of the former being much greater than those of the latter. On the whole the story is one of prosperity, with irregular movements in 1924, 1927, and 1928. In the fiscal year 1930 comes a substantial decline, and in 1931 a tremendous drop.

Of the reaction in business which occurred between the spring of 1923 and the fall of 1924, and the slighter reaction that occurred in the last half of 1927 and the first half of 1928, Chart 2 gives no evidence except the slight decrease recorded by combined exports and imports in the fiscal year 1928 which included the very months affected by the slight reaction that began in the latter part of 1927. Thus imports, more accurately than combined exports and imports, reflect the reaction of 1923-24 which has been regarded by Thorp and some others as a mild depression.[45] Both Chart 2 and Chart 3 record the reaction which began in the latter part of 1927; but Chart 3 records this development more clearly than Chart 2. Thus in this last period, as in a number of others, imports reflected more sensitively than combined exports and imports the changes that occurred in general business conditions.

This survey of the available data reveals, as might have been expected, a fair correlation between changes in the volume of foreign trade and the cyclical movements of business in the United States. This correlation is somewhat greater for imports than for combined exports and imports, but for both series it is significant. For the first forty years, foreign trade probably exerted a greater influence on the economic life of the country than in any of the subsequent periods except the last. Then, chiefly if not wholly as a result of the Great War, it seems to have recovered something of its original primacy. During the next two or three decades, it will be interesting to observe whether foreign trade retains the importance it has had for the last ten years, or again, as in 1820, enters upon a decline in the importance of its contribution to business prosperity or depression.

[45] Thorp, *idem*, p. 145.

INTERNATIONAL COLLABORATION IN THE STUDY OF ECONOMIC CONJUNCTURE[1]

I

MORE than seventeen years have passed since the Harvard University Committee on Economic Research began the study of current economic conditions and established the Review of Economic Statistics devoted principally to the study of economic conjuncture. Today in many leading countries there are committees, institutes, or societies, pursuing this line of scientific investigation with such vigor as their resources permit and with sufficient success to give the world a record and appraisal of current economic conditions such as no previous generation of economists ever knew or would have regarded as possible. These organizations have already held four international conferences; others I trust will follow. International cooperation in the study of economic conjuncture is now *fait accompli;* and it has all come to pass in the brief period of seventeen years.

As my contribution to the symposium, I shall present some observations concerning the extraordinary conditions under which scientific men have had to study this difficult and important subject during the last seventeen years. This I shall do, not as a matter of historical interest, but rather for the help it can give those who must try to understand the economic difficulties of the world in which we economists now live and move and have our scientific being. Perhaps from the lamp of experience there may fall some rays that will light the tortuous channels through which, for another decade or more, we must steer

[1] Reprinted by the generous permission of the Institut für Konjunkturforschung (Berlin) from Beiträge zür Konjunkturlehre (1936), a memorial volume in celebration of the twentieth anniversary of its founding.

the fragile but immensely valuable craft committed to our charge. I have nothing new to present either in the way of facts or principles, yet from a review of obvious conditions and familiar events I hope to obtain a final conspectus that will prove to have value.

Many of the subjects I discuss are highly controversial; but I shall not offer proofs of any statements of fact, or much argument in support of any conclusions I present. To do these things would require that I write not an article, not even a book, but a library. I shall therefore present my own views, briefly and very dogmatically, knowing that concerning many things nothing like general agreement is yet possible; but comforting myself with the reflection that even if I, or any one else, should write a whole library, a universal consensus of opinion would not be much nearer. To the *"quot homines, tot sententiae"* of the Latin poet, we do well in these days to add: *quot libri, tot sententiae.* A further comforting reflection is that, with the passage of the years, economic phenomena, like other human events, come to be seen in truer perspective; while finally a point is reached where trees no longer prevent one from seeing the forest, and foothills no longer obstruct one's view of the mountain range. Finally, truth has a way of getting a hearing, whereupon controversy disappears. Ten years ago I should not have dared to undertake my present task; but today I am confident that there is sufficient agreement among economists to make it worth while to present quite dogmatically a general survey of conditions and events; and then to offer, not dogmatically, but with full knowledge that in such difficult matters it is given to no one to see the whole truth, what seem to be some fairly obvious conclusions.

II

We must begin with the basic, far-reaching, and unpleasant fact that the World War did not actually end in 1918. The Treaty of Versailles, whatever its merits or demerits, did not restore real peace to distracted and impoverished Europe. For a few years actual warfare continued; after that came frequent threats of war; and in 1936 it is hard for any of us to see how another European war can be averted eventually. Some still hope that it may not come, among whom I am numbered; but it is difficult to find rational grounds for this hope, perhaps never more so than at the present moment. The last fifteen years have brought many critical developments which have somehow been adjusted, at least temporarily; and it may be that, if Europe goes on meeting periodic crises in this way, the general situation will gradually improve. I trust that it will; but I find nothing in history to justify such an expectation, and the only raional ground for entertaining it seems to be that another war might bring the end of our present European, and indeed western, civilization. Polybios, we recall, in his account of the cycles of change in political institutions, thought that from time to time flood, famine, pestilence, or other calamities decimate mankind, reducing it to a small, brutish remnant knowing none of the arts of civilization or conditions of social existence. To most moderns, his words had little meaning twenty years ago, because we had come to accept progress as a natural and almost inevitable thing which seemed securely buttressed by all the scientific discoveries and material improvement of the last four or five centuries. Today, while we may still hope, we should read and ponder the words of this Greek historian.

For my present purpose it is unnecessary to account for the fact that Europe today is war-minded and not peace-minded; nor need I undertake to assess and apportion responsibility therefor or to determine degrees of responsibility. I wish only to base my subsequent observations upon the unescapable fact that for the last seventeen years the scientist currently investigating economic conjuncture has pursued his studies with a sword of Damocles suspended from the ceiling of his library or laboratory. More than this, the materials with which he works have been disturbed, from time to time, by sudden tremors of non-economic and distinctly political origin. Finally, many objects the economist studies are not what he knew them to be twenty years ago. Some seem to have undergone permanent change of structure and even of some of the elements of which they are composed. Others show signs of reverting to pre-war types. Still others have completely reverted, but show themselves to be unstable, easily affected by war or rumor of war, and incapable of easy readjustment to conditions of peace. To an investigator interested only in economic annals, or in writing accurate descriptions of economic changes that come with kaleidoscopic frequency, these conditions present no serious difficulty. But he who would interpret current events, and on his interpretation try to base a scientific forecast, finds his investigations disturbed, limited, and complicated, to a degree incapable of being realized by any one who has not carried on such studies currently since 1918.

From the fact that the War did not really end in 1918, it has inevitably followed that all the forces making for nationalism have been greatly intensified throughout the world. By "nationalism" I mean, of course, not that regard for the welfare of one's country that is rightly recognized as a duty by every man who knows the meaning of loyalty, but that extreme pursuit of national interests which grows either out of the desire for endless aggrandizement at the expense of others or out of the fear of suffering from the ambitious designs of other nations. All history shows plainly whither such extreme nationalism leads. Whatever we may think of Hobbes's theory of human nature and of the political philosophy based upon it, we must all agree with him that, in their relations with each other, the nations of the world have to a large extent lived

"in continual jealousies and in the state and posture of gladiators, having their weapons pointing, and their eyes fixed on one another, that is, their forts, garrisons, and guns, upon the frontiers of their kingdoms, and continual spies upon their neighbours: which is a posture of war."

Of course we have heard more of internationalism since 1919 than at any other time since the rise of national monarchies in Europe; and in many countries there are people who, with fine spirit and the best motives, have tried to improve and extend international relations and have hoped for world peace. But the fact remains that nationalism of an extreme form is dominant today, and that thereby the economic life of the world is vitally and, in some ways, disastrously affected. With this condition modern economists must reckon quite as much as did their Mercantilist predecessors of the seventeenth and eighteenth centuries. In spite of wars and injurious commercial restrictions, the commerce of the world had very greatly and fairly steadily increased from the time of the First Crusade to the outbreak of the World War, a period of something more than eight centuries. To this constant and substantial increase in the volume of international trade, the life of the world had become so thoroughly adjusted that, like the fact of progress, it was finally accepted as a matter of course. The last few years have seen this process arrested by a tremendous shrinkage in the amount of such trade, which is one of the outstanding developments and major contributing causes of the present great depression.

Today the student of economic conjuncture, looking out upon a nationalistic world, must try to determine as best he can whether even world-wide recovery from the present depression will bring such a revival of commercial intercourse as will restore international trade to its former volume and then permit it to resume its former upward trend. On this point, I suppose, we cannot for many years reach anything like certainty; and yet, in our interpretation of current events and in our economic forecasts, we must either leave out a factor of vital importance or make our best estimate of the probabilities of the case. There is great wisdom in an observation made by Sir William Petty in his remarkable treatise on *Political Arithmetick.* Writing at a time when many Englishmen seemed doubtful about the future of their country and were contending that French competition and other things were destroying British trade, Petty undertook a thorough survey of the available data, with a view to determining the truth of the matter. His task was far easier than that confronting the modern economist, and the words I quote were easier for him to write than they would be for us in this year of grace. They are as follows:

"Forasmuch as Men, who are in a decaying condition, or who have but an ill opinion of their own Concernments, instead of being (as some think) the more industrious to resist the Evils they apprehend, do contrariwise become the more languid and ineffectual in all their Endeavours, neither caring to attempt or prosecute even the probable means of their relief. Upon this Consideration, as a Member of the Common-Wealth, next to knowing the precise Truth in what condition the common Interest stands, I would in all doubtful Cases think the best, and consequently not despair, without strong and manifest Reasons, carefully examining whatever tends to lessen my hopes of the publick Welfare."

Beside making our best estimate of the probable trend of international trade, we economists will inevitably have our views about what the commercial policies of the nations should be, and especially the policies of our own countries. These, of course, must not affect our estimate of the probable trend; but they will affect materially our views concerning the rapidity and completeness with which the world can recover from the present depression, and so should influence our forecasts. Believing, as I do, that commerce among nations has been an important factor in the progress of civilization, and believing also that restoration of freer commercial relations is a prime requisite for complete recovery from this depression, I am content to make no further statement or explanation of my views. I have mentioned the subject merely for the purpose of emphasizing the difficulties which beset the student of economic conjuncture at the present time, but I cannot leave it without going back to the eighteenth century and drawing upon the wisdom of David Hume. In his essay *Of the Jealousy of Trade*, the great philosopher remarked that nothing was more usual,

"among states which have made some advances in commerce, than to look on the progress of their neighbours with a suspicious eye, to consider all trading states as their rivals, and to suppose that it is impossible for any of them to flourish but at their expence."

In opposition to "this narrow and malignant opinion," which he knew to be prevalent in his own country as in others, Hume asserted that

> "the increase of riches and commerce in any one nation, instead of hurting, commonly promotes the riches and commerce of all its neighbours; and that a state can scarcely carry its trade and industry very far, where all the surrounding states are buried in ignorance, sloth, and barbarism."

The essay closes with these noble words, which all may well consider:

> "I shall therefore venture to acknowledge, that, not only as a man, but as a British subject, I pray for the flourishing commerce of Germany, Spain, Italy, and even France itself. I am at least certain, that Great Britain, and all those nations, would flourish more, did their sovereigns and ministers adopt such enlarged and benevolent sentiments towards each other."

War-mindedness and nationalism are old and familiar phenomena which I have felt obliged to discuss briefly because they have such basic importance for the scientific student of economic conditions at the present day. A third factor which has greatly and fundamentally disturbed the economic life of nations, so far as our present knowledge goes, is probably unique. The War left a fearful legacy of international debts, some of them known as reparation payments and others resulting from loans between the allied nations. With the rights and wrongs of reparations and of interallied debts, I am not here concerned. This statement, like others already made or presently to be made in this essay, will not, I trust, be taken as evidence that I am indifferent to the moral aspects of the many issues left by the War. It means simply that my present task is to appraise the economic consequences of certain hard and terribly difficult facts.

For some centuries the rapid growth of commerce had bound the nations of the world into a great trading society. Not only commodities but capital had come to move with considerable freedom from country to country; and all this required the establishment of monetary systems stable enough to permit commercial and financial intercourse to proceed without undue risk. Finally, the use of credit had been greatly extended in modern times, so that international dealings were carried on chiefly through the agency of a complicated and delicate mechanism which, if rightly used, was a valuable servant of mankind, but, if abused, became an avenging power inflicting retribution upon transgressors. In ordinary times the movement of capital into permanent foreign investments proceeded smoothly, and the flow of short-time loans and funds for current payments was largely a matter of routine; while shipments of gold were so far avoided that they constituted but a very small item in the total volume of international transactions. Of course wars and economic crises sometimes strained the delicate machine severely, even shaking it to its foundation; but necessary repairs and readjustments could always be made, so that a breakdown was averted; and international finance seemed never so securely buttressed and never functioned so well as in the first thirteen years of the present century.

The nearest parallel to the present condition of the world's monetary systems and credit relations was that which followed the termination, in 1815, of the long war which had finally involved most of Europe, all of North America, and even parts of Asia and Africa. Commercial relations had been greatly dislocated, monetary and credit systems had been thrown into confusion, governmental finances had been deeply involved, and the economic life of the entire world had been so greatly unsettled that it was necessary to begin at the very bottom and construct some parts of the edifice anew, while many years were required for repair and readjustment of other parts of the structure. Yet Europe in 1815 desired peace, and the Congress of Vienna had not insisted upon economic or financial settlements so impossible as to constitute a bar to the resumption of normal commercial relations between the countries of Europe, or between Europe and the rest of the world. Under such circumstances, the governments of the former belligerent nations could gradually put their houses in order, balance their budgets, and restore monetary stability. With this assured, the people of all countries could and did proceed, step by step, to work out their own salvation, without being advised, directed, or assisted very much by rulers eager to assume tasks "for the proper performance of which," as Adam Smith long ago remarked, "no human wisdom or knowledge could ever be sufficient," and in attempting to perform which they "must always be exposed to numerous delusions." The result was that the ties of commercial intercouse were reknit, the trade of the world recovered, and international financial relations entered upon those developments which by the end of the nineteenth century had given us our intricate and delicate mechanism of international credit and finance which, when rightly used, was such a powerful factor in economic progress.

If this picture seems a veiled attack upon the financial provisions of the Treaty of Versailles, I can assure you that I have endeavored to make it square at every point with the outstanding facts of the historical record. That treaty imposed upon Germany reparation payments in an amount which was not to be determined for some years but, according to optimistic estimates of Germany's ability to pay, would be of fantastic proportions. One of the principals in the negotiations that resulted in the adoption of the Dawes Plan described the situation accurately when he said that the Plan had at least reduced the amount of the indemnity from astronomical to mundane dimensions. Even so, when brought down from the fixed stars to the earth's surface, the amount of the reparations finally demanded so far exceeded the economic possibilities of the case that it constituted a complete barrier to the recovery of Germany and a menace to the economic welfare of the world. Any one who will examine the statistics of German trade in 1913 and roughly estimate the possibilities of increasing exports and decreasing imports will see that by no human effort could Germany have converted her moderate pre-war balance of imports into the colossal balance of exports necessary for the payment of the annuities finally required under the Young Plan. This would have been true even for pre-war Germany, with territory intact and with foreign investments which accounted for the balance of imports she received at that time; but for Germany of 1919 the reparation figures were an economic absurdity fraught with terrible consequences.

The interallied debts were never of astronomical proportions. If Germany could have met the payments required even under the Young Plan, they would have presented no economic difficulties, since payment in full would have meant, in last analysis, transferring to the United States, the principal creditor, a considerable part of the reparation payments. Politically the thing would not have been so simple. It was easy for Great Britain, whose debit and credit items nearly balanced, to suggest that these troublesome debts be cancelled; but it was not so easy for the debtor countries to shoulder their burden, and quite impossible to persuade the United States that Germany's creditors could not meet obligations much smaller than the anticipated reparation payments. Today, with reparations at an end and the commerce of the world reduced to its present proportions, the interallied debts are an economic as well as a political impossibility. They have helped to deepen and prolong the depression, and now make more difficult the restoration of normal commercial relations which would so greatly aid the process of recovery.

With the rights or wrongs of reparations and interallied debts, we are not here concerned, but we are obliged to reckon with their consequences. International payments flow through the delicate mechanism of the foreign exchanges, which are quite capable of taking care of any transactions resulting from ordinary commercial and financial intercourse. They can do this because such dealings are two-sided, so that a debtor on foreign account, or his banker, can ordinarily find persons having exchange they desire to sell; and the result is that gold shipments are reduced to a minimum and are insignificant in comparison with the total volume of international transfers. But such colossal payments as were now proposed were one-sided in character, and so far beyond the capacity of the complicated machine through which they must pass that they stand today a fearful and shameful indictment of the economic intelligence of the modern world. The truth was finally recognized in some measure when provision was made for the payment of reparations in marks to an agent of Germany's creditors, who received the funds in Berlin and was to remit them to creditor countries only so far as this could be done without threatening the stability of German exchange. This solved the immediate financial difficulties of reparations, but did not enable Germany to build up the excess of exported commodities and services by which alone real payment could have been made.[2] In the nationalistic, and therefore protectionist, world in which we live, there was never any possibility of such a development of Germany's export trade; and therefore the last chapter of the Great Delusion was written at Lausanne in 1932.

But the baleful legacy of intergovernmental debts had thrown out of balance the international accounts of many leading countries, and had thereby produced a general state of economic instability such as no former generation of economists has known. Particular countries, of course, have often had their exchanges rudely shaken, and in 1815 great commercial and financial disturbances were world-wide. But never, so far as the record goes, has there been a period of seventeen years in which an impossible burden of intergovernmental debts produced a disequilibrium so serious that even two depressions, both world-wide and one the greatest in history, have not been able to force the general readjustments that are so necessary. From this fundamental *malaise* have inevitably come other evils the chief of which will be discussed hereafter. For science, however, has come one gain—more thorough study and more accurate determination of the foreign balances of the leading commercial nations, a work to which students of economic con-

[2] For the writer's present purpose, it is unnecessary to refer to the deliveries in kind; or to the loans made to Germany by creditor countries, especially the United States, by which, in form but not in fact, substantial payments on reparation account were made possible for a few years.

juncture have been able to make their contribution. In this development, history repeats itself. Economics perforce concerns itself chiefly with problems of the day, with the result that a complete and classified bibliography of the economic writings of any period could always serve as a catalogue of economic ills or complaints. Just as Italy two or three centuries ago was said to have the worst money and the best books about money, so today the generation that has witnessed the worst of all disturbances in the world's exchanges have produced the best balances of international payments.

The fourth great factor contributing to economic unsettlement since the War has been the disordered currencies of most belligerent countries and of many non-belligerents. That great wars lead to inflation, to suspension of specie payments, and to currency disorders, we all know. But never before has it been so hard for so many countries to return to a specie basis, whether by devaluation or otherwise; and never before have so many countries found it impossible to remain upon the specie bases so painfully regained. For this the unbalanced state of the world's exchanges has been responsible. All will agree that the disequilibrium was due chiefly to the enormous intergovernmental debts; I myself am inclined to place the sole responsibility upon them. It is true, of course, that a great mass of private international debts created since 1918 has contributed to the disordered state of the exchanges; but a large part of such indebtedness would never have come into being if it had not been for the impasse to which intergovernmental debts of all descriptions had brought us. If at Versailles in 1919, the amount of reparation payments could have been fixed at a figure consistent with economic realities, and if the interallied debts could have been either cancelled or reduced to modest proportions consistent with political as well as economic realities, some of the private debts would never have been contracted; and improvement of economic conditions would have greatly reduced the amount of other borrowings. In such case, therefore, the world might well have weathered the next depression without running into currency disorders; so that I incline rather strongly to the view that in last analysis the intergovernmental debts *are solely responsible* for the fact that only a few countries are on a gold basis today and that their position sometimes appears none too secure. It will be observed that three words in the last sentence are italicized.

A fifth topic of vast importance for the student of economic conjuncture was the general return to a gold or a gold-exchange standard in so many countries between 1925 and 1927. That in principle it was very desirable for nations to extricate themselves from the maze of fluctuating paper currency and get back to gold, I have never doubted, that the commodity dollar, bimetallism, or symmetallism would have been preferable, I have never believed: but whether this view is correct or not is of little consequence, because, with conditions as they were in 1925, the gold standard was the only expedient which had any chance of being adopted. In any case, the immediate effect of the return to gold was beneficial.

Of course the general adoption of a gold standard could not remedy all ills; but the economic indices then or a little later constructed for various countries show general improvement, though naturally in varying degrees. Many nations, indeed, remained far from prosperous, and some continued in sore distress; but by and large we can now see that things had taken definitely a turn for the better, and that there was some reason for hoping that improvement would continue. To students of economic conjuncture, the years just mentioned were, I suppose, the happiest they have seen since 1919, because the economic structure of most countries had been given greater stability, and, therefore, economic functions were proceeding more nearly in a manner which, without offering a definition, I shall venture to call "normal." In most countries at this time economic indices seemed easier to construct and easier to interpret; and some of us, for the first time since 1914, indulged in the hope that we were returning to an economic world very much like that in which we had lived in other and happier days.

It was not long, however, before disquieting developments appeared. The chief of these was that in 1925 commodity prices in gold-standard countries began to decline. This was accepted by many as a natural and desirable thing. I do not wish to suggest here that anything could or should have been done to prevent it, for that would carry me too far afield; but is it not true that, as we review the events of the last nine years with that hindsight which is so much easier than foresight, the decline of commodity prices which began soon after the return of Great Britain to the gold standard ought to have disquieted us more than it did? Whether it was due wholly to the operation of that standard, or partly, or not at all, in various countries, especially the United States, it has developed a suspicion and dislike of any gold standard, which are leading to a desire to try monetary experiments, some old and others new, that confuse, disconcert, and tend to delay that return of general confidence upon which recovery so largely depends. It is with no little satisfaction, therefore, that I can here recall that, at the first general conference of the various committees and institutions collaborating in international studies of economic conjuncture, held in London in 1928, the subject of the future course of commodity prices received especial attention, and the consequences to a debt-ridden world of a long-continued decline were fully realized. Economic theorists might speculate about the possibility of the world enjoying considerable prosperity in an era of declining commodity prices, as it undoubtedly did in the latter part of the nineteenth century. But no student of economic conjuncture who had studied the great depression of the 1870's and that of the 1890's could take an optimistic view of the probable consequences of a long decline of commodity prices in a world as deeply indebted as that in which we lived in the year 1928.

Since Great Britain was really the leader in the return to the gold standard, and her experience so well illustrates the conclusions which I am obliged to present, so briefly and dogmatically, I shall, in these observations, refer chiefly to the course of events in that country. In the first place, it now seems clear that it was a great mistake to try to return to the former gold standard, and that it would have been better to resume gold payments at some lower figure. We can all appreciate the very strong reasons which led the government and financial leaders of Great Britain to desire restoration of the old pound; we can admire the integrity which in no small share contributed to this decision, and the courage and determination with which the experiment was carried out. None the less, it is now clear that too high a valuation had been placed upon the pound. In previous periods of war inflation, it was possible for developed commercial nations to supplement the natural liquidation, which always follows inflation, with measures of credit contraction that finally resulted in reducing commodity prices, wages, and most other things, to levels so related to each other that pre-war relations could be reknit and trade could begin to recover. In the general liquidation, some reduction of debts would occur, as well as of government expenses and taxes. No perfectly equal and satisfactory readjustment of all things was ever reached; but most things could be so nearly restored to their former relations with each other that a tolerable state of equilibrium would result, and economic conditions would then improve. This, I take it, was the economics of the situation; but unfortunately political conditions in the twentieth century so far differ from those obtaining in the nineteenth that politics, both national and international, proved too strong for economics.

Restoration of the old standard involved, first of all, a decline in commodity prices. This might have been accepted by merchants and manufacturers, even though opposition to revaluation was developing among British industrial leaders. But with wages, the case was different. A powerful and well-organized Labor Party had developed, and there was no likelihood that labor would willingly accept reductions in rates of wages, even from the high levels reached during the period of inflation. Then, in Great Britain as in the United States and probably many other countries, rates of wages were, in popular thought and even in the thinking of many economists, confused with wage payments to workers actually employed. The fact that rates higher than the economic situation warrants will certainly lead to unemployment, and may even result in reducing the total amount paid to laborers in the form of wages, was, and is, insufficiently appreciated almost everywhere; and ignorance of it had much to do with developments in Great Britain after 1925, just as in the United States and doubtless other countries, it has contributed to the unusual severity and length of the present depression.

Reduction of wage rates was not the only adjustment required although it was among the things that were necessary if the restoration of the former gold standard was to prove beneficial. Industry might increase its efficiency, might improve its organization, might "rationalize" itself. In the United States, in the 1920's, manufacturers, faced by inflated wage rates and deflated commodity prices, managed, as a rule, to cope with the situation by using more machinery and increasing general efficiency so that the output per workman was greatly increased and profits restored to a satisfactory level. Railroads and some other industries could make somewhat similar readjustments, though not to a degree sufficient to bring real prosperity; but agriculture naturally was less able to readjust itself to post-war conditions, and therefore enjoyed only a partial recovery and in some of its branches remained depressed. Of course increased output per man meant decreased employment, at least temporarily; and therefore in the 1920's much was heard in the United States of technological unemployment. In Great Britain reconstruction of popular ideas was extremely difficult; industry was slow to change its ways, partly on account of the opposition of strongly organized trade unions; and output per laborer employed showed no increase adequate to the needs of the situation. Therefore costs of production remained high, export trade suffered, and sterling exchange from 1925 onward was much less secure than it would have been if gold payments had been resumed with a pound sufficiently devalued to cope with this and other handicaps to the satisfactory operation of a gold standard.

Another trouble was that government expenses and taxes proved hard to deflate. Of course the huge war expenditure had come to an end; but the army of the unemployed had to be maintained, and doles became a major item of expenditure. Then came a number of other demands, for education and a variety of things called "social service," which were expensive even at their inception and were bound to grow in number and importance. Therefore taxes remained high, and, added to an excessive labor cost, imposed on industry a heavy burden which could not but have a restrictive effect on all save the exceptionally fortunate trades. In all other countries of which I have knowledge, something of the same sort occurred—certainly it did in the United States;—but, for a nation endeavoring to maintain a gold standard higher than economic realities justified, the maintenance of wages and taxes at high and fixed levels, after commodity prices had been deflated, could only spell disaster unless some powerful compensating factor intervened to balance the international accounts. This was not, and could not be, forthcoming. Many changes in many countries had injured British export trade; other conditions might be mentioned which did not favor the success of the experiment undertaken in 1925; and it is impossible to discover a single favorable development sufficient to compensate in any substantial degree for the handicaps under which Great Britain labored.

Indeed, not long after gold payments had been resumed, an important new development occurred which, while favorably regarded at the time, proved ultimately a source of weakness. After the War, London, as soon as possible, became a lender of short-term money, but was in no position to resume the export of capital for permanent investment. With gold payments successfully resumed and the pound sterling in an apparently secure position, it then seemed both possible and necessary to return to the foreign investment field in which London had been supreme before the War. In a short time the net export of capital assumed large proportions, and at the end of 1927 was found to have exceeded the net export from the United States. But this had been accomplished partly through a substantial flow of short-term capital to London; and to this extent Britain, as our colleague Maynard Keynes then expressed it, was borrowing short and lending long. It became evident, too, that, with death duties eating into accumulated wealth and the heavy supertax diminishing substantially the amount of new accumulation, Great Britain no longer had as large a surplus for new investment as she had enjoyed before the War; so that, without borrowing short, foreign investments on the existing scale could not continue. Finally it came to be realized that England was exporting more capital than her rate of annual accumulation and her balance of international payments really justified; such a development imposed an additional strain upon the pound sterling.

Another circumstance which intensified the difficulties of the situation, not only for Great Britain but for other countries on the gold standard, was that, ever since the War, sudden shifts of liquid funds from one currency to another had become quite the order of the day. The wild fluctuations of exchange rates in the period of currency inflation immediately after the War had opened a vast field for speculators and brought into existence a large amount of migratory capital. The general return to the gold standard temporarily diminished such movements; but nevertheless, whenever any country ran into difficulties, a flight of capital was sure to begin and frequently assumed proportions quite unknown before the War. To the same result also the gold-exchange standard contributed, since its inevitable effect was to lead the banks of countries adopting it to carry a large part of their reserves in foreign bills. It was inevitable that such funds would be immediately withdrawn to the greatest extent possible from any currency that seemed to be in a difficult situation. For all countries on a real gold standard, sudden, swift, and extensive shifts of migratory capital constituted a serious problem; and to none was the danger greater than to Great Britain, because, while the pound had been overvalued when gold payments were resumed, the franc had been somewhat undervalued, and the principal market for the franc was in London.

Two things, we know, create difficulties that are almost insuperable for the student of economic conjuncture. These are war and monetary upheavals. From 1919 to 1924 we had wild inflation in several countries, to which were added several wars and many rumors of war. Then followed five years of comparative stability of the world's currencies, as one country after another adopted a gold or gold-exchange standard. During this time our tasks became easier, but were always of more than normal difficulty, because the movement of gold was not really free in many countries, certain security markets were not open to the same degree as before the War, and certain exchanges were known to be weak. Therefore we realized that it was a somewhat precarious gold standard to which many countries held; and we always knew that the monetary data with which we dealt were subject to sudden shocks and tremors that could not well be foreseen and might bring to naught the results of our most careful investigations.

A sixth factor of far-reaching importance is the state of disequilibrium in which the markets for many, if not most, of the world's great commodities were left by the War, to which must be added the disequilibria in industry resulting from the forced expansion of certain trades of vital military importance. It is surely unnecessary to go into details. We all know that the War rudely broke established commercial relations, and left many markets glutted and many industries overexpanded. Even in 1936 the economist can read with greater interest than at any time in the century that followed their publication the words in which, in 1817, David Ricardo described the condition of the Europe in which he lived. In the fourth chapter of his *Principles of Political Economy and Taxation,* he described the manner in which "market" prices differ from "natural" and pointed out that fluctuations in market prices control the flow of capital into and out of the various employments open to it. He then remarked:

"The present time appears to be one of the exceptions to the justness of this remark. The termination of the war has so deranged the division which before existed of employments in Europe, that every capitalist has not yet found his place in the new division which has now become necessary."

Of course there were scarcities as well as surpluses in 1919, and the former to some extent helped to care for the latter. But at no time did important disequilibria cease to exist, and presently it became evident that many governments were pursuing policies which could tend only to make conditions worse. Military reasons led various importing countries to stimulate the production of wheat in order to increase their future supply in the event of war. Military and economic reasons led coal-importing countries to electrify railways and other industries, thereby intensifying the glutted condition of the markets of another overexpanded industry. Then, when the unbalanced condition of the world's exchanges caused numerous countries to seek to improve their position on international account, it naturally happened that tariffs were raised, import quotas were established, and domestic production was encouraged in every possible way. Rationalization of industry was much discussed and sometimes attempted; but it seldom brought reduction in operating costs through the discharge of unnecessary workmen or otherwise, and the usual result was more or less successful price-fixing. Thus the volume of world trade was reduced, old surpluses became more serious, and new surpluses developed. With the return to the gold standard, careful consideration had to be paid to the balance of international payments; and in a war-minded, nationalistic world this could only bring still higher tariffs, stricter exchange restrictions, smaller quotas, and other measures which reduced international trade and increased the menace of commodity surpluses. Finally, since 1930, as monetary disturbances have broken out in one nation after another and gold payments have been suspended, old restrictions have been tightened, new ones have been contrived, commerce naturally has suffered, and commodity markets have been further demoralized.

The plight of the producer and merchant was serious enough in Ricardo's time to serve for a century as the classic example of the economic disorder caused by a great war involving many belligerents; but it was far less serious than that of their successors in 1919. In the world of our great-grandfathers, a general recovery presently began, because the world was peace-minded and governments, setting their own houses in order, did comparatively little to help or to hinder the natural healing process. In our time the world has not been peace-minded, the economic problems left by the War have been too great for the economic intelligence of rulers or peoples, theories of governmental functions have changed, and the result has been that about all the powers of human malevolence and economic misunderstanding have joined in carrying through policies which have brought it about that the ordinary producer or merchant, in the words of David Ricardo, has "not yet found his place in the new division which has now become necessary." Until he does this, commodity surpluses and the disequilibria they create will constitute formidable problems for students of economic conjuncture. They owe their existence to a variety of causes—military, political, agricultural, industrial, monetary, and financial—and can be neither understood nor solved when approached on any single front. Whether nature could solve them for us, we shall not know; because it is evident that she will not be given a chance. The patient is in the hands of political, economic, and social doctors who are going to try all the remedies in all known systems of therapeutics, and perhaps others, not yet known, which their powers of planning, regulating, prohibiting, encouraging, negotiating, and coördinating may enable them to devise. I am not suggesting that surgery and medicine are not needed, for I think they are; but I do believe that students of economic conjuncture will do well to recall the words of Sir William Petty, perhaps the greatest of seventeenth-century economists, who gave the following counsel to the political doctors of his age:

"We must consider in general, that as wiser Physicians tamper not excessively with their Patients, rather observing and complying with the motions of nature, than contradicting it with vehement Administrations of their own; so in Politicks and Oeconomicks the same must be used."

A seventh fact of great importance for an understanding of the history of the last seventeen years and the problems sure to develop during the next decade is the resort to large international loans as a means of relieving distress and promoting recovery. That some such loans should have been made was inevitable, that they afforded temporary relief and accomplished some permanent good can hardly be doubted. Yet, with fundamental conditions such as I have outlined above, it was impossible for the loans to have the helpful, stabilizing effects that were anticipated; and it was certain that they could not cure the world's unbalanced exchanges, which were the root of so many of the evils the loans were expected to remove. Lending money to debtor nations for the purpose of enabling them to pay reparations or other governmental debts merely concealed from the people of the world, and apparently from most of the rulers, the truth about the unbalanced condition of the exchanges; and therefore it postponed the day when the unpleasant truth would have to be faced, and delayed the settlement of the most fundamental economic problem that confronted the world in 1919. That some of the loans grew out of the deliberations of international commissions and conferences, that others were made by bankers at the instance of governments interested in various political objectives, and that still others—and these among the largest—came from a new reservoir recently created in the United States and competed with the capital of other countries in a field where experience, circumspection, and avoidance of excessive competition are very necessary, made it certain that some loans would be so large in amount that ultimately they would injure the borrower as well as the lender, and so contribute to the general unsettlement which prolongs and intensifies the present depression.

The eighth outstanding development of the last fifteen years was coöperation between the central banks of leading countries on a scale hitherto unknown. Of course differences of interest and policy existed; and in 1931 coöperation came to an end, being followed by a period in which the prevailing maxim seemed to be *sauve qui peut*. Nevertheless from 1924 until 1931 one of the major factors for the student of economic conjuncture was that the central banks of leading nations were conferring and, upon occasion, taking common action to accomplish definite ends. Perhaps the most striking illustration is the understanding reached by the Federal Reserve System of the United States and the Bank of England, by which the resumption of specie payments in Great Britain was greatly facilitated and subsequent occasional strains were materially eased. Finally came the establishment of the Bank for International Settlements, which, although it grew out of the final arrangements made for reparations, was believed to provide a means for securing better understanding and greater coöperation than had yet been attained. That good was accomplished in this way, we can hardly doubt; but the fact always remained that the exchanges of the world were unbalanced, that currencies of debtor countries were weak, that creditor countries like Great Britain had resumed gold payments at too high a figure, that the franc was probably undervalued—with the result that gold had a natural tendency flow to Paris,—and that the United States, as the principal creditor, tended to receive excessive imports of gold unless favorable conditions abroad and easy money at home—sometimes kept easy by action of the Federal Reserve System—encouraged the export of capital in the form of large loans made to European and South American countries. The one fundamental and really important fact was that so many of the world's exchanges were unbalanced. Until broken bones could be set and have time to knit, it was useless for central banks to apply poultices or administer stimulants. The helping hand extended by the Federal Reserve System to Great Britain between the summer of 1924 and the spring of 1925 appears now to have wrought evil, and not good, as intended, because the pound sterling was given too high a rating. Again, some, perhaps many, of the foreign loans made by the United States and other countries had decidedly injurious effects; and could not possibly have accomplished some of the things expected of them, because of fundamental disequilibria in the world's foreign exchanges.

Along with coöperation between central banks came another development, ninth in order of mention. In the last part of the nineteenth century, with gold moving freely between countries, exchanges functioning normally, and economic relations becoming increasingly international in scope, there were worked out in Europe, very largely by the Bank of England, methods of central-bank control which at the opening of the twentieth century were operating smoothly and helpfully. They are so familiar to economists that I need not describe them; there was little mystery about them; and they were fundamentally, though not in all details of application, automatic in character. Central-bank control meant, substantially, following the movements of the exchanges. Overexpansion of credit usually led to an outflow of gold; and at the proper time the central bank, chiefly by selling securities and raising its discount rate, could correct the credit situation and check the outflow before it had taken on dangerous proportions. In times of crisis the purchase of securities and reduction of the discount rate would provide the necessary remedies, and stability would again be reached. The system was not wholly automatic; but it was chiefly so, and therefore imposed no superhuman task on human intelligence. Neither extraordinary prescience nor genius for effecting grand combinations was required; complete fidelity to the task, sufficient practical experience, mastery of financial technique, and high but not supernatural intelligence, were sufficient. Those responsible for the operation of central banks did not need a grand "plan" of national economy, or a still grander design for a regulated and regimented economy for the entire world, devised either by themselves or by some supreme board of planners. Under such circumstances, men of ability, experience, and wisdom developed the helpful methods of central-bank control with which we are all familiar.

But the War had left foreign exchanges unbalanced, and gold movements were no longer under the control of central banks. Instead of the moderate balances on visible and invisible items in national balance sheets, which had grown so gradually as to permit other things to become adjusted to them, the world now had to deal with enormous surpluses and deficits in international accounts, which, if intergovernmental debts and interest thereon were ever going to be paid, would become still more colossal. By one means or another which camouflaged the real situation, temporary settlements prevented all the gold in the world from being concentrated in a few countries which, on balance, were overwhelmingly in creditor positions. But, in spite of all that was done, concentration of gold in a few huge reservoirs steadily went on; and, in years when temporary adjustments failed, actual gold shipments took on prodigious proportions. In the ocean of international finance, elemental forces, created by unbalanced exchanges, whipped up tidal waves that swept gold out of banks and treasuries of debtor countries and threw it into the coffers of creditor nations. Against such titanic agencies, central banks, governments, international conferences and committees, all were powerless; and following the exchanges was no longer a satisfactory rule of action. The best of the world's bankers understood the difficulties of the situation, as did some, at least, of the politicians in whose hands rested responsibility for governmental action. But any remedy that could go to the bottom of the difficulty always required some nation or nations to make sacrifices so unpleasant as to be certain to cause popular discontent that would threaten the political life of the ministries, the presidents or other great rulers with whom lay the final decision. Therefore no fundamental remedy was found, and the result was what we all know.

Under these circumstances no central bank, even in a creditor country, could make the customary methods of control effective. In a debtor country suffering from deep depression and endeavoring to keep itself on a gold standard, easy money was obviously the one thing which domestic industry called for; but from time to time situations arose which threatened the stability of the foreign exchanges and required sharp increases in discount rates. In a creditor country like the United States, the Federal Reserve authorities in 1923, when they thought that a sharp upturn in business activity, commodity prices, and stock speculation threatened speculative excesses and inflation of prices, found that they could not raise discount rates without inviting gold imports which were both undesired and unwelcome. They were not wanted, because our gold supply already exceeded our normal proportion of the world's stock; and they were unwelcome because, first, they provided a basis for further speculative and inflationary activity, and, in the second place, they drained other countries of resources which would be needed if the gold standard was to be reëstablished. Between 1925 and 1927, with the reëstablishment of the gold standard, it developed that wholesale commodity prices in the world's markets were vitally affected by the discount rate in New York, so that regulation of the American money market became a very delicate and difficult matter. Obviously the gold standard was not working, and could not work, as it had in the days before the War. Gold imports might be averted by a policy that encouraged American bankers to make foreign loans, which, of course, after the year in which they were made, would increase further the annual charges which were already beyond the power of the debtor countries to meet. Such loans were no permanent solution; but, on the contrary, increased the disequilibria in the world's exchanges.

No monetary standard that was a real standard, to which other things must conform, could operate well under such conditions. If silver had been chosen instead of gold, if a bimetallic standard had been adopted, if a commodity dollar had been set up, the final result would have been different in no material respects. If the new standards permitted more expansion of credit than was possible under the gold standard, and time were given for that expansion to take place, a point would finally be reached at which the brake would have to be applied; and this would certainly precipitate a panic if the check proved effective and the standards turned out to be standards and not ropes of sand. During the period of expansion, creditor nations might have made more loans to debtor than they did when the gold standard was operative; but this would simply have increased the amount of disequilibrium in the foreign exchanges, and the final reckoning would have been even harder. Nor could most of the emergencies which threatened to drain debtor countries of all their money have been avoided, while some new ones might have been generated. No standard can work satisfactorily in a world that suffers from such economic maladjustments as resulted from the Great War. Not the gold standard, but the fundamental disequilibrium out of which so many other difficulties have come, is responsible for the situation in which we find ourselves today. We cannot blame our central banks, and should not blame the gold standard; neither of them ought to have been expected to carry us safely through a period involved in problems that have proved too great for the intelligence of the rulers and peoples of the world.

This completes my survey of the chief economic developments from 1919 to 1933. My tenth and last venture will be to present a few observations concerning the last thirty-six months which have brought us to a new phase of the Great Depression in which the world is painfully liquidating the consequences of the Great War. The events of this period have been so many and so momentous that my treatment of them will necessarily be even more fragmentary and inadequate than that accorded the other subjects I have tried to review in this essay. It may, although I trust it will not, prove less objective, because nothing can yet be viewed in historical perspective, novel factors have become operative for which we have no precedents to serve as guides, and the investigator's emotions are bound to be aroused because his own economic, and even scientific, future may be in question. Usually, for example, he is a salaried man with a modest fortune, if any, who, since he has a fixed income and a "white-collar" job, will be one of the chief victims of whatever inflation may occur in his country as a result of monetary upheavals, in the United States or elsewhere. Nevertheless I shall act upon the principle that I have already run so many hazards that no great additional harm can come from taking chances on a few more. After all, for an economist who lives in a country that has adopted a deliberate policy of currency inflation, life becomes very much of a gamble, the nature and proportions of which he understands better than any other sort of man.

Viewing with as much detachment as I can the tremendous developments which have occurred since the opening of 1933, it seems to me that three things of major importance stand out so conspicuously that they may well prove to be what the future historian will regard as most fundamental. The first is deliberate devaluation of the dollar. Against foreign demands in the fall of 1931 and spring of 1932, the dollar had proved impregnable; and in July of the latter year a few signs of improvement in economic conditions began to appear. But fall trade proved disappointing; and the demand for inflation, which for about two years had been gradually increasing, became so strong that runs on banks, which had occurred to some extent in the fall of 1931 and spring of 1932, started up again with greater force than before. The whole situation was epitomized by the experience of one of the Federal Reserve Banks in a district then one of the storm centres. After Congress adjourned in June, 1932, the bank saw the withdrawal of currency and hoarding of gold come practically to an end. Then in December, when Congress reconvened and the voice of the inflationist was heard in legislative halls, the demand for currency and gold —and this time chiefly gold—was renewed with increased intensity, so that within a few weeks it was evident that the country's banking troubles had only begun. When general suspension occurred on the 5th of March, 1933, it was not foreign but, rather, domestic demands that caused the final crash. Then an embargo on gold exports and the amazing inflation legislation of May, 1933, launched the United States upon a deliberate experiment with inflation. Up to that time, most if not all countries that had suspended gold payments seemed to be endeavoring to stabilize their exchanges as well as they could; while countries still upon a gold basis seemed determined to remain there. Now the United States, which had appeared to be in the strongest position of all, deliberately adopted the policy of inflation.

Upon other currencies the effect of devaluation in the United States was somewhat slow in developing, because of the enormous strength of the dollar which resisted the attempt to debase it. Omitting details, important and interesting as they are, the passage of the Devaluation Act in January of the following year was soon followed by an adjustment of exchange rates which brought the devalued dollar into its due relation to other currencies; and at that point it was possible for other countries to consider what, if anything, they might need to do in order to meet the situation caused by American devaluation. Since war and post-war inflation in Europe brought home to all classes of people the misery it causes and the iniquities it works, the tendency has been to try to protect exchanges by increased tariffs, redetermination of quotas, and restrictions on international movements of money, bills, and securities. Whether these measures will suffice is not yet clear; but it is evident that devaluation of the dollar, if it does not initiate competitive debasement of the world's currencies, has certainly increased greatly the forces that had been operating for several years to reduce the ability of the nations to trade with each other, and so has deepened and prolonged the depression. When, in June of 1933, the President of the United States, reversing his earlier position, announced that his country was not yet prepared to stabilize its currency, he abandoned the policy which, more than any other at that moment, would have laid a secure basis for future prosperity. Of course the intergovernmental debts would have remained, and many other problems would have had to be solved. Of course, too, international conferences seldom accomplish very much; but here was something definite which might have been done, and I am compelled to view the failure of the London Conference as one of the great tragedies of the last seventeen years. With other aspects of American devaluation, I cannot undertake to deal; but I may remark in passing that it has been slow and uncertain in producing the desired rise in domestic commodity prices because it did not, of itself, put any more money in circulation. Thus far credit has expanded only to the extent that banks have increased their holdings of securities, chiefly government obligations; and there has been practically no increase of loans, because the many other things attempted, accomplished, or threatened by the political doctors at Washington have made men intelligent enough to be in good credit quite unwilling to borrow more money for any purpose whatsoever.

The second development of major importance has been the extraordinary increase of governmental control over private industry. From Italy, Fascism, crossing the Alps, has brought political revolutions which have established or are in process of establishing authoritarian direction of industry. In the United States the National Recovery Act and other measures relating to agriculture, banking, security issues, stock exchanges, and other things, have brought about temporarily a regimentation which has already proceeded very far and is regarded by some, perhaps many, people as an economic revolution that marks the passing, or the serious modification, of what is called "capitalism." Justified at the start chiefly on the ground that it was needed to promote economic recovery, the extraordinary legislation of the last three years has disclosed more and more clearly that the desire for "social reform" has been at all times an important, and at some times the dominant, motive for measures enacted by the American Congress upon recommendation or insistence of the President and with apparent public approval. Sometimes the reform has been stronger than the recovery motive. It cannot be questioned, for example, that the securities Act of 1933 so far restricted the flow of private capital into industry, especially the so-called "heavy industries" which require large amounts of fixed capital, that the government has been obliged to turn public money into such channels. Even so, our heavy industries, which are peculiarly dependent upon the capital market and in times past have usually led in the process of recovery, are now more depressed than most other branches of trade. The course of events in the United States since March, 1933, cannot be understood unless it is realized that the government has been trying to carry out a large number of policies which are sometimes inconsistent with each other and so have frequently failed to produce the desired results.

Authoritarian direction of economic life, regimentation of industry, Fascism, the New Deal, and other economic measures, methods, and systems, designed to reform, promote, or control private industry, I cannot discuss in this paper except as they affect the work of the student of economic conjuncture. Seventeen years ago we studied the economic life of a world which, up to the Great War, had been under the control of individual enterprise operating in most countries with a minimum of public regulation. In 1919 we saw the emergence of the pre-war order, although with an increased degree of governmental control. The older order was largely self-regulating; and upon the actions of millions of men producing and transporting, buying and selling, employing and laboring, depended the economic conjuncture. We must now—many of us in our own countries, all of us in our study of other countries—deal with a new factor, or perhaps I would better say agent, because he is a man whom, with etymological accuracy, we may call the "conjoiner." We know that he has historical predecessors; but as yet we have not had much experience with him, and we do not know who will be his successors, or how they may improve, impair, or, conceivably, wreck his work. We also know that all things change, and that only in the philosophy of the Eleatics do we find unchanging Being. However well we may come to know the conjoiner of today and to understand how he affects our economic conjuncture, we must ever be alert to observe tomorrow's new conjoiner, because, acting alone or with colleagues, his business is to "direct." Indeed, we can be sure that, with authoritarian control, the very centre of the problem of economic conjuncture is the economic conjoiner.

History provides us with one method of approach to this new problem. For example, the study of Colbert and his great system would be helpful; and from this we can proceed to Colbert's successors, and determine, if possible, to what extent it is true, as has been alleged, that they developed his system into a straight-jacket. In political history we can also study the almost inevitable effect of autocratic power upon the human beings who possess and therefore must exercise it. In the United States at all times the President possesses great power; but in time of war we have sometimes found it necessary to make him a virtual dictator. This Lincoln was; and this, too, was Woodrow Wilson; this Franklin D. Roosevelt is today. As I read his life, the most conclusive, striking, and touching evidence of Abraham Lincoln's greatness was that dictatorial power, while bravely and intelligently used when necessary, was to his mind and heart absolutely repugnant. As a temporary war measure he accepted it; but, even when compelled to use it to the utmost, he looked forward with longing to the day when he could lay it down and resume his status as chief executive of a free people. I do not desire to press the analogy, and especially do not desire to convey the suggestion that I believe the economic dictatorships of the present day are certain to prove temporary. On that subject, indeed, I disavow possession of anything that a scientist should call knowledge. But one thing I know—a thing not gleaned from statistics but from the study of history, biography, and the sayings of the philosophers and sages who in all times and places have studied human nature and recorded their observations. Unless our conjoiners today have the greatness of heart, humility of spirit, dislike of unlimited power, repugnance to dictatorial methods, and the wisdom, the justice, the kindliness, and the humor of Abraham Lincoln, they will fall considerably short of attaining the objectives at which they now aim; and may fall so far short that their conjunctural dictatorships will prove temporary phenomena. Indeed, does not history teach that, among people—for example the ancient Greeks—accustomed to regard themselves as freemen, dictatorship is certainly as subject to change as other forms of government, and perhaps more subject than forms which admit freemen to participate in determining political conjuncture? This conclusion, I hasten to add, is based chiefly on what I have learned from the study of Greek history and from observation of American conjoiners.

The third and final development is one recorded by most of the economic indices that are now available to the student of economic conjuncture. In the spring of 1936 they show that, at some time between the middle of 1932 and the middle of 1933, the process of economic recovery got gradually under way. Even in the United States it is clear that, during these twelve months the general direction of movement of most of the curves reflecting economic conditions was horizontal, in spite of the increasing financial difficulties and the final collapse of the country's banking structure. It is pleasant to refer to this fact, because students of economic conjuncture developed the first of these indices and are now actively carrying on such work in the various committees, institutes, and societies who are glad to number Ernst Wagemann among their collaborators. If our research had accomplished nothing else, it would have justified a thousandfold the very modest sums we have had to spend upon it. In any prior depression, the political party in power in the United States would have claimed for itself entire credit for all the improvement in economic conditions that has taken place since March, 1933. Today, while, naturally enough, it claims as much as possible, and attributes to the previous administration all responsibility for the depression, some of its representatives take account of the fact that economic indices of all nations show, first, that recovery is world-wide, and, second, that not all of it occurred subsequent to March 4, 1933. Students of economic conjuncture can justly claim that they have already done something to moderate partisan discussion of economic problems and to introduce into political controversy some respect for scientific truths capable of statistical demonstration. If my view of the inflation policy of the United States is wholly unfavorable; if I have been unable—with my present knowledge—to present a favorable view of authoritarian control of industry; if, therefore, I am greatly disturbed by one of the outstanding developments of the last three years and am not reassured by the second; I can at least discern one favorable development of great significance and importance, concerning which disinterested scientific study of economic conjuncture is now able to give the world convincing evidence.

III

I have concluded a hazardous undertaking, and offer this brief, inadequate, and imperfect summary of events of the last fifteen years as I have observed them in a scientific laboratory and have sought to interpret them with the aid of history, personal contacts at home and abroad, and, best of all, with the assistance of trusted and valued collaborators in other countries. I rejoice that it has been given to me to have some part in a new scientific movement which, having surmounted many initial difficulties and achieved substantial successes, is, in this year 1936, giving us a book which will be an important milestone in the progress of international collaboration in economic research. To this symposium I should have been glad to bring a better contribution; but time was too short to permit me to offer anything more than some general observations upon certain aspects of the work of students of economic conjuncture who have lived through seventeen memorable years.

I am impressed, as I write these closing words, with the fact that, in this particular field of research, economic science today has a more international character than in any other. If this is true, then it follows that our studies have set an example which in the course of time must affect the work of investigators in other parts of that discipline which we call economics; and in this we have a right to rejoice, for science is always international. In the nationalistic world in which, for a time at least, we must live and conduct our research, we must remember that great scientific research is always the work of a great mind operating freely, impartially, impersonally, and fearlessly; and that such a mind presupposes a free man, that is, a free soul. If our studies are to prosper, they must be carried on in an atmosphere of freedom which may not be easy to preserve in a nationalistic state in a world which seems to be war-minded. However good authoritarian control may be in economic life, it can but blight and wither economic science. Indeed, the best evidence we shall have in the immediate future of the probable success or failure of authoritarian experiments may be the course that rulers pursue toward scientific research in the field of economic conjuncture. If that is shackled, scientific progress stops and decay begins. For a state in which industry is free and economic life has been gradually fashioned by a process of trial and error, neglect or suppression of economic research might be a matter of less importance; but, for an authoritarian state, retrogression in economic science might well prove fatal. If authoritarian conjoiners of the present day respect the scientific freedom of students of economic conjecture, we shall have important evidence that they may be equal to the huge tasks they have set themselves; but if freedom is denied, we shall have persuasive evidence to the contrary. From the policy it follows in respect to economic research we may presently learn the fate of economic authoritarianism.

II

DIRECT TAXES UNDER THE CONSTITUTION[1]

WHEN the Supreme Court of the United States decided that the income-tax law of 1894 was unconstitutional, interest was necessarily revived in that clause of the federal Constitution which requires that direct taxes shall be apportioned among the states "according to their respective numbers." Previous judicial interpretation had for nearly a century limited the application of this provision so narrowly that it had been rendered incapable of causing serious public injury or of arousing general public interest. But our highest tribunal has now decided that hundreds of millions of dollars have been collected in the past by taxes that were unconstitutional and that, for the future, Congress cannot reach property or income except by taxes apportioned according to the rule of numbers. These circumstances seem to justify an inquiry into the genesis and original purpose of the constitutional rule concerning direct taxation.

Such an investigation will be found to raise questions that cannot be answered satisfactorily without a careful study of all the clauses of the Constitution that relate to the powers of Congress in matters of taxation. It will become necessary to consider the experience of the United States, even during the period of the Confederation, before all the facts relating to the direct-tax clause can be seen in their true light. These considerations have determined the form and scope of this article.

I

For twelve years prior to the assembling of the constitutional convention, Congress had been attempting to wage war and

[1] Reprinted from *Political Science Quarterly*, Vol. XV (1900), pp. 217-39, 452-81. Reproduced by generous permission of the publishers.

provide for the ordinary expenses of a league of states without possessing the power to levy or collect taxes. Public expenses had been apportioned among the members of the Confederation, and each had been expected to provide for the payment of its quota of the common charges. The failure of the states to comply with the requisitions made by Congress reduced the United States to bankruptcy and demonstrated the need of a central government that should possess the power of taxation.

Meanwhile Congress experienced the greatest difficulties in securing a satisfactory apportionment of the quotas. This question had arisen when paper money was issued in 1775. Congress allotted to each state a certain quota of the bills of credit and requested that the currency should be redeemed by suitable taxes. These amounts were determined by a provisional assessment, based upon the number of inhabitants of all ages, including negroes and mulattoes.[2] When the system of requisitions was adopted as the method of raising the revenues of the Confederation, the question of apportionment occasioned much debate. The first draft of the eleventh article of the plan of union provided that the public treasury should "be supplied by the several colonies in proportion to the number of inhabitants of every age, sex, and quality, except Indians not paying taxes, in each colony. . . ." The Southern states immediately objected to having the slaves counted equally with the whites. Chase proposed that the requisitions should be apportioned according to the number of white inhabitants. John Adams insisted that all the slaves should be included. Harrison suggested "that two slaves should be counted as one freeman." It is probable that the Southern states would have preferred to have the quotas proportioned to numbers, if Harrison's plan could have been adopted. But the Northern states would not accede to this arrangement and defeated Harrison's amendment by a strictly sectional vote. Later it was proposed to proportion the requisitions to the ascertained value of all property within each state, but this motion failed to

[2] Journals of Congress, July 29, 1775.

pass. Finally, in October, 1777, Congress accepted a suggestion that Witherspoon had made during the debates of the previous year and resolved that the quota of each state should be fixed according to the ascertained value of the land, with the buildings and improvements thereon. This was the plan finally incorporated into the Articles of Confederation; and in 1778 Congress rejected all amendments which some of the states desired to make to this provision.[3]

Such an apportionment of the requisitions proved to be utterly impracticable. Few, if any, of the states took steps to secure a valuation of their lands; and Congress seems to have given the matter little attention until, early in 1783, it requested the states to make the necessary assessments.[4] But this action was soon followed by a proposal to change the method of apportioning the requisitions. The committee on revenue reported an amendment to the Articles of Confederation, providing that the requisitions should thenceforth be divided among the states "in proportion to the number of inhabitants, of every age, sex, and condition, except Indians not paying taxes. . . ."[5] Then followed the inevitable discussion concerning the propriety of including all the slaves in the enumeration. It was suggested that only one-half of the blacks should be counted, then one-fourth and later three-fourths; finally, Madison proposed three-fifths, and Congress at length adopted this proposition, "influenced by the conviction of the necessity of the change, and despair on both sides of a more favorable rate of the slaves."[6]

It proved impossible, however, to induce all the states to accept the amendments which Congress submitted for approval in April, 1783. In 1786 a second attempt was made to secure the acceptance of the amended plan of revenue, but without

[3] Elliot, Debates on the Federal Constitution (Philadelphia, 1836), Vol. I, pp. 70, 72-74, 85-92; Vol. V, p. 79; Works of John Adams (Boston, 1856), Vol. I, p. 496; Journals of Congress, October 13 and 14, 1777; Poore, Federal and State Constitutions of the United States (Washington, 1877), Vol. I, p. 9.

[4] Elliot, Vol. V, pp. 5, 21, 24, 25, 43, 45-47; Journals of Congress, February 17, 1783.

[5] Journals of Congress, March 20, 1783.

[6] Elliot, Vol. V, pp. 79, 81; Journals of Congress, April 1 and 18, 1783.

success; and hence the original plan of assessing quotas was retained until the end of the old Confederation.[7]

II

In the proceedings of the constitutional convention it will be convenient to study first of all the grant of the general power of taxation, which it was decided to confer upon the new government. We may then consider the direct-tax clause and all the other provisions by which Congress was to be restrained in its exercise of the general power. In this manner the purpose of the framers of the Constitution may be set forth in the clearest light possible.

The first proposals concerning the general taxing power of the new government are found in the second and sixth resolutions introduced by Randolph as early as May 29.[8] Of these, the first provided that "the rights of suffrage in the National Legislature ought to be proportioned to the quotas of contribution, or to the number of free inhabitants, as the one or the other rule may seem best in different cases." This suggestion does not imply necessarily that Randolph contemplated the continuance of the requisition system as a means for supplying the public treasury. It is compatible with any plan of federal taxation in which the quota of each state could be ascertained in advance—that is, with any system of apportioned taxes such as prevailed in all the states north of Maryland and Delaware.[9] But the proposi-

[7] In his decision in the income-tax cases, Mr. Justice Fuller falls into a singular error of fact at this point. He bases an argument upon the assumption that the amended plan of apportionment was adopted, whereas it failed of adoption by the votes of one or two states. (158 U. S. Reports, 620, 621.) All the men who discussed the subject in 1787 and 1788 state that the amendment was approved by only eleven or twelve states. See Elliot, Vol. I, p. 485; Peirce and Hale, Debates in the Convention of Massuchsetts (Boston, 1856), p. 299; Ford, Essays on the Constitution (Brooklyn, 1892), pp. 84, 102, 239; Boutell, Life of Roger Sherman (Chicago 1896), p. 174.

[8] Elliot, Vol. I, pp. 143-145, Vol. V, p. 127; the Papers of James Madison (Gilpin's ed., Mobile, 1842), pp. 731, 732. The plan of government proposed by Charles Pinckney is entirely overlooked in this paper, because we have no knowledge as to what its original provisions were.

[9] See Wolcott's report on taxation in the various states in 1796, in American State Papers, Finance, Vol. I, pp. 418-436.

tion would have prevented the use of import and excise duties. Accordingly, when it first came before the convention, King and Madison objected to it, because "the revenue might hereafter be so collected by the general government that the sums respectively drawn from the states would not appear, and would besides be continually varying."[10] The sixth of Randolph's resolutions gave to the national legislature "the legislative rights vested in Congress by the Confederation," with the additional power to legislate "in all cases to which the separate states are incompetent," and "to call forth the force of the Union against any member of the Union failing to fulfill its duty unto the Articles thereof." This plan was evidently intended to give to the federal government adequate powers of taxation, the necessity for which was evident to all who desired to remedy the real weaknesses of the Articles of Confederation.[11]

The resolutions submitted by Patterson, on June 15,[12] conceded to the United States the power to raise revenues from duties on imports, stamp duties and postal charges, in addition to the old requisitions upon the several states. Such requisitions, whenever levied, were to be apportioned according to numbers, in the ascertainment of which all the free inhabitants and three-fifths of all others were to be included. The inadequacy of such a plan was strongly urged by Hamilton, who offered another plan of government. He boldly proposed to give the legislature of the United States "power to pass all laws whatsoever," subject only to the negative of the executive.[13] But, though "praised by everybody," his plan was "supported by none."[14]

In committee of the whole house, Randolph's resolutions were adopted with some amendments; and then, on June 19, were reported to the convention. The amended resolutions did not suggest the quotas of contributions as the basis of representa-

[10] Elliot, Vol. V, p. 134; *cf.* 178.

[11] On this point see references given by Story, Commentaries on the Constitution, Secs. 932-948 (fifth edition, Boston, 1891).

[12] Elliot, Vol. I, pp. 175-177; Vol. V, pp. 191, 192.

[13] *Ibid.*, Vol. I, p. 179; Vol. V, pp. 201, 205.

[14] From Johnson, in Yates's Minutes.—Elliot, Vol. I, p. 431.

tion, but the general grant of legislative powers remained practically as drafted by Randolph, except for the omission of the words, "to call forth the force of the Union against any member of the Union failing to fulfill its duty under the Articles thereof."[15]

From June 19 to July 26, the report of the committee of the whole was considered by the convention. During the controversy over the question of representation in the national legislature, it was voted that "direct taxation ought to be proportioned to representation."[16] In connection with other questions, a few additional limitations were imposed upon the taxing power of Congress; but it will be shown in subsequent pages that all these restrictions were the result of some special interest or exigency, and were not due to a general desire to limit the new government in its right of taxing its citizens. After the rejection of Patterson's proposal to concede to the United States merely the right to levy impost and stamp duties, there is no evidence of any general desire in the convention to withhold from Congress all necessary powers of taxation.

On July 26, the convention referred to a committee of detail twenty-three resolutions, embodying the results of its deliberations. The right of levying taxes was conceded to the national legislature in the sixth resolution, which was retained largely in the form in which it was submitted by Randolph.[17] Eleven days later, the committee of detail submitted the first draft of a constitution. In conformity with the decision of the convention, the committee had enumerated carefully the specific powers that should be conferred upon Congress. The first section of article eight provided: "The legislature of the United States shall have the power to lay and collect taxes, duties, imposts, and ex-

[15] Elliot, Vol. I, pp. 180-183; Vol. V, pp. 189, 190, 212.

[16] *Ibid.*, Vol. I, p. 201; Vol. V, p. 302.

[17] *Ibid.*, Vol. I, p. 221; Vol. V, p. 375. The resolution was as follows: "That the national legislature ought to possess the legislative rights vested in Congress by the Confederation; and moreover, to legislate, in all cases, for the general interests of the Union, and also in those to which the states are separately incompetent, or in which the harmony of the United States may be interrupted by the exercise of individual legislation." Compare Story, Commentaries, Sec. 928.

cises; . . ."[18] This power was limited in certain directions, as will be shown elsewhere; but the grant was broad enough, expressed as it was in terms that included all four of the common names for taxes,[19] to confer upon the new government adequate powers of taxation. When Luther Martin proposed to allow Congress to levy and collect direct taxes only after a failure to secure from the states a compliance with its requisitions for the necessary revenues, his motion secured the approval of only one state.[20]

On August 23, this grant of the power to levy taxes was amended, in order to make more secure provision for the public debt. In its amended form, this section of the drafted constitution stood as follows:[21] "The legislature shall fulfill the engagements and discharge the debts of the United States, and shall have the power to lay and collect taxes, duties, imposts, and excises." Two days later, this was reconsidered, and Randolph moved to postpone the clause, in favor of the following resolution:[22] "All debts contracted, and engagements entered into, by or under the authority of Congress, shall be as valid against the United States under the Constitution as under the Confederation." When this had been adopted, Mr. Sherman insisted that it was still desirable "to connect with the clause for laying taxes, duties, *etc.*, an express provision for the object of the old debts. . . ." He moved, therefore, to add to the clause giving the right to levy taxes the words, "for the payment of said debts, and for defraying the expenses that shall be incurred for the common defense and general welfare." This proposal was rejected, on the ground that it was unnecessary. But, on August 31, this section of the constitution, together with some others, was referred to a grand committee, of which Sherman was a member. Four days later, this committee reported the following amended resolution: "The legislature shall have power to lay and collect taxes, duties, imposts, and excises; to pay the debts

[18] Elliot, Vol. I, p. 226; Vol. V, pp. 378, 379.
[19] Story, Commentaries, Sec. 950.
[20] Elliot, Vol. I, p. 255; Vol. V, p. 453.
[21] *Ibid.*, Vol. I, p. 260; Vol. V, p. 469.
[22] *Ibid.*, Vol. I, p. 264; Vol. V, p. 476.

and provide for the common defense and general welfare of the United States." This resolution was adopted by the convention without dissent.[23] In the final draft of the constitution, a clause was added requiring uniformity in the assessment of duties, imposts and excises. This may be passed over for the present. In other respects, the resolution of September 4 stands unaltered in the completed Constitution, except for the substitution of the word Congress for the word legislature.[24]

Thus, finally, Sherman's amendment was added to the grant of the power to levy taxes. Without entering further into a discussion of the interpretation of the "general welfare" clause, it may be pointed out that the procedure of the convention shows conclusively that the words were inserted originally as a qualification of the grant of the taxing power. By this amendment, the right to levy taxes was limited to the purposes specified—namely, "to pay the debts, and provide for the common defense and general welfare of the United States."[25]

III

Postponing for the moment the constitutional provisions concerning direct taxes, it is now in order to consider various other proposals for limiting the taxing power of Congress in certain directions. On August 18, Pinckney urged that the committee of detail should prepare a resolution restraining the legislature of the United States from establishing a perpetual revenue; and, upon a motion of Mr. Mason, this suggestion was adopted.[26] Four days later, the committee recommended that the following words should be added to the clause giving Congress the power to levy taxes: "for payment of the debts and necessary expenses of the United States; provided that no law for raising any

[23] *Ibid.*, Vol. I, pp. 280, 283, 284; Vol. V, pp. 503, 506.

[24] Poore, Federal and State Constitutions, Vol. I, p. 15.

[25] On the subject see Story, Commentaries, Secs. 911-931; Curtis, Constitutional History (N. Y., 1889), Vol. I, pp. 518-521. Note also the amendment to this clause proposed in Congress, shortly after the adoption of the constitution.—H. V. Ames, Amendments to the Constitution of the United States, p. 242. (Washington, 1897.)

[26] Elliot, Vol. V, pp. 440, 441.

branch of revenue, except what may be specially appropriated for the payment of interest on debts or loans, shall continue in force for more than —— years." This proposal had not received the attention of the convention when, on August 31, such parts of the constitution or amendments as had not been considered were referred to a general committee.[27] On September 4, this committee reported a revenue clause which did not contain a prohibition of tax laws that should remain in continuous operation.

The ninth section of the first article of the constitution prohibited Congress from taxing exports and limited the amount of the duties that could be imposed upon the importation of slaves. These two limitations of the taxing power had a common origin, and were closely connected in the deliberations of the constitutional convention. On June 12, Pinckney expressed a desire that the legislature might be prohibited from taxing exports, since such imposts would strike chiefly the products of the labor of the slaves.[28] It was not strange that such a question arose. During the colonial period, tobacco had been almost the only article that could bear an export duty,[29] and the Southern colonies had been the only ones that could make much use of such an impost. In the fiscal years 1790 and 1791, tobacco, rice and indigo, produced almost exclusively in the slave states, constituted nearly one-third of the total exports from the United States,[30] and would have offered almost the only promising field where export duties could have been applied without destroying the possibility of further exportations. On July 23, Pinckney asserted that, "if the committee should fail to insert some security to the Southern States against an emancipation of the slaves, and taxes on exports, he should be bound by his duty to his state to vote against their report."[31]

[27] Elliot, Vol. I, pp. 256, 285; Vol. V, pp. 462, 503.

[28] *Ibid.*, Vol. V, p. 302.

[29] W. Hill, First Stages of the Tariff Policy of the United States, pp. 23-26 (Publications of the American Economic Association, Baltimore, 1893).

[30] See American State Papers, Commerce and Navigation, Vol. I, pp. 23-33, 103-146.

[31] Elliot, Vol. V, p. 357.

In the report submitted by the committee of detail, on August 6, the following provisions were inserted:

No tax or duty shall be laid by the legislature on articles exported from any state; nor on the migration or importation of such persons as the several states shall think proper to admit; nor shall such migration or importation be prohibited.[32]

In the discussions that followed, the restriction on the power of Congress to tax exports was opposed by Morris, Wilson and Madison. Of the Southern members, Mason, Butler, Carroll, Mercer and Williamson favored it; while, of the Northern delegates, Gerry, Sherman and Ellsworth considered the restriction necessary.[33] Sherman and Ellsworth urged that exports could not be taxed without injuring trade and arousing sectional jealousies. While a number of Northern delegates were inclined to Sherman's opinion, that "the complexity of the business in America would render an equal tax on exports impracticable," the debates make it evident that the real moving force back of this prohibition was the fear of the South that the value of the negroes might be decreased by export duties on the peculiar products of slave labor.[34] The clause was finally passed by seven states against four.[35] Massachusetts and Connecticut voted in the affirmative with the five Southern states, while New Hampshire, New Jersey, Pennsylvania and Delaware were counted in the negative.

The other clauses reported by the committee of detail, on August 6, prohibited the imposition of duties on slaves imported into the United States and prevented Congress from interfering with the external slave trade. These aroused fierce debates upon the question of slavery, and did not pass until they had been materially amended. As the result of a compromise, in which the South conceded the right of Congress to regulate commerce, the convention finally adopted the following provision:

[32] *Ibid.*, Vol. I, p. 227; Vol. V, p. 379.

[33] Elliot, Vol. V, pp. 432-434, 454-456; Gilpin, pp. 1339-1343, 1382-1387.

[34] On this subject see Curtis, Vol. I, pp. 495-498, 504; Bancroft, History (author's last revision, 1891); Vol. VI, pp. 315-316.

[35] Elliot, Vol. I, p. 255; Vol. V, p. 457.

The migration or importation of such persons as the several states now existing shall think proper to admit shall not be prohibited by the legislature prior to the year 1808, but a tax or duty may be imposed on such importation, not exceeding ten dollars for each person.[36]

In the revised draft of the constitution, submitted by the committee of revision on September 12, the clause prohibiting the taxation of exports is separated from that which relates to the taxation of persons imported into the United States.[37] But the proceedings of the convention show that both of these restraints upon the taxing power of Congress grew out of the anxiety of the South for the safety of its peculiar institution.

Another restriction upon the power of Congress to levy taxes was proposed for the first time on August 25. Upon the previous day the committee appointed to consider the slave trade and the regulation of commerce had reported in favor of allowing the legislature to pass navigation acts by a simple majority vote. In the discussions that followed, anxiety was expressed lest the legislature should favor the ports of some states in preference to those of others. Two sets of resolutions were then introduced, in order to prevent such discriminations.[38] Of these, the latter provided, among other restrictions, that "all duties, imposts, and excises, prohibitions or restraints, laid or made by the legislature of the United States, shall be uniform and equal throughout the United States." These resolutions were referred to a grand committee, which, on August 28, reported the following clause:

Nor shall any regulation of commerce or revenue give preference to the ports of one state over those of another, or oblige vessels bound to or from any state to enter or pay duties in another. And all tonnage, duties, imposts, and excises, laid by the legislature, shall be uniform throughout the United States.

Three days later, the convention, after striking out the word tonnage, adopted this provision.[39]

36 *Ibid.*, Vol. I, pp. 256, 261, 265; Vol. V, pp. 461, 470, 471, 477, 478.

37 Elliot, Vol. I, p. 301; Vol. V, p. 561.

38 *Ibid.*, Vol. I, pp. 227, 261, 265, 266; Vol. V, pp. 379, 471, 479.

39 *Ibid.*, Vol. I, pp. 270, 279, 280; Vol. V, pp. 483, 484, 502, 503.

On September 14, while the final draft of the constitution was under consideration, these resolutions were placed in separate sections. It was voted that, to the clause conferring on Congress the power of taxation, should be added the words, "but all duties, imposts, and excises shall be uniform throughout the United States." The origin of the clause shows that it was intended to secure territorial uniformity in the imposition of duties, imposts, and excises, and "to cut off all undue preferences of one state over another, in the regulation of subjects affecting their common interests."[40]

IV

We are now ready to study the proceedings of the constitutional convention on the subject of the apportionment of direct taxes. It has already been shown that Randolph's original resolutions had proposed to apportion representation in the national legislature according to either the quotas of contribution or the number of free inhabitants in the several states. When the convention went into committee of the whole to consider Randolph's resolutions, the question of representation engrossed a large portion of its attention. Out of the disputes occasioned by this troublesome subject sprang the proposal to limit the powers of Congress in levying direct taxes. It is necessary, therefore, to study the entire controversy over the question of representation.

After the convention had determined that the national legislature should consist of two branches, it was voted that the lower house should be elected by the people and that the upper house should be chosen by the legislatures of the states. Then came the critical question: What shall be the basis of representation? This brought on the well-known controversy between the smaller states, which demanded equal rights, and the larger states, which advocated proportional representation.

On June 11, the committee of the whole voted[41] that the

[40] Elliot, Vol. I, p. 311. See Story, Sec. 957; Curtis, Vol. I, p. 522.

[41] Elliot, Vol. I, pp. 168, 169; Vol. V, p. 181. See Bancroft, Vol. VI, p. 228; Curtis, Vol. I, pp. 340, 343; Hildreth, History of the United States (New York, 1856), Vol. III, pp. 486-489.

rights of suffrage in the lower house should be proportioned to the whole number of free inhabitants and three-fifths of all other persons, except Indians not paying taxes, in each state. This, it will be remembered, was the basis adopted by Congress in its resolution of April 18, 1783, concerning the apportionment of requisitions. Upon the same day, by a vote of six against five, the larger states carried a motion that the right of suffrage in the upper house of the legislature should be according to the rule established for the lower; and then, on June 19, the committee of the whole made its final report to the convention. After discussion of this report, the convention finally voted, June 29, that the right of suffrage in the lower house "ought not to be according to the rule established in the Articles of Confederation, but according to some equitable ratio of representation." Then the small states made a determined struggle to secure equal representation in the upper house. But a motion conceding this point was defeated by a tie vote, Georgia's delegates being divided.[42] Thus it seemed that a deadlock must ensue. But the entire subject of representation was finally referred to a grand committee for further consideration. On July 5, this committee reported a plan brought forward by Franklin, proposing that in the lower house each state should have one representative for every forty thousand inhabitants, including all the whites and three-fifths of the blacks, while in the upper house each state should have an equal voice. But this arrangement failed to satisfy the convention at that moment, and a long debate ensued. Some members did not like the proposed scheme for regulating representation in the lower house, though little was said at the moment concerning the representation for three-fifths of the slaves. Others still opposed equal representation in the upper house, and a warm discussion followed between delegates from the larger states and those from the smaller. On July 6, the convention resolved to refer to a committee of five the question of the proper basis of representation in the lower house. On the next day it was agreed that the

[42] Elliot, Vol. I, pp. 169, 181-183, 192, 193; Vol. V, pp. 182, 259, 269, 270.

states should have equal votes in the upper branch of the legislature. This decision tended to allay the strife between the larger and the smaller states, although one more attempt was made, a few days later, to destroy the equality of suffrage in the upper house. Mutterings of discontent were, indeed, heard up to July 16, when, Madison tells us, the delegates from the larger states finally decided that such a concession to the smaller states was an absolute necessity.[43]

But the question of representation in the lower house was not so easily settled. When the convention agreed that in this branch proportional representation should be the rule, the difficulties had merely commenced. For several days interest centered around the basis of representation in the lower house. In the course of the deliberations the parties of the large and the small states almost disappeared, and distinct Northern and Southern parties were formed.[44] Madison declared, July 14:

> It seemed now to be pretty well understood that the real difference of interest lay, not between the large and small, but between the northern and southern states. The institution of slavery, and its consequences, formed the line of discrimination.[45]

In this controversy the direct-tax clause of the constitution originated.

It has been shown that, on July 6, a committee of five was instructed to devise a plan for settling the question of representation in the lower house of the national legislature. On July 9, this committee reported a scheme by which, for the first meeting of the new legislature, fifty-six members should be apportioned among the several states. It was further recommended that, in future apportionments, the legislature should "regulate the number of representatives, in any of the foregoing cases, upon the principles of their wealth and numbers." This latter recommendation was considered first by the convention, and was adopted.[46] It is important to remem-

[43] Elliot, Vol. I, pp. 195, 196, 205; Vol. V, pp. 280, 281, 285, 286, 311, 319.

[44] This is best appreciated by Hildreth. See his History, Vol. III, pp. 496-501.

[45] Elliot, Vol. V, p. 315. *Cf.* the words of King to the same effect.—Elliot, Vol. V, pp. 290, 291.

[46] *Ibid.*, Vol. I, pp. 197; Vol. V, pp. 287, 288.

ber this fact, because the discussions of the next few days need to be interpreted in the light of this decision.

At this point a new consideration was brought into the debate. A few members of the convention entertained some jealousy toward the growing power of the West. Three of these delegates, Morris, Gorham and King, were members of the committee of five. When asked for the reasons that had induced the committee to combine wealth and numbers in the basis of representation, Gorham stated that such a provision was necessary, in order to prevent the Western states from outvoting the Atlantic states at some future time.[47] Like arguments were advanced by Gerry, King and Morris during the next few days, and were answered promptly by Mason, Randolph, Madison, Wilson and Sherman.[48] When, July 14, Gerry moved that the number of representatives should be so regulated that states subsequently admitted could never outvote the original members of the Union, the convention rejected the proposal. Massachusetts, Connecticut, Delaware and Maryland were the only states to favor Gerry's motion; and, of these, the votes of Delaware and Maryland were probably nothing more than "the dying expression of old regrets about the proprietaryship of western lands."[49] It is probable that the extent and importance of the jealousy of the West has been exaggerated; but, in any case, the discussion of the subject centered around the question of representation, not that of taxation.

The first recommendation contained in the report of the committee of five did not meet the approval of the convention. The committee's scheme of apportionment awarded twenty-six members to the Southern states and thirty members to the Northern. Upon the motion of Sherman, the subject was referred to another committee consisting of one member from each state; and on July 10 this committee recommended that the first lower house should consist of sixty-five representatives, of which number thirty-five were allotted to the North and thirty to the

[47] Elliot, Vol. V, p. 238.
[48] See Elliot, Vol. V, pp. 288-318, *passim*.
[49] *Ibid.*, Vol. I, p. 204; Vol. V, p. 312. See Bancroft, Vol. VI, p. 264.

South.[50] After various unsuccessful attempts to reduce the representation of New Hampshire and to increase that of the Southern states, the convention finally adopted the distribution recommended by the committee. The discussions of the subject more and more brought the question of slavery to the front,[51] from July 10 to 12 nearly all debate turned on the opposing interests of the Northern and the Southern states.

After the final vote on the distribution of members, Randolph proposed an important amendment to the second paragraph of the report that the committee of five had submitted on the previous day (July 9). This paragraph, which had been accepted by the convention, provided that the national legislature, whenever occasion might arise, should be "authorized" to augment the number of representatives, following numbers and wealth as the rule of apportionment. The control of future representation was thus left wholly to the discretion of the legislature. As the Northern states were to have thirty-five out of the sixty-five members in the lower branch of the first legislature, this plan would enable the North to control all future representation. The delegates from the South were alarmed at such a prospect. Randolph proposed, therefore, that the paragraph should be amended, so as to oblige the legislature "to cause a proper census and estimate to be taken once in every term of——years." This reasonable suggestion was opposed, especially by Morris and King, on the ground that it would be unwise to fetter the legislature by any rigid constitutional requirement.

Sectional lines having been most sharply drawn, the debates became more heated and excited. On July 11, Randolph's proposition was withdrawn in favor of the following resolution, introduced by Williamson, of North Carolina:

Resolved, That, in order to ascertain the alterations that may happen in the population and wealth of the several states, a census shall be taken of the free inhabitants of each state, and three-fifths of the

[50] Elliot, Vol. I, p. 198; Vol. V, p. 293. See Bancroft, Vol. VI, p. 258; Curtis, Vol. I, p. 407.

[51] Elliot, Vol. I, p. 199; Vol. V, p. 293. See especially the speech by King, Vol. V, pp. 290, 291.

inhabitants of the other description, on the first year after this form of government shall have been adopted, and afterwards on every term of —— years; and the legislature shall alter or augment the representation accordingly.[52]

This resolution not only made periodical apportionments obligatory, but marked the return to numbers as the sole rule for representation. In including three-fifths of the slaves, Williamson followed the expedient that had been previously recommended. But this device no longer satisfied the extremists of either the North or the South. Butler and Pinckney moved that all the slaves should be enumerated for the purpose of determining each state's representation, but their demand was refused. Then the convention adopted that part of Williamson's resolution which provided for the enumeration of all the white inhabitants. This brought the members to the single question, whether three-fifths of the slaves should be included also. King and Morris antagonized the proposition most strenuously. Finally, the extremists on both sides—those who desired to have all the slaves counted and those who refused to allow any blacks to be enumerated—combined to defeat the three-fifths clause. After this, Williamson's entire resolution was rejected by a unanimous vote,[53] and the delegates seemed more widely divided than ever. The defeat of Williamson's motion left before the convention the amended report of the compromise committee of July 5, providing that the lower house of the first legislature should consist of sixty-five members and that the legislature might adjust future representation according to the rule of wealth and numbers.

When the convention assembled on the morning of July 12, the sole question of immediate interest was that of representation for slaves. For the time being, the controversy between the large and the small states was entirely forgotten. At this juncture, Gouverneur Morris came forward with a proposal which he designed "as a bridge to assist" the convention "over

[52] Elliot, Vol. I, p. 199; Vol. V, p. 295.

[53] Elliot, Vol. I, pp. 199-201; Vol. V, pp. 296, 300-302. *Cf.* Curtis, Vol. I, pp. 410, 411; Bancroft, Vol. VI, p. 265; Hildreth, Vol. III, p. 500.

a certain gulf."[54] He moved to add to the clause authorizing the legislature to regulate representation according to wealth and numbers, the provision that "taxation shall be in proportion to representation."[55] This proposal was intended to make the South less desirous of securing representation for all the slaves, since its share of public burdens would be increased proportionally. On the other hand, such a plan would tend to decrease the opposition of the North to admitting some portion of the slaves into the rule for representation.[56] But, contrary to Morris's expectation, Butler, of South Carolina, immediately demanded representation for all the slaves, although he conceded the justice of the new proposition. On the other hand, Mason and Wilson objected that the provision advocated by Morris "might drive the legislature to the plan of requisitions." This criticism was regarded as a serious one, for no member manifested a desire to restrict the taxing power in such a way as to cripple its effectiveness for purposes of revenue. Accordingly, Morris "admitted that some objections lay against his motion, but supposed they would be removed by restraining the rule to *direct* taxation." With regard "to indirect taxes on exports and imports, and on consumption, the rule would be inapplicable."[57] Therefore, the motion was amended; and, without dissent, it passed the convention in the following form: "*Provided always*, That direct taxation ought to be proportioned according to representation."

Two conclusions stand out clearly from the foregoing recital

[54] These are Morris's own words.—Elliot, Vol. V, p. 363.

[55] Elliot, Vol. V, p. 302. This seems to have been an entirely novel suggestion. Precedents might have been found for the reverse proposal—to proportion representation to taxation. In the Continental Congress Middleton had proposed, in 1776, that the colonies should vote according to the amounts they paid in requisitions. (Works of John Adams, Vol. II, p. 499.) The following year a similar motion was defeated. (Journals of Congress, October 13, 1777.) In the convention Randolph had originally proposed the quotas of contribution as a basis for determining representation. (Elliot, Vol. V, p. 127.) On June 11 it was twice proposed to take the actual contributions of the states as the "equitable ratio of representation." (Elliot, Vol. V, pp. 179, 181.)

[56] Such is Madison's explanation.—See Elliot, Vol. V, p. 363, note.

[57] Elliot, Vol. V, p. 302.

of facts. First, the resolution of Morris was intended simply as a means of harmonizing differences between the free and the slave states. Second, it was not designed to injure, much less to cripple, the taxing power of the new government.[58] There is no reason for thinking that any such measure would have been suggested, if the dispute over the representation for the blacks had not taken the turn that it did. One other consideration should be emphasized. Morris's amendment was added to a resolution which provided for representation according to wealth and numbers. It did not contemplate originally an apportionment of direct taxes upon the basis of population alone.

After Morris's motion had been passed, the Southern delegates desired to have the rule of wealth and numbers more explicitly defined. Pinckney urged that the clause, as it stood, left the legislature entire freedom in the manner of ascertaining the wealth of the states, and he demanded protection for property in slaves. Randolph urged the same considerations that he had presented the previous day, against leaving the future regulation of representation entirely to the discretion of the legislature: "Express security," he argued, "ought to be provided for including slaves in the ratio of representation"; he "lamented that such a species of property existed; but, as it did exist, the holders of it would require this security." In accordance with these demands, a motion, made by Randolph and amended by Wilson, was passed in the following form:

Provided always, That representation ought to be proportioned according to direct taxation; and, in order to ascertain the alterations in the direct taxation which may be required, from time to time, by the changes in the relative circumstances of the states, . . . *Resolved,* That a census be taken within six years from the first meeting of the legislature of the United States, and once within the term of every ten years afterwards, of all the inhabitants of the United

[58] This is well shown by the fact that the motion passed unanimously, securing the support of those members who opposed most strenuously all proposals that seemed likely to make the taxing power of Congress ineffective. Thus, the motion was supported by Morris, Madison and Wilson, all of whom had opposed the proposal to prohibit Congress from taxing exports.—Elliot, Vol. V, pp. 432, 433, 454-456.

States, in the manner, and according to the ratio, recommended by Congress in their resolution of April 18, 1783; and that the legislature of the United States shall proportion the direct taxation accordingly.[59]

The reader will remember that the resolution of April 18, 1783, provided that all free inhabitants and three-fifths of the slaves should be included in the basis of apportionment of the requisitions. The motion passed by the convention was purposely worded so as to avoid the actual mention of slaves.

On July 13, Randolph proposed another amendment. The resolutions adopted on the previous day had all been in amendment of the original proposition that the legislature might regulate representation in the lower branch according to the rule of wealth and numbers. The convention had now decided that representation should be proportioned to direct taxation and that direct taxation should be divided among the states in proportion to population. In order to secure entire clearness, Randolph moved that the word "wealth" should be stricken out of the original motion.[60] This was agreed to by a nearly unanimous vote. Thus the original proposal was made to read that future representation should be adjusted to the number of inhabitants of the respective states; while amendments provided that representation should be proportioned to direct taxation and that direct taxation should be divided among the states according to the rule of numbers, including three-fifths of the slaves.[61]

This was the final form of the compromise between the North and the South over representation in the lower house.[62] With this difficult question settled, the large and the small states found time, on July 14, to indulge in one more controversy over the equal vote of the states in the upper branch of the legislature.[63] Upon July 16, the report of the grand committee, as

[59] Elliot, Vol. I, pp. 201-203; Vol. V, pp. 303-306.

[60] Elliot, Vol. I, p. 204; Vol. V, pp. 307-309.

[61] These final resolutions may be found most easily in Elliot, Vol. I, pp. 202-204, 222, 223.

[62] On August 8, Morris moved once more to strike out the provision allowing representation for three-fifths of the slaves, but he secured the vote of only one state.—Elliot, Vol. I, p. 233; Vol. V, p. 392-394.

[63] Elliot, Vol. V, pp. 310-316.

amended, was finally adopted, but by the narrowest of majorities; and this was generally accepted as a final settlement of differences over the question of representation.[64]

In the first draft of the constitution,[65] submitted by the committee of detail on August 6, these resolutions relating to representation and direct taxes were separated. The provision regarding the number of representatives in the lower house of the first Congress and that concerning the apportionment of future representatives by the prescribed rule of population were placed in the fourth article. The provision concerning the apportionment of direct taxes was placed in the seventh article, which enumerated the powers of Congress.[66] This arrangement was changed by the committee of revision. All the provisions concerning the apportionment of representatives and direct taxes were brought together in section two of article one:[67]

Representatives and direct taxes shall be apportioned among the several states which may be included within this Union, according to their respective numbers, which shall be determined by adding to the whole number of free persons, including those bound to servitude for a term of years, and excluding Indians not taxed, three-fifths of all other persons. The actual enumeration shall be made within three years after the first meeting of the Congress of the United States, and within every subsequent term of ten years, in such manner as they shall by law direct. The number of representatives shall not exceed one for

[64] *Ibid.*, Vol. I, pp. 205, 206; Vol. V, pp. 316, 317, 319, note. Upon July 24, Morris endeavored to induce the convention "to strike out the whole of the clause proportioning direct taxation to representation." He said that he had intended it merely as a bridge over a certain gulf, and he believed the bridge could be removed now that the gulf had been crossed. He thought that the rule was open to strong objections. But it was too late to disturb the compromise that had been effected with so much difficulty.—Elliot, Vol. V, pp. 362, 363.

[65] On August 25, while this draft was under discussion, Luther Martin proposed an amendment, which provided that the United States should not possess the power to levy and collect direct taxes until requisitions for the amounts due should have been made upon the several states and should have been refused. It is not recorded that the members of the convention considered this proposal worth discussion. At any rate, the motion was defeated by an overwhelming vote, in which Martin secured the support only of one of his Maryland colleagues and of the state of New Jersey.—Elliot, Vol. I, p. 255; Vol. V, p. 453.

[66] Elliot, Vol. I, pp. 224, 227; Vol. V, pp. 377, 379.

[67] *Ibid.*, Vol. I, p. 298.

every forty thousand, but each state shall have at least one representative; and until such enumeration shall be made, the state of New Hampshire shall be entitled to choose three, Massachusetts eight, Rhode Island and Providence Plantations one, Connecticut five, New York six, New Jersey four, Pennsylvania eight, Delaware one, Maryland six, Virginia ten, North Carolina five, South Carolina five, and Georgia three.

While the final draft of the constitution was under consideration, Dickinson and Wilson moved to strike out the words "direct taxes" from this clause, on the ground that the expression was out of place in an article which related merely to the constitution of the House of Representatives. The motion was defeated, however, by a vote of eight states to three; and the clause, without amendment, became a part of the constitution.[68]

Before leaving this subject, mention must be made of a second constitutional provision concerning direct taxes. On July 13, after the rule for apportioning representatives and direct taxes had been established, the convention adopted a resolution which required that, until the first census should be taken, direct taxes should be divided among the states in proportion to the number of representatives allowed to each in the first Congress.[69] This resolution does not appear among those referred to the committee of detail on July 26.[70] That committee, however, submitted the following proposition in their report of August 6: "No capitation tax shall be laid, unless in proportion to the census herein before directed to be taken."[71] This prohibited Congress from levying one kind of a direct tax before the census should be completed; and the purpose of the provision was to make it impossible for Congress to render slavery unprofitable by heavy taxation of the slaves.[72] It seems strange that such a clause should have

[68] Elliot, Vol. I, p. 308; Vol. V, p. 540. Gilpin, pp. 1569, 1570.
[69] Elliot, Vol. I, p. 203; Vol. V, pp. 306, 307.
[70] *Ibid.*, Vol. I, pp. 221, 222; Vol. V, pp. 375, 376.
[71] *Ibid.*, Vol. I, p. 227; Vol. V, p. 379.
[72] See explanation made by Baldwin, a member of the convention, in the House of Representatives, on February 12, 1790. (Annals of Congress, First Congress,

been deemed necessary; for the rule for direct taxation had been established, and it was never doubted at any time that capitation taxes were direct, within the meaning of the constitution. But the Southern members may have feared that, before a census could be taken, Congress might make an arbitrary estimate of population and might apportion a capitation tax unfairly, in such a manner as to lay disproportionate burdens upon owners of slaves. Gerry made an effort, on August 20, to have the convention adopt the original motion concerning the assessment of direct taxes before the taking of the first census. His proposition was rejected as unnecessary, but the clause reported by the committee of detail was accepted.[73]

An amendment was adopted by the convention on September 14, when the final draft of the constitution was under consideration. Read suggested that the words "or other direct tax" be inserted after the word "capitation," and the motion was carried.[74] His purpose was to prevent Congress from attempting "to saddle the states with a readjustment, by this rule, of past requisitions of Congress."

V

This study of the procedure of the federal convention has shown that there was manifested no general desire to limit the taxing powers of the new government. Patterson's plan, which would have restricted Congress to impost and stamp duties, received the support of only two states; while Randolph's propositions were reported to the convention by a vote of seven states to three, Maryland's delegates being equally divided.[75] But in a few directions limitations were finally imposed. When

---

Vol. I, pp. 1242, 1243.) In the Virginia convention this subject came up for discussion. (Elliot, Vol. III, 456-458.) Mr. George Mason urged that this clause was "a mere confirmation of the clause which fixed the ratio of taxes and representation." In the subsequent debates of the federal convention, this clause was always grouped with those relating to taxation of the slave trade, navigation acts, etc.

[73] Elliot, Vol. I, pp. 253, 254, 261, 265; Vol. V, pp. 451-453, 471, 478.

[74] *Ibid.*, Vol. I, p. 311; Vol. V, p. 545.

[75] Elliot, Vol. I, p. 180; Vol. V, pp. 211, 212.

the power of regulating commerce was granted, the convention provided that duties, imposts and excises should be uniform throughout the United States. Then the institution of slavery required and secured protection in three provisions—namely, the limitation of the duties that could be imposed upon the importation of negroes, the prohibition of taxes on exports and the specific provision concerning capitation taxes. Finally, out of the controversy over representation for the slaves in the apportionment of members of the House of Representatives, there came the requirement that direct taxes and representatives should be apportioned according to the rule of numbers. Thus it seems that the constitutional requirement concerning direct taxes originated in the struggle to effect a compromise on the question of representation for the slaves. It had no basis in any rational scheme for regulating taxation, and could have had none. There is no reason for thinking that such a plan would have occurred to any one, had the convention not been at its wit's end for some method of effecting an adjustment of the question of representation. Historically, the provision must be viewed as a relic of the great compromise upon the subject of slavery.

But different views have been advanced. Mr. George Ticknor Curtis argued, in 1866, that the direct-tax clause was an intentional limitation of the power of Congress. He held that, after the states gave up to the general government the exclusive right of levying customs duties, they refused to concede full powers of direct taxation concurrent with their own.[76] In the income-tax cases, in 1895, Chief Justice Fuller gave a somewhat similar explanation. "The men who formed and adopted that instrument," he said, "had just emerged from the struggle

[76] *Harper's Magazine*, Vol. XXXIII, p. 359. Mr. Curtis also advanced a second reason. He said that the people "had never been accustomed to have a direct tax imposed without apportionment among the local subdivisions of the state." Nothing could be further from the truth. In all states south of Delaware, "taxes were laid directly on persons or the property of individuals by the state." (R. T. Ely, Taxation in American States and Cities, p. 123. See Wolcott's report on direct taxes, State Papers, Finance, Vol. I.) In the states north of Delaware, taxes were apportioned among counties and towns, but according to assessed valuations, not according to the absurd and inequitable rule of numbers.

for independence, whose rallying cry had been that 'taxation and representation go together.' " This principle was incorporated in the constitution, so that whenever Congress should vote a tax, "it would fall proportionately upon the immediate constituents of those who imposed it." More than this, the states surrendered their power to tax imports. Therefore, in giving Congress "power to tax persons and property directly," they did so "in reliance on the protection afforded by restrictions on the grant of power." "If, in the changes of wealth and population in particular states, apportionment produced inequality, it was an inequality stipulated for, just as the equal representation of the states, however small, in the Senate, was stipulated for."[77]

Again, Mr. Justice Field, in his tirade against the legislators who passed the income-tax law, found time for a few remarks concerning the origin of this constitutional provision. He said that the convention was greatly embarrassed, first, by the disinclination of the importing states to give up their right to levy import duties and, second, by the fear on the part of the small states that the larger states might impose unequal burdens upon them, if the power to tax directly real and personal property should be surrendered to Congress. This embarrassment, he declared, was so great as to threaten the dissolution of the convention, and the direct-tax clause was finally formulated as a compromise on this important point.[78] Justice Field confined himself to generalities, and did not refer in detail to the proceedings of the convention. This was fortunate for the argument; for an examination of the debates shows that no member of the convention was inclined to question the propriety or expediency of giving Congress power to levy import duties;

[77] 157 U. S. Reports, pp. 556, 557; 158 U. S. Reports, pp. 620, 621.

[78] 157 U. S. Reports, p. 587. There is no doubt that Justice Field formed this opinion as a result of a correspondence with the late David A. Wells. The writer is informed by a friend, who holds the chair of political economy in a well-known university, that he saw one letter which Wells wrote to Field, and that this letter was incorporated almost literally in Field's opinion. In the *Popular Science Monthly* (Vol. LIII, pp. 385, 386), Mr. Wells discusses the purpose of the direct-tax clause in language which is almost the same, word for word, as that used by Justice Field.

that the fears of the small states concerned the general influence of the large states in matters of legislation, not in taxation, as a principal source of danger; and that the direct-tax clause was introduced in the middle of a heated controversy over representation for slaves, and without any reference to questions of taxation. There is not one word in the proceedings of the convention to justify the claim that difficulties on the subject of taxation threatened to bring its efforts to naught.

Views similar to those of Justices Fuller and Field were advanced by the counsel in the income-tax cases. It was urged that the older and richer states had been jealous of the growing power of the West, and had inserted this clause in order to prevent a combination of Western states from imposing heavy burdens on the richer communities of the Atlantic coast; and even that this provision was "designed for the protection or advantage of some set of persons or some particular interest or interests," and that the rule "was manifestly designed for the protection and advantage of property holders, as a class."

All these views may be fairly summarized in two theories of the origin and purpose of the direct-tax clause. The first is that it was a check upon the powers of Congress in direct taxation, devised for the purpose of compensating the states for conceding to the general government the right to levy customs duties. The second is that it was intended to prevent oppressive taxation of any one section of the country by a combination of representatives from other sections.[79]

In the proceedings of the convention there seems to be nothing to support either of these theories. The direct-tax clause was proposed at a time when the members were inter-

[79] In this connection, allusion has been made to the jealousy of the growing power of the West; and it has been intimated that the direct-tax clause was intended to protect the property of the Eastern states from combinations of Western representatives. Nothing could be more incorrect. It has already been shown in this article that jealousy of the West was confined to a few members of the convention, who were promptly outvoted when they made a definite proposal to restrict the representation of new states. Moreover, the fears expressed with regard to the future power of the West concerned general matters of legislation, taxation never being mentioned in this connection. No one dreamed of crippling the government's powers of taxation in order to restrict the future power of the West.

ested solely in the question of representation for the slaves. It was manifestly intended as an expedient for cooling the ardor of the South in insisting upon such representation or for reconciling the North to a concession of at least a part of what was demanded. For data with which to settle this question we are not dependent solely upon the votes and debates of the convention. We have the express testimony of the very man who proposed to proportion direct taxation to representation, and this is confirmed by the explicit statement of James Madison. On the twenty-fourth of July, just before the resolutions of the convention were referred to the committee of detail, Gouverneur Morris expressed the hope that

> the committee would strike out the whole of the clause proportioning direct taxation to representation. He had only meant it as a bridge to assist us over a certain gulf: having passed the gulf the bridge may be removed. He thought the principle laid down with so much strictness liable to strong objections.

This was sufficiently explicit, but Madison, in his report of the debates, added an explanatory note at this point.[80] He wrote:

> The object was to lessen the eagerness on one side for, and the opposition on the other to, the share of representation claimed by the Southern States on account of the negroes.

The obvious interpretation suggested by the proceedings of the convention is, therefore, corroborated by the testimony of the men who were in the best position to know the exact reason for the introduction of the direct-tax clause. The most careful reading of the journal of the convention and of Madison's report of the debates fails to show anything that contradicts this explanation or lends support to any other. We have but one other account of the proceedings of the convention at the time when the direct-tax proposition was brought forward. This is contained in the papers of Rufus King.[81] It is not

[80] Elliot, Vol. V, p. 363; Gilpin, p. 1197. This note was clearly in the original minutes taken by Madison. The writer examined the original manuscript to determine this point, and found that the color of the ink, the writing and the position of the note leave no doubt that it was a part of the original minutes. See Madison Papers, Vol. III, p. 75, in State Department Library.

[81] The Life and Correspondence of Rufus King, Vol. I, p. 615 (New York,

satisfactory in many respects, but it deserves mention at this point. King gives an account of the famous controversy over representation for the slaves, and says:

The Representation was twice recommitted altho' not to the same Committee; finally it was agreed yt Taxation of the direct sort & Representation shd. be in direct proportion with each other. . . .

This makes it clear that, in the mind of King, the provision concerning direct taxation was connected with the compromise over the representation for the slaves.

The proceedings of the convention, therefore, as interpreted by Morris, Madison and King, should leave no room for doubt concerning the origin and purpose of the direct-tax clause. If, however, the subsequent discussions concerning the constitution are examined, the case is not, at first sight, so perfectly clear. Statements were made concerning the probable effects, if not the original purpose, of the clause, which seem to lend support to other views. Some of these facts are perhaps the basis for the theories advanced by Mr. Curtis and by Justices Fuller and Field.

We may consider first the theory that the states were unwilling to give the general government the right to levy customs duties, without having the powers of Congress narrowly restricted in matters of direct taxation. This theory seems to be entirely unsupported by any explicit statements of the men who framed and adopted the constitution. It is based upon inferences from certain well-established facts, and its truth or falsity depends upon the correctness with which the inferences have been drawn.

In its support it is pointed out that, when the constitution was before the people, much criticism was directed against the power of direct taxation;[82] that fears were expressed lest the

---

1894). The minutes kept by Robert Yates cover only the period from May twenty-fifth to July fifth. (Elliot, Vol. I, pp. 389-479.) The notes taken by William Pierce cover only a small portion of the debates in June.—*American Historical Review*, Vol. III, pp. 317-324.

[82] Elliot, Vol. I, p. 369; Vol. II, pp. 71, 160, 332, 333, 374; Vol. III, pp. 29, 56, 57, 166, 167, 214, 280, 320; Vol. IV, p. 75; Ford, Essays on the Constitution, p. 53; Ford, Pamphlets on the Constitution (Brooklyn, 1888), pp. 102, 304.

new government would seize upon all sources of revenue, leaving the states with no means of support;[83] and that the friends of the constitution often declared that direct taxes would probably be a last resort of Congress, and would be used only in case of some great emergency.[84] But, on the other hand, it may be answered conclusively that the leaders in the fight for a national government unfalteringly insisted that the United States ought to possess complete powers of taxation, and that they carried the day against the timid conservatives and the paper-money repudiators who desired to deprive the new government of all adequate means of support. He who reads the ringing words of Hamilton, Jay, Ellsworth, McKean, Randolph, Wilson and a host of others cannot doubt that the constitution was intended to confer upon Congress complete powers of taxation.[85] Ellsworth, for instance, argued:

> It is necessary that the power of the general legislature should extend to all the objects of taxation, that government should be able to command all the resources of the country; because no man can tell what our exigencies may be. . . . A government which can command but half its resources is like a man with but one arm to defend himself.

More than this, the opponents of the constitution explicitly stated that its adoption would confer upon Congress the most complete powers of taxation. These men never doubted the intention of the new instrument on this point.[86] William Patterson, the man who proposed in the federal convention the plan of government that sought to limit Congress to impost and stamp duties,[87] has left us a judicial opinion upon this very subject. In 1796 he declared: "It was, however, obviously

[83] For example, see a report of a committee of the Massachusetts legislature in 1790. Published in *American Historical Review*, Vol. II, p. 104.

[84] Elliot, Vol. II, pp. 42, 57, 60, 61, 64, 76, 106, 132, 191, 192, 211, 243, 333, 343, 501; Vol. III, pp. 40, 95, 109, 300; Vol. IV, pp. 77, 78, 189, 190, 220, 260; Vol. V, pp. 373, 417, 433, 455; Ford, Pamphlets, pp. 160, 253; Ford, Essays, pp. 239, 404; Lodge, Works of Hamilton (New York, 1885-1886), Vol. IX, pp. 69, 123, 125, 183.

[85] See especially Elliot, Vol. II, pp. 190, 191, 367, 380, 466, 535; Vol. III, p. 127.

[86] Elliot, Vol. II, pp. 71, 330-332, 378; Vol. III, pp. 29, 57, 263; Vol. IV, p. 75; Ford, Pamphlets, pp. 102, 304; Ford, Essays, p. 53.

[87] Elliot, Vol. I, p. 175; Vol. V, p. 191.

the intention of the framers of the constitution, that Congress should possess full power over every species of taxable property, except exports." And in this opinion all of Patterson's associates upon the supreme bench concurred.[88] Upon other questions the framers of the constitution were sometimes obliged to resort to compromises, but in the matter of taxation this was not the case. The men who were willing to have Congress incur debts, but unwilling to provide adequate means for their honest payment, were squarely met and totally defeated. Except in the case of exports, it is clear that the constitution was intended to give to the general government full power to command the resources of the country in its exercise of the right of taxation.

But it has been argued that a number of states proposed amendments by which it was to be provided that Congress should not levy direct taxes until it should first make requisitions upon the states for the quotas of money due according to the rule of apportionment, and should fail to secure a compliance with its demands.[89] Furthermore, it may be said that friends of the constitution recognized the strength of the opposition to direct taxation, when they intimated that the states would probably be given an opportunity to collect, in the manner most convenient, their quotas of direct taxes, before Congress would proceed to exercise the right of taxing citizens directly.[90] But these facts do not prove the theory that the states insisted upon the direct-tax provision, as a necessary protection for their own revenue powers after import duties were conceded to the national legislature. These proposals do indicate an opposition to direct taxation by the federal government, and part of this opposition did certainly come from jealousy concerning the safety of state revenues. But these proposals were opposed in the state conventions by the

[88] 3 Dallas, pp. 173, 176, 181.

[89] Elliot, Vol. I, pp. 322, 323, 325, 326, 329, 335; Vol. III, p. 31; Vol. V, p. 453.

[90] Elliot, Vol. I, p. 492; Vol. V, p. 316; Pierce, Debates in the Convention in Massachusetts, pp. 304, 311; Ford, Essays, pp. 235, 236; Ford, Pamphlets, p. 49.

leading friends of the new plan of government;[91] the constitution was actually adopted without the suggested alterations; and when an amendment to secure them was introduced in the first House of Representatives, it was rejected by a vote of 39 to 9.[92] It is submitted that the failure of the attempt to oblige Congress to resort to requisitions does not support the theory that the direct-tax clause was intended as a safeguard of the revenues of the states.

According to the second theory, the rule for apportioning taxes was intended to prevent oppressive taxation of any state or section by a combination of other states or sections. Various passages from the speeches of such men as Madison, Randolph, Hamilton, Nicholas, Pendleton and Williamson may be cited in support of such a view. We may begin with extracts from the *Federalist*. Hamilton, after discussing the difficulties of securing accurate assessments for the apportionment of direct taxes, wrote:

> In a branch of taxation where no limits to the discretion of the government are to be found in the nature of things, the establishment of a fixed rule, not incompatible with the end, may be attended with fewer inconveniences than to leave the discretion altogether at large.[93]

This was intended as a defense of the rule of apportionment according to numbers. It will be noted that Hamilton considered that rule not incompatible with the end of giving the government complete powers of taxation. He did not consider the adequacy of direct taxation for purposes of revenue to be limited by the constitutional requirement, but simply thought that abuse of the power might be prevented by the apportionment rule. Elsewhere he wrote that this provision "effectually shuts the door to partiality or oppression."[94] Similar ideas were advanced in the Virginia convention, where Patrick Henry,

[91] Elliot, Vol. II, pp. 59, 60, 342, 343, 367, 368, 380, 381, 536; Vol. III, pp. 40, 41, 100, 101, 118, 119, 122, 181, 228, 229, 245, 250-252, 328, 329; Vol. IV, pp. 77, 78, 82, 85, 92.

[92] Annals of Congress, First Congress, p. 807.

[93] Lodge, Works of Hamilton, Vol. IX, p. 125.

[94] *Ibid.*, Vol. IX, p. 210.

George Mason and others attacked vigorously the proposal to give Congress the right to levy direct taxes. In reply to such objections, Madison said:

> Our state is secured on this foundation. Its proportion will be commensurate to its population. This is a constitutional scale, which is an insuperable bar against disproportion, and ought to satisfy all reasonable minds.

Randolph and George Nicholas also urged strongly that the provision fixed the amount which could be drawn from Virginia by direct taxation.[95]

These statements, if they stood by themselves, would seem to support strongly the theory under discussion. But they need to be considered carefully, with reference to the circumstances under which they were made. Hamilton, Madison, Randolph and Nicholas were in the midst of a controversy, and were defending the power of direct taxation from the criticisms that were raised against it. It will be noticed that none of these statements are *express explanations of the purpose of the clause relating to apportionment*. They may be considered merely as declarations concerning its incidental effects upon the position of the states in the matter of direct taxation. In the case of Madison, it will be remembered, we have his express statement, made in his minutes of the debates of the convention, that Morris offered his proposals concerning the apportioning of taxes in order to hasten a settlement of a dispute over representation for the slaves. Special pleading in the course of a heated controversy cannot stand against the deliberate records which are found in the proceedings of the convention.

Upon later occasions we find two express statements that the object of the direct-tax clause was to safeguard a state or section against oppressive taxation. Hugh Williamson said in Congress, in 1792, that this clause was intended to prevent the imposition of unequal burdens.[96] Four years later

[95] Elliot, Vol. III, p. 307; *cf.* pp. 121, 244.
[96] Elliot, Vol. IV, p. 427.

Edmund Pendleton advanced a similar argument.[97] Such evidence is of importance, especially when added to that furnished by the words of the statesmen previously quoted. But it needs to be weighed against the express statements of Morris, Madison and King, made in the accounts of the debates of the federal convention, and against all the other materials that can be drawn from the discussions of the period when the constitution was being ratified. It will be shown in subsequent paragraphs that the explanation which Morris, Madison and King made concerning the purpose of the direct-tax clause is confirmed by evidence drawn from later sources.

Besides the two theories already presented, there was suggested a third explanation of the purpose of the apportionment clause. In support of this third theory, James Madison may be quoted. In the Virginia convention he urged that, "from the modes of representation and taxation, Congress cannot lay such a tax on slaves as will amount to manumission."[98] In North Carolina it was argued by Spaight, who had been a member of the federal convention, that the apportionment rule was "meant for the salvation and benefit of the Southern States."[99] Without this provision the South might be oppressed, since "an acre of land in the Northern States is worth many acres in the Southern States." In the Hylton case, in 1796, Judge Patterson advanced the same explanation.[100] He held that the constitutional rule was made in the interest of the South. This section had many slaves and large tracts of land thinly settled. The other states had few slaves, and their territory was limited and well settled. Without this constitutional requirement, Congress might have taxed slaves arbitrarily, and might have taxed land in all parts of the country at a uniform rate. This would have been highly oppressive to the South.

Madison's words are not an express statement of the pur-

[97] In Bache's *Aurora General Advertiser* for February 11, 1796.
[98] Elliot, Vol. III, p. 453.
[99] Elliot, Vol. IV, pp. 209, 210.
[100] 3 Dallas, p. 177.

pose of the constitution, and may be merely an opinion concerning its incidental effects. But Spaight and Patterson clearly advanced explanations of the object of the direct-tax clause. Two things may be said concerning the theory here presented. First, it ought not to stand against the evidence found in the debates of the federal convention, supported, as we shall find it to be, by later testimony. Second, it seems certain that Patterson and Spaight were misled by what they undoubtedly remembered concerning the provision that no "capitation or other direct-tax shall be laid, unless in proportion to the census or enumeration herein before directed to be taken." We have seen that so much of this clause as refers to a capitation tax was introduced for the sole purpose of protecting slave owners from an arbitrary tax upon the blacks. Knowledge of this fact might easily lead to the conclusion that the original apportionment rule was likewise intended for the benefit of the South.

Having considered all the evidence in favor of these three divergent theories, we may now inquire what facts can be drawn from subsequent discussions to support the theory which seems to be the only one justified by the proceedings of the federal convention, as explained by Morris, Madison and King. In the New York convention Hamilton referred to the direct-tax clause in a manner that corroborates the view that this provision was intended to reconcile both the North and the South to representation for three-fifths of the slaves. Hamilton was called upon to meet the contention that it was unfair to allow the South any representation whatever for men who were held as property, with no political rights and no "will of their own." He argued:

> But representation and taxation go together, and one uniform rule ought to apply to both. Would it be just to compute these slaves in the assessment of taxes, and discard them from the estimate in the apportionment of representatives?[101]

In the same state, George Clinton objected to the rule for apportioning direct taxes according to numbers. He held

[101] Elliot, Vol. II, p. 237.

that property should be the basis for the assessment of public burdens, and said: "You are told to look for the reason for these things in accommodation."[102] Hamilton's argument and Clinton's objection alike make it clear that in New York the requirement of direct taxation for three-fifths of the slaves was used, as Morris had intended, for the purpose of reconciling the people of the North to the concession of a three-fifths representation.

In the Massachusetts convention, when the provision for apportioning direct taxes was under discussion, the record states[103] that "Messrs. King, Gore, Parsons, and Jones, of Boston, spoke of the advantage to the Northern States the rule of apportionment in the third paragraph (still under debate) gave to them." Unfortunately these speeches are not reported; but the drift of the argument is, nevertheless, sufficiently plain. Better still is the reply which James Warren made to the plea that the taxation for the three-fifths of the slaves compensated the North for the concession of a three-fifths representation. Warren asked whether Massachusetts ought to give up her right of equal representation for her white inhabitants "to any State that would pay our whole proportion of direct and indirect taxes."[104] He declared that no financial consideration could compensate for a concession of unequal representation. Moreover, he thought that the burdens avoided by Massachusetts would be merely nominal, because the South, enjoying slave representation, could prevent the imposition of direct taxes and confine the federal government to indirect taxation. Here again both the argument and the reply show that the direct-tax clause was actually used in precisely the manner contemplated by Morris and explained by Madison.

We find therefore, four conflicting views of the purpose of the constitutional provision for apportioning direct taxes. The proceedings of the constitutional convention, interpreted fairly

[102] Ford, Essays, p. 273.

[103] Elliot, Vol. II, p. 42.

[104] Letters of a Republican Federalist, quoted by S. B. Harding, The Contest over the Ratification of the Federal Constitution in Masschusetts (New York, 1896), pp. 157, 158.

and explained by Morris, Madison and King, give countenance to only one theory—that the apportionment rule was merely a bait for extremists in the North and in the South, thrown out in order to secure the adoption of the compromise over representation for the slaves. This consideration should be of decisive weight. Three other theories find more or less support in the discussions of the period that witnessed the adoption of the constitution. But the theory based upon the proceedings of the federal convention finds important corroborating testimony. Can there be any doubt as to which explanation has the weight of evidence on its side?

This particular question has not attracted much notice from the writers upon American constitutional law and history. But it will be well to consider the views of the few authorities who have in any way referred to the subject. Joseph Story has treated at length the great controversy over the concession of representation for three-fifths of the slaves. After explaining the real nature of the compromise between the free and the slave states[105] upon this point, he shows that, in order to reconcile the non-slaveholding states to this provision concerning representation, another clause was inserted, requiring that direct taxes should be apportioned in the same manner as representatives. Thus the weight of his authority can be invoked in support of the theory clearly indicated by the proceedings and debates of the federal convention. James Kent treated of this subject very briefly.[106] He considered the objections that could be advanced against allowing representation for the slaves and the reasons for such a concession. Then he pointed out that these same slaves served to increase the burdens of direct taxation—a fact which he regarded in the light of a compensation to the non-slaveholding states. W. A. Duer noted that the apportionment of direct taxes upon the same basis as representatives increased the burdens of direct taxation to be borne

[105] Commentaries, Sec. 642.

[106] Commentaries on American Law (fourteenth edition, Boston, 1896), Vol. I, p. 231.

by the South.[107] Mr. Justice Swayne, in a decision delivered in 1880,[108] called attention to the origin of the direct-tax clause in the compromise over representation for slaves. Mr. George Ticknor Curtis, who advanced in 1866 a different theory of the purpose of the apportionment rule, presented in his *Constitutional History*[109] an account of the genesis of this provision that is identical with that offered in the present essay. Finally, George Bancroft has given us a history of the proceedings of the convention, in which he explains most clearly that the provision concerning direct taxes originated in the attempt of Gouverneur Morris to effect a compromise of the dispute over representation for the slaves.[110] With the exception of George Ticknor Curtis, in his article of 1866, it is believed that no writer can be quoted in support of the views advanced by Justices Fuller and Field in 1895. It thus appears that the weight of authority has always been on the side of that theory which alone finds justification in the records of the constitutional convention.

VI

It remains for us to consider the character and the effect of this constitutional rule, which had its origin, as has been shown, in an attempt to compromise differences of opinion concerning the justice of allowing representation for the slaves.

This clause of the constitution requires that direct taxes shall be divided among the states according to their respective numbers, and provides for what Bancroft would have called a "collective poll tax."[111] Such a rule of apportioning public burdens is repugnant to every principle of just taxation. It is open to the further objection that direct taxes assessed upon this basis must prove almost valueless as a source of revenue. When

[107] Constitutional Jurisprudence of the United States (second edition, Boston, 1856), p. 56.

[108] 102 U. S. Reports, p. 596.

[109] Constitutional History, Vol. I, pp. 408-414.

[110] History of the United States, Vol. VI, pp. 265, 266.

[111] History of the United States (fifth edition, Boston, 1863), Vol. VIII, p. 58.

public burdens are apportioned in such a manner that the weakest communities must bear as great a burden as the strongest, the fruitfulness of any tax is measured by the ability of the weakest state to contribute to the support of the general government.[112] Both the injustice and the unproductiveness of such imposts ought to be so clear as to require no further discussion. But in the income-tax cases it was argued by counsel, and explicitly stated by the court, that there is no real difficulty in apportioning taxes, even upon income, according to the rule prescribed by the constitution. The Chief Justice gravely raised the question:

> Cannot Congress, if the necessity exists of raising thirty, forty, or any other number of million dollars for the support of the government, in addition to the revenue from duties, imposts, and excises, apportion the quota of each State upon the basis of the census?[113]

Elsewhere, he seemed to admit the possibility of inequalities arising from the operation of the apportionment requirement; but he claimed, nevertheless, that the clause conferred upon Congress "a power just as efficacious" as any form of taxation "to serve the needs of the general government."[114] These statements may perhaps warrant a historical and statistical investigation of the justice and efficacy of taxes apportioned according to the constitutional rule.

1. *Opinions of the framers of the constitution.*—It must be said that most of these men had no idea that the direct-tax clause would seriously impair the power of the government to draw forth the resources of the country. Such men as Hamilton, who desired Congress to possess all necessary authority, considered the provision "not incompatible with the end" of conferring upon the United States a general revenue power.[115]

[112] This was well stated by George Nicholas in the Virginia convention: "If we be wealthier, in proportion, than other states, it will fall lighter upon us than upon poorer states. They must fix the taxes so that the poorest states can pay; and Virginia, being richer, will bear it easier." (Elliot, Vol. III, p. 243.) Nicholas urged this fact as an argument in favor of the constitution. Such a consideration would have made no friends for the constitution in the poorer states.

[113] 158 U. S. Reports, pp. 632, 633.

[114] *Ibid.*, p. 621.

[115] Lodge, Works of Hamilton, Vol. IX, p. 125.

The clause was not accepted in the constitutional convention, until it had been amended so as to appear incapable of causing injury to the financial powers of Congress.[116] Sufficient other evidence has already been offered to support the conclusion that all, or nearly all, of the friends of the constitution held the same views as Hamilton. But one important consideration should not be overlooked. It is probable that the inequalities in the comparative wealth of the different states were not so marked in 1787 as they are today. At that time, the ability of the weakest state to contribute may not have fallen so far short of the ability of the richest as to make an apportioned tax so ineffective for revenue purposes as it would be at the present time.

Concerning the justice of the apportionment rule, opinions were divided. It will be well to consider first the arguments advanced in favor of numbers as a basis for apportioning direct taxes. Perhaps a majority of those who defended the provision did so because they believed it impossible to secure an equal and uniform assessment of property in all the states and preferred numbers as a "more practicable" rule, possessing greater "simplicity and certainty."[117] Thus, in the *Federalist,*[118] it is stated that numbers are not "a precise measure" of wealth and ordinarily are "a very unfit one"; but the constitutional provision is called the "least objectionable among the practicable rules." Other leaders seemed to endorse more fully the principle of the apportionment clause.[119] But when reasons were advanced for such an opinion, nothing better was offered than a statement that "population, industry, arts, and the value of labor, would constantly tend to equalize themselves," or some other equally vague explanation.[120]

On the other hand, many statesmen believed that the require-

[116] Elliot, Debates, Vol. V, p. 302.

[117] See Works of Hamilton, Vol. IX, p. 125; Elliot, Vol. I, pp. 70, 71; Vol. II, p. 42; Vol. V, p. 295.

[118] Works of Hamilton, Vol. IX, p. 339.

[119] Elliot, Vol. I, p. 72; Vol. IV, p. 210; Vol. V, pp. 281, 299, 303, 309; Pelatiah Webster, Political Essays (Philadelphia, 1791); p. 55; Ford, Essays, p. 193.

[120] Elliot, Vol. V, p. 299. *Cf.* Works of Hamilton, Vol. IX, p. 125.

ment was unjust. Opponents of the constitution naturally did not neglect such an opportunity as this clause offered, and insisted, with George Clinton, that property should be the basis of taxation.[121] But King and Morris also expressed their hostility to selecting numbers as a measure of wealth.[122] Moreover, Wilson and Hamilton can be quoted in opposition to the proposition that numbers are a fair rule for taxation.[123] Hugh Williamson asserted: "It is impossible to tax according to numbers. Can a man over the mountain, where produce is a drug, pay equal with one near the shore?"[124] Gouverneur Morris, as we have seen, declared, before the convention closed, that the provision was "liable to strong objections." In 1789 he wrote that the difficulties caused by the direct-tax clause would probably "force Congress into requisitions."[125] In 1796 Justice Patterson declared that "numbers do not afford a just estimate or rule of wealth," and that the apportionment clause was "radically wrong."[126] In 1797 it was argued in Congress that a direct tax would be inexpedient, because its distribution among the states would, of necessity, be extremely unequal and unjust.[127] In 1807, and again in 1812, Gallatin urged the same considerations.[128]

In proof of the assertion that the constitutional rule of apportionment was considered entirely just and satisfactory, it is pointed out that eleven or twelve states had voted to amend the Articles of Confederation in such a way as to permit the quotas of the requisitions to be determined by a similar rule. But this was not done until all attempts to assess the requisitions upon the basis of the value of real property had failed. So far as

[121] Ford, Essays, pp. 272, 273.
[122] Elliot, Vol. V, pp. 297, 304.
[123] Elliot, Vol. I, p. 77; Vol. V, p. 25; Works of Hamilton, Vol. IX, pp. 122-124.
[124] Elliot, Vol. I, p. 459.
[125] Sparks, Life of Morris (Boston, 1832), Vol. III, p. 471.
[126] 3 Dallas, p. 178.
[127] Annals of Congress, 4th Congress, Vol. II, pp. 1866, 1906, 2196.
[128] State Papers, Finance, Vol. II, p. 249; Writings of Gallatin (Philadelphia, 1879), Vol. II, p. 506.

the old Confederation was concerned, there can be no doubt of the absolute impracticability of any other rule of apportionment than that of numbers. But when a new government was formed and endowed with a general power of taxation, there was no longer any necessity for apportioning requisitions among the states, and there was no justice in selecting numbers as the basis of direct taxation. The direct-tax clause was accepted by most of the friends of the constitution with the best grace possible, and was defended as well as its manifest injustice allowed. But it prescribed a rule of taxation that would have secured the assent of few, if any, of the framers of the constitution, under circumstances of less dire necessity.

Many of the expressions that can be quoted in favor of the apportionment rule are labored arguments in support of a compromise measure that could be neither rejected nor defended. In justification it was often said that "taxation ought to be in proportion to representation," or that "taxation and representation ought to go together." These phrases were on the surface akin to the watchword of the Revolution, "no taxation without representation"; but in essence they were, of course, totally dissimilar. That taxpayers should have a voice, through their representatives, in the imposition of taxes, is one principle: that every man should be taxed in proportion to the representation that he enjoys, is a very different proposition. The last principle would lead to a uniform poll tax as the sole source of public revenue, whenever citizens have an equal voice in the choice of representatives. Such a rule of taxation would have been universally repudiated in state affairs, where the poll tax had either been abandoned or had been supplemented by taxes upon property. In all quarters the very suggestion of a poll tax aroused bitter opposition,[129] and no one defended such an impost as a principle source of revenue, except in cases of direst emergency. The Maryland constitution of 1776 had condemned "levying taxes by the poll" as "grievous and oppres-

[129] Elliot, Vol. II, pp. 43, 105, 106, 135, 340, 391, 502; Vol. III, p. 364; Ford Essays, pp. 272, 273; Works of Hamilton, Vol. IX, pp. 213, 214.

sive."[130] Two states proposed to amend the federal constitution so as to prohibit Congress from ever levying a poll tax.[131] It is difficult to believe that the fathers would have chosen freely to limit the government's powers of direct taxation to what is practically a collective poll tax.

Finally, the constitution did not provide for equality of representation; for the whites of the South were given representation for three-fifths of their slaves. When the expression "taxation according to representation" is interpreted in the light of this fact, it may be taken to mean that the South should bear an additional share of direct taxation, to compensate for the increased representation that its white population was to enjoy. This brings us back to the true explanation of the purpose of the direct-tax clause. In view of the representation conceded for three-fifths of the slaves, it may have seemed a fair compromise that the South's quota of direct taxation should be proportioned to its share of representation.

2. *The experience of the federal government.*—Five years after the new government was established under the constitution, the necessary expenditures of the United States had increased to such an extent that it was perceived by the best financiers that indirect taxation ought to be supplemented by other revenues. A direct tax was proposed in 1794 and in 1796,[132] but Congress did not come to a decision until 1798. One of the reasons assigned for the reluctance to pass such a measure was the inequality and injustice of the constitutional requirement. The act of 1798 apportioned among the states a direct tax of $2,000,000.[133] This was assessed upon dwelling-houses, lands and slaves, and was collected by federal officers, without reference to state authorities. The tax was to be paid

[130] Poore, Federal and State Constitutions, Vol. I, p. 819.

[131] Elliot, Vol. I, pp. 330, 336.

[132] State Papers, Finance, Vol. I, pp. 276, 409, 414-441.

[133] 1 Statutes at Large, pp. 580, 597. See also C. F. Dunbar, in *Quarterly Journal of Economics,* Vol. III, pp. 441, 442; Bolles, Financial History of the United States, Vol. II, pp. 116-122 (New York, 1879-1886); Howe, Taxation in the United States, pp. 30-34 (New York, 1896).

in 1800, but only $734,000 was raised in that year. In 1801 the collections amounted to $534,000, and in 1803 $207,000 was paid in.[134] Thus, less than three-quarters of the tax was raised in three years. Small payments dribbled into the treasury until 1813, when $238,000 still remained uncollected. The amount of the tax had been extremely small, when compared with the apparent needs of the government in 1798, but the difficulties of collection rendered it still more insignificant as a source of revenue. It will be seen that, if other imposts had been equally "efficacious to serve the needs of the general government," the United States would have been reduced to practical bankruptcy.

Congress did not attempt to levy another direct tax until the country became involved in the second wàr with Great Britain. Then the blockade of our ports caused the revenue from customs duties to fall off so heavily that internal taxes became absolutely necessary. So in 1813, Congress imposed, among other taxes, a direct levy of $3,000,000 upon the states.[135] This was assessed upon lands, houses and slaves, but the states were allowed to assume their quotas and collect the money for the United States by means of their own taxes. Seven states[136] availed themselves of this privilege, and in the other eleven the tax was collected by the federal government. This was a most favorable opportunity for proving the efficacy of direct taxes apportioned in the constitutional manner. The emergency was alarming, the necessities of the federal treasury were perfectly clear, and no one could deny the propriety of attempting to collect the small amount of money called for under the law. The result was a deficiency of nearly $800,000 out of the total levy of $3,000,000 for the year 1814. Congress felt obliged to establish, in 1815, an annual direct tax of $6,000,000. But this measure was repealed in 1816, when, however, a tax of

[134] These figures may be found in Scribner's Statistical Atlas, plate 81. (New York, 1883.) The amounts are stated in the nearest thousands of dollars.

[135] 3 Statutes at Large, pp. 22, 53; *Quarterly Journal of Economics*, Vol. III, pp. 442, 443; Bolles, Vol. II, pp. 254, 259; Howe, pp. 41-49.

[136] State Papers, Finance, Vol. II, pp. 860, 861.

$3,000,000 was required for that year.[137] These later acts differed in no essential feature from the law of 1813. The amounts required had been as follows: $3,000,000 by the act of 1813, $6,000,000 by the act of 1815 and $3,000,000 by the act of 1816. By the close of the fiscal year 1817, the payments had amounted to $10,470,000. Small collections continued until the year 1839, when the total receipts had risen to $10,984,000. The efficacy of this power of apportioned taxes can be judged from the fact that, during the years 1814, 1815, 1816 and 1817, when the returns were largest, direct taxes upon property had yielded only $10,470,000 out of a total of $100,486,000 which the government had drawn from the people by taxation.[138] Worse even than the failure of these direct taxes for purposes of revenue were the hardships caused by their unequal assessment.

Congress made no further attempts to use this efficacious power until the nation was convulsed in the throes of a life and death struggle with domestic insurrection. In the first war revenue act of 1861, there was a provision for an annual direct tax of $20,000,000.[139] This followed closely the lines laid down by the laws of 1813 and 1815. It was assessed upon lands and dwelling-houses, and the states were allowed to assume their quotas, if they should prefer to do so. The seceding states were included in the apportionment, so that the loyal states were asked for only $15,000,000. This was a very small amount, when compared with the resources of the country and the needs of the federal government. All the loyal states but two assumed their quotas. The payments made, however, consisted largely of the settlement of accounts which the states held against the federal treasury for their expenses in equip-

[137] 3 Statutes at Large, pp. 164, 255; *Quarterly Journal of Economics*, Vol. III, p. 444.

[138] These figures may be found in Scribner's Statistical Atlas. The results are stated in the nearest thousands.

[139] 12 Statutes at Large, p. 294; *Quarterly Journal of Economics*, Vol. III, p. 445 *et seq.;* Bolles, Vol. III, pp. 17, 18, 160, 161; Howe, pp. 81-90. See also House Report, No. 552, 50th Congress, first session, February 21, 1888.

ping troops. By an act of 1862[140] the duration of the tax was limited to a single year and all further assessments were suspended until 1865; and in 1864 the tax was practically repealed.[141] Thus, $20,000,000 represents the total amount which Congress attempted to draw from the country by means of apportioned taxes during a struggle which required an increase of all other taxation to an extent that would have seemed absolutely impossible at the opening of the war. It will be instructive to present in a single table the payments made under the law of 1861 during the years when they were largest, and to contrast them with the receipts of the federal government from other taxes. The results, stated in the nearest thousands of dollars, are as follows:[142]

YEARS.	ALL OTHER TAXES.	DIRECT TAX.
1861	$ 39,582	
1862	49,056	$ 1,795
1863	106,701	1,485
1864	212,057	476
1865	294,392	1,201
1866	488,274	1,975
1867	442,446	4,200
1868	355,553	1,788
Totals	$1,988,061	$12,920

Long after the close of the war, small payments kept dribbling into the treasury, the last being credited in 1888. The total amount paid or credited up to February 18, 1888, is stated at $15,360,000.[143] After allowing $2,125,000 for the cost of collecting the tax in the states where the quotas had been assumed, there remained an unpaid balance amounting to $2,554,000. The tax had been but partially collected in the seceding states; and this circumstance, with others, led Congress in 1891[144] to

[140] 12 Statutes at Large, p. 489.
[141] 13 Statutes at Large, p. 304.
[142] Scribner's Statistical Atlas, plate 81.
[143] House Report, No. 552, 50th Congress, first session, p. 45.
[144] 26 Statutes at Large, p. 822.

vote to return to the states the amounts that had been paid and to remit the quotas that still remained due. Under this law, about $14,222,000 had been returned to the states by the close of the fiscal year 1895.

The direct tax of the Civil War, then, did not prove a more brilliant success than its predecessors. An exhibit of the net results to the United States from the exercise of the power of levying apportioned taxes may not prove uninstructive. The five direct taxes levied in 1798, 1813, 1815, 1816, and 1861 called for a total of $34,000,000. Of this amount, the government succeeded in collecting, within periods varying from thirteen to twenty-six years, the surprising sum of $28,100,000. From this, however, we must deduct the $14,222,000 returned to the states under the law of 1891. When this is done, it will be seen that, in the course of the one hundred and nine years that have elapsed since the federal government has possessed this valuable power, Congress has been able to collect the net sum of $13,880,000 from these apportioned taxes. Upon a liberal estimate, this is much less than one-tenth of one per cent of the total ordinary revenues of the United States since 1789, exclusive of the postal receipts.

3. *The inequalities caused by the constitutional rule.*—The direct tax of 1861 was assessed upon lands and dwelling-houses; but, since all the loyal states except two assumed their quotas, it became practically a general property tax. The federal census gives the assessed value of property in each state in 1860, as well as the *per capita* assessed valuation.[145] In order to show the inequality of assessment, Massachusetts, Rhode Island and Connecticut are compared with Michigan, Kansas and Minnesota. The results are embodied in the table on the opposite page, in which the *per capita* assessed valuation of all property is stated in the nearest number of dollars.

Thus it appears that a hundred dollars' worth of property was taxed in Minnesota nearly four times as much as in Connecticut; while the three Western states, in general, paid at

[145] Eleventh Census: Report on Wealth, Debt and Taxation, Vol. II, p. 59.

three and one-half times the rate that was imposed upon the three Eastern states.

STATES.	QUOTAS OF TAX.	AMOUNT OF TAX *per capita.*	VALUE OF ALL PROPERTY *per capita.*	AMOUNT OF TAX *per* HUNDRED DOLLARS OF PROPERTY.
Mass.	$825,000	$0.67	$631	$0.106
R.I.	117,000	.67	716	.093
Conn.	308,000	.67	742	.090
Minn.	109,000	.63	186	.338
Kan.	72,000	.67	210	.318
Mich.	502,000	.67	218	.307

We may next compute the largest possible yield of a direct tax in the United States at the present time, and the inequalities that would be caused by the attempt to levy such an impost. The census of 1890 showed the smallest *per capita* valuation of assessed property to be in North Carolina.[146] The amount that could be collected by a direct tax must be gauged by the ability of this state to contribute to the support of the general government. In order to make the estimate of the yield of the tax as large as it could possibly be, under any circumstances, let us assume that the United States decides to ask from North Carolina an amount equal to all the taxes, state and local, which the property of the state was compelled to bear in 1890. As a matter of fact, to double the direct taxes, state and local, which property is now compelled to bear, would be a political impossibility in any section of the country; but we will suppose this to be done in North Carolina. In 1890 that state raised, for state and local purposes, the sum of $2,151,835 by *ad valorem* taxes on real and personal property.[147] This amounted to $1.33 for each person in the state. This figure sets the limit which Congress could not exceed in imposing the collective poll taxes which the constitution calls direct taxes. In 1890, such an apportioned tax of $1.33 would

[146] Eleventh Census: Wealth, Debt and Taxation, Vol. II, p. 59.
[147] *Ibid.*, p. 412.

have yielded $83,287,000. If we assume a population of 70,000,000 at the present moment, we should get about $93,000,000 as the largest conceivable amount of a direct tax.

This estimate is probably two or three times as large as any tax that Congress would dare to ask for. It would impose upon the poorer states a crushing burden, and would cause an amount of injustice that cannot be readily described. Moreover, it could never be collected, even in times of direst need, as the history of previous direct taxes has shown. If the tax should be needed for more than a single year, Congress would not venture to impose upon the poorer states more than one-third or one-fourth of the amount of their present property taxes. Thus, if we suppose a war, lasting four years, to call for all the resources of the country, Congress might hope to raise from twenty to thirty million dollars annually by means of this efficacious power conferred by the constitution. This, it will be remembered, presupposes that enormous inequalities would be tolerated and that a crushing burden would be imposed upon the poorer states. It also assumes, contrary to all previous experience, that such an unjust tax could be promptly collected.

The inefficacy of the power of apportioned taxation may be further shown by another comparison. In 1890 the state and local governments raised $443,096,574 by *ad valorem* taxes upon real and personal property. If Congress could reach this property uniformly with a tax only one-third as large as that imposed by state and local authorities, it could raise $147,697,000 by this means. If, on the other hand, the property of the poorest states should be taxed at one-third the rate imposed for local purposes and the other states should be taxed the same *per capita* amount, as required by the constitution, the yield would be but $31,000,000.

We may conclude this subject by examining the extent of the inequalities that would be perpetrated, if Congress should attempt to raise $93,000,000 by an extraordinary levy of $1.33 for each person in every state. For this purpose we may use the census figures of the *per capita* amounts of property assessed for taxation. At this point it may be objected that the assessed value of property is not, for all the states, a uniform proportion of the true valuation. It would be better to use figures of the true valuation of all property, if any such could be found that were anything more than the most conjectural estimates. As it is, we have only the statistics of assessed valuation for scientific purposes. But these are sufficient in this case, because a comparison is to be made of the richer Eastern states and the poorer states of the West and South. Now it may happen, although nothing definite can be said upon the subject, that real property, in the poorer states selected for our table, is assessed at a smaller per cent of its true value than is the case in the richer states selected. For the sake of argument, this may be conceded. But it is perfectly certain that the amount of personal property that escapes the assessor in the richer states is far greater than in the poorer states. In Kansas, Nebraska, North Carolina and South Carolina, a far larger proportion of personal property consists of farm stock and household goods, which are readily found for the purpose of assessment. The intangible forms of personalty, which escape taxation almost wholly, are far more common in the richer states.[148] These forms of intangible wealth have probably escaped taxation in an increasing degree; for the census shows that the *per capita* amount of personal property assessed in Massachusetts had increased by only two dollars between 1860 and 1890. In Rhode Island the *per capita* assessment of personalty had decreased by nine dollars during the same period, and in New York it had decreased by eighteen dollars. We are safe in concluding that the census tables of property assessed

[148] "The taxation of personal property is in inverse ratio to its quantity: the more it increases, the less it pays." (Seligman, Essays in Taxation [New York, 1895], p. 27.) See the statistics presented by Professor Seligman, pp. 27-30. A single fact may be cited here. From 1860 to 1890 the assessed value of real estate increased from $6,973,000,000 to $18,957,000,000. During the same period the assessed value of personal property increased only from $5,112,000,000 to $6,516,000,000.—Eleventh Census: Report on Wealth, Debt and Taxation, Vol. II, pp. 59, 60.

for taxation cannot exaggerate the differences in wealth between such states as are chosen for our table. The probability is that such differences are even greater than are shown by the figures of the census; so that our results will underestimate, rather than overestimate, the extent of the inequalities.

The subjoined table shows the *per capita* amount of assessed property in each state selected for comparison, the figures being stated in the nearest number of dollars. It also shows the amount of the tax that must be assessed upon each hundred dollars of property, in order to raise each state's quota, estimated upon the basis of $1.33 *per capita*.

STATES.	AMOUNT OF TAX. *per capita.*	VALUE OF ASSESSED PROPERTY *per capita.*	AMOUNT OF TAX *per* HUNDRED DOLLARS OF PROPERTY.
Mass.	$1.33	$962	$0.138
R.I.	1.33	931	.142
Kan.	1.33	244	.545
Neb.	1.33	174	.764
N.Car.	1.33	145	.917
S.Car.	1.33	146	.910

Thus the rate of taxation in Nebraska would be more than five times the rate in Rhode Island; while property in the Carolinas would bear about seven times the burden imposed in Massachusetts. It is not likely that Congress will ever attempt to perpetrate such an injustice, which would be not taxation, but robbery—a robbery of the weakest for the benefit of the strong; a robbery none the less because sanctioned by a constitutional rule begotten of the old strife over slavery.

4. *Opinions of various writers.*—Judge Story, writing long before the abolition of slavery, expressed the belief that the direct-tax clause was unjust. In view of the existence of slavery, however, he thought that "some artificial rule of apportionment" might be "indispensable to the public repose."[149] George Bancroft, after explaining the manner in which the direct-tax

[149] Commentaries, Secs. 993-997.

provision was introduced by Morris, said: "In this short interlude, by the temerity of one man, the United States were precluded from deriving an equitable revenue from real property."[150] Francis Bowen, in his discussion of the finances of the Civil War,[151] called the article obsolete, and held that it should be repealed. He wrote:

> This article was adopted only as part of a compromise, being intended as compensation for the rule which ascertains the representative population, by adding to the whole number of whites three-fifths of the slaves. As there are no slaves now, this rule for apportioning the number of Representatives in Congress is obsolete, and ought to be abrogated, together with its appendage and offset, the rule for the apportionment of direct taxation.

More recently, three other writers have considered the subject. Professor C. F. Dunbar, discussing the experience of 1861, has written:[152]

> The direct tax had, in fact, far less to recommend it in 1861 than at the beginning of the century. The inequality of apportionment according to population, serious enough at first, had been increased by the concentration of wealth in the commercial and manufacturing States.

Then he narrates the miserable failure of the tax levied as a war measure, and concludes as follows:[153]

> The direct tax provided for by the constitution has at last been effectually discredited as a source of revenue, and it has also been too prolific of misconception and confusion to have any interest henceforth as a practical measure of finance.

Dr. Howe, after reviewing the history of apportioned taxes, wrote:[154]

> Even admitting that the tax conformed roughly to justice a hundred years ago, when population was a rough criterion of the ability of the states to pay, it must be apparent that the unequal territorial dis-

[150] History, Vol. VI, p. 266.
[151] American Political Economy, p. 438 (New York, 1870).
[152] *Quarterly Journal of Economics*, Vol. III, p. 445.
[153] *Ibid.*, p. 461.
[154] Taxation in the United States, p. 84.

tribution of wealth at the present time renders even an approximation to justice impossible.

Finally, Francis A. Walker discussed the subject in one of his last books. He said:

The provisions of the constitution regarding direct taxes, again, are such that it might just about as well have declared that such taxes should not be imposed at all.

And then he explains:

If the amount of the tax were to be made large enough really to bring out the resources of the older and richer states, the newer and poorer states could not pay their share. If, on the other hand, the amount is kept so low as to be within the means of the frontier states, the proceeds for the whole country will be insignificant.

Mr. Walker's conclusion is as follows:

Three times has the general government undertaken to levy such a tax; but in each case the amount raised was small in proportion to receipts from other sources. In each case the collection of the tax excited bitter opposition. In each case large portions of the tax were left uncollected, after the lapse of years. It would not be a very hazardous prediction that the United States government will never again resort to this mode of raising revenue.[155]

Against the opinion of Chief Justice Fuller may be placed that of one of the dissenting judges in the income-tax cases. Mr. Justice White declared[156] that the rule of apportionment, especially as interpreted in 1895, prescribes "the most flagrantly unjust, unequal, and wrongful system of taxation known to any civilized government." In the light of all our experience of the operation of the direct-tax clause, the reader will have no difficulty in deciding between the opinions of Justices Fuller and White.

The writer is unable to dismiss this subject without referring to the experience of the Confederate States in trying to secure revenue by apportioned direct taxation. Fortunately for the cause of the Union, the constitution of the Confederacy bor-

[155] The Making of the Nation, pp. 145, 146 (New York, 1895).
[156] 158 U. S. Reports, p. 713.

rowed from that of the United States the provision that direct taxes should be apportioned according to the rule of numbers. The result was what reason and experience could have foretold. On account of the blockade of its ports, the Confederacy was obliged to depend very largely upon internal taxation as a support for its loans and paper money. A direct war tax was apportioned among the states, which were given the privilege of assuming its payment. Some of the states then issued bonds, in order to secure the means for paying their quotas. In these cases the tax was converted into a loan, at a time when the public credit was beginning to be strained to a perilous point. Elsewhere the tax was only partially collected. The net result was that direct taxes furnished only one-third of one per cent of the total revenue of the Confederacy in one year, and two-thirds of one per cent in another.[157] Jefferson Davis has left us a melancholy record of the failure of the Confederate States to reach their principal sources of wealth, land and slaves, by means of apportioned taxes.[158] It need not surprise us, therefore, to find the direct-tax clause of its constitution assigned as an important cause of the downfall of the Confederacy.[159] Yet this was the exact provision whose application has been so widely extended by the recent decision of our Supreme Court that, apart from customs, excise and some other duties, the United States has no clear power to reach the wealth or income if its citizens, save by taxes apportioned according to the rule of numbers.[160]

[157] See J. C. Schwab, "The Finances of the Confederacy," *Political Science Quarterly*, Vol. VII, pp. 38-56 (March, 1892).

[158] Rise and Fall of the Confederate Government, Vol. I, pp. 495, 496 (New York, 1881).

[159] See the *Century*, Vol. LIII, p. 38.

[160] The probable historical meaning of the words "direct taxes" as used in the Constitution of the United States is treated by the author in articles published in the *Yale Review*, February, May, and August, 1901.

A CLASSIFIED PROPERTY TAX[1]

I

THE general property tax, which is in this country the mainstay of State and local finances, has been the object of incessant criticism for more than forty years. Discontent with its workings undoubtedly existed in the early part of the nineteenth century, but it was not until the period following the Civil War that State and local taxation acquired the status of a "problem." Between 1867 and 1876, six States appointed tax commissions to investigate the subject, and their example has been followed by many others, until the student of taxation is now confronted by the reports of scores of such commissions, which constitute in the aggregate a literature of financial discontent without parallel in any other country. Everywhere the story is the same: existing laws are either unenforced, or, if enforced, prove destructive to industry and highly unjust in their operation upon individual taxpayers. The outcome usually is that personal property evades assessment to an increasing extent, so that the burden of taxation falls more and more heavily upon real estate. The system as a whole is inadequate, and was long ago discarded by most other countries; so that in the United States we have the proud distinction of possessing about the worst methods of local taxation to be found in any part of the civilized world.

Ever since discussion of the subject began, critics of the general property tax have maintained that our troubles arise from attempting to tax all, or substantially all, forms of property. Proposed reforms have generally contemplated the total exemption of certain kinds of property, such as intangible wealth or even all forms of personalty, and the retention of taxes on

[1] Reprinted from *National Tax Association, Addresses and Proceedings,* Vol. III (1909), pp. 95-105. Reproduced by generous permission of the publishers.

real estate supplemented by corporation, inheritance, income or business taxes. That a practicable system might be worked out in some such fashion, I will not question; but it must be apparent that the proposal to exempt important classes, not to say all classes, of personal property has thus far failed to gain the popular approval necessary for its adoption, and is not likely soon to command such approval. In view of this fact, I ventured a year ago to call the attention of this Association to the merits of a moderate uniform tax upon intangible property, such as now prevails in two of our commonwealths; and I desire this year to carry the discussion a stage farther, and outline a general plan for a classified property tax.

The root of our difficulty, I believe, is not that we have attempted to tax all classes of property, but that we have tried to tax them all at a uniform rate high enough to meet public expenditures at the present day. During the first half of the nineteenth century, when expenditures were smaller and tax rates but a fraction of their present figures, the general property tax, while occasioning more or less friction, did not lead to the intolerable conditions that have existed since the Civil War. In my own State the average rate of taxation could not have exceeded 40 or 50 cents per $100 in the year 1820; in Boston it was 36 cents per $100 in 1822. As late as 1860 the general level was from 60 cents to $1 throughout the State, and in 1861 the average was approximately 83 cents. It is to be further observed that the rate of interest on good investments was considerably higher at that time than at the present day, so that a tax of 60 cents per $100 represented less, rather than more, than 10 per cent of the taxpayer's income; and the evidence shows that under such conditions the tax could be levied upon all property with reasonable success.

In the City of Boston in 1794, when the rate of taxation was 30 cents per $100, personal property constituted more than half of the total assessment; and as late as 1850, when the tax rate was 65 cents per $100, it formed 41 per cent of the total valuation; but after 1850 conditions changed, public expenditures greatly increased, and the rate of taxation rapidly advanced. Whereas in Boston the per capita tax levied in 1850 was about $8, by 1874 it had risen to $35.70. In the State of Massachusetts between 1860 and 1870 the per capita taxes upon property increased from $6.04 to $17.10. The tax rate in Boston, which in 1850 had been 65 cents per $100, advanced to $1.56 in the year 1874; and in Massachusetts the average tax rate, which was 83 cents in 1861, stood at $1.57 a decade later. The result of this great increase in rates was widespread evasion of taxes upon personal property, which brought it about that personalty thereafter formed but a small proportion of the total assessment, leaving the burden to fall chiefly upon real estate. It was under such conditions that Massachusetts appointed its first commission to investigate the working of its laws relative to taxation.

While the situation may not have been the same in every other State, it appears that in the country at large the same thing happened that occurred in Massachusetts. The Census shows that the average tax rate in 1860 in all the States was 78 cents, whereas in 1870 it was $1.98 and in 1902 was $2.05. It further discloses that in 1850 personal property throughout the United States was assessed at $2,125,000,000, and realty at $3,899,000,000; while in 1902 personalty was assessed at $8,923,000,000, and realty at $26,415,000,000. The evidence points to the conclusion, therefore, that it was mainly the progressive increase of tax rates after 1860 which caused the disintegration of the general property tax and produced the intolerable conditions with which we are all familiar.

Nor should this conclusion surprise us. While some forms of taxation may be more convenient and flexible than others, the most important thing about any tax is the proportion it bears to the income of the taxpayer. If this proportion is small, the burden is more cheerfully borne and the collection of a tax correspondingly easy; while as it increases, the temptation to evade becomes stronger and the process of collection more difficult. I would by no means minimize the other considerations which have contributed to the unsatisfactory working of the general property tax in the United States, but I believe the thing of greatest moment is the unparalleled increase of tax rates which occurred during the last half of the nineteenth century. For forty or fifty years we have been endeavoring to collect from all classes of property a tax amounting to some such figure as 2 per cent of the selling value. Such a tax can and will be paid by no property that can manage to evade it, and its only effect must be to drive personalty into hiding and impose a constantly increasing burden upon real estate. In the eighteenth century and early part of the nineteenth, when the tax rate was but 50 or 60 cents per $100, it may have been possible to tax all property at a uniform rate; at the present time, when the average tax rate is $2 per $100, it is absolutely impossible to do so; and no reform of the property tax is possible until we learn that the rate of taxation upon any class of property should be adjusted to what that class can bear. If we are to continue to tax property, as apparently we must for a long time to come, it is under modern conditions imperative that we should classify property in a scientific manner and pass from a general to a classified property tax.

II

A scientific method of classification must be based upon facts, and the first fact which it must recognize is that the heavy taxes needed at the present day to defray the increased cost of local government must fall chiefly upon real estate. This is actually the result of our present system, although it is reached through the devious channel of evasion of taxation by personal property, and not by the process of classification. In 1902 the total State and local taxes amounted to $860,600,000. Of this sum, $153,900,000 came from miscellaneous taxes on polls, business, inheritances and corporations; while $706,700,000 came from taxes assessed on property. Of the taxes on property, as nearly as can be estimated, 75 per cent fell upon real estate, so that the total contribution of real property to the State and local revenues amounted to $529,000,000, out of a total of $860,600,000 raised by taxation. In reality, however, the contribution of real estate was somewhat larger, since a portion of the inheritance and corporation taxes represented realty values. In recognizing, therefore, that the basis of a classified property tax must be a tax upon realty, I am not proposing so much a change in actual conditions as a different and better method of bringing such conditions about. Indeed, there is room for thinking that, by scientifically classifying personal property, the contribution it makes toward public charges may be somewhat increased so that a natural result of the change would be to diminish somewhat the actual burdens on real estate.

Not only is it a fact that real estate is and must be the chief source of local revenues, but is it further true that under modern conditions this ought to be the case. Nearly nine-tenths of the taxes levied upon property in the United States are for the use of local governments, and little more than one-tenth are for the support of States and Territories. The local taxes are expended in large measure for objects that tend to enhance or maintain the value of real property. Allow streets, sidewalks, and sewers to fall into decay, and you reduce real estate values in any locality. Withdraw police and fire protection, extinguish street lights, and otherwise diminish municipal services, and you undo the owner of real property. Personal property can usually be removed or sold, so that its value will not be greatly affected; and it is not, like land, the permanent beneficiary of municipal growth and development. It is but just, therefore, that real property should be taxed for local purposes at a higher rate than personalty; and this principle is frequently recognized in special assessments levied by various American cities to defray the cost of certain kinds of improvements.

The heavier burden which falls upon real estate is greatly alleviated by the fact that, whenever real property changes hands, existing taxes are capitalized, so that the purchaser buys upon what is practically a tax-exempt basis. Every buyer of real estate, at the time of his purchase, takes into account the taxes falling upon the property, and adjusts accordingly the price he offers. The result is that, at any time, the value of real estate is diminished by the existing taxes capitalized at the current rate of interest, so that these taxes are no real burden for the subsequent purchaser. If the taxes increase during the time he holds the property, the additional burden of course falls upon him, since it diminishes by so much the price obtainable at the next transfer. In this manner from generation to generation the burden of real estate taxation is diffused among successive owners, each of whom bears only such increases in the tax rate as occur during his period of tenure.

While real estate must be the basis of the system, a classified property tax can draw substantial revenues from personal property if it rightly classifies the objects to which it applies. Personal property has sometimes been considered to form a single class, and it has been proposed either to exempt it from all taxation or to tax it at a uniform rate, though not at the rate levied upon real estate. But this ignores the well-defined distinction between tangible and intangible personalty, a distinction which must be recognized by any reasonable scheme of classification.

Intangible property is easiest of all to conceal or remove from one jurisdiction to another. It can be taxed successfully only by making the rate moderate and uniform throughout the widest possible area. For this reason it is desirable not only that the rate should be the same throughout an entire State, but that the various commonwealths should, so far as practicable, bring their rates to a common standard. In the next place, intangible property consists of investments from which the owners on an average derive but simple interest; perhaps 5 per cent is a fair average in most parts of the United States. In a reasonable system of classification, then, it would seem that the rate for intangibles should not exceed such a figure as a government can collect with reasonable certainty from property that is easily concealed and yields only an income of 5 per cent. Experience shows that from 5 to 6 per cent of the income is a reasonable figure for any tax upon intangible wealth; and that taxes exceeding this rate, by causing evasion, are less productive than those which do not exceed it. Pennsylvania and Maryland have learned this lesson and have demonstrated that a tax of 30 or 40 cents per $100 is the safe limit in the taxation of intangibles.

Tangible personalty, on the other hand, consists either of personal effects or of capital employed in agriculture, manufactures, and commerce. A tax upon personal effects bears no determinate relation to the taxpayer's income, and is of the nature of a tax on consumption. Capital actively employed in trade may be presumed, on an average, to yield the ordinary trade profit, which is twice the rate of simple interest. It, therefore, can and should pay a higher tax than intangible property, and its tangible character makes the collection of such a tax possible. If 30 or 40 cents per $100 is the correct figure for the taxation of intangible wealth, it would seem that the tax on tangible personalty should be placed at some such figure as 60 or 80 cents per $100.

How such a limitation of the tax rate on tangible personalty would affect the revenue from this source cannot yet be ascertained from actual experience, as can be done in the case of the moderate uniform rate on intangible property. But it appears that throughout the country merchandise and manufacturing capital are greatly undervalued. Investigations have shown that the assessed value may not exceed one-half or one-third of the true value, and in the State of Ohio the assessment of "merchants' and manufacturers' stock" declined from $70,442,000 in 1870 to $52,446,000 in 1906. It would seem, therefore, that at the reduced rate of taxation the assessed value of this class of property might double or treble, and that the taxes collected might well equal the present revenue from such sources. And if it should be said that such a result would leave merchants and manufacturers about where they are to-day, the sufficient answer is that they would then be paying all the law requires, and would no longer be dodging their taxes.

Since the classification of personal property is undoubtedly the crux of the problem, it may be well to emphasize the fact that the method I have proposed would give the same average result as a general tax on incomes. If we assume that the average rate of interest in any community is 5 per cent, and that the income tax is levied at the rate of 6 per cent, then $100 invested in intangible wealth will yield, on an average, an income of $5 per annum and pay a tax of 30 cents; while $100 invested in manufactures or trade will yield an average trade profit of $10 and pay a tax of 60 cents. If the rate of the income tax is 8 per cent, intangibles will, on an average, pay a tax of 40 cents, and capital invested in manufactures or trade, a tax of 80 cents. Clearly, if average results alone are considered, the result is the same whether the tax is levied on income or levied on property under a correct system of classification. In individual cases, it must be admitted, the results would differ, since all property of any given class is not equally productive. But for such differences in individual incomes from investments of the same class no property tax can make provision; indeed, it is a commonplace with students of finance that such inequality is inherent in any method of property taxation. This may be, and in my opinion is, a sufficient reason for substituting income for property taxes whenever practicable; but whenever such a change is impracticable, the most that can be expected is to adjust taxation to average conditions, and that can be done only by some system of classification such as I have proposed.

Forest property would also need to be dealt with in a scientific scheme of classification. In papers read at earlier meetings of this Association it has been made sufficiently clear that forests are unlike ordinary real estate and cannot be taxed in the same manner. The Forest Service of the United States is now investigating this problem, and will be in a position eventually to recommend a scientific method of taxing forests. Since the problem is primarily one for the forest expert, I may be excused from making any definite suggestion concerning the taxation of forests, and refer to the subject merely for the purpose of emphasizing the need of a proper classification of property for taxation.

I am compelled to leave untouched many other questions that

naturally suggest themselves, and must content myself with this brief discussion of the chief problems involved in a reasonable classification of property. I may refer, however, to the fear sometimes expressed that, if the rule of uniformity is abandoned, we shall fall into a chaos of diverse and bewildering classifications. Such fear I believe to be groundless. Property falls into certain natural classes of which the economic characteristics are tolerably plain, and our legislatures would be decidedly averse to making classifications except for sufficient cause. Ordinary real estate, forests, tangible personalty, intangible property,—these classes are well established and recognized by all. Some others may need recognition—I do not profess to offer a final classification; but experience shows that our legislatures are slow to diversify methods and rates of taxation, and that there is more danger that they will not go far enough than that they may go too far.

III

We have been so long accustomed to a tax upon all property that the proposal to classify and adjust rates to the economic nature of each class gains acceptance but slowly, even though it is surely finding increased favor. It may help to overcome dissent if I suggest that nothing is here proposed that is inconsistent with accepted principles of legislation and business procedure.

All successful legislation is based upon a reasonable discrimination between the classes of things with which it deals, and laws that ignore necessary distinctions between classes prove ineffectual or pernicious in their results. Uniform regulations for the transfer of all classes of property, a uniform penalty for all crimes, and absolute uniformity in the treatment of persons, without discrimination of age, sex, or condition, would be no more unreasonable than a uniform rate of taxation for all property, irrespective of its nature or class.

Diversification of rates of taxation agrees with the ordinary business principle of adjusting charges and prices to "what the traffic will bear." No railroad charges as much for carrying logs as for carrying furniture; but the discrimination in favor of logs, by enabling that traffic to move, contributes to the revenue of the road and decreases the charges upon furniture and other traffic of higher grade. When the average rate of taxation was 50 cents per $100, it was possible to tax all property at a uniform rate because the tax was not higher than any important class of property could bear; but under modern conditions the rate of taxation is so high that it is necessary to classify property and adjust methods and rates of taxation to the needs of each important class.

Reasonable discrimination between the objects of taxation is the principle upon which our customs tariff and internal taxes upon commodities are now adjusted. We tax beer at one rate, spirits at another, and tobacco at another; and no sensible man would propose to tax all three commodities at a uniform rate. Our tariff taxes cut diamonds at the rate of 10 per cent, and levies upon sugar a duty equivalent to 60 per cent *ad valorem*. This discrimination is both just and expedient, since a duty of 60 per cent upon diamonds would lead to so much smuggling as to produce little revenue; while the duty of 10 per cent yielded, in 1905, $2,500,000. This illustration not only makes clear the necessity of adjusting taxation to "what the traffic will bear," but points to the reason therefor. The duty of 10 per cent can be collected from any dealer in diamonds, because the government succeeds in collecting it from practically all dealers. If the duty were raised to 60 per cent, and a few dishonest dealers were tempted to evade payment of it, the honest dealers, who would have no objection to paying duties uniformly collected upon all persons engaged in their trade, would have no choice but to resort to smuggling or go out of business. Evasion of taxation, when it becomes general, is not due to dishonesty on the part of the average taxpayer, but to the sheer inability of the honest man to pay his taxes when other persons succeed in evading theirs.

Not only in the indirect taxes levied by the national government, but also in the taxes levied in certain States upon deposits in savings banks can we find a noteworthy illustration of the advantage of adjusting taxation to what property will bear. In 1862 Massachusetts made deposits in savings banks subject to an excise duty which for many years has been nominally one-half of 1 per cent, and actually one-fourth of 1 per cent of the total deposits. This duty has been collected from banks, and there has been no possibility of evasion, yet the deposits in those institutions have increased very much more rapidly than any other class of taxable property in the State, with corresponding benefit to the revenue derived therefrom. Far from injuring owners of other classes of property, the moderate tax upon savings deposits in Massachusetts and some other States has greatly benefited them, and their taxes would to-day be higher than they are if we had undertaken to collect a tax of 2 per cent.

Then, finally, we have the experience of Maryland and Pennsylvania, with their present taxes on intangible wealth. Their experience has shown that a rate that can be collected is far more productive than a higher rate that cannot be enforced, and they have pointed out a way to remove some of the worst abuses in our system of local taxation. We have had, then, even in this country, some practical object lessons of the benefit of classification, so that the proposal I make finds a basis in experience as well as in reason.

The platform of this Association commits us to the policy of removing obsolete constitutional restraints upon the classification of property for taxation, and has further recognized the impossibility of taxing forests under the general property tax. Our action gives rise to the natural question, Whither are we moving, and where are we likely to come out? May I suggest that we are tending toward a classified property tax, under which both rates and methods of taxation will be adjusted to the needs of each class of property. In such a system no rate upon any class will be higher than can be collected with reasonable certainty; none will be so high as to drive out of a community persons or capital or industry; and it will be recognized that any rate exceeding what the property will bear must result in loss of revenue, injury to industries and such general demoralization as accompanies widespread evasion of law. If we move in this direction, may we not devise a system of taxation suited to the conditions of modern life, just in its operation upon individuals, and beneficent in its effect upon the industry and commerce of our common country?

SEPARATION OF STATE AND LOCAL REVENUE[1]

SUMMARY

I. The advantages claimed for the plan of separation, 323.—II. First criticism: separation would not necessarily ensure a just distribution of state taxation, 325.—Second criticism: separation would not necessarily lead to a full valuation of property subject to local taxation, 329.—Third criticism: separation would not end diversity of local interests in tax legislation, 332.—Fourth criticism: local option in taxation is undesirable, 333.—Fifth criticism: it is undesirable to abolish direct state taxation, 335.—III. Conclusion, 337.

I

AMONG plans for the reform of American taxation the proposal to separate the sources of state and local revenues holds a conspicuous place. Eminent authorities declare it the "necessary starting point of reform," and "the indispensable initial step" to any substantial progress. In one commonwealth complete separation has already been effected, and in a number of others the process is thought to be well advanced. Yet there has always been dissent, and of late the plan has encountered increasing criticism from persons sincerely interested in the cause of tax reform.

As the name implies, the proposal is that state and local revenues shall be drawn from separate sources. When first advanced, the plan was that the states should derive their income wholly from taxes on inheritances, corporations, and some other independent sources, and that local revenues should be raised by taxes on property. More recently, and as an alternative, it has been proposed that only part—though perhaps the greater part—of the state revenues shall be raised by independent taxes, and that the remainder shall be obtained by a direct tax appor-

[1] Reprinted from *Quarterly Journal of Economics*, Vol. XXIV (1909-10), pp. 437-58. Reproduced by generous permission of the publishers.

tioned among the local bodies in proportion to their respective local revenues or expenditures. In both the original and the alternative forms, plans for separation usually, though I believe not necessarily, contemplate that the local governments shall be left comparatively free to determine what property shall be taxed and what exempted from local taxation. And in both, the essential feature is declared to be that there shall be no direct state tax apportioned among local units according to their assessed valuation.

The advantages claimed for the plan of separation are numerous, but the more important are four in number. The first is that existing inequalities in state taxation would be removed, and substantial justice reached in the distribution of the burden. Boards of equalization have signally failed to secure a just apportionment of direct state taxes distributed according to valuation, and must always fail, since they have imperfect knowledge of local conditions, are subject to pressure of local interests or the vicissitudes of politics, and in any case would be impotent to overcome the mutual mistrust and antagonism of local taxing authorities. But if the states, following natural lines of demarcation between central and local functions, create independent revenues from inheritances, corporations, and other sources, it is said that a just distribution will be automatically secured—the states retaining what properly belongs to them and leaving to the localities the general mass of property naturally subject to local jurisdiction. And if more money is needed than the states can conveniently obtain from independent taxes, it is believed that the plan of apportioning a direct tax according to local expenditures or revenues offers a just method of distribution requiring for its administration nothing but the collection of accurate statistics.

The second advantage is said to be that the abolition of the state tax apportioned according to local valuations will remove the inducements to undervalue property subject to local taxation, and lead automatically to full and fair valuations. In any event, boards of equalization will no longer be necessary, since it will be immaterial to the taxpayers of one county whether property in other counties is assessed at fifty, sixty, or one hundred per cent of its true value. And it is sometimes added that for purely local taxation it makes no difference to any one whether there is a low valuation of property with a high tax rate or a high valuation with a low tax rate.

The third benefit expected to result from separation is that such an adjustment of state and local revenues would remove that diversity of local interests which in our legislatures blocks most attempts to modify tax laws, and would open the way for other desirable changes. The direct state tax, apportioned according to valuations, binds each locality to every other in a single system which is hard to alter since any change may affect adversely the interests of particular localities, or, what is the same thing so far as legislation is concerned, may be feared to affect those interests adversely. With this tax either removed or apportioned according to local expenditures, it is believed that local suspicions and antagonisms would largely disappear, and that progressive legislation would become possible. It is chiefly for this reason, I take it, that separation of state and local revenues has been considered "the necessary starting point of reform."

And the fourth advantage usually, though not always, claimed for the plan is that, under it, the various local governments might be granted either partial or complete freedom in selecting methods of taxation. This I believe to be no necessary part of the scheme, since it is conceivable that a state, after establishing independent revenues for its own use, might consider it safer to prescribe the methods by which local revenues should be raised. But it is usually set forth as one of the chief advantages of separation, and under the caption "local option," "home rule in taxation," or some other attractive name of supposedly popular character, figures prominently in plans of tax reform. The chief reason advanced in its favor is that, since local conditions differ, each community should be free to adjust its fiscal system to its own needs and should be free to work out its own salvation in matters of taxation. Uniformity in tax laws is considered undesirable, and the need of the time is declared to be freedom of experimentation.

II

This is the case in favor of separation. Its strength at some points must be frankly conceded, and it is supported by weighty authority. I must add that formerly, and largely through respect for authority, I fully accepted the proposal. Further study, however, has brought change of view, and compels me to join the dissenters.

In the first place I can see no guarantee, or even probability, that separation would ensure a just distribution of the burden of state taxation. It is proposed to create independent sources of revenue in conformity with the natural division of state and local functions, and it is thought that in this manner a just distribution will be reached automatically. But there is no necessary and automatic connection between the division of governmental functions and the apportionment of sources of revenue. The former should be determined primarily with reference to convenience and efficiency of administration; the latter should depend chiefly upon comparative fiscal needs and resources. The national government charters and regulates national banks, but concedes to the states, under proper restrictions, the power to tax the capital stock and real estate of these institutions; and if it ever grants charters of incorporation to companies engaged in interstate commerce, we cannot doubt that the states will retain power to tax the property of such corporations. In these cases the governmental function is of a national character, but the property remains subject to state and local taxation because fiscal, and doubtless political, conditions require that it shall so remain. And similarly with the relations between the states and the local governing bodies. The State of New York administers the liquor license tax and shares the revenue with the local bodies; in Massachusetts the towns and cities administer this tax and share the revenue with the commonwealth. What natural and automatic connection is there in these cases between the division of functions and the apportionment of revenue? So far as any rational principle controlled the latter, it was probably the consideration of fiscal needs; but it is probable also that politics was the chief factor controlling the division. I do not say that there is never a coincidence between the allotment of functions and the allotment of revenues,—indeed, the customs revenue of the national government furnishes an example of such coincidence; but I do maintain that the controlling factor in the distribution of functions is administrative convenience, that the controlling factor in the assignment of revenues should be comparative fiscal need, and that between the two there is no necessary and automatic connection.

This conclusion is readily confirmed by study of the particular sources of revenue which it is proposed to allot the states. The inheritance tax is always on the list, and in the United States the propriety of such allocation cannot be questioned at the present day. But this is because the tax takes from the local bodies nothing that they formerly possessed, and because, further, the yield is not large as compared with the needs of the states. If fiscal conditions were different, it might be convenient to divide the proceeds between the central and local governments, as is done in Great Britain with the proceeds of the death duties. Fiscal convenience, evidently, is the controlling factor, and not an automatic connection between governmental functions and sources of revenue.

Taxes on corporations, particularly though not exclusively public-service corporations, are considered also to belong peculiarly to the states. If the taxes in question are confined to small annual payments for the franchise, as in New Jersey, I have no quarrel with the convenience of the arrangement. But if, under whatever guise or name, they are collected practically from property thereby withdrawn from local taxation, I deny that the arrangement is necessarily convenient or just. I do not question in the least the desirability and even necessity of the assessment of many kinds of corporations by state boards, or even the collection of corporation taxes by the states. But when a state appropriates to its own use the revenue from such sources, it is distributing the burden of state expenditures among the local units in proportion to the number and extent of the incorporated enterprises in each district, and this process results in a hit-or-miss distribution that accords with no conceivable principle of justice. True, the taxable values of some corporations, as railroads, are hard to localize; but this does not justify the state in assessing no tax upon districts not reached by railroads, a light tax upon localities where the roads occupy land of little value, and a tax of crushing weight upon a terminal city. It may well be that the tax should not be allotted wholly to the localities traversed by the roads—I cannot undertake in this paper a solution of the problem; but I maintain that the state has no natural and necessary right to the entire tax, and that the proper solution must be distribution in accordance with fiscal needs, and not distribution in conformity to governmental functions.

Many other examples might be given; I have time to cite but a few. If I deposit money in a national bank in Cambridge, I am required to pay the regular local tax on such deposit, but if I cross the street and place the money in a savings bank the tax will be paid by the bank and appropriated for the use of the state. If Smith, Jones, and Brown form a partnership to conduct some form of mercantile business in Boston, they will pay a local tax on their merchandise and other stock in trade. But if they incorporate under the laws of the commonwealth, the tax, according to the advocates of separation, naturally belongs to the state and not to the city in which the business is carried on. Search as you will, you will find no necessary and natural connection between the action of the state in chartering or regulating corporations and the just allocation of taxes assessed on the property or business of incorporated companies.

And the same is true of the other proposed sources of independent revenue for the use of the states. The controlling consideration always should be of a fiscal character, though in practice it is quite as likely to be political. The withdrawal of property from local taxation, either partly or wholly, merely distributes the state taxes in proportion to the respective interests of the different localities in such property, and can give no assurance of a just distribution.

There remains the alternative plan that a substantial part of the state revenue be raised by a direct tax apportioned according to local expenditures or revenues. In support of this it is said that the amount of money expended for local government is a fair index of a community's wealth and of its ability to contribute to the support of the state government. With individuals it would probably be admitted that expenditure is not a satisfactory index of ability, but with communities the case is thought to be otherwise; and the further suggestion is made that a state tax apportioned according to expenditures would be a salutary restraint upon local extravagance.

I must admit that when this proposal was first advanced it impressed me as attractive in many ways; but I now believe that there is a better remedy for existing inequalities in the apportionment of state taxes, and that this method of distribution is unjust and in other ways undesirable. It is unjust because communities, like individuals, differ in need and in disposition to adopt a liberal scale of expenditure. Their needs differ on account of differences in situation and in the character of their population; and to tax in proportion to expenditures absolutely necessary for public works, public schools, and protection to life or property, is to tax the more necessitous communities for the benefit of the more fortunate. Again, communities differ in their disposition to provide improved forms of public service which modern conditions make highly desirable. Better schools, improved highways, increased care for public health and sanitation, more intelligent and humane treatment of dependent, defective, and delinquent classes—these things are imperatively required by the conditions of our age; and to impose a larger share of state taxation on the communities that exhibit the most progressive spirit would be extremely short-sighted and objectionable. By so doing we might, indeed, curtail local expenditures, but we should certainly repress many desirable improvements in public service. Extravagance, no doubt, exists, and is always to be deplored; but I am not anxious to see it checked in any way except by improvement in the spirit and methods of government, and least of all by a method that taxes progressive communities for the benefit of unprogressive. For these reasons I hold that apportionment by expenditure would overtax the least fortunate, place a penalty on progress, and divert attention from the true method of dealing with local extravagance.

To meet such criticism it has been said that, after all, the state taxes are comparatively light, so that the objection has little force. This is true in some states, as in Massachusetts, but is absolutely untrue in others where the outlay of the commonwealth is a very large part of the total expenditure. It can be true in very few states that levy a state tax for the support of public schools; and wherever such a levy is made, apportionment by expenditure would be likely to defeat the very purpose of the school tax, which is to equalize educational opportunities. Since another remedy can be found for existing evils, I believe that the proposed method of apportioning the state tax must be rejected without reservation or qualification.

My second general criticism of the plan of separation is that it will not remove all inducements to undervaluation of property subject to local taxation, or lead automatically and surely to full and fair valuations. Abolition of the state tax or apportionment of expenditures would undoubtedly remove one inducement to undervaluation, but unfortunately there are others. First there are the county taxes, which in the United States in the year 1902 exceeded by seventy-five per cent the direct taxes levied for the use of the states and territories. There may be states in which conflicts of local interests do not arise within the separate counties, but in many, if not most, county assessments are now vitiated by the same forces that affect so unfortunately the apportionment of the state levy. In all such cases separation would hardly reach the roots of our present difficulties. A second reason for the continuance of local undervaluation is the fear of taxpayers that, if property is assessed at its true value, the ultimate result will be not a lower tax rate but larger expenditures and an increase in the actual burden of taxation; and the experience of some communities that have raised valuations with a view to reducing tax rates lends some force to this apprehension. And a final reason is that the full and fair assessment of all property, even real estate, is not a simple task, as sometimes assumed; but a work requiring skill, experience, and freedom from political or personal influence. In the State of Wisconsin the opinion of the best judges is that the practical separation of revenues there accomplished has not affected appreciably the work of local assessors. The truth is that the evils of which complaint is made are more deep-seated than the advocates of separation have ever realized, and would not be removed by the plans they propose.

But it is said that undervaluation, even if it were to continue, would not be a thing of much importance after the state tax had been abolished, since it would work no injustice between different counties. And, for local purposes, there is said to be no difference between a low valuation with a high tax rate and a high valuation with a low tax rate. This I believe to be a great mistake. In the first place if the law now prescribes assessment at the true value, it should be either obeyed or amended; and boards of assessors who willfully disregard the statutes at one point are almost certain to violate them at others. Can the habitual disregard of laws relating to taxation be admitted to be a matter of little moment? And in the second place it seems clear that the true rule is assessment at the full value, if we wish to secure equality of individual assessments within the same community. Investigations have shown that when assessors with the best intentions, undertake to undervalue all property at some uniform percentage, say seventy per cent, they will value some parcels of real estate as low as twenty per cent of the true value and others as high as one hundred and twenty per cent. For this there is a simple explanation. If the practice is to assess realty at its true value the assessor has a definite mark at which to aim, and the taxpayer a definite standard by which to compare his own assessment with his neighbor's; but when undervaluation prevails the work is beset with uncertainty, the detection of errors is difficult, and glaring inequalities escape notice.

Not only should local officials aim at a full valuation of taxable property, but it is becoming increasingly clear that in this work they should have the advice, support, and, when necessary, compulsion of the state. Experience shows, both in this and other countries, that local assessments of property, income, or business need constant supervision and control by some central authority. I do not refer to mere "equalization" by boards of the old-fashioned type, but to genuine supervision, by commissions clothed with necessary authority over the methods and, when necessary, the details of local assessments. This raises a question too large to be considered adequately here; and I can only refer you to the work accomplished by such commissions in Indiana, Wisconsin, Minnesota, Washington, and a few other states, which has been described in various papers contained in the Proceedings of the International Tax Association. I am aware that centralization has its disadvantages as well as advantages; I could even wish that in this case it were not necessary; but I am convinced that local boards of assessors need to be supervised by a central body of experts, specialists in their appropriate field, and free from personal local, or political influences. Instead of abandoning the effort to secure full and fair valuation, the duty of the state, after enacting a rational system of tax laws, is to insist upon the strict enforcement of those laws in letter and in spirit. This may be a difficult task; it certainly will not be accomplished in a day. But this is no reason for discouragement, and certainly no excuse for taking what can plainly be seen to be a step in the wrong direction.

The third criticism of the program of the separationists is that it would not put an end to diversity of local interests in tax legislation. At some points, I concede, it might do so; but at others the old antagonisms would remain, and would lead to most unfortunate consequences. For the independent revenues of the states must come from somewhere, and most of the special taxes which it is proposed to assign the commonwealths can be seen clearly to burden some localities more than others. All of the plans with which I am familiar would have for their net result the shifting of a considerable share of state taxation from rural districts to urban, and particularly to the larger urban centers. Indeed this is frankly avowed by leading advocates of separation, and considered to be one of the merits of the plan. Whether, in view of the problems confronting the modern city, such a result is desirable, I cannot now consider; but the transfer of burdens must arouse the same local antagonisms that attend the apportionment of our present state taxes, and in the process city interests would be arrayed against country as they so often are in our legislatures and boards of equalization.

In Massachusetts the problem of distributing the proceeds of the general corporation tax has for years arrayed the residential towns and cities against the manufacturing and commercial centers, principally the city of Boston. In Connecticut, during the past winter, it is reported that the problem of raising additional revenue for the state brought on a contest between city and country interests. In the state where complete separation has been accomplished, the division of the liquor license tax and the enactment of a tax on stock transfers seem to have arrayed the virtuous and unselfish "up-state" counties against the wicked city of New York. If you will read the reports of tax commissions that have recommended plans for separating state and local revenues, you will find that although appeal is made to abstract justice or scientific principles of taxation, care is usually taken to construct statistical tables showing that a majority of counties, or towns and cities, will pay less under the new arrangement than under the old. And as for the average legislator, you may rest assured that, while he will cheerfully agree with you that what we want is fair play and a square deal all around, his first, and usually last, question will be, How does your scheme affect my district? Until you can devise taxes that come from nowhere and are paid by no one, you may depend upon it that the quest of new sources of state revenue ordinarily means a search for taxes that some other fellow or other district will have to pay, and that imposts of most objectionable character may be established if thereby a combination of towns or counties can unload state charges on one or more large cities as convenient beasts of burden. If the time has come or ever shall come when taxes resting upon country districts must be transferred to large cities, I submit that the transfer should be effected according to some rational principle, and not by the hit-or-miss methods contemplated by the advocates of separation; and venture the further suggestion that we cannot expect to effect the change without arousing local jealousies and antagonisms.

A fourth criticism concerns the proposal usually made by separationists to confer upon local governments freedom to devise their own systems of taxation. This is advocated by those who believe that taxes on personal property ought to be abolished, and think that if local option were permitted, some communities, perhaps many, would grant such exemption. It is favored also by our friend the single taxer, who hopes that some communities would elect to place all their taxes upon land values. Neither the merits of the single tax nor the desirability of exempting personal property can be considered in this paper; I can only state my opinion that the remedy for the shocking evils that now exist is to be found in a proper classification of property for taxation, coupled with state supervision of the work of assessment. From my own point of view, therefore, local option, or home rule in taxation, has no attractions; and it must be still less attractive to those who believe that all property should be taxed at a uniform rate.

The reason usually assigned for the proposal is that local conditions differ very widely, and that each community is the best, indeed the only, judge of its own needs. But I believe that there are few advocates of local option who, after prolonged consideration of such diversities, would not in any concrete case recommend either total exemption of all personalty or the single tax. And I have often heard the opinion expressed that if any locality should hold out to investors the prospect of total exemption of personal property,—to say nothing of exemption of improvements on land,—capital and industries would migrate to that district in such volume that other places would be forced to grant similar exemptions if they desired to retain any part of their movable wealth. I cannot, then, believe that the real purpose of most advocates of the plan is anything but the ultimate establishment of a uniform system of exemption of certain classes of property, and the concentration of local taxes on real estate or on land values alone. Such a program is difficult to carry through state legislatures where the farmers have a voice, but it might readily be accepted in large cities where only a small fraction of the voters are owners of real estate. Until we are prepared to accept state-wide uniformity in the concentration of local taxes upon real estate or land values, we are bound to oppose local option as a remedy for real or alleged diversities of local conditions and needs.

If, however, I am wrong in believing that the purpose and possible result of local option is what I have represented it, and if the outcome of the experiment would be the establishment of diverse local methods of taxing many or most kinds of property and business, it is easy to show that such diversity, unless narrowly restricted by state law, would give rise to undesirable, even intolerable conditions. Suppose that one county should decide to tax mortgages as an interest in real estate where the land lies, that another continues to tax mortgages as personal property, and that the state, in its quest of independent revenues, establishes a recording mortgage tax. Then the interest the mortgagee has in the land would be taxed in the first county, the mortgage note might be taxed in the second, and the state would impose a third tax at the time the mortgage was recorded. In the assessment of taxes on business enterprises owning property and conducting operations in two or more places, similar opportunities would exist for double or multiple taxation; and other cases would probably arise in which similar injustice would be perpetrated. So far as I know, no country permits any such degree of local option, and the only result in the United States would be local chaos, assuming still that most forms of property and business would remain on the list of taxables. This is not to say that no latitude whatever should be allowed local governments. Such a tax as the habitation tax, which does not affect the distribution of capital or offer opportunity for unjust double taxation, might be introduced, if any community desired it, in connection with other taxes; and there may be one or two other taxes the use of which could safely be made permissive. But with such possible exceptions, the forms and methods of local taxation should be prescribed by state law, and few things could be more undesirable than the wide discretion it is proposed to grant local governing bodies.

A fifth and final criticism lies against that form of separation which contemplates drawing all the revenue of the states from independent sources, without a direct tax of any sort or description. To this the objection is that it leaves the states without an elastic tax which can readily be increased when more revenue is needed, and reduced when a surplus is foreseen. Taxes on inheritances ought to be levied at unchanging rates in order to secure equality in the distribution of their burden; nothing can be more unequal than to tax at a high rate an estate probated in a year of a deficit, and to tax at a low rate one that is transferred in a year that shows a surplus. Taxes on corporations are either levied at fixed rates, or at rates depending on the aggregate of local taxation. They might be made to vary with the needs of the commonwealth, but such a proposal would probably encounter so much opposition as to postpone to the Greek Kalends a plan of separation contingent upon its acceptance. And so with the other sources of independent income; they should not, or probably could not, be made variable taxes.

There may be states in which inelasticity of revenue would

cause no embarrassment; in which expenditures would not outstrip the natural increase of the income from established taxes, and in good years a surplus would be set aside to provide for the lean ones. This has been said to be true of New Jersey and Pennsylvania. But I apprehend that in most states the abolition of the direct tax would remove a necessary check on public expenditures. Experience shows that legislative bodies will usually spend all the revenue drawn from indirect taxes or from taxes on inheritances and corporations, since these are not felt sensibly by the average taxpayer; and in good years will regard a surplus merely as a reason for increased appropriations. This is not mere speculation. It has been, notoriously, the experience of our national government, and is confirmed by the experience of not a few states.

For it should not be forgotten that during the first half of the nineteenth century separation of revenues was attempted in a number of states. The experiment has never been fully studied, and the results were complicated by the fact that at the same time extensive public works were undertaken with borrowed money. But I think it can be shown that in most cases, even when allowance is made for unwise use of public credit, the usual result of abolishing direct state taxation was an unprecedented increase in ordinary expenditures. My own state (Massachusetts) affords a particularly good field for study, since the experiment was hardly affected by the use of loans; and it is too clear to admit of doubt that from 1825 to 1853 the attempt to dispense with direct taxation resulted in loss of control over state outlay.

Concerning the present working of complete or partial separation in the states where it now prevails, I speak with diffidence, for I have been unable to study the situation at first hand. But it is a fact that in New York expenditures increased from $12,934,000 to $34,589,000 during the fifteen years ending in 1908, and that, although opinions differ, there are well-informed persons who believe that abolition of direct taxation is responsible for a considerable part of the increase. In New Jersey the condition of the state's finances was the object of a special message from the Governor last January, and although that document denies that expenditures have been extravagant, it states that the condition of the treasury is such that the legislature ought either to appropriate to the use of the state certain revenues formerly distributed to the counties or levy a direct tax. In Connecticut I find that during the decade ending in 1908 expenditures rose from $2,530,000 to $4,741,000, that the official best qualified to judge declares "the abolition of a direct state tax has led to extravagance in expenditure," and that the present year the legislature was obliged to levy a direct tax, the first since 1890. And finally it is a significant fact that whereas the original proposals of the separationists contemplated the abolition of direct taxation for the support of the state, the plans now current usually provide for a direct tax apportioned according to local expenditures.

III

Thus far, and not without regret, I have offered you little but destructive criticism. I trust, however, you have not formed the impression that I am satisfied with existing methods of taxation, either state or local; or that I think there is no remedy for the evils admitted to exist. Will you permit me to state in the fewest possible words what I believe to be a wise and practicable solution of the problem?

There are, undoubtedly, certain taxes which should be reserved for the use of the states. One of these is the inheritance tax, which takes from the localities nothing in the way of revenue which they formerly possessed and is collected with approximate equality from property in all parts of a commonwealth. A second may well be a light tax an the franchises of all corporations, which is a reasonable payment for something which the state confers and is not in derogation of the taxing power of counties or municipalities. Third in order are the usual taxes on insurance companies, which reach taxable values distributed with some approach to equality and never, so far as I recall, subject to local taxation. Further than this the question is less clear, though perhaps the states may reasonably claim a portion of the taxes collected from railroads and from telegraph, telephone, express, and parlor-car companies, since these fall in part upon intangible values hard to localize and belonging naturally to no one district rather than another. And finally, in view of their increasing outlay for dependents, defectives, and delinquents, the commonwealths may fairly claim part of the liquor license taxes, since the business taxed contributes in some degree to the production of pauperism, disease, and crime.

After this allocation of revenues to the states, the remainder of their income should be drawn from direct taxation. If, in any case, the revenue from the specified independent sources equals or exceeds the needs of the treasury, a larger part of the taxes on transportation companies should be assigned to counties or municipalities, in order that the legislature may not be freed from the restraints imposed by an annual or biennial accounting with the people. The apportionment of the state tax may not be an easy task, but an intelligent revision of our laws relating to the taxation of property will remove all serious difficulties.

As the source of local taxation we must assign property and business generally, undiminished by the hit-or-miss reservation of important classes for the exclusive service of the state. But I speak not of a general property tax, levied as at present at a uniform rate; for that has proved the abomination of abominations, and cannot be amended until we learn to classify property in a rational manner and adjust the rates and methods of taxation to the economic nature and needs of each class of taxable objects. The method of classification, I need hardly add, should be prescribed by the state; and the process of assessment should be under strict and direct state supervision, though performed by local officials. The result, I believe, will be a reasonably full and fair assessment of taxable property; not instantly, perhaps, since new methods are not learned perfectly in a day, but ultimately and at no distant time. It is obvious, too, that such a consummation will solve the problem of the just distribution of the direct state tax.

THE GENERAL PROPERTY TAX IN SWITZERLAND[1]

SUMMARY

I. History of Swiss property taxes.—Federal and cantonal taxation.—Income from property and industries.—Cantonal and local taxation is diversified: the various taxes employed. II. Constitutional status of the property taxes.—The property taxable.—Deduction of debts.—Methods of assessment.—Penalties.—Tax rates.—Taxation of corporations.—Communal taxation. III. The workings of the property taxes: (*a*) real estate; (*b*) mortgages; (*c*) forests; (*d*) personal property; (*e*) the prevailing rates of taxation.—The taxation of incomes.—State supervision of local assessments.—Popular lawmaking. —Conclusion.

FOR an American the property taxes of the Swiss cantons have peculiar interest. Switzerland is the only country of Europe in which direct taxes upon property hold such a position in the fiscal system as they occupy in the United States. It has a federal form of government; and therefore, like the United States, must adjust federal finances to state and local, while readjusting the latter to the conditions created by the formation of a federal union. In political institutions, also, fundamental similarity exists, since both countries are democratic. Evidently, then, the property taxes of the Swiss cantons operate under conditions closely resembling those with which the American student is familiar; they are in most, though not all, cases the mainstay of the state and local finances; they have been adjusted more or less perfectly to the relations that exist under a federal system of government; and they have been shaped in accordance with the popular will of some of the most democratic communities in the world.

[1] Reprinted from *National Tax Association, Addresses and Proceedings*, Vol. IV (1910), pp. 53-84. Reproduced by generous permission of the publishers.

I

The property tax in Switzerland is a very old institution; it is also, as we now find it, mainly the product of the nineteenth century. In the Middle Ages the German emperors levied direct taxes upon the property of their Swiss subjects. In the thirteenth and fourteenth centuries, as various cantons secured fiscal autonomy, property taxes were employed whenever occasion demanded, as in Schwyz, for example, where as early as 1294 there was a tax on the capital value of property, and each citizen was required to make "a loyal and true" declaration of his entire fortune. These imposts were, however, an occasional and extraordinary form of revenue, since in ordinary times the governments were expected to subsist upon the income from public property and the produce of indirect taxes. Glarus and Geneva seem to have been the first cantons to make direct taxes upon property a regular and ordinary resource; in the former the present general property tax, and in the latter the "*taxe mobilière*" have been in continuous operation since the last half of the seventeenth century. Elsewhere the property taxes remained an extraordinary expedient, and early in the eighteenth century completely disappeared. In 1798 the Helvetic republic introduced taxes on land and movables; but when the cantons regained their autonomy in 1803, most of them abolished these taxes,[2] and undertook to finance themselves in the eighteenth-century fashion. But conditions were changing, and with the growth of democratic institutions were to change still more until direct taxation in some form or other became an absolute necessity. Then, and only then, were direct taxes upon property or incomes reëstablished. Zurich led the way in 1832, and by 1856 had been followed by eleven other cantons. Between 1867 and 1879 four others reintroduced direct taxation; Solothurn, the last to reconcile itself to the new order of things, postponing its evil day until 1894, when a series of deficits compelled the people to accept a combined property and income tax. Except

[2] Glarus, Geneva, and six other cantons continued to levy property taxes. The last mentioned were newly created cantons which had no other resources.

in two cantons, therefore, the existing Swiss property taxes are of comparatively recent origin, and are a reluctant concession of Swiss democracy to the financial exigencies of the nineteenth century.

The present status of these taxes is both similar to the status of the property tax in the United States, and at the same time different from it. In Switzerland, as in our own country, the revenues of the federal government are derived chiefly from indirect taxes; and direct taxation is reserved for the use of the state and local governments. There is not, however, in Switzerland such a separation of the federal from the state and local taxes as prevails in the United States. The Swiss alcohol monopoly is administered by the Confederation, but the profits, which correspond to our tax on spirits, are divided among the cantons in proportion to their population; and the same is true of an unimportant tax on commercial travelers. The military exemption tax, imposed upon all persons liable to military service who do not perform such duty in any year, while regulated by federal law, is administered by the several cantons; and the proceeds—a very substantial sum—are divided equally between the cantons and the Confederation.

Prior to the establishment of a federal bank under the Act of 1905, most of the cantons derived a substantial revenue from a tax on the note issues of the cantonal banks. Since that event, these issues have gradually disappeared, and with them the revenue from the bank taxes; but the cantons, by way of compensation, are now receiving from the federal treasury an annual grant of over two million francs, which will be assumed by the federal bank as soon as it is able to do so. And finally, the Confederation, out of the surplus accruing from very productive duties on imports, has granted subventions to the several cantons for the development of agriculture, promotion of education, conservation of forests, and the improvement of roads and rivers. As a result, the cantons now receive from the federal treasury, and from the military tax collected under federal law, a considerable part of their income. In 1900 not less than 13 per cent of the gross revenues of the cantons, and a materially larger percentage of the net revenues, came directly from the federal treasury or from the military exemption tax. It goes without saying that such an arrangement materially lightens the pressure of cantonal taxation, even though, under the subvention system, the federal grants are usually conditioned upon further expenditure by cantonal or local authorities.

It is further to be observed that the weight of cantonal and, more particularly, local taxation is considerably reduced by revenues derived from public property and industries. The income-yielding property of the cantons does not greatly exceed, if it exceeds at all, the cantonal debts; and the income from this source is largely, if not wholly, offset by interest payments. From the cantonal banks substantial profits are realized, while from forests the revenues are small, since most of the public forests of Switzerland are owned by the local governing bodies and not by the cantons. The net result is that in some of the richer cantons the pressure of state taxation is materially reduced by the revenue from such sources, and that the average canton is more favorably situated than the average American State. Among the local governing bodies conditions differ widely. In the cities the income-yielding property is generally much less than the municipal debts; but municipal industries, with the exception of street railways, usually yield a substantial profit and sometimes a very large one. In rural districts, on the other hand, communal industries are less important, but income-yielding properties far exceed communal indebtedness.

A large part of the forest area of Switzerland is owned by the communes, and the revenues from forests and other productive property materially lighten the weight of local taxation. There are, in fact, not a few communes where the income from public property and miscellaneous sources suffices to defray all local expenses, and communal taxation is unknown. Lest, however, I give you a false idea of average conditions, I hasten to add that the number of communes levying no taxes is steadily decreasing, and that in many localities taxes are exceedingly high.

Both cantons and communes, it appears, are increasingly dependent upon taxation, since other revenues have not in general kept pace with the growth of public expenditures. But up to the present the federal subventions and the revenues from public property or industries have made the financial conditions materially different from those which prevail in the United States, where both state and local governments are dependent almost exclusively upon taxes.

Not only is taxation a relatively smaller factor in the revenues of Swiss state and local governments, but its sources are far more diversified than in the United States. In 1902, according to our last census, not less than 82 per cent of the tax revenues of American state and local governments was derived from *ad valorem* assessments upon property. For Switzerland no similar statistics are available, but it is certain that the property tax, while usually more important than any other, furnishes a much smaller proportion of the aggregate tax revenues than in our own country. The various imposts employed are numerous and difficult to classify, but for our purpose it will suffice to divide them into personal, sumptuary, license or privilege, transfer, income, and property taxes.

Our first group includes poll, household, and habitation taxes. Cantonal poll taxes are usually levied at moderate rates; but local poll taxes are sometimes very high, and, what is more, are rigorously collected. In the canton of Zurich there are many communes where the local poll tax ranges from eight to fourteen francs, to which must be added the cantonal tax of one and one half francs; and there are other cantons in which these figures are approached or even exceeded. In Vaud, where the tax is graduated according to the resources of the taxpayer, the rates in some places rise to five or six hundred francs. Household taxes, imposed on heads of housholds, are in use locally in a number of cantons, and range from one to sixteen francs per houshold. Where poll and household taxes coexist, as is frequently the case, every head of a household, even though he be a small farmer or common laborer, may have to pay a poll tax of from ten to sixteen francs and a household tax of from eight to fourteen. The habitation or rental tax is used by the canton of Geneva and some of the larger cities of other cantons. Altogether it is evident that these taxes on persons, though not found everywhere, have in Switzerland a scope and rigor quite unknown in our own country, with the possible exception of a few of the Southern States.

Sumptuary taxes on servants, horses and pleasure carriages, billiard tables, automobiles, bicycles, and dogs, are extensively employed by the canton of Geneva; and elsewhere are represented chiefly by taxes on automobiles, bicycles, and dogs, with here and there a tax on billiard tables or pianos. With these we may include the monopoly of the sale of salt, from which all of the cantons derive a certain amount of revenue. The produce of these taxes is nowhere very important, but it helps to reduce the pressure of direct taxes on property or income. In Geneva, at the present time, personal and sumptuary taxes furnish about 10 per cent of the tax revenue of the canton.

License or privilege taxes are represented in all cantons by peddlers' licenses and the very interesting licenses for hunting and fishing; also by innkeepers' licenses and licenses to sell intoxicating liquors at retail, which in most cantons, on account of the customs of the people and political power of the licensees, are not as high as they ought to be, and very far below the rates now charged in many American States. Some cantons, too, impose taxes, or concession fees, on water-power privileges, and are beginning to derive a substantial revenue therefrom. And finally, in lieu of a tax on business profits, a few cantons impose a general license tax, modeled more or less closely after the French "*patente*," on all occupations, industries, or professions.

In practically all cantons certain transfer taxes yield a substantial revenue, and in a few a general system of transfer and transaction taxes affords a very large income. First in importance are the taxes on inheritances and gifts, which are found in nearly every canton and are relatively more productive than the inheritance taxes of the American States; in 1900 they yielded about one sixth as much as all the direct taxes levied by the cantons. Then come taxes on transfers of real estate, which are found in about two thirds of the cantons, and sometimes, as in Geneva, Vaud, Bern, and Zurich, afford a very large revenue. Two thirds of the cantons also impose stamp taxes on various commercial or legal transactions, and three tax transfers on the stock exchanges. In 1900 the cantons derived from transaction and transfer taxes other than inheritance taxes over one sixth as much as they received from all direct taxes; with the inheritance taxes included, the yield of the transfer and transaction taxes amounted to approximately one third of the direct taxes.

Geneva, which has developed these imposts into a general system of registration duties, after the French model, derives about as much revenue from them as it does from direct taxes; in 1909 the canton received 3,353,200 francs from transfer and succession duties and 3,437,800 francs from taxes on real and personal property. In all such comparisons, I should add, it is to be remembered that the taxes of the Swiss cantons constitute a very large proportion of the total levied for state and local purposes, whereas in our own country the revenues of the States are but a small fraction of the combined county and municipal revenues. When Geneva, therefore, raises a third or more of her cantonal revenues by transfer taxes, she greatly lightens the burden resting upon property subject to taxation; whereas the average American State, in a similar case, would not very greatly reduce the total taxes falling upon property.

The income tax is employed by twenty out of the twenty-five cantons. Usually it is designed to reach only incomes not derived from taxable property, such as business profits in excess of the current rate of interest on the invested capital, wages, salaries, and professional earnings. But in four cantons it extends to all incomes, so that there exists in these cases a so-called double taxation of property and the income therefrom. In one canton, Bern, the property tax is applied only to real estate and the mortgage indebtedness resting thereon, and the income tax reaches all incomes other than those derived from land and mortgages.

The result is that the function and financial importance of the income tax vary greatly from canton to canton. Where its function is merely to reach personal, industrial, and professional incomes, which pay nothing under the property tax, the tax on incomes produces, on an average, perhaps one third as much as the tax on property. Its precise yield depends not only upon the comparative rates of income and property taxation, but also upon the comparative completeness of the assessment of incomes and property. Where about one half of the taxable property evades assessment, as in Zurich, and there are large industrial or commercial centers in which the income tax is reasonably productive, the yield rises to 60 or 70 per cent of the income from the tax on property; and where the conditions are reversed, as in Fribourg or Vaud, the income tax may yield but 12 or 15 per cent of the amount collected from property.

Upon the other hand, in the four cantons where the function of the income tax is not only to reach personal, industrial, and professional incomes, but also to bring about the so-called double taxation of property and income, the yield usually exceeds that of the property tax. In Baselstadt, for instance, in 1909, the cantonal and local income taxes yielded 4,081,000 francs, while the property tax, which is not used for local purposes, yielded but 2,124,000 francs. According to their function, therefore, according to the comparative rates of income and property taxation, and according to the relative completeness of income and property assessment, the Swiss income taxes produce from 12 to 190 per cent of the yield of the taxes on property. In general, it may be said that in the average canton a substantial revenue is derived from taxes on incomes, and that the burden resting upon property is thereby materially reduced. The situation is clearly different from that of the American States, in which the income tax seldom exists, and never produces enough revenue to make the average taxpayer or public official conscious of its existence.

This excessively long introduction will have justified itself, perhaps, if it has made clear the fact that, although the status of the Swiss property taxes greatly resembles that of the property taxes of the American States, there are nevertheless important points of difference. Federal grants and subventions lighten the weight of cantonal and local taxation; revenues from property and public industries further reduce it; the burden that remains is not thrown almost wholly upon property, as in the United States, but is distributed among a variety of direct and indirect taxes, so that the share finally falling to the property tax, while usually the largest,[3] is relatively much smaller than in our own country. This fact I consider to be of capital importance. As will later appear, it goes far toward explaining the further fact that in Switzerland the property tax has not in general produced such intolerable conditions as attend its operation in the United States.

II

The constitutional status of the property tax in Switzerland is not unlike its status in our own country. The cantons are, generally speaking, sovereign in the matter of internal taxation; but, like the American States, are limited by certain provisions of the federal constitution. There is, in the first place, the general guarantee of the equality of all Swiss before the law, which somewhat resembles the fourteenth amendment to our federal Constitution. This has been invoked in at least one case of alleged discrimination in taxation, but has not yet received the wide extension given to the fourteenth amendment by our Supreme Court. There is also a general guarantee of freedom of industry and commerce from restrictive taxation, which in theory, and to some extent in practice, prohibits taxes so laid as to operate as a restraint on the trade or occupation concerned. And then, of far greater practical and theoretical importance,

[3] In Geneva the extraordinary development of transfer and miscellaneous taxes reduces the property taxes to an almost subordinate position. In Baselstadt, Solothurn, and Tessin the so-called double income tax is more important than the property tax.

there is a clause authorizing such federal legislation as may be needed to prevent double taxation. As yet no such legislation has been enacted; but the federal court, somewhat against its will, has been obliged to take cognizance of a large number of cases brought before it, and has formulated certain general principles which now control cantonal legislation at a number of points. The court has ruled that real property is taxable only at its situs, so that the cantons have no power to tax land outside their borders. Movables have been declared taxable only at the domicile of the owner, but this principle has been modified so far as to make taxable at its situs capital invested in a branch establishment, industrial or commercial, and the investment of a limited partner in a *"société en commandite."* With joint-stock companies, however, the court has held that to tax the companies at their seat and then tax the shareholders at their domiciles is not double taxation in the sense contemplated by the federal constitution. Other decisions concern persons successively domiciled in two cantons during a given year, and hold that only a proportionate part of any tax shall be paid in each canton. In general, the court has held to the theory that the double taxation contemplated by the constitution is that arising from intercantonal relations, and not that resulting from the legislation of a single canton.

The constitutions of the several cantons, like those of most American States, contain more or less extensive provisions concerning taxation. The constitution of Baselland contains about all the law that exists in that canton concerning the taxation of property and income; at the other extreme are constitutions that merely prohibit progressive taxation, fix the proportions that shall subsist between different taxes, limit the rates of direct taxation, or prescribe other general regulations. So far as I have yet found, none of them contains a requirement that everything must be taxed in the same way and at the same rate. In general, it is within the power of the cantonal authorities to classify property for taxation, and this is not infrequently done. Compared with the average American State, the Swiss canton is somewhat less trammeled by constitutional limitations, and therefore better able to adjust its tax laws to present-day needs.

The laws of the various cantons naturally enough differ at many points, but, like those of the American States, exhibit a general family resemblance. They either make all property subject to taxation, and then proceed to allow certain exemptions, or else proceed by process of specification, exempting all that is not made specifically taxable. By the one process or the other such things as personal effects, household goods, artisans' tools, and agricultural implements are usually exempted in whole or in part. Thus far the laws run like those of the American commonwealths, but now begin exemptions quite foreign to the practice of most of our States. Cattle are wholly exempted in several of the cantons. In French Switzerland two cantons tax no personal property except interest-yielding investments. Bern exempts all personalty other than mortgages, preferring to reach the income therefrom through her income tax. Appenzell (I. Rh.) knows nothing of the general property tax, and confines direct taxation to real estate. A most interesting class of exemptions concerns real property. Geneva exempts buildings used for agricultural purposes, Schwyz exempts capital necessary for agricultural operations, and three other cantons tax agricultural buildings at only one half or three quarters of their value. One provides that all buildings shall be valued at two thirds of their actual worth. Personal exemptions granted to the sick, aged, or infirm, and to widows and orphans, find their counterparts in the United States; but I know of no American State that, like Lucerne, accords a special exemption to heads of families; or, like St. Gall, acts upon the theory that the property of widows and orphans is more likely to be discovered than that of other persons, and therefore provides that it shall be assessed at only three quarters of its value. About half the cantons, finally, exempt a certain minimum amount of property, real or personal, the exemption ranging from two hundred to five thousand francs; so that in many cases even small estates in land are freed from taxation.

The deduction of debts is permitted on a far larger scale than in the United States, and it may be said that in Switzerland people are usually taxed upon their net fortunes. In cantons where the rates of taxation are progressive, this is the only logical course, since the absurdity of taxing a person progressively upon his debts is apparent to any one possessed of even a rudimentary sense of humor. A distinction is, however, made in most cantons between mortgage and other debts, and the treatment accorded the former is less liberal than that extended to the latter. Ordinary debts, not secured by mortgage, can be deducted from the gross value of one's entire estate in all cantons except Fribourg, where, however, the tax rate is proportional, and interest-yielding investments are the only form of personalty subject to taxation. Valais permits such deduction for the cantonal tax, but not for local taxation; Tessin forbids it if the creditor lives outside the canton; and Geneva limits it to fifty thousand francs. Concerning mortgage debts, the laws of the cantons vary about as widely as those of the American States. Appenzell (I. Rh.), which does not tax personal property, naturally enough refuses to allow the deduction of mortgages; but all the others now permit deduction to a greater or less degree. Two of them authorize it in all cases. Some allow deduction only in case the landowner is a resident of the canton; others permit such resident landowner to deduct only in case the creditor lives in the canton and is taxed on the mortgage. Several allow nonresidents as well as residents the deduction, provided the creditor lives in the canton and is taxed there. Others extend the privilege of deduction to nonresidents upon conditions which cannot be enumerated here. Geneva limits the amount deducted to fifty thousand francs. A further complication arises from the fact that in some cantons where deduction of mortgages is permitted in connection with the cantonal tax it is not allowed in local taxation. And finally, the canton of Vaud, which permits deduction even for local taxation, authorizes the communes to levy, in addition to the regular tax, a special realty tax for which no deduction is permitted. The result is that in Switzerland resident landowners can usually deduct their mortgaged debts, and that proprietors not resident in a canton are sometimes granted the deduction; but that for local taxation the laws are somewhat less liberal. The general situation is in striking contrast with that of most American States, which tax real estate without deduction and then endeavor to tax mortgage notes as personal property.

Most of the cantons require taxpayers to make a return of their taxable property, but a few cling to the method of official assessment, and ask for no declarations. About half confine the declaration to personal property, and tax real estate according to official estimate. Declarations are required annually in some cantons; in others, at periods of from two to six years. Usually they must be in writing, but two cantons still accept oral statements. In two cases declarations are demanded only when a person settles in the canton, and thereafter assessments are revised annually by the officials. When real estate is assessed by official estimate, general revaluation takes place at such periods as from five to twenty years; but in a few cases no definite time is set, and as a result land is sometimes taxed on the basis of cadastral valuations made half a century ago. The forms of declaration prescribed in the various cantons differ widely. Sometimes the taxpayer is required to submit a very detailed statement resembling those which most Americans conscientiously abstain from making; in other cases, including cantons where personal property is most successfully taxed, nothing is required but a bare declaration that the net taxable property amounts to a certain sum, and that thereof a certain part represents the value of real estate. In Geneva, where personal estates are taxed with conspicuous success, the taxpayer makes no declaration of his property, but states merely the amount of the tax due from him. So far as I can learn, no canton requires the declaration to be under oath, but in some cases oaths are required if a person wishes to appeal from an assessment made by the officials. The statements of taxpayers are subject to official revision, and persons who make no declaration are assessed by the officials and frequently lose their right of appeal.

For recalcitrant or dishonest contributors the laws provide the usual terrors, together with some that are not usual. Persons who make no declaration, besides being assessed by the officials and losing the right of appeal, are sometimes fined. For continued recalcitrancy at least one canton prescribes cumulative doomage. False returns are punished by fines of larger or smaller amount, and one canton even authorizes imprisonment. Where evasion is detected, nearly all the cantons promptly proceed to recover back taxes for periods varying from two to twenty years, and add thereto fines varying from 100 to 2000 per cent of the amounts withheld. Back taxes for five years and a penalty of five times the amount of the taxes represent, perhaps, the average rigor of the laws. For the detection of evasion there are two principal agencies. One is the returns of estates subject to the inheritance tax, which may be made in the first instance by heirs, but are naturally subject to official control. The other is the compulsory official inventory made at the taxpayer's death, and pending which his books and papers are placed under seal. Seven cantons now have the official inventory; the others content themselves with returns of property subject to the inheritance tax and such other information as the assessors are able to gather. In general, the Swiss laws are more severe than those of most American States, but no canton has yet hit upon the Ohio expedient of dragging bank officials into court and compelling them to testify concerning the affairs of their customers. On the contrary, Swiss banks can refuse to give information about their customers' affairs, and uniformly would refuse to do so if the request were made.

Tax rates are much more stable in Switzerland than in the United States. Sometimes the rate of the cantonal tax is fixed by the constitution or by a general law not easily changed. Even when it is nominally variable, it does not fluctuate much from year to year, and in practice is likely to remain stationary over considerable periods. Variable rates are generally considered an evil, while proposals to increase existing rates must often be submitted to popular vote and are usually rejected;

so that the cantonal authorities must ordinarily content themselves with a stationary tax rate for property and income, and adjust their budgets accordingly. For local taxation the rates are subject to more variation, but probably fluctuate less than local tax rates in the United States. A few cantons have established maximum rates which communes are under no circumstances permitted to exceed; some others fix a rate which the communes cannot exceed without permission of the cantonal authorities.

The rate is usually the same for real and personal property, but this is not always the case. Four cantons impose a lighter rate on real estate than on personalty. In a number of others the rate is nominally the same, but realty is in fact less heavily taxed than personalty by virtue of provisions that it shall be assessed for only 70 or 80 per cent of its value, or that buildings shall be assessed at two thirds of their value, or that agricultural land shall be assessed at 70 per cent of its value, or that buildings devoted to agricultural purposes shall be exempted in whole or in part. Upon the other hand, one canton, after taxing land and movables equally under the property tax, imposes on real estate a second tax based upon the income it yields. It should be said, however, in this connection, that many cantons tax transfers of real estate; and that such taxes sometimes, as in Vaud and Geneva, go far to offset the lower rate of taxation for real property. At least one canton, finally, gives to forests a separate classification, and assesses them either at one half their present exchange value or at twelve and one half times their average net yield for the last ten years.

Switzerland has been called the home of progressive taxation, and much has been written about the progressive rates of her property, income, and inheritance taxes. While sometimes practiced in the Middle Ages, progression was not extensively employed until the last half of the nineteenth century, during which it steadily grew in favor. In some form or other it is now found in nearly all the cantons, but not necessarily for all taxes, and in the taxation of property is less used than in the taxation of incomes and inheritances. In eleven out of the twenty-five cantons the property tax is proportional, and in six of the others local taxes must be proportional, although the cantonal taxes are progressive. The methods of applying progression are various, and have been variously classified by different writers. All have their respective advantages and disadvantages, a discussion of which would carry me too far afield. The important thing for present purposes is that the scale of progression, while sometimes sharp, does not suggest a desire to confiscate large fortunes; and that, wherever the taxes on large estates seem excessive, this result is due not so much to the progressive scale as to the fact that the taxes are too heavy all along the line. I am of the opinion, however, that some of the cantons have carried progression quite as far as is safe or financially profitable. For this country Swiss experience can offer nothing of present profit, since, until we have a tolerably complete assessment of taxable property, progression would mean nothing but graduating a person's tax rate according to his ability or inclination to dodge his taxes.

The taxation of corporations offers such a favorable field for diversity of methods that Swiss lawmakers would have been more than human if they had failed to take advantage of it; and the decision of the federal court that the constitution of the Confederation does not prohibit double taxation of the property of a corporation and its capital stock, has left them entirely free to do their best—or worst. About one third of the cantons tax corporations domiciled within their borders, usually in the same manner as natural persons, and exempt the shares of these companies, shares of companies not domiciled within the canton remaining subject to taxation. Nearly a third more tax the shares like other personal property, and then tax the company on some part of its property, or on its income, or in some other way that results in the company paying something less than the ordinary assessment on all its property. Vaud seeks to avoid double taxation by making the shares taxable to the holders for their par value, and then taxing the companies on their reserve and other surplus funds, including sinking funds. Double taxation of stockholders and the property of the corporation is practiced in a few cantons, but in at least one of these, Baselstadt, the tax levied on the corporation is so moderate that it leads to no complaint, and may perhaps be defended as a franchise tax.

What has been said applies particularly to cantonal taxes; for local taxation some cantons suspend all rules of the game, and allow the communes to pluck as many feathers as they please from any portion of any goose that may chance within their reach. Not unnaturally, this results in more squawking than is consistent with sound principles of finance. Other cantons suspend only part of the rules, and thus extend partial protection. Vaud applies to communal taxation the same regulations that govern cantonal, and so prevents double taxation. If cantonal taxation is diverse, communal is chaotic; and in general it may be said that in this matter our American States, although sufficiently in need of instruction, have little to learn from the laws of most of the Swiss cantons.

In a majority of the cantons the taxes levied for local purposes exceed those for the use of the cantons, but in no such overwhelming proportion as in the United States, while in a number of cases cantonal taxes exceed communal. One canton confines communal taxation to a tax on incomes, and in the city of Geneva the municipal tax is a combined income and occupation tax. But elsewhere the property tax is used for local purposes, though usually in combination with income, poll, household, habitation, and even other taxes. In most, if not all, cases the tax on property is more important than any of the others, and the rates are sometimes very high, here and there approaching those prevailing in the United States. In French Switzerland, where communal administration in any locality is centralized in the hands of a single governing body, the political commune, the citizen pays but one tax in respect of his property. But in the German cantons, where local administration is parceled out among a number of different sorts of communes, we find separate school taxes, church taxes, poor taxes, and finally "police" taxes which are for the general expenses of civil government. In former times the communes, like the Massachusetts towns during the seventeenth century, were allowed great freedom in matters of taxation; and in a few cantons today they are subject to little regulation. But the chaotic conditions resulting from such "local option" have led most of the cantons to regulate local taxation by general law. Sometimes the rules prescribed for the local taxation of property are the same as for cantonal; but frequently they differ at certain points, as we have had occasion to remark. The deduction of mortgage debts is not so generally permitted for local taxation as for cantonal, since it would leave some communes very little taxable property. In dealing with corporations the cantonal laws designed to prevent double taxation are often suspended —perhaps for a similar reason. And finally, progressive taxation is frequently prohibited, even in cantons that make their own taxes progressive, either because deduction of mortgage debts is not permitted, or because it is realized that the taxable property which a citizen owns in a single commune may be only a part of his fortune.

III

Such in outline are Swiss methods of taxing property. Now, how do they work?

It will be convenient to begin with the taxation of real estate. Land is supposed to be assessed either at its selling value or according to the capitalized average yield. In cities the former basis is naturally the one generally adopted, but in many rural districts, where transfers are infrequent, the latter is easier to apply. There are undoubtedly many cases where assessment according to the selling price gives a higher valuation than assessment according to the capitalized average yield. A generation ago, when expenditures were smaller and taxes lower, the assessment of land was considerably below the true value; but more recently the need for increased revenue has obliged assessors to raise the valuation. In the cities, generally, assessments are now tolerably close to the true values, but in rural districts they are probably on a relatively lower basis. There are, doubtless, exceptions to the rule; but in most of the cantons it appears that, in respect of real estate, the cantonal taxes fall with undue weight on the urban districts. Large tracts of forest and pasture land belonging to rural communes are assessed for state taxation at only a third or a half of their value. Local assessors sometimes deliberately aim at low valuations in order to reduce the commune's contribution to the cantonal tax. In a few cantons there has been no general revaluation for an absurdly long time, and some other conditions exist which resemble those known in the United States. I incline, however, to the opinion that the inequalities in the valuation of land in Switzerland are seldom as great as in our own country, that the average conditions are considerably better there than among us, but that in some localities in the United States the assessment of real estate is quite as satisfactory as in any of the Swiss cantons.

Buildings are usually assessed at about the figure for which they are insured, though special conditions sometimes warrant a departure from this rule. Since in most of the cantons insurance is compulsory, this part of the assessors' task is a comparatively simple matter. The partial or total exemption of buildings used for agricultural purposes tends sometimes to reduce the share of the cantonal tax falling upon rural districts, and there is reason for thinking that in rural communes assessors sometimes deal more leniently with all buildings than city officials are wont to do.

Some cantons, as we have seen, impose a lower rate of taxation on realty than on personalty; and others, by exempting a part of the value of buildings, or land and buildings, accomplish substantially the same result. This is occasionally justified on the ground that inasmuch as some personal property evades taxation, it is only fair that realty should have a lower rate. The usual justification is that it is a necessary concession to the agricultural interests, which stand in special need of the fostering care of government. The actual reason, however, for the favored position accorded to real property is that in most of the cantons a majority of the voters are small proprietors and are able to help themselves to anything they may desire. With the growth of public expenditures and the need of additional revenue the subject is beginning to attract attention. In the cities, and sometimes elsewhere, taxation of the increment of land values is frequently proposed; and one small commune has recently voted to introduce such a tax. Whatever the outcome of the present discussions concerning land taxation, it seems clear that the favors accorded to real estate in some of the cantons are without justification, and invite correction at the earliest possible moment.

The deduction of mortgages is a topic of peculiar interest. In most, if not all, of the cantons the mortgage indebtedness resting upon the land is surprisingly large. Although it is sometimes as low as 25 per cent of the assessed valuation of real estate, the average for all Switzerland is probably as high as 40 per cent; while there are not a few cantons where it exceeds 50 per cent of the realty valuations, and considerable districts where it rises to 60 or even 70 per cent. It is not strange, therefore, that, for local taxation, the deduction of mortgages is frequently prohibited, even when it is permitted for the cantonal taxes. Several causes have contributed to produce this large mortgage indebtedness, and it is not easy to say how important a factor tax laws may have been; but it is clear that the right to deduct mortgages, so generally granted in Switzerland, has been a material factor in the situation. In cantons where the tax on personal property is widely evaded, and we shall see presently that there are such, a person can mortgage his land and invest the proceeds in securities which will partly or wholly escape taxation. Then, too, when the local tax on real property is progressive, it is obviously to the advantage of a nonresident proprietor to mortgage his land, since he thereby reduces the net value of his property and gains the advantage of a lower tax rate. Even when the tax on personalty is not evaded, and the rate is proportional, it is evident that exemption from double taxation, while it offers no special inducement to borrowing, removes an obstacle to the conversion of a part of one's real estate into personal property promising a higher rate of interest than is paid upon the mortgage.

There has been in Switzerland some complaint of excessive taxation of forests, and in 1889 the Society of Swiss Foresters turned for relief to the federal government, which could take no action, since the matter was one in which the cantons are sovereign. At least one canton has provided a special method of taxing forests, but usually private forests are subject to the property tax. Yet conditions are widely different from those prevailing in the United States, and the general result is much better. In the first place, a very large proportion of the forest area is owned by the communes, and is therefore exempt from local taxation. Then the law prohibits indiscriminate cutting, so that the value of a forest depends upon its sustained yield rather than on the profit that can be made from stripping the land of every stick of timber. And finally, the method of assessing land according to the capitalized average yield results in a lower valuation and is more favorable to rational utilization than the usual provision of American laws that land shall be assessed at its selling value. Swiss methods of taxing private forests may not be all that could be desired—upon that subject I am prepared to express no opinion; but it is clear that the Swiss property taxes are far less injurious than those of the American States in so far as the latter are enforced.

We turn to the taxation of personal property. The results achieved in different cantons vary all the way from bad to satisfactory, through a variety of intermediate grades which I will not undertake to characterize. At the worst, conditions are better than in most American States; at the best, they are about as good as under any system of personal property or income taxation, and I do not except the income taxes of Great Britain and Prussia. While I am not yet prepared to assign a definite status to every canton, I believe that, in respect of the taxation of personal property, the Swiss states may be divided into four groups.

The first includes the two city cantons, Geneva and Baselstadt, and perhaps canton Vaud, where the taxation of personal property is conspicuously successful. Declarations are actually made by practically all taxpayers, as required by law, and the proportion of incorrect returns is comparatively small. Such evasion as exists is confined largely to the smaller properties, while the large estates are in general returned with scrupulous fidelity. In official reports of Geneva one may find such statements as the following: "Half of the revenue from the tax on personalty, or about 600,000 francs, is turned in by about one hundred contributors, who, it should be recognized, have fulfilled their obligations with absolute correctness and loyalty. It is not among them, but rather elsewhere, that one must look for evasions that cause loss to the treasury." In Baselstadt, where there is a double property and income tax, less than 4 per cent of the taxpayers paid 74.4 per cent of the income tax for 1908; and statistics of the property tax, if they were available, would probably make an equally remarkable showing. In both Geneva and Basel a progressive rate of taxation contributes largely to the results just stated, but it is also clear that, without a substantially complete return of the larger properties, the progressive rates would not be as productive as they are. Equally significant is the fact that in Geneva, in 1909, the tax on personalty yielded 2,135,900 francs, and that on realty 1,301,900. After making allowance for the circumstance that the rate of taxation on personal property is higher than that on realty, it remains true none the less that the assessment of the former is larger than that of the latter. I do not wish to overdraw the picture. I know very well that no taxation of income or personal property can be wholly free from evasion, and am sure that some evasion exists at Geneva and Basel. But it is probable that in those cities not less than 80 or 90 per cent of the taxable personalty is returned for taxation, and it is certain that public opinion condemns tax dodging and supports the strictest enforcement of the law. There is, then, no reason for thinking that the tax on personal property in Geneva or Basel is less successful than the income taxes of such countries as Great Britain or Prussia. Whether Vaud does equally well may perhaps be doubted. Geneva and Basel are practically city states, and a uniform enforcement of the law is comparatively easy. Vaud, however, presents a variety of local conditions, communal tax rates are sometimes high, and the canton has reached its present fairly satisfactory position only after a bitter struggle over progressive taxation, the marks of which are not yet wholly effaced. That she is tolerably successful in enforcing the taxation of personal property cannot be doubted; I hesitate, however, to accord her the same rank as Geneva and Basel.

The second group includes a number of cantons, like Aargau and Solothurn, where severe laws, accompanied by vigorous efforts to enforce them, result in a fairly complete assessment of personal property, but unfavorable conditions in many localities render impossible such results as are obtained in Geneva and Basel. The cantons of this group probably tax from 60 to 70 per cent of the personalty subject to assessment, but in some communes the local tax rates are so high as to make it impossible for a person to pay his taxes upon a full valuation of his property. The result is that the law is not strictly enforced in such communes, or else that wealthy taxpayers take up their residence in localities where the rates are lower. The conditions that exist resemble at many points those which in the United States attend attempts to enforce vigorously the taxation of personal property; but in general these cantons have done very much better than any American State of which I have knowledge, and in them the tax on personalty, if not a conspicuous success, is far from being an utter failure.

In the third group belong a number of cantons in which conditions somewhat resemble those which prevailed in Massachusetts, and perhaps other American States, before the Civil

War. Here the terrors of the official inventory are unknown, and in other respects the laws are less severe than those of Vaud, Aargau, or Solothurn. Methods of enforcement, also, while not deserving to be called lax, are usually less rigorous than in the cantons of the first and second groups. Yet the rates of taxation are low; and, despite milder laws and administration, a substantial amount of personal property is actually assessed, perhaps as much as 50 or 60 per cent of that liable to taxation, and occasionally somewhat more. In this class I should place Neuchâtel, Zug, Uri, Nidwald, Obwald, and perhaps three or four others. Forty years ago the majority of the cantons employing the property tax might have answered to this description, but in some of these the growth of expenditures and taxes has either forced a change of methods of administration or produced the conditions that prevail in cantons of the next class.

To this fourth group belong notoriously Zurich, St. Gall, Appenzell (A. Rh.), Tessin, and probably Thurgau. In these cantons conditions approximate, though perhaps they seldom equal, those common in the American States. Few people make declarations, as required by law, and even fewer make honest ones. Personal property either evades assessment or tends to concentrate in localities where tax rates are low. Officials hesitate to enforce the law, because under existing conditions it is practically unenforcible, and public opinion will not sanction strict enforcement. Small properties or incomes and the estates of widows or orphans are heavily taxed, being required to contribute one fourth or one third of the income, while wealthy persons, able to evade the law, escape with a relatively small assessment. To an American audience it is unnecessary to describe in greater detail conditions so very similar to those prevailing in the United States.

How are we to account for the widely divergent results obtained by the various cantons in the taxation of personal property? Clearly not on the ground of differences in the character of the people, for in point of general honesty and respect for law it does not appear that the people of Zurich or St. Gall are inferior to those of Basel or Geneva. Nor is it a mere matter of severity in the provisions of the laws or of rigor in their execution. The milder laws and administration of the third group of cantons yield better results than more drastic measures employed by cantons of the fourth group. Zurich and St. Gall provide quite as heavy penalties as Basel and Geneva, yet do not get the same results. Appenzell (A. Rh.) has the dreaded official inventory, as has Thurgau for certain cases, yet personal property largely escapes them; while it is well taxed in cantons that, like Basel and Geneva, content themselves with the returns of estates subject to the inheritance tax and such casual information as may come to the officials. Even state supervision of local assessments, while good in itself and productive of excellent results, is powerless to secure the enforcement of the laws under the conditions that exist in the fourth group of cantons, as the experience of Zurich, St. Gall, Thurgau, and Appenzell (A. Rh.) sufficiently demonstrates. Upon all these points Swiss experience teaches the same lesson as American: Draconian laws and drastic administration are of no avail under conditions that make rigid enforcement of the law disastrous, and therefore intolerable.

No single cause has produced the diverse conditions prevailing in the different groups of cantons, but beyond question the most important factor in the problem is the rate of taxation. Wherever in Switzerland personal property is taxed with reasonable success, the rate is comparatively moderate; and wherever the rate exceeds the bounds of moderation, the severest laws fail to prevent general evasion. The cantons of the first group impose rates that vary from 40 cents per $100 to 70 cents per $100 for the largest estates, and for smaller properties, subject to the lowest rates of the progressive scale, are decidedly less. Those in the second group suffer from high rates of communal taxation in certain localities. When the combined state and local taxes range from 40 to 60 cents per $100, the property tax may be said to work well; and in communes where it rises to $1 or $1.20 per $100, the attempt to reach personal property utterly fails. The cantons of the third group, by reason of their economic and financial positions, get along with a low rate of taxation for property, and their combined state and local taxes range from 30 to 60 cents per $100, seldom exceeding the higher figure, and sometimes not reaching the lower. As a result, their less drastic laws and milder administration suffice to reach a substantial proportion of the taxable personal property, as was the case in Massachusetts and perhaps other American States during the first half of the nineteenth century. And finally, the cantons of the fourth group are vainly endeavoring to enforce taxation of personal estates at rates which, for combined cantonal and local purposes, usually range from 80 cents to $1.20 per $100, and in many cases rise to $1.50 or $2 per $100. The only possible result is hopeless failure.

This point is so important that you will bear with me if I make my illustrations more specific. In Geneva the *mobilière,* or personal property tax, is used only for cantonal purposes, although in the city of Geneva there is a light local tax on the income of personal as well as real property. The rate, moreover, is fixed, and for the largest estate is at present 38 7/10 cents per $100. In Baselstadt the rate of taxation on property and income is also fixed, and for estates of the largest size the combined property and income tax in 1909 amounted to 62 cents per $100. In Vaud the *mobilière* is used for local purposes, and in some communes the rate is fairly high. The combined state and local rates usually range from 60 to 70 cents per $100 for large estates; and precisely because they sometimes rise to 70 cents or even higher, the canton is probably not in as good a position as Geneva and Basel. At the other end of the scale, in the fourth group, the canton of Zurich levies a state tax at a rate exceeding 40 cents per $100 for the larger estates, to which are added communal taxes averaging more than 80 cents per $100. In some cases the communal rates rise to $1.40 per $100, so that a large property will be taxed at a rate of $1.80 per $100. In the second group local conditions are worse than in Vaud, and seldom so bad as in Zurich, which accounts for the intermediate position of these cantons. In the third group the cantonal taxes vary from 3 to 25 cents per $100, and the local range from zero to 40 or 50 cents per $100. Thus, in Neuchâtel, the cantonal tax is 20 cents per $100, while local rates usually range from 20 to 30 cents per $100, and by law are limited to a maximum of 40 cents, so that the total tax levied on property is usually from 40 to 50 cents per $100, and can never exceed 60 cents. In Obwald the cantonal rate is but 3 cents per $100, and the local rates range from 20 to 30 cents per $100; in Uri and Zug both cantonal and local taxes are usually higher than in Obwald, but the total seldom exceeds 50 cents per $100, and is often considerably less. In most parts of Switzerland the local taxes are higher than the cantonal, and the excessive rates sometimes prevailing are the chief cause for the unsatisfactory working of the property tax in some of the cantons.

Perhaps some of you may ask whether I have not put the cart before the horse; and whether the high rates of taxation in certain cantons are not the result of evasion of the tax on personal property rather than the cause of it. I reply that historically they have been both cause and effect; but that, once established and accepted by the taxpayer as inevitable, they become the cause of a chronic state of evasion which nothing but a radical change in the system is likely to cure. This point I can make clear by the example of my own State. Prior to 1850, when rates of taxation in Massachusetts were less than one third of their present average, which is in excess of $1.70 per $100, a substantial proportion of the property assessed consisted of personal estates; in Boston the proportion of personalty varied from 40 to 50 per cent of the total assessment. But when growing expenditures subjected the property tax to a pressure it was not able to stand, personal property began largely to escape taxation; and this increasing evasion then became a second factor contributing to the further rise of tax rates. By the early seventies, when the average rate in the commonwealth had advanced to $1.50 or $1.60 per $100, taxpayers had adjusted themselves to the changed conditions; and, therefore, when they made or abstained from making returns of their taxable property, acted upon the reasonable and inevitable assumption that the tax rate would be about $1.50 or $1.60. Thirty years of added experience have now hardened this assumption into an accepted fact, and it is therefore correct to say that the high rate of taxation makes a full assessment of personal estates impossible in Massachusetts.

It is by a generally similar process that the property tax in certain Swiss cantons has broken down. In Switzerland, as in the United States, the last fifty years have witnessed an unprecedented increase of public expenditures. According to Schanz and Cérenville, the total federal and cantonal taxes of Switzerland increased from 18,800,000 francs in 1856 to 51,200,000 francs in 1876 and 109,000,000 francs in 1896, more than doubling in each period of twenty years. At the present time they exceed 160,000,000 francs, and are still rising. If the total communal taxes could be ascertained, the showing would be even more striking, since almost everywhere they have increased by leaps and bounds. Thanks to abundant revenues from custom duties, the Confederation until recently has been little embarrassed by the rising tide of expenditure; but the cantons and communes have had no similar resource at their command. Some of them, by voluntary or enforced economy, have restrained, but not altogether prevented, the increase of outlay. Some, by thrifty husbandry, contrive to draw larger revenues from property or industries. Some have made large use of transfer and transaction taxes, and most have laid heavier hands on inheritances and successions. Here and there local taxes on polls and households have risen to extraordinary figures. But most cantons and a majority of communes have been unable to avoid increased pressure on property and income. Income taxes have been introduced where formerly only property taxes existed, and in one case a property tax where there had been only a tax on incomes. Withal there has been a sharper assessment of taxable property or incomes, with a sharper graduation of rates designed to secure more revenue from the larger contributors. In proportion as expenditures have been held in restraint or other sources of revenue developed, pressure on the property tax has been reduced, and a breakdown averted. The cantons where personal property is successfully taxed to-day are those which have managed to keep the pressure within reasonable bounds, and those which fail to do so are the ones that have done what the American States did during the last half of the nineteenth century. Not a few cantons have improved their methods of administration and imparted increased rigor to their tax laws. These measures have had excellent results when other conditions were favorable, but they have utterly failed to bring about a satisfactory assessment of personal property for taxation at the rates of $1 or $1.50 per $100. The fundamental factor in every canton has been the tax rate. A property tax levied at the rate of 50 cents per $100 is one thing, a tax levied at the rate of $1 or $1.50 per $100 is quite another. The former, as Swiss experience shows, may be enforced with conspicuous success; the latter never has been, nor can be, enforced in respect of any kind of property capable of concealment or undervaluation.

The taxation of incomes is in most cantons so closely connected with the taxation of property that I am constrained to refer briefly to the results attained. Speaking broadly, there can be no question but that the Swiss cantons have found the supplementary income tax on personal, professional, or industrial incomes a useful adjunct of the tax on property. It is enforced with at least tolerable success, yields a substantial revenue, and places under contribution a class of incomes, which, under a pure property tax, would pay nothing. At this point Swiss experience has been absolutely different from that of the handful of American States that have experimented with a tax on incomes, but with so little success that the average taxpayer hardly knows of its existence. Concerning the working of the double system of property taxation in Baselstadt, Baselland, Tessin, and Solothurn, I prefer within the necessary limits of this paper to say nothing. The picture, however, is not all light;

it undoubtedly has shadows which sometimes are rather dark. In agricultural districts taxation of incomes partly or almost wholly breaks down. The farmer believes that the use of his house, the living which his family gets off the farm, and everything else except the savings he puts into the bank are not—or at least should not be—included under the head of taxable income; and accordingly he does not include them. Where agricultural earnings are taxed on the basis of taxpayers' declarations, entire districts of great fertility contribute little or nothing; and the burden of taxation falls, therefore, with undue weight on industrial or commercial centers where incomes can be better ascertained and assessed. Thus, a city that pays 16 per cent of the cantonal tax on property may pay 36 per cent of the tax on incomes, and one that pays 13 per cent of the former may pay 39 per cent of the latter. To meet this difficulty, one canton arbitrarily fixes the taxable income from agriculture at a certain percentage of the value of the land, and another fixes the tax on agricultural incomes at three eighths of 1 per cent of the value of the land. Nor is the difficulty of taxing agricultural incomes the only one encountered. Small merchants and manufacturers frequently do not know the size of their incomes, and, like the farmers, think they should be taxed only on what they save. In Baselstadt, where the larger incomes are supposed to be pretty fully returned, it is evident that smaller incomes evade assessment to a considerable extent. Naturally enough, persons receiving fixed salaries or wages are unable to escape, and in some cantons, particularly Bern, it is believed that this class of contributors is considerably overtaxed. Altogether Swiss experience, while not unfavorable to state taxation of incomes, shows that such taxes present difficulties much like those encountered in taxing personal property, and for their successful operation require the very best methods of administration.

A subject that I cannot wholly ignore is state supervision of the assessment of property and income. In Switzerland, as in our own country, the assessment of property is, in the first instance, intrusted to local officials; and there, as here, it has been found advantageous to bring the process of assessment under state supervision or control. Swiss communes, like American municipalities and counties, naturally desire to attract or keep wealthy residents and large employers of labor; and to do so are often willing to make concessions inconsistent with both spirit and letter of the law. Actual bargains between assessors and taxpayers have probably been rarer in the Swiss cantons than in the American States, yet they are not unknown. Still more common are cases where local officials are unable to withstand the threat of withdrawal of property to some other commune where tax rates are lower or the officials more given to hospitality. In cantons where local tax rates are usually high, there seem always to be cities of refuge where oppressed taxpayers are assured of a cordial welcome. On Lake Constance and on the Rhine there are said to be colonies of wealthy people, who in selecting their places of domicile have considered, among other things, the advantages of a low tax rate and perhaps a moderate assessment. Then there are cases where a small commune is dominated by a large corporation which employs a majority of the inhabitants. In one canton there is a commune in which all voters and officials are employees of a large company which, as a consequence, used to enjoy a kind and amount of "home rule" in taxation inconsistent with the interests of the cantonal treasury.

To meet such conditions, state supervision and control have been introduced. Most of the cantons now provide for revision of the local assessments by a special commission appointed by the cantonal authorities. I hesitate to compare these commissions with the boards of equalization known to most American States; but in some cantons at least it appears that the commissions of revision have failed to revise just as our boards of equalization have usually failed to equalize, and for the same reason—lack of authority, time, and knowledge necessary for the task. I believe, however, that there have been cases in which the Swiss commissions have been able to accomplish valuable results. Not a few cantons go farther, and appoint members of the local assessment boards. One adds to each communal board a cantonal representative with merely consultative powers; three appoint a district chairman, very much like the county assessor of Indiana and some other States, who supervises the communal boards within his district; one appoints two members of each local board, and another appoints a majority of the members; one appoints the chairman of each board, intrusts the appointment of two members to the district, and allows the commune to appoint the other two; and one intrusts the whole work of assessment to district commissions appointed by the canton. The general results of cantonal supervision and control have been quite as good as those achieved by the tax commissions recently appointed by various American States, though perhaps not so striking, since the original conditions in Switzerland were generally better than in the United States, and the chance for improvement correspondingly less.

My last topic is popular lawmaking in its application to tax legislation. By the initiative and referendem the tax laws of most cantons are directly under popular control, and in financial matters the referendum has been very widely employed. I speak with hesitation of this subject, and am not yet ready to express an opinion as to whether, on the whole, popular lawmaking has worked badly or well. Some things, however, are too clear for dispute, and will be questioned by no one acquainted with the facts. The chief result has been everywhere to make a change of the tax laws exceedingly difficult, since most proposals are certain to be defeated. Laws imposing taxes on transportation companies, increasing the rates of the inheritance tax, or graduating more sharply the taxes on large fortunes or incomes are not infrequently accepted by the people, since the average voter knows that the result will be to increase some other fellow's taxes. But a general income tax affecting the mass of the voters, a reform needed to increase the effectiveness of the property tax, or a proposal to raise the rate of taxation in order to avoid recurring deficits, has about four chances in five of being rejected, and will be accepted only in cases of dire financial need. The introduction of property and income taxes during the last half of the nineteenth century was a work of the greatest difficulty, and the people of some cantons absolutely refused to accept a direct tax until their governments were on the road to bankruptcy. In Aargau the people bestowed upon themselves in 1870 the right of fixing the rate of the direct state tax, and then proceeded to fix it at zero. They were at length persuaded to divest themselves of this right, but they will not to-day consent to a slight increase in the rate of the state tax needed to meet a chronic deficit in the cantonal budget, and the canton has been obliged to borrow money in order to provide for accumulated deficits. Baselland had a somewhat similar experience, and secured the establishment of a state tax in 1892 only by reducing the rates of various indirect taxes and making certain concessions to the communes. The rates of taxation then authorized by the constitution have never been adequate, and the government to-day is at its wits' ends, since it knows well that it is useless to propose an increase. St. Gall's experience is equally interesting. Her antiquated tax laws had brought the canton to a pass where amendment was absolutely necessary, but in 1900 the people rejected a reform measure. Three years later, knowing that a new project would meet with a similar fate, the leaders of all parties agreed to enact a law and then endeavor to avoid a referendum. This was actually done, petitions for a referendum failing to receive the necessary number of signatures; but it is doubted by no one that if a referendum had been ordered, the new law, which has greatly improved the finances of the canton, would have been summarily rejected. Upon the other hand, it is clear that the difficulty of securing the adoption of new laws has made the cantonal governments extremely careful, and has tended to retard somewhat the increase of expenditures. In not a few cantons new laws have been accepted during the past ten or twelve years; and some persons, in an excellent position to judge, are of the opinion that, with a few conspicuous exceptions, the people have judged fairly well concerning the necessity of proposed legislation. Upon the basis of my present studies I am unwilling to accept or reject this opinion.

Concerning the taxation of property by the Swiss cantons, I submit, somewhat tentatively, the following conclusions. General conditions in Switzerland are more favorable than in the United States to the successful operation of direct taxation. There is less making of law, and very much more enforcement; consequently, respect for law is undoubtedly greater than in our own country, and the enforcement of tax laws far less difficult. Then the business of cantons and communes alike is conducted with reasonable efficiency, great economy, and absolute honesty; so that taxpayers know that their money will be well expended, and therefore contribute more willingly. State and local taxation, besides being reduced in amount by revenues from other sources, is more diversified than in the United States; and the pressure of the property tax is relatively less severe. In many respects the tax laws of the cantons are open to serious criticism. Some of them are antiquated statutes which, under popular lawmaking, it seems impossible to change. In America such laws would break down from mere weight of years without the slightest assistance from taxpayers or courts. Yet in Switzerland, with lower tax rates, efficient administration, and more favorable general conditions, they frequently work better than the most up-to-date revenue code ever adopted by a newly organized American State. In taxing real property the average Swiss canton probably avoids such gross inequalities as frequently occur in the United States, but a few of our commonwealths and not a few cities manage quite as well as any of the Swiss cantons or communes. And finally, Swiss experience shows that, with good administration and a moderate rate of taxation, personal property can be taxed with reasonable success. It also demonstrates that the most Draconian laws and rigorous administration are powerless to reach the great mass of personalty when the tax rate exceeds the bounds of reason and moderation. In Switzerland this fact finds general recognition; if American States would take it to heart, they could speedily solve the most difficult problem in the whole realm of taxation.

LOCAL OPTION IN TAXATION[1]

I

LOCAL option in taxation has received little attention from this Association since the first conference in 1907,[2] and various events of the last four years invite further consideration of the subject. As you are aware, the proposal is to grant local governing bodies more or less freedom in determining the methods of local taxation. Sometimes complete freedom is advocated; but often, and perhaps usually, it is proposed to reserve certain taxes for the exclusive use of the States, and to confine the choice of the local governments within limits consistent with the plan of segrating the sources of revenue.

Obviously complete freedom for the local bodies is inconsistent with segregation of state and local revenues, since it would permit local taxation of the objects which it is desired to reserve for the States. Beyond this, however, there seems to be no necessary relation between separation of the sources of revenue and local option. Complete freedom might be granted to localities, and the States might raise all their taxes by apportionment among the local governments upon the basis of local expenditures or revenues; in which case state taxation would in every locality fall upon the objects selected for local taxation. Upon the other hand, the sources of state and local revenue might be separated, either completely or partially, and at the same time the methods of local taxation might be rigidly prescribed in every detail by the State; in which case there would be no local option. Since, therefore, there is no necessary connection between the two proposals, I need not in this paper con-

[1] Reprinted from the Addresses and Proceedings of the Fifth National Conference on State and Local Taxation held at Richmond, Virginia, September 5-8, 1911. Reproduced by generous permission of the publishers.

[2] Addresses and Proceedings of the First National Conference, 73, 107, 495, 516.

sider the merits of the plan of separating the sources of state and local revenue; and shall confine myself to the single remark, that while complete freedom for the local governments is inconsistent with complete segregation of state and local revenues, separation does not necessarily imply that the local bodies shall be given the least freedom in selecting their methods of taxation.

In behalf of local option[3] the argument is advanced that freedom is good for communities, as it is for individuals. It manifestly awakens interest in local affairs, creates a feeling of responsibility for the welfare of one's city or county, and necessarily promotes good citizenship. Local option, it is said, accords with what is called the "American" idea of local self-government, and for it the attractive name "home rule in taxation" has been devised.

A second argument is that local governments are better fitted than the State to deal with local taxation since they have greater knowledge of local conditions, which differ very widely, and obviously are the parties most interested in the subject. Legislatures, it is said, cannot be expected to have sufficient acquaintance with diverse local conditions, or to have the time and interest necessary for solving local tax problems.

In the third place it is argued that uniform methods of local taxation are undesirable and that diversity is highly advantageous; for physical and social conditions differ so widely that a system that suits one locality is certain to be poorly adapted to the needs of another. This is usually illustrated by contrasting urban with rural districts, small cities with large, and agricultural with mining regions. It is further said that public opinion varies greatly from one locality to another, and that such differences are as important as physical and social.

[3] For arguments in behalf of local option, see Report of Committee on State and Municipal Taxation of the New York Chamber of Commerce, January 3, 1901; National Conference on Taxation, of the National Civic Federation, 1901, 114-115, 123-127; Report of New York City Advisory Commission on Taxation and Finance, 70-77; Report of the Tax Commission of Louisiana, 1908, 15-21; Addresses and Proceedings of the First National Conference of the National Tax Association, 73, 107, 495.

Laws, in order to be respected, must be supported by public sentiment; and tax laws, no less than others, should accord with the public sentiment of the localities within which they are to be enforced. Indeed, failure to conform to the diversities of local sentiment is considered to be an important cause of the breakdown of the general property tax.

It is further argued that local option will break up the rigid uniformity of our tax system, and greatly facilitate desirable changes. Under it the various sections of a State will not be bound together by a rigid tax law which cannot be altered without readjusting the burden of state taxation, and so arousing opposition from localities likely to be adversely affected. Moreover, local option would permit any county to experiment with novel methods, thus demonstrating their worth by actual trial; and in this manner useful object lessons would be furnished to other counties, and even the world at large. Such conditions, it is believed, would be highly favorable to progress, and would greatly accelerate desired reforms in American taxation.

More than this, it is suggested, local option would permit each community to foster by exemption from taxation any interest it desired to encourage, and to repress by heavy taxation any that it desired to discourage. So far as I can ascertain, no one has yet offered a list of the interests that should be encouraged or repressed by local governments, and we are, therefore, left to form our own conjectures upon this point.

And finally it is contended that one community cannot possibly injure another by the methods it adopts in raising local revenues. Under existing systems, conflicts of local interests too frequently arise, and obstruct the best-laid plans of reform; but with local option, such controversies will immediately disappear, and each community will go its own way unmolesting and unmolested.

These are the arguments for local option, or at least the arguments that usually figure in public discussion. There is another which for many advocates of the plan is the weightiest of all; but for equally weighty reasons it is frequently reserved for private consumption, and in public discussion is sometimes declared irrelevant. Local option is believed by many to be the shortest road to the single tax, and most, though not all, partisans of the former are advocates of the latter. Campaigns for state-wide adoption of the single tax have for the present little hope of success, particularly in States where the farmers are an important political force. Obviously, then, the best tactics are to secure reference of the question to the local governing bodies, and then to concentrate the attacking forces upon a few localities where the conditions are most favorable for success. It is evident, also, that at this point the case in favor of local option turns upon a mere question of tactics rather than upon a question of principle. If political control of any State ever passes into the hands of the single taxers, it is probable that the principle of home rule in taxation will lose much of its present popularity.

II

Criticism of the arguments for local option[4] may follow conveniently the order of presentation, and so begin with the laudation of local self-government. I suppose we all agree that it is desirable in every practicable way to foster interest in local affairs and create a livelier responsibility for them. I believe, also, that we all find it necessary to draw a line between purely local interests and matters that concern the entire State. The only question is where the line shall be drawn, and in determining that no help is to be derived from mere eulogies of local freedom or even captivating phrases like "home rule." For our purpose the important thing is to know whether local taxation is a matter of purely local concern, or one in which the State is interested, as well as the community.

[4] For criticisms of local option, see Addresses and Proceedings of the First National Conference, 516-518; *Quarterly Journal of Economics,* XXIV, 451-453; Report of the Joint Special Committee on the Taxation Laws of Rhode Island, 1910, 71-74; Annual Report of the State Board of Tax Commissioners of New York, 1911, 17-19; First Biennial Report of the Board of State Tax Commissioners of Oregon, 1911, 21-32.

The second argument for local option brings us squarely to the issue: Are local governments better fitted than the State to deal with the problem of local taxation? That they may have in many things greater knowledge of local conditions must be admitted; but that the conditions affecting local taxation present so many and minute differences that it is impossible, or even unusually difficult, to draft a general law regulating the matter is certainly untrue. I think that few advocates of local option would admit that they themselves do not understand tolerably well the conditions to which local taxation must be adjusted; I am persuaded that most of them, if invited to do so, would draft you a very perfect law prescribing a system of local taxation for any State; and I know that many of them are prepared upon short notice to instruct any community concerning the things it must do to work out its salvation in fiscal affairs. Therefore, until the advocates of local option conform practice to precept, we need not take too seriously the claim that only the people of a locality possess sufficient knowledge to draft an appropriate law concerning local taxation. I will only add that the experience of various foreign countries shows that it is practicable to regulate by general law even such a difficult matter as this.

It is further true, as alleged, that, generally speaking, the people of any locality are the persons most interested in local taxation, but it is far from true that they are the only persons concerned. There may be large amounts of property belonging to non-residents, and it is evident that such persons have an interest in taxation quite as real and direct as that of residents. It is true that rights of property, or at least landed property, are not regarded with much favor by many advocates of local option; but it is clear that all who believe that such rights deserve consideration, along with the other factors in the problem, cannot admit that the people of a locality are the only persons concerned with local taxation. Then there is the question of the rights of minorities, which leads to the further question whether the entire State has an interest in the treatment accorded to the minority of the residents of a community. The unrestrained power to tax means the power to destroy, and we shall deal somewhat less than frankly with this subject if we overlook the fact that many, and probably most, of the partisans of local option desire to destroy certain rights now connected with the institution of landed property. We cannot, therefore, admit that local taxation is a matter of purely local concern unless we believe that the institution of landed property is not a thing that interests the State as a whole. Another important consideration is the financial interest of the State itself. No State will or can permit its own revenues to be adversely affected by vagaries of local taxing authorities; and many plans for local option provide for reserving certain revenues for the exclusive use of the State, thus limiting the principle of home rule and conceding that local taxation is not a purely local affair.

If from argument we turn to authority, we find that writers uniformly hold that the State is intimately concerned in this matter. I find none who favor anything remotely resembling complete local option; on the contrary, there is general recognition of the dangers of local class interest or party spirit, local vagaries in the use of the taxing power, and interference with the financial policy of the State. There is, therefore, agreement that local taxation should be regulated by general law; and those who favor granting a certain freedom to the local authorities would have such discretionary power carefully defined and strictly limited. The idea that local governments are better fitted than any other to deal with local taxation appears to be the outgrowth of the campaign for the single tax on land values; and it seems reasonable to suppose that if in any of our commonwealths the single taxers should secure political control, there would be an immediate restoration of confidence in the ability of the state government to regulate local taxation in every county, city, or town. In fact it already appears that in New Zealand, where local option prevails, the single taxers favor it only as a means to an end, and, if possible, "would make rating on unimproved values not optional, but mandatory, in every rating district."[5]

The third argument for local option is that uniformity is undesirable in local taxation and diversity advantageous, on account of differences in physical and social conditions or the state of public opinion. Here again it is pertinent to say that most partisans of local option, after prolonged consideration of these diversities, would in all places recommend a uniform and simple method—the single tax; and that a few others, without going so far as this, would advise the exemption of most or all personal property and the cencentration of local taxation chiefly on real estate. When it comes, therefore, to such a practical matter as a definite program, local option in taxation turns out to mean, in most cases, local option in exemption. It is perfectly true that, as a temporary concession to public opinion, advocates of local option might content themselves with proposing the exemption of intangibles, dwelling houses, farmers' or mechanics' tools, and the like; but this would be merely a recognition of the need of diversity in tactics, and not of varying economic and social conditions which make diversity of local taxation inherently desirable. We are justified, therefore, in entertaining skepticism concerning the need and advantages of diversity in taxation.

Indeed it seems pratically certain that diverse methods of local taxation, unless carefully defined and narrowly restricted by general law, would produce undesirable and even intolerable conditions. Suppose, for example, that one county elects to tax mortgages as an interest in real estate where the land lies, another continues to tax them as personal property, and the State, in its quest of independent revenues, establishes a recording mortgage tax. Then the interest of the mortgagee would be taxable in the first county, the note would be taxable in the second, where the mortgagee resides, and the State would impose a third tax at the time the mortgage is recorded. Consider,

[5] Le Rossignol, "State Socialism in New Zealand," 141-142.

also, how diverse methods of local taxation would affect any business enterprise owning property and conducting its operations in several or many counties, and think what opportunities for multiple taxation such conditions would present. Then, too, it seems most undesirable to allow localities to enter into competition with one another to attract capital by offering exemption from taxation. It must be admitted that a few localities may profit in this manner, but if all offer similar inducements, the advantage disappears. The result is that capitalists are given an effective weapon by which they can extort unnecessary and unreasonable concessions, and that localities make unthrifty bargains by which they may later be embarrassed. In New Hampshire, where since 1860 the State has permitted towns to exempt new manufacturing establishments for a period of ten years, a recent commission has reported that "the law now serves as a cudgel rather than a bait";[6] and in the long run the like effect will everywhere follow the like cause. No country in the world permits any such degree of local option, and the only result in the United States would be chaos, unless, as is sometimes hoped and predicted, the ultimate result would be the exemption of everything but land values.

In fact some of the advocates of local option have expressly stated that what is wanted is freedom to exempt and not freedom to tax,[7] and measures proposed in several of our States have carefully restricted the option of the localities to granting exemptions to certain kinds of property or reducing the rate of taxation levied upon them. Even the constitutional amendment recently adopted in Oregon, which apparently gives the counties unrestricted power for the time "to regulate taxation and exemption," provides that this power shall be "subject to any general law which may be hereafter enacted." While, therefore, attractive pictures have been drawn of one locality introducing this device and another adopting that, it appears

[6] Report of the Taxation Commission of 1908, 154.

[7] *E.g.* National Conference on Taxation, of the National Civic Federation, 126.

that few partisans of local option, if any, really desire freedom for diverse experiments in taxation; the thing actually sought is local option in exemption.

The fourth argument is that if the connecting cord that now binds localities together in a uniform system of taxation is cut, the progress of tax reform will be greatly accelerated. We must all admit the difficulty of persuading Legislatures to amend tax laws that relate to the assessment of property in every district of a State. But has the fault been wholly with the Legislatures? When the reform movement began early in the seventies, the Legislatures were told that personal property *could not* be taxed at all. Today we are discussing methods of classifying it, advocating state control, and studying the experience of Maryland and Pennsylvania. For a long time it was considered sufficient merely to tell our lawmakers that the tax on personal property should be repealed; now this Association is considering practicable substitutes for the tax. A generation ago it was seriously argued that state taxation could be equalized only by complete separation of the sources of revenue, and that local real estate assessments could not be brought up to the full value of the property until such separation was secured. It is now evident that complete separation of the sources of revenue does not insure full valuation of real estate, and that control of assessments by a state commission clothed with adequate authority may do so. Clearly the fault has not been all on one side, and recent years have afforded gratifying evidence that Legislatures are willing to consider plans of reform which take account of all the facts and pay due regard to the practical needs of the case. The legislation secured in various States the present year should convince us that it is not necessary for Legislatures to delegate their authority to local governments, and that the thing really necessary is more care in drafting reform programs.

The suggestion that reform will be hastened by freedom to experiment on a small scale with different methods of local taxation is more interesting than convincing. The experiment which most advocates of local option wish to try is the taxation of land values; and this is being worked out for us in other countries, while, of our own States, Oregon promises to afford us an object lesson. Such other experiments as reducing the rate of taxation on buildings or exempting dwellings valued at less than $3000 can be tried, if it is desired to do so, without conferring upon localities broad discretion in other directions. But it is always to be remembered that experimentation may prove expensive, and that the expense of object lessons which are thought to have value for an entire State should not be thrown thoughtlessly upon helpless minorities in a few localities. Therefore, instead of encouraging experimentation for experimentation's sake, we should insist that discretionary power given the local governments be carefully defined; and before favoring any such grant should be satisfied that the experiment has reasonable prospects of success. Our Legislatures should never permit temporary majorities in any district of a State to try reckless experiments with the property or business of minorities.

The fifth argument is that with local option a community can foster any interests it desires to encourage and repress others. In the absence of specifications it is difficult to say just what is advocated, but it is certain that great danger lurks this way. Do we wish to have our cities and counties encouraging one branch of industry and discouraging another? Do we wish them to discriminate in favor of local business and against out-of-town competition? Or do we wish them to legislate against nonresident owners of property? Such policies should be undertaken, if at all, by a government of a higher order, in which there is necessarily a broader outlook upon the questions involved and a better balance of divergent business, class, or political interests.

The final argument, that local option insures harmony of interest among local governing bodies, remains to be considered. Is it true, as alleged, that under this plan one community cannot injure another? Will conflict of local interests disappear, and harmony everywhere prevail? Confining the question to the United States, where conditions are most familiar to us, and judging the future by the past, these things seem most improbable. Proposals for local option authorize a variety of exemptions, most of which are well calculated to involve the local governments in competition to attract capital and industries by such inducements. May not one locality in this manner injure another, and even compel it, against its will, to enter upon a demoralizing contest to avert further loss? Conditions less likely to prevent conflict and produce harmony can hardly be imagined if American experience is taken as a guide. And if, instead of competition in exemptions, local option should lead to diverse experiments with new methods of taxing business or personal property, conflicts of jurisdiction would immediately arise and there would be constant controversy upon this subject. As the Oregon Board of Tax Commissioners has well said:[8]

> "The natural tendency under local option in taxation will be toward disorganization of the revenue system of the State. Permitting the counties to adopt different classifications of the property to be taxed or exempted and different standards of value in assessment is reasonably certain to be destructive of any general and orderly plan of tax reform. Under such a system controversies and jealousies between counties are apt to be engendered and principles of intercounty comity perverted."

In fact it is upon just such conflicts that the foremost partisans of local option rely to bring about the results they have at heart. Those who desire the total exemption of personal property have often declared that if any community should offer investors such an inducement, capital and industries would pour into that locality in such volume that other places would be obliged to adopt the same policy if they desired to retain any part of their movable wealth. And our friends the single taxers believe that even buildings would follow personal property in the mad rush to any locality that confines taxation to land

[8] First Biennial Report, 1911, 24.

values. In short, it is believed that, while the law might extend local option to all localities, economic forces would effectually deny it to any community that did not desire to exempt all personal property or adopt the single tax. I can see how the advocate of either policy can contemplate such a result with entire satisfaction, but cannot take him seriously when he says that local option would not enable one community to injure another, and would insure such harmony as ought to prevail among the different taxing districts of a commonwealth. His own arguments prove the contrary.

III

This critical survey of the arguments advanced in favor of local option leads to the conclusion that, except for the single taxer, the plan has few advantages and many dangers. It is further to be observed that the proposal to turn over from state to local governments the great problem of taxation runs directly counter to the experience of the last five or six centuries.

For Europe once enjoyed local option in taxation. The towns that grew up in such numbers from the twelfth century onward possessed financial autonomy and devised their own systems of direct and indirect taxation. Elsewhere, when the growth of community needs led to the development of local taxation, there was either no regulation by the central government or only regulation of the most general character, which left details to the local authorities. Gradually, however, the financial needs of the State and the inconveniences attending diverse local systems, led to the transference of most forms of indirect taxation to the central governments. Regulation of local direct taxation came later, and in some places, as the Swiss cantons, was deferred until the nineteenth century; but in the end the forces of centralization carried the day. At present, in the leading countries of Europe, the methods of local taxation are more or less minutely prescribed by law, the rates are frequently limited, and the tendency is toward increased supervision and control. In some cases, indeed, as in Prussia, the local authorities retain certain discretionary powers, but these are carefully defined by general law.

Our own country has had a similar experience. In Massachusetts taxation for town purposes was a thing of independent local growth, having no connection with colonial taxation. During the seventeenth century it was little regulated by the colonial government, and not until the close of the eighteenth does it appear to have been controlled in all details by general law. Whether similar conditions existed in other colonies I am unable to say, but it appears that all of them permitted another kind of local option, namely, freedom to enforce or not enforce the general laws relating to taxation. For the machinery of assessment was from the beginning purely local in its character. The need of centralization was not felt seriously until the last half of the nineteenth century, when the growth of large corporations obliged us to turn over the taxation of certain, or even all, corporations to state boards or commissions. Still later it was realized that the methods of enforcing locally the general tax laws are a matter with which the State itself is concerned, and the result was the establishment of commissions possessing supervisory powers. The number of such commissions is rapidly increasing; some of them have power to revalue property in any district where the laws are not enforced, and one State has this year created centralized machinery for the assessment of an income tax. This movement toward state control of taxation is rightly regarded as one of the most hopeful signs of the time. It is the outgrowth of dearly bought experience, and in accord with tendencies that have long manifested themselves in Europe. Yet if the arguments for local option are sound, centralization is a great mistake; and we must declare that, except for certain taxes reserved for its own use, the State has no concern with the great problem of taxation.

To consider why European countries and American States have been impelled to unify tax laws and centralize administration would but traverse the ground already covered in our examination of the arguments for local option. One important reason is the need of preventing interference with the revenues and financial policy of the central government. A second is the necessity of safeguarding the rights of minorities or non-resident property owners.[9] The third, and in some ways the most important of all, is the fact that the great facility of transport and ease of communication which characterize modern times have broken down the barriers that used to isolate communities and confine them to a self-contained life. A few centuries ago the methods by which one community raised its taxes were of little concern to another; today they are of direct and vital interest. They may affect the movement of population and industry, may work injustice to persons who have no voice in local affairs, and may run counter to the established policy of the State. No locality now lives of itself, or can claim the right to act as if it did. In these facts we find the explanation and justification of centralizing tendencies, and sufficient warrant for rejecting the proposal to grant practical autonomy in the matter of local taxation.

But if autonomy is to be denied, does it follow that limited powers of local option are to be refused? Indeed, as a practical matter, it is often proposed to grant only limited power, although the arguments generally adduced lead logically to the demand for complete autonomy. Here, as elsewhere, we shall derive little help from mere laudation of the principle of home rule; and cannot safely agree first to approve the principle and after that pass to definite proposals. Least of all can we accept the argument used last fall in Oregon that consideration of specific measures is irrelevant in a discussion of local option. Until we know what is proposed and have formed some opinion concerning its merits, we are, obviously, in no position to pass upon the question. The very desire to avoid definite plans suggests strongly that there are ulterior designs which it is inexpedient to reveal too plainly during the discussion of home rule.

The limited powers of local option which have been proposed are so numerous that adequate consideration of them is

[9] On the first and second reasons see Schanz, "Die Steuern der Schweiz," I, 205; Wagner, "Finanzwissenschaft," I, 3d edit., 105.

impossible within the necessary limits of this paper. The list includes power to exempt personal property or to tax it at a reduced rate, power to impose a habitation tax and a tax on store rentals, power to exempt manufacturing plants for a period of years or to exempt machinery and manufacturing capital generally, power to exempt dwelling houses up to such a value as $2000 or $3000, and power to exempt all buildings or to tax them at a reduced rate. The various proposals may be divided into two groups: those which aim to remedy evils arising in the taxation of personal property, and those designed to exempt improvements made upon land.

Concerning the first group of projects, it is evident that in so far as they propose merely the exemption of personal property they involve all the dangers of local competition, which have been already discussed. So far, however, as they propose adequate substitutes for the present tax on personal property, they minimize this danger. They nevertheless raise the further question whether the inconvenience of diverse local methods of taxing personality does not make it preferable to postpone action until a uniform method can be prescribed by the State. This question I have not time to answer; I desire merely to indicate the considerations upon which intelligent decision of the matter must turn.

The second class of proposals is variously motivated. The exemption of dwelling houses is advocated on the ground that it will encourage home-building and reduce the weight of taxation upon persons of small means. Exemption of all buildings, or taxation at a reduced rate, is favored as a means of stimulating construction and remedying congestion of population. Another consideration is that such measures may prove the first step toward concentration of all taxes upon land values, for it seems that the single taxer is never far distant from the scene whenever it is proposed to exempt anything, save land, from taxation. Our decision concerning these projects should depend upon three considerations: the probability that the measures will accomplish useful ends, the danger of undesirable local competition in offering exemptions, and the possibility that they might lead to further exemptions which we should approve or disapprove according to the view we entertain concerning the single tax on land values. Here, again, I must content myself with defining the issues, and cannot undertake further consideration of them.

The outcome of my argument, then, is this: Local autonomy, or the general power to tax or exempt from taxation, should not be granted local governments; and the wisdom of granting limited discretionary power cannot be determined except after careful consideration of specific proposals. I should have preferred to take all this for granted, and to deal with the specific proposals that have been offered; but the drift of current discussion made such a course impracticable. One of our States has already adopted a constitutional amendment which makes the counties autonomous in regulating taxation and exemption; and others are urged in a similar manner to establish local option and then consider particular plans of action. It seemed necessary, therefore, to invite attention to the issue thus presented, and to show that reason and experience condemn what is called "home rule in taxation."

The subject is of importance to this Association, since one of the resolutions adopted at the Conference of 1907 contains a qualified indorsement of local option, which has already been misconstrued and is likely hereafter to be misunderstood or misrepresented. That resolution recommends that state and local revenue systems "should be so far divorced," that, by general laws, the local governing bodies "may, *if deemed expedient,*[10] be granted certain limited and carefully prescribed powers" in regulating local taxation. This has been quoted in support of the complete separation of state and local revenues, whereas it merely recommends such a measure of separation as will permit the grant of certain powers to the local governments; and has been cited also in behalf of very broad and indefinite grants of "home rule," whereas it refers only to "certain limited and carefully prescribed powers." Since we are not now considering the separation of state and local

[10] The italics are the writer's.

revenues, I invite your attention only to that part of the resolution which relates to local option.

The published Proceedings of the Conference[11] show that when this resolution was reported at the final session, objection was made immediately to the "home-rule" feature. This brought from the chairman of the committee on resolutions the explanation that the resolution, as drafted, did not recommend that limited powers of local option "*shall* be granted," but merely that state and local revenues should be so far divorced that "such powers *may* be granted." Another delegate then suggested that the resolution, as worded, might easily be misconstrued; and that it would be well to insert the words "if deemed expedient," which was promptly done. Clearly then the whole question of the expediency of local option was waived before the resolution was accepted by the Conference, and those who were present will remember that laughter and applause greeted the delegate from North Carolina, who closed the debate by urging adoption of the resolution on the ground that it was "very clear, to the point, and entirely noncommittal." Why it was thought worth while to refer to local option at all after the resolution had been so amended as to reserve judgment concerning its expediency, is not apparent. Perhaps the explanation is that the hour was very late, the members were extremely fatigued, and no one thought of the matter. My own vote in the affirmative was given because it was represented that the brethren in Missouri would be extremely glad to have the resolution for use in their State, and it seemed a pity to deny them whatever satisfaction they could extract from such a noncommittal affair. I believe, too, that few of us realized what influence the Tax Association would later attain, and what importance would attach to resolutions adopted by its Conferences.

In view of recent developments in the campaign for local option, it seems necessary to raise the question whether this Association, in justice to itself and the growing constituency that looks to it for guidance, can afford to retain in its platform a resolution which refers to local option only to withhold judg-

[11] Pages 664-665.

ment concerning its expediency. When carefully read, and interpreted in the light of the debate concerning its adoption, the resolution may appear so noncommittal as to be harmless; but to the average reader it undoubtedly conveys the idea that the Association has indorsed the principle of local option. It has been misunderstood, and, as long as retained in our platform, will give rise to continued misunderstanding.

The matter is one in which reasonable caution is necessary if we are not practically to commit the Association to the single-tax propaganda. It should be clearly understood that the local-option movement in this country originated in the State of New York, some twenty-five years ago, under the leadership of Henry George and Thomas G. Shearman. It has, in New York and elsewhere, sometimes enlisted the support of persons who are not advocates of the single tax; but its foremost partisans are usually single taxers, and the progress of the movement is carefully recorded in all single-tax papers. While much is said about the advantages of diverse experiments in taxation, the real objective point turns out everywhere to be the single tax; while the principle of "home rule" is extolled, local option is nothing but a temporary device, which will be quickly discarded if it ever becomes possible to enact a state-wide law. This has been avowed in New Zealand, and it is interesting to observe that the constitutional amendment adopted in Oregon, while making the counties autonomous for the time being, provides that they shall be subject to "any general law" hereafter enacted. Last fall in Oregon the people were asked to pass upon the general question of home rule, without considering particular plans of taxation; indeed, discussion of such details was declared to be irrelevant. But after the election the victory was hailed as a triumph for the single tax, and that, too, in spite of the fact that the slender majority in favor of the amendment was probably secured by attaching to it a provision, delightfully inconsistent with the principle of "home rule," by which it was declared that no poll tax should be levied in Oregon. Manifestly we cannot afford longer to invite misunderstanding of our position.

TAXATION OF PROPERTY AND INCOME IN MASSACHUSETTS[1]

SUMMARY

I. Taxation in Massachusetts in the seventeenth and eighteenth centuries, 391.—II. The period, 1800-1850, 394.—III. The critical period, 1850-1874, 396.—IV. Gradual disintegration of the general property tax, 406.—V. Attempts at stricter enforcement, 1908-1916, lead finally to change of the system, 418.—VI. An income tax proposed: constitutional amendment of 1915, 430.—VII. The income tax act of 1916, 433.

I

IN PRINCIPLE the general property tax was established in Masachusetts by the well-known law of 1634 which provided that in all "rates and public charges" the towns should tax everyone according to his estate and with reference to "all other his abilities whatsoever." The first detailed tax law, enacted in 1646, established a system of taxation upon "visible estate" real and personal, supplemented by a tax upon incomes of laborers, artificers and others, which in time developed into a tax upon incomes not derived from property. With these levies upon estates and incomes went the poll tax which had existed in the colony from the very beginning. The act of 1646, therefore, definitely established a system of direct taxation upon property, income, and polls, which continued in operation without fundamental changes until 1862, and for the most part lasted until the twentieth century.

The operation of this tax system in the seventeenth century has been exhaustively studied by Professor Day,[2] who finds that it was customary to levy upon polls from 35 to 40 per cent

[1] Reprinted from *Quarterly Journal of Economics*, Vol. XXXI (1916-17), pp. 1-61. Reproduced by generous permission of the publishers.

[2] E. E. Day, History of the General Property Tax in Massachusetts, 1630-1688. (Unpublished thesis, in Harvard University Library.)

of the direct taxes imposed for colonial and local purposes. In some communities the proportion was frequently greater than this, sometimes rising to 50 and even 60 per cent of the tax levy. Property, therefore, paid but 60 or 65 per cent of the direct taxes, and sometimes contributed 50 per cent or less.

Until the very end of the century the property tax was confined to *visible* estates, which term, however, probably included money. In practice this meant that land, buildings, and live stock accounted for nearly the whole of the assessments. Since land values were low and there were few expensive buildings in the colony, the proportion of the taxes falling upon live stock was very heavy. Professor Day finds that such property often accounted for one-half, two-thirds, and even three-fourths of the whole assessment placed upon estates, with the result that personalty frequently paid a larger proportion of the taxes than did realty. It may be estimated roughly that of every £100 of direct taxes levied in a representative Massachusetts town in the seventeenth century, some £35 to £40 was levied upon polls, and that the remaining £60 to £65 was contributed by real estate and live stock in proportions which varied but may not have been very unequal.[3] Personal property other than live stock constituted in most towns an unimportant part of the assessment, and incomes usually were a negligible factor.

The eighteenth century brought new conditions which gradually wrought material changes in the practical operation of the tax system. The proportion of direct taxation falling upon polls slightly decreased, since it became the general rule to levy one-third of the direct taxes upon polls and two-thirds upon property. Peculiar conditions sometimes made the poll taxes considerably higher or a little lower than this figure, but in the average town conditions probably conformed pretty closely to the intention of the law.

The great change, however, was the advance of real estate

[3] In Boston, for instance, Day finds that in 1676 real estate accounted for 62 per cent of the total assessment of property, while in 1687 personalty accounted for 53 per cent.

to a commanding position upon the tax rolls. The frontier of settlement had been pushed forward into the Connecticut valley, and eastern Massachusetts was becoming a fairly populous and prosperous community. Land values were rising, and houses better than American architects ordinarily produced in the nineteenth century were becoming common. As a result, the assessed value of real estate steadily rose, and personal property became of much less relative importance. In 1792, the assessment placed upon realty was £713,600, that upon personalty was £144,400, while property "doomed" by the assessors, which was largely personalty, was assessed at £81,100. If we assume all the "doomed" property to be personalty, we may compute that personal property accounted for 24 per cent of the total assessment and real estate for 76 per cent.[4] Since one-third of the direct taxes was levied upon polls, we may compute that of every £100 of taxes levied in a Massachusetts town, £33⅓ fell upon polls, £50⅔ fell upon real estate, and £16 fell upon personalty, including income which was almost everywhere a negligible factor.

Wolcott's Report enables us to divide the £144,400 of property recorded as personalty into its component parts. Of this sum £66,300 represented live stock, £42,600 represented other tangible personalty, and £35,500 intangibles. What the £81,100 of "doomed" personalty consisted of, we can only conjecture; but we may believe that it was composed chiefly of merchants' stocks, money at interest and other intangibles, and perhaps incomes. In considering these figures it should be remembered that at this time property was placed upon the assessment roll at 6 per cent of its true value, with the exception of unimproved real estate, which was assessed at 2 per cent.

Money was, doubtless, included in the visible estates, for which inhabitants of Massachusetts were taxable in the seventeenth century. At the very end of that period money at interest is mentioned by the annual tax acts, and during the eighteenth century intangible property became subject to taxation. When

[4] See Wolcott's Report on Direct Taxes. State Papers, Finance, Vol. I, p. 451.

corporations developed, their shares were taxable, like other personalty; but, as a gentle reminder to local assessors, the tax act for 1793 specifically mentioned bank stock. During the next decade shares of bridge or turnpike companies and other moneyed corporations received similar mention. The commercial development of the state was greatly increasing the amount and the importance of this class of property, and the growth of a considerable body of public securities at the same period tended to the same result. In 1790, Massachusetts had merchant princes whose fortunes were counted by the hundred thousands, and in some cases approached the figure of $1,000,000. The money made in commerce soon overflowed into banking and manufacturing, and into bridge, turnpike, and canal companies, with the result that the amount of intangible personal property rapidly increased.[5]

II

From 1800 to 1850 the financial problems confronting Massachusetts were few and comparatively simple. When the Federal government in 1790 assumed the greater part of the state debt, the burden of state taxation was reduced to an almost nominal figure.[6] By 1850 conditions had somewhat changed, but the pressure of taxation was still comparatively light. In Boston the tax rate for that year was $6.80, and this figure was probably not far from the average for the state at large. In interpreting these figures it is necessary to consider the further fact that real estate assessments were undoubtedly at a lower percentage of the true value than they are at the

[5] This period is being exhaustively studied by Dr. H. H. Burbank, and will be treated in his book dealing with the history of the general property tax in Massachusetts since 1775.

[6] I have treated this subject in my monograph upon The Finances and Financial Policy of Massachusetts, chs. 2-4. The local governments were as yet undertaking few new functions so that their expenses were comparatively light. The result was that the pressure of taxation was light and the general property tax met fairly well the requirements of the period. In Boston the tax levy of 1820 amounted to no more than $3.60 per capita, and the tax rate was but $3.50. In 1840, after Boston had been a city for eighteen years and had greatly increased her expenditures, the tax levy was but $6.30 per capita and the tax rate $5.50.

present day. While the matter has not been fully investigated, such evidence as we have indicates that in the average city or town prior to 1860 realty was probably not assessed at more than 50 per cent of its true value.

Under such conditions an easy-going administration of the tax laws sufficed to place a substantial amount of personal property upon the assessment rolls. In Boston in 1794 over 57 per cent of the assessment appears to have consisted of personal property. In 1810 the proportion of personalty was over 45 per cent, in 1822 it was over 44 per cent, and as late as 1860 it was nearly 41 per cent. The per capita assessment of personal property in Boston was approximately $540 in 1804, and $635 in 1860. For the state at large no figures are yet available between the years 1792, when we have Wolcott's Report, and 1850, when we have the figures of the United States Census. In the former year, as we have seen, if the property "doomed" by the assessors is counted as personal, 24 per cent of the total assessment consisted of personalty. In 1850 the Census figures showed a total assessment of $551,000,000 of which nearly $202,000,000 was personal property, the percentage of personalty being 36.6. It appears, therefore, that between 1792 and 1850, at the time when intangible property first became an important factor in Massachusetts, the proportion which personal property bore to the total assessment rose from 24 to 36.6 per cent.

What proportion of the increased assessment of personalty consisted of intangibles and what proportion consisted of merchants' stocks, machinery, live stock, and the very important item of ships and vessels, has not yet been ascertained. It may be that intangible property accounted for only a small part of the increase; but so far as our present knowledge goes, we can say that there is no evidence that it was the growth of intangible property in Massachusetts which broke down the general property tax. Upon the contrary, during the period when intangibles became an important factor in the situation, the assessment of personal property showed both an absolute and relative increase. With low tax rates the assessors succeeded in reaching a sufficient amount of personal property to account for 40 per cent of the total assessments during the period.

An important change in the distribution of the whole tax burden occurred in 1814 when the proportion of direct taxes assessed upon polls was reduced to one-sixth of the total levies. In 1850 we may estimate[7] that of every $100 of local taxation, $16.67 was levied upon polls, $52.80 was levied upon real estate, and $30.50 was levied upon personal property and income, the latter still being a negligible factor. If these figures are compared with those computed for 1792, it will be seen that the proportion which real estate formed of the total assessment had slightly increased, and that the decrease in the levy upon polls was made up chiefly by the increase in the assessment of personal property.

III

The twenty-four years following 1850 were the critical period in the history of the general property tax in Massachusetts. The tax had met fairly well the requirements of the first half of the nineteenth century, but proved wholly inadequate for subsequent needs. All the evidence justifies the conclusion that it was the increase of public expenditures which caused the breakdown.

The growth of cities, the emergence of new public needs, the unusual demands of the civil war, and the period of public and private extravagance which continued until the panic of 1873, combined to produce an unprecedented increase in expenditures. The outlay of the state government was $566,100 in 1850, while in 1860 it had increased to $1,193,000, and in 1868 had risen to $5,159,000. Thereafter it decreased to some extent, but at the end of a period of severe retrenchment stood at $3,907,000 in 1880. Local expenditures followed the same

[7] If the bank tax, which yielded the state $354,700 in 1850, were added to the local taxes, the proportion of personal property in the total would be increased by perhaps six or seven dollars. But as we have no data concerning the taxes raised for local purposes, no accurate calculation can be made on this point.

general course. For 1850 no data are available, but we know that in 1861 the taxes levied upon property in Massachusetts amounted to $7,145,000, and that by 1874 they had risen to $27,830,000. The total taxes of all descriptions levied in the Commonwealth amounted to $8,284,000 in the former year and to $33,674,000 in the latter; while the per capita tax burden had risen from $6.69 to $20.87.[8] To make the situation worse, both state and local debts had shown a portentous increase, so that interest and sinking fund charges were certain to complicate the financial problem of the future.

The only possible result was a sharp increase of tax rates. In Boston the rate advanced from $6.80 per $1000 in 1850 to $9.30 in 1860 and to $15.60 in 1874. In the entire state the average tax rate, which was $8.29 in 1861, was $15.18 in 1874. The strain of such high rates was greater than the existing system could possibly endure, and therefore taxation immediately became a "problem" in Massachusetts.

One of the first readjustments required in the tax laws was a reduction of the poll tax. Since 1829 the law had provided that one-sixth of the state tax should be assessed upon polls, and that the same proportion should be followed in local taxes, provided, however, that the total poll tax levy for city, town, and county purposes should not exceed $1.50. If one-sixth of the heavy taxes levied for state purposes during the civil war had been levied upon polls, and the assessments for local purposes had approximated $1.50, the aggregate poll taxes would have risen to high figures. Therefore in 1862 it was enacted that the aggregate poll tax for all purposes, state and local, should not exceed $2, with a possible exception in the case of highway taxes separately assessed. Even under this law the poll tax, which in 1861 had averaged $1.62, increased to $2.50 and $3.00 in many towns in 1864 and 1865; while such a rate as $4.25 was reported in one instance. For the entire state the average poll tax in 1865 was $2.11. With the tax limited in this manner,

[8] These figures may be found in The Finances and Financial Policy of Massachusetts, pp. 46, 63, and 135.

increases in local taxation thereafter fell wholly upon property; and the poll tax became a factor of decreasing importance.

The principal change that occurred during this period was the introduction of an extensive system of corporation taxes. In 1812, Massachusetts had imposed a tax of one per cent upon the capital stock of state banks, and twenty years later had levied a retaliatory tax upon the agents of foreign insurance companies chartered in states that taxed the agents of Massachusetts companies. The bank tax soon yielded a handsome revenue, and was the mainstay of the state's finances during the civil war. It seems to have been looked upon as a tax upon the privilege of issuing notes, since the shares of the banks remained taxable in the hands of the stockholders. The insurance taxes never produced enough revenue to make them of financial significance. Up to 1862 Massachusetts had made no fundamental departure from the general property tax; and, except for comparatively unimportant exemptions, all property was subject to local taxation.

But in the year just mentioned a law was enacted which exempted from taxation deposits in savings banks, and then imposed upon the banks themselves an excise tax of one-half of one per cent. Although this rate was subsequently increased, then reduced, then increased, and finally restored to the original figure, it was always less than the average rate imposed upon other property in Massachusetts; and as local tax rates increased, it finally fell to less than one-third of the average rate of taxation. It therefore established a separate classification for savings bank deposits, justified no doubt upon the theory that such property was entitled to special consideration, but marking none the less a deliberate departure from the principle of the general property tax. It also raised interesting and important constitutional questions.

The earliest tax laws of the colony of Massachusetts had been based upon the English system of local taxation. That system had been based upon the principle of equal, proportionable, and ratable taxation according to the abilities of the citizens, but had not always employed the same measure of ability.[9] The earliest Massachusetts tax laws provided in almost identical language for equal and proportionable rating of the inhabitants of Massachusetts, and selected visible estates as the measure of the citizens' contributions. It, therefore, naturally happened that the province charter of 1691 contained a provision authorizing the general court to levy "proportionable and reasonable assessments, rates, and taxes." What the word "proportionable" meant to the person who inserted it in the charter, we do not know; but we do know that the word was never so construed as to prevent the province from classifying property for taxation. On the contrary, the provincial tax laws repeatedly classified property and continued to do so down to the time of the revolution. Real estate was usually required to be assessed at six times the annual income. Live stock was assessed at arbitrary valuations fixed by law, and other personal property practically according to the judgment and discretion of the assessors.

The constitution adopted by Massachusetts in 1780 took over from the provincial charter the provision that the general court should have the power to levy "proportional and reasonable assessments, rates and taxes." If it had stopped there, it might never have been so construed as to prevent classification of the objects of taxation, because the colony and province had always levied excise and import duties, and the state continued to do so. It would probably have been evident to any court that the framers of the constitution had not intended to invalidate the existing system of excise and customs taxes, and it is therefore unlikely that the constitutional requirement that taxes shall be "proportional" would have been construed so strictly as to make excise and customs duties unconstitutional. But after conferring upon the general court the same taxing power that the province of Massachusetts had always exercised, the fram-

[9] Cannan's History of Local Rates in England gives sufficient evidence concerning the sources upon which the authors of the earliest Massachusetts laws drew.

ers of the constitution inserted an additional provision authorizing the levy of "reasonable duties and excises." This action may have been due to a fear or belief that, without specific authorization of duties and excises, the general court might be unable to levy such imposts. But this caution was probably unnecessary. The taxation system of Massachusetts had never been proportional in any mathematical sense, and it had always included excise and customs duties, to which it would have been practically impossible to apply any requirement of proportionality. The excise clause, therefore, was probably unnecessary, and could have no other effect than to oblige the courts to find a reason for the inclusion of the word "proportional" in the clause relating to direct taxes and for its exclusion from the clause relating to duties and excises.

Whatever the framers may have intended, the second tax act[10] enacted after the adoption of the constitution, provided that all property except unimproved lands should be assessed at 6 per cent of its real value, and that such lands should be assessed at 2 per cent. This was obviously a classification of property, and it continued to be the law of the Commonwealth until its repeal in 1828 without any question being raised concerning its constitutionality. Another law of 1781[11] levied a duty upon coaches, chariots, and carriages, and required the inhabitants of the Commonwealth under oath to make returns of such property to the local assessors. This was in everything except name a direct tax upon property, and could not have been upheld as an excise or duty except under such a broad construction of those terms as to render meaningless the distinction between the taxing power and the excise power. It also passed without question.

The meaning of the word "proportional" was considered by the Supreme Court for the first time in the case of Portland Bank *v.* Apthorp (12 Mass. 252), which involved the constitutionality of the tax levied upon state banks in 1812. The

[10] Ch. 16 of 1781.
[11] Ch. 17 of 1781.

court upheld this tax as an excise, but took occasion to say that it could not be sustained as a tax because it was not proportional. Although this was a mere dictum, it inevitably carried great weight fifty years later when the next case arose; and yet if the dictum of the court was correct, it followed that the province of Massachusetts had never had anything remotely resembling a proportional system of taxation, and that the legislature of the state only a year after the adoption of the constitution had established an unconstitutional classification of real estate which was still in force, and under the guise of an excise had levied an unconstitutional tax upon certain other classes of property.

When the savings bank tax came up for consideration, the court, following the reasoning of Portland Bank *v.* Apthorp, upheld it[12] as an excise or duty on the franchises of the banks, even though, unlike the bank tax of 1812, it was in lieu of local taxation of the deposits. The earlier decision had merely upheld an excise that was in addition to the property tax. The latter, however, made it possible for the legislature, wherever it could levy a valid excise, to exempt from local taxation the property which in effect had been excised. The door was opened, therefore, for a considerable extension of the excise power, and the legislature soon took advantage of the opportunity. Another important effect of the decision was to commit the court to the general line of reasoning followed in the earlier case, and to make it probable that, if the question ever arose, the dictum laid down in Portland Bank *v.* Apthorp would become a decision to the effect that a tax, in order to be constitutional, must be proportional in the strictest sense of that word.

Cases involving this question were not long in coming before the court, and it was presently held that the constitution required taxes on property to be so laid that, "taking 'all the estates lying within the Commonwealth' as one of the elements of proportion, each taxpayer should be obliged to bear only such part of the general burden as the property owned by him

[12] 5 Allen, 428, 431, and 433.

bore to the whole sum to be raised."[13] Thus the tax clause of the constitution was finally interpreted in such a manner as to make it prescribe strict uniformity in taxation.

In 1864, the general corporation tax was enacted, and, like the savings bank tax, was sustained by the court as a valid excise. As is well known, it left the real estate and machinery of corporations subject to local taxation, and then imposed upon corporations a franchise tax which was to be assessed upon the so-called "corporate excess," or the amount by which the value of the capital stock exceeded the value of the real estate and machinery locally assessed. As the shares of the corporations were thereafter exempt from local taxation and the corporation tax was administered by the state, the law of 1864 introduced another radical change in the tax system of Massachusetts. But since the rate of taxation on the corporate excess was the average rate levied upon property in the Commonwealth, the law involved no departure from the principle of the general property tax, and in this respect differed radically from the tax on savings banks. Except for the arrangement by which double taxation of the stock and of certain tangible property of corporations was avoided,[14] the only real change wrought by the law of 1864 was that thereafter the state dealt directly with corporations and the stockholders were exempted from local taxation. The change effected, therefore, was chiefly of an administrative character, and there was no intention that corporations should pay either more or less taxes than the general mass of property subject to local taxation.

The establishment of the national banking system was followed by the conversion of state into national banks, and this required changes in the tax law. The final outcome was the establishment in 1873 of the present tax upon the shares of

[13] Oliver v. Washington Mills, 11 Allen 275. See also 12 Allen 298 and 312; 118 Mass. 386; 133 Mass. 161; 134 Mass. 424; 195 Mass. 607.

[14] Manufacturing corporations had been relieved from double taxation in 1832 by a law (ch. 158 of 1832) which provided that, in assessing the stock of such corporations, the local assessors should make a suitable deduction for the value of real estate and machinery already taxed.

national banks, which, being levied at the local rates of taxation, results theoretically in taxing banks in the same manner as other property. In 1874, therefore, Massachusetts was collecting from the savings bank, the general corporation, and the national bank taxes $4,875,000 of revenue, which was over seven times the revenue derived from the old bank tax in 1861. The system had begun to be diversified, but except in the case of savings banks no departure had been made from the principle of the general property tax.

Without doubt the new taxes were more effective in reaching corporate property than the old methods of local assessment, so that perhaps the greater part of the revenue derived therefrom in 1874 represented an increase of financial resources. But this increase had not been sufficient, as we have seen, to prevent a rise of local tax rates under which conditions were rapidly going from bad to worse.

Boston was probably the first and also the chief sufferer. Mr. Thomas Hills, an able and determined advocate of the general property tax, was made one of the principal assessors in 1865, and in 1866 became chairman of the board. He increased greatly the efficiency of the assessing department, and inaugurated a vigorous search for taxable property under which Boston valuations rapidly increased. In 1860, the real estate of the city had been assessed at $163,891,000, and the personal property at $112,969,000. In 1865, these figures had been increased, respectively, to $201,628,000 and $170,263,000. By 1870, Mr. Hills had raised the real estate assessment to $365,593,000 and the personal to $218,496,000; and in 1872, had raised the former to $443,283,000 and the latter to $239,440,000. Account must be taken, of course, of the annexation of Roxbury and Dorchester, which added materially to the total valuation; but even when this is done, the results secured by Mr. Hills were sufficiently striking.

But things were not working out as expected because personal property was rapidly migrating from Boston. Removals to the suburbs had been going on for many years, as is evidenced by the fact that before the middle of the eighteenth century it was necessary to amend the tax laws by providing that merchandise employed in any city or town should be taxable in that city and not at the domicile of the merchant. But under Mr. Hills there ensued a veritable hegira under which the attractive suburbs of Boston were rapidly built up at the expense of the city's tax rolls. The most striking case was that of Nahant, which in 1865 had assessed $513,000 of real property and $12,710 of personal, its tax rate standing at $15 per $1000. In 1870, however, thanks to Mr. Hills, its realty was assessed at $985,000, and its personalty at $4,160,000, while its tax rate had dropped to $2.50 per $1000. Between 1869 and 1873 not less than $13,900,000 of taxable personal estate was removed from Boston to eight suburban towns and to Newport, Rhode Island. Naturally enough, in time, such removals more than offset the diligence of Mr. Hills and his minions. The assessment of personal property reached high water mark in 1874 when it stood at $244,554,000. Thereafter it steadily decreased until it reached low water mark in 1879 at $184,545,000. But even in 1874 Mr. Hills had failed to increase the proportion of the taxes paid by personal property. In 1860, personalty constituted over 40 per cent of the total assessment and in 1865 formed even a larger percentage. But in 1874, although the total personal assessment had increased by some $74,000,000, the assessment of real estate had been raised 175 per cent, with the result that personal property formed less than 31 per cent of the total assessment.

In the entire state, as we have seen, personal property had constituted over 36 per cent of the local assessments of $551,000,000 in 1850. By 1874, however, it accounted for 29.6 per cent of the total assessment of $1,831,600,000. Allowance should be made for the fact that the savings bank, the general corporation, and the national bank taxes had removed a large amount of property from the category of "taxables," but only a small proportion of such property had ever been placed upon the assessment lists, and therefore the corporation taxes made comparatively little difference with the local assessments. In 1861, for instance, the deposits in the savings banks of Massachusetts amounted to $44,785,000, and of this sum the local assessors had taxed only $9,655,000. No similar comprehensive data concerning local taxation of the stock of Massachusetts corporations and of national banks are available; but in 1864 when, under the operation of the general corporation tax, the shares of Massachusetts corporations were exempted from taxation, the local assessments upon personal property decreased only from $343,500,000 to $324,600,000. In 1873, also, when the bank tax went into operation, the local assessments upon personal property decreased from $565,294,000 to $537,388,000. While, therefore, the total assessment of personal property for local taxation in 1874 would have been somewhat larger but for the changes wrought by the new corporation taxes, there had been a gradual shifting of taxation from personalty to real estate. Even if we estimate the reductions caused by the corporation taxes at the very generous figure of $70,000,000, there would still remain a shrinkage of some 2 per cent in the proportion which personal property bore to the total local assessments. For a time, however, this tendency was probably offset by the fact that the new corporation taxes succeeded in reaching taxable values which would have eluded local assessment.

Since the poll tax was now fixed at what was practically a uniform charge of $2.00, the burden of taxation had shifted very greatly from polls to property. In 1874, polls were assessed for $877,700 in a total of $33,556,000, or for no more than 2½ per cent, which contrasts strikingly with the proportion of 16⅔ per cent established by the law of 1814.[15] The taxes paid by corporations amounted to $4,875,000 in 1874, and constituted 14½ per cent of the total. Local taxes upon personal property amounted to $8,229,000, or 24.6 per cent; and those

[15] Of course the limitation placed by the Act of 1829 upon the local levy on polls tended to reduce appreciably the proportion of the total taxes falling upon polls, but up to 1850 the increase in the amount of taxes levied had probably not been sufficient to reduce the poll tax to a negligible factor.

assessed upon real estate were $19,573,000, or 58.4 per cent. Thus it appears that the reduction in the proportion of the taxes falling upon polls had been made up by the new corporation taxes; polls and corporations were paying in 1874 fully 17 per cent of the total taxes, whereas polls were required to contribute 16⅔ per cent under the law of 1814, and somewhat less than that under the law of 1829. But the corporation taxes were in effect taxes levied upon property, so that what the figures really show is that the proportion of the total taxes falling upon property had increased from 83⅓ per cent in the early part of the nineteenth century to 97½ per cent in the year 1874.

If we assume that the whole of the corporation taxes were levied in respect of personal property,[16] and therefore combine them with the taxes levied locally upon personalty, we find that the total contribution of personal property was $13,105,000, or 39.1 per cent of all the taxes levied in the Commonwealth. This left 58.4 per cent of the total taxes to be paid by real estate. Compared with 1850, therefore, we find that the contribution of personal property to the total public revenue, state and local, had increased to 39.1 per cent, while the contribution of real estate had increased to 58.4 per cent.

IV

Following the critical period which ended in 1874, came thirty-three years of comparative calm during which disintegration of the general property tax gradually and quietly continued. In 1874, dissatisfaction with the working of the tax laws led to the appointment of the first special commission to investigate the subject. This commission was composed of able

[16] In fact some part of the general corporation tax represented real estate values, since, under a decision of the Supreme Court, the right of way of railroads and some other classes of public service corporations is exempt from local taxation. This decision had relieved such property from taxation up to 1864, but after that it merely increased the taxable corporate excess upon which the general corporation tax was levied. See *Quarterly Journal of Economics*, Vol. XXI, pp. 185 and 218.

men and submitted in January, 1875, a report that is replete with information. It was, however, dominated in its thought by Mr. Hills, who seems to have been the most influential as well as the most active member. The report recognizes existing evils, but does not understand their cause. It assails vigorously the proposal, made by the New York tax commission of 1871, to exempt personal property from taxation, and recommends merely changes in various details of the tax laws. For the evils attending the taxation of personal property the commission could make no more hopeful recommendations than that certain changes be made in the provisions of the law relating to offsets for indebtedness and the matter of domicile.[17] It was unfortunate for the Commonwealth that its tax laws could not be radically altered in 1875, but the principle of the general property tax was undoubtedly approved by all but a small minority, and that minority had little more to propose than exemption measures designed to relieve certain kinds of personal property from taxation. All things considered, it seems probable that Mr. Hills and his associates voiced very faithfully the prevailing opinion of the state.

In the years that followed, discussion of tax problems was confined principally to the subject of double taxation. An organized effort was made to bring about the exemption of mortgages secured by Massachusetts real estate; and this was practically accomplished in 1881, when the present law upon that subject was enacted. Under that act a note secured by a mortgage of taxable real estate in Massachusetts is exempt from taxation as personal property; and the interest of the mortgagee in the real estate is taxable to him as real estate in the place where the land lies, while the mortgagor is taxable only for his equity in the property. Since, however, the law does not prohibit contracting out, mortgages invariably provide that the mortgagor shall assume all taxes; and the prac-

[17] Report of the Commissioners Appointed to Inquire into the Expediency of Revising and Amending the Laws Relating to Taxation and Exemption, pp. 101, 121. H. Doc. 15 of 1875.

tical result is that real estate is taxed to the mortgagor at its full value, while the mortgage note is exempt. This law had the effect of exempting from taxation about $48,000,000 of mortgage debts reported as assessed for taxation in 1881. But the assessment of personal property throughout the state decreased by only $3,600,000 in 1882, and the following year it was $6,900,000 larger than it had been before mortgages were exempted.[18]

Advocates of the general property tax interpreted these figures as meaning that the loss of $48,000,000 of taxable mortgages was offset by the natural increase of other personal property, and reasoned as if the assessment for 1883 might have been not $6,900,000 but $54,900,000 greater than the assessment for 1881 if mortgages had not been exempt. In fact, however, things would not have worked out that way. The exemption of mortgages nominally relieved $48,000,000 of personal property from local taxation. But, in reality, very few of the owners of such property had previously been assessed for their entire personal estates as the law directed, or had made returns of their taxable property. Except in cases where a person's property consisted largely of mortgages and he could therefore make a return to his assessors that reduced his taxable personalty below the amount for which he was assessed in 1881, taxpayers who had been "doomed" for a given amount of personal property in 1881 had no interest in coming forward in 1882 with statements of their taxable personalty. They were presumably assessed for as much personal estate as in 1881, and therefore received no benefit from the mortgage exemption. The situation was like that which developed later when, in order to encourage forestry, new plantations were exempted from taxation for a stated period of years. This exemption was of absolutely no benefit to the average farmer because his farm was usually assessed for somewhat less than it was worth and

[18] These figures, as well as those given above concerning the operation of the corporation taxes, may be found on pp. 36-38 of the Report of the Commission on Taxation of 1907.

the assessors could add to the rest of the farm all that they were obliged to take off from the plantation. We are not to suppose, therefore, that, if mortgages had not been exempted in 1881, the assessment of personal property in 1883 would have increased by $54,900,000 instead of $6,900,000 as it actually did.

After 1881 few changes in the tax laws occurred for many years. Until 1906, indeed, the only significant development was the introduction, in 1891, of a tax upon collateral inheritances and successions. In point of fact, tax legislation in Massachusetts was in a state of deadlock.

Advocates of change, who were increasing in numbers, labored to secure the exemption of foreign corporation stocks, and sometimes urged the total exemption of all intangible property. Upon the other hand, the assessors of the state, who numbered considerably more than 1000, had been organized by Mr. Hills and others into a state-wide association which was able to offer determined resistance to any and all exemption measures.

Advocates of the existing system proposed various measures to make the tax laws more effective, of which the most important were the appointment of assessors by some state authority and the taxation of personal property at a uniform rate which should be the average imposed upon real estate subject to local taxation. Either of these measures would have wrought havoc to the state, since the time had passed when it was possible to enforce the taxation of personal property at the prevailing local rates or at an average state rate. Such taxation would have meant confiscation of one-third or one-fourth of the taxpayers' incomes, and would have led to wholesale removals of property from Massachusetts. As things stood, the tax laws resulted in what was aptly described as a "system of confiscation tempered by favoritism." The legislature was not disposed to grant further exemptions that might increase the burdens falling upon taxable property; and, upon the other hand, it probably realized that the existing laws were not capable of strict enforcement, and therefore was not disposed to adopt the drastic measures favored by the assessors.

In 1893, a joint special committee of the legislature was appointed to revise the laws relating to taxation; and the following year reported against radical changes in the taxation of property.[19] But conditions were going from bad to worse, so that in 1896 a special commission was appointed to inquire into the expediency of revising the tax laws. The following year this commission submitted a noteworthy report which grappled squarely with the problem confronting the Commonwealth. It investigated searchingly the practical operation of the existing system, and recommended that intangible property be exempted from taxation. It realized, however, that a substitute or substitutes should be found for the tax upon intangibles, and therefore recommended that the inheritance tax should be extended to direct inheritances, and that a habitation tax should be introduced which should be levied upon house rentals in excess of $400.[20]

Although this plan provided substitutes for the existing tax upon intangible property, the legislature was not ready for radical departures from the existing system, and therefore the recommendations of the commission bore no immediate fruit. But the report effectively exposed the evils of the existing system, and pointed out their cause. It therefore served as the starting-point for subsequent discussion, and proved to be a document of great educational value. In 1906, another joint-special committee on taxation was appointed which recommended no radical changes in the property tax but advocated the taxation of direct inheritances, which was finally carried into effect by an act of 1907.[21] A minority of the committee,

[19] Sen. Doc. 9 of 1894. The above statement relates to the majority of the committee. Minority reports favored the exemption of stock of foreign corporations and the exemption of state and municipal bonds.

[20] Report of the Commission Appointed to Inquire into the Expediency of Revising and Amending the Laws of the Commonwealth Relating to Taxation, 120 (Boston, 1897). The Commission also recommended that the state should retain in its treasury the revenue from the general corporation tax, and should then assume county expenses.

[21] Report of the Joint-Special Committee on Taxation (Boston, 1907).

reverting to the recommendations of the commission of 1896, advocated the exemption of intangible property from taxation but proposed no substitute.

Meanwhile, the general property tax was steadily disintegrating and producing conditions which were certain to lead ultimately to revision of the tax laws. Public expenditures, which had greatly declined during the period of retrenchment following 1874, were again upon the increase. The total taxes of all descriptions levied in the Commonwealth had decreased from $33,674,000 in 1874 to $25,714,000 in 1879, but by 1890 they had risen to $39,731,000, and by 1905 had reached the imposing total of $72,121,000. The per capita tax burden, which in 1874 had been $20.87, in 1905 was $24.01, and local tax rates were again increasing. From 1874 to 1879, during the period of enforced economy, the average tax rate in the state had declined from $15.51 per $1000 to $12.78. During the next fifteen years the average hovered around $15, but by 1900 it had risen to $16.14, and in 1905 it stood at $17.25. Under such conditions the evils which were serious enough in 1874 were gradually becoming intolerable.

One result of the heavier pressure of taxation was an increase in real estate valuations, especially in the cities. The mere desire to obtain revenue without undue increase of tax rates would have led, in any event, to somewhat higher valuations; but this tendency was increased by the operation of the law of 1875 limiting city debts, and that of 1885 limiting city tax rates. Under these acts many cities were obliged to increase real estate valuations in order to provide the necessary margin for loans and to keep tax rates within the specified limit. If this had resulted merely in changing the old-fashioned practice of valuing property at "about" one-half or two-thirds of what it was worth, it would have been a matter for congratulation. But in some cities it finally resulted in valuations so high as to be clearly excessive. There are today within the metropolitan district not a few municipalities in which it is difficult to sell real estate for its assessed valuation and transfers are frequently made at much lower figures.

Tangible personal property was seriously affected by the high rates of taxation, but in many cases had a comparatively easy method of escape, namely, incorporation. Merchants and manufacturers who found themselves more heavily taxed upon their goods, wares, or merchandise than their competitors in other states could incorporate under the laws of the Commonwealth and come under the general corporation tax. Under this tax, real estate and machinery remained subject to local taxation, and the rest of the property of corporations was supposed to be fully reached by the tax which the state levied upon the so-called "corporate excess." In practice, however, it developed that whereas an individual or a firm was taxable upon all property without deduction of debts except against the item of credits, the corporation was able to deduct the whole of its indebtedness from its assets taxable under the corporation tax. This circumstance, with others, brought it about that in 1902 the manufacturing and mercantile companies subject to the corporation tax owned merchandise valued at $143,604,000, and had a taxable corporate excess of no more than $104,238,000. It is clear, therefore, that the effect of the corporation tax was even at that time to enable incorporated companies to reduce the tax upon their merchandise, or at any rate to reduce it below what it would be if the local assessors assessed it at its true value. In 1903, a maximum limit was placed upon the corporate excess, which had the effect of enabling many concerns to secure a further reduction of their taxes. While in individual cases the corporation tax was fully as heavy as the local tax upon unincorporated enterprises, and in some cases even heavier, there can be no doubt that, upon the whole, manufacturing and mercantile concerns found incorporation an easy method of escape from increasing burdens of local taxation.[22] In extreme cases it was

[22] The operation of the tax upon the corporate excess of manufacturing and mercantile companies is so complicated that it cannot be adequately treated in this paper. I may refer to my article upon the taxation of corporations in Massachusetts, published in the *Quarterly Journal of Economics* for February, 1907. The subject has been fully discussed in recent annual reports of the tax commissioner and in a special memorandum prepared for the legislative committee on taxation in May, 1916 (H. Doc. 2133 of 1916).

possible to arrange matters so that an incorporated mercantile concern secured exemption from local taxation upon its merchandise, and then, after deducting its debts, had no corporate excess to be taxed by the state.

Other kinds of tangible personalty did not fare so well. Live stock is employed in an industry where incorporation is highly uncommon. Machinery is expressly excepted from the operation of the corporation tax, and is very heavily taxed in some localities. In textile centers it sometimes forms a very large percentage of the total valuation, as may be seen by looking at the assessments of personal property in such cities as Fall River and New Bedford.[23] In some cases it is supposed that manufacturers and assessors have working agreements under which machinery is assessed at a certain proportion of its actual value, and in other localities it is probable that machinery is taxed upon something less than a full valuation. But, upon the whole, it is reasonable to conclude that machinery is very heavily taxed in Massachusetts, and probably more heavily than in most other states.

Intangible personalty found several avenues of escape. In the first place, it tended more and more to leave communities where tax rates were high, and to concentrate in a number of attractive residential towns where taxpayers could virtually fix their own assessments. Between 1871 and 1891 not less than $75,000,000 of personal estates assessed in Boston through the diligence of Mr. Hills were removed to fifteen favorite towns. In the former year these towns had assessed $26,750,000 of personal property; in the latter their personal assessments had advanced to $52,558,000—an increase of $25,808,000. Even if we assume that during the interval there had been no increase

[23] Of a total valuation of $106,691,000 in 1915, the personal property of Fall River accounted for $42,707,000, or slightly over 40 per cent. In New Bedford, in the same year, out of a total valuation of $111,346,000, personal property accounted for $41,845,000, or approximately 37 per cent. These percentages are to be compared with an average of about 25 per cent in the total assessment in the state. Fall River and New Bedford do not tax very large amounts of intangible personal property, so that it is probable that the greater part of the taxable personalty in those cities consists of machinery.

of personal property except the $75,000,000 gained by the removal of certain taxpayers from Boston, it would appear that the local assessors had taxed but one-third of these estates. In 1882, one town received an estate assessed in Boston at $800,000, and in the following year increased its assessment of personal property by no more than $281,000, but was able nevertheless to reduce its tax rate from $11 to $7 per $1000.[24]

In this connection it should be noticed that the method which the state followed in distributing among the cities and towns the revenue from the corporation and the bank taxes tended still further to give taxpayers the whip hand over the assessors. The general principle was to divide this revenue according to the residence of the stockholders;[25] and this brought it about that, when a wealthy taxpayer changed his residence, the town to which he removed received an increased share of the corporation and bank taxes. The result was that assessors knew that strict enforcement of the tax on intangible property would not only lead to the removal of such property to some other jurisdiction, but would decrease the amount of corporation and bank taxes received from the state treasury.

As years passed, the distribution of intangible property, and of the corporation and bank taxes, became more and more favorable to the wealthy towns. In 1865, before the process of concentration had begun, the fourteen wealthiest towns had derived a revenue of $6.87 per capita from local taxes on personal property and the corporation and bank taxes, while in the rest of the state the revenue from these sources amounted to $5.81. Twenty years later these fourteen towns were receiving $14.28 per capita, while the average for the rest of the state had fallen to $4.48. In 1905, the revenue of the fourteen towns had increased to $24.01 per capita, while that of the rest of the state amounted to $5.35, a trifle more than the figure for

[24] See Report of the Commission on Taxation (1908), pp. 45-46.

[25] In 1898, the first departure from this principle was made when it was provided that the tax paid by street railroads should be distributed among cities and towns where the tracks were located. Subsequently, the distribution of the tax on other corporations was modified in the interest of the industrial towns where such enterprises were located.

1885 but materially less than the amount received in 1865. Somewhat similar conditions can doubtless be found in other states and countries, but it is probable that the student of taxation would have difficulty in finding elsewhere such extreme concentration of taxable resources as was gradually brought about in Massachusetts after 1865. The only possible result was the creation of inequalities by which the rates of taxation in the cities and industrial towns were greatly increased, while they were lowered to almost nominal figures in a handful of wealthy communities.[26]

But overburdened taxpayers had still another method of escape; they could change their investments. Prior to 1862 this opportunity had not been open to them, since practically every form of investment was taxable. But when savings deposits were exempted from taxation, it was possible for people of means to make increased use of the savings banks. That this was done almost from the outset, there can be little doubt;[27] and it is certain that no small part of the very large deposits of Massachusetts savings banks today are held by people of means. Another door was opened by the great increase of the Federal debt during the civil war, which supplied investors with upward of two billions of non-taxable securities. The establishment of the corporation tax in 1864 placed the stocks of Massachusetts corporations in the list of so-called non-taxables. At first this may not have affected the situation, but in time there was created an artificial demand for tax-exempt stocks which were bought in large quantities by trustees and some others who were not in a position to change their domicile and could not well avoid making returns of personal property. The exemption of mortgages in 1881 created another class of untaxed investments, so that altogether a rather wide range of opportunities was open to persons acquainted with the provisions of the law.

In many cases untaxed securities were bought for permanent investment, so that no evasion of the tax laws was either contem-

[26] This subject was first carefully studied by the Tax Commission appointed in 1896. See Report, pp. 63-68.

[27] See the Report of the Tax Commission appointed in 1874, p. 61 *et seq.*

plated or practised. But it was now possible to invest temporarily in non-taxables for the purpose of escaping assessment upon taxable securities. This could be done only a day or two before the date of assessment in any year, and there developed a regular spring demand for securities that could be held over assessment day and then returned to their former—perhaps one might say actual—owners. In other cases the practice was different but the result the same. Comparatively few investors ordinarily made returns of their personal property, and intangibles were usually taxed by "doomage." This meant that assessors would begin with a small assessment, and then, if the taxpayer did not make a declaration of his property, would subsequently increase it. In time the assessment might reach a figure that would compel the taxpayer to seek relief, and this could be had by shifting his investments from taxables to non-taxables until he could make a full return of his personal property under oath. Such a statement would probably satisfy the curiosity of the assessors for a number of years, so that after making it the taxpayer could at the first favorable opportunity sell his non-taxables and reinvest in taxable securities. There has probably been comparatively little downright lying in the taxation of personal property in Massachusetts; perjury is an ugly thing, and the law did not make it necessary. Intangible property nevertheless managed to evade assessment, and could do so in many cases without change of the taxpayer's domicile.

The next result was that personal property paid a constantly decreasing proportion of the local taxes. In 1907, out of a total local assessment of $3,512,000,000 in the state of Massachusetts, personal property accounted for no more than $766,600,000, or 21.8 per cent; whereas in 1891 it had constituted 25.2 per cent of the total valuation, and in 1871 had constituted 33.8 per cent. At the end of this period it can be estimated that about half of the personal property actually taxed consisted of intangible personalty.[28]

[28] See Report of Commission on Taxation (1908), pp. 40 and 67. Compare also the data found on pp. 50-51 of the Report of the Commission of 1896.

In the distribution of the total burden of state and local taxation some changes had occurred since 1874. In 1907, polls were assessed for $1,758,000 of taxes, or 2.4 per cent of the entire amount. The tax, however, was not so easy to collect as in former years, and the actual contribution made by polls was somewhat less than the percentage just stated. Since 1874 the liquor license tax had come into operation, and this, with some minor business taxes, amounted in 1907 to $3,453,000, or 4.7 per cent. The collateral inheritance tax introduced in 1891 now yielded $772,000, or about one per cent of the total. The corporation taxes amounted to $9,761,000, or 13.2 per cent. The taxes levied locally upon personal property stood at $12,386,000, or 16.8 per cent; while those levied upon real estate amounted to $45,794,000, or 61.9 per cent. Comparison with the figures for 1874 shows that polls were assessed in 1907 for substantially the same proportion as in 1874, that personal property and corporations accounted for 30 per cent of the total against 39 per cent in the former year, and that real estate paid 61.9 per cent of the total taxes against 58.4 per cent at the beginning of the period. The net result was that the proportion of the taxes paid by personal property and corporations had decreased by some 9 per cent, and that this had been made up by business and inheritance taxes, which now contributed 5.7 per cent, and by an increase in the real estate taxes of something more than 3 per cent.

A new chapter in the history of taxation in Massachusetts opened in 1908. In the previous year the inheritance tax was extended to direct inheritances, and this brought the whole property of inhabitants of the state under review by the tax commissioner's department. Up to that time the local assessors had not infrequently gained information from probate returns. But since no tax was imposed upon direct inheritances, it was often possible for executors to avoid disclosing the amounts of probated estates, a request from all the heirs that no inventory be filed being sufficient to accomplish this end. With a direct inheritance tax in operation it was no longer possible to avoid filing inventories, and this fact alone would have altered materially taxation conditions in the Commonwealth.

V

Another law enacted in 1908 hastened the inevitable crisis. The tax commissioner, in 1898, had been given certain supervisory powers over the local assessors,[29] and thus the first step had been taken toward the establishment of central control over the assessment of property. The commissioner, however, was given but a single assistant to carry on the work of supervision, and there was no direct inheritance tax which enforced the filing of inventories of all estates; so that prior to 1908 his supervisory power had not been effective enough to alter materially the situation. But in that year a law was enacted[30] by which the powers of the tax commissioner were extended, and he was authorized to appoint three supervisors of assessors to assist him in the performance of his new duties.

The act stopped short of authorizing him directly or through the supervisors to revise local assessments, and merely authorized him to direct the local authorities to assess property in the manner prescribed by law. In case local assessors failed to comply with such directions, the commissioner could merely notify the mayor of the city, or the selectmen of the town, of such failure, a provision which becomes almost humorous when one recalls that in many of the towns the selectmen are also the assessors. The tax commissioner was indeed authorized to cause an assessor, guilty of any violation of law for which a penalty was imposed, to be prosecuted in the county courts, but for various reasons this did not meet the needs of the case. It therefore happened that in some instances the local officials refused to obey the directions of the commissioner; but in a majority of cases his recommendations met with substantial compliance, so that the Act of 1908 proved fairly effective. It at least created

[29] Ch. 507 of 1898.
[30] Ch. 550 of 1908.

machinery by which information coming to the probate courts under the operation of the direct inheritance tax was systematically gathered by the supervisor of assessors and transmitted to the taxing authorities of the cities and towns. After 1907, therefore the local taxing authorities were continually supplied with more information about taxable personalty than they had ever possessed before, and in some cases more than they desired to possess. Up to this time the general property tax had been undergoing a gradual process of disintegration; it might have lasted many years longer if no provision had been made for stricter enforcement. But the law of 1908 rapidly produced conditions under which a fundamental change in the system soon became inevitable.

Another factor that contributed to the same result was the growth of private agencies for collecting and distributing information concerning the ownership of corporation stocks. Foreign corporations doing business in Massachusetts were required to file lists of their stockholders with the secretary of state, and these lists supplied a mine of interesting information. Others could sometimes be reached by examining lists filed in other states, or by purchasing a share of stock and then demanding the right to examine stock books. In recent years, therefore, Massachusetts assessors have been able to procure, if they desire it, a large amount of information concerning taxable corporation stocks; and the result has been a fuller assessment of such property than was formerly possible.

There naturally followed a substantial increase in local assessments of personal property. From $766,600,000 in 1907 the figures advanced to $930,817,000 in 1910, to $1,033,000,000 in 1912, and to $1,195,100,000 in 1915. During the entire period of eight years the total increase was $428,500,000, which was practically equal to the total increase in local assessments of personal property between 1861 and 1907. The following table shows the facts for significant years:

STATISTICS OF TOTAL AND PERSONAL PROPERTY ASSESSMENTS IN MASSACHUSETTS

Year	Total Valuation	Valuation of Personal Property	Percentage of Personal Property
1850	$ 551,106,000	$ 201,977,000	36.0
1861	861,500,000	309,400,000	35.9
1874	1,831,600,000	542,300,000	29.6
1881	1,642,200,000	498,300,000	30.2
1907	3,512,600,000	766,600,000	21.8
1915	4,769,900,000	1,195,100,000	25.1

It will be seen that, after declining for fifty-seven years, the proportion of personal property in the total valuations increased from 21.8 per cent in 1907 to 25.1 per cent in 1915. This was a substantial achievement for the supervisors of assessors, but its effect was not what was anticipated. In the first place, the property thus listed tended to disappear from the tax rolls in a comparatively short time through changes in investments or domicile. Prior to 1908 domiciliary changes had been mostly within the state, and the tax laws had probably driven little property out of Massachusetts, although they had doubtless prevented a certain amount from coming here. But after that year removals became increasingly frequent, and presently threatened serious injury to the Commonwealth. Precise data on the subject are, of course, very difficult to obtain; but by 1914 it was estimated, and generally believed, that the property removed from Massachusetts in that year was not less than $100,000,000. Whatever the exact amount may have been, it was now large enough to attract public attention, and to affect materially the attitude of lawyers and bankers who were in a position to know what was going on.

The second natural result was to increase greatly the demand for non-taxable investments; and, inevitably, a greater demand began to create a greater supply. The manufacture of non-taxable preferred stocks of Massachusetts corporations became a regular industry; and, as was natural under the circumstances, some of the new securities proved to be of doubtful solidity. In

1907, the number of new corporations organized under the business corporation law was 1,234, having a total capital of $63,372,000. By 1912, the number of such corporations was 1,453, having a capital of $213,466,000. Thereafter there was somewhat less activity among promoters, but both the number of companies and the total capital remained much larger than had ever been known. In 1913, 1914, and 1915, the business corporations organized were, respectively, 1,504, 1,604, and 1,700; while the figures of the total capital were, respectively, $172,103,000, $123,211,000, and $113,509,000. Unfavorable business conditions may have been partly responsible for the decrease that followed 1912, but another probable cause was a growing distrust of the new securities.

A third result was to stimulate greatly migration to the favored residential towns. Whenever the assessors in the ordinary city or town, acting upon the information furnished by the supervisors, increased materially the assessment of personal property, some favored town immediately acquired new inhabitants. The average rate of taxation in the state was gradually increasing from about $17 per $1000, the figure for 1907, to $18, and finally $19. But in the wealthy residential towns tax rates were often less than $10 per $1000, and valuations were low. Such conditions could not be permanent.

Some of the developments in particular localities during this period deserve to be mentioned. The town of Norwood in 1908 had a tax rate of $26.50, and at that juncture the assessors received information concerning $2,000,000 of taxable estates, which amounted to more than one and one-half times the existing assessment upon personal property. If matters had taken the usual course, these estates would have been taxed for a sum that would have absorbed fully half of the income, and would presently have been removed from the town. But under exceptionally fortunate and able leadership Norwood decided to try to assess all property at its full value, and thereby reduce the rate of taxation to a tolerable figure which would not drive any citizen away. Accordingly, in 1909 the valuation of real estate was increased from $4,739,000 to $7,680,000, while that of personalty was raised from $1,361,000 to $6,118,000. This resulted in an increase of over 125 per cent in the total valuation, and, together with a reduction in the tax levy, reduced the rate of taxation to $8.50. For the moment the crisis was averted. But the tax rate was still higher than intangible property could bear permanently; and in subsequent years the assessment of personal property gradually declined, while, despite further increases in the valuation of realty, the tax rate began to increase. In 1915, the assessment upon personalty was half a million less than in 1909, while the tax rate had increased to $12.80. Norwood had shown that exceptional conditions might enable an industrial town to enforce the tax laws without inviting immediate disaster; but its subsequent experience demonstrates that not even such conditions will avail in the long run.

Stimulated by the example of Norwood or urged by the supervisors of assessors, a few other localities sought to enforce strictly the existing tax laws, but with very different results. The city of Malden in 1909 increased the assessment of personalty from $6,734,000 to $12,751,000, and reduced its tax rate from $19.20 to $15.70; but by 1912 the assessment of personalty had declined to $8,438,000, and the tax rate had returned to the figure for 1908. Meanwhile, a number of wealthy residents had changed their domicile, and the city had lost a substantial amount of revenue from corporation taxes. Between 1909 and 1911, the city of Quincy increased the assessment of personalty from $5,813,000 to $7,830,000, and reduced its tax rate from $20.40 to $19.50. But two years later the personal assessment had sunk to $6,254,000, while the tax rate had advanced to $23.70. Salem tried the same experiment between 1909 and 1912, increasing its personal assessment from $9,821,000 to $10,617,000, and reducing its tax rate from $18.60 to $18. But in 1913, nearly a million of personal property disappeared from the tax roll, and the tax rate advanced to $20.50. Such examples were sufficient to deter other localities from attempting to emulate the example of Norwood.

The other side of the picture may be seen by turning to some of the small residential towns. In 1908, Dover had assessed $470,000 of personal property and $931,000 of realty, and had a tax rate of $9.80. In the following year the assessment of personal property jumped to $4,296,000, and the tax rate fell to $4.30. This suddenly acquired wealth was thereafter retained, and, in fact, increased to $6,925,000 in 1914, in which year the tax rate was $5.50. The town of Rowley in 1912 assessed $170,000 of personal property, and had a tax rate of $13.00. But in the next year the assessment of personalty rose to $2,088,000, and the tax rate decreased to $5.50. Though subsequently changes occurred, Rowley continued to tax a large amount of personalty, and remained in affluent circumstances.

The most striking case was that of the town of Orleans, which in 1910 had taxed $181,000 of personal property at a rate of $15 per $1000. The next year the assessment of this class of property increased to $968,000, and the tax rate fell to $3. With its reputation thus established, the town continued to increase its taxable wealth until in 1915 the valuation of personalty amounted to $3,941,000, and the tax rate was prevented from reaching the vanishing point only by liberal outlays for improvements. In this case corporation and bank taxes were an especially important factor in the situation. In 1910, Orleans had raised $10,259 from taxes upon property, and had received only $1,085 from the state treasury on account of corporation and bank taxes. In 1911, the levy upon property declined to $4,557, while the revenue from corporation and bank taxes increased to $10,302. In 1914, the taxes upon property had increased to $11,509, as a result of the inflow of personal estates, while the revenue drawn from the state treasury had risen to $24,883. In that year Orleans enjoyed a revenue of $37,108 from all sources, including polls, whereas in 1910 it had an income of $11,982.

In 1915, Orleans showed a tax rate of $3 per $1000, the lowest in the state, and seven other towns had tax rates that were less than $10; fifty-two towns showed rates ranging from $10 to

$14.80; nine cities and one hundred forty-seven towns showed rates ranging from $15 to $19.90; while twenty-six cities and one hundred and eleven towns had rates that ranged from $20 to $30. These inequalities persisted in spite of certain changes in the distribution of the corporation taxes, by which the revenue from mercantile and manufacturing corporations was allotted to the localities where the plants were situated and business carried on. Further changes in the distribution of the corporation and bank taxes might improve somewhat the position of the cities and the ordinary agricultural or manufacturing towns, but the distribution of taxable personal property had become so unequal as to make the situation worse than it had been prior to the introduction of the direct inheritance tax and the enactment of the law creating supervisors of assessors. In 1905, the fourteen towns previously mentioned had received $24.01 of revenue per capita from corporation taxes and the local tax on personal property; while in the rest of the state the revenue was but $5.35 per capita. In 1915, the figures were, respectively, $29.50 and $7.54.[31] Nothing but a radical change in the laws relating to taxation held out any prospect of relief.

From 1907 to 1915 only slight changes occurred in the distribution of the total burden of taxation. Of the total of $112,280,000,[32] polls were assessed for $2,055,000, or 1.8 per cent, which is to be compared with 2.4 per cent for 1907. Liquor licenses and minor business taxes contributed $3,678,000, or 3.3 per cent, which is 1.4 per cent less than in the earlier year. Corporations paid $12,484,000, or 11.1 per cent, as against a percentage of 13.2 eight years earlier. The inheritance tax yielded $3,104,000, or 2.8 per cent of the total, which is an increase of 1.8 per cent over 1907. The taxes assessed upon

[31] It is worth while to notice the changes that occurred over the whole period from 1865 to 1915. In the former year fourteen favored towns derived a per capita revenue of $6.87 from the stated sources, and the rest of the Commonwealth $5.81. In 1915, the figures were, respectively, $29.50 and $7.54. Thus the fourteen towns had gained $22.63, while the rest of the state had gained $1.73.

[32] From this total automobile licenses are excluded.

personal property stood at $22,180,000,[33] which was 19.8 per cent of the total, the proportion of personalty being 3 per cent greater than at the beginning of this period. Finally, real estate taxes contributed $68,776,000, or 61.2 per cent, which was 0.7 per cent less than in 1907.

As was to be expected, the introduction of a tax upon direct inheritances led to renewed efforts to secure a better method of taxing personal property. In response to a petition from leading business interests, and upon the recommendation of the governor, another tax commission was authorized in 1907. In the following year this commission recommended[34] changes in the distribution of the corporate franchise tax, the exemption of future issues of county and municipal bonds, the appointment of supervisors of assessors, and the introduction of a flat tax upon intangible property—the so-called "three-mill tax."

The first proposal was promptly carried into effect by a law which provided that thereafter the taxes paid by manufacturing and mercantile corporations and distributed among the several cities and towns should be divided equally between the localities where the stockholders resided and those in which the business was carried on.[35] Since previously the whole amount not retained by the state had been allocated to the towns where the stockholders were domiciled, this act tended to mitigate somewhat the growing inequality between the wealthy residential towns and the rest of the state. Subsequent acts[36] turned over to the towns where business was carried on the whole of the revenue from ordinary business corporations except that part, representing the proportion paid in respect of stock owned by non-residents, which was retained by the Commonwealth. The result was that between 1905 and 1915 the whole amount of revenue received from corporation taxes by the fourteen favored

[33] In this item is included $76,644 of revenue paid into the state treasury under the operation of the bond registration tax.

[34] Report of the Commission on Taxation appointed under the provisions of ch. 129 of the resolves of 1907 (Boston, 1908).

[35] Ch. 614 of 1908.

[36] Chs. 456 of 1910 and 198 of 1914.

towns previously referred to, decreased from $10.36 per capita to $6.20, whereas in the rest of the state it increased from $1.62 to $1.93. In 1916, a final act[37] provided that the taxes paid by all remaining classes of corporations, except that part representing non-resident stock, should be allocated to the cities and towns where the business is carried on. This leaves only the revenue from the bank tax subject to the old rule of distribution according to the domicile of the stockholders.

The second recommendation of the commission also was accepted. In 1905, the state treasurer had urged that future issues of bonds of the Commonwealth should be exempt from taxation. He showed that of $84,580,000 of registered bonds then outstanding 70 per cent were held outside the state, 24 per cent were held by corporations and institutions within the state but exempt from taxation thereon, and only 6 per cent were in the hands of individual inhabitants subject to local taxation.[38] The legislature, accordingly, passed an act exempting future issues of state bonds,[39] under which it was estimated that the state gained ¼ of 1 per cent in the interest rate upon the next issue.[40] The cities and towns now came forward with the request that their securities also should be made tax exempt, and the legislature exempted from taxation future issues of county and municipal bonds.[41]

This step was stoutly opposed by most of the remaining advocates of the general property tax. But the practical situation confronting the cities and towns called loudly for a change. No investor would purchase a bond yielding 4 per cent interest with the expectation of paying a tax amounting to 1½ or 2 per cent, and accordingly city and town treasurers withheld from the assessors information concerning the ownership of municipal bonds. In some cases, indeed, they made it their policy to inform investors that this was their practice. Little

[37] Ch. 299 of 1916.
[38] Treasurer's Report, 1905, pp. 6-7.
[39] Ch. 493 of 1906.
[40] Treasurer's Report, 1906, pp. 8-9.
[41] Chs. 464 and 594 of 1908.

or no revenue was actually derived from the tax upon municipal bonds, while the fact that such bonds were legally taxable tended to limit somewhat the demand and so to increase the rate of interest. Neither the state nor the towns could expect a reduction of interest equivalent to the average rate of taxation, since so many of the bonds were held by corporations and exempted institutions and so few of the remainder were ever taxed, but it is probable that the broader market opened to public securities in consequence of exemption resulted in an immediate reduction of about ¼ of 1 per cent in the interest basis.

In time, the exemption of municipal securities opened the door to serious abuse. The city and town officials soon learned that there was a regular demand for tax-exempt securities just before the first day of April in each year, and began to accommodate their offerings to this situation. In January, February, and March, increasing quantities of short term notes maturing after April 1st began to come into the market, which commanded very low rates of interest. In 1911, the total amount of short term notes issued by the towns was $9,700,000, while by 1915 it had risen to $15,363,000, an increase of approximately 60 per cent. But the striking fact was that the notes issued in January, February, and March, which were those utilized over the first day of April, increased from $2,580,000 to $5,180,000, or more than 100 per cent; while the amount of notes issued in April, May, and June, which could not be so utilized, remained practically stationary, the increase being less than 10 per cent. Complete data for the cities are not available, but the issues of notes recorded in the leading financial papers show the same conditions that developed in the towns. In 1911, these papers reported the issue of $4,667,000 of city notes during the months of January, February, and March, while in 1916, they reported a total of $9,870,000, an increase of over 110 per cent. The March issues, which were especially sought around tax day, rose from $1,460,000 in 1911 to $5,590,000 in 1916, an increase of nearly 300 per cent. Interest rates upon these issues were very low, sometimes falling below 2 per cent, and in some cases reaching such figures as 1.3 per cent, or even ¼ of 1 per cent; while one city actually received a small premium for accommodating an investor with $100,000 of notes maturing just around tax day. Thus an exemption intended to apply to permanent investments in municipal securities came to be a means of facilitating temporary changes in investments with a view to evading taxation.

The third recommendation of the commission resulted in the enactment of the law, already discussed, by which three supervisors of assessors were appointed and provision was made for distributing among the local boards information about property uncovered in the probate courts. This proposal originated in connection with the plan for a flat tax on intangible property, but was presented separately by the commission with the suggestion that the establishment of a three-mill tax upon intangible property "will remove all reasonable ground of objection to the proposal for state supervision of the assessment of property." Since it has been supposed by not a few people that the supervisor law was proposed with the deliberate intention of forcing a crisis in taxation affairs, it is important to recall the fact that it originated in connection with a plan for establishing a fair and practicable method of taxing intangible property.

The fourth recommendation was that intangible property should be exempted from other taxation, and should then be taxed at the uniform rate of three mills upon each dollar of the fair cash value, or $3 per $1000. Since such a tax would be levied at the same rate in every city and town, taxpayers would have no inducement to change their domicile; and since it would substitute a reasonable for a confiscatory exaction, it could be strictly enforced without driving people out of the state. It was based upon a plan which had been tried in Pennsylvania and Maryland with no little success, and was subsequently adopted by Minnesota, Iowa, Rhode Island, and North Dakota. The commission realized, however, that it was open to objection upon constitutional grounds, and therefore recommended that the legislature secure the opinion of the Supreme Court concerning its constitutionality. In case the opinion of the court should be adverse, the commission pointed out that the constitution of the Commonwealth ought to be amended.

In due course the legislature submitted the question to the Supreme Court, which pronounced the three-mill tax unconstitutional.[42] Thereupon, an amendment was proposed striking out of the constitution the requirement that taxes must be proportional, but this failed to secure the two-thirds vote required in the House of Representatives. The following year a similar amendment passed the legislature, but with a provision that it should be referred to a special commission for further investigation. This commission submitted to the next legislature an adverse report,[43] which in 1910 resulted in the defeat of the proposed amendment, so that the project of a three-mill tax had to be abandoned.

Opposition to the proposed constitutional amendment was based upon a number of grounds. In the first place, Mr. Hills, Mr. Henry Winn, and most of the local assessors opposed it because they still desired to have all property taxed at the same rate. Many of them would have favored the taxation of personal property at the average rate prevailing throughout the Commonwealth, but they were unwilling to make any further concessions. A second group of remonstrants would have favored the establishment of a uniform tax upon intangible property at some such rate as $10 or $12 per $1000, but contended that a rate of $3 was altogether too low and would tend to increase the burden upon other classes of property. A third ground for objection was the belief that a reduction of the tax upon bonds and upon stocks of foreign corporations would affect adversely the value of non-taxable securities. And, finally, a fourth reason for opposition was the fear that the removal of the requirement that taxes must be proportional would open the door to favoritism and to radical legislation.

[42] 195 Mass. 607.

[43] Report of the Commission Appointed to Investigate the Laws Relating to Taxation (December, 1909).

Taxation conditions in Massachusetts were then so bad that it is probable that the opposition of the first two classes of remonstrants would not have availed to defeat the amendment. But the arguments advanced by the other objectors raised a number of new questions which seemed to many people to require further time for consideration, and divided the forces which otherwise might have favored a better method of taxing intangible property.

VI

In 1911, Governor Foss directed the attention of the legislature to the subject of taxation,[44] and recommended the establishment of a state income tax and the adoption of a better method of taxing wild and forest lands. Prior to 1910 it would probably have been useless to propose in Massachusetts such a measure as a state tax upon incomes, since here, as elsewhere, the people had long been accustomed to the taxation of property and were inclined to regard an income tax as inquisitorial. But the situation suddenly changed when congress submitted to the states the sixteenth amendment to the federal constitution. This brought up for consideration the whole question of income taxation, and required every one in active political life to define his attitude upon it. Those who advocated immediate ratification of the amendment could not urge that a state income tax would be inquisitorial; while those who opposed such ratification usually did so upon the ground that the income tax should be reserved for the states, and were not in a position to argue that Massachusetts ought not to employ it. Governor Foss's proposals, therefore, met with very general support; his amendment authorizing a special forest tax was immediately adopted, and nothing but differences of opinion concerning the proper form of an income tax amendment prevented acceptance of his other recommendation.

These differences, however, proved difficult to harmonize; the more so because they offered a convenient reason for opposi-

[44] See H. Doc. 1900 of 1911. Also Sen. Docs. 255 of 1912 and 39 of 1913.

tion to any change in the method of taxing intangible property. They turned chiefly upon the questions, whether the amendment should authorize a progressive income tax, and whether it should provide that property taxed upon its income should be exempted by constitutional requirement from other taxation. In 1912 and 1913, as in 1911, controversy over these points was chiefly responsible for the defeat of proposed income tax amendments.

But while such controversy continued, conditions were becoming increasingly serious. Orleans had a $3 tax rate, other favored towns were receiving large accessions of taxable personalty every spring, and it was becoming evident to the people of the rest of the state that they could not hope to retain even their existing revenue from intangible property. Moreover, removals of large amounts of personalty to neighboring states were becoming increasingly common, and were causing well-founded alarm. These conditions finally led the mayor and the assessors of Boston to favor the income tax project, and elsewhere tended to disintegrate the opposition of local assessors. Moreover, the tax commissioner had become convinced of the necessity of reform, and the annual reports of his department were dealing vigorously with the subject in a manner which could not fail to impress both the legislature and the public. Finally, Wisconsin in 1912 introduced a state income tax which proved an immediate success and furnished an impressive object lesson to Massachusetts.

In 1911, at the suggestion of Governor Foss, the tax commissioner instituted an investigation of the data furnished by the inheritance tax returns, and found that in estates passing through the probate courts the personal property amounted to between three and four times as much as the realty. From September 1, 1907, to August 31, 1908, the returns of all estates, whether taxable or not, showed that the real property brought under review was valued at $22,462,000 and the personalty at $70,715,000. From September 1, 1908, to December 1, 1911, the returns showed real property amounting to $97,734,000 and personal property valued at $368,741,000. Upon the assumption that the total personalty of the inhabitants of Massachusetts was more than three times the total realty, and that at least one-half of the personalty was taxable under existing law, the tax commissioner estimated that there must be from $4,000,000,000 to $5,000,000,000 of taxable personal property within the Commonwealth, whereas the local assessors in that year had assessed but $984,300,000.[45] Up to that time it had been possible to argue that, although much intangible property evaded taxation, the assessors were able to secure the greater part of it. But thereafter it was usually accepted as a fact that the untaxed personalty, chiefly intangibles, was three and perhaps four times as great as the amount actually taxed. This tended to give a somewhat new turn to discussions of the tax problem.

In 1914, the need for a change in the method of taxing intangible property become so apparent that, without waiting for a constitutional amendment, the legislature established a registration tax upon certain classes of bonds.[46] It provided that holders of bonds secured by mortgage upon tangible property actually taxed in Massachusetts or elsewhere might register such bonds with the tax commissioner and pay a registration tax of three mills on the dollar. Bonds so registered were to become exempt from other taxation. As a property tax, of course, this measure would have been wholly invalid, but the legislature acted upon the theory that it might be upheld as a valid excise. Doubts about the constitutionality of the measure were sufficient to prevent most investors from taking advantage of the act, but substantial amounts of bonds were registered with the tax commissioner up to the repeal of the law by the Income Tax Act of 1916.

Agitation for a better method of taxing intangible property was becoming increasingly active and influential. In 1908, a committee of prominent citizens was organized to advocate the adoption of the three-mill tax, and the following year the Boston

[45] See Sen. Doc. 255 of 1912, pp. 2-3.
[46] Ch. 761 of 1914.

Chamber of Commerce took up the subject in vigorous fashion. In 1910, a state-wide organization known as the Merchants' and Manufacturers' Committee on the Tax Laws came into the field, so that the movement was no longer confined to Boston and its immediate vicinity. In 1914, the Massachusetts Tax Association was organized, with Lucius Tuttle as its first president and a board of directors representing many of the important business interests of the Commonwealth as well as organized labor. Upon Mr. Tuttle's death, Ex-Governor Curtis Guild succeeded to the presidency, and an active campaign was instituted under most favorable auspices. With the coöperation of Governor Walsh and the tax commissioner's department, a constitutional amendment permitting the levy of a proportional income tax, but not requiring that property taxed upon its income *must* be exempted from other taxation, was drafted and submitted to the legislature which ratified it by decisive votes in both branches. This amendment passed the legislature of 1915 even more decisively, and in the following November was adopted at the polls by an overwhelming vote. The way was now open for a reform of the tax on personal property.

VII

The legislature of 1915, anticipating the ratification of the amendment, authorized the appointment of a special commission on taxation which was instructed to investigate the advisability of changes in existing tax laws and to draft an income tax act. In January, 1916, this commission[47] submitted the draft of a well-considered act which, under the impetus of the overwhelming ratification of the income tax amendment at the polls, was enacted after much discussion but with little effective opposition.

The income tax law of 1915 was designed primarily to provide a better method of taxing intangible property. It therefore exempts such property from local taxation, and imposes upon its income a tax of 6 per cent, from which, however, $300 of

[47] Report of the Special Commission on Taxation (1916).

taxable income is exempt for persons whose total income from all sources does not exceed $600. But for the tax levied since 1646 upon personal, trade, and professional incomes, the law of 1916 might have been confined to the income from intangible property. Since, however, that tax was in existence and was not likely to be repealed, it was necessary for the new act to take cognizance of this fact. It would have been clearly undesirable to have two income taxes: one levied by the state and strictly enforced; the other levied by local assessors and almost a dead letter. The obvious and expedient solution was the transfer of the old local tax to the Commonwealth, and therefore the law of 1916 includes a tax upon income from personal, trade, and professional earnings. Finally, the act imposes a tax of 3 per cent upon profits derived from dealings in intangible personal property.

The new law, therefore, is much narrower in scope than the Federal income tax, which applies to income from all sources, and somewhat narrower than the Wisconsin income tax, which reaches practically all incomes except dividends from certain classes of corporations. It follows, however, what was undoubtedly the line of least resistance for Massachusetts. There was no popular demand for a new method of taxing real estate and tangible personal property, and the problem before the legislature was that of finding a better method of taxing intangible personalty. The result is a perfectly logical adjustment by which personal, professional, and trade incomes, and income from intangible property are taxed by the state; while tangible property continues to be subject to local taxation upon its capital value.

Following antecedent practice, the Massachusetts income tax is imposed upon "inhabitants" of the Commonwealth. It is, therefore, a personal tax payable by people who are inhabitants of the Commonwealth at any time between the first day of January and the thirtieth day of June in any year. Persons who are not inhabitants within the meaning of that word as defined by the Supreme Court are not subject to the tax, even though they may carry on business in Massachusetts; and, upon the other hand, inhabitants of Massachusetts are taxable upon income derived from business carried on outside of the Commonwealth. The working of this feature of the law will be watched with interest.

The tax upon the income from intangible property substitutes a reasonable and uniform tax for one levied at rates that ranged from $3 to $30 per $1000. Under the old system many people evaded taxation, some compounded with the local assessors for a reasonable tax, and still others paid one-fourth or one-third of their incomes. The intention is that the new tax shall be enforced upon every one, and the act accordingly provides adequate methods of administration.

The first thing, of course, is the requirement of sworn returns of income from taxable intangible property, which must be made on or before the first day of March in each year and relate to the income of the preceding calendar year. Failure to file such a return renders a taxable person liable to an additional tax of $5 for every day he is in default. Continued failure after receipt of a notice from the tax commissioner makes a person liable to be assessed by the commissioner for twice the amount of his taxable income, and subjects him to a further penalty of fine, imprisonment, or both. Conviction for refusal to make a return works the forfeiture of a person's right to hold public office within the Commonwealth for such a period, not exceeding five years, as the court may determine. Similar penalties are provided for making fraudulent returns, the law making no distinction between persistent refusal to file a return and the filing of a return found to be fraudulent. Since the enforcement of the act is to be wholly in the hands of the state tax department, these penalties should prove adequate.[48] No careful lawyer or responsible banker will advise a client or customer to trifle with

[48] The act, of course, makes suitable provision for preventing disclosure of the details of tax returns. It provides, however, that the names of the persons who have filed returns shall be open to public inspection. It permits taxpayers to file their returns either with the tax commissioner or with the income tax assessor of the district in which they live.

the new law; and there is every indication that the income tax, with its requirement of sworn returns, has been accepted by the business community, and will be strictly complied with. It will not be people of wealth, but those of smaller means and little or no business experience, who will cause most difficulty.

The tax upon the income of intangible personalty applies only to such property as was formerly subject to taxation; thus incomes from mortgages upon taxable Massachusetts real estate, deposits in savings banks, tax-exempt state and municipal bonds, national bank stock, and the stock of Massachusetts corporations, are all exempted. The same is true of income from so-called "stocks" of most of the voluntary associations which are so common in Massachusetts. In general, owners of securities will find that they are taxable only upon income derived from sources that were taxable under the old law. About the only exception is found in the case of trusts or other voluntary associations not owning real estate exclusively, or shares in Massachusetts corporations, and not doing business principally in Massachusetts.

A very important and interesting feature of the tax on the income from intangibles is that it provides for a deduction on account of indebtedness. The property tax had authorized such deduction only against certain credits, that is, it allowed the taxpayer to deduct money he owed from debts due him. The new law does not indeed permit the deduction of interest paid upon any and all debts from the income received by the taxpayer from taxable intangible property. To do so would have been wrong in principle and would have opened the door to wholesale evasion. Deduction of all debts from taxable income is necessary as well as proper under a general income tax applicable to income from all sources, but under a partial income tax it is manifestly impossible. The new law, therefore, follows what may be called the principle of granting the taxpayer a proportional offset or deduction. It provides in effect that, from the income received from taxable intangible property, the taxpayer may deduct such a proportion of the interest paid on his total indebtedness as the income which he derives from taxable intangible property bears to his total income.

The provisions of the law at this point are necessarily complicated, but their practical operation may be shown by the three following cases: a person receiving $99,000 of income from taxable intangible property and $1000 of income from other sources may deduct from his taxable income derived from intangible property 99 per cent of the interest paid upon his indebtedness; a person receiving $50,000 of income from taxable intangibles, and $50,000 from other sources will be able to deduct one-half of the interest which he pays upon his debts; and, finally, a person receiving $1000 from taxable intangible property and $99,000 from other sources will be permitted to deduct but one per cent of the interest upon his obligations. These cases do not take account of all the provisions of the law and are intended merely to illustrate the principle which is eminently fair and in practice should offer no serious difficulties.

Another departure from former practice is the provision which grants an exemption of $300 of income from intangible property to persons whose total income from all sources does not exceed $600 during the year in respect of which the tax is assessed. Under the old law a person owning taxable securities, received no exemption, and in many cases where small estates were uncovered in the probate courts great hardship arose. There was, indeed, a provision that the assessors might exempt the polls and any portion of the estates of persons who by reason of age, infirmity, or poverty were deemed to be unable to contribute toward the public charges. But this did not meet the needs of the case, since a person with a capital of five or ten thousand dollars was not in a position to plead "poverty." Thus it came about that persons deriving small incomes from taxable property were frequently taxed for twenty or twenty-five per cent of such incomes. The new law not only reduces the rate of taxation to 6 per cent of the income from intangibles, but provides an exemption of $300.

The tax imposed upon income derived from annuities and

from "professions, employments, trade, or business" will be levied at the uniform rate of 1½ per cent. This is a trifle less than the average of the local tax rates to which such incomes were subject under the old law. It is expected, however, that the assessments made by state authorities will be so much more complete that the revenue will be considerably greater than formerly. The new law continues the exemption of $2000 of professional, personal, or trade incomes, and provides the further exemption of $500 for a married person and $250 for each child under the age of eighteen years, or for a parent dependent upon the taxpayer for support; but provides that the total exemption shall in no case exceed $3000. Income from annuities received no exemptions under the old law, but under the new has an exemption of $300 if the total income of the annuitant from all sources does not exceed $600.

In its provisions concerning professions, employments, trade, or business, the new law is noteworthy because it carefully defines taxable income. The old law merely provided that the "income" from such sources should be taxed, and that income derived from property subject to taxation should not be taxed. The Supreme Court held, however, that this permitted the taxation of the entire income of a merchant even though his merchandise might be subject to local taxation,[49] so that in fact double taxation of merchandise and the income derived therefrom was possible. The new law imposes the tax upon the net income of a business, determined substantially as any good accountant would compute it; and then provides that a taxpayer may deduct from such net income a sum equal to 5 per cent of the assessed value of the tangible property, real and personal, owned by him and used in the business.

The tax of 3 per cent imposed upon profits derived from dealings in intangible personal property is levied upon all inhabitants of the Commonwealth whether or not they are engaged in the business of dealing in such property. It also applies to dealings in all classes of securities, taxable and non-taxable. The

[49] Wilcox v. Middlesex County Commissioners, 103 Mass. 544.

tax is to be levied upon the "excess of the gains over the losses," and is to be assessed annually. But the law provides that trustees or other fiduciaries shall be assessed at the time a trust is terminated unless it continues for more than five years, in which case the assessment shall be made at least in every fifth year.

This provision of the act occasioned considerable discussion. Without it gains from dealings in intangible property would have been taxable at the rate of 1½ per cent if they formed part of the income of any business carried on by inhabitants of the Commonwealth; but they would not have been taxable to individuals who speculated in securities. Now an income tax differs from a property tax in that it exempts from taxation property yielding no income, which, if it has any value, would be taxable under a property tax. It is obviously the intention of the new law that persons who speculate in non-dividend-yielding stocks shall be taxed upon their speculative gains, even though they may not be engaged in the business of buying or selling intangible property. That the rate was placed at 3 per cent instead of 1½ per cent was perhaps due in part to the desire to tax the "speculator"; but it is also explicable on the ground that intangible property is now exempt from taxation as property, so that persons who deal in it may fairly be required to pay a somewhat heavier rate than persons who deal in merchandise or other taxable tangible property.

As already stated, the administration of the income tax is placed in the hands of the state tax commissioner. It was not to be expected that the tax would work well if administrated in approximately three hundred and fifty different ways by approximately three hundred and fifty local boards of assessors; and Massachusetts acted wisely in turning the work over to the Commonwealth. During the fifty years of its existence, the tax commissioner's department has been administered in a manner that has commanded general confidence, and all that needed to be done was to add to its equipment a new bureau charged with the assessment and collection of the income tax.

The tax commissioner accordingly is authorized to appoint an income tax deputy who will have general charge of the taxation of incomes. He is also to divide the state into districts, and to appoint an income tax assessor for each district. Thus the administration will be in some measure localized, but the number of districts will probably not exceed ten or twelve, and responsibility will rest with a single ultimate authority, the state tax commissioner. Under this arrangement there will undoubtedly be intelligent and even-handed enforcement of the law in every city and town, so that taxpayers will have the assurance that all citizens are being treated alike. The tax commissioner is authorized to make necessary rules and regulations for the assessment and collection of the income tax, and will undoubtedly be given a generous allowance for necessary expenses. Upon the administrative side, therefore, the law of 1916 seems to make adequate provision for strict enforcement of the tax upon incomes.

Information at the source is also required in certain cases. Every employer of labor must report to the tax commissioner the names and addresses of all regular employees who are inhabitants of Massachusetts, and have received wages, salaries, or other compensation in excess of $1800 during the previous calendar year. Also corporations doing business in the Commonwealth and voluntary associations having transferable shares are, unless their stocks fall within the class of tax-exempt securities, required to report the names of their shareholders. They are further required to report the names of all inhabitants of Massachusetts to whom they have paid annuities or interest upon their bonds, notes, or other evidences of indebtedness, except interest on coupon bonds and incomes exempt from taxation under the act. Neither of these requirements is unduly burdensome, so that no such difficulties will arise as have developed under the federal income tax.

A final provision of interest is that concerning the taxation of personal property in the year 1917 when the new law goes into effect. Since intangible property is hereafter to be exempt from local taxation, many taxpayers will be entitled to reductions of the local assessments upon their personalty; but since tangible personal property today is frequently under-assessed, it is important that such persons should not receive greater reductions than they are entitled to. The law, therefore, provides that in 1917 no local assessment of personal estate shall be reduced below the amount assessed in 1916, unless the taxpayer makes a return of his tangible personal property. This means that, in order to benefit by the exemption of intangible property or income formerly subject to local taxation, taxpayers must file with their local assessors in 1917 a return of their taxable personalty. For the average citizen this will mean household furniture in excess of $1000, automobiles, carriages, horses, and live stock; and for merchants and manufacturers it will mean a return of merchandise and machinery. In this manner there will be secured a much fuller assessment of tangible personalty than ever before; so that the new law, by providing a just and practicable method of taxing intangibles, will remove many of the difficulties that have hitherto attended taxation of tangible personalty. In this respect it is probable that the experience of Massachusetts will be the same as that of the few other states that have adopted fair and efficient methods of taxing intangible property.

The new law is calculated to yield a revenue somewhat greater than is now derived from intangible property and taxable incomes, and there can be little doubt that it will fulfil expectations. It should be remembered, however, that Massachusetts has been taxing some $500,000,000 or $550,000,000 of intangible personalty, so that the results of the new act cannot be as spectacular as those secured in other states where intangible property had formerly contributed little or nothing.

The intangible property taxed in 1914 probably paid somewhat less than the average rate of taxation because of its concentration in wealthy towns. If we estimate that it paid $16 per $1000, it yielded a revenue of $8,000,000 to $8,800,000. The amount of incomes now taxed is not known, but it probably does not exceed $20,000,000, and the taxes collected from this source cannot exceed $350,000 or $400,000. The new income tax, therefore, must yield from eight to nine millions of dollars in order to offset the loss of revenue occasioned by the exemption of intangible property and income from local taxation. It ought to do so, since all the estimates show that there are in the state enough taxable intangibles, and professional, personal or trade incomes, to give the desired result. This calculation assumes that the exemption of intangibles and income from local taxation will decrease local assessments of personal property by some $550,000,000. But this will not be the case, because of the provision that such assessments shall not be less in 1917 than in 1916 unless taxpayers bring in returns of their taxable property. The law, therefore, is certain to produce a larger revenue from tangible personal property, an important factor of safety in calculations of the probable result of the new income tax.

Greatly in favor of the new act is the fact that it was adopted only after some years of serious discussion which familiarized the people of the Commonwealth with the evils of the existing system and the need of having reasonable and enforcible tax laws. It represents a fairly general consensus of opinion reached after thorough consideration, and therefore promises to solve the most vexatious of taxation problems. This has been the experience of other states that have introduced reasonable methods of taxing intangible property, and there is little ground for doubt about the result in Massachusetts.

INCREASE OF TAXES ON REAL ESTATE IN AMERICAN CITIES[1]

I

AS FAR back as the record runs, taxes upon urban real estate have only one direction of movement, and that is upward. A hundred years ago a tax of 30 or 40 cents per $100, levied upon realty valued at half or two-thirds of its true worth, probably sufficed for the requirements of most cities and towns; and as late as 1860 the average rate of taxation imposed for state and local purposes was no more than 78 cents per $100 throughout the United States. Then followed a great increase in state and local taxation which, by the end of the nineteenth century, made a rate of $1.50 per $100 very common and a rate of $2 not very exceptional. Today we find ourselves asking whether a rate of $2.50 or $3 has come to stay, and whether a rate of $3.50 or $4 is not in prospect.

These rates are mentioned as fairly representative, but are not true averages, which would be very difficult to compute. Where the basis of valuation is less than 50%, much higher nominal rates of taxation are found; and where a genuine effort is made to approximate full value, the rates are naturally lower. I am dealing merely with the general trend, and can fairly represent it by contrasting the tax rates of 30 or 40 cents which prevailed a century ago with those of $2.50 or $3 which now frequently occur and may be subject to further increase.

Under ordinary conditions, the increase of taxes upon real estate is gradual; but there have been two periods in our history when it became extremely rapid. Between 1860 and 1870 the per capita taxes levied on property for state and local purposes increased from $3 to $7.28, and the average rate of taxation

[1] Reprinted from *Harvard Business Review,* Vol. VI (1927-28), pp. 129-42. Reproduced by generous permission of the publishers.

rose from 78 cents to $1.98 per $100. For this great change the rapid growth of cities, the emergence of new economic and social needs, municipal misgovernment, and the inflation of commodity prices resulting from the Civil War were responsible. The second period is that which was ushered in by the World War and may not yet have reached its end. Between 1913 and 1925, the latest year for which statistics are available, the per capita taxes levied upon general property in American cities having a population of over 30,000 rose from $17.82 to $39.20, while special assessments increased from $2.40 per capita to $4.52. For all taxes and assessments the total increase was from $22.16 per capita to $47.14 in the twelve years ending in 1925. Preliminary data for the year 1926 indicate a further increase; and anyone whose local taxes decrease in 1927 may count himself an exceptional as well as a fortunate man. We have been living in times as unusual as the decade which saw our Civil War; and the increase of local taxation which has recently taken place is due to somewhat similar causes, especially to the inflation of commodity prices such as results from any great war.

Since times are so exceptional and resemble in so many important respects the decade of the 1860's, is it reasonable to expect that the increase of local taxation will come to an end as it did in the former instance? No certain answer can be given to the question. In the nineteenth century the increase of public expenditures, and therefore of taxes, was sometimes checked by a period of enforced economy and retrenchment following severe commercial depressions such as occurred in 1837 and 1873. The hard times following the panic of 1893 checked the increase of public expenditures for a few years, but brought little enforced retrenchment; and the panic of 1907 did not check in any appreciable degree the upward movement of expenditures and taxes. Even before the war, therefore, there was reason for thinking that the forces making for increased state and local taxation had gathered such momentum that industrial depressions had little effect upon them. The same conclusion must be drawn from our experience with our last depression, which broke upon the country in 1920 and ran its course by the end of 1921. In the year 1919 the ordinary expenses (including interest) of cities having a population of over 30,000 amounted to $28.19 per capita, and in 1922 such expenses had increased to $41.42 per capita. Moreover, capital outlays, which were $7.38 per capita in the year first named, had increased to $15.95 in the second. Naturally enough, therefore, during this period of three years taxes levied upon property increased from $23.13 per capita to $34.54. We have, therefore, even more reason today than we had in 1913 to doubt whether the forces making for continued increase of local expenses and taxes can be checked even by the severest industrial depression.

The continued increase of local, and especially city, expenditures since 1919 is the more striking because it contrasts so sharply with the decrease which has been effected in the expenditures of our federal government. I do not refer, of course, to the reduction in military expenditures immediately after the war, but to the decrease of ordinary civil expenditures following the establishment of a national budget system and an efficient bureau for carrying that system into effect.

The divergent movements of federal and local expenditures are not difficult to understand. Few local governments, if any, have a budget system and organization that compare in efficiency with those which our national government has developed. Few local governments, indeed, have chief executives who dare to practice, preach, and enforce economy at a time when politicians are afraid of the word and prefer to campaign for office on their records as liberal spenders. And, finally, there is the obvious fact that local governments touch more closely the personal, business, and social life of the people, with the result that the unpleasant side of enforced economy is brought more closely to the average voter. Abolishing useless bureaus, reducing pay rolls, eliminating waste, and moderating ambitious plans for public works and "improvements" are more or less thankless jobs anywhere, but are especially difficult and troublesome among friends and neighbors.

The revenue required to finance increased municipal expenditures has come chiefly from the property tax. Attempts have been made to diversify the sources of municipal revenue, but nevertheless the percentage which taxes on property bore to all revenue receipts increased from 62.1% in 1913 to 63.7% in 1925. What proportion of the taxes levied upon property fell upon real estate, we do not know. Statistics showing the assessed valuation of different classes of property indicate that the proportion which real estate bore to the total assessed valuation declined from 84.5% to 81% between 1913 and 1925. But this does not necessarily mean that the proportion of the property taxes falling upon real estate declined, because some of the property classified as personal, especially intangibles, was in some cities taxed at rates much lower than those imposed on real estate, so that the figures showing the separate valuations of real and personal property do not tell the whole story. We are thrown back upon the simple fact that taxes levied upon general property increased from $525,000,000 to $1,597,000,000, or 201%, during the twelve years covered by the latest available report, and that, therefore, taxes upon real estate increased rapidly and sharply.

II

Under these circumstances, it is natural that city administrators, owners of real estate, and others should be seriously concerned with the growing burden of taxes on urban real estate. It is also natural that they should inquire whether there is not some fairer method of distributing taxes which would afford the desired relief.

Of plans for reforming state and local taxation there are many; devising such plans has been a favorite pastime in the United States for over fifty years. There are probably few of us who, if given the necessary authority, could not get up a plan satisfactory to ourselves and put it into operation in comparatively short order. But tax reform is one thing, and reforming taxes is something very different. Tax reform may be a game of solitaire (and it frequently is); it may be a committee, a commission, or an organization activity, which affords outlet for superfluous energies and supplies mild diversion and excitement, of which most of us feel the need; or it may be a theme for endless oratory of the platform, soap-box, or after-dinner variety.

Reforming a tax, however, means passing from generalities to a definite project of law which will affect the pocketbooks of many people and inevitably arouse conflict of interest and opinion. It means, therefore, that, in proportion as one gets away from generalities and deals with definite projects, the number of supporters will diminish and the number of opponents will increase.

Both with tax reform and the reform of taxes I have had sufficient experience to incline me to conservatism in estimating what may be accomplished in the way of securing a very different distribution of state and local taxes from that which now prevails. Please note that I said conservatism, not pessimism.

Adequate presentation of any of the plans which have been, and today are, proposed is so impossible within the space at my disposal that I shall be obliged to confine my discussion to a few outstanding facts and considerations particularly relating to the taxation of urban real estate.

1. *Separation of State and Local Sources of Revenue.* When serious study of state and local taxation began in this country over fifty years ago, the proposal which gained immediate favor was that of separating the sources of state and local revenues. It was clearly seen that the levy of a direct state tax upon property gave local assessors a strong inducement to undervaluation, since they could thereby reduce the proportion of the levy falling upon the localities they served. State boards of equalization had never succeeded in remedying this condition, and therefore the conclusion was natural that, since equalization did not equalize, the true remedy was to provide state governments with independent revenues by levying separate taxes upon corporations, inheritances, business licenses, in-

comes, and possibly other objects. It was then argued that, if this could be done, local governments could derive ample revenue from taxes upon property, chiefly real estate, not segregated for exclusive taxation by the state; and, under such conditions, it was said that either local assessors would discontinue the practice of undervaluation or that the practice would do no harm, since it would affect equally all taxpayers in a given locality.

But in reality the separation of state and local revenues was not a new plan. It had been tried by various states early in the nineteenth century, and in most cases had been abandoned; and the more recent experiments have not been generally reassuring. Abolition of the direct state tax has not led automatically to the assessment at full value of property subject to local taxation, and it is now evident that undervaluation has other and more deeply seated causes. Moreover, we have learned that undervaluation is not unimportant even when property is taxed only for local purposes, since it means that individual assessments in a given community may vary as widely as from 10% to 120% of the true value of the property. Such a condition in local taxation is not a thing of indifference to the state at large. The property overburdened may be that of a small minority which has no effective voice in local affairs, and it may be, and often is, the property of nonresidents who have no representation whatever in the government of the locality. The state has an obvious duty in the premises which cannot be justly or honorably evaded.

Moreover, the total abolition of the direct state tax destroys a desirable check upon state expenditures. Legislatures quickly spend revenues originally segregated, and then look around for more. At such times they are disposed to grasp at almost any expedient that may be proposed, and ultimately it has happened in a number of cases that a direct tax on property has been reestablished and that the plan of complete separation has broken down.

Nor has real estate necessarily benefited by the abolition of the direct state tax, for it has happened that whatever slack is let out by the state is speedily taken up by increased municipal tax rates. It is certainly a fact that a high rate of municipal taxation does exert a deterring effect upon proposals for increased expenditure, and it is also a fact that, if the rate is reduced on account of the abolition of the direct state tax, local authorities are likely to proceed with plans that would otherwise be held in abeyance.

In this respect segregation resembles all other plans for redistributing the present burden of taxation: it is not likely to reduce permanently the rates of taxation levied upon real estate unless local expenditures can be brought under better control than has hitherto been found possible.

2. *Classification of Property.* Another proposal which has found many advocates is that of classifying property for the purpose of taxation and imposing different methods of taxation. This is reasonable, because property is not homogeneous in character but falls into well-recognized classes which differ widely in economic character. Real estate, tangible personal property, and intangible property are classes well known to the law and the world of business. The general property tax, by ignoring the economic differences of the three kinds of property and seeking to tax them by a uniform rule, has never secured, in practice, anything remotely resembling uniformity of results.

Intangibles have largely escaped; tangible personalty evades to a considerable extent, and when listed is usually assessed at a fraction of its true value; while real estate, which cannot be hidden or removed, pays the greater part of the total taxes. Though the lawmaker may ignore the economic difference of the things he seeks to tax, the assessor and the taxpayer will not and cannot ignore them.

By classifying intangibles and subjecting them to a moderate rate of 3, 4, or 5 mills upon the dollar, some states have substantially increased the revenue derived from this class of property and obtained far greater equality among taxpayers.

None of these states, however, has ever yet provided such methods of administration as are needed for securing the best results from the classified tax on intangible property. Other kinds of property besides intangibles have been given separate classification, with what results I cannot appraise because we lack adequate information.

Classification has undoubtedly been found to have difficulties as well as advantages, and cannot be expected to produce its best results unless proper methods of administration are provided. Like segregation, it will not reduce taxes upon real estate if new revenues derived from the flat tax on intangibles, or other sources, are absorbed by increasing public expenditure.

3. *The State Income Tax.* A third and more recent proposal is the adoption of a state income tax. Between 1911 and 1919 three states, Wisconsin, Massachusetts, and New York, enacted well-considered income tax laws, which have operated with general satisfaction because they exempted intangible property from other taxation, imposed moderate rates, and were administered by state and not local officials. Their example was subsequently followed by a few other states, which have not done so well because they did not provide the conditions necessary for the successful administration of such a tax.

We now know that an income tax may be a useful part of a system of state and local taxation, but that, unless intelligently handled, it will prove a disappointment and may even make a bad situation worse.

The state income tax is sometimes opposed on the ground that it means double taxation since the federal government levies a similar tax. This argument is not well founded, because under our federal system of government the citizen has a double obligation in taxation. Where such an obligation exists, it is not of itself objectionable that income, property, or any other object of taxation should be twice taxed, provided that the thing is done without discrimination and the total burden is reasonable.

So far as I have been able to judge, the recent opposition to a state income tax is largely a by-product of the natural reaction against the excesses of federal taxation of incomes during and immediately after the recent war. Prior to 1911 the state income tax was in general disfavor; thereafter for some years the success achieved by Wisconsin, Massachusetts, and New York led many to overestimate its advantages; today it is temporarily unpopular. But we now know that any state that is willing to enact a proper law and make adequate provisions for administration can make good use of a state tax upon incomes; and this fact had not been demonstrated sixteen years ago. Another thing we know is that the introduction of an income tax will not reduce the burden resting upon real estate if it is followed by an increase in public expenditures.

4. *The Gasoline Tax.* The slow and halting progress of all plans of tax reform stands in striking contrast with the rapid growth of taxes upon gasoline. At first thought, these gasoline taxes seem an interesting confirmation of Adam Smith's statement that there is "no art which one government sooner learns of another, than that of draining money from the pockets of the people."

But in this instance Smith's generalization is inadequate, for it would probably be equally true to say that the tax on gasoline has been widely approved because it afforded the American people increased facilities for draining money out of their own pockets. For weal or woe, every man, woman, and child in the United States seems determined to own an automobile and to have expensive roads upon which to drive it. The gasoline tax offered so many people a chance to secure something which they wanted at once, and might otherwise have to wait for, that it is easy to understand its general acceptance. It amounts, after all, to a trifling addition to the cost of owning and operating a car; the method of collection is practically painless, and the tax is soon forgotten in the joy of getting somewhere quickly and then getting somewhere else.

To some extent the new tax law may have reduced local levies upon property for road construction, but this has not helped urban real estate, since the money is usually spent outside the city limits. So far as the city dweller is concerned, the gasoline tax is a comparatively painless method of making him finance the building of country roads, a thing which otherwise he would have to do in some other way if the improved roads were to be had at all. In short, the owner of urban real estate is interested in a gasoline tax in his capacity as joy rider rather than as taxpayer.

III

It will not have escaped attention that in this account of plans for readjusting the burden of state and local taxation I have been unable to record anything which has made much permanent difference to urban real estate. Temporarily, such readjustments may have reduced local taxation of property, but the final result of tapping new sources of revenue has usually been increased expenditure. For this reason it has become increasingly true that our problems of taxation are really problems of expenditure. If the cost of maintaining state and local governments continues to increase as it has done for a generation past, it is difficult to see how real estate, urban or rural, is going to secure any permanent relief.

I have had something to do, in Massachusetts and a few other states, with drafting laws providing new sources of revenue which might have resulted in moderate reductions of local taxes on property, chiefly real estate, but I have never seen that result follow the enactment of such laws. I have therefore lost some of the interest I used to feel in plans for *readjusting* tax burdens, and have been forced to the conclusion that the first and principal problem is not one of readjustment but of *control.*

Forty years ago, when I commenced the study of economics, the doctrine was still taught, and was supported by eminent authorities, that, while the total expenditure of any community must increase with the growth of population, the per capita expenditure ought to decrease. It was supposed by those who held this view that a law of decreasing cost applied to public expenditure and that therefore, as a community grew in wealth and population, new wants could be readily financed by the surplus resulting from the reduced per capita cost of existing governmental departments and services.

Of course there were dissenters, who pointed out that increasing density of population and other factors, such as the increase of wealth, might produce new wants and require more expensive provision for old ones. The next decade proved that the dissenters were right; and the old doctrine has not only dropped out of the books but even out of our memories. Today there is a general disposition to accept an increased per capita cost of government as a thing not only natural but desirable and an indication of social progress.

It is certainly true that, as wealth has increased and standards of living have risen, there has come a demand for higher standards of public service. It is also true that the progress of science and invention has not only demonstrated the need of such higher standards but has provided the means of attaining them. The discovery of the microbe has revolutionized the provision governments make for public health and sanitation; the internal combustion engine has revolutionized the construction of our highways and increased greatly the cost of policing them; increased interest in education has greatly increased expenditure for schools and colleges. City and town planning has become a new art; the splendid work of our architects now gives us public buildings which stimulate community pride and lead to emulation or competition in luxurious expenditure. There is no need of multiplying examples. We all know that times have changed and that public expenditures are not necessarily governed by a law of decreasing cost.

But, while we can all see that the increased expenditures of the present day are due in large part to scientific, economic, and social progress, other factors are involved which seldom receive sufficient consideration and ought not to be left out of account. We should not forget that when any organization, public or private, doubles or trebles its expenditure, the percentage of money wasted increases at an even greater rate unless financial control keeps pace with the expansion in the volume of business.

Business executives know that in a period of rapid expansion many things creep in which have to be eliminated in the following period of depression. Reduction of swollen overhead and drastic measures of economy are things which come with hard times because they are difficult and even impossible in days of prosperity. In this respect governmental business cannot differ from private. Between 1913 and 1925 the total government cost payments of American cities having a population of over 30,000 increased from $32.59 per capita to $71.46. This increase is due, of course, in considerable measure to the decreased purchasing power of the dollar; there is no doubt also that it brought a higher standard of public service in many directions. But it would be contrary to reason and experience to suppose that in this period of rapid expansion many things have not crept into the administration of city governments which can and should be eliminated.

Here and there a courageous executive has tackled this problem. Recently one city, by saving a few thousands here, tens of thousands there, and scores of thousands in enforced reduction of school expenditures, has reduced its tax rate 36 cents per $100 in a single year. Incidentally, it is worth noting that investigation showed that a score of grocers were delivering liquor to the city's poor under authorization of the department of public charities. Another and larger city in 1925 wiped out an inherited deficit of $1,100,00 and reduced the tax rate 49 cents per $100. That similar opportunities do not await the right sort of executive elsewhere, it is impossible to believe.

Another factor with which we have to deal is the natural desire of governmental departments to expand. Within reasonable limits, determined of course by the needs of the whole organization, no good executive would have things otherwise in either a public or a private corporation. But it is also true that this tendency needs to be carefully watched, and in government business control of the department that spends public money is often difficult.

If a department has much patronage to bestow, it may easily become *imperium in imperio,* and its head may defy the chief executive and even wreck well-considered plans of administrative organization. When the work of a department is of a sort that interests large numbers of voters, whether they be farmers, laborers, educators, or any other class of people, it is likely to receive about what it asks for; neither a legislator nor an executive welcomes a contest with it.

There is even more truth than humor in the definition given to a congressional committee by an experienced administrator, who stated that a scientific agriculturalist is a man who can make two dollars grow on an appropriation bill where but one has grown before.

Mutatis mutandis, the definition is equally applicable to the educator, road builder, city planner, welfare worker or other governmental agent carrying on an activity that is, or is supposed to be, popular with many voters. Economy is always difficult when large numbers of public employees are concerned or when the work of a small body of experts enlists active outside support.

IV

This brings us to a third factor, which for ten or twenty years past has become increasingly important—the organized activity of groups of citizens interested in securing new or enlarged expenditures for a variety of causes and projects. In itself this may be a good thing, and to it we doubtless owe a large number of improvements which otherwise we should not now enjoy. But it is undeniably expensive, and it frequently leads to confusion between real public demands and demands that result from mere propaganda which does not really enlist public support. Civic and commercial bodies interested in the improvement of their communities naturally and properly endorse projects calling for increased expenditures. But such agencies for developing and directing public opinion have become so numerous and they are now so highly organized that it is difficult for public officials and boards of estimate and appropriation to "cut the coat according to the cloth." Most, if not all, of us, I suppose, in sundry times and places have done our part in organizing demand for increased expenditure, but mounting municipal budgets and increasing tax rates have brought us to a point where we ought to count the cost of new and attractive projects for spending public money. On every hand, I believe, we find evidence that in this respect the country is over-organized and that we are breaking down all control over the public purse.

Such control is always difficult, for it is so much easier for the man in public life to say "yes" than to say "no." As President Coolidge remarked last December, "Nothing is easier than the expenditure of public money. It does not appear to belong to anybody. The temptation is overwhelming to bestow it upon somebody." To the same general purport, a clever journalist has observed that the business man reasons that money is flat and therefore should be stacked; while the politician reasons that money is round therefore should be kept rolling along. Economy may be popular in the abstract, but when reduced to concrete proposals for saving public money it is usually anything but popular. When the chairman of the appropriations committee of the national House of Representatives addressed the chamber of commerce of a large city, he received enthusiastic applause for his plea for reducing national expenditure. But he subsequently wrote, in an article published in *The Nation's Business,* that on his way out of the dining hall he was met by at least a dozen members of the chamber who wanted to say a good word for particular appropriations that interested them. As the governor of Massachusetts expresses it, in these days a public official who practices and enforces economy receives very little help and feels very lonesome most of the time.

Governor Fuller's remark is the more significant because it

comes from the chief executive of a state which has always provided liberally for real public needs and for some years past has been adhering resolutely to the sound policy of "pay as you go." Within the past decade we have reorganized the administrative departments of Massachusetts, introduced a good budget system, established adequate financial control, and refrained from contracting new loans. We have been financing necessary improvements out of current revenues, and can look forward to the time when the direct debt of the state will be completely extinguished. There may have been cases of unwise economy, but they have not been important or more numerous than should be expected. Economizers sometimes err, but so also do magnificent spenders, and our state, while following the straight and narrow path of financial rectitude, has been able to make reasonable provision for permanent improvements. Yet, in spite of this splendid record the "pay as you go" policy has been under constant attack and will be maintained only so long as we have governors who refuse to yield to the pressure of state employees and organized outside propaganda.

In ancient Greece, we are told, the city of Thurii had a law which provided that anyone who sought to abolish any existing law or establish a new one should come into the popular assembly with a rope around his neck and there present his proposal. If his innovation was accepted, he could go on his way rejoicing; but if it was rejected, the rope was tightened and he departed for that bourne whence no innovator or other traveler returns. The result may have been that Thurii was an unprogressive town which had to worry along without public improvements, and the punishment meted out to unsuccessful innovators was certainly extreme. But suppose that, in place of the rope, we required projectors of new enterprises to provide definite plans for raising additional revenue, and stipulated that new projects should not be undertaken until additional revenue had been actually authorized. Bond issues, of course, would not be considered revenue, but the new revenue might be used for interest and sinking fund purposes.

This would not discourage projectors unduly, but would help us to distinguish between real and manufactured public demands. In a number of states something like this was actually done when taxes on gasoline were introduced. If there is a genuine demand for an improvement, public opinion ought to approve the necessary ways and means, whether by increase of existing taxes or introduction of new ones. We need improvements and shall always need them, but we need also some better method than we now have of obliging the public that calls for new expenditures to reckon seriously and intelligently with the cost.

No private business could keep its head above water if its budget of expenditure was dictated by the pressure of more or less irresponsible and interested groups of employees, stockholders, or even directors. Yet this is precisely the condition which confronts us in the business of government. For a decade or more, municipal budgets have been subject to increasing pressure of interested groups professing to voice public demands and urging their claims under conditions which make coordination difficult and intelligent control well-nigh impossible. Public officials often realize this, but feel themselves swept along by an uncontrollable movement which seems to have popular support. So long as this condition continues, it is hard to see how real estate can hope for relief.

This is the appropriate place for the observation that commercial bodies, including real estate boards, have no little responsibility for the conditions I have set forth and that they can do much to make them better. We shall always need improvements, and with such things commercial organizations are properly concerned. But we want improvements that really improve, and we need to coordinate and moderate demands upon the public purse. With our city planning and all our other planning that tends to increase expenditures, we need also financial planning and careful consideration of ways and means.

In our private and business affairs we know that it is possible to go too fast and too far with expenditures that are in themselves desirable. We should realize that the same is true with the business of government and that we cannot go on increasing public expenditure indefinitely without reckoning the cost.

V

Since the chief difficulty arises from the amount of public expenditure, there are some devices that should be avoided because they direct attention away from the real problem and produce results worse than the disease they are designed to cure. One of these is the limitation of rates of taxation. When unaccompanied by effective control of municipal borrowing, this device has generally had disastrous results. Municipalities soon increase tax rates to the maximum figures permitted, and then proceed to borrow such money as cannot be raised within the tax limit, even using it, in fact if not in form, for meeting current expenditures. Few American cities, if any, have not at one time or another borrowed money improvidently, and laws limiting tax rates have tended in no small degree to intensify this evil, which is the most dangerous in the whole domain of municipal finance. Current expenditures, as we all know, should be financed from current revenues, and limitation of tax rates has frequently resulted in financing some part of them with borrowed money.

Another device has been to limit not the rate of taxation but the amount of the tax levy, by requiring that no levy shall exceed by more than a certain percentage, say 5% or 6%, that of the previous year. When first adopted, this plan seemed partially effective, but further experience showed that the percentage of increase fixed as a maximum came to be accepted as the proper and even necessary rate of increase, with the result that, as an Oregon official expressed it, "The maximum became a minimum." Moreover, under the percentage limitation, there is the same danger of obtaining by bond issues money that cannot be raised within the limits imposed upon the tax levy. It would seem too much to say that tax limitations have always proved ineffective and injurious, but it is certain that they are pernicious unless they are accompanied by effective control of municipal borrowing.

From the preceding considerations it follows that readjustments in state and local taxation, diversification of revenue systems, and limitation of tax rates or levies are things to be entered upon with care and circumspection and with full realization that the principal problem in these days is the insatiate demand for more and more and more expenditure. I have said nothing in disparagement of tax reform, but have warned that it will not help real estate unless public expenditures can be brought under control. If the prospect is unpleasing, it is all that the facts warrant. The fundamental problem, I repeat, is one of expenditure and not of taxation.

The outlook for real estate is not brightened by another factor, to which all too little attention is usually given, namely, competition between states and competition between municipalities to attract people and wealth and industry, by offering more favorable conditions of taxation. This tendency is nothing new, but it seems to have gained force in recent years as a result of organized activity similar to that which has helped to increase public expenditure.

Tax laws intended to attract manufacturing industries, incorporated companies of all descriptions, and monied capital are no novelty in the United States, and efforts of municipalities to secure residents and industries by offering inducements, authorized or not authorized by law, are all too familiar to students of taxation. One state has recently amended its constitution so as to prohibit its legislature from ever imposing taxes on incomes and inheritances, and the influence of this action has been felt in many others which had been trying to improve their system of taxation. It is also a fact that in towns and cities in all parts of the country there are committees, councils, boards, chambers, and foundations, many of them, I suppose, receiving the support of real estate interests, which are working industriously to attract industries, and in this laudable effort are advertising as never before the advantages offered in the way of taxation. Low valuations on buildings, total exemption of machinery and stocks of goods, "cooperation" between tax officials and new industries, exemption of such industries for periods of five or ten years, exemption of manufacturing capital employed within the state, and other things with which many of us are familiar, are the bait offered by booklets, circulars, and newspaper advertisements broadcast throughout the nation.

We are faced, therefore, not only with organized effort to increase public expenditure but also with organized activity directed toward narrowing and reducing the basis of taxation.

Since no state and no municipality would benefit by such measures if all states and municipalities offered inducements exactly similar in nature and degree, it is obvious that the net effect is to attract industries, people, and wealth to those places which outdo the others. Competition, therefore, tends to become increasingly severe; and in proportion as the work becomes better organized and financed it constitutes more and more of an obstacle to tax reform. When a city can advertise that a manufacturer with $200,000 of capital will receive exemptions and other advantages in taxation which will save him $40,000 in ten years, it is easy for him to figure that by locating in that city the taxes he will save will, with the accumulating interest, amount to $50,000 and will enable him to write off 50% of his plant within a decade. In cities that play this game with the most success, some advantage doubtless accrues to real estate, but for real estate the country over the final outcome must be a loss.

What used to be a condition of no great importance and of a sporadic nature is tending to become a systematic and widespread movement which bodes no good for the future. If it continues the basis of taxation will be continually narrowed, and there can be no doubt as to what class of property will be injuriously affected thereby. Looking at the matter broadly and ignoring the advantage that may accrue in some localities, we see that the exemption game, whatever its momentary attraction, is not one which the owner of real estate can play with advantage to himself. For many years state and local taxation has been honeycombed with exemptions that reduce the amount of taxable property and increase the burden falling upon real estate.

With such forces, owners of real estate have no community of interest, and against them they should, both in the interest of real estate and in the public interest, make ceaseless war. Even at some immediate cost, real estate interests should insist that the exemption of property yielding private gain is contrary to public policy and should be brought to an end. This does not mean that all property should be subject to a general property tax levied at a uniform rate, for such a method of taxation has never worked to the advantage of real estate or the community at large. It does mean that what we need is reasonable and practicable methods of getting from everyone a fair contribution to public charges by such diversified methods as best suit the nature of the case. In this direction certainly, as well as in that of controlling the amount of public expenditure, the true interest of real estate owners lies.

The Problem Before the Real Estate Owner

He who buys real estate gives hostages to fortune. His property cannot be removed to another locality and cannot be concealed; he must, therefore, bear scot and lot with the community of his choice. Since his interests are localized, he must deal with local conditions as he finds them, and he is therefore vulnerable to attack by local projectors, planners, exempters, boomers, boosters, and advertisers. National conditions and the nation-wide results of financial policies affecting real estate may interest him in the abstract, but it is the concrete situation facing him in his home town that chiefly concerns him. Only by cooperation on a national scale, through organizations capable of taking the broadest point of view and considering the nation-wide effect of policies of local expenditure and taxation, can real estate owners avoid being picked off in detail by the organized forces now campaigning for increased public expenditure and continued narrowing of the basis of taxation.

Seven years ago, the country was in the midst of a great industrial depression. There was a shortage of buildings in most American cities, but construction costs were very high, and money was difficult to obtain. At that moment the real estate owner and operator had so many troubles that municipal taxation constituted one of the least of his problems. However, as the war receded further into history and real estate readjusted itself to peace conditions, real estate owners found that their tax problems were more important than ever before. Today it is safe to make the forecast that, if existing conditions in municipal expenditure and taxation continue for another seven years, urban real estate will find peace as onerous as war.

Instead of the shortage of buildings which existed in 1920, we now have buildings in plenty, and even to spare. Yet, under the influence of easy money, high-powered salesmanship of security dealers, and a highly organized construction industry which has service to sell and a large overhead to carry, the boom in building construction has continued. How long it will go on, I do not know. This year has brought a decline of activity in cities, which is a healthy symptom, but until money conditions change radically I shall expect to see a large volume of construction maintained.

During boom times the increase of real estate taxes has not been felt so seriously as it will be some day when our cities become further overbuilt and rentals and values move as they always have moved under such conditions as will then exist. Just as, in regions affected by the present agricultural depression, farmers are finding their substance devoured by high taxes required to pay for good things in which they indulged during the flush times that ended in 1920, so in many of our cities it is easy to foresee a pressure of real estate taxes not pleasant to contemplate.

Somehow, no doubt, the situation will be dealt with when

it arises; but I am old enough to recall that forty years ago, in the decade of the 1880's, cities were still writing off inflated values and were liquidating debts that ought never to have been contracted, although the boom conditions which had made these things necessary had come to an end in 1873 and the worst of the resulting liquidation was probably over by 1879. History never repeats itself precisely, but it does exact severe penalties from those who ignore it. We have been living through the most tremendous boom the construction industry has ever experienced in the United States. Such things always have been followed by a period of reaction; and the only prudent course is to put our house in order while there is yet time.

III

THE LEGACY OF REHOBOAM: AN OLD TESTAMENT LESSON IN TAXATION[1]

AND King Solomon was king over all Israel," records the First Book of Kings; but his succession had been attended with difficulty. King David introduced the oriental institution of the harem, and "favorite sons" of different wives inevitably developed conflicting ambitions. Absalom, indeed, the favorite of favorites, revolted against his father and had been slain by the darts of Joab; so that he was out of the way. But Adonijah, the son of Haggith, said unto himself, "I will be king," provided himself with chariots and horsemen, and secured the support of the mighty Joab and of Abiathar the priest, while his father lay "old and stricken in years." Without Bathsheba, his mother, who acted on the timely warning of Nathan the prophet, Solomon almost certainly would have missed the main chance. However, Bathsheba's intercession came in time; and, while she was yet talking with the dying king, Nathan entered opportunely to inquire whether David had really decided that Adonijah should succeed him. "For," the resourceful prophet went on, Adonijah this day "hath slain oxen and fatlings and sheep in abundance," and hath called "the captains of the host, and Abiathar the priest"; and "behold, they are eating and drinking before him, and say, Long live King Adonijah." This aroused the dying lion who called Bathsheba and declared: "As I swore unto thee by Jehovah, the God of Israel, saying, Assuredly Solomon thy son shall reign after me" . . . even "so will I do this day." The royal order hurriedly issued. Solomon was taken to Gihon upon his father's steed and anointed by

[1] Reprinted by generous permission of the publisher, from Barron's *The National Financial Weekly,* April 2 and 9, 1928, with additional comment on the Old Testament narrative.

Zadok, the priest, with oil out of the tabernacle; then a trumpet was blown, and all the people cried: "Long live King Solomon."

Nathan, the prophet, on that day became Nathan the master politician. It was harem politics, of course; but that was a brand in which counselors of oriental despots had to be well versed. One who doubts this may seek enlightenment from the English adviser of an Indian prince; moreover, the brand does not differ so widely from politics of the court or salon. Nathan's achievement was truly great, since he had no resource but his keen wit and the time was short because Adonijah had really "started something." Among king-makers, Nathan for all time should rank with the great Warwick and his peers.

This may seem to have nothing to do with taxation or the legacy which Solomon left to Rehoboam, his son; but it is a necessary prelude to our Old Testament Lesson. Royalty was a new institution among the Hebrews. King Saul had fallen upon his sword, and the upstart David fought every step of the way to the eminence and security he finally achieved. When Solomon began to rule, great affairs of state pressed upon his attention, which must be arranged before he could begin to improve his kingdom and embark upon a career as financier. In the first place, like many a new prince, he had his own and his father's personal enemies to deal with. The second chapter of First Kings tells how he accomplished this task with expedition and due regard to all proprieties set forth much later in the Gospel according to Machiavelli.

Adonijah, who had heard the sound of the trumpet acclaiming Solomon king, precipitately fled to the horns of the altar; but was coaxed away from that place of safety by the promise that "there shall not a hair of him fall to the earth" if he "show himself a worthy man." Then, presently, as Solomon sat upon the throne of David, he decided that Adonijah had acted unworthily in requesting that Abishag the Shunammite be given to him for his wife, and gave orders that he "be put to death this day." Abiathar the priest, who had followed Adonijah and helped him, fared better. But he was told that he was worthy of death, was "thrust out . . . from being priest unto Jehovah," and banished to his "own fields" at Anathoth; while Zadok, the priest who had not conferred with Adonijah and had anointed Solomon with a horn of oil out of the tabernacle, was "put in the room of Abiathar." As for Joab, the "captain of the host," who had erred in backing the wrong candidate, it is recorded that, when the "tidings" came to him, he stood not upon the order of his going but "fled unto the tent of Jehovah, and caught hold on the horns of the altar."

If the story of Solomon is ever filmed at Hollywood, this tableau certainly will not be missed; and it is equally sure that the title will read: "It will not be long now." And it was not, although the proprieties of the situation were strictly observed. Solomon immediately sent Benaiah, the son of Jehoiada, to the tent of Jehovah, with the order: "Come forth." Joab replied: "Nay; but I will die here." The situation was beyond a soldier; and Benaiah reported it to the king, who, in his wisdom, recalled that Joab was really a man of blood whose presence defiled the altar, because he had slain "two men more righteous and better that he." Their "blood," he declared, shall "return upon the head of Joab"; whereupon Benaiah returned to the tent of Jehovah and slew Joab, so that the altar and its horns were no longer defiled. Then we read: "the king put Benaiah the son of Jehoiada in his (Joab's) room over the host."

Thus Solomon disposed of his half-brother, a possible claimant to the throne, promoted religion pure and undefiled by substituting his backer Zadok for Adonijah's friend Abiathar, and secured control of the army by killing Joab and placing Benaiah in command. He then found sufficient cause for punishing his father's enemy Shimei, turning him over to Benaiah who "went out, and fell upon him, so that he died." With these good works accomplished, the chapter ends abruptly with the remark that "the kingdom was established in the hand of Solomon." All this, be it noted, was twenty-five hundred years before Machiavelli. Though it reads like a chapter in "The Prince," it is actually an Old Testament Lesson—in practical politics.

With his personal safety and that of his mother assured, Solomon turned to other affairs of state. Chapter three records, first of all, that he made an alliance with Pharaoh, king of Egypt, and took Pharaoh's daughter to wife. That this was a diplomatic as well as a matrimonial arrangement will be evident to anyone who recalls that Palestine lay athwart the natural lines of communication between the two great river valleys, the Nile and the Tigro-Euphrates, to which we trace our civilization. It had been a meeting place for the civilizations of Africa and Asia, and also for their armies. Too small and poor in natural resources to become a world power, it had been subject to Egypt for many centuries, just as later on it was to be subject to Assyria, Chaldea, and Persia. Under David, the Hebrew kingdom fought its ways to independence, Jerusalem was seized and fortified, and the boundaries of the realm extended. His son inherited a position temporarily secure; but it behooved him to think of foreign relations, and this he did at his first opportunity. It is then recorded that he besought the Lord for "an understanding heart," that he might "discern between good and evil" and be able to judge "this thy great people." Then came the two women with the child whose possession they disputed; and he rendered the celebrated judgment of which "all Israel heard," and, hearing, "feared the king." Thus foreign relations were improved, administration of strict justice assured, and domestic tranquillity could reasonably be expected. This brings us back to the first verse of the fourth chapter, with which we started: "And King Solomon was king over all Israel."

But as yet he had done nothing more than provide conditions necessary for success; as an administrator he was practically untried. In perfect logical sequence, chapter four supplies all essential details. First of all, he set up his civil list by appointing the necessary princes, scribes, recorders, generals, priests, and other officers of state. In passing, it should be noted that the reliable Zadok was made high priest, and that his son Azariah succeeded him; that the mighty Benaiah was placed in charge of the army; and that Azariah, the son of resourceful Nathan, was placed "over the officers," while another son, Zabud, became "chief minister and the king's friend." Thus he provided for the administration of public affairs, and forgot neither his friends nor their sons.

At this point it is necessary to take account of the fact that modern scholars have found First and Second Kings to be compilations of earlier relations of the history of the Hebrews, in which the purely factual narratives of the original chroniclers were pieced together by later editors who endeavored, not only to produce a continuous history of their people, but also to give a theological and moral interpretation of the events they recorded. If evil befell King Solomon, these pious editors could see in it only a just retribution for violation of Jehovah's command; so that, naturally enough, they could not perceive that the financial difficulties of the Hebrew Monarchy were the natural and logical result of royal extravagance and excessive taxation. Thus we are here dealing with a quaint and fascinating *mélange* of ancient factual tradition and later theological interpretations, in which the constituent elements need to be carefully separated from each other.

Fortunately in this case the constituents can be readily distinguished. The Hebrew text itself shows that the original narrative of events is of very ancient origin, and may well be assigned a date not long after the time of Solomon. But even more important for our purpose is the fact that the story is the work of an ancient chronicler who saw things so clearly and understood them so well that he could draw a perfect picture, true to life in every essential detail, artistic in the way a simple historic record is charged with both scientific and dramatic values, and unexcelled—perhaps unequalled—by any later writer who has ever undertaken to depict the rise and fall of a famous country that went to shipwreck on the rock of unsound finance. No pious editor, no clever anecdotist, produced this narrative which could have come only from a man endowed with profound insight into politics and finance. It is easy therefore to distinguish historical realities from theological emendations, even without the aid afforded by the ancient text itself.

We now come to the royal finances. Adoniram, the son of Abda, "was over the men subject to task-work"; and twelve officers were appointed to secure "victuals for the king and his household." These twelve providers were assigned to twelve districts into which the kingdom was divided, and Solomon then "ruled over all the kingdoms from the River unto the land of the Philistines, and unto the border of Egypt," to which may be added the interesting detail that "they brought tribute, and served Solomon all the days of his life."

Judah and Israel, we are then told, "dwelt safely, every man under his vine and under his fig-tree"; and the next verse adds that Solomon "had forty thousand stalls of horses for his chariots, and twelve thousand horsemen." Evidently Solomon did not have a Federal Council of Prophets to tell him that this was reprehensible militarism, and that Judah and Israel would dwell more safely if they would disarm or, at least, hamstring the army and cut military expenditures to the bone. Perhaps the higher criticism of the pacifists can extract some different meaning from the fourth chapter of First Kings. Possibly some unknown scribe in the pay of the horse breeders or chariot makers tampered with the text; but, as the record stands, we read about the twelve thousand horsemen, the ample provision of horses and chariots, and the safety enjoyed by Judah and Israel; as well as that Solomon's wisdom "excelled the wisdom of all the children of the east, and all the wisdom of Egypt"; and also that "there came of all peoples to hear the wisdom of Solomon, from all kings of the earth, who had heard of his wisdom."

The next chapter continues the logical and orderly development of the story. Securely established on the throne, Solomon had provided the fundamental requisites of good government: friendly foreign relations, good administration of justice, an adequate system of administration, a strong army, and sufficient revenues. This was a great achievement; and not the least remarkable feature of the record is that everything was done in the proper order, the whole program of governmental necessities being completed before Solomon allowed attention to be diverted to luxuries. To maintain and operate the kingdom cost money; but expenditures thus far had been confined to necessary purposes, and there is no evidence of complaint about taxes. Chapter five records a new epoch in the financial history of Solomon, an epoch of grand "improvements" and luxurious expenditure all along the line.

Piety and ambition conspired to make the transition easy. To Hiram, king of Tyre, whose city then held hegemony among the Phœnicians (or Sidonians, as they are commonly called in the Old Testament), Solomon sent a message saying: "Thou knowest how that David my father could not build a house for the name of Jehovah his God for the wars which were about him on every side. . . . But now Jehovah my God hath given me rest on every side; there is neither adversary, nor evil occurrence. And, behold, I purpose to build a house for the name of Jehovah, my God, as Jehovah spake unto David my father, saying, Thy son, whom I will set upon thy throne in thy room, he shall build the house for my name. Now therefore command thou that they cut me cedar-trees out of Lebanon; and my servants shall be with thy servants; and I will give thee hire for thy servants according to all that thou shall say." The last clause of this contract was sufficiently liberal; but to it Solomon added a delicate touch, "for thou knowest that there is not among us any that knoweth how to cut timber like unto the Sidonians." That the work was carried through on a scale commensurate with the liberality of the beginning is sufficiently known; and it is needless to recount the hewn stone, the bronze, the gold, and other costly materials that went into the structure, or the huge number of workmen required. The years that followed must have brought prosperity to many industries.

But we read also that "King Solomon raised a levy out of all Israel; and the levy was thirty thousand men." Presently Solomon had "threescore and ten thousand that bare burdens, and fourscore thousand that were hewers in the mountains." And, in addition to this corvée, which provided merely the common labor, there was the necessary overhead, consisting of "Solomon's chief officers that were over the work, three thousand and three hundred, who bare rule over the people that wrought in the work."

Seven years was Solomon in building his splendid temple, as we read in the sixth chapter; the seventh tells us that, not content with fulfilling the desire of his father concerning "a house for the name of Jehovah," Solomon "was building *his own* house *thirteen* years." The incident well illustrates how the spirit of "improvement," once aroused, tends to spread and enlarge the ideas of those possessed by it. Seven years were enough for the first project, a house for the Lord; but thirteen were required for the next which was a house for Solomon. The palace naturally had to be built of the same costly materials, and in it there had to be "a house for Pharaoh's daughter," and a great court ornately constructed "like as the inner court of the house of Jehovah." It had a "porch of judgment," where Solomon "was to judge" in regal state, as well as a porch of the throne and other necessaries. That all was done upon a grand scale might be taken for granted without other evidence; but, in the eleventh chapter, we read that Solomon presently "had seven hundred wives, princesses, and three hundred concubines," who must have required accommodations suited to their state. Obviously, the plan of improvements for Jerusalem included provision for a "bigger and better" harem. Moreover, it appeared that his consorts insisted upon burning incense and sacrificing unto their strange gods, which inevitably increased the household budget.

When the temple was built, there naturally had to be a solemn and expensive dedication, at which there were sacrificed sheep and oxen "that could not be counted nor numbered for multitude." Later on came peace offerings, "two and twenty thousand oxen, and a hundred and twenty thousand sheep"; after which we read: "So the king and all the children of Israel dedicated the house of Jehovah." Of course, somebody would have to pay the bills; but possibly few spectators considered this at the time, because Solomon held a feast, "and all Israel with him," which is said to have lasted seven days. When, on the eighth day, the king, "sent the people away," we read that "they blessed the king, and went unto their tents joyful and glad to heart."

So far, so good. To the necessary expenditures of government, Solomon had now added splendid improvements, which had made his people joyful and increased his fame. He was still on friendly terms with Hiram, to whom he gave twenty cities in the land of Galilee; and Hiram, coming out from Tyre to see the cities, was so pleased that he sent Solomon six score talents of gold. That this was something more than an exchange of expensive compliments, and that Solomon was realizing upon some real estate in order to meet his bills, would be mere conjecture, though quite as reasonable as much of that in which "higher criticism" indulges; but it is perfectly clear that the *result* was an exchange of twenty cities for six score talents of gold, so that Solomon, if he had had no liabilities hanging over him, would have found himself "in funds," at least temporarily. But the very next verse runs, "And this is the reason of the levy which King Solomon raised, to build the house of Jehovah, and his own house, and Millo, and the wall of Jerusalem, and Hazor, and Megiddo, and Gezer."

Thus, after receiving six score talents of gold, Solomon had to levy a tax, for which the historian felt it appropriate and pertinent to give "the reason," which is practically in the form of a bill stating items but not amounts. Items I and II (the temple and palace) would not be there if the improvements had been paid for when completed. Item III (Millo) was either a part of the fortifications of Jerusalem or a sanctuary, which the twenty fourth verse tells us that Solomon built. Item IV (the wall of Jerusalem) meant a strengthening of the defenses of his capital, which was better worth attacking now that it contained magnificent buildings full of splendid furnishings. Item V may have been the town which Joshua had taken from King Jabin, but we cannot be sure of this because five towns named

Hazor are mentioned in the Bible. Item VI (Megiddo) we recognize as Armageddon, the stronghold commanding the plain where the nations have been coming to battle from the time of Thutmose III to that of Lord Allenby. The seventh item (Gezer) is almost too good to be true. Pharaoh, king of Egypt, so we are told in the next verse, "had gone up, and taken Gezer, and burnt it with fire, and slain the Canaanites that dwelt in the city, and given it for a portion unto his daughter, Solomon's wife." But he omitted to reconstruct the city; and therefore, in the seventeenth verse, we read that his son-in-law "built Gezer." Whether Solomon did that because the city was worth having or in order to keep peace in the family, we are not told; and the question may be referred to the higher critics.

Other expenses followed, for Solomon went on building. Store cities for supplies he built, and cities for his chariots, and cities for his horsemen, as well as what he "desired to build for his pleasure in Jerusalem, and in Lebanon, and in all the land of his dominion." Therefore he found himself in need of new sources of revenue, which play so large a part in the history of taxation. This time he discovered an ideal tax, which, as all know, is a tax paid by some other fellow. He and his predecessors had warred for years with the Amorites, Hittites, Perizzites, Hivites, and Jebusites, "who were not of the children of Israel." But it seems that they had not been able "utterly to destroy" them. From such survivors and their children as were found in the land, "of them did Solomon raise a levy of bondservants," which was so highly esteemed by the children of Israel that the historian records that it continued unto his day.

The new tax provided Solomon with additional laborers, but it did also another thing which new sources of revenue have continued to do "unto this day." It increased Solomon's overhead, for the twenty-third verse records that Solomon had five hundred and fifty chief officers, "who bare rule over the people that wrought in the work." The historian knew nothing of the word "overhead,'" and his remark may be nothing more than a tribute to the greatness of Solomon, who had so many people working for him. But obviously a "levy of bondservants" is useless without "officers" to direct the work and hold unwilling labor to its task.

Solomon's kingdom was now both improved and taxed; but one thing it yet needed, and from this it seemed, like Switzerland, to be debarred by nature; it had no navy. Of the coast of Palestine, only the northern part had good harbors; and these belonged to the king of Tyre, a friend, indeed, but one who had naval interests of his own. Therefore Solomon turned to "the shore of the Red Sea, in the land of Edom" and "made a navy of ships in Ezion-geber." From the friendly Hiram he procured "shipmen that had knowledge of the sea," and thus nature was circumvented so long as no enemy cut the line of communication through the desert to the distant seaport. What other uses the navy had, we are not informed; but we are told that it was sent to Ophir and brought thence "gold, four hundred and twenty talents," as well as "plenty of almug-trees and precious stones." Whether the returns equaled the cost of the enterprise, we do not know; but if the navy really yielded a profit we can be sure that Solomon needed it.

Of this we can be perfectly certain, because the next chapter (I Kings, 10), after telling us that "the weight of gold that came to Solomon in one year was six hundred threescore and six talents," in addition to all which the merchants and others brought into the country, also informs us that "King Solomon made two hundred bucklers of beaten gold" and "three hundred shields of beaten gold," which he placed "in the house of the forest of Lebanon," which "house" was (I Kings, 7) one of the various structures included in the royal palace. Thus the revenue from the mines of Ophir did not lighten the taxes paid by the children of Israel but was absorbed by new expenditures, as has usually been the case.

By this time Solomon had become a great spender, and, like other potentates reputed to be rich and lavish, was under the necessity of living up to his reputation. The ancient world made much of royal liberality, of which classical literature supplies abundant proof. Not until the time of Machiavelli, so far as we know, did anyone consider philosophically the comparative advantages of liberality and meanness, and point out that a ruler who wishes to maintain among men the name of liberal is obliged to avoid no attribute of magnificence. A prince thus inclined, as Machiavelli observed, will not only consume his own substance but "will be compelled in the end, if he wish to maintain the name of liberal, unduly to weigh down his people, and tax them, and do everything he can to get money." This will naturally tend to "make him odious to his subjects," and may lead him into serious trouble; whereas, if he tries to avoid this danger by practicing economy, "he runs at once into the reproach of being miserly." Nothing "wastes so rapidly as liberality," says Machiavelli; "for even while you exercise it you lose the power to do so, and so become either poor and despised, or else, in avoiding poverty, become rapacious and hated." Of course, you can bequeath your troubles to your successor, as Solomon did; but this is postponement and not solution. *"Après nous, le déluge"* were the words of a monarch whose house was tottering toward bankruptcy and revolution.

Whether Solomon in his wisdom ever thought of changing his financial policies, we are not informed; had he done so he would have discovered how hard it is to substitute economy for prodigality in public expenditure. All the record yields is the last chapter of the "Rake's Progress," which, as usual, was the wildest of all. There had been "a great throne of ivory," overlaid "with the finest gold," reached by six steps and surrounded by lions, of which "there was not the like made in any kingdom." And now we read that "all King Solomon's drinking vessels were of gold, and all the vessels of the house of the forest of Lebanon were of pure gold; none were of silver; it was nothing accounted of in the days of Solomon." As for the white metal, "the king made silver to be in Jerusalem as stones." It is not strange, therefore, to read of the royal spendthrift that he "exceeded all the kings of the earth in *riches* and in wisdom."

A few minor details should not be omitted. Solomon's navy

brought him not only gold, silver, and ivory, but also apes and peacocks. Whether these animals adorned his palace or were consigned to a national zoo, we are not told. But we are informed, in chapter four, not only that Solomon was "wiser than all men"; that "he spake three thousand proverbs," and that "his songs were a thousand and five": but also that "he spake of trees, from the cedar that is in Lebanon even unto the hyssop that springeth out of the wall"; and that "he spake also of beasts, and of birds, and of creeping things, and of fishes." Since the king was interested in natural history, it is reasonable to conjecture that the imported apes and peacocks may have served some other purpose than idle display. We read, further, that "cedars made he to be as the sycamore-trees that are in the lowland, for abundance," an expenditure that testified to an interest either in sylviculture or landscape architecture. His horses "were brought out of Egypt"; and "the king's merchants received them in droves, each drove at a price." In a city where silver was "as stones" and was "nothing accounted of," it is not probable that the king's merchants bargained and haggled sharply over mere matters of price. In Solomon's day, as in that of Lorenzo di Medici, it was probably true, as Adam Smith puts it, that the "agents of a prince regard the wealth of their master as inexhaustible; are careless at what price they buy; are careless at what price they sell; are careless at what expense they transport his goods from one place to another." Solomon's merchants, like the servants of the East India Company after it acquired sovereignty in India (again using the words of Adam Smith), must have considered themselves "the ministers of sovereigns" rather than "the clerks of merchants."

To finance all his grandeur, Solomon developed extraterritorial revenue, or tribute. As his fame spread, we read of the presents he received from King Hiram and the Queen of Sheba; but for these he made due return out of "his royal bounty." Later the twenty-third to the twenty-fifth verses of the tenth chapter tell us something more: "So King Solomon exceeded all the kings of the earth in riches and in wisdom. And all the earth sought the presence of Solomon, to hear his wisdom, which God had put in his heart. And they brought every man his tribute, vessels of silver, and vessels of gold, and raiment, and armor, and spices, horses, and mules, a rate year by year."

In this passage, the last five words are the most significant. After extolling Solomon for his riches and wisdom, and recounting how all the earth came to hear his wisdom and brought "tribute," all of which might mean nothing but the free-will offering of occasional pilgrims, the historian lets drop the words "a rate year by year." One familiar with the history of taxation will more than surmise that we find here another instance of occasional free-will offerings hardening into fixed annual exactions.

To the end of the remarkable story told in First Kings, Solomon maintained his reputation for wisdom and riches. As a magnificent spender and also a tax gatherer, he had been a conspicuous success. The sequel shows, however, that he had been laying up financial wrath; most of this he bequeathed to his son, Rehoboam. When trouble came, toward the end of his reign, it is represented to be a visitation from Jehovah. Solomon, we are told, had allowed his "many foreign women," Moabites, Ammonites, Edomites, Sidonians, and Hittites, to turn "away his heart after other gods" and had done "that which was evil." His sins involved further expenditure for building high places for the gods of the Moabites and Ammonites, as well as for the incense and sacrifices which he offered unto the gods of his "foreign wives." But his punishment was for forsaking the God of his fathers; and it took the form of numerous revolts which must have cost him dear, and of the dread words which "Jehovah said unto Solomon," that after his death his kingdom should be rent asunder so that only a remnant would be left to his son.

Here we have no difficulty in recognizing the hand of the pious editor who worked the marvellous ancient narrative, which is κτῆμα ἐς ἀεί, into the historical compilation in which it has come down to us. To him the evils which finally befell Solomon and then overwhelmed his son would readily appear to be a divine visitation for the King's sin of forsaking the God of his fathers, and so they are represented in First Kings. In subsequent passages where Jehovah's acts and purposes are brought into the story of Solomon I shall accept them, usually without comment, as part of the composite work with which we have to deal. The reader will have no trouble in identifying the separate historical and theological strands in the splendid fabric, and to remove the latter would change the familiar form of an historical classic without serving any useful end.

Immediately after the dire judgment of Jehovah comes the fourteenth verse of the eleventh chapter: "And Jehovah raised up an adversary unto Solomon, Hadad the Edomite: he was of the king's seed in Edom." Years before, King David had sent Joab, the captain of the host, to "cut off every male in Edom," a transaction which is reported to have required six months. But Hadad, then a child, had escaped into Egypt where he grew up an enemy to David and all his house. And then "God raised up another adversary" unto Solomon, namely, Rezon, the son of Eliada, who had been obliged to flee to Damascus when David slew the men of Zobah. Thus two suitable men, whom we might call King David's "omissions," were ready at hand; and all that Jehovah had to do was to stir them up, a very happy emendation by the pious editor. So we read, in the twenty-fifth verse, that Rezon "was an adversary to Israel all the days of Solomon, besides the mischief that Hadad did."

Hadad's "mischief" is not described, but it is easy to see that there was one thing which a mischievous Edomite would surely do to Solomon, and without needing any suggestion from Jehovah. It was through Edom that the long trail ran from Jerusalem to the naval base "in Ezion-geber, which is beside Eloth" on the Red Sea. When Solomon in his youth chose wisdom rather than riches, Jehovah had bestowed upon him riches and honor as well as an understanding heart. When in later life Solomon "turned away his heart after other gods," Jehovah raised up an enemy who could easily cut off Solomon from his navy and intercept the treasure from Ophir. If Jehovah's judgment upon Solomon was just, his economics was impeccable. Wealth he had given, and wealth he took away surely and expeditiously.

Finally, Jeroboam, the son of Nebat, "also lifted up his hand against the king," because, after the prophet Ahijah had declared that he should be king of the ten tribes which were to be taken from Solomon's successor, the king "sought therefore to kill Jeroboam." What mischief, if any, Jeroboam did, we are not informed; for the narrative states simply that he fled unto Egypt, where he remained until the death of Solomon.

For forty years Solomon "reigned in Jerusalem over all Israel." In spite of his wisdom, riches and women finally "got" him, so that his end was like unto that of many magnificent spenders. As financier he had achieved great fame; but when he "was buried in the city of David his father," his financial condition was far from enviable, as will presently appear. Yet things might have been worse.

Solomon's financial problems were those of an oriental despot, who, besides fortifying and defending his kingdom, must, if possible, make a display of wealth and spend money liberally. He knew nothing about "modern improvements" and the difficulties of democratic finance. He had no city planners urging him to tunnel the hills of Jerusalem, widen its streets, throw ornamental bridges across the surrounding valleys, convert Bethesda and Siloam into municipal swimming pools, and erect war memorials of a purely sentimental (and in no way utilitarian) character to the memory of those who had fallen in the wars against the Amorites, Canaanites, Hittites, Hivites, Jebusites, and Perizzites. The gas engine had not yet been invented, and the children of Israel were content to dwell quietly, "every man under his vine and under his fig-tree." They therefore had no desire to demonstrate the possibility of perpetual motion, by touring through all Palestine over hard-surfaced roads expensive to construct and maintain. Of professional "educators" and boards of education, he knew nothing. He therefore was never told that he must provide unlimited money for "new departures," or that he must have a school board with an independent budget which he, since he was a politician, could not understand and therefore ought not to control, even to the extent of determining its total amount. Since his government was a despotism, he did not have to reckon with the votes of municipal or national employees, organized in associations of professional tax eaters. Neither, so far as we can judge, did he have to deal with chambers, boards, leagues, federations, committees, associations, and other organizations, employing secretaries and other agents, who must justify their existence by organizing "movements" designed to benefit and uplift Palestine at public expense. His situation was simply that of a despot with a world-wide reputation for wisdom and wealth, and therefore obliged to justify that reputation by public display of both attributes. Had he lived in the age of the gas engine and organized propaganda for spending public money, he might not have been able to leave his troubles as a legacy to his successor.

This interpretation of the story of Solomon is not offered as adequate for all purposes, but as substantially correct so far as it goes, according to the record in First Kings. That there are some inconsistencies even in this book is very true; but these are of minor importance compared with the powerfully dramatic and scientifically correct story of Solomon, the magnificent spender, which cannot fail to impress anyone acquainted with human nature, public finance, and the teachings of history. That the First and Second Books of Chronicles present a narrative different at some points is also true; but few of the differences are of major importance, and upon the whole the latter book offers more confirmation than discrepancy. Chronicles lacks the logical sequence and dramatic power of the first eleven chapters of Kings, which carry their own credentials and testify either to the marvelous skill of the original narrator or the essential truthfulness of the story. It is easier to believe that the relation is substantially true, in spite of the theological and moralizing emendation of the pious compiler, than to suppose that the ancient scribe invented the details presented with such dramatic force and scientific accuracy.

The forty-first verse of the eleventh chapter tells us that "the rest of the acts of Solomon, and all that he did, and his wisdom," are "written in the book of the acts of Solomon"; but here the editor erred. For the grand finale is found in the twelfth and fourteenth chapters of First Kings, which give a truthful account, carrying its own credentials, of the legacy of Rehoboam. Economic chickens always come home to roost; but if you are sufficiently wise or fortunate, you may, like Solomon, "sleep with your fathers" before the birds return.

After Solomon had been "buried in the city of David his father," we are told that "Rehoboam his son reigned in his stead." Harem politics in this instance seem to have led to no quarrel over the succession, a fact which may be a tribute to the wisdom of Solomon. But, after all, Rehoboam was a product of a harem, and certainly acted the part of a spoiled child. Of the legacy his father left him, he was either not informed, or, being informed by advisers, gained no understanding. Yet the time had come when his choice lay between knowing the condition of his finances or losing the greater part of his kingdom. Of course, the judgment of Jehovah stood: the kingdom was to be rent "out of his hand"; and therefore Rehoboam had no chance of preserving it. Yet, even if the pious editor had left Jehovah out of the case, the student of public finance can readily perceive that nothing but an understanding mind and very resolute heart could have saved the weak son of a great sire.

Solomon now slept with his fathers; but he left his son a legacy well calculated to "murder sleep." Reboboam was the son of a man renowned for his wealth; but he inherited liabilities as well as assets. Impressive as the assets undoubtedly were, the liabilities were so large that, even if Jehovah had not been determined to visit the sins of the father upon the son, the only thing that could have saved Rehoboam was a general house-cleaning. To understand this, we need only to consider well-known facts of public finance.

If one thing ever leads to another, if one step is ever difficult to retrace and practically certain to be followed by a second, if a snowball gains in mass as well as velocity when it rolls down hill, so a shekel devoted to new or increased public expenditure involves the spender in further outlays. When Solomon entered upon his first building project, he inevitably committed himself to others. When he appointed "king's merchants" to bring him horses "in droves, each drove at a price," he created a new class of tax eaters who would extol his wisdom as long as the employment lasted and curse his parsimony if he ever sought to economize. When he made silver so plentiful in Jerusalem that "it was nothing accounted," he established an awkward precedent for the son who succeeded to the "great throne of ivory" overlaid with the finest gold and surrounded with carved lions. If Rehoboam inherited "two hundred bucklers of beaten gold" and "three hundred shields of beaten gold" and a palace in which "all the vessels" were "of pure gold," he also succeeded to a scale of living which he must keep up if he would be counted a worthy son of a renowned sire. If Solomon had tried to economize, he would have realized the truth which Machiavelli later formulated when he wrote that the prince who wishes "to draw back" from a policy of liberality "runs at once into the reproach of being miserly." For the heir of a king renowned for wealth and magnificence to reverse gears would have made the royal chariot skid most dangerously.

At this point the scribe who wrote the original story of Solomon gives his reader no help and compels him to fall back upon his knowledge of public finance and human nature. Dramatists there have been to portray the private spendthrift; but where is the drama that presents adequately the royal, or for that matter the democratical, spendthrift? Who has fully appreciated the dramatic interest of Turgot's thwarted plans for curing financial ills that were destroying France but were not yet beyond remedy? Who has ever limned or filmed the solid combination of tax eaters and publicans, fattening upon corruption and extravagance, which wrecked the plans of the faithful minister who, tactless though he may have been, could have saved King Louis's throne and head? And who has drawn the contrasting figure of Calonne willing to borrow and expend? We should not, therefore, he surprised at the shortcomings of the Hebrew scribe, but rather thank him for the remarkable picture he presents of Solomon, the magnificent improver and taxer.

Assets such as constituted Rehoboam's legacy bring little income and constant expense of maintenance and operation. If Solomon left no other liabilities, he bequeathed to his successor a spendthrift habit which must continue if a reputation for magnificence was to be retained and the reproach of meanness avoided. If Jehovah designed the destruction of Rehoboam, his plan of operation was faultless. If the new prince turned back, he would be destroyed by the army of tax eaters which had fattened on the magnificence of Solomon; and if he went forward, as we shall see, he faced destruction at the hands of angry taxpayers.

Chapter twelve informs us that "Rehoboam went to Schechem," where all Israel had assembled to make him king; and "it came to pass" also that Jeroboam, the son of Nebat, who had returned from Egypt, came as spokesman for "all the assembly of Israel . . . and spake unto Rehoboam, saying, Thy father made our yoke grievous: now therefore make thou the grievous service of thy father, and his heavy yoke which he put upon us, lighter, and we will serve thee." Here we have the reverse side of Solomon's grandeur. The taxpayers were in revolt, and their spokesman did not mince words; yet there was an offer of continued service if the yoke were lightened. Both the dramatic and political requirements of the situation were met by the new king: "Depart yet for three days, then come again to me." Rehoboam may have been merely "stalling," but there was need for careful consideration: his request was reasonable, and he had disposed of the deputation for the time being.

That Rehoboam was in a thoughtful mood is indicated by the fact that he "took counsel with the old men, that had stood before Solomon, his father, while he yet lived, saying, What counsel give ye me to return answer to this people?" And the friends and counselors of Solomon, full of years and experience, advised wisely, saying: "If thou wilt be a servant unto this people this day, and wilt serve them, and answer them, and speak good words to them, then they will be thy servants forever." That the "good words" which the elders counseled meant reduction of taxes and all that might go with it, we cannot doubt, since they stand in stark contrast with the course the king followed. Immediately Rehoboam "forsook the counsel of the old men" and "took counsel with the young men that were grown up with him, that stood before him." With superior wisdom and the advantage their inexperience gave them, the young men replied: "Thus shalt thou say. . . . My little finger is thicker than my father's loins. And now whereas my father did lade you with a heavy yoke, I will add to your yoke: my father chastised you with whips, but I will chastise you with scorpions."

To some of the commentators, Rehoboam's turning to the "young men" is considered to "give an impression of youth" and possibly to throw doubt on the subsequent statement that he "was forty and one years old when he began to reign." But we should not assume community of ideas between the ancient scribe and the modern critic as to the meaning of "young." The narrative brings out in sharp contrast the group of older men "that had stood before Solomon" and the younger group "that were grown up" with Rehoboam. That the young men were "flaming youth" advising a boy king to "express himself," would be a silly inference. They were simply men of Rehoboam's generation, who doubtless looked young to the old-timers who knew Solomon. They were young in political and financial experience; but it is perfectly consistent to conceive of them as "youths" of forty making their first contact with public affairs. We may conjecture also that they had more to gain than had Solomon's old cronies, by continuation of the policy of lavish expenditure and heavy taxation.

This last surmise admits of modern application. When some person in authority tells us that we need never expect to have our taxes reduced and will be lucky if they are not increased, it is well to inquire who are his advisers and whether he be not a well meaning executive entirely surrounded by gentlemen who know exactly what they want. When an educational politician informs us that the chief trouble with the public schools is that they do not cost enough, it is not unwise to look into building contracts, school supplies, and the expensive overhead devoted to telling the teachers how it all ought to be done. He who proclaims that taxes yield a larger return than any other "investment" may think so because his return comes to him in very tangible form as the direct result of the outflow of money from the public treasury. To the Hebrew scribe, Rehoboam's advisers may have seemed "young," but in interpreting that word one needs to draw upon the philosophy of relativity.

On the third day, Jeroboam and "all the people" returned, as arranged; but "the king answered the people roughly, and forsook the counsel of the old men which they had given him, and spake to them after the counsel of the young men, saying, My father made your yoke heavy, but I will add to your yoke: my father chastised you with whips, but I will chastise you with scorpions." Then we read: "For it was a thing brought about of Jehovah," that he might "establish his word" concerning the partition of the kingdom—a passage recalling a Greek chorus driving home the meaning of the tragedy, but wholly the work of the pious editor.

The action of the drama is now rapid. When "all Israel saw that the king hearkened not unto them," they made answer "saying, What portion have we in David? neither have we inheritance in the son of Jesse: to your tents, O Israel." The scene ends as "Israel departed unto their tents."

The Hebrews had been nomads when they drifted into Palestine from the Arabian desert, but they had long led a settled life in towns and villages. The cry, "to your tents," is merely reminiscent of earlier times and has dramatic rather than descriptive value. It meant that Jeroboam's followers turned away from Rehoboam, whose kingdom thereby was rent asunder. Revolution was now complete. Jeroboam, the spokesman of the taxpayers, became king over the ten seceding tribes; and his dominion extended over the larger and more fertile and prosperous part of the kingdom builded by David and Solomon. There was then "none that followed the house of David but the tribe of Judah only," in habiting the southern and least productive part of the land.

Rehoboam, dissatisfied with the work of Jehovah, made one effort to win back the lost tribes. He "sent Adoram, who was over the men subject to task-work," to essay the role of conciliator. Whether the idea of sending a tax collector on this delicate job originated with the king or with his young advisers, we are not told; but we can be sure that none of the old men who had "stood before Solomon" would have counseled anything so futile—and humorous. Adoram's mission ended abruptly when "all Israel stoned him to death with stones," and thus passed conciliation and the conciliator. Whether Rehoboam was more pained or surprised by the news, we are not told; perhaps there was no time for introspection, because it is stated that he "made speed to get him up to his chariot, to flee to Jerusalem." Thus "Israel rebelled against the house of David unto this day."

Arrived at Jerusalem, Rehoboam assembled "chosen men, that were warriors, to fight against the house of Israel" and reunite his kingdom. But here Jehovah (and the editor) interposed a veto, to which "they hearkened." "They" must have included both Rehoboam and his clever young men; so the younger generation "returned and went their way, according to the word of Jehovah." Rehoboam had reaped the first fruits of his legacy; but there were others. That he and his kingdom are reported to have sinned and to have done "that which was evil in the sight of Jehovah" had happened before and was to happen again, in Palestine as in other lands; but the resulting punishment involved the inheritance received from Solomon.

It soon "came to pass" that "Shishak, king of Egypt, came up against Jerusalem." Moreover, he came up so violently that "he took away the treasures of the house of Jehovah, and the treasures of the king's house." In fact, "he even took away all"; and in particular "he took away all the shields of gold which Solomon had made." Rehoboam had inherited two liabilities: extravagant habits of expenditure and an incipient revolt of taxpayers; these rent his kingdom asunder. The remnant could not withstand Shishak who despoiled the chief asset: the hill-town of the Jebusites, which David had conquered and Solomon had filled with gold and silver and jewels and ivory and apes and cedars and peacocks and women and other things, which made him famous for his wealth and wisdom and looked interesting to the king of Egypt. With assets and liabilities both behaving this way, Rehoboam could hardly have repeated his grandfather's psalm: "The lines are fallen unto me in pleasant places; Yea, I have a goodly heritage." (Psalm XVI, 6).

The worst had now befallen; but, even so, consequences remained inexorable. After recounting the loss of the shields of gold, the chronicler adds: "And King Rehaboam made in their stead shields of brass, and committed them to the hands of the captains of the guard, who kept the door of the king's house." Solomon's assets were gone and his liabilities were now liquidated, all save one. His successor must reduce his scale of living, but must also consider appearances. The golden shields had testified to the magnificence of Solomon, and the bare places they had occupied now gave mute witness to the abasement of his son. Something had to be done, and shields of brass were perhaps the best solution. To procure them occasioned additional expenditure; but the improverished son of the magnificent spender evidently considered them necessary, because we read that, thereafter, "as oft as the king went into the house of Jehovah" his guards carried the shields; and that, when he left the temple, his soldiers "brought them back into the guard-chamber." Thus the age of gold is followed by that of brass, tawdry display succeeds regal splendor, and the last account in the legacy of Rehoboam is "well and duly" paid.

If an epilogue is desired it may be found in the ninth and tenth verses of the first chapter of Ecclesiastes: "That which hath been is that which shall be; and that which hath been done is that which shall be done: and there is no new thing under the sun. Is there a thing whereof it may be said, See, this is new? it hath been long ago, in the ages which were before us."

BANK ADVERTISEMENTS: ANCIENT AND MODERN[1]

THE art of banking followed hard upon the trade which developed in remote antiquity between the Valley of the Nile and that of the Tigris and Euphrates rivers. Like navigation, accounting, and commercial law, concerning which archeologists have learned so much in the last sixty years, it was a necessary ancillary to the extensive commerce of Southwestern Asia and the Eastern Mediterranean. At Babylon, where the temples, possessing vast wealth, trafficked in merchandise and controlled extensive lands, we read that they also loaned money; and we can hardly doubt, though historical proof is lacking, that Babylonian merchants, so powerful that they were sometimes called rulers, naturally found themselves custodians of customers' funds which they put out to use, as did the merchants who founded great banking houses in modern Europe. At any rate, we know that in Asia Minor, before the invention of coined money, merchants or bankers impressed their seals upon ingots of precious metal, thereby certifying fineness and increasing acceptability; while it seems probable that they also instituted private coinages by placing their stamps upon early coins of electrum. We know also that goldsmiths, silversmiths and money changers, plied their trades whenever and wherever opportunity offered.

When, therefore, the Greeks went down to the sea in ships and turned to trade, their bankers, as they appeared, could look to Asia Minor for guidance, and obtain there not only instruction in an old art but well-trained servants to carry it on. Whether from the East they acquired also their knowledge of advertising, we do not know, since the earliest recorded bank advertisement

[1] Reprinted from *Barron's*, Vol. VIII (1928, July 30), pp. 3 and 8. Reproduced by generous permission of the publishers.

was written by a Greek poet for a Greek banker, doubtless of Syracuse, not far from the middle of the third century B.C. The twenty-third "Epigram" of the Sicilian poet, Theocritus, translated almost literally, runs as follows:

> "To citizens and foreigners this bank gives equal dealing;
> Deposit and withdraw, when your account is correctly made up.
> Let another make excuse: but Caicus even at night
> Pays foreign money to those who want it."

In the first line, the pronoun "this" is that particular demonstrative (*hede,* or, in Doric, *hade*) which suggests the presence of the subject, in this case none other than Caicus the banker, who in the third and fourth lines speaks in the third person, exactly as an advertising writer would make his principal do. Therefore, in the first line, for "this bank" we might well substitute "this bank of mine"; and in the third and fourth we really have Caicus "pointing with pride" to the fact that his depositors are paid foreign money if they want it, even at night.

That this is an advertisement of a bank which, if it lived up to its professions, was managed exceedingly well, cannot be doubted. Why, then for twenty-two centuries, have these verses passed for an epigram? An easy answer would be that editors and commentators have been men of such gross wits that they did not know a good advertisement when they saw one. But this would reveal the inadequacy of the critic rather more than that of his victims, and it is necessary to look further into the matter.

In the first place, those who turn to the poetry of Theocritus, whether readers or editors, have not been much interested in this epigram. Some editors omit it, and in this they have been followed by many translators. This is easy to understand. The verses are not poetry of a high order; in fact, the author's muse in this instance was compelled to travel on the solid ground of practical banking and could not for an instant stray into the realms of imagination and emotion. Since those who read Theocritus look to him for real poetry, it is not strange that the twenty-third "Epigram" has been treated with neglect.

In the second place, there is a troublesome question about authorship, such as arises in connection with so many Greek epigrams. A majority of the editors, indeed, attributes these verses to Theocritus; but a respectable minority gives them to Leonidas of Tarentum, reputed author of a hundred or more epigrams in the Doric dialect and a contemporary of the Syracusan poet. Obviously an editor of Theocritus who doubted the authenticity of this metrical, but hardly poetical, composition would not be likely to discover the real import of the lines.

In the third place, the Greek word "epigram" is the exact equivalent of the Latin word "inscriptio," from which we have derived our word "inscription." It was a "writing on" a temple, a statue, a tomb, or any object calling for description, explanation, or embellishment. To the Greek it meant a few verses expressing some thought appropriate to the object, occasion, or place. Not until Roman poets, especially Martial, sharpened the point of the inscription and inserted therein a sting, did epigram begin to connote a sharp saying, so well described by the unknown Latin author of the lines cleverly reproduced by an English translator:

"The qualities rare in a bee that we meet
In an epigram never should fail;
The body should always be little and sweet:
And a sting should be left in its tail."

The Greek epigram (inscription) had point but no sting. On temple, statue, tomb—or bank—it merely expressed some appropriate thought in well-turned verses. If Theocritus had been asked to state the requisites for an inscription (epigram) on a bank, he might, with apologies to the unknown and unborn Latin poet, have written something which an English translator would reproduce as follows:

The quality chief in a bee that we meet
In such epigram never should fail;
For honey draws customers in from the street,
And there must be no sting in its tail.

If we extract the sting from our conception of an epigram and remember that to the Greek it meant nothing but an inscription, it will be tolerably clear that, whoever may have written these lines, they were intended to be inscribed in a conspicuous place on the bank of Caicus, and that for such an advertisement the Greek language had no better word than "epigram." That the verses were inscribed on the bank and not in some other public place is plainly indicated by the fact that, in the phrase "this bank," the demonstrative is the very pronoun which implies the presence of the person speaking. The letters of *hade*, like nails of bronze, fasten the inscription securely on the façade of the house in which Caicus, after the manner of his time, doubtless lived and also carried on his bank. Though bank and banker are gone, the epigram remains, recalling the lines Theocritus wrote on the statue of Peisander (Epigram XX):

"In solid brass that shall endure
Through many a month and year."

But would the muse of Theocritus, "creator of pastoral poetry," have permitted him to indulge in the urban and hardly poetical pursuit of inscribing an appropriate inscription on a bank? We cannot doubt that she would. Poets who love to describe lyrically and idyllically the beauties of the countryside are not above hankering for the flesh pots of the city, and often enough have preferred to live and compose their verses not far from the maddening crowd. We know that Theocritus proclaimed himself a Syracusan by birth; and he lived for a time in Alexandria, a favorite resort of Greek *literati* in the age of the Ptolemies and well located in a country famous for flesh pots. That, as Wilamowitz-Möllendorf suggests, he may have ended his life in retirement on the island of Cos, does not alter the fact that he was an urban (see his fifteenth "Idyll") as well as a rural poet.

But, some one further asks, would Theocritus have employed his poetic talents for lucre such as may have come to the author of this bank advertisement? Again, we cannot doubt that he would. In his day the one thing a poet seemed to require was a wealthy patron; and the encomium he wrote on Hiero II exhibits a needy poet in quest of a sympathetic friend possessed of a commodious palace and accomplished chef. If this does not settle the matter, we need only recall that, having gone to Alexandria, Theocritus could flatter King Ptolemy and even write in celebration of the monarch's incestuous marriage with Arsinoë. Poets, like other artists, have to live; and we cannot doubt that the Theocritus who could pay court to Hiero and Ptolemy would not hold himself above writing an inscription for a bank. Indeed, Theocritus himself (Idyll XVI) wrote concerning the uses of wealth (following Mr. Calverley's free translation):

"Yet what if all your chests with gold are lined?
Is this enjoying life? Oh fools and blind!
Part on your heart's desire, on minstrels spend
Part; and your kindred and your kind befriend."

That poets should not be overlooked when bankers were spending their money on "minstrels" and their "kind," particularly if they desired inscriptions for their banks, would clearly have been the opinion of the father of pastoral poetry.

But, still a third time, is there anything in the other writings of Theocritus to justify the belief that he could have written an inscription which described so accurately and practically the characteristics of a first-rate bank? Of course his pastoral poetry furnishes no evidence that he could. Out of stories, songs, and scenes of country life, he developed bucolic verse into a new and distinctive form of Greek poetry. His lines abound with lambs, rams, ewes, goats, bulls, cows, bees, crickets, and wolves; with birds of all descriptions, and now and then lions which he can produce as naïvely and ungeographically as Shakespeare at the precise spot where their presence is required. They are fairly cluttered up with pipes, reeds, flutes, crooks, spears, and shepherds' scrips; while his measures weave their way through grasses, flowers, and fruits, with inevitable emphasis on ivy and asphodel, and favorable mention of lotus and all the other "properties" which after his time formed the stock in trade of pastoral poets. His hills and vales, cool rills and fountains, grottoes fair and nymphs fairer still, shepherds and shepherdesses, goatherds and cowherds, testify further to his command of the materials of bucolic verse, but qualify him in no respect as a writer of bank advertisements.

But, even a fourth time, conceding that we should not turn to a writer's pastoral verse for evidence of ability to write bank advertisements, is there in the rest of his poems anything to show that Theocritus may well have turned out these lines? Unquestionably there is—not only some, but sufficient, evidence to show that the Sicilian poet was just the fellow to whom a banker might have turned for an inscription. First of all, there is Idyll XV, a clever and thoroughly sophisticated mime, dealing with the visit of the two Syracusan women to the temple of Adonis at Alexandria where their husbands, perhaps Greek merchants, had taken them to reside. Here the domestic affairs of a well-to-do city household, the chatter (birdlike and feline) of the two "ladies of Syracuse," the crowds in the city streets, the rearing horses that threatened pedestrians at crossings, the jam at the temple gate, the torn muslin veil, the solicitous stranger nearly brushing away a shawl but retrieving himself and thanked for assistance rendered at the final squeeze through the door, the beauties of the temple decorations, the other stranger rebuking the ladies for their endless talk in the broad vowels of the Doric dialect and receiving "what was coming to him," the distinguished woman singer who won last year's prize for dirge singing and now breaks forth in praise of Adonis for whom the party is being "thrown," the delight of the fair Syracusans in hearing so sweet a voice, and then the sudden recollection that hungry husbands must have their dinners (and are not fit to be approached while waiting), which sends them scurrying home with a farewell to beloved Adonis,—all this, and much more, is set forth in a manner that proves the poet well acquainted with cities and city folk.

Indeed, it might fairly be argued that he knows more of city than country, because his treatment of it is realistic and true, while his treatment of the countryside and country folk is often romantically unreal, as good pastoral poetry has to be. One must know his city, and know it well, in order to write the fifteenth Idyll and some of the other poems attributed with great certainty to Theocritus. But pastoral poetry may be written by a city dweller who, assuming him to have the divine gift, is able to make occasional romantic and sentimental journeys in the country. Indeed, in later days it required hardly more love for rural life or knowledge of it than was needed by Watteau when he mixed up court ladies in garden-party costume, impossible shepherdesses with crooks bearing gorgeous streamers, courtiers with lace neckwear and kerchiefs, and the wherewithal for a first-class city lunch, on a canvas depicting a *fête champêtre* with scenic effects such as never were on sea or land, and fortunately never will be. There is, however, no need of pressing the argument that Theocritus really knew city better than country. It is enough to say that he knew it full well—perhaps too well.

More important, however, than such generalities, is the very definite evidence his other epigrams supply of his skill in the difficult art of writing inscriptions. While the authenticity of many of the epigrams is disputed, there is no doubt that he wrote the seventh, an inscription for a statue of Aesculapius, set up at Miletus by the great physician Nicias, friend of Theocritus, to whose wife, fair yet noted for her housewifely care, he gave a distaff carved of ivory with verses (Idyll XXVIII) as graceful as ever accompanied gift, and ending: "Great friendship with a small gift: All things are valued that come from friends." With this may be compared Epigram XXI, almost certainly authentic, which is an epitaph on the grave of Hipponax and as fine a tribute as one poet ever paid another.

In quite different vein, but no less to the point, is the epitaph (Epigram VIII) to Ortho of Syracuse, which reads for all the world like the monitory or minatory inscriptions often found on old New England tombstones:

"Friend, Ortho of Syracuse gives you this word:
Ne'er walk out when drunk on a cold winter's night,
For this was my fate; and now here abroad
I lie clad in soil which is strange to me quite."

Equally reminiscent of New England graveyards is another epitaph (Epigram IX) on Cleonicus, who launched his boat in the stormy season and was unable to "walk back." "Man, value existence," it begins; "Think of poor Cleonicus, for Phasos sailed he," it continues; and "When the Pleiades were sinking" so "he sank with them," it ends.

That one who could write such inscriptions for statues and tombs could have written inscriptions for stores and other business establishments, we cannot doubt. For a draper, dealing in fine lingerie and desirous of advertising a consignment of Coan robes, Theocritus might well have written: "In this shoppe ye smart Syracuse flapper procures her diaphanous wrapper"; and for an undraper, purveyor of Sicilian Scandals of B.C. 260, Theocritus might have picked these lines out of the fifteenth Idyll: "Having loosed our hair, and let our robes drop upon our ankles, with bosoms bare, we will sing our shrill songs." For Theocritus *redivivus* steady employment might await today in writing inscriptions for temples of Folly, Scandal, and Review.

Yet, even if we admit that Theocritus might have written other kinds of advertisements, is it reasonable to suppose that he could have written a bank advertisement which shows such knowledge of the fundamental principles of banking? To this question there is but one answer. Neither Theocritus nor any other poet, unless he happened also to have been a banker, and an exceptionally good one at that, could ever have written this inscription—unless the banker, or his manager, told him exactly what to say and trusted the versifier only to clothe the ideas in good literary form and give the inscription the necessary point. We can conceive of Theocritus, translated to a modern bank, bursting out in lyrical praise of the generosity of the paying teller who gladly gives people good money for worthless pieces of paper, which, since he studies them with such care and puts them so carefully away, he must have some insane desire to "collect." And, similarly, we can readily imagine him bursting into imprecations at the meanness of the receiving teller who apparently makes a business of taking the joy out of customers' lives and then withdrawing it from circulation. That any poet, ancient or modern, from his own observation should understand that the paying teller is really the man who brings depositors into the bank, it is quite unreasonable to suppose. Therefore, concerning the authorship of the twenty-third Epigram, we can only assert that Theocritus could have done it as well as any other Greek poet who had been told what to say.

Some items in our literary inheritance from the remote past carry their own credentials and must simply be accepted as true. Over twenty-two centuries this inscription from the bank of Caicus conveys, to those who understand, the indubitable fact that Caicus, or his manager, comprehended fully the "mystery" of banking. This bank, it begins, gives equal treatment "to citizens and foreigners." To appreciate this, one needs merely to know that the commerce of Greek cities was very largely carried on by foreigners, and that in such cities a foreigner had no *rights* that anyone was *bound* to respect. When Pasion, the great Athenian banker whose credit was good throughout all Hellas, leased his bank to his trusted manager, originally his slave but then a freedman, he did not turn over his loans to his successor, but kept them in his own name, because he, as a citizen, could enforce the payment of debts due the bank. It is clear, then, that the first line of this inscription offers fair dealing to the class of people who would naturally be the best customers of a banker in ancient Syracuse. Then the second line displays a knowledge of the whole "mystery" of banking, when it says: "Deposit and withdraw, when your account is correctly made up." A good bank is built upon the credit of the banker, which is nothing else than the confidence people have in his ability and willingness to pay depositors upon demand exactly what he owes them. "Let another make excuse," the third line begins; but not Caicus, who knew that credit is not built upon excuses, difficulties, or technicalities, but is founded solely and everlastingly on readiness to pay.

Simple as this seems to the modern reader, history records that it has been a hard lesson for most of those who, in divers times and places, have tried to learn in the school of experience how to run a bank. Of this our own country affords instances too numerous to recount. Early in the last century bank notes sent to New York for redemption were once seized by the collector of the port, on the pretext of preventing a run on New York banks. Between 1855 and 1859, in Massachusetts, Ohio, Indiana, Missouri, and other states too numerous to mention, messengers sent to demand payment of notes issued by local banks were arrested on frivolous charges, threatened with lynching, or given coats of tar and feathers. At such a time a banker who, like Caicus, met all obligations on demand might well advertise the fact. At this very day there is, in our own Northwest, where for some years bank failures have been epidemic, a bank which used ordinary good sense in the loans which it made in 1919 and 1920, and during the following period of depression and liquidation met every demand of its depositors. As a result of such comprehension of the "mystery" of banking, this institution today holds most of the surplus funds of the circumjacent territory. The thing seems simple enough; but it has been a hard lesson for men to learn. When the modern world, three or four centuries ago, began to develop credit institutions, it had to purchase, by dear experience, such knowledge of the "mystery" of banking as today in any commercial center is regarded as so simple and elementary that it can be taken for granted and needs no mention in bank advertising.

We come finally to the last line and a half, in which Caicus, speaking in the third person, advertises that he pays *foreign* money to anyone who wants it *"even at night."* Why those words: "foreign" and "night"? For several years after the writer found the epigram and used it in lectures on Greek economics, this question never occurred to him. A square deal to foreigners and prompt payment of depositors were things that "registered"; but the last line and a half conveyed no real meaning. In the summer of 1917 the significance of the words suddenly dawned upon the economist as he was paddling a canoe up the Kennebunk River past old shipyards, idle for forty years, where wooden vessels were again being built for credulous folk who thought they might meet some wartime need. New life stirring in the old yards and revived interest in an art long forgotten aroused in memories of the older folk recollections of the days when Kennebunkport was a noted center of the shipbuilding industry and not only built but owned many ships. As tongues wagged, memories were further stimulated; and presently, as was inevitable, imagination was invoked when it was impossible to recall tales equal to those last told. By the close of the summer, all the things that had ever happened in Kennebunkport, in books, or elsewhere, had been soberly narrated as veracious narratives of the days that had been and, in various particulars, never were.

Certain things, however, the tales had in common. Many of them related to ships which had sailed out of the tortuous river and never returned. With ordinary ships there was apparently, no common time or set procedure for departure; but for those which sailed into the "Great Unknown" it was accounted bad form to leave the wharf much before 12:00 P.M. Conformity to fashion apparently required that severe storms, or at least adverse winds, should have delayed the vessel for many days, during which the captain fussed, fumed, and indulged in language which seemed strong on the quarter-deck but today on golf links would pass as commonplace. Finally, some evening, "about sunset," the wind would be good enough to change, and it would be consistent with ordinary decency for the skipper to send around word that all hands must be ready to sail at midnight.

Then the canoe passed through the narrows, where blocks of cut granite mark the location of the lock built before ships could be constructed on the upper reaches of the river, and the meaning of the inscription flashed clear as sunlight. Theocritus had inserted no sting in the tail of the epigram; this was not the Greek fashion; but he had conveyed to foreign merchants waiting at Syracuse for the right turn of wind and tide such additional information as ought to be decisive in the choice of a bank: Caicus, *even at night*, pays foreign money to those who want it. If otherwise this epigram were not entitled to rank as one of the best bank advertisements ever written, this finishing touch would establish its claims beyond doubt or cavil. Honest treatment to all customers, payment of depositors on demand without excuse, and providing foreign money even at night for merchants who must take advantage of favoring elements—these were the things which the banker, or his manager, told his advertising man to put into the inscription; and these not only constitute its claim to distinction but guarantee modernity so long as banking and the art of advertising endure.

On the front of the house in which Caicus carried on his banking we have now located with tolerable certainty a wonderful advertisement which some clever versifier (not improbably Theocritus) put into form well contrived to secure the desired effect. In this respect ancient Greek advertising differed not from modern. The essential ideas must be derived from the man who runs the business, and cannot be purchased ready-made from advertising agents. Certainly no poet—epic or septic, lyric or idyllic, dramatic or epigrammatic, bucolic or alcoholic, erotic or neurotic, frivolous or serious as the expert with leather brief-case who makes a "survey" of your business—ever supplied a banker with advertisement reaching down so deeply into the fundamentals of good banking and therefore entitled to immortality.

Nor is this the limit to which we can push reasonable inference. This inscription makes excellent professions; but, after all, did Caicus live up to his promises? No one capable of valuing this inscription at its true worth can doubt seriously that he did. A banker intelligent enough to provide such ideas for a poet to embody in a well-turned inscription on the façade of his bank was almost certainly intelligent enough to reap the profit that would flow from living up to his advertisement. Like the banker in the little town of our great Northwest, who refused to make bad loans when farm lands were selling for twice their worth and then met every demand of depositors when evil days came, Caicus had fathomed not only the "mystery" of banking but the very best method of making a bank profitable. The fundamentals of the arts do not change. Banking is always banking, credit is always credit, and excuses are no substitute for money in the paying teller's cage. Old Caicus knew full well, and advertised to the world, that in good banking there is no "equivalent" for cash.

DIONYSIUS OF SYRACUSE—FINANCIER[1]

BY THE opening of the fifth century B.C. a fortunate combination of land and sea power had made Syracuse the first city in Sicily, and not long afterward factional controversies brought it under the sway of a series of tyrants who ruled it most of the time until it came under Roman dominion in 212 B.C. Of these usurpers the outstanding figure was Dionysius the Elder, born about 432 B.C., who, after becoming scribe or secretary to the generals commanding the army, served with distinction in wars against the Carthaginians who then held the western part of Sicily and continually threatened the Greek cities in the rest of the island. By intrigue and demagogy Dionysius finally secured his election as generalissimo and made himself master of Syracuse; whereupon he first got rid of his principal adversaries and then disarmed his friends, "the people," by searching their houses while they were in the fields at harvest time. Thus, says Diodorus Siculus, a clerk and man of mean origin got control of the greatest city among the Greeks and maintained his dominion for thirty-eight years.

Taking advantage of his strategic position, Dionysius created a navy which swept the Tyrrhenian and Adriatic Seas, founded various cities on the Adriatic, secured control, though not direct rule, of the southern end of Italy, made a league with the Illyrians, and contracted an alliance with the Lacedaemonians that proved advantageous in many ways. In 387 B.C. he may have reached the height of his power, and at that time he was one of the outstanding figures in the Greek world. Historians have sometimes attributed to him greater power and influence than were possessed by any other Greek prior to Alexander. Though

[1] Reprinted from *Classical Journal*, Vol. XXV (1930), pp. 260-76. Reproduced by generous permission of the publishers.

he never succeeded in driving the Carthaginians out of Sicily and left them in possession of about a third of the island, there can be no doubt of his ability as a warrior and of his right to rank as the greatest of the Greek tyrants except, perhaps, Pisistratus of Athens.

Such a mighty and colorful figure could not fail to make a deep impression upon the Greek world. Though Hellenes hated tyrants, they were greatly interested in what they said and did, as Greek literature abundantly testifies. Diodorus Siculus, upon whom we depend chiefly for knowledge of the great Syracusan, is not a very satisfactory historian, although he collected materials extensively if not always critically. But if we turn from historians to collectors of anecdotes current in the Greek world, we find in their repositories of fact, fable, wit, and wisdom, ample evidence corroborating the general account given by Diodorus, as well as many additional details that give force and clarity to the picture. What value should be placed upon any particular story is in most cases impossible to determine; but taken as a whole the tales about Dionysius, told and retold by Aristotle, Athenaeus, Diodorus, Diogenes Laertius, Plutarch, Polyaenus, the author of the *Economics* wrongly attributed to Aristotle, and others who need not be recounted, give evidence of value concerning the character of the man. If the *Acts of Dionysius* written by Polycritus had come down to us, we might have still more valuable details but would probably be left with a picture not very different from that derived from writings now extant. Whereas a single story from Greek antiquity may have little probative value, a large collection of anecdotes, such as we have concerning Dionysius, may with proper interpretation yield evidence of great worth.

Who can doubt that a complete anthology of American humor of the last two decades would give the future historian considerable information concerning the life and achievements of Henry Ford? If the book were provided with a good index, even the casual reader would quickly learn that few Americans, if any, of the present day had more stories told about their factory output and personal affairs than the great industrialist of Detroit. And since there is no humor where there is not a modicum of truth, such an anthology would transmit to posterity evidence which, if better sources of information were lacking, the historian of A.D. 3929 could not afford to ignore.

If from the twentieth century we revert to the eighteenth and from Detroit turn to Philadelphia, we find Matthew Carey publishing his *American Museum*, the first American magazine, which was launched in January, 1787. If in 1800 some Herodotus or Plutarch had gone through Carey's twelve volumes and excerpted all references to Benjamin Franklin, he would have collected materials which, if they constituted today all the information we had, would give us a tolerably complete picture of that distinguished man. In the first place, the fact that references to Franklin vastly outnumber those to any other person except Washington would have much significance. The principal events in his public career, his scientific interests and achievements, his inventions, "Poor Richard's" philosophy of common sense, his political and economic opinions, his family affairs, and personal characteristics, including his sense of humor, and, finally, his death and the esteem in which he was held by contemporaries, would be clearly enough set forth to enable the historian to write a satisfactory account of Benjamin Franklin the man. So we must judge it to be with the stories about Dionysius.

Without making an exact count, it is easy to determine that the Syracusan was one of the favorite subjects in antiquity. Philosophers, poets, and rulers clearly lead the list, with aesthetes, epicures, courtesans, artists, actors, parasites, and flatterers trailing far in the rear and in order not worth determining. Among rulers Dionysius ranks with the favored few, among whom Alexander was perhaps the chief, followed by such worthies as Philip, Agesilaus, Lysander, Themistocles, and a few others. By the votes of the anecdotists, therefore, the eminence of Dionysius is securely attested.

We are here concerned with Dionysius the financier, magnificent spender of public money and ruthless but successful tax gatherer. On these points the testimony of the stories is clear and consistent. Not only as a tyrant, strong, treacherous, and cruel, was the Syracusan eminent in the opinion of the Greek world, but also as a money-getter and money-spender. Two treatises upon what the Greeks called economics have come down to us; and one of these consists chiefly of a collection of stories about expedients employed by men of former times to provide themselves with money, the men in all cases being rulers and not private citizens. Among these worthies, Dionysius clearly leads, with a record of nine successful "drives" to his credit, while the second "collector" has a record of five, and third place is divided among three contestants with scores of four each. Moreover, we have many stories from other authors about the tyrant's money-getting exploits, so that we cannot well doubt his eminence.

Like other tyrants, Dionysius always needed money. His first act as generalissimo was prophetic, for he doubled the pay of the army and told the Syracusans that there would be plenty of ways to meet the bills. Besides the army, recruited largely by mercenary troops, upon which his power depended, he had to maintain a multitude of spies; while he must look well to the fortifications of his city against Carthaginians without and secret enemies within. His navy which swept adjoining seas, his docks and storehouses, his new instruments of war, and all the paraphernalia for numerous campaigns entailed expense that could not be avoided. But beyond such absolute necessities of a great career, he sought to enlarge and embellish his city on a magnificent scale that should interest his subjects, testify to his greatness, and make his fame secure. Then, like others of his kind, he must patronize the arts and maintain his retinue of poets, philosophers, and artists, to give distinction to his court. Accounts seem to agree that the tyrant was fond of great luxury and personal indulgence; but in this respect he was reputed inferior to the Persian king, who had all Asia to supply him with luxuries, beside which those available to Dionysius seemed limited enough.

In all his spending, he was under the necessity of maintaining a tradition of royal liberality. His city must be adorned with temples and other splendid edifices. For the people there must be magnificent feasts and spectacles. On the death of his first wife he proceeded to marry at about the same time Doris, daughter of an eminent citizen of Locris, and Aristomache, a noble lady of Syracuse. The former he brought home in a quinquereme adorned with gold and silver flags, and the latter was conveyed to his palace in a chariot drawn by four white horses. In celebration of this matrimonial "double-header" he feasted both soldiers and citizens, and for a time ruled less cruelly and bore himself more courteously. Not content with the rôle of patron of art, the tyrant turned his hand to poetry and caused his poems to be sung at the Olympian Games. There he sent skillful singers to recite his verses and four-horse chariots to compete in races, his delegation being provided with tents adorned with gold and silver embroideries. Though his verses were ridiculed and his chariots fared badly in the races, Dionysius continued his literary endeavors, being told by flatterers that envious critics would at length admire what they professed to despise. In Syracuse criticism of his poetry brought the same hazards that attended criticism of his government. The poet Philoxenus was bold enough to comment adversely upon some of the tyrant's lines, and was straightway sent to the quarries to work as a slave. Through the good offices of friends he was presently released; but at another feast, when Dionysius praised his own poetry and recited some of it, Philoxenus, being asked his opinion, bade them take him back to the quarries.

That the tyrant understood well the philosophy of liberality is sufficiently shown by the rebuke he gave his son, the younger Dionysius. Entering the young man's house one day, he beheld a large number of gold and silver vessels, and cried out: "There is in you no mind of a tyrant, you who have made no friends for yourself with all these drinking cups received from me." No other tradition than that liberality helps to secure and maintain a kingdom could have been transmitted by a Greek despot to his son. Indeed, in all antiquity no one seems to have questioned the efficacy of liberality as an aid to statecraft. The great Alexander spoke for all when, having offered fifty talents to Persillus, who replied that ten would suffice, he said: "Sufficient for you to receive, but not for me to give."

In the age of the tyrants, questions of "ways and means" were frequently settled in mean ways. Dionysius did not differ from his kind, except in the number of his recorded exploits and perhaps the greater ingenuity exhibited in some of them. His numerous wars sometimes brought rich booty, while tribute he may have received from conquered cities. Then there was the levy made upon unfortunate Rhegium after he captured it. Calling an assembly of the inhabitants, Dionysius told them that, instead of enslaving them, he would permit them to go free if they reimbursed his war expenses and in addition paid three minae per head. The Rhegians drew upon their concealed wealth, and paid the sum demanded. Then Dionysius sold them into slavery, and seized the hidden treasures which had been brought to light.

On occasion he plundered temples which, in Greece as elsewhere, sometimes acquired riches that attracted the attention of needy rulers. From the temple of Leucothea he is reported to have taken much gold and silver, besides many ornaments of many kinds. As a reprisal against the Etruscans, he captured the town of Pyrgi and plundered a wealthy temple in that vicinity. The temple of Hera at Lacinium also felt his heavy hand; and it was there that he may have secured the costly garment which Athenaeus says he sold to the Carthaginians for a hundred and twenty talents. At home, it is related, also by Athenaeus, that Dionysius stood at a golden table before the statue of Aesculapius to drink a pledge, and then ordered the table carried away. The anonymous treatise on *Economics* states that whenever, in making a round of the temples, Dionysius saw a gold or silver table displayed, he would order a libation to be poured and the table to be removed. In the same place we read that he was accustomed to strip gold raiment and silver crowns from the statues of the gods, saying that he would give them substitutes, lighter and more fragrant, which he caused to be fashioned with white cloth and white violets. Such things he is reputed to have done light-heartedly and sometimes with accompaniment of ready wit. When sailing away from plundering the temple of Proserpina in Locris, he noticed that his fleet enjoyed a favoring breeze, and called attention to the prosperous voyage which the immortal gods gave to those committing sacrilege. When he took a heavy golden mantle from the statue of Olympian Zeus and replaced it with one of wool, he remarked that gold was too heavy for summer and too cold for winter. And again, when he appropriated golden drinking cups and crowns that were held in the outstretched hands of statues of the gods, he said he was not *taking* anything but merely *receiving* what was offered. In respect of the number of "drives" against temples, the name of Dionysius leads all the rest; and this habit furnished ground for one of the accusations hurled against the tyrant on the day when his opponent, Theodorus, "cut loose" in the public assembly.

Debasement of the coinage was a fairly common expedient in Greek times, and it did not escape the attention of Dionysius. Having borrowed money from citizens of Syracuse and being pressed for repayment, he ordered all the coin in the city to be brought to him, under penalty of death. After taking up the collection, he restamped the coins, giving to each drachma the value of two drachmae, so that he was enabled to pay back both the original loan and the money he had ordered brought to the mint. At another time he coined money of tin and, calling an assembly, praised the new coinage and secured an unwilling vote that it should pass current at the same rate as silver. Heavy fines and confiscations of property must have been in his repertoire, though the chief evidence we have is the statement of Diodorus that the reason why he wished to have exiles called back to Syracuse was that he considered them to be people naturally inclined toward change, who would like to see their enemies killed and their enemies' property confiscated. That he failed to resort to expedients often practised by tyrants, as recorded in the treatise on *Economics* and known to be common in Greek cities, can hardly be believed. Another of his devices suggests the practice known to English law as "wardship." He is said to have ordered all estates of orphans to be registered, and then to have made what use he could of such properties until the owners became of age.

Whatever other means he may have employed, Dionysius resorted to heavy taxation. One of the arts of the tyrant, says Aristotle, is to impoverish his subjects in order that he may thus provide for the support of his troops and, by keeping the people hard at work, prevent them from conspiring against him. Dionysius, he states, resorted to heavy taxation of property and, in a period of five years, contrived to have brought into his treasury the whole substance of his people. Just what this means is not clear; but it may be that the Syracusan merely improved on the device of Cypselus of Corinth, who listed the property of his subjects and took away the tenth part thereof, telling the people to trade with what was left them and thus restore their fortunes. This he is said to have repeated for ten years, with the resulth that he collected as much as the Corinthians originally owned, while they endeavored by hard work to keep their fortunes intact. But the story admits of other interpretations: listing all property at its full value was apparently as difficult in ancient Greece as it is in the United States. At Athens, in a law court, Demosthenes offers evidence that the taxable value of his estate is three talents as proof that it is really worth fifteen, which would indicate that property was assessed at twenty per cent of its true value. This may have been true in Syracuse. Certainly the people of that city would be inclined to conceal their wealth; in fact, one of the interesting stories about the tyrant relates to a citizen who buried money. But even if we assume a great deal of evasion, the levy described by Aristotle would certainly appear too heavy to be endured as a permanent tax. In Greek cities the tax on property was universally hated, so much so that in Athens the original name was dropped and a more agreeable euphemism substituted. The general tendency was to finance a Greek city by other revenues in time of peace, and reserve the property tax for emergencies. This may have been the practice of the tyrant of Syracuse; and the levy mentioned by Aristotle, like the similar tax of Cypselus at Corinth, may well have been a capital levy for war expenses.

In a community as heavily taxed as Syracuse, Dionysius had abundant opportunity to display his resourcefulness as financier. Once he wanted to increase his navy, and thereupon called an assembly before which he appeared with the statement that a certain city was on the point of being betrayed to him and that he needed money for the enterprise. He therefore asked each citizen to contribute two staters, which was done. After two or three days, he pretended that the project had gone wrong and returned the money, praising the citizens, apparently collected in the assembly, for their generosity. Having won the good will of his subjects, he later asked and received another contribution, given in the expectation that it would be returned. Obviously, if the tyrant took a city, the booty would enable him to reimburse those who advanced the necessary capital. Like participants in a modern shell game, the Syracusans had been allowed to win the first time; but the second time Dionysius kept the money and built his triremes.

Besides this popular loan, which turned out to be ship money, Dionysius tried an interesting experiment with taxation of live stock. When taxes became so heavy that people stopped raising cattle, Dionysius announced that his needs were now satisfied and that thereafter those who acquired cattle should be free of tax. Soon, the story continues, many people acquired many cattle in reliance on the promised exemption; and then, at the fitting moment, Dionysius ordered that cattle should again be valued and taxed. Angry at the deception, the people started to slaughter their herds and sell the meat; whereupon the tyrant decreed that they should kill only as many cattle as were needed for daily use. To meet this order, the people devoted their cattle to sacrifice in honor of the gods, upon which the tyrant prohibited the sacrifice of any female animal.

Popular resistance to new taxes is the theme of two anecdotes, or perhaps variant versions of the same original. According to the *Economics*, when Dionysius in want of money demanded a contribution, the citizens replied that they had nothing to give. The tyrant then brought out his own household effects and, pretending poverty, offered them for sale. When the Syracusans came forward to purchase, he recorded what everyone bought and then, after receiving payment, ordered every purchaser to bring the articles back. According to Polyaenus, Dionysius, in need of money, demanded a contribution. When the people replied that they had been contributing altogether too frequently, he ordered his officers to take from the temple of Aesculapius all offerings of silver and gold and place them on sale in the market place. The Syracusans purchased the treasures with avidity, so that a large sum of money was raised. This Dionysius appropriated and then made proclamation that whoever had bought of the sacred objects should immediately take them to the temple and restore them to the god, under penalty of death. Thus Aesculapius received his due and Dionysius was left in funds. Since such an expedient would hardly succeed more than once, it is reasonable to regard these stories as variant versions of the same occurrence, and reasonable also to accept them as fairly trustworthy evidence that upon occasion the tyrant secured payment of taxes by stratagem rather than distraint of goods and chattels.

Dionysius the tax gatherer believed in equal rights, at least to the extent of not denying the women of Syracuse the privilege of paying taxes. In this he was not original, because Periander, tyrant of Corinth, at a solemn festival where he knew the women would be present in their best apparel, sent officers who despoiled them of their jewels, thus raising money for a golden statue he had vowed to erect if he won his chariot race at the Olympic Games. Moreover, the *Economics* records that the Ephesians, needing money, passed a law that women should not wear gold ornaments and should lend to the city what they then possessed. While the narrative is far from clear, it further appears that those whose contributions equaled a certain sum in silver money (presumably the coin current) should have their names inscribed upon pillars of the temple as dedicators, a detail which suggests that the forced loan was for the purpose of constructing, refitting, or embellishing the temple which made the city famous.

The exploit of Dionysius is thus set forth in the *Economics*. Needing money, he summoned the Syracusans to an assembly, wherein we may assume that mere men were the only persons in attendance. As was his custom, he appeared and presented his story, which was that he had seen the goddess Demeter, who bade him bring to her temple the ornaments of the women. As for himself, he stated, he had already contributed the ornaments of the women of his household. He desired, therefore, that the rest of the citizens should do likewise in order to avoid the vengeance of the goddess, adding, naturally, that anyone who refused would be guilty of sacrilege. When all the ornaments were brought to the temple, through fear of the goddess and of the tyrant himself, as the narrative puts it, he dedicated them to Demeter and then bore them away as a loan from the goddess. No doubt the dedication was as public as his communication to the assembly, and it is touching to contemplate the despoiler of temples helping his fellow townsmen avoid the crime of sacrilege; concerning the loan the narrative merely tells us that it was from the goddess, and says nothing about the rate of interest or terms of repayment. But the *Economics* does add that, after some time had elapsed and the women had again begun to wear ornaments, the tyrant gave orders that anyone who wished to deck herself with gold should offer a stated sum to the temple. Conceivably such offerings were to repay the loan which the tyrant received from the goddess. But if this view be rejected, it is clear that the temple in the course of time would again acquire funds which would enable it to make further loans.

Thus far the tales exihibt Dionysius in the guise of a clever but utterly rapacious tyrant, spending money without limit and gathering it without regard to consequences in this world or in the lower regions where dwelt the spirits of the dead. Whatever he secured abroad by spoiling temples, looting cities, and exacting tribute may be set down as gain to Syracuse; but within that city his fines, confiscations, and heavy taxes, if employed as ordinary measures, must have tended to repress enterprise, discourage accumulation, and dry up sources of future revenue. Yet the tyrant ruled for thirty-eight years and left his throne to his son, so that the economist wonders whether his financial measures could always have been so uneconomic as most of the anecdotes depict. All this is mere conjecture, though based on just inference from the correct principle that in the long run excessive taxation defeats its primary purpose, which is of course to provide revenue to defray the charges of government. But we are not left wholly to conjecture, for there are three anecdotes which throw upon the character of Dionysius the financier quite a different light from that shed by the other stories. In Greek antiquity, as at the present day, the picturesque, the startling, the conspicuous must have been noised abroad and preserved in anecdote much more readily than the quiet, sober, and well-considered acts which arouse less popular interest but tend to preserve cities and dynasties. Three such actions of Dionysius are recorded in tales which have come down to us.

The first is related by no less a person than Aristotle, whose *Politics* dates to the period immediately following the death of Dionysius. It is narrated soberly, with serious purpose, and obviously with confidence in its authenticity. But more than this, it is one of those stories which, rightly understood, carry their own credentials because they contain truths beyond the ken of the maker of tales or the wielder of a ready calamus. "And in Sicily a certain man who had money on deposit with him bought up all the iron from the mines; and afterward, when the merchants came from the markets, he was the only seller. Without greatly increasing the price, he nevertheless on his outlay of fifty talents received a hundred. Now when Dionysius learned this, he ordered the man to take his money away and remain no longer in Syracuse, because he had discovered ways of making money opposed to his own interests." The exploit of the banker was nothing extraordinary. Aristotle relates that the philosopher Thales cornered the supply of olive presses in a season when the harvest was especially abundant, and the anonymous treatise on *Economics* relates that various cities created monopolies of grain and other commodities. But the most interesting detail of the story of the banker of Syracuse, and the hall mark certifying its essential veracity, is the permission freely given by the tyrant to take so much money away frim his city. Can this be our Dionysius the rapacious, plunderer of cities, despoiler of temples, tax gatherer with a scourge of scorpions? Even though his treasury overflowed at the moment, he must have known that the tyrant of Syracuse could never have enough. Why, then, these words that stand out so clearly in the narrative: "He ordered the man to take his money away and remain no longer in Syracuse"? For such a departure from ordinary form, which the recorder of the tale apparently desired to emphasize, there is one, and so far as I can see but one, plausible explanation. As a financier, Dionysius was big enough to appreciate skill in a fellow craftsman, even when exhibited in his own city and adversely to his interests. In effect, he said to the poacher on his domain: "You are a clever worker, and I am not going to rob you. Keep your money, but get out of Syracuse. There isn't room enough for two of us in one town."

Another tale, preserved in Plutarch's *Apophthegmata,* has less color but no less interest. "And having heard that a certain citizen had gold concealed in his house, he ordered the man to bring it to him. But when the man, having managed to conceal a little of the treasure, moved to another city and purchased land there, Dionysius sent for him and told him to take back all his gold, enjoining him to keep his money employed and never again allow it to lie idle." Again we ask, Can this be Dionysius? And again we confront the question of reconciling this tale with others of a different purport. If the mystery admits of solution, I think we must begin with the simple fact that, grasping as the tyrant was, he ruled Syracuse for thirty-eight years while the city grew in wealth and power. This could not have been if his financial policies had always been repressive, destructive, and uneconomic. We must indeed, believe that his taxes were sometimes heavy, that he devised cunning and severe methods of collection, and that the people of Syracuse often complained. But revenue was necessary for the defense and development of his city; in spite of his taxes, the community grew and prospered; and complaints about taxation are as old as the hills and as recurrent as the fifteenth day of March. If most of the tales that have come down to us reveal Dionysius the rapacious, this story presents him as a financier who desired that citizens of Syracuse should keep their capital employed, by which course, obviously, they would increase the sources of public revenue.

That there was a limit to his exactions, and one fixed with financial wisdom, is indicated by a final tale, also preserved by Plutarch: "When, levying taxes upon the Syracusans, he found them lamenting, entreating, and saying that they had no money, he ordered still another tax to be levied. And this he did twice and thrice. But when he was preparing another levy and heard that the people were laughing and jesting as they went around in the market place, he ordered his officers to desist. 'For now,' he said, 'they have nothing left, since they hold us in derision.' " In the last sentence the word "nothing" should be understood to refer not to property but to ready money for the payment of taxes. While all property was laid under contribution, the tyrant knew that payment must be made out of current and not fixed assets. The point of the story is that, so long as the Syracusans lamented, entreated, and declared they had no money for taxes, Dionysius knew that they protested too much and that more revenue could be secured by another twist of the screw. Upon the other hand, when current assets were reduced to a point that brought them face to face with ruin, the Syracusans perforce became resigned to the situation and proceeded to extract what amusement they could from it; whereupon the tyrant stayed his hand.

This tale conveys a lesson not found, so far as I am aware, in any treatise on public finance, and one that escaped me until I observed the last years of the excess profits tax in the United States. In 1917, when the measure was before Congress, few realized what it was going to mean. Then in the spring of 1918, when the first returns must be made, came curses both loud and deep. For this, of course, the confused language of the law, the inevitable complexity of its provisions, and the bureaucratic administration it received were to a considerable extent responsible; but presently the destructive and uneconomic nature of the measure began to be realized. Then came 1920, when the post-war boom collapsed; but liability for taxes, assessed, reassessed, and overassessed for the war years, did not disappear along with the hectic prosperity which came to an end when inflation was followed by inevitable deflation. By 1921, a year of deep depression, when it came to paying taxes, back taxes, and further back taxes, on paper profits never realized in money but estimated to have been made in the previous three or four years, the situation had become too serious for curses or imprecations; and there was nothing to do but accept it in the best humor possible. Then came jokes about "tax hounds," the distress profits tax, the red ink-come tax, the taxation of deficits, and the conversion of frozen inventories into taxable sunshine. Then, and only then, did I appreciate the wisdom of Dionysius, who found out twenty-two centuries ago that when a tax becomes a joke it should be repealed, and that quickly. In this instance the wisdom of Dionysius so far surpassed that of the American Congress and our Department of Internal Revenue, as then constituted, that comparison would be not only difficult but odious.

This is the story of Dionysius, financier. Syracuse found him expensive but became a bigger and perhaps a busier city, so that it must have received some return for the money contributed during the thirty-eight years of his rule. In finance, as in other things, the tyrant was ruthless, and his methods were often characterized by severity, impiety, and deceit; but he did nothing that differed generically from the expedients to which Greek cities, whether ruled by tyrants or not, resorted in time of financial stress. As revealed by the anecdotes, he was simply more resourceful and successful than ordinary tyrants, while some of the stories, as we have seen, indicate that he had some grasp of principles of sound finance. In the main, his conduct seems to have been governed chiefly by the inexorable conditions of the great game he elected to play, that of usurping rule in Syracuse, mastering the island of Sicily, and, from this strategic base, making himself arbiter of the western part of the Greek world.

Among the conditions of this game was the necessity of carrying on activities involving great expense which must be on a regal scale. This habit of magnificent expenditure he inevitably bequeathed his son, the younger Dionysius, who presently ruled in his stead. The young man, reared in luxury and indolence, was not allowed to participate in public affairs and so prepare himself for ruling a city. In fact, no tyrant with two wives could safely allow a son to take a hand in affairs of state; and in the case of Dionysius we have Plutarch's story of the attempt of Dion to intervene in the interests of the children of the tyrant's Syracusan wife, and of the physicians, friendly to the younger Dionysius, son of the Locrian wife, who gave the dying tyrant a potion which brought him not only sleep but death. Yet there are at least two tales that testify to the desire of the father to educate the son to his responsibilities. When the young man debauched the wife of a citizen and was called to account, he replied, with the cleverness of the younger generation, that his father did not know what it was to be the son of a tyrant. To this the elder replied: "Nor will you have a tyrant for a son unless you stop doing such things." Like Machiavelli, the great Syracusan knew that it was prudent for a tyrant to respect the wives and daughters of his subjects. And again, we have the story, presented above, of Dionysius remonstrating with his son for selfishly keeping golden treasures instead of distributing them among his friends and securing their friendship by royal liberality. Whatever the responsibility of the father may have been, the younger Dionysius proved easy-going and pleasure-loving, swayed by the influence of flatterers and boon companions, and incapable of wearing the heavy mantle of the great tyrant.

The rest of the story is quickly related. The legacy of magnificence, in expenditure and taxes, turned out to be one of the causes of the ruin of the son and heir. Like Rehoboam, who inherited the grandeur and taxes of Solomon, the younger Dionysius found himself plagued with financial problems. The splendor of the court must be maintained, and real economy would have raised up a host of enemies from those who profited by great public expenditure. That he felt financially embarrassed is indicated by a vain attempt to reduce the pay of his father's veteran soldiers. The road to ruin was easy and broad; and when, despised for his indolence and debauchery, he rejected the advice of his best counselor, the inevitable uprising occurred. Sending secretly to Dion, the popular leader, the young tyrant tried to make terms with him, but was told to treat publicly with the Syracusans, now a free people. The father would have dared to go in person to the assembly; but the weak son sent representatives who promised *moderation in taxes* and easy military service, both of which should be determined by vote of the people. Coming too late, this offer was derided by the Syracusans, who replied that they would not confer with their ruler unless he first abdicated, in which case he might expect personal immunity and reasonable treatment. In the end, negotiating proving fruitless and treachery unavailing, Dionysius the Younger escaped from his citadel on the little island of Ortygia and sailed away with such persons and property as he valued most, eluding the Syracusan fleet. The financial requirements of the great tyrant could not be readily reduced, or safely financed by his weak and less resourceful son. For this, among other reasons, the younger Dionysius lost his city, just as Rehoboam saw the kingdom of Solomon rent asunder. Thereby history repeated itself, as nearly as it ever does; and from the tale the student of finance may learn lessons of universal interest and of modern as well as ancient application. "Financial science," as Leroy-Beaulieu once remarked, "has a terrible fashion of avenging itself upon governments which ignore or defy it."

THE NEW DEAL IN ANCIENT GREECE[1]

THE Greek political world was the most marvellous a political scientist ever had spread before him for observation and study. It was made up of hundreds of little city states, in which things happened quickly. It was a three- or four-hundred ring political circus, with something happening in some of the rings all the time and frequently several major acts going on in different rings at the same time.

Out upon that world the great political philosophers of antiquity looked, and from their studies and observations Plato, Aristotle, and Polybius wrote their immortal works. Modern historians have had much to say about it, but frequently they have been people who call themselves liberals or people who call themselves conservatives; and they have gone back to Hellas to fight their battles over the merits and demerits of democracy. The discussion has centered largely around Athens, the most interesting of all the Greek city states, which has been the exposed salient on which this controversy between historians has centered. There Mitford goes, for example, in his day, to find examples of the horrible workings of democracy, with the result that in the next generation George Grote repairs to the same city and the same sources of information to write a glorified history of Athenian democracy.

I am going to say nothing more about the historians, and shall say but little about the ordinary sources of information. But I am going to lay before you some materials which, over a period of forty years and more, I have gathered, a bit now and

[1] An address delivered at the annual meeting of the American Association of Collegiate Schools of Business, at the Harvard Graduate School of Business Administration, Soldiers Field, Boston, Massachusetts, April 24, 1936. Reprinted from *Harvard Business Review* (Summer, 1936), pp. 389-404. Reproduced by generous permission of the publishers.

a bit then, from sources that were to me most interesting and seemed to have the greatest probative value. I shall draw chiefly upon Greek anecdotes, upon Greek plays, and upon the orations of the great Attic orators.

Greek Anecdotes

Beginning with anecdotes: If we had a complete classified collection of all the anecdotes ever in circulation among the ancient Greeks, and preserved by Plutarch and others because they were such good anecdotes, we could perhaps construct from them a history of Greece better in some ways than any historian has ever written, and we should be especially helped by anecdotes of a humorous character.

I will begin with the story of King Archelaus and his barber. The king sits down one morning and his barber inquires: "How shall I cut your hair?" to which comes the terse answer: "In silence." Now, of course that doesn't *prove* that there ever was a King Archelaus; and, if there was such a king, it doesn't *prove* that *he* ever made that reply. Some good story-teller may have made it up and fastened it on King Archelaus. Many stories ten or a dozen years ago were made up and fastened onto Henry Ford and his celebrated product. But it does demonstrate one thing beyond the reach of doubt or peradventure, something that the most confirmed historic skeptic cannot question; namely, that the Greeks not only had barbers, but that such tonsorial artists sometimes tired their patients by their loquacity.

There is no historical evidence of greater probative value than a humorous story, properly interpreted. If you have never studied Greek originals and if you grew up after our "educators" debased American education by eliminating the classics, your Greek education might well begin with that story.

If time permitted I should like to go on with stories about barbers that were current among the Greeks. You can learn much of politics from them, and the same is true of stories about barbers that were current in Rome. The Greek stories turn frequently on the same point; namely, what tyrants' barbers might do to tyrants' throats. When Plato was visiting Dionysius, tyrant of Syracuse, he expressed various unfavorable views about tyranny and tyrants. Finally Dionysius said, in substance: you will admit that at least a tyrant has courage. Plato replied, in substance: I don't know about that; he is always afraid of his barber. And Dionysius was afraid because there is another story to the effect that one day his barber expressed the happy thought that it would be very easy for him to cut the tyrant's throat. This remark came to Dionysius, who, like other tyrants, lived in fear of edged or pointed tools; and straight-way he sent the man—his own barber—to the celebrated quarry where he kept political and other prisoners.

Greek stories about barbers tend in that direction; Roman stories in quite another. They tend in the line we find in the great Roman satirists, and relate to the wealth that barbers frequently acquired in ancient Rome and what they did with it. Emperor Julian one day is said to have sent for his barber, and when the man came in elaborately and ambitiously arrayed, he said: "I didn't send for my High Treasurer. I sent for a barber."

From barbers, who take us fairly deeply into Greek and Roman life, let us turn to politicians and begin with a fable of Aesop's which I found in a public place, namely, in Aristotle's *Rhetoric* (2:26) only a year ago, but have not yet found in any collection of Aesop's fables. The story is that Aesop, who not only made fables but also was a politician and advocate in Samos where he lived, told this story while he was defending a Simian demagogue accused of a capital political offense. Aristotle tells this story in a part of his book in which he is setting forth how public speakers may use stories effectively in their arguments. He says that Aesop, defending this demagaogue in the assembly, told the people of Samos that they should remember the fox who was caught in a cleft in some rocks, from which he was unable to extricate himself. While lying there he suffered greatly from fleas, and finally a hedgehog came by and took pity on him, asking him if he could not remove the tormentors. This the fox refused, saying: "They are already full of me and they are not now sucking much more blood but if you take these away, others will come and, being thirsty, will drink what little blood I have left." And then Aesop concluded: "O men of Samos, you, like the fox, will suffer no more harm from this man because he is already wealthy. But if you put him to death, other demagogues will come who will be poor, and they will steal and squander the public money."

When you laugh at this, you enter into the feelings, the life, and the thought of the ancient Greeks. That this was a good story about Greek politicians is evidenced by the fact that Aristotle put it in his *Rhetoric* as an example for political speakers, again the best sort of historical evidence.

There are many more. There is the story of Themistocles and Aristides, who weren't the best of friends. Themistocles, having made a "crack" at his rival, received this in reply from Aristides the Just. He was arguing that what a great general most needed to know was how to anticipate the plans of the enemy, and Aristides replied: "That is indeed necessary, Themistocles; but the honorable thing, and that which creates a real general, is control over his fingers." Now, to understand that, remember that when a Greek general was put in command of an army he was expected to march with his army and somehow to finance it; with the result that he not only financed the army, but frequently financed himself. Themistocles, who was worth only three talents when he came into office, when he was finally banished and after he had managed, with the aid of friends, to sequester a good part of his ill-gotten gains, nevertheless left something like eighty talents which the government succeeded in confiscating.

There is plenty of other evidence. After these stories we are prepared to accept what Polybius, the great philosophic historian, wrote about Greek officials. He said the Romans in his day still respected their solemn oaths of office and that their magistrates were honest, but the Greeks had emancipated themselves from old-fashioned religious superstitions. They had, therefore, no regard for oaths; and the result was that men handling public money, if entrusted with only a single talent and given ten checking clerks, ten seals, and twenty witnesses, could not keep their faith. It is hard, he remarked, to find a man who keeps his hands off public money and maintains a clean record. To one who really knows Polybius that statement is good historical evidence; but to one who does not know, Aesop's fable is very much better. When you put the two together the case is closed, and you know a good deal about Greek politicians. This will give you a pretty fair introduction to the New Deal in ancient Greece.

Greek Plays

Passing from anecdotes to plays, we find in several of Aristophanes' comedies some indubitable bits of evidence concerning Greek political and economic life. For example, in *The Peace* there is a scene in which, after the conclusion of the Peloponnesian War, the people pour into the Athenian market place rejoicing and conversing in a manner that compels the attention of the modern reader: Hermes begins: "Look here! See how the reconciled cities greet and blend in cheerful intercourse and laugh for joy." And Trygaeus replies: "Yes, and survey the people; by their looks you can discern their trades." Then Hermes: "Oh dear! Oh dear! Don't you observe that man that makes the helmet crests tearing his hair? And there is a pitchfork seller. See how he fillips the sword cutler there." Evidently the munition makers are out of luck and Athenian manufacturers of agricultural implements are going to do some business. The farmers had all been driven into Athens during the war, while the munition makers were doing all the business and agricultural implement makers had been out of luck.

Then Trygaeus continues: "See how pleased the sickle maker looks, joking and poking the spear burnisher! If there be any that delights in war, King Dionysius, may he never cease picking spear heads from his funny bones." Then as now there was nothing funny about a spear head hitting a funny bone, and here is the reaction, as a great dramatist saw it, of the Athenian audience to the return of peace. It tells you much about the ancient Greeks, how much they were like ourselves, and how the munition business and agricultural implement business in Greece resembled the munition business and the agricultural implement business in our own time.

New Deals

Now we come to New Deals. Of course, anything that is trumpeted abroad as new is always old. There really isn't anything fundamentally new. And if it is called a deal—then you know a lot more about it. If a fellow sits down at a little square table covered with green cloth and says he is going to give everybody an honest deal, somebody is sure to call for a new deck of cards. Nobody who intends to deal the cards honestly ever says anything about his dealing; he just sits down and deals, without talking about it. If he begins talking about his square dealing or new dealing or any other kind of dealing, the other players will want a new deck of cards, and then will watch subsequent operations very closely. So much for dealing.

We can begin with Solon. A deal in politics always means that people who have money or other valuables in their pockets will do well to button up their coats tightly because something is likely to be coming their way. In Solon's time the city of Athens was in a very bad condition. It had changed from a small city into a great commercial center. A great deal of wealth had been made there, and inevitably it was very unequally distributed. Men having wealth evidently undertook to rule the city. Reverses of some kind in economic and commercial conditions had reduced many people to want, while many were in debt; so that a political revolution threatened. Out of such things revolutions have often come and probably often will.

Solon himself said in some of his verses: "But of themselves in their folly, the men of the city are willing our great city to wreck, being won over by wealth. . . . Great men ruin the city: for lack of understanding under a despot's yoke lie the people enslaved." And that was written not so many years before Pisistratus did establish himself as despot in Athens.

Finally, at the opening of the sixth century, Solon was invited to mediate between the contending factions, and he carried through his famous reforms, which I cannot discuss in detail. But one of his reforms was that he cancelled at least a large part of the outstanding debts, which entitles it to the name of deal. There were two plans for reform, both of which might have been called new and progressive. One was cancellation of debts and the other was redistribution of lands. Solon took both under consideration and everybody naturally was speculating as to which one of these new deals he would adopt; or whether he would try both; or first try one and, if that didn't work, try the other; but always try something. While he was considering the matter he had to do what practically everybody under such circumstances does—he had to confide his real designs to somebody; nobody can keep such a secret one hundred per cent to himself. So Solon told this to three friends in whom he especially confided, informing them that he was going to cancel debts and that he was not going to redistribute lands. Then the three friends, like actors in our movies, evidently said: "That's all I want to know!"

Athens was a commercial city. A thing like that couldn't be proposed without merchants speculating on which particular reform was going to be adopted. These three fellows went out and borrowed a lot of money with which they bought a lot of land before the story leaked out. If they hadn't got ahead of the leak, of course the land would have gone up and the operation would not have been so attractive. They then held their lands bought with borrowed money, and finally debts were cancelled. The story presently got out, and naturally made a sensation which reacted on Solon; but he was able to show that he had himself cancelled debts owing him, and that he was the first man to do that in Athens, so that he saved the situation.

Now, that is the story. It may not be true, but some things are true about it. It is the sort of thing that must have happened somewhere. Even a clever story-teller could never have made that up out of whole cloth. No man contemplating that sort of thing could keep it absolutely to himself. He would have had to confide his secret to some of his friends who were absolutely to be trusted, and absolutely sure to go out and act upon it. So much for the first New Deal of which we have any very clear record. It was perhaps an old thing when Solon tried it, but after his time it became pretty common in Greece. Now we pass to Greek liberality.

Greek kings had always maintained the tradition of liberality; many of their subjects were free to come and dine at the royal tables. After the Persian Wars were over and the Athenian conservatives, or oligarchs as they were called, and the Athenian democrats squared away for another tussle over "social justice," the leader of the conservatives was Cimon, a very wealthy man. Cimon was liberal—in a conservative way. Perhaps you laugh too soon. What I was going to say was that he was liberal with his own money. He took down his fences and invited his fellow countrymen to come into his fields and help themselves. He provided a meal every day for anybody who wanted it. He was very liberal and very popular in a conservative way, with his own money.

Pericles, the leader of the popular party, could not possibly meet such competition. He had inherited a comfortable estate which he managed in thrifty fashion. He is credited with having been one of the few Athenian statesmen who were absolutely honest, like Aristides and Phocion. They are a fairly lonesome trio in the Grecian gallery of famous politicians. But Pericles had to compete with Cimon; and since he couldn't be liberal himself, he inaugurated a new kind of liberality—with other people's money. That is the progressive way of doing it.

He began by instituting a system of paying citizens for every public duty. Up to that time Athenians had served in the army without pay. They had served on juries without pay. They had come to the popular assembly without pay. They had held public office without pay and for the honor of the thing. Pericles began by paying for jury duty and to this he added various amusements at public expense. After his time payment for attending the popular assembly was instituted. Presently, of course, the attendance at assemblies increased greatly; and it was observed by Aristotle that, when cities began to pay people for attending assemblies, the poor always had more leisure than the rich to whom two obols were nothing while they had other uses for their time.

In these ways and others a large part of the population of Athens came onto the city. In order that as many people should be on the payroll as possible, they increased the number of jurors to six thousand. There were then thirty thousand citizens; one in five was a juror on pay, and you have popular liberality. It was Pericles who introduced this particular New Deal. Once established, of course, there was no end to it; and presently pay had to be increased, and was increased.

To finance these things at first was easy, because, in the Confederacy of Delos, Athens had become the leader. Whereas the treasury had once been on the Island of Delos, the Athenians presently brought it to Athens where it would be perfectly safe. They put it up on the Acropolis in the temple of the goddess where it was perfectly inaccessible to others, but of course they themselves could borrow from the goddess if they had to.

But although easy to finance at first, the system grew with what it fed on; and the time came, after they had got into the wars with Lacedaemon and Pericles had passed from the scene, when Cleon, the best representative of the Greek demagogue of the worst type, increased the pay and the other distributions. Pericles was a demagogue or popular leader of the best type, able, honest, and very patriotic, but playing politics in the way he had to play it in order to match the conservative liberality of Cimon. Cleon increased the pay and the other distributions, and then had to increase the tribute from the allies in order to pay the bills. Financing the doles, the pay of six thousand jurors, and all that sort of thing was easy as long as the tribute lasted; but when the allies revolted and the tribute declined, then the money had to be raised at home and everything was different. The Athenians had not only levied tribute on the allies, but they made them come to Athens to conduct their law suits. That meant that the revenue of the law courts was increased, as Xenophon pointed out in his *Revenues of Athens*, and also that the yield of port dues was increased because when these people came they brought their provisions and other things with them. Moreover, since the law suits were not always decided quickly, there was a considerable demand for living accommodations as well as other things, and the city prospered greatly.

Athenian finances were never well managed. There was no central treasury into which all revenues were turned and out of which all expenditures were made, but there were separate treasuries for the different departments of government. For example, there was a separate treasury for the courts; fines and confiscations went there, and out of it came the pay of the judges. If there wasn't enough money in any year, because the fine and confiscation business wasn't good, the judges just didn't get their pay. So the administration of justice in the law courts was poisoned by this very fact of the existence of a separate treasury.

Moreover, there was an old custom which existed not only in Athens but everywhere else, a custom which long antedated payments for service or the institution of the system of doles. Greek states, if in any year they came out with a surplus, were accustomed to distribute it among their people; and in Athens a surplus in any of the separate treasuries was likely to be distributed even though other treasuries showed a deficit which had to be made good somehow.

To remedy that, a capable politician and good financier devised what appeared to be a great reform. Under it, surpluses originating in any of the treasuries, instead of being distributed, went into a special treasury which, it was hoped, would be prudently managed. But, unfortunately, this was not what happened; and the result was that the change created a central reservoir to which the people of Athens more and more looked for regular distributions.

Now I come to public works, as a measure of relieving distress and beautifying the city. There hadn't been many such things in Athens prior to the time of Pericles; but he, a man of ideas and with the revenues of the Confederacy to draw upon, was able to institute and carry through those magnificent improvements that made Athens so famous, both in antiquity and even down to the present day. I will not go into them except to point out, first, that they were made largely out of the money of the Confederacy; and second, that Phidias, the master builder and master architect, came out of the great enterprise badly smirched.

The story isn't clear. One version is that, when he was accused of having made away with gold, the authorities took down all the gold plates on the enormous image of the goddess, weighed them, and found that no gold had been stolen. But there were complaints about ivory and other things, and Phidias presently left town. The whole story is very obscure; he may have been unjustly accused, but there is the story, nevertheless.

Solon could not cancel debts without stories arising about his friends taking advantage of their opportunities, and the great work of Pericles couldn't have been done without stories like this one. Moreover, the great expenditures, of course, led to opposition. His opponents, the conservatives, who were permitted to look at the improvements but had to pay the cost in so far as the revenues of the Confederacy didn't suffice, naturally opposed him, and Pericles twice had to resort to a plebiscite.

That, in Athens, was simple; he just called the people to the general assembly: Greek tyrants did that also. The institution of the popular assembly was deeply rooted; and when Dionysius or many another tyrant had something particularly difficult that he wanted to put across, he would call the people into the assembly for a little fireside talk and tell them what was coming. That is what Pericles did, and I will present a few lines from some remarks attributed to him. Having called the people into the assembly he asked them whether they thought he had spent too much money. The conservatives evidently declared that he had, and he said: "All right then, let it not have been spent on your account, but on mine; and I will make the inscription of dedication in my own name." This recalls the speech that Daniel Webster is said to have made after he had dined and wined not wisely but too well. The United States debt at that time had been practically wiped out, and the country owed only fifty or a hundred thousand dollars. Webster in the course of his address referred to this small debt, and said that it was such a trifle he could pay it himself.

Thus Pericles to his critics. But the fellows who were getting the jobs were present and the matter didn't end there. On the contrary, "they cried out loudly and told him to draw freely from the public funds and spare naught whatsoever." And Plutarch, who preserved the story, tells it without any appreciation of its humor.[2]

Of course I have stated it this way because I wanted to make you laugh, even as I laughed when I read Plutarch's story. You have to go over such stories year after year, and then let current events supply you with modern parallels. Here we have Pericles asking Athenian tax-eaters whether he had been too extravagant; whereupon they cried out loudly, telling him to spend freely and spare nothing whatsoever. How much that is really new can there ever be in alleged innovations which politicians miscall *New* Deals?

When the Confederation of Delos was turned into an Athenian empire, and former allies became subject states which

[2] Only a few days after I had this material typed and filed away I read an account of meetings which Secretary Wallace caused his agents to hold with farmers in various parts of this country, at which the recipients of agricultural benefits were asked to vote whether they wished to get some more checks the next year. When, strangely, they voted in the affirmative, Wallace promptly issued one of his effusions about this wonderfully democratic method of taking the sense of the people. I leave to you the question, whether the Secretary of Agriculture is a great statesman like Pericles; or whether Pericles, the great statesman, on occasion could be as funny as Henry Wallace.

were cruelly exploited, revolts began to occur and finally the great empire was destroyed, so that Athens was left to pay its own bills. Then, of course, the Athenians had to finance with their own resources whatever fine things they might elect to do and enjoy. The result was that public works could never again be carried on as in the age of Pericles, and, what was still worse, the great navy and army were never thereafter maintained at their former strength. The reason was simple. Little things like temples, fleets, and armies could be neglected, but not King Demos, to whose will statesmen had to bow and whose appetite for distributions of public money had become insatiable. So bread and meat and festivals and doles of money had to continue; and, as we shall see, the result was what might have been expected.

The Law Courts

And now I turn to some of the stories which have come down to us about the law courts and what they were doing to the rich. These courts provided wages for six thousand judges, and when the number of citizens, as a result of the Peloponnesian Wars, declined from thirty thousand to twenty, there was no reduction in the number. What the people had actually done was to raise the requirements for citizenship so as to make it very difficult for more people to become citizens and so qualify as judges. They didn't call that unemployment insurance, but that is what it really was.

A court consisted of several hundred judges so as to distribute employment widely and abundantly; there might be four hundred and one or five hundred and one. One of the archons acted as president, but he was not a judge. No orderly legal procedure was provided. Suitors appeared to present their own cases, but could go to the orators and get arguments written for them if they preferred. Later the custom of allowing an advocate to come in and plead for a client was instituted.

In the orations of the Attic orators we have materials which, properly interpreted, give us all we need to know about the procedure in these law courts. The penalties were severe and frequent. Banishment, death, confiscation of goods, all these things were common; these penalties, of course, being directed against the wealthy. There naturally grew up a class of blackmailers, called sycophants, who brought these prosecutions. Under the law the person who preferred charges received a percentage of the fine or the property confiscated, so that one historian has very justly said that at first they confiscated in order to punish but later punished in order to confiscate. These sycophants became a well-recognized class and we read much about them.

Now what an orator will write for a client to present in court, or what a good trial lawyer in our day will say before a jury, may frequently wander pretty far from the facts in the case; but there are some things that no lawyer would say to a jury, because if he said them he would lose his case. No Cambridge lawyer would say, defending a man accused of bootlegging, that such a thing couldn't happen in Middlesex County because everybody knows there never was a case of bootlegging here. There are some things that even an advocate in a trial cannot and will not say. Lysias, for example, arguing against confiscation of a client's property, says: "You know that some of the property is disappearing in the hands of those who are holding it,"—that is, the conservators of the property. Moreover, the rest of the estate, although of great value, "is being sold at a low price." So he tells the judges that the city will profit little by this confiscation, but will be taking property from people who are doing well here, paying taxes and making special contributions, while the sycophants and the people who sell the property will get most of it. That, by the way, is what usually happens with confiscated property. When the French confiscated the property of the congregations, the transaction was going to produce huge sums; but it never has yielded such amounts and never will. That is the history of confiscations.

In another case he argued that it would be disadvantageous to the city to condemn a man, because the city would profit much more by letting him live than by confiscating his estate.

And again he remarks that he has to argue a difficult case because the judges have exaggerated ideas as to how wealthy the defendant is; and, besides, the city is in financial difficulties, with no money in the treasury. Repeatedly Athenian orators say that it is a bad time to argue a case because the treasury is empty.

In another case Lysias shows that a certain man started without any wealth and acquired property in spite of the fact that he paid taxes and performed various public services. He gives in detail his investments, showing that the money went mostly into land and houses and that he could not have left much movable property when he died. Later a suit was brought against a relative and friend of the deceased, who was accused of having sequestered a part of the man's confiscated estate. Lysias's job was to prove that no property had been sequestered, and he argued that, as soon as the man was condemned, his house was placed under guard in order that none of his goods and chattels should be taken out. Moreover, from the sale of his household effects the city had realized a thousand drachmae, which was more than it had received in any previous case. Now a thousand drachmae wasn't much money, but he declared that in cases of confiscation usually no sale of furniture is reported, that house furnishings simply disappear, and that, incidentally, doors are torn out of the houses. Now, you wouldn't say that to a jury in Cambridge. You know that when we collect taxes or other debts here by distraint and sell a man's movables, the doors of his houses do not figure as movables and are not torn out and made away with. No advocate would say such a thing to a jury unless it was true.

I will say nothing about the liturgies, the trierarchies, the choruses. The Athenians had the habit, something like that which survives at New Orleans in the Festival of Mardi Gras, of electing wealthy citizens leaders of choruses in the annual competitions in the drama, music, and dancing. They also, when they had to outfit warships, appointed some wealthy men trierarchs, and allowed them to perform and finance the job. Such things were very expensive, and they had unpleasant consequences which I will presently mention: the general result was that the resources of Athens were squandered. If it hadn't been that much of her trade was in the hands of people who were not citizens and, therefore, although they contributed to the city in regular taxes and made gifts, were not subject to the special attentions of the law courts, the city's wealth might have declined sooner than it did. In time you find, for example, that their property tax, when they levied it, although it was supposed to be levied upon all people, was collected in the first instance from the three hundred wealthiest men in town, who were supposed to collect from all the other people who were subject to taxation but not required to pay directly to the city.

Aristophanes, in his *Wasps,* devotes a whole play to judges of the law courts. The wasps are jurors and they swarm onto the stage in large numbers, dressed as wasps. Each one has a stylus, such as he would write his verdict with, but it is in the form of a dart with a wasp's sting for the point. The whole play turns on the way the jurors "stung" the wealthy people of Athens, and it received the prize for that year. In one of the scenes an old judge is talking with his son who tells him that the total revenues of the city are two thousand talents, and the old man asks how much is paid to the judges. He is told that they get one hundred and fifty talents; whereupon the old judge gets up angrily and exclaims: "Then it's not a tenth of the revenue that constitutes our wages." And where, he asks, does the rest of the money go; to which the son replies: "It goes to those who say, 'I shall never betray the Athenian populace, but I shall always fight for the people.' "

Turning to another of Aristophanes' plays, *The Knights,* where he satirizes Cleon, he makes a sycophant in court say in his argument to the judges, "No barley meal for you, judges, unless you decide upon condemnation in this case." That was a good joke for a great comedian to put in a comedy submitted in public competition, the play which won the prize for that year, and it is good historical evidence as to what happened in cases involving heavy fines and confiscation of property.

All such evidence is minimized and discounted by the historians who have eulogized or glorified Athenian democracy. There were occasional cases, they admit, in which rich men were unjustly treated; but in fourth-century Athens they tell us that a rich man who paid his taxes and did his part as a good citizen came off fairly well. To the statement of Isocrates that the Athenians have seen fellow citizens stripped of their property while sycophants and blackmailers have become rich; or that the demagogues, while professing to be so devoted to the commonwealth that they cannot attend to their own affairs, have in fact become wealthier than they had ever dreamed of being, while the rich have been impoverished and the city as a whole has become poor—they reply that Isocrates was a disappointed old man who had outlived his usefulness and influence. Sometimes they have got down to cases and have referred to the two characters Xenophon introduces in his *Economics,* Critobulus and Ischomachus, who are represented as men of wealth who had managed to do well enough in democratic Athens. But they do not read the whole of this dialogue, or else do not note that Critobulus is told by Socrates that he isn't really rich, but is poor, because of the large contributions he must make, the strangers he must entertain, the public feasts he must give, and the heavy contributions the city is ever exacting. If in any of these things he fails, Socrates tells him, the Athenians will certainly punish him as if they had caught him robbing the city; so that in fact he really stands in danger of being reduced to poverty or coming to some fate even worse than that. And so far as Ischomachus is concerned, it appears that he is continually being required to equip a warship or provide a chorus, and all this in an abrupt and peremptory way; and it also appears that he has been obliged to practice oratory in order to be able to defend himself in the courts, and that he finds it a public duty to watch the sycophants and note the wrongs they do. So far, however, the sycophants haven't yet "got him," but of course he knows that some day they may be able to do so.

So much for the *Economics*; Xenophon's *Symposium* these liberal historians of course overlook. In this dialogue you will find an interesting account of the conversation at an Athenian banquet where the guests are asked in turn to tell the company what one thing they value more highly than any others. Charmides, a rich man who has been wholly impoverished, when it came his turn, told the banqueters that he valued his poverty above everything else. In explanation, he says that he finds it far better to feel secure than to live in fear as he used to do when he was rich; to be free rather than a slave; and to be trusted rather than distrusted. When he was rich he had lived in continual fear that his house might be broken into, his money stolen, and his life forfeited on account of his wealth. More than that, he used to be obliged to court the good will of the sycophants and was unable to leave Athens when he desired on account of the public duties he was required to perform, meaning liturgies which obliged him to spend a great deal of money. Now, however, with his property gone and even his household goods sold, he can sleep in peace. He is no longer suspected by the government and no longer threatened by the sycophants. He is free to come and go as he pleases; while men who are still rich now defer to him and give him precedence because, since he is a poor man, he may be supposed to be ready to practice blackmail. As a result he now lives like a king and no longer like a slave. Formerly he was always losing property; but now he has nothing to lose and on the contrary can live in hope of sometime acquiring something—of course, he means, by some New Deal. Finally he remarks: "I formerly paid taxes to the city, but now the city pays taxes to me because it supports me."

Here again the testimony of a story which Xenophon puts into the mouth of a character in a dialogue is worth more than all the labored arguments of liberal historians. Xenophon may or may not have had any actual case in mind; but he was writing a dialogue which he hoped would at least interest his contemporaries, and he would not have inserted this story if he had not known that it was fundamentally true to life and therefore would make Athenians who read it smile, just as we smile today when we hear good losers speaking jocosely about their losses in the famous stock market of 1929, or the things that have happened to their industries and investments since 1933. Xenophon, while a writer of great merit in many ways, was not a man of lively imagination; and he was an intelligent reporter and historian rather than a maker of tales. The story told by Charmides would never have been written if Xenophon had not known it would be recognized as so nearly true to life as to possess the genuine humor which we can recognize in it even seven years after the stock market debâcle of 1929.

Now what was the final result? It was, of course, that public works declined, and that, in the end, the Athenians could not even keep up their fleet and their army. They had in their harbor a large number of triremes, but they couldn't send out more than thirty or forty in proper condition for a battle, and couldn't send these out in time. Their fleets declined, were always too small, generally arrived too late, and usually lost their battles.

Moreover, their people wouldn't fight any more. They preferred to stay at Athens to get the doles and attend the festivals. The situation would be humorous if it were not so tragic; the sovereign citizens of Athens couldn't be invited to go to a play without being paid for it, and the musical and religious festivals took so long that Demos became hungry and had to have a free lunch. It was really a liberal and progressive age. Thus their allies fell away, their fleets declined, their armies were composed chiefly of mercenaries; and the rich, of course, knowing that every war would mean heavy war taxes, were always opposed to war.

The Greek Orators

When Macedonia rose to power, Demosthenes, as you know, undertook in his *Olynthiacs* and *Philippics* to arouse his countrymen to an appreciation of their danger. Now, Demosthenes is often a very poor witness. He was a man who, to carry a point in an assembly or law court, would say anything; but in this case he is trying to arouse his countrymen to avert a great danger. His sincerity cannot be questioned, for his opposition to Macedonia ultimately cost him his life. These orations have a force and a majesty that carry conviction of the sincerity of the man, and compel translators not to write in colloquial English but to give you the orator's periods in true oratorical style, even though no translation can do justice to a great Greek oration.

And what does the orator tell his countrymen? Well, he deplores the fact that Athenian orators in the general assembly make such fine speeches and are considered to have said exactly the right thing, while nothing of the needed action, which alone would make the speeches worthwhile, ever results from them. The Athenians, he says, are doing exactly what Philip would pray that they might do: "You are behind time, and you waste your money; you look around for some one to lead your enterprise and then you quarrel with him," lest perhaps you "blame one another." Never yet, "Athenians, have you instituted or organized a single plan of action properly from the start, but you always follow in the train of every event, and then when you find yourselves too late, you give up the project." Subsequently, when another trouble arises Athenians again work themselves up into a perfect bustle of preparation.

When the question of opposing Philip arises, the oraters immediately begin to discourse on what a fine thing peace is and how expensive it is to support a large army, even suggesting that someone is trying to rob the city. Finally he gets around to the struggle between the rich and the poor, and says that Athens is always weakened in time of a crisis because the wealthy complain that the people will not allow their doles to be discontinued when war taxes become necessary. To this topic of reconciling the rich and the poor, in the face of a common danger, he then devotes himself. So far, so good. Here we find what we must accept as an accurate description of the final result of the financial and social policies of Athenian democracy.

And what is the orator's solution? Well, of course, as a member of the popular party and a demagogue or popular leader, Demosthenes cannot conceive of stopping the distributions from the Theoric Fund, even in time of war. The Athenians, he said, ought to banish the idea that any reproach or obloquy attends the receipt of distributions or of free tickets to plays and festivals with free lunches thrown in and even payment for the time required for attendance. Earnestly does he chide the rich for objecting to these distributions, and he tells them that they ought rather "to regard the whole body of citizens as the common parents of the whole state." and never think of depriving the people of anything the state is accustomed to bestow—not even in time of war. Yes, the rich must pay their war taxes; and what should be the contribution of the poor?

The answer of Demosthenes is that the poor ought to "abolish the grievance which makes property owners discontented . . . and gives them just cause for complaint against the government of Athens." The rich have a grievance, but it is not the distributions of public money to the poor or the war taxes they are required to pay; it is, rather, the distribution of their remaining private fortunes through the fines and confiscations of the law courts. The rich have a real grievance when they see either the popular assembly or a court of judges applauding a defendant who speaks well in his own cause, but then voting against him when they come to casting their ballots in secret. The wealthy ought to be given security, and ought not to be haunted by fears for their lives and property when in time of danger they are called upon to pay heavy taxes for the defense of the state. And the poor ought to realize that, while the money of the state is common property and may well be shared with them, nevertheless, private property belongs to the possessor. Thus the best he can suggest is continuance of the doles, heavy war taxes for the rich, and that the poor shall make their patriotic contribution by desisting from spoliation of the rich. Indeed in one passage he appears to suggest, though he may not have intended to do so, that it is only when the rich in time of danger are compelled to pay their war taxes, that the poor should give them security for their lives and property.

He also declares that, while Macedonia has been increasing,

Athens has declined not only in military power but even in domestic affairs. The parapets were still whitewashed and roads in good repair, while fountains and similar trumpery had been provided; but—observe, he says, the politicians who have controlled the city, some of whom have risen from obscurity to eminence and others from poverty to wealth, while still others have made their own houses more magnificent than the public buildings. As the city has declined, the fortunes of the politicans have increased, while the people have become underlings and hangers-on, content if they receive their share of the meat from the sacrifices and the money that admits them to public spectacles. A people thus made tame and submissive by the demagogues who have become their masters cannot have a high and noble spirit. Even freedom of speech, he declared, is denied them on some subjects.

This is not an anecdote or a play, but the word of a great politician, a successful demagogue, and one of the world's greatest orators, who knew full well the men he was addressing and is earnestly endeavoring, even at the risk of his life, to place before his countrymen a plan which he thinks may save them from a great danger which finally engulfed them. Stories properly interpreted are valuable historical evidence; the play of a great comedian may give you indisputable evidence concerning the political and social life of a people; but the sincere appeal of this consummate orator obliged to tell his countrymen unpleasant truths which he hoped would awaken them to a great danger, gives historical evidence that cannot be gainsaid. The eloquence of Demosthenes failed to arouse the Athenians, but it ought to instruct intelligent students of contemporary economics and politics.

The End of the Road

The end of the road was reached in 323 B.C. when, having learned of the death of Alexander the Great, the Athenians concluded that a good time had come for a revolt against Macedonian rule. There were still the two parties in Athens: the popular party consisting of those who were not going to pay the war taxes, but were going to continue to receive their doles, though they might possibly be asked during the duration of the war to refrain from spoliation of the rich. Then there were the conservatives led by Phocion, statesman, general, and one of the absolutely honest men in Greek public life—a man withal who had great power of brief, pithy, and deadly statement. He is the man, you may recall, whom Demosthenes called the pruner of his periods, the man who, after the orator had delivered himself of a mighty effort, could arise in his place and in a few words say something that would wreck the best Attic oratory.

In 323 B.C. the popular leaders were all for the war and Phocion as usual was against them. To the general who expected to lead the expedition he said: "Young man, you are like a beautiful cypress tree. You are very beautiful but you produce no fruit." But then they asked him under what conditions he would favor a war, to which he replied: "Whenever I see the young men willing to take their places in the ranks of the army, the rich men disposed to pay the war taxes, and the politicians ready to keep their thievish hands out of the public treasury." Thus Phocion the conservative and Demosthenes the democrat agreed in their final diagnosis of political conditions in Athens.

Nevertheless, the Athenians decided on the war and Leosthenes, the handsome cypress tree, led an expedition intended to inaugurate a general revolt of the Greek states against Macedonian dominion. When the ships and soldiers for the expedition had been assembled, Phocion looked them over and remarked that they seemed sufficient for a short campaign, but inadequate for a long struggle because the city had no reserves of money, of ships, of troops. So it turned out: after an initial success Leosthenes was killed, and then his successor won a single battle; but Macedonian reinforcements continued to arrive and at last the Athenians were overwhelmed exactly as Phocion had foreseen. Presently a Macedonian garrison was placed in Athens and demand was made for the surrender of Demosthenes and other agitators. This was the end of Athenian independence.

Under Macedonian control the democratic constitution of the city was changed and the 12,000 poorest citizens were disfranchised, so that only 9,000 were left and control passed to the conservative or oligarchical party. Under the new constitution the jury courts were pretty well emptied. Many offices were abolished and expensive boards were replaced by single magistrates. A superintendent was appointed to receive and disburse revenues, and financial administration generally was centralized.

With these changes naturally enough, distributions of surplus revenues to the people disappeared and pay for attending the assemblies, for jury service, and possibly even for holding office was abolished. Thus disappeared the whole system of doles, and Athenian citizens thereafter were expected to support their government and not to be supported by it. Two years later the death of the Macedonian regent was followed by democratic reaction in Athens, in the course of which the conservative party was overthrown and Phocion was killed. But this lasted less than a year and then the Macedonians set up a new government under the leadership of Demetrius of Phalerum, the last of the great Attic orators and an administrator of great ability with sound views of finance and general economic policy. Demetrius did not persecute the democratic leaders and restored political tranquility for a time. He abolished the liturgies and transferred to the state the cost of choruses, festivals, and other public functions which had previously been saddled upon the rich. With Athenian independence gone, there was now no need of a great fleet, and public expenditures could be greatly reduced. Within ten years a policy of prudent economy had restored the prosperity, and so the revenues, of Athens to such an extent that some historians have supposed that the city was more prosperous than at any time after the Peloponnesian Wars. When a democratic reaction occurred in 307 B.C. and Demetrius was driven from power, the liturgies were not reestablished and the city did not revert to the old regime. Conditions simply did not permit the restoration of doles and the other abuses of fifth-century and fourth-century finance. Of course independence was gone, but Athens long remained the center of Hellenic culture, even though in all that concerned the world of politics it must content itself with memories of a great past.

Before he disappeared from the scene Demetrius, upon some fitting occasion, delivered the best of all possible epilogues to the story of the New Deal in ancient Athens. He had not only reduced expenditures and taxes, but also had introduced sumptuary regulations designed to discourage the wealthy from impoverishing themselves. East of the Acropolis a long street led to the theater, and along this, wealthy citizens, victors in the annual artistic and other contests, had erected expensive monuments upon which were placed the bronze tripods given each year to those Athenians whose productions, which cost them so dearly, had been victorious in the annual competitions. The fortunate recipient of a prize, although he had already undergone the heavy outlay of the competition, could do no less than vie with his predecessors in erecting a handsome monument, somewhere along the Street of the Tripods, upon which to place his prize, thus running into further extravagance which many could ill afford. Understanding this all too well, Demetrius, the last of the great orators who had adorned Athens, upon some occasion unknown to us, uttered wingèd words so true and striking that they could hardly have come from any other Athenian of his time. Such a monument, he declared, was "not a votive offering to victory," but "a libation over a wasted fortune and a cenotaph of a deserted home."

BOOKS AND ARTICLES BY PROFESSOR BULLOCK

Finances of the United States from 1775 to 1789, with especial reference to the budget. Madison, Wis.: The University, 1895. viii, 117-273 pp. (Bulletin of the University of Wisconsin. Economics, political science and history series, Vol. 1, No. 2).

Introduction to the study of economics. Boston: Silver, Burdett and Co., 1897. 511 pp.

Introduction to "A Discourse concerning the currencies of the British plantations in America," by William Douglass. *American Economic Association* (October, 1897).

Introduction to the study of economics. Boston: Silver, Burdett and Co., 1898. 511 pp.

Direct and indirect taxes in economic literature. *Political Science Quarterly*, Vol. XIII (1898), pp. 442-476.

Contributions to the history of wage statistics. *American Statistical Association, Publication, New Series*, Vol. VI (1898-1899), pp. 187-218.

Wage statistics and the federal census. New York: Published for the American Economic Association by the Macmillan Company, 1899. (American Economic Association, Publications, New Series, No. 2, pp. 343-68).

Direct taxes under the constitution. *Political Science Quarterly*, Vol. XV (1900), pp. 217-239, 452-481.

Essays on the monetary history of the United States. New York: Macmillan, 1900. x, 292 pp.

Introduction to the study of economics. Boston: Silver, Burdett and Co., 1900. 511 pp.

Introduction to the study of economics; new edition, revised and enlarged. Boston: Silver, Burdett and Co., 1900. 581 pp.

Unity in the life and work of the university. *Boston University Notes*, Vol. II, No. 2 (July, 1900), pp. 1-12.

Theory of the balance of trade. *North American Review*, Vol. 173 (July, 1901), pp. 111-133.

Trust literature: a survey and a criticism. *Quarterly Journal of Economics*, Vol. XV (1900-01), pp. 167-217.

Trusts and public policy. *Atlantic Monthly*, Vol. 87 (1901), pp. 737-745.

Direct taxes and the federal constitution. *The Yale Review,* Vol. IX (1900-01), pp. 439-449; Vol. X (1901-02), pp. 6-29, 144-158.

The variation of productive forces. *Quarterly Journal of Economics,* Vol. XVI (1901-02), pp. 473-513.

Concentration of banking interests in the United States. *Atlantic Monthly,* Vol. 92 (1903), pp. 182-192.

Growth of federal expenditures. *Political Science Quarterly,* Vol. XVIII (1903), pp. 97-111.

Closed shop. *Atlantic Monthly,* Vol. 94 (1904), pp. 433-439.

History of economic and political studies in Williams College. *Education,* Vol. XXIV (1904), pp. 532-537.

The variation of productive forces: a rejoinder. *Quarterly Journal of Economics,* Vol. XVIII (1903-04), pp. 437-439.

Cost of war. *Atlantic Monthly,* Vol. 95 (1905), pp. 433-445.

The elements of economics. New York: Silver, Burdett and Co., 1905. vii, 378 pp.

Tariff reform. *North American Review,* Vol. 180 (Jan. 1905), 64-73.

Life insurance and speculation. *Atlantic Monthly,* Vol. 97 (1906), pp. 629-648.

Selected readings in public finance. Boston: Ginn and Co., 1906. viii, 671 pp.

Historical sketch of the finances and financial policy of Massachusetts from 1780 to 1905. New York: Published for the American Economic Association by the Macmillan Company, 1907. 144 pp. American Economic Association, Publications, Third Series, Vol. VIII, No. 2.)

The position of the inheritance tax in American taxation. *National Tax Association, Addresses and Proceedings,* Vol. I (1907), pp. 231-240.

Selected readings in economics. Boston: Ginn and Co., 1907. ix, 705 pp.

The taxation of corporations in Massachusetts. *Quarterly Journal of Economics,* Vol. XXI (1906-07), pp. 181-246.

Introduction to the study of economics; third edition, revised and enlarged. Boston: Silver, Burdett and Co., 1908. 619 pp.

The taxation of intangible property. *National Tax Association, Addresses and Proceedings,* Vol. II (1908), pp. 127-137.

Argument in favor of the proposed constitutional amendment permitting the General Court to classify property for the purpose of taxation; by Charles J. Bullock, for the Taxation Committee, Boston Chamber of Commerce, October 26, 1909. Boston, 1909. 58 pp.

A classified property tax. *National Tax Association, Addresses and Proceedings,* Vol. III (1909), pp. 95-105.

The general property tax in the United States. Columbus, Ohio: International Tax Association, 1909. 21 pp. (Reprinted from the *Boston Transcript*, January 13, 20, and 27, 1909.)

Taxation in New Hampshire. *Manchester Union*, February 3, 1909.

Control of the capitalization of public service corporations in Massachusetts. *American Economic Association, Publications*, Vol. X, No. 1 (April, 1909), pp. 384-414.

The general property tax in Switzerland. *National Tax Association, Addresses and Proceedings*, Vol. IV (1910), pp. 53-84.

The separation of state and local revenues. *Quarterly Journal of Economics*, Vol. XXIV, (1909-10), pp. 437-458.

Inheritance taxes and swollen fortunes. *Bankers' Magazine*, Vol. 82 (1911), pp. 755-757.

Local option in taxation. *National Tax Association, Addresses and Proceedings*, Vol. V (1911), pp. 271-287.

Quarterly Journal of Economics, 1886-1911. *Harvard Graduates' Magazine*, Vol. XX (1911), pp. 281-284.

The elements of economics; second edition. Boston: Silver, Burdett and Co., 1913. vii, 378 pp.

Introduction to the study of economics; fourth edition, revised and enlarged. Boston: Silver, Burdett and Co., 1913. 621 pp.

Report of committee on taxation of public service corporations. *National Tax Association, Addresses and Proceedings*, Vol. VII (1913), pp. 372-383.

Federal income tax. *National Tax Association, Addresses and Proceedings*, Vol. VIII (1914), pp. 264-279.

New York's taxation problem. *Real Estate Magazine*, Vol. IV, No. 1 (April, 1914), pp. 73, 95, 97-98.

Practicable reforms in state and local taxation. *University of Washington, Bulletin*. No. 84 (1914), pp. 224-239.

The single tax in Vancouver. *Boston Transcript*, June 27, 1914.

The taxation of forests in Massachusetts. *Forestry Quarterly*, Vol. XII (1914), pp. 544-545.

Need of endowment for economic research. *Harvard Graduates' Magazine*, Vol. XXIII (1915), pp. 601-610.

Adam Smith's views on national defence. *Military Historian and Economist*, Vol. I (1916), pp. 249-257.

The state income tax and the classified property tax. *National Tax Association, Addresses and Proceedings*, Vol. X (1916), pp. 362-384.

The Harvard University department of economics. *Harvard Crimson*, May 9, 1916, pp. 1, 3.

The taxation of property and income in Massachusetts. *Quarterly Journal of Economics*. Vol. XXXI (1916-17), pp. 1-61.

Conscription of income. *North American Review,* Vol. 205 (1917), pp. 895-904.

Financing the war. *Quarterly Journal of Economics,* Vol. XXXI (1916-17), pp. 357-379.

Report of the committee upon a model tax system. Prepared in collaboration with Charles V. Galloway and others. *National Tax Association, Proceedings,* Vol. XI (1917), pp. 183-184.

War finance. *National Tax Association, Proceedings,* Vol. XI (1917), 146-157.

The operation of the Massachusetts income tax. *Quarterly Journal of Economics,* Vol. XXXII (1917-18), pp. 525-532.

War taxes and our industrial situation. Cambridge, Mass.: 1918.

Sidelights on the model tax system committee report. *National Tax Association, Bulletin,* Vol. IV (1918-19), pp. 169-175.

The balance of trade of the United States. Written in collaboration with John H. Williams and Rufus S. Tucker. *Review of Economic Statistics,* Vol. I (1919), pp. 215-266.

Economic conditions since the armistice: review of the year. *Review of Economic Statistics, Monthly Supplement* (December, 1919), pp. 9-13.

The economic background: a review of business conditions since November, 1918. *Review of Economic Statistics, Monthly Supplement* (September, 1919), pp. 9-12.

The elements of economics; revised and enlarged. Boston: Silver, Burdett and Co., 1919. vii, 406 pp.

The elements of economics; third edition. Boston: Silver, Burdett and Co., 1919. vii, 406 pp.

The imperative need of financing exports. *Review of Economic Statistics, Monthly Supplement,* (November, 1919), pp. 17-18.

Preliminary report of the committee appointed by the National Tax Association to prepare a plan of a model system of state and local taxation, by C. J. Bullock and others. *National Tax Association, Proceedings,* Vol. XII (1919).

Introductory remarks on model income tax acts. *National Tax Association, Bulletin,* Vol. VI (1920-21), pp. 100-101.

Review of the first, second and third quarters of the year. *Review of Economic Statistics,* Vol. II (1920), pp. 73-75, 178-180, 284-286.

Selected readings in public finance; second edition. Boston: Ginn and Co., 1920. x, 920 pp.

The taxation of urban real estate. *Thirteenth Annual Convention of the National Association of Building Owners and Managers,* Proceedings (1920), pp. 73-90.

Review of the first, second and third quarters of the year. *Review of Economic Statistics*, Vol. III (1921), pp. 83-87, 219-222, 334-336.

Review of the year 1920. *Review of Economic Statistics*, Vol. III (1921), pp. 7-10.

Review of the year 1921. *Review of Economic Statistics*, Vol. IV (1922), pp. 1-6.

The business man and the business cycle. *National Association of Cotton Manufacturers, Transactions*, No. 113 (October 5, 1922), pp. 208-222.

Commodity prices during the present decade. *Harvard Economic Service, Weekly Letters*, Vol. I (1922), pp. 133-140.

Federal reserve bank policy—the need of a definite statement. *Harvard Business Review*, Vol. I (1922-23), pp. 132-138.

Business opinion and business conditions. *Harvard Economic Service, Weekly Letters*, Vol. II (1923), pp. 1-8.

The elements of economics; revised and enlarged. Boston: Silver, Burdett and Co., 1923. vii, 406 pp.

Selected readings in public finance; third edition. Boston: Ginn and Co., 1924. x, 982 pp.

The future of estate and inheritance taxes in the United States. *National Tax Association, Conference on Inheritance and Estate Taxation* (1925), pp. 128-146.

The construction and interpretation of the Harvard index of business conditions. Written in collaboration with W. M. Persons and W. L. Crum. *Review of Economic Statistics*, Vol. IX (1927), pp. 74-92.

The increase of taxes on real estate in American cities. *Harvard Business Review*, Vol. VI (1927-28), pp. 129-142.

Bank advertisements: ancient and modern. *Barron's*, Vol. VIII, No. 31 (July, 1928), pp. 3, 8.

The legacy of Rahoboam: an Old Testament lesson in taxation. *Barron's*, Vol. VIII, No. 14 (April 2, 1928), pp. 3, 8; Vol. VIII, No. 15 (April 8, 1928), pp. 3, 8.

The American money market. Cambridge, Mass.: Harvard Economic Society, 1930. 12 pp.

Dionysius of Syracuse; financier. *Classical Journal*, Vol. XXV (1930), pp. 260-276.

Economic research at Harvard University. *Harvard Alumni Bulletin*, Vol. XXXII (1929-30), pp. 459-463.

Foreign trade and the business cycle. *Review of Economic Statistics*, Vol. XIII (1931), pp. 138-159. Written in collaboration with H. L. Micoleau.

Postal revenues and the business cycle. Written in collaboration with

B. Fox and A. R. Eckler. *Review of Economic Statistics,* Vol. XIII 1931), pp. 47-58.

The Harvard index of economic conditions, 1919-31. Written in collaboration with W. L. Crum. *Review of Economic Statistics,* Vol. XIV (1932), pp. 132-148.

The United States as a creditor nation. *Review of Economic Statistics,* Vol. XIV (1932), pp. 178-180.

Second report on a plan of a model system of state and local taxation. Prepared in collaboration with A. W. Bliss and others. *National Tax Association, Proceedings,* Vol. XXVI (1933), pp. 353-420.

Devaluation. *Review of Economic Statistics,* XVI (1934), 41-44.

Gold. *Review of Economic Statistics,* Vol. XVI (1934), pp. 148-152.

Inflation. *Review of Economic Statistics,* Vol. XVI (1934), pp. 104-108.

Inflation by public expenditure. *Review of Economic Statistics,* Vol. XVI (1934), 213-216.

Reform versus recovery. *Review of Economic Statistics,* Vol. XVI (1934), pp. 261-264.

The securities act of 1933. *Review of Economic Statistics,* Vol. XVI (1934), pp. 17-20.

Reform, recovery and the budget. *Review of Economic Statistics,* Vol. XVII (1935), pp. 49-52.

The New Deal in Ancient Greece, *Harvard Business Review,* Vol. XIV (1935-36), 389-404.